T0331650

Handbook of Research on Intrusion Detection Systems

Brij B. Gupta
National Institute of Technology, Kurukshetra, India

Srivathsan Srinivasagopalan
AT&T, USA

A volume in the Advances in Information Security, Privacy, and Ethics (AISPE) Book Series

Published in the United States of America by
IGI Global
Information Science Reference (an imprint of IGI Global)
701 E. Chocolate Avenue
Hershey PA, USA 17033
Tel: 717-533-8845
Fax: 717-533-8661
E-mail: cust@igi-global.com
Web site: http://www.igi-global.com

Copyright © 2020 by IGI Global. All rights reserved. No part of this publication may be reproduced, stored or distributed in any form or by any means, electronic or mechanical, including photocopying, without written permission from the publisher. Product or company names used in this set are for identification purposes only. Inclusion of the names of the products or companies does not indicate a claim of ownership by IGI Global of the trademark or registered trademark.

Library of Congress Cataloging-in-Publication Data

Names: Gupta, Brij, 1982- editor. | Srinivasagopalan, Srivathsan, 1974-
   editor.
Title: Handbook of research on intrusion detection systems / Brij B. Gupta
   and Srivathsan Srinivasagopalan, editors.
Other titles: Intrusion detection systems
Description: Hershey, PA : Information Science Reference, 2020. | Includes
   bibliographical references. | Summary: "This book explores recent
   developments and applications in intrusion detection systems and
   intrusion detection security"-- Provided by publisher.
Identifiers: LCCN 2019037710 (print) | LCCN 2019037711 (ebook) | ISBN
   9781799822424 (h/c) | ISBN 9781799822431 (eISBN)
Subjects: LCSH: Computer networks--Security measures. | Intrusion detection
   systems (Computer security)
Classification: LCC TK5105.59 .H33 2020 (print) | LCC TK5105.59 (ebook) |
   DDC 005.8/2--dc23
LC record available at https://lccn.loc.gov/2019037710
LC ebook record available at https://lccn.loc.gov/2019037711

This book is published in the IGI Global book series Advances in Information Security, Privacy, and Ethics (AISPE) (ISSN: 1948-9730; eISSN: 1948-9749)

British Cataloguing in Publication Data
A Cataloguing in Publication record for this book is available from the British Library.

All work contributed to this book is new, previously-unpublished material. The views expressed in this book are those of the authors, but not necessarily of the publisher.

For electronic access to this publication, please contact: eresources@igi-global.com.

Advances in Information Security, Privacy, and Ethics (AISPE) Book Series

Manish Gupta
State University of New York, USA

ISSN:1948-9730
EISSN:1948-9749

Mission

As digital technologies become more pervasive in everyday life and the Internet is utilized in ever increasing ways by both private and public entities, concern over digital threats becomes more prevalent.

The **Advances in Information Security, Privacy, & Ethics (AISPE) Book Series** provides cutting-edge research on the protection and misuse of information and technology across various industries and settings. Comprised of scholarly research on topics such as identity management, cryptography, system security, authentication, and data protection, this book series is ideal for reference by IT professionals, academicians, and upper-level students.

Coverage

- IT Risk
- Electronic Mail Security
- Telecommunications Regulations
- Global Privacy Concerns
- Security Classifications
- Access Control
- Technoethics
- Risk Management
- Security Information Management
- Tracking Cookies

IGI Global is currently accepting manuscripts for publication within this series. To submit a proposal for a volume in this series, please contact our Acquisition Editors at Acquisitions@igi-global.com or visit: http://www.igi-global.com/publish/.

The Advances in Information Security, Privacy, and Ethics (AISPE) Book Series (ISSN 1948-9730) is published by IGI Global, 701 E. Chocolate Avenue, Hershey, PA 17033-1240, USA, www.igi-global.com. This series is composed of titles available for purchase individually; each title is edited to be contextually exclusive from any other title within the series. For pricing and ordering information please visit http://www.igi-global.com/book-series/advances-information-security-privacy-ethics/37157. Postmaster: Send all address changes to above address. © © 2020 IGI Global. All rights, including translation in other languages reserved by the publisher. No part of this series may be reproduced or used in any form or by any means – graphics, electronic, or mechanical, including photocopying, recording, taping, or information and retrieval systems – without written permission from the publisher, except for non commercial, educational use, including classroom teaching purposes. The views expressed in this series are those of the authors, but not necessarily of IGI Global.

Titles in this Series

For a list of additional titles in this series, please visit: https://www.igi-global.com/book-series/advances-information-security-privacy-ethics/37157

Digital Investigation and Intrusion Detection in Biometrics and Embeddd Sensors
Asaad Abdulrahman Nayyef (Sultan Qaboos University, Iraq)
Information Science Reference • © 2020 • 320pp • H/C (ISBN: 9781799819448) • US $235.00

Applied Approach to Privacy and Security for the Internet of Things
Parag Chatterjee (National Technological University, Argentina & University of the Republic, Uruguay) Emmanuel Benoist (Bern University of Applied Sciences, Switzerland) and Asoke Nath (St. Xavier's College, University of Calcutta, India)
Information Science Reference • © 2020 • 315pp • H/C (ISBN: 9781799824442) • US $235.00

Internet Censorship and Regulation Systems in Democracies Emerging Research and Opportunities
Nikolaos Koumartzis (Aristotle University of Thessaloniki, Greece) and Andreas Veglis (Aristotle University of Thessaloniki, Greece)
Information Science Reference • © 2020 • 200pp • H/C (ISBN: 9781522599739) • US $185.00

Quantum Cryptography and the Future of Cyber Security
Nirbhay Kumar Chaubey (Gujarat Technological University, India) and Bhavesh B. Prajapati (Education Department, Government of Gujarat, India)
Information Science Reference • © 2020 • 343pp • H/C (ISBN: 9781799822530) • US $235.00

Impact of Digital Transformation on Security Policies and Standards
Sam Goundar (The University of the South Pacific, Fiji) Bharath Bhushan (Sree Vidyanikethan Engineering College, India) and Vaishali Ravindra Thakare (Atria Institute of Technology, India)
Information Science Reference • © 2020 • 300pp • H/C (ISBN: 9781799823674) • US $215.00

Handbook of Research on Intelligent Data Processing and Information Security Systems
Stepan Mykolayovych Bilan (State University of Infrastructure and Technology, Ukraine) and Saleem Issa Al-Zoubi (Irbid National University, Jordan)
Engineering Science Reference • © 2020 • 434pp • H/C (ISBN: 9781799812906) • US $345.00

Security and Privacy Issues in Sensor Networks and IoT
Priyanka Ahlawat (National Institute of Technology, Kurukshetra, India) and Mayank Dave (National Institute of Technology, Kurukshetra, India)

701 East Chocolate Avenue, Hershey, PA 17033, USA
Tel: 717-533-8845 x100 • Fax: 717-533-8661
E-Mail: cust@igi-global.com • www.igi-global.com

Dedicated to my wife Varsha Gupta and daughter Prisha Gupta for their constant support during the course of this handbook
-B. B. Gupta

Dedicated to my family for their constant support during the course of this handbook
-Srivathsan Srinivasagopalan

Editorial Advisory Board

Dharma P. Agrawal, *University of Cincinnati, USA*

Mohd Anuaruddin Bin Ahmadon, *Yamaguchi University, Japan*

Nalin A.G. Arachchilage, *University of New South Wales, Australia*

V. C. Bhavsar, *UNB, Canada*

Kuan-Ching Li, *Providence University, Taiwan*

Ahmad Manasrah, *Yarmouk University, Jordan*

Nadia Nedjah, *State University of Rio de Janeiro, Brazil*

Francesco Palmieri, *University of Salerno, Italy*

Gregorio Martinez Perez, *University of Murcia, Spain*

T. Perumal, *Universiti Putra Malaysia (UPM), Malaysia*

Konstantinos Psannis, *University of Macedonia, Greece*

Yogachandran Rahulamathavan, *Loughborough University, UK*

Seungmin Rho, *Sungkyul University, Republic of Korea*

Michael Sheng, *Macquarie University, Australia*

Jie Wu, *Temple University, USA*

Shingo Yamaguchi, *Yamaguchi University, Japan*

List of Contributors

Table of Contents

Detailed Table of Contents

    Pedro Miguel Sánchez Sánchez, Universidad de Murcia, Spain
    José María Jorquera Valero, Universidad de Murcia, Spain
    Alberto Huertas Celdran, Waterford Institute of Technology, Ireland
    Gregorio Martínez Pérez, Universidad de Murcia, Spain

Continuous authentication systems are considered as a promising solution to secure access to mobile devices. Their main benefit is the improvement of the users' experience when they use the services or applications of their mobile device. Specifically, continuous authentication avoids having to remember or possess any key to access an application or service that requires authentication. In this sense, having the user authenticated permanently increases the security of the device. It also allows the user interaction with applications to be much more fluid, simple, and satisfactory. This chapter proposes a new continuous authentication system for mobile devices. The system acquires data from the device sensors and the GPS location to create a dataset that represents the user's profile or normal behaviour. Then, the proposed system uses Machine Learning algorithms based on anomaly detection to perform user identification in real time. Several experiments have been carried out to demonstrate the performance and usefulness of the proposed solution.

    Reinaldo Padilha França, State University of Campinas (UNICAMP), Brazil
    Yuzo Iano, State University of Campinas (UNICAMP), Brazil
    Ana Carolina Borges Monteiro, State University of Campinas (UNICAMP), Brazil
    Rangel Arthur, State University of Campinas (UNICAMP), Brazil

To anticipate threats, the Intrusion Detection System (IDS) enables the collection and use of information from various types of attacks to defend an entire network infrastructure. Therefore, this chapter develops a method of data transmission based on discrete event concepts, due to the fact that in this digitally globalized world, networks deal with a huge set of data all the time. Data refers to facts, events, actions, activities, and transactions which have been and can be recorded, i.e., the raw material from which information is produced, nurturing the infrastructure and components that enable modern computing. This methodology was named CBEDE and experiments were matched in the MATLAB software, where the memory consumption was evaluated, presenting great potential to intermediate users and computer systems. Results showed better computational performance related to memory utilization related to the compression of the information, showing an improvement reaching up to 114.39%.

Tameem Ahmad, Department of Computer Engineering, Z. H. College of Engineering and Technology, Aligarh Muslim University, Aligarh, India
Mohd Asad Anwar, Department of Computer Engineering, Z. H. College of Engineering and Technology, Aligarh Muslim University, Aligarh, India
Misbahul Haque, Department of Computer Engineering, Z. H. College of Engineering and Technology, Aligarh Muslim University, Aligarh, India

This chapter proposes a hybrid classifier technique for network Intrusion Detection System by implementing a method that combines Random Forest classification technique with K-Means and Gaussian Mixture clustering algorithms. Random-forest will build patterns of intrusion over a training data in misuse-detection, while anomaly-detection intrusions will be identiðed by the outlier-detection mechanism. The implementation and simulation of the proposed method for various metrics are carried out under varying threshold values. The effectiveness of the proposed method has been carried out for metrics such as precision, recall, accuracy rate, false alarm rate, and detection rate. The various existing algorithms are analyzed extensively. It is observed experimentally that the proposed method gives superior results compared to the existing simpler classifiers as well as existing hybrid classifier techniques. The proposed hybrid classifier technique outperforms other common existing classifiers with an accuracy of 99.84%, false alarm rate as 0.09% and the detection rate as 99.7%.

Mouhammd Sharari Alkasassbeh, Computer Science Department, Princess Sumaya University for Technology, Jordan
Mohannad Zead Khairallah, Computer Science Department, Princess Sumaya University for Technology, Jordan

Over the past decades, the Internet and information technologies have elevated security issues due to the huge use of networks. Because of this advance information and communication and sharing information, the threats of cybersecurity have been increasing daily. Intrusion Detection System (IDS) is considered one of the most critical security components which detects network security breaches in organizations. However, a lot of challenges raise while implementing dynamics and effective NIDS for unknown and unpredictable attacks. Consider the machine learning approach to developing an effective and flexible IDS. A deep neural network model is proposed to increase the effectiveness of intrusions detection system. This chapter presents an efficient mechanism for network attacks detection and attack classification using the Management Information Base (MIB) variables with machine learning techniques. During the evaluation test, the proposed model seems highly effective with deep neural network implementation with a precision of 99.6% accuracy rate.

Chapter 5

Cyber crime is a serious threat for day-to-day transactions of the digital life. Overexposure of the personal details in social networks will lead to the cyber crime case. Therefore, detection and monitoring of cyber crime are challenging tasks. The cyber criminals are continually flooding the various intrusions all over the network. The cyber safety team should have a noteworthy challenge of filtering various such information. Continuous nonstop cyberattacks or intrusion examinations by security tools will significantly improve the threat alerts. However, cyber security becomes more expensive in the case of the above methods. The chapter provides systematic survey of various cyber security threats, evolution of intrusion detection systems, various monitoring mechanisms, open source cyber security monitoring tools, and various assessment techniques. The chapter also proposes a model of Cyber security detection and monitoring system and its challenges.

As the number and sophistication of cyber threats increases year after year, security systems such as antivirus, firewalls, or Intrusion Detection Systems based on misuse detection techniques are improved in detection capabilities. However, these traditional systems are usually limited to detect potential threats, since they are inadequate to spot zero-day attacks or mutations in behaviour. Authors propose using honeypot systems as a further security layer able to provide an intelligence holistic level in detecting unknown threats, or well-known attacks with new behaviour patterns. Since brute-force attacks are increasing in recent years, authors opted for an SSH medium-interaction honeypot to acquire a log set from attacker's interactions. The proposed system is able to acquire behaviour patterns of each attacker and link them with future sessions for early detection. Authors also generate a feature set to feed Machine Learning algorithms with the main goal of identifying and classifying attacker's sessions, and thus be able to learn malicious intentions in executing cyber threats.

Chapter 7

Multi-cloud storage offers better Quality of Service (QoS) such as availability, durability, and users' perceived latency. The exploitation of price differences across cloud-based storage services is a motivate example of storing data in different Geo-graphically data stores, where data migration is also a choice to achieve more cost optimization. However, this requires migrating data in tolerable time from the perspective of users. This chapter first proposes a comprehensive review on different classes of data stores inspiring data migration within and across data stores. Then, it presents the design of a system prototype spanned across storage services of Amazon Web Services (AWS) and Microsoft Azure employing their RESTful APIs to store, retrieve, delete, and migrate data. Finally, the experimental results show that the data migration can be conducted in a few seconds for data with a magnitude of Megabytes.

    Gayathri K. S., Mar Baselios College of Engineering and Technology, India
    Tony Thomas, Indian Institute of Information Technology and Management, Kerala, India

Internet of things (IoT) is revolutionizing this world with its evolving applications in various aspects of life such as sensing, healthcare, remote monitoring, and so on. These systems improve the comfort and efficiency of human life, but the inherent vulnerabilities in these IoT devices create a backdoor for intruders to enter and attack the entire system. Hence, there is a need for intrusion detection systems (IDSs) designed for IoT environments to mitigate IoT-related security attacks that exploit some of these security vulnerabilities. Due to the limited computing and storage capabilities of IoT devices and the specific protocols used, conventional IDSs may not be an option for IoT environments. Since the security of IoT systems is critical, this chapter presents recent research in intrusion detection systems in IoT systems.

    Saurav Jindal, Punjab Engineering College, India
    Poonam Saini, Punjab Engineering College, India

In recent years, data collection and data mining have emerged as fast-paced computational processes as the amount of data from different sources has increased manifold. With the advent of such technologies, major concern is exposure of an individual's self-contained information. To confront the unusual situation, anonymization of dataset is performed before being released into public for further usage. The chapter discusses various existing techniques of anonymization. Thereafter, a novel redaction technique is proposed for generalization to minimize the overall cost (penalty) of the process being inversely proportional to utility of generated dataset. To validate the proposed work, authors assume a pre-processed dataset and further compare our algorithm with existing techniques. Lastly, the proposed technique is made scalable thus ensuring further minimization of generalization cost and improving overall utility of information gain.

    Brij B. Gupta, National Institute of Technology, Kurukshetra, India
    Amrita Dahiya, National Institute of Technology, Kurukshetra, India
    Chivesh Upneja, National Institute of Technology, Kurukshetra, India
    Aditi Garg, National Institute of Technology, Kurukshetra, India
    Ruby Choudhary, National Institute of Technology, Kurukshetra, India

DDoS attack always takes advantage of structure of Internet and imbalance of resources between defender and attacker. DDoS attacks are driven by factors like interdependency of Internet's security, limited resources, fewer incentives for home users and local ISPs, flexibility of handlers to control multiple compromised systems at the same time, untraceable nature of malicious packets and unfair distribution of resources all over the Internet. This survey chapter gives a comprehensive view on DDoS attacks and its defense mechanisms. Defense mechanisms are categorized according to the deployment position and nature of defense. Comprehensive study of DDoS attacks will definitely help researchers to understand the important issues related to cyber security.

Chapter 11

Veli Durmuş, Marmara University, Turkey
Mert Uydaci, Marmara University, Turkey

This chapter provides a holistic general overview of the data protection regime in Turkey. Authors present the principal rights of data protection and transmission in health law and latent ethical concerns by specifying decisions of the Supreme Court in Turkey and the European Court of Human Rights on using personal data. The research describes data protection law for health care setting in Turkey. Primary and secondary data have been used for the study. The primary data includes the information collected with current national and international regulations or law. Secondary data include publications, books, journals, and empirical legal studies. Privacy and data protection regimes in health law show there are some obligations, principles, and procedures which shall be binding upon natural or legal persons who process health-related personal data.

Chapter 12

Brij B. Gupta, National Institute of Technology, Kurukshetra, India
Somya Ranjan Sahoo, National Institute of Technology, Kurukshetra, India
Vaibhav Bhatia, National Institute of Technology, Kurukshetra, India
Adil Arafat, National Institute of Technology, Kurukshetra, India
Abhik Setia, National Institute of Technology, Kurukshetra, India

This chapter discusses a model that allows the user to access social networking sites through login using smart phone-based biometric authentication. Currently, social networking websites permit the user to access their page through login and some sites provide auto fill system to login into users account through browser by permit. The browser saves the password in password protected space and automatically auto fills the password to access the account by user. This facility is not highly reliable due to the auto fill system for laptop users. When someone uses the laptop of others and visits any website, the auto fill system opens the content with saved password. Secondly, elderly people have problems logging into today's websites. To remember the password for every account is very difficult for elderly people. This chapter describes a model for security and authenticity. Authors used a hybrid model with android as the application with fingerprint authentication and chrome extension as the auto fill process for user access.

Chapter 13

Mamta , National Institute of Technology, Kurukshetra, India
Brij B. Gupta, National Institute of Technology, Kurukshetra, India

Attribute based encryption (ABE) is a widely used technique with tremendous application in cloud computing because it provides fine-grained access control capability. Owing to this property, it is emerging as a popular technique in the area of searchable encryption where the fine-grained access control is used to determine the search capabilities of a user. But, in the searchable encryption schemes developed using ABE it is assumed that the access structure is monotonic which contains AND, OR and threshold gates. Many ABE schemes have been developed for non-monotonic access structure which supports NOT gate, but this is the first attempt to develop a searchable encryption scheme for the same. The proposed scheme results in fast search and generates secret key and search token of constant size and also the ciphertext components are quite fewer than the number of attributes involved. The proposed scheme is proven secure against chosen keyword attack (CKA) in selective security model under Decisional Bilinear Diffie-Hellman (DBDH) assumption.

Chapter 14

Cryptography is a progression where message correspondences are intelligently sent from one abuser to an additional abuser which endows with frequent defense services like privacy, data truthfulness, or verification to the wireless transportation structure. An encryption method keeps exceptional crucial contribution to communication safety measures. Here we mentioned characteristics of various Symmetric and Asymmetric encryption techniques along with inclusion of optimization techniques in cryptography for decrease computation difficulty. Moreover, advanced encryption techniques such as Zero-knowledge, Multi-party, Homomorphism encryptions, and Cognitive cryptography, Blockchain with their associated protocols are described. The present day's extensive research practices on quantum computer machines explain mathematical tribulations which are complicated or stubborn for classical computers. Quantum cryptography, challenges, Goal of Quantum resistant cryptography with associated literature work is described.

Chapter 15

The applications and software using cloud computing as a base have significantly increased, and cloud computing is nowadays developed as a scalable and cost-effective technique. It facilitates many features in the computing environment like resource pooling, multi-tenancy, virtualization, etc. The cloud environment has led to the proliferation of various attacks that affect the security of applications and software developed by using cloud services and also cloud user's data. Data security is the main concern in cloud computing because it is stored in data centers provided by service providers. The chapter presents the background history of cloud computing and different challenges faced by the cloud environment, especially in terms of providing security for customer data stored in data centers. Authors also discuss the case studies on Microsoft Azure (i.e. a cloud platform) and Aneka (i.e. a cloud development and management platform).

Cybersecurity is generally considered as an information security topic, often associated with personal data and information databases: collecting, exposing, corrupting, or deleting these data. However, it is a more global problem, and related to broader aspects, such as controlling cyber-systems. In ICS, the topic of cybersecurity is considered at the operational and responsible level as a secondary threat, and much more as an IT problem. This premise has proven to lead to substantial losses. For example, dangerous aspects in some installation can stress the cybersecurity in ICS, for instance, plants dealing with hazardous materials, as the attackers can take over control of the production lines. This chapter encapsulates points in common on the topic of cybersecurity in IT and ICS. IT has already devoted significant resources into cyber-threats. ICS has yet to do so. To do so, authors review a number of papers dealing with the same topic.

Smart cards have gained popularity in many domains by providing different facilities in every domain. Such cards are beneficial for storing credentials and access information. The cards are easy to carry and provides easy and fast computations. The cards have certain limitations due to the possible attacks on them. This chapter gives an overview of the smartcards including its history, physical design, life cycle. It also provides an overview of the possible threats on smartcards and its application area.

Preface

Cyberspace has become a fact of daily life. Its pervasiveness and the wide variety of ways in which it is used has changed and continues to change the way we live. From its humble beginnings in ARPANET, it has come a long way, outpacing even the most optimistic expectations of the scientists at ARPANET, in helping us in communication, search, education, healthcare, aerospace, agriculture, wildlife-protection and plenty of other areas where we have successfully used and where we are just beginning to. Like any other technological advancement, the history has seen, cyberspace and all the means it provides, has proven to be a double-edged sword. In one hand, it continues to immensely help humanity progress in various ways we either never thought of or we never thought possible. On the other hand, though less anticipated, it has grown into a potent weapon for cyber-criminals; who continues to gain unauthorized access to systems across the world and perform a variety of nefarious activities. The mere number of new malwares being registered everyday (~400,000), the growth of pesky adwares, rise of ransomware attacks across the world, the darknet underworld and the establishment of syndicates and state-sponsored organization to systematically target entities of choice. In 2019, Emotet botnet spread its malicious payloads (such as Trickbot, Qakbot, IcedID) wider, firmly establishing its presence not only as a fearsome malware, but also for its potent 'malware-as-a-service' style of operation (Miles, Ferguson & Warner, 2019). Furthermore, the cyber criminals have not only used the technology for their malicious activities, but also, have been successful in innovating novel ways to disrupt and distort cyber portals. The frequency and audacity with which such attacks are perpetrated are a testament to the multitude of vulnerabilities we have today, to the rise of adoption of advances in science, especially in Artificial Intelligence by the cyber-criminals and finally, to the lack of cooperative efforts by industries for effective threat reduction strategies.

It is quite clear that in the past decade, the level of cyber threats across the globe has intensified both in frequency and in severity leading to billions of lost dollars. Both government and industry (affected and non-affected) have elevated their efforts to develop solutions and minimize the breaches. Understanding the issues that are related to developing a well-rounded solution to cybersecurity and how this will spur the necessary technological innovations and more importantly, galvanize industries such as financial and healthcare sectors to cooperate and coordinate in their common goals. This requires cyber intelligence – the process of acquiring, processing, analyzing and disseminating information that identifies, tracks and predicts threats, risks and opportunities in the cyber space to enhance decision making. Enterprises, in most cases, operate with insufficient resources thereby leading to poor intelligence, and on top of that, they are driven by the perceived need to respond to critical breaches in a way more appropriate to the stakeholders rather than focusing on the core problem.

As the digital transformation of global economy continues to rapidly evolve the way we conduct business, there lies a secondary shift that is more subtle but equally important – their cyber risk profiles. This growing issue is yet another reason why cyber risk management, threat intelligence sharing and threat hunting is of utmost priority with an added focus to raise the bar on preparedness for the day when the strike happens.

This handbook is positioned to provide a panoramic view of the threat landscape enterprises face today and potential solutions to minimize or thwart the threats. This handbook focuses on various cyber-vulnerabilities (government networks and regular networks that citizens use on a daily basis), survey for defense mechanisms, mechanisms to monitor networks, IDS for IoTs and frameworks for different security applications that employ big data technologies. In this age of automation and intelligence, we take a good look at the impact of directed attacks against specific organizations, DNS compromises, the growth of defense mechanisms against such intrusions, non-direct attacks where it is more of a numbers game for cybercriminals., where they try to hit as many victims as possible with total disregard for the consequences. Furthermore, we will see a plethora of tools cybercriminals use – called as cybercriminal toolkit – such as Remote Access Trojans, encryption schemes, evasion techniques etc., in various chapters. Students, researchers and IT security professionals will find this handbook educative and interesting. This handbook is organized into 17 chapters.

Chapter 1 endeavors to encapsulate points in common on the topic of cybersecurity in IT and ICS and were they converge. Since IT has already devoted significant resources into cyber-threats, whereas ICS, has yet to do so. In order to do so, the authors review a number of papers dealing with the same topic, of cybersecurity, from both the ICS and IT side, and draw parallels. Furthermore, a list of potential threats is detailed and recommended practices on preventing them are listed. Chapter 2 provides a comprehensive view of various IDSs for IoTs, details of several methods, features and mechanisms besides touching upon their vulnerabilities. This overall view of IoTs and various IDSs will help the designers to design better IoTs systems (be it in hardware, secure communication protocol, energy-aware algorithms and more) that will go a long way in preventing such systems to be compromised. Chapter 3 gives an overview of the smartcards including its history, physical design, communication aspects and built-in security mechanisms. It also provides an overview of the possible threats on smartcards and its application area.

Chapter 4, a new continuous authentication system for mobile devices is proposed. The system acquires data from the device sensors and the GPS location to create a dataset that represents the user's profile or normal behaviors. Then, the proposed system uses Machine Learning unsupervised algorithms based on anomaly detection to perform user identification in real time. Finally, to demonstrate the performance and usefulness of proposed solution a use case based on a banking app and several experiments have been carried out. Chapter 5 presents an efficient mechanism for network attacks detection and attack classification using the Management Information Base (MIB) variables with machine learning techniques. During the evaluation test, the proposed model seems highly effective with deep neural network implementation with a precision of 99.6% accuracy rate.

Chapter 6 proposes the various cyber security threats, monitoring mechanisms, monitoring tool and various assessing techniques. In Chapter 7, authors firstly discuss various existing techniques of anonymization. Thereafter, a novel redaction technique is proposed for generalization in order to minimize the overall cost (penalty) of the process being inversely proportional to utility of generated dataset. To validate the proposed work, the authors assume a pre-processed dataset and further compare proposed algorithm with existing techniques. Lastly, the proposed technique is made scalable thus ensuring further minimization of generalization cost and improving overall utility of information gain. In Chapter 8, authors use honeypot systems as a further security layer able to provide an intelligence holistic level in detecting unknown threats, or well-known attacks with new behavior patterns. Since brute-force attacks are increasing in last years, the authors opted for an SSH medium-interaction honeypot to acquire a log set from attacker's interactions. The proposed system is able to acquire behavior patterns of each attacker and link them with future sessions for early detection. Finally, the authors generate a feature set to feed Machine Learning algorithms with the main goal of identifying and classifying attacker's sessions, and thus be able to learn malicious intentions in executing cyber threats.

In Chapter 9, authors present the background history of cloud computing and different challenges face by the cloud environment especially in terms of providing security for customer's data stored in data centers. Moreover, the authors also discuss the case studies on Microsoft Azure (i.e. a cloud platform) and Aneka (i.e. a cloud development and management platform). Chapter 10 first proposes a comprehensive review on different classes of data stores inspiring data migration within and across data stores. Then, it presents the design of a system prototype spanned across storage services of Amazon Web Services (AWS) and Microsoft Azure employing their RESTful APIs to store, retrieve, delete, and migrate data. Finally, the experimental results show that the data migration can be conducted in a few seconds for data with a magnitude of Megabytes. Chapter 11 presents a comprehensive view on DDoS attacks and its defense mechanisms. Defense mechanisms are categorized according to the deployment position and nature of defense. Comprehensive study of DDoS attacks will help researchers to understand the important issues related to cyber security. Chapter 12 aims to provide a holistic general overview of the data protection regime in Turkey. Furthermore, authors present the principal rights of data protection and transmission in health law and latent ethical concerns by specifying decisions of the Supreme Court in Turkey and the European Court of Human Rights on using personal data. The research is descriptive on data protection law for health care setting in Turkey. Primary as well as secondary data has been used for the study. The primary data includes the information collected with current national and international regulations or law. Secondary data include publications, books, journals, empirical legal studies. Privacy and data protection regimes in health law show there are some obligations, principles, and procedures which shall be binding upon natural or legal persons who process health-related personal data.

In Chapter 13, authors aim to implement DES (Discrete Event Simulation) based model. This model is called CBEDE (Coding of Bits for Entities by means of Discrete Events) and aims to improve the transmission of information in communication systems, further enhancing the structure of the Intrusion Detection System. DES is an effective tool to approach a wide variety of communication issues, discrete event mainly relates to the model representing the system as a sequence of operations performed on entities (transactions) of certain types such as data packets, bits, among others. The discrete events are derived from the results of actions taken in a system, and can be classified as an occurrence responsible for the change in the state of the system in which they act, and may be of all kinds, where they are generally capable of producing state changes at random intervals of time, generating data and consequently the information. Being the differential of this research the use of discrete events applied in the physical layer of a transmission medium, the bit itself, being this a low-level of abstraction, the results show better computational performance related to memory utilization related to the compression of the information, showing an improvement of 65%. The objective of this research is in the use of discrete events being applied at the lowest level of abstraction possible within a communication system, as is done in bit generation, and as a result make the Intrusion Detection environment more productive, faster and with better performance.

In Chapter 14, characteristics of various Symmetric and Asymmetric encryption techniques along with inclusion of optimization techniques in cryptography for decrease computation difficulty are elaborated. Moreover, advanced encryption techniques such as Zero-knowledge, Multi-party, Homomorphism encryptions, and Cognitive cryptography, Blockchain with their associated protocols are described. In present days' extensive research practices on quantum computer machines to explain mathematical tribulations which are complicated or stubborn for classical computers. Quantum cryptography, challenges, Goal of Quantum resistant cryptography with associated literature work is described. Chapter 15 revolves around Intrusion Detection using Machine Learning Techniques. High false-alarm and Low detection rates are major problems encountered by intrusion detection systems (IDS). IDS with high efficiency and fewer false positives and false negatives were proposed that uses unsupervised machine learning with k-means algorithm. In this work, the authors apply a machine learning algorithm named random forest for the hybrid-based network IDS. In recent research, the Intrusion Detection system in Machine Learning has been giving good detection and high accuracy on novel attacks. The major purpose of this work is implementing a method that combines Random-Forest classification technique and K-Means clustering Algorithms. Random-forest algorithm will build patterns of intrusion over a training data in misuse detection, while in anomaly-detection intrusions will be identified by the outlier-detection mechanism.

Chapter 16, the authors have designed a system which monitor different happening in social park-like gardening, fogging, and lightning and security issues in any of the park in a residential society. Atmel micro-controller AT Mega 328P is used to control the devices connected with the systems and ESP 8266 Micro-controller is used to provide the interfacing with the Internet and outside world. In Chapter 17, authors discuss a model that allow the user to access social networking sites through login using smart phone based biometric authentication. Currently, social networking websites permit the user to access their page through login and some sites provide auto fill system to login into users account through browser by permit. The browser saves the password in password protected space and automatically auto fills the password to access the account by user. This facility is not highly reliable due to the auto fill system for laptop users. When someone uses the laptop of others and visits any website, the auto fill system opens the content with saved password. Secondly, elderly people have problem logging into today's websites. To remember the password for every account is very difficult for elderly people. For security and authenticity, authors describe a model in this article. In this article, the authors used a hybrid model, which uses android as the application with fingerprint authentication and chrome extension as the auto fill process for user access. So, at the time of visit to any website, certain pre-configured rules are met by the user and a notification is sent to the user android mobile containing auto fill as a request. After fingerprint authentication, the auto fill fills the required login details for access the web content. Also, to protect the user content from various attacks like fake profile attack, the authors developed a self-reliant fake profile detection mechanism which can be used to identify identity clone attack as well as forbid users from falling into various scams, which can lead non-legitimate users to gain access to user password. After merging both of these techniques the overall security of the OSN user enhanced.

REFERENCES

Miles, E., Ferguson, P., & Warner, J. (2019, March 5). Three Families in Three Days – Revisiting Prolific Crimeware To Improve Network Detection: Emotet. Retrieved January 1, 2020, from https://atr-blog. gigamon.com/2019/02/28/revisiting-prolific-crimeware-to-improve-network-detection-emotet/

Acknowledgment

Many people have contributed greatly to this Handbook of Research on Intrusion Detection Systems. We, the editors, would like to acknowledge all of them for their valuable help and generous ideas in improving the quality of this handbook. With our feelings of gratitude, we would like to introduce them in turn. The first mention is the authors and reviewers of each chapter of this handbook. Without their outstanding expertise, constructive reviews and devoted effort, this comprehensive handbook would become something without contents. The second mention is the IGI Global staff, especially Ms. Morgan Brajkovich, assistant development editor and her team for their constant encouragement, continuous assistance and untiring support. Without their technical support, this handbook would not be completed. The third mention is the editor's family for being the source of continuous love, unconditional support and prayers not only for this work, but throughout our life. Last but far from least, we express our heartfelt thanks to the Almighty for bestowing over us the courage to face the complexities of life and complete this work.

Brij B. Gupta
National Institute of Technology, Kurukshetra, India

Srivathsan Srinivasagopalan
AT&T, USA
December 18, 2019

Chapter 1
Intelligent User Profiling Based on Sensors and Location Data to Detect Intrusions on Mobile Devices

Pedro Miguel Sánchez Sánchez
Universidad de Murcia, Spain

José María Jorquera Valero
Universidad de Murcia, Spain

Alberto Huertas Celdran
iD https://orcid.org/0000-0001-7125-1710
Waterford Institute of Technology, Ireland

Gregorio Martínez Pérez
Universidad de Murcia, Spain

ABSTRACT

Continuous authentication systems are considered as a promising solution to secure access to mobile devices. Their main benefit is the improvement of the users' experience when they use the services or applications of their mobile device. Specifically, continuous authentication avoids having to remember or possess any key to access an application or service that requires authentication. In this sense, having the user authenticated permanently increases the security of the device. It also allows the user interaction with applications to be much more fluid, simple, and satisfactory. This chapter proposes a new continuous authentication system for mobile devices. The system acquires data from the device sensors and the GPS location to create a dataset that represents the user's profile or normal behaviour. Then, the proposed system uses Machine Learning algorithms based on anomaly detection to perform user identification in real time. Several experiments have been carried out to demonstrate the performance and usefulness of the proposed solution.

DOI: 10.4018/978-1-7998-2242-4.ch001

Copyright © 2020, IGI Global. Copying or distributing in print or electronic forms without written permission of IGI Global is prohibited.

1. INTRODUCTION

Nowadays, the use of mobile devices has become a daily activity for the majority of the population of industrialized countries, for example, there are 2.71 billion smartphone users in the world today (2019) (Deyan, 2019). Within this wide range of mobile devices, there is a huge variety in terms of usage, from a private and personal usage such as social networks, take pictures or videos, online banking or entertainment, to a professional usage as the generation of invoices or consult customer data. The sensitive information stored in the devices and its usage is extremely important (Huertas, García, Gil & Martínez, 2016) so several knowledge management measures (Turulja & Bajgoric, 2018; Zenko, Mulej & Potocan, 2017) must be taken. The private information should be protected, so, most users restrict access to this information by controlling the access to the device. For that, it is necessary to make use of authentication mechanisms.

The fact of securing or protecting devices is usually done by establishing unlock patterns, pins or passwords that only the owner (or persons authorized to use the device) knows. The password gives access to the device until it is locked again by the user. In this way, an unauthorized person who has managed to know the password can access the content of the device without major impediment (Winkler, 2016). The companies that manufacture mobile devices are aware of the previous problem, thus, current devices implement new access control mechanisms and techniques. These techniques are related to biometric aspects (Wayman, Jain, Maltoni & Maio, 2005), such as fingerprint or facial recognition. They allow unlocking the device without having to enter a password. Besides, authentication is done using something that the user "is" and not something that "knows", which complicates unauthorized access and impersonation of the owner's identity. However, these methods are not 100% functional and there are situations in which they do not work properly such as low light devices, dirty fingers, or hardware restrictions. Thus, it is still necessary to have a password set as an auxiliary measure for these cases.

Aware of this situation, in recent years, numerous cybersecurity researchers have made efforts to solve the problems mentioned above. In this context, a possible solution is to perform periodic evaluation of the actions that the user is performing with the device to identify anomalous behaviours that allow to determine that the device is being used by an unauthorized external person. This new authentication system is called continuous authentication (Deutschmann, Nordström & Nilson, 2013), and its main objective is to identify the user who uses the device constantly and not in a timely manner as the traditional authentication systems mentioned above. In order to identify the user continuously as intended, it is necessary to determine a dataset that models the behaviour of the user or users. This dataset is called the user profile and is used to compare with the current usage or behaviour of the mobile device. Thus, if the behaviour is known, the user will be someone authorized. In contrast, if it is an anomalous behaviour, the user will be taken as intruder.

Nowadays, the current continuous authentication systems present several open challenges. Among them, the following ones are highlighted:

- The systems obtaining the best results in terms of precision using supervised ML algorithms cannot detect intruders whose data are not previously available.
- Most of the current solutions do not adapt to gradual changes in the behaviour of the user who owns the device.
- No existing solution takes into account changes in user's behaviour relative to the time of day or day of the week.

- Some solutions do not combine different dimensions, or they do not perform an optimal combination of them.
- It is not taken into account the usability of these systems and the battery consumption.

Intending to improve the above limitations, this chapter focuses on the design and development of a continuous authentication system that collects data from two dimensions of mobile devices: sensors and location. The proposed system is adaptive to changes in user behaviour. To do this, when the evaluation is positive, the data used will become part of the dataset modelling the user's behaviour profile. Besides, the oldest dataset vectors will be removed to forget old behaviours and ensure an acceptable execution time of the algorithm. Sensors and location dimensions have been chosen since they will be available on any mobile device. The selected ML algorithm is Isolation Forest (Fei, Ming & Zhou, 2008) since it is an unsupervised algorithm based on anomaly detection. This fact allows to identify the anomalous behaviour performed by any other user even if he has never used the device before. Finally, a series of experiments are carried out in the evaluation phase to determine which data are the most significant when evaluating to achieve the highest possible accuracy. These experiments consist of checking if all the data collected are useful in the system or instead give non-relevant information and if filtering the user's behaviour for hours will improve the accuracy of the system.

The rest of this chapter is structured in the following way. Section 2 explains the operation process of a continuous authentication system and also reviews previous works in the same field, focusing attention on solutions that obtained good results in terms of accuracy. Section 3 highlights the main dimensions considered to model the behavior profiles of users and explains the design and implementation details of the proposed solution. This section also details the data making up the users' profiles. The implementation of the proof of the concept of the system. Next, the different experiments performed to improve the final solution are explained in Section 4. Then, Section 5 compares the system with the literature and comments its possible limitations. Finally, Section 6 summarizes the work carried out and also proposes different future steps to continue with the development of the system.

2. LITERATURE REVIEW

In this section, the main components and operational phases of a continuous authentication system will be mentioned. Besides, the current state of the art will be analyzed with the objective of extracting the initial ideas to develop a continuous authentication system.

The user profile must be created from data collected by mobile devices, and the data needs to be different when the devices are used by diverse persons. On mobile devices, there are some relevant dimensions that can provide data useful to create behaviour profiles. Some of the most important dimensions are:

- **Sensors**: Such as accelerometer, oscilloscope, or magnetic sensors.
- **GPS Location**: To determine if the location is known.
- Data transfer rates of Cellular and WIFI.
- **Touch on the Screen**: With a touch on the screen, various aspects such as pressure, area, speed, time, start and end points can be measured.
- **User Writing**: The writing speed, the usage rate of each character, or the number of errors, among others.

Figure 1. Continuous authentication system phases simple scheme

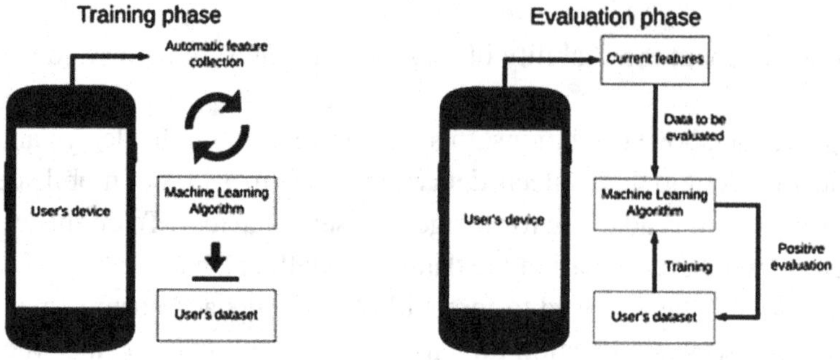

- **Use of Applications**: Number of open applications, opening order, time of use, or the number and name of background applications.
- **Call History**: Calls to known contacts, duration, or the number of them.

Once the dimension or dimensions have been selected, the user's profile is generated by collecting data of these dimensions for a time period called the training phase. During this training phase, the system collects data, which is saved in a dataset that represents or models the user's profile. These data, also called features, are modelled in the form of vectors, so that the dataset that represents the user (dataset) will be a set consisting of all these vectors. When the training phase concludes, a new phase called evaluation begins. During this phase, vectors collected after the training period are compared with the set of data that make up the user's profile to determine if they conform to the normal behaviour of the user who owns the device. In this way, it is possible to perform a real-time authentication of the user based on the behaviour he is having at each moment. The evaluation of user behaviour is carried out periodically and automatically using non-supervised Machine Learning (ML) algorithms (Broownlee, 2016). Those algorithms look for anomalies (Omar, Asri, Jebur & Bengdara, 2013) in the user's current behaviour in comparison with the profile defined during the training phase. The training and evaluation phases are outlined in Figure 1.

Next, other works which address continuous authentication from different points of view will be analysed, using different dimensions present in mobile devices and ML algorithms. In addition, some companies that have managed to develop a continuous authentication system and launch it to the market will be mentioned.

Thus, the literature review is started with one of the most outstanding academic works in the discipline, which is the one carried out by (Bo, Zhang, Li, Huang and Wang, 2013). This work proposed a continuous authentication system that makes use of two dimensions: screen touches and motion sensors. This article also contemplates the training and evaluation phases discussed in the introduction to the developed prototype (See Figure 2). As ML algorithm to classify the user as legitimate or not, one-class Support vector machines (SVM) are used (Omar, Asri, Jebur & Bengdara, 2013). This system achieves a final accuracy of 72.36% with a FAR (False Acceptance Rate) of 24.99%.

On the other hand, in this work it is verified that if instead of using a single class in the SVM algorithm, two classes are used, being this second class corresponding to a guest profile, the accuracy of the system increases up to 80% of success in the recognition of classes with a FAR and FRR of around 20%.

Figure 2. Execution phases defined in SilentSense

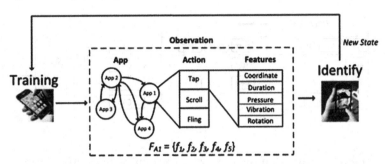

Another reference article in the field is that published by Ehatisham-ul-Haq et al. (2017). This work was focused on developing a continuous authentication system that makes use of the sensors present in the device to identify the user. The used sensors are the accelerometer, gyroscope, and magnetometer. The results showed that the SVM algorithm has the best accuracy when recognizing mobile position, with 99.18%. However, the average computing time of this algorithm is 25 seconds, while Decision Tree and Bayesian Networks algorithms have an average computing time of 10 and 6 seconds and an accuracy of 97.38% and 96.82% respectively, results very close to SVM with a much lower computational cost. Shi, Yang, Jiang, Yang & Xiong (2011) proposed the SenGuard system, which uses data from the movement (accelerometer), voice (microphone), location (coverage cell and GPS) and touches on the screen. The evaluations of the 4 dimensions are combined to provide a final result (See Figure 3). The system uses training data from 4 different users and is able to correctly classify the user who is using the device with an accuracy of 95-97%, depending on the user. This work used classification algorithms since the information of the 4 users is previously available.

Patel, Chellappa, Chandra & Barbello (2016) performed an interesting analysis of the different dimensions and ML algorithms that can be used in continuous authentication systems. Authors detailed and compared different studies in the field. In this way, the following conclusions are drawn from the comparison made:

Figure 3. Evaluation process in SenGuard

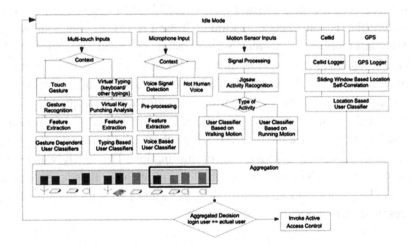

Figure 4. Classifier result fusion architecture

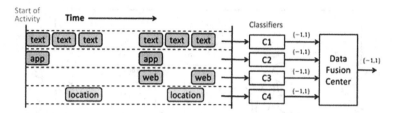

- The fusion of different dimension data allows to obtain better results in terms of accuracy and error rate.
- There is a lot of variety in the ML algorithms used depending on the datasets that handled each study, although it is appreciated that SVM stands out for its accuracy in many studies.
- The use of the camera as a dimension when performing continuous authentication shows low results due to possible lighting conditions, device orientation and the calculations necessary to extract data from images/videos.

Gascon, Uellenbeck, Wolf & Rieck (2014) developed a continuous authentication system in which information is collected through a keyboard application which collects data from device sensors while writing. A vector of 2376 dimensions is created and an SVM algorithm is used to evaluate the data. The results show 92% accuracy when recognizing authorized users. Fridman, Weber, Greenstadt & Kam (2017) considered a method to combine different dimensions in continuous authentication systems which consists of evaluating each dimension separately and then combine the results of the different evaluations into a final result (see Figure 4) to determine whether the user is authorized or not. In this work, the devices of 200 voluntary users are monitored for 5 months observing the following dimensions: writing, used applications, visited websites and GPS location. Then, to test the system a device is delivered to the users to verify if the system, using the SVM algorithm, is able to recognize and classify the 200 training users. The obtained results are an EER of 5% after first minute of use of the device and an EER of 1% after 30 minutes.

Another work of special interest is Parreño, Moorsel & Castruccio (2017), where calculations of ML algorithms are performed in the cloud (Marston, Li, Bandyopadhyay, Zhang & Ghalsi, 2011). This improves the device resource consumption and makes possible to run more complex algorithms. In this way, the selected algorithm is Autoencoder, a kind on Neural Network, which allows to obtain greater accuracy, while the consumption of resources is also greater. The used dimension to obtain the data is the accelerometer. The obtained results show an EER (Equal Error Rate) of 2% with an auto-encoder training time ranging from 40 to 105 seconds depending on the dataset and an evaluation time of only 5 milliseconds. Another interesting work that is worth considering was performed by Li, Clarke, Papadaki and Dowland (2011). This work compared the results of using phone calls, text messages and used applications as dimensions to recognize the user. Also, the generated vectors on each of these dimensions include data about device location to provide extra information. This study was carried out with 76 volunteers and the vectors of each of them were labelled with the user ID so the study used supervised learning algorithms. The results show an EER of 5.4%, 2.2% and 13.5% for the dimensions of telephone calls, text messages, and used applications, respectively.

An interesting comparison of different used algorithms to perform anomaly detection is performed in (Goldstein & Uchida, 2016). In this article, authors made an exhaustive execution of different ML algorithms on different datasets, to later compare the results in terms of accuracy and execution speed. In the final results of global anomaly detection, One-Class SVM and k-NN stand out, among others. Jorquera et al. (2018) proposed an intelligent and adaptive continuous authentication system for mobile devices. The proposed system enabled real-time users' authentication by considering statistical information from applications, sensors and Machine Learning techniques based on anomaly detection. Several experiments demonstrated the accuracy, adaptability, and resources consumption of their solution. Finally, there was proposed an online bank application as proof of concept, which allows users to perform different actions according to their authentication level. (Nespoli et al., 2019) proposed the PALOT framework, which leverages IoT to provide context-aware, continuous and non-intrusive authentication and authorization services. Specifically, authors proposed a formal information system model based on ontologies, representing the main source of knowledge of the framework. Furthermore, to recognize users' behavioral patterns within the IoT ecosystem, they introduced the confidence manager module. The module is then integrated into an extended version of their early framework architecture, IoTCAF (Nespoli et al., 2018), which is consequently adapted to include the above-mentioned component. Sánchez, Huertas, Fernández, Martínez & Wang (2019) proposed a continuous and intelligent authentication architecture oriented to Smart Offices. The architecture was oriented to the cloud computing paradigm and considers ML techniques to authenticate users according to their behaviors. Some experiments demonstrated the suitability of the proposed solution when recognizing and authenticating different users using a classification algorithm.

Within the industrial field, there are several companies that have developed continuous authentication systems. Currently, BehavioSec (2019) is the existing product on the market that best addresses the problem of continuous authentication. This company offers both a web solution and SDKs for Android and iOS (Degtyar et al., 2008). On mobile devices, the dimensions from which data is extracted are the sensors, touches on the screen and pressed keys. In addition, the evaluation can be done both on the device and in the cloud. This company has received 17.5 million dollars this year as financing to boost its global expansion, the financing has come from a consortium of companies formed by Cisco and others.

Another product that addresses continuous authentication is Zighra (2019). This solution evaluates 6 elements such as location, networks, typing or device sensors. However, no further details on its operation are offered, it is only specified that used ML algorithms are proprietary and the system is patented. In turn, the company BioCatch (2019) offers a continuous authentication module available for both mobile devices and computers, authentication is done through a series of "invisible challenges" to which the user is subjected while using the devices and that they evaluate their behavior. Another commercial solution is Veridium (Veridium Ltd., 2019), which provides an SDK to be incorporated into any business or consumer application. The product offered is based on user recognition through the following dimensions: use of sensors, camera, and device flash, face, thumbprint and 4 fingers TouchlessID (finger identification through interaction with the screen).

Although commercial solutions do not provide much information about their operation and only give information that can serve as marketing for their products, they allow demonstrating the viability of this type of systems in commercial environments since there is a market demand for these types of solutions.

3. METHODOLOGY

One of the key aspects to enable a precise authentication system is the selection of data in charge of creating the users' profiles. This section gives an overview of the most relevant dimensions of mobile devices that can be considered to create accurate users' profiles. Once the dimensions and data are selected, it will be assessed how to treat them to extract relevant information from them and then enter this information as input to the selected ML algorithm. After that, this section will discuss the design of the proposed continuous authentication system and the main scheduled classes and their functionality.

3.1 Input Data or Dimensions

I. Sensors

This dimension is one of the most exploited by previous studies that seek to develop a continuous authentication system. This fact is due to the heterogeneity of the sensors available in a mobile device today, the large amount of data that these sensors can collect and the simple code integration of the operating system operations to access this data. The most common sensors (Android Developers, 2019a) that incorporate mobile devices are:

- **Accelerometer**: This sensor measures the acceleration of the movements that the device is experiencing in an instant, it is measured in m/s2. It obtains data from the three spatial dimensions X, Y, Z. This sensor can be used to detect the inclination and movements, so it can provide information about how the device is held. For this reason, it is considered that the data provided by this sensor could be interesting for the continuous authentication system.
- **Gyroscope**: This sensor measures the device rotation. The collected data is measured in rad/s and obtains data from the three dimensions of space X, Y, Z. This sensor allows obtaining the turning movements to which the device is subjected while it is being used so it is also considered of interest at the time of differentiating the user.
- **Barometer**: This sensor measures the atmospheric pressure the device is receiving. It allows to calculate the height above sea level. It is measured in hPa or mbar. This information is not considered a factor that will be decisive when identifying the user since the values are not defined by who is using the device.
- **Magnetometer**: This sensor measures the intensity of the magnetic field in which the device is located. It is measured in µT and obtains data from the three dimensions of space X, Y, Z. Determining whether this sensor will provide information to identify the user is not as simple as in the previous cases, because this sensor has been used in other projects found in the state of the art (Bo, Zhang, Li, Huang and Wang, 2013) in an initial approach it will be considered as a differentiator. Then, it will be checked whether this data is useful or not.
- **Proximity Sensor**: This sensor measures the relative position, in centimeters, of an object in front of the mobile phone's screen. This data is not considered important since this sensor is usually used to turn off the screen when using the phone in the head during a call or when keeping it in the pocket and it does not provide information that differentiates an abnormal behavior from a common one.

- **Light Sensor**: This sensor measures the brightness of the environment in which the device is located, the data collected is measured in lux, that is, lumen/meter2. This information is usually used to automatically adapt the brightness of the screen and it is not considered differentiating information.
- **Fingerprint Reader**: This sensor collects information about the fingerprint placed on the sensor. It is mainly used to increase the security level of the device when unlocking it. Although this sensor allows to achieve an extra level of security, in continuous authentication environments it is not useful since the user does not use the fingerprint reader once the device has been unlocked and it will not be able to collect data about the user.

In addition, there are other types of sensors in mobile devices, although they are less common, these sensors can be a thermometer, pedometer, heart rate sensor, or humidity, among others. In this work, these sensors are discarded since the data they provide is not considered relevant when differentiating the user.

II. Location

In the location dimension, the variety of data available is much smaller than in the sensor dimension. In this context, the location of the device can be determined in two ways:

- **GPS Coordinates**: Through the device's GPS sensor and the Wi-Fi and telephone networks, it is possible to determine its latitude and longitude geographical location. These two values are basic when establishing the geographic location and therefore indispensable in a system that uses the dimension of the location as a data source.
- **Public IP Address**: Through the public IP of the device it is possible to know if the device has been previously connected to the network, and therefore, know if the location is known. However, to exploit this data there are two fundamental problems. On the one hand, it is necessary to have an Internet connection to know the public IP. On the other hand, the public IP usually is not static and most public IP addresses are dynamic and change from time to time.

Thus, the data extracted from the location dimension will be the geographic coordinates determined by latitude/longitude values through the device's GPS. The acquisition of this data can mean a high battery cost if it is done continuously so it will be necessary to carry out a system design that takes this factor into account.

III. Application Usage Statistics

Application usage statistics is not one of the usual dimensions that different scientific articles and market products found use to check for anomaly detection in user behaviour. After reviewing the state of the art, only two works make use of this dimension, (Patel, Chellappa, Chandra & Barbello, 2016) and (Fridman, Weber, Greenstadt & Kam, 2017). One of the reasons which determine application usage statistics as a dimension to determine the anomalous user behaviour, is due to daily habits and routines that people usually carry out unconsciously, allowing to create a user profile adapted to the use of the device applications.

Some characteristics which can determine the behaviour can be the number of applications opened in the last minute, hour and day, the number of uses of the most used app in the last minute, hour and day, the most used app in the last minute, hour, day, the same/different apps open at the last minute, hour, day, the number of application changes, the bytes sent and received, etc.

In addition, for each of the features mentioned above, there are many combinations that will be carried out in the experiments of the next sections. For example, you can divide the days of the week into working days and holidays. Within this division, it is possible to differentiate between the use of applications during working hours and the use outside working hours.

3.2 Proposed System Design

Once it is determined that relevant features can recognize the user's behavior, next step is to design a system capable of collecting data.

The proposed system has been implemented like a proof of concept developed in Android using Android Studio version 3.0.1 and Java development version JDK8 has been used. One of the fundamentals of system is that it is compatible with all or almost all current Android devices, therefore, after studying the use percentage of each version of the system (Android Developers, 2019b) it is determined that the minimum Android version required will be the 5.0 (API 21). This version is decided on the basis that almost 85% of Android devices use this version or a higher version and that from API 21, and to include previous APIs, numerous code adaptations would have to be made depending on the version. In addition, devices currently leave factory with a minimum version of Android 6.0, so the percentage devices that meet the condition of being higher than API 21 will increase.

I. Services for Data Collection and Modelling

First, it is necessary to model obtained data from sensors and location dimensions to determine vectors' morphology that will be used by Isolation Forest to form a dataset that represents the user and evaluate user's behaviour. Therefore, the provided information by each dimension will be analysed and the calculations that will be carried out on this information will be determined to extract features that characterize the user.

The vectors of each dimension will be evaluated separately and then the result of each evaluation will be normalized and combined. This is because a study has been carried out that has provided satisfactory results on evaluating data separately versus evaluating all data together, and also, this evaluation type has had good results in previous studies (Shi, Yang, Jiang, Yang & Xiong, 2011). This evaluation type also favors the system's extensibility to add new dimensions in the future. In addition, to enrich the generated dataset, so that it better represents the user, two extra fields will be added both in the sensor vectors and in the location vectors: weekday and time. Thus, final dataset can be filtered by schedules, so that training dataset can be better adjusted to user's behaviour under certain conditions.

Next, the morphology of both the sensor vector and the vector with location data will be defined.

On the one hand, the three selected sensors, accelerometer, gyroscope and magnetometer, collect data from three spatial dimensions. Therefore, each reading of each sensor will have 3 coordinates: X, Y, Z. In addition to these three coordinates, in (Ehatisham-ul-Haq et al., 2017) an extra coordinate called "Magnitude" (Mag) is considered, this coordinate is calculated from the 3 collected from the sensor as

$\sqrt{X^2 + Y^2 + Z^2}$. This new coordinate allows quantifying "how big" the other three are. That is, it allows to detect if there have been many movements in all coordinates at the same time (the Mag value is high), or if all coordinates have remained with few changes (the Mag value is low). This work will also calculate this coordinate to later verify its impact by including it in the vectors that make up the dataset.

In this way, the readings on the sensors will give 4 fields: X, Y, Z, Mag. Thus, to detect movements in the device it is not enough to perform a single reading of each sensor from time to time, but it would be necessary to be monitoring continuously all sensors at the same time (Kenda & Mladenic, 2018). This fact is important since it is necessary to find a balance between the number of readings made on the sensor to obtain information and battery consumption. So many readings continuously could cause the device's battery to run out quickly.

Therefore, the proposed solution proposes to carry out periodic cycles of sensors reading along with periods in which no information is obtained, such as monitoring the sensors for 5 seconds and waiting 10 seconds before monitoring again. These 5 seconds of reading the values of the sensors will only be done if device is unlocked, since the objective is to observe user's behaviour and if data were read when the device is locked, strange readings would be registered corresponding to when the device is for example in a pocket, on a table, etc.

During reading time, numerous sets of coordinates will be collected, this number is not fixed and depend on the sensors reading frequency and changes that occur in them. To reduce noise and randomness in coordinate sets, each set will be averaged with the previous and next set, in order to normalize data and peaks in the measurement values.

Although the number of values in the readings set is not fixed, it is necessary to extract a fixed data size to form the sensor data vector from a variable number of coordinates. Therefore, it is decided to calculate from the measurements set that the following elements are carried out periodically:

- Average of each of the coordinates.
- Maximum of each of the coordinates.
- Minimum of each of the coordinates.
- Peak to peak distance (Max-Min) of each of the coordinates.
- Variance of each of the coordinates.

Thus, 20 values are extracted from each reading period on each sensor (4 coordinates * 5 fields). From each of these readings a vector will be generated with the 20 fields of each sensor plus 2 fields of weekday and time. Therefore, each vector with information related to the sensors will have 62 fields in total.

On the other hand, there is the formed vector by the location data. This vector is simpler than the sensor vectors and contains only 4 fields: latitude, longitude, weekday and time. The vector will be generated each time the location of the device is read. It is estimated that a suitable period to read the coordinates of the location is every 5 minutes.

Once the shape of vectors and frequency have been determined, the programming on Android about processes necessary to collect vectors described above will be described in order to form a dataset that models the user. To outline the set of the most important programmed classes in the system, and the relationship among them, Figure 5 shows a diagram of these classes.

To program the services that run periodically it is necessary to make use of the AlarmManager class, which is responsible for launching each service when the waiting time is up, and IntentService, which

Figure 5. Diagram of the main system classes

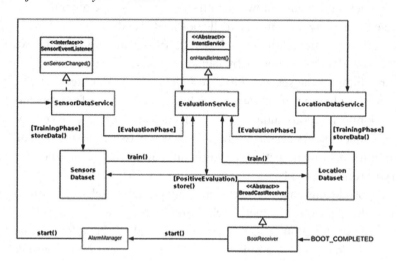

is responsible for the service execution necessary to collect data, model the information in vectors and store them together on the dataset (Android Developers, 2019c).

On the one hand, the classes that inherits from IntentService implement the methods of the Sensor-EventListener class to record the sensor updates that the sensors send to the system. In this class, for 5 seconds the readings from the accelerometer, gyroscope and magnetometer sensors are collected. On the other hand, there is a class collecting the data from the device location and inherits from Intent Service. To launch services automatically when the device is turned on, it is implemented a class that inherits from BroadcastReceiver and receive the BOOT_COMPLETED event, which represents the device's power on.

II. Training and Evaluation of the Proposed System

After collecting data for two weeks, Isolation Forest algorithm will be trained and subsequently evaluate new data that is collected. Therefore, it is necessary to find a library that implements the algorithm.

The reference library in Machine Learning area is Scikit-learn (scikit-learn developers, 2019), written in Python. However, Android uses Java as a programming language, so to use Scikit-learn it would be necessary to use an additional interpreter that would make the algorithm's execution process more complex.

Therefore, another solution is sought to run Isolation Forest in Java. After an investigation into the available libraries, it is concluded that Weka (Weka 3, 2019) is the bookstore that best fits the project. Weka is a free software library that implements numerous algorithms and procedures related to ML, developed and maintained by the University of Waikato, New Zealand.

Another Java service inherits from IntentService and runs every minute. In this class, the last and penultimate collected vectors with sensor information and the last collected vector relative to the location will be obtained, and each vector will be evaluated separately. For this, the service will train an instance of Isolation Forest with each dataset and evaluate with each of them the corresponding vectors.

From each evaluation using Isolation Forest, a value of 0 to 1 will be obtained, which will represent the "normality" of the vector against the vectors set in the dataset. So, a value closer to 1 will indicate that the vector looks more like those present in the dataset than one whose evaluation result is closer to

0. The IF implementation calculates this value by calculating 1-vector anomaly. Each evaluation will have its own range of values, this range will depend on the training dataset that has been used and the anomalies present in it. Thus, to combine different evaluations of different dimensions it is necessary to normalize them according to:

- Once the Isolation Forest algorithm is trained, the set of training vectors is evaluated to verify the values range that the evaluation function can yield as result. This range will go from the maximum to the minimum of the training vector's evaluation results.
- Once the range have been determined, it is estimated that 90% of the training values will represent normal user behaviour. The 10% will correspond to the anomalous situations occurred during the two weeks of training. Then the value that delimits the upper 90% of the range is chosen and set as anomaly threshold.
- Finally, to standardize each evaluation carried out by the system, the following formula will be applied to the result produced by the Isolation Forest algorithm:

$$StandarizedValue = \frac{(EvaluationResult - RangeMin)}{(RangeMax - RangeMin)}$$

If the results of the three evaluations were added directly, the result would be a value of 0 to 3. However, it is decided to weigh the evaluation values since it is considered that the location value has less weight than that of the sensors. This is decided because a user who travels a lot can be usually in new places, which will harm the evaluation result even if it is the authorized user. Therefore, the value of the final result of the evaluation is given by the following equation:

$$FinalEvaluation = (0.4 * uvs) + (0.4 * pvs) - (0.2 * uvl)$$

Being *uvs* the normalized result of the evaluation of the last collected vector from the sensors, *pvs*, the normalized result of the evaluation of the penultimate sensors vector and *uvl*, the normalized result of the evaluation of the last location vector. In this way, the final result will be a value of 0 to 1, much more intuitive to be able to be represented as a percentage if necessary and more precise when identifying the user by the weighting made.

III. Adaptive Continuous Authentication

The system adaptability arises from two different points of view, one of them is the optimization of the dataset that models the user's profile and the other is the filtering of this dataset by schedules to accurately capture routines in the user's behaviour.

To guarantee the adaptability of the user profile to the user's behaviour, when the result value obtained when carrying out the evaluation is high enough and it is above the threshold determined, the evaluated data will become part of the corresponding dataset (the sensor's vectors will go to the sensor dataset and the location vectors will go to the location dataset). In addition, the oldest dataset vectors will be removed at the same rate at which new vectors are added. In this way, the dataset will reflect the last behaviour

Figure 6. Prototype battery consumption

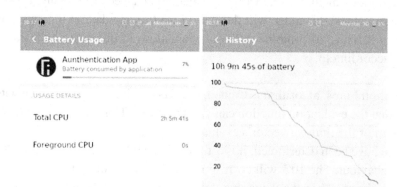

of the user, and thus the performance of the algorithm will not be weighed down by having too much training data. The user's privacy is also preserved by not storing more data than is really necessary for the system to work (Huertas, Gil, García & Martínez, 2014a, 2017, 2014b, 2016).

The other way of the system to adapt itself to the user's behaviour will be to filter the training datasets by hours/days so the datasets can reflect routines such as work or free time. To do this, each vector generated will have a field with the time and another with weekday in which it was generated. These two fields will be used to filter the data and then they will be discarded when performing the model training. In this way, the time and day fields will only be used to filter the dataset and will not harm the final evaluation result.

4. RESULTS

As mentioned in previous sections, battery consumption is a key point in a continuous authentication system, since if consumption is very high, the availability of device will be delayed, and user can end up getting rid of the system to increase device use time. Therefore, once the two weeks of training time is over, battery consumption of prototype application that contains data collection and evaluation services running periodically is monitored.

The average battery consumption is between 7-9% of the total. In Figure 6, there is an example where a device has operated 10 hours and has consumed 7%, having a device battery of 4180 mAh, this is an hourly expense of 4180*0.07/10 = 29 mAh. This consumption is considered acceptable since it is below 1% of the total per hour. In addition, in devices with a smaller battery size, such as 3000mAh, this consumption is still below 1%.

About storage, at the end of the training period there are two files that contain the sensor's dataset and the location dataset, respectively. These files have the following characteristics:

- The sensor vector dataset has a size of 4 MB and contains 13,000 data vectors.
- The location vector dataset has a size of 80kB and contains 3300 vectors.

Figure 7. Dimension normalization graphs. Up sensors, down location

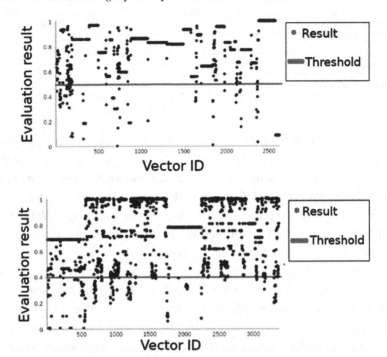

I. First Experiment

In this first experiment, it is desired to check the initial system performance to verify if it is able to successfully identify the user. To do this, after completing the training phase, the evaluation phase results are observed.

With the gathered datasets during training phase, evaluation service calculates the equation which returns the authentication value periodically every minute. In this first experiment, the weekday and hour values are eliminated from both vectors, since the filtering by hours will be done once there is a solid basis about the system performance. Thus, Figure 7 shows two graphs with the results of the training vectors' evaluation (See section 4) for the two dimensions used. This evaluation is carried out to identify the threshold of anomalies, so the vectors that remain below the red line (a threshold that represents the upper 90% value of the range, see section 4), will be the ones that the system treats as anomalies.

The training dataset contains anomalies since for example, during the training phase the system can pick up movements such as taking the phone out of the pocket and add them to the training dataset, so this movement would be abnormal compared to the device normal use. The blue dots in Figure 7 represent each of the evaluated vectors, the value in the Y-axis being the obtained score and the X-axis shows the ID of evaluated vector. In the case of sensors, threshold is defined at 0.501 and in the location case the threshold will be 0.405, for this reason, user authentication threshold will be 0.4818 (0.8 * 0.501 + 0.2 * 0.405).

Table 1. Result values for the first experiment

Person Using the Device	Score
Owner	~0.60-0.95
Owner with anomalous behavior	~0.30-0.70
User moving the smartphone randomly	~0.20-0.55

Once the threshold from which the user is authenticated is defined, the next step is to verify system accuracy. In these tests, different device usages are made, then the result given by the continuous authentication system is checked. After a few tests evaluating user vectors and anomalous conditions, the obtained values in each case are recorded (Score = (0.4 * uvs) + (0.4 * pvs) + (0.2 * uvl)), these results are shown in Table 1. These values represent the obtained results range by each type of user and device usage. Thus, to authenticate a user, the evaluation result must be greater than the authentication threshold determined by combining the threshold of each dimension.

The tests to emulate an anomalous behavior are: 1) hold the device with the left hand when in the training phase it has been used with the right hand, and 2) hold it in a different position than usual. The results of this first experiment are not satisfactory since the result value shows great randomness and is not able to distinguish a legitimate user from an illegitimate one. An illegitimate user can get a score above the threshold, so it would be authenticated by the system. Even random movements of the device show result that can coincide with both a legitimate and illegitimate user and are above the calculated threshold. For this reason, the values that make up the sensor vector are analyzed, as it is the most important dimension when identifying the user.

After studying the values of sensor vector fields, it is observed that data related to the magnetic sensor are completely random in their values. So, the presence of these data in the vector will negatively affect the system performance as the evaluation results become unstable.

II. Second Experiment

After a review on the available data, it is found that the offered data by magnetic sensor are almost random values. So, it is decided to remove the magnetometer data and perform a new system test to check whether the accuracy of this improvement.

Weka has a graphical interface that allows to eliminate and filter fields, so it is not necessary to repeat two weeks of training completely to perform new experiments. With these changes, the evaluation process is repeated to see if the results change and new conclusions can be drawn. After normalizing the new sensor dataset, its threshold is 0.53 (90% higher value), the evaluation plot of all sensor vectors is shown in Figure 8. The location dimension dataset is maintained as in the previous experiment. Therefore, threshold to authenticate the user will be 0.53*0.8+0.405*0.2 = 0.505.

The new obtained results when using the system under different conditions, in the same way as in the first experiment, are those shown in Table 2:

These results are better than ones from the first experiment since there can be seen a bigger difference between when the owner uses the device and if he has an anomalous behaviour.

Figure 8. Normalization dataset graphic of sensors without magnetometer

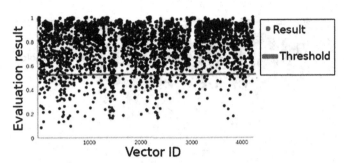

Table 2. Final values of the second experiment

Person Using the Device	Score
Owner	~0.55-0.95
User with anomalous behaviour	~0.25-0.45
User moving the devices randomly	~0.05-0.30

This system shows a sensitive reaction to the changes in the user behaviour. Based on the obtained values in the second experiment, it is confirmed that user will be authenticated when the evaluation result has a value equal to or greater than 0.505, that is, the determined threshold by values normalization.

To improve and guarantee the system adaptability, when evaluation results in a positive value (> 0.505), the evaluated vectors will be added to the training dataset, in this way the continuous authentication system will adapt to changes in behaviour that the owner of the device progressively does. The oldest training vectors will also be eliminated, so the training dataset size is controlled and does not damage evaluation time of a large dataset size.

III. Third Experiment

In the third experiment, the performed tests consist of eliminating different values in the sensor vector and verify the change in the system performance. When eliminating the values referring to the peak to peak distance and variance, it is observed that evaluations results vary tenths up or down compared to the original vector evaluation, but it does not change the result significantly (See Figure 9). Sensor dimension threshold is set at 0.48 in this case. This may indicate that these fields do not offer too much information about anomalies, however, by influencing the final result even if it is slightly decided to keep them in the system, although results will be taken into account for future optimizations.

If the fields relative to the average of the coordinates in each sensor are eliminated, the sensor threshold remains at 0.494 (See Figure 10). However, the evaluation stops working correctly, and the results become much more erratic, as evaluation result of both normal and anomalous behaviour varies by several tenths.

Figure 9. Normalized dataset graph without variance and peak to peak distance

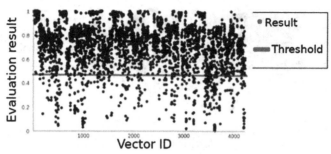

Figure 10. Normalized dataset graph without variance, peak to peak distance and mean

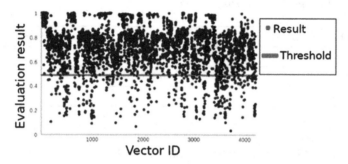

IV. Fourth Experiment

In this fourth experiment, it is pretended to verify if the weekday and time features present in the dataset vectors provide decisive information when performing user evaluation. The next test carried out is to use the date and time data as a feature of the sensor and location vectors. In this case, the threshold for sensor vector is 0.507 and for location vector is 0.415, that is, threshold to authenticate user will be 0.488 (0.8 * 0.507 + 0.2 * 0.415) (See Figure 11).

In this case, system accuracy is negatively affected since known anomalous vectors generated in weekdays and hours when the device had a lot of activity during the training phase get a higher score than in the previous experiment. Even looking at the location normalization graph (Figure 11), peaks in the evaluation result can be observed with the naked eye. This happens because this vector has few fields (only latitude and longitude), so by adding new features, these will greatly affect result. Thus, hours with more activity (phone turned on) will have a higher score regardless of whether location is common or not. In the same way, the legit vectors of the device owner generated in more unusual hours are also impaired. The obtained result values when using system under different conditions, in the same way as in the first experiment, are shown in Table 3:

Therefore, after observing result of this experiment, it is ruled out to use the fields of the hour and day of the week when evaluating the vectors. These fields will be reserved to filter the training dataset at runtime. Therefore, these fields will be removed from the training instances and the evaluated vector when the algorithm will perform the evaluation.

Figure 11. Normalized dataset graphics with time fields as features. Sensors (above) and Location (below)

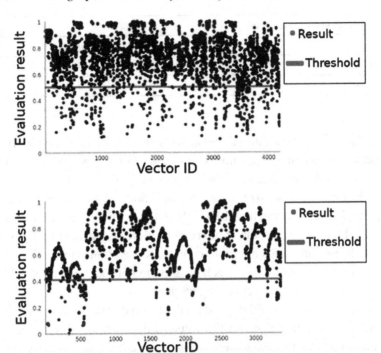

V. Fifth Experiment

The last carried out experiment consists of filtering the training dataset to train the algorithm only with the vectors that belong to the same weekday and have been generated in a range between next hour and the one before the vector to be evaluated. It is sought to check if filtering the dataset by schedules improves the system accuracy by recognizing user routines.

In this case, the result of vectors evaluation shows considerable changes compared to when it is not filtered. In this case, it is more complicated to show the graph with the normalized dataset values since depending on the dataset resulting from the filtering, the algorithm will be trained with a different dataset and this will have a different threshold. To find an average threshold value, 100 generated vectors in different days and hours are evaluated, in order to obtain 100 filtered datasets of each type and check the generated average threshold.

Table 3. Final Values of the fourth experiment

Person Using the Device	Score
Owner at a normal schedule	~0.55-0.95
Owner at an unusual schedule	~0.45-0.75
User with anomalous behaviour at a normal schedule	~0.35-0.65
User with anomalous behaviour at an unusual schedule	~0.05-0.35

Table 4. Final Values of the fourth experiment

Person Using the Device	Score
Owner	~0.60-0.95
Owner with an anomalous behaviour	~0.25-0.45
User moving the devices randomly	~0.05-0.30

In the case of the filtered location dataset, threshold is very unstable and varies from ~0.30 to ~0.70. This situation is because when filtering by hours and days of the week, the size of the training dataset greatly decreases, for example, in the case of the location dataset the size goes from 3300 instances to 21/24. Due to this reduction in dataset size, values concentration of vector fields will present a different pattern when using the dataset set, which will be different according to the time and day.

In the case of filtered sensor dataset, threshold is much more stable between 0.49 and 0.60. The average threshold is 0.54. These thresholds are more constant since phone is usually used in the same way regardless of time. Thus, since thresholds of each dataset are not fixed, the threshold for authenticating the user will not be fixed and will vary depending on them.

As mentioned, score result values will depend on the filtered dataset in each evaluation, however, in the case of a user with anomalous behaviour the values are shown lower in proportion to those of the owner. Thus, it is determined that filtering datasets in proposed way gives the system greater precision for being able to identify more easily whether it is a known user or not. Table 4 shows the values obtained after different executions with different schedules performing the different test cases:

Following the result of this experiment, it is decided to filter dataset when evaluating by weekday and time since difference between score with anomalous behaviour and the owner's score becomes larger and therefore there is less similarity in the outcome. This allows to better differentiate anomalous behaviour from the common one and optimizes the system again.

5. DISCUSSION

The system proposed in this chapter is a novelty in the state of the art since there is no other work that combines data from the sensors with data from the location. As can be seen in Table 5, despite the achieved advances by the previous solutions, these present a series of shortcomings. For example, most systems use classification ML algorithms instead of anomaly detection algorithms. This fact means that the systems cannot detect any intruder and only identify users whose data they have about their behavior. In addition, those that perform anomaly detection do not have as good results as those that use classification algorithms.

In this sense, the proposed solution in this work seeks to improve existing solutions. To do this, it combines two dimensions, such as location and sensors, which are evaluated using unsupervised algorithms to detect anomalies. In addition, it is a system which adapts to changes in user behavior, without forgetting a key aspect such as the consumption of mobile device resources.

Bo, Zhang, Li, Huang and Wang (2013) does not propose system adaptability to new behaviours and does not analyze the resource consumption. In Parreño, Moorsel & Castruccio (2017), mobile device should be connected to the Internet and this is a situation that is not always met. In contrast, the pro-

Table 5. Comparison of the most current solutions

Proposal	Considered Dimensions	Adaptability	Machine Learning Techniques	Results
SilentSense (Bo, Zhang, Li, Huang and Wang, 2013)	Movement and touches on the screen	No	OneClass-SVM SVM	Accuracy: 72.36% FAR: 24.99%
(Ehatisham-ul-Haq et al., 2017)	Sensors accelerometer, magnetometer and gyroscope	No	SVM, Bayes Net (BN), Decision tree (DT), K-Nearest Neighbors (K-NN)	Accuracy: 99.18-93.30% depend on algorithm
SenGuard (Shi, Yang, Jiang, Yang & Xiong, 2011)	Movement, location, voice and touches on the screen	No	Bayesian Networks	Accuracy: 97-95%
(Fridman, Weber, Greenstadt & Kam, 2017)	Location, used applications, web navigation and writing	No	SVM	Accuracy: 95% EER: 5%
(Parreño, Moorsel & Castruccio, 2017)	Accelerometer	Yes	Autoencoder	Accuracy: 97.8% EER: 2.2%
(Li, Clarke, Papadaki and Dowland, 2011)	Calls, text messages and applications	Yes	Classification algorithm	EER: 5.4%, 2.2% y 13.5%, for each dimension, respectively
(Jorquera et al., 2018)	Applications' usage statistics and sensors	Yes	Isolation Forest	Precision: 77% Recall: 92%

posed solution on this work can work offline as it is self-contained on the device. Li, Clarke, Papadaki and Dowland (2011) is the only work which provides information about energy consumption, being this consumption higher than the one on the present work.

Note that the work presented is based on Jorquera et al. (2018) but using other dimensions, so the results are similar regarding the consumption of resources and the algorithms used.

As practical implications, the developed system can be used to improve security on mobile devices, complementing traditional authentication systems and granting an extra level of user privacy. The system is suitable for virtually any smartphone since the data used belongs to sources present in any modern device.

As system limitations, GPS coordinate location does not always work in all environments. Thus, in large cities with buildings that surround the user, the coordinates may be more inaccurate or difficult to determine. Besides, the use of motion sensors can cause the system to not work properly if the user is making unusual movements such as running or other sports.

6. CONCLUSIONS

This work proposes a continuous and adaptive authentication system for mobile devices capable of authenticating a user according to data obtained from the GPS location and the sensors of the device. In turn, the proposed solution can detect changes in the user's normal behaviour to recognize unauthorized persons. The designed system uses unsupervised ML algorithms based on anomaly detection to evaluate user's behaviour concerning its previously known actions. Besides, the system is able to adapt itself over time to changes in the user's behaviour. A proof of concept has been implemented in Android and, after several experiments, data vectors with which the system works have been optimized for correct authentication. In addition, the proposed system adapts to changes in user behaviour depending on the time of day. The resource consumption of the final system is satisfactory in terms of battery consumption (below 1% per hour) and runtime. Complete training and evaluation processes for both dimensions are completed in less than 5 seconds, plus 8 seconds required to read the files that contain the dataset.

As a future route of work, we plan to develop an accurate and efficient continuous authentication system that can be launched as a product that covers a real market need. As a road map to achieve this objective, new dimensions will be analysed to achieve a solution that adapts to different reality scenarios. Possibilities that improve system performance are also assessed, such as calculating ML algorithms in the cloud to save battery and computational resources of mobile devices. Finally, a system evaluation is proposed on a larger scale by using a real environment with voluntary users. The possibility of extending continuous authentication system to other systems such as iOS or desktop environments is also valued in the future.

ACKNOWLEDGMENT

This work has been funded by the Fundación Séneca - Agencia de Ciencia y Tecnología de la Región de Murcia, through the AUTHCODE (AUTHentication for Continuous access On DEvices) project (grant code 20549/PDC/18), and the Government of Ireland, through the IRC post-doc fellowship (grant code GOIPD/2018/466).

REFERENCES

BehavioSec, Inc. (2019). Continuous Authentication through Passive Behavioral Biometrics. Retrieved October 1, 2019, from http://behaviosec.com

BioCatch. (2019). Less friction, Less fraud. Retrieved October 1, 2019, from https://www.biocatch.com/

Bo, C., Zhang, L., Li, X. Y., Huang, Q., & Wang, Y. (2013). SilentSense: Silent User Identification Via Touch and Movement Behavioral Biometrics. In *Proceedings 19th Annual International Conference on Mobile Computing & Networking*, 187-190. 10.1145/2500423.2504572

Broownlee, J. (2016, March 16). Supervised and Unsupervised Machine Learning Algorithms. Retrieved October 1, 2019, from https://machinelearningmastery.com/supervised-and-unsupervised-machine-learning-algorithms/

Degtyar, R., Peri, J. M., Thakkar, J. B., Whittenberger, K. M., Miller, M., Thadani, N. I., & Zaytsev, A. A. (2008). Method and apparatus for building metadata driven software development kit. U.S. Patent 7, 321, 894.

Deutschmann, I., Nordström, P., & Nilsson, L. (2013). Continuous Authentication Using Behavioral Biometrics. *IT Professional*, 15(4), 12–15. doi:10.1109/MITP.2013.50

Developers, A. (2019). Sensors Overview. Retrieved October 1, 2019, from https://developer.android.com/guide/topics/sensors/sensors_overview

Developers, A. (2019). Distribution Dashboard. Retrieved October 1, 2019, from https://developer.android.com/about/dashboards/

Developers, A. IntentService. (2019). Retrieved October 1, 2019, from https://developer.android.com/reference/android/app/IntentService

Deyan, G. (2019, March 28). 60+ Smartphone. *Stat, 2019*. Retrieved from https://techjury.net/stats-about/smartphone-usage/

Ehatisham-ul-Haq, M., Azam, M. A., Loo, J., Shuang, K., Islam, S., Naeem, U., & Amin, Y. (2017). Authentication of Smartphone Users Based on Activity Recognition and Mobile Sensing. *Sensors (Basel), 17*(9), 2043. doi:10.339017092043 PMID:28878177

Fei, T. L., Ming, K., & Zhou, Z. (2008). Isolation forest. In *Proceedings Eighth IEEE International Conference on Data Mining (ICDM)*, 413-422. Academic Press.

Fridman, L., Weber, S., Greenstadt, R., & Kam, M. (2017). Active Authentication on Mobile Devices via Stylometry, Application Usage, Web Browsing, and GPS Location. *IEEE Systems Journal, 11*(2), 513–521. doi:10.1109/JSYST.2015.2472579

Gascon, H., Uellenbeck, S., Wolf, C., & Rieck, K. (2014). Continuous Authentication on Mobile Devices by Analysis of Typing Motion Behavior. *Lecture Notes in Informatics (LNI), Proceedings - Series of the Gesellschaft fur Informatik (GI)*. Academic Press.

Goldstein, M., & Uchida, S. (2016). A Comparative Evaluation of Unsupervised Anomaly Detection Algorithms for Multivariate Data. *PLoS One, 11*(4). doi:10.1371/journal.pone.0152173 PMID:27093601

Huertas, A., García, F. J., Gil, M., & Martínez, G. (2016). SeCoMan: A Semantic-Aware Policy Framework for Developing Privacy-Preserving and Context-Aware Smart Applications. *IEEE Systems Journal, 10*(3), 111–1124.

Huertas, A., Gil, M., García, F. J., & Martínez, G. (2014). Precise: Privacy-aware recommender based on context information for cloud service environments. *IEEE Communications Magazine, 52*(8), 90–96. doi:10.1109/MCOM.2014.6871675

Huertas, A., Gil, M., García, F. J., & Martínez, G. (2014). *What Private Information Are You Disclosing? A Privacy-Preserving System Supervised by Yourself* (pp. 1221–1228). Paris, France: IEEE Intl Conf on High Performance Computing and Communications.

Huertas, A., Gil, M., García, F. J., & Martínez, G. (2016). MASTERY: A multicontext-aware system that preserves the users' privacy. In *Proceedings NOMS IEEE/IFIP Network Operations and Management Symposium*, 523-528.

Huertas, A., Gil, M., García, F. J., & Martínez, G. (2017). Preserving patients' privacy in health scenarios through a multicontext-aware system. *Annales des Télécommunications, 72*(9-10), 577–587. doi:10.100712243-017-0582-7

Jorquera, J. M., Sánchez, P. M., Fernández, L., Huertas, A., Arjona, M., De Los Santos, S., & Martínez, G. (2018). Improving the Security and QoE in Mobile Devices through an Intelligent and Adaptive Continuous Authentication System. *Sensors (Basel), 18*(11), 3769. doi:10.339018113769 PMID:30400377

Kenda, K., & Mladenic, D. (2018). Autonomous Sensor Data Cleaning in Stream Mining Setting. *Business Systems Research*, *9*(2), 69–79. doi:10.2478/bsrj-2018-0020

Li, F., Clarke, N., Papadaki, M., & Dowland, P. (2011). Behaviour Profiling for Transparent Authentication for Mobile Devices. In *Proceedings 10th European Conference on Information Warfare and Security, ECIW. (p. 307). Academic Conferences International Limited.*

Marston, S., Li, Z., Bandyopadhyay, S., Zhang, J., & Ghalsasi, A. (2011). Cloud computing—The business perspective. *Decision Support Systems*, *51*(1), 176–189. doi:10.1016/j.dss.2010.12.006

Nespoli, P., Zago, M., Huertas, A., Gil, M., Gómez, F., & García, F. J. (2018). A Dynamic Continuous Authentication Framework in IoT-Enabled Environments. In *IoTSMS'18: Proceedings of the 5th International Conference on Internet of Things: Systems, Management, and Security*, Valencia, Spain. 10.1109/IoTSMS.2018.8554389

Nespoli, P., Zago, M., Huertas, A., Gil, M., Gómez, F., & García, F. J. (2019). PALOT: Profiling and Authenticating Users Leveraging Internet of Things. *Sensors. Special Issue on Sensor Systems for Internet of Things*, *19*(12), 2832.

Omar, S., Asri, Md., Jebur, H., & Benqdara, S. (2013). Machine Learning Techniques for Anomaly Detection: An Overview. *International Journal of Computers and Applications*, *79*(2).

Parreño, M., Moorsel, A., & Castruccio, S. (2017). Smartphone Continuous Authentication Using Deep Learning Autoencoders. In *Proceedings 15th International Conference on Privacy, Security and Trust*, 147-1478. Academic Press.

Patel, V. M., Chellappa, R., Chandra, D., & Barbello, B. (2016). Continuous User Authentication on Mobile Devices: Recent Progress and Remaining Challenges. *IEEE Signal Processing Magazine*, *33*(4), 49–61. doi:10.1109/MSP.2016.2555335

Sánchez, P., Huertas, A., Fernández, L., Martínez, G., & Wang, G. (2019). Securing Smart Offices through an Intelligent and Multi-device Continuous Authentication System. In *Proceedings of the 7th International Conference on Smart City and Informatization*. Guangzhou, China: Springer Computer Science Proceedings.

scikit-learn developers. (2019). Scikit-learn: machine learning in Python. Retrieved October 1, 2019, from http://scikit-learn.org/stable/index.html

Shi, W., Yang, J., Jiang, Y., Yang, F., & Xiong, Y. (2011). SenGuard: Passive user identification on smartphones using multiple sensors. In *Proceedings IEEE 7th International Conference on Wireless and Mobile Computing, Networking and Communications (WiMob)*, 141-148. IEEE.

Turulja, L., & Bajgoric, N. (2018). Knowing Means Existing: Organizational Learning Dimensions and Knowledge Management Capability. *Business Systems Research*, *9*(1), 1–18. doi:10.2478/bsrj-2018-0001

Veridium Ltd. (2019). Biometric Authentication Technology - Fingerprint, Face, Camera, Sensors. Retrieved October 1, 2019, from http://veridiumid.com/biometric-authentication-technology/mobile-authentication

Wayman, J., Jain, A., Maltoni, D., & Maio, D. (2005). An Introduction to Biometric Authentication Systems. In *Biometric Systems* (pp. 1–20). London, UK: Springer. doi:10.1007/1-84628-064-8_1

Weka 3. (2019). Data Mining Software in Java. Retrieved October 1, 2019, from https://www.cs.waikato.ac.nz/ml/weka/

Winkler, I. (2016, January 13). The threat of shoulder surfing should not be underestimated. Retrieved October 1, 2019, from https://www.csoonline.com/article/3021882/security/the-threat-of-shoulder-surfing-should-not-be-underestimated.html

Ženko, Z., Mulej, M., & Potocan, V. (2017). Knowledge-cum-values Management belongs to the Way out from Global Crisis. *Business Systems Research*, 8(1), 113–123. doi:10.1515/bsrj-2017-0009

Zighra. (2019). Smart Identity Defense. AI-Powered Continuous Authentication and Fraud Detection. Retrieved October 1, 2019, from https://zighra.com/

Chapter 2
Improved Transmission of Data and Information in Intrusion Detection Environments Using the CBEDE Methodology

Reinaldo Padilha França
State University of Campinas (UNICAMP), Brazil

Yuzo Iano
State University of Campinas (UNICAMP), Brazil

Ana Carolina Borges Monteiro
State University of Campinas (UNICAMP), Brazil

Rangel Arthur
State University of Campinas (UNICAMP), Brazil

ABSTRACT

To anticipate threats, the Intrusion Detection System (IDS) enables the collection and use of information from various types of attacks to defend an entire network infrastructure. Therefore, this chapter develops a method of data transmission based on discrete event concepts, due to the fact that in this digitally globalized world, networks deal with a huge set of data all the time. Data refers to facts, events, actions, activities, and transactions which have been and can be recorded, i.e., the raw material from which information is produced, nurturing the infrastructure and components that enable modern computing. This methodology was named CBEDE and experiments were matched in the MATLAB software, where the memory consumption was evaluated, presenting great potential to intermediate users and computer systems. Results showed better computational performance related to memory utilization related to the compression of the information, showing an improvement reaching up to 114.39%.

DOI: 10.4018/978-1-7998-2242-4.ch002

Copyright © 2020, IGI Global. Copying or distributing in print or electronic forms without written permission of IGI Global is prohibited.

INTRODUCTION

The popularization of the computer in the 80's and 90's made the world go through a real "technological revolution", where such a machine came to play a fundamental role in the lives of all people. In this way, large companies using financial networks and communication systems became increasingly dependent on computer systems, and to this day the advancement of technology has brought innumerable benefits and facilities to society as a whole (Amichai-Hamburger, 2017)

Cloud Computing is a technology that has come to improve the quality and interaction of communication, revolutionizing the way organizations, and people consume technology where no effort is required on the part of users in the management or maintenance of the applications in use, the cloud is effectively infinite in size, so you do not have to worry about running out of capacity, and access to cloud-based applications and services can be done from anywhere, all you need is a device connected to the internet, so such as the use of memory and the storage and computing capacity of computers and servers can be hosted in online datacenter and interconnected through the Internet.

Another current modern technology is Internet of Things, which has been growing rapidly in the field of telecommunications, related to wireless telecommunications, where its main goal of the interaction and cooperation between things and objects send data through the wireless networks with the objective set to them as a combined entity. However, one should not forget or even lose focus on the security issues of both technologies, in particular, examining the common features, and in order to discover the benefits of their integration (Gupta, Agrawal & Yamaguchi, 2016; Stergiou, Psannis, Kim & Gupta, 2018).

There are several tools that contribute significantly to improving the security of a network, ranging from encryption, establishing a real level of protection for data; to the use of Firewalls, which establish logic in the input and output of the network controlling the traffic at the level of data packets [2]. Thus, the Intrusion Detection System (IDS) deserves special mention because it encompasses the process of monitoring, identifying and reporting the occurrence of malicious activities, unauthorized activities that put at risk and target technology assets of a network of computers (Kenkre, Pai & Colaco, 2015).

The constant evolution of computer technology and telecommunications is making Internet access increasingly broad and fast, since these innovations and increasing popularity of smart cities, video analytics (ie in this modern world of media eocial, entertainment, surveillance, smart health monitoring, crowd management, among others) are used in a range of application domains to provide safety, security, and wellness for residents, creating a scenario with perfect conditions for cloud computing (Gupta, Agrawal & Yamaguchi, 2016; Hossain, Muhammad, Abdul, Song & Gupta, 2018).

With cloud computing, many applications, as well as files and other related data, no longer need to be installed or stored on the user's computer or on a nearby server. Where such video analytics, for example, are shared through highly interconnected devices, sensors, and other smart city stakeholders, security and integrity is concerned with secure video content, and provided there is no proper techniques to address the security threats of such transmission and sharing, is very difficult for the smart city government to provide safety and quality-of-life to its residents, where their personal and private contents become available in the clouds, that is, in the internet (Hossain, Muhammad, Abdul, Song & Gupta, 2018; Gupta, 2018).

By migrating such information to a cloud platform, the first concern for managers is the security of everything that has been archived. The cloud, on the other hand, stands out in the ease of access, and can happen at any time through several platforms, from notebooks and desktops to mobile devices such as tablets and cell phones (Dutta et al., 2018).

In the same way, intrusion prevention system (IPS) are tools that are used to sniff out malicious activity occurring over a network and / or system, having among its main functions to find malicious activity, recording and reporting information about the malicious activity, and trying to block / stop the activity from occurring, which expand on the capabilities of intrusion detection systems (IDS), which serves the fundamental purpose of monitoring network and system traffic (Peng, Choo & Ashman, 2016).

Thus, the first IDS model, called IDES (Intrusion Detection Specialist System), was developed in the 1990s, based on the hypothesis that the basis of an intruder's behavior is not the same as that of a legitimate user. Thus, the model attempts to create a pattern of user behavior in relation to programs, files, and devices, both in the long term and in the short term. And after the IDES, were developed many other systems were developed, based on an approach that combined statistics and expert systems. Conceptually, the IDS refers to a mechanism capable of identifying or detecting the presence of intrusive activities, and in a broader concept, encompasses all the processes used in the discovery of actions and unauthorized uses of devices contained in the network or even computers. However, we must point out the difference between IDS, Intrusion Prevention System (IPS). While the former is software that automates the process of intrusion detection, the latter does intrusion prevention, which aims to prevent possible attacks (Kenkre, Pai & Colaco, 2015; Peng, Choo & Ashman, 2016; Duhan & Khandnor, 2016).

Information security is an increasingly important issue, which over the last few years has gone behind the scenes to become a news bulletin in various media outlets. Business is increasingly connected, people are increasingly connected. Being a universe of data, information, knowledge, and experiences being transited, transmitted, stored, centralized or not, highly distributed, by small and large content providers, and digital infrastructure. The benefits brought by the internet, the evolution of the devices, where there is no reason to go back, are unquestionable. With each passing day, new techniques for compromising computing environments are created, and it is increasingly a challenge for the information security market to keep up with that speed, and even to be on the front line reactively (Peltier, 2016).

Therefore, the implementation of a good IDS policy is fundamental in security architecture. This resource must be constantly updated, being able to keep the infrastructure away from opportunistic attacks, either from a network perspective, or by the very commitment of a computer within the organization. So, combining so many network-based and host-based intrusion detection and prevention systems is essential for good security health, be it organization, institution or company. Focusing this protection prioritizing the three aspects of the information being confidentiality, integrity, and availability.

Based on this, the present chapter aims to show the development and performance of a model of information transmission based on discrete event concepts, the methodology employed aims to increase the performance in sending and receiving data between environments protected with IDS or IPS, if it is an application in the transmission channel, results to consuming less computational memory during this process. Next, we will discuss the concepts of methodologies that contribute to the development of the CBEDE methodology (Coding of Bits for Entities by means of Discrete Events).

INTRUSION DETECTION SYSTEM (IDS)

Network security is a topic that is always well discussed by Information Technology managers and analysts, since every year that happens, large investments are made to protect the privacy, integrity, and availability of information. All this because of the increasing attacks and kidnappings of data that reaches to diverse people and companies around the world, being this with each passing day becomes more and more digital

(Kenkre, Pai & Colaco, 2015; Hossain, Muhammad, Abdul, Song & Gupta, 2018; Snapp et al., 2017).

Intrusion Detection System (IDS) is an intrusion detection system that allows the collection and use of information of the various types of attacks to defend an entire network infrastructure, allowing the identification of points or attempted intrusions, allowing registration and enabling the continuous improvement of the security environment (Kenkre, Pai & Colaco, 2015).

IDS refers to the technical means of discovering in a network the unauthorized accesses that may or may not indicate the action of a cracker in execution, installed or sent by external third parties to the organization or even of malicious employees. Related to the strong growth of digital infrastructure technologies in both services and network protocols, it is becoming increasingly necessary to deploy an intrusion detection system, is closely linked not only to the speed with which technologies advance, but the complexity of the means used to increase the security of data transmissions. Thus, IDS refers to a mechanism that stealthily hears the traffic on the network to detect abnormal or suspicious activity and, thus, reduce the risks of intrusion [7]. Intrusion detection systems can be categorized into four groups, ranging from the type of event they monitor to the way they are deployed. There are two distinct families of IDS: Network-Based Intrusion Detection System, which guarantees security within the network and the Host-Based Intrusion Detection System, which ensure security on the host (Hossain, Muhammad, Abdul, Song & Gupta, 2018).

Network-Based IDS are those that monitor network traffic on a segment or device, and analyzes the network and protocol activity to identify suspicious behavior, malicious activity on the network, such as service-based attacks, port scans, and so on. Being effective and able to detect numerous types of events of interest. They are usually deployed in a security topology as a border between two networks, where traffic is tapered, often being directly integrated into the firewall (Subba, Biswas & Karmakar, 2016; Meng, Tischhauser, Wang, Wang, & Han, 2018).

They are installed on machines responsible for identifying attacks directed at the entire network, monitoring the contents of data packets or traffic and their details as header and protocol information. Acting with major goals to detect if someone is trying to enter the system or if any legitimate user is misusing it. They need unique hardware and constitute a system capable of checking the information packets that circulate in one or more network connections to find out if any malicious or abnormal activity is taking place, for this type of IDS one or more network adapters are placed system in anonymous mode so that they do not have an IP address or an associated protocol stack. In general, they operate as "probes" outside the network to study possible attacks, as well as operate in the same way as internal "probes" to analyze queries that have passed through the firewall or that were carried out internally (Subba, Biswas & Karmakar, 2016; Meng, Tischhauser, Wang, Wang, & Han, 2018).

Host-based IDSs are computers or servers working as hosts to alert and identify attacks and attempts to gain access to the machine itself, being more employed in cases where security is focused on information contained in a server and users are not need to be monitored, since the term refers to equipment or asset itself. Its detection, in this format, monitors device characteristics and the events that happen with it in search of suspicious activity (Chawla, Lee, Fallon & Jacob, 2018; Zaidi, Milojevic, Rakocevic, Nallanathan & Rajarajan, 2016; Deshpande, Sharma, Peddoju & Junaid, 2018)

They can be installed individually for both corporate computers within a corporate network and endpoints. Its main features include network traffic to the device, processes running, system logs, and access and change in files and applications, and are essential for the security of the organization. However, it does not observe the traffic passing through the network, its use is to verify the information related to the events and logs and filesystem records (permission, change, etc.), being applied in networks where the transmission speed is very high as in "Gigabit Ethernet" networks or when you do not trust the corporate security of the network where the server is installed (Chawla, Lee, Fallon & Jacob, 2018; Zaidi, Milojevic, Rakocevic, Nallanathan & Rajarajan, 2016; Deshpande, Sharma, Peddoju & Junaid, 2018).

In general, host-based IDS is a specific host and is related to software that covers a large part of today's operating systems, such as Windows, Solaris, Linux, and more. Usually by analyzing the specific information stored in the logs (syslogs, messages, lastlog, wtmp, etc.) and capturing network packets that enter / leave the guest to detect signals and possible signs of intrusion (such as denial of service attacks, backdoors, Trojans, attempts of unauthorized access, execution of malicious code, attacks by profusion of buffer, among others) (Chawla, Lee, Fallon & Jacob, 2018; Zaidi, Milojevic, Rakocevic, Nallanathan & Rajarajan, 2016; Deshpande, Sharma, Peddoju & Junaid, 2018).

Knowledge-based IDS (or by Signature), is based on a database that recognizes the signature of previously identified vulnerabilities. It is of the utmost importance that the structure has a policy of continuous and uninterrupted updating of this database, guaranteeing the continuity of environmental security. On the principle that what is not known cannot be protected. This type of IDS parses system activities by looking for events that match predefined patterns of attacks and other malicious activities, such patterns are known as signatures, and each signature generally corresponds to an attack. A disadvantage of this detection technique is that it can detect only known attacks, that is, that are included in the set of subscriptions (database) that the IDS has, thus needing constant updating in view of the speed that new attacks appear (Kazanjian, Drazin & Glynn, 2017).

Differently, from the above, the behavior-based IDS (or by Anomalies), analyzes the traffic behavior and follows a standard line of normal system activity. In case of occurrence, there are deviations from this pattern, with the possibility of being an intrusion, some actions can be taken, such as temporary blocking of traffic or alarms to a network operating nuclei, thus enabling a better investigation of the anomaly, being released or permanently blocked (Saracino, Sgandurra, Dini & Martinelli, 2018; Mitchell & Chen, 2015).

This type of IDS assumes that attacks are actions other than the normal activities performed by the systems, assembling a profile that represents the routine behavior of a user, Host and/or network connection. Monitoring the network and using multiple metrics to determine when the monitored data is out of order, i.e., bypassing the profile. A disadvantage of this type of IDS is the generation of a large number of false alarms related to the unpredictable behavior of users and the system itself (Saracino, Sgandurra, Dini & Martinelli, 2018; Mitchell & Chen, 2015).

An active IDS is defined as one that is programmed to automatically block suspicious attacks or activities that are known to you without any need for human (external) intervention, and proper standardization is necessary and important in protected environments in order to minimize false positives (blocking connections that are legitimate, thus causing disruptions to the organization, for example). Acting in an automatic mode, not only detecting suspicious or malicious traffic and alerting the administrator, but also having predefined actions to respond to the appearance of threats. In general, it means blocking all traffic from the suspicious IP or from the malicious user (Rathore, Ahmad & Paul, 2016).

A passive IDS performs the monitoring of the traffic passing through it and thus identifies potential attacks or abnormalities, generating alerts for network administrators and security, but unlike the active one, without affecting in any aspect in the communication, that is, taking no attitude towards the possible attack itself. Regardless of not directly acting on prevention, it has the utility of acting as a good thermometer for attacks and possible unauthorized attempts to access the infrastructure of an organization (Maske & Parvat, 2016).

Finally, an intrusion detection system (IDS) is a system that monitors network traffic for suspicious activity and issues alerts when such activity is discovered, while they are capable of taking actions when malicious activity or anomalous traffic is detected, and others can take action based on rules when malicious activity is detected for example blocking certain traffic. Having as benefits from the ability to identify security incidents, giving companies greater visibility across their networks, making it easier to meet security regulations, can be used to help analyze the quantity and types of attacks, and thus organizations can use this information to change their security systems or implement more effective controls, in the same way, that they can also help companies identify bugs or problems with their network device configurations, helping in the evaluation of possible future risks (Kenkre, Pai & Colaco, 2015; Carlin, Hammoudeh & Aldabbas, 2015).

Intrusion Prevention System (IPS)

An intrusion prevention system (IPS) also monitors network packets for damaging network traffic by observing packet flow across the network and acting similarly to an Intrusion Detection System (IDS), attempting to identify suspicious data in network packets with based on a database of signatures, or detect anomalies compared to what is predefined as "normal" traffic. But where an intrusion detection system responds to potentially malicious traffic by logging the traffic and issuing warning notifications, intrusion prevention systems respond to such traffic by rejecting the potentially malicious packets (Farhaoui,2016).

In addition to its IDS functionality, an IPS can do more than just generate logs and alerts. It is possible to program it to react to what it detects, and its ability to react to detections is what makes IPS more desirable than IDS. IPS is a system of prevention and protection against intrusions and not just a simple system of recognition and alerts, like most IDS. However, IPS and IDS are branches of the same technology because they have no way to have prevention without detection (Anwar et al., 2017).

Unlike an intrusion detection system (IDS), network intrusion prevention systems (IPS) are capable of dropping or blocking network connections that are determined to be risky for the organization. The difference between a network-based IDS and a network-based IPS resides mainly in two main features, the IPS lies on a line within the IPS network and does not passively listen to the network as an IDS (usually placed as a ports on the network) and still have the ability to immediately block intrusions without worrying about the type of transport protocol used and without reconfiguring an external device, and can filter and block packets in native mode using techniques such as dropping offensive packets or the blocking of an intruder (drop connection, drop offending packets, block intruder, among others) (Nagasundaram et al., 2017; Rathore et al., 2016).

The main functions of IPS are to monitor network traffic, identify malicious activity, generate log information about such activities and try to block or stop them. In an active system, IPS responds to suspicious activity by terminating a user session or by reprogramming the firewall to block network traffic from a malicious source considered suspicious. IPS technologies provide several benefits to organizations, such as detects and stops attacks that other security controls can not; supports customization of detection capabilities to stop activity that is only of concern to a single organization; and reduces the amount of network traffic reaching other security controls, which both lowers the workload for those controls and protects those controls from direct attacks (Peng, Choo & Ashman, 2016; Farhaoui, 2016).

Unlike an IDS which simply detects and reports on threats, an IPS is meant for what its name implies, i.e., prevent intrusions, adding a layer of security works as a complement to other network security components. Usually getting directly behind the system's native firewall and providing a complementary layer of analysis that negatively selects harmful content. IPS has a number of detection methods to find explorations, but signature-based detection and anomaly-based detection are the two dominant mechanisms (Peng, Choo & Ashman, 2016; Farhaoui, 2016; Anwar et al., 2017).

However, there are some disadvantages to an IPS because it is designed to block certain types of traffic, identified as potentially dangerous. It does not have the ability to understand the logic of the web application protocol. Thus, it can not completely distinguish whether a request is normal or malformed at the application layer (considering the OSI layer). Where such a limitation could potentially allow the passage of some types of attacks without being detected or prevented, especially new types of attacks more sophisticated and without signatures. IPS, usually do not implement solutions directly, and thus they interact with firewalls and applications by adjusting settings, automatically implement defense strategy on detection of an alert condition. However, incorrectly setting up an IPS or leaving it poorly calibrated can cause havoc and bring your legitimate network activity to a standstill (Aziz, Amin, Ismael & Bu, 2017).

Discrete Events

Discrete events encompass the study of simulation models whose variables change state instantaneously at specific points of time, that is, the state of the system changes only at the instant that an event occurs, for all other instants of time, nothing changes in the system, in contrast to continuous models, whose variables can change state continuously over time. Systems with discrete events encompass systems with medium to a high level of detail, is generally applied for modeling systems with a low level of abstraction (Brito, Trevisan & Booter, 2011).

The event is defined as the instant occurrence that can change the state of the system, represented in system as a sequence of operations performed on entities (transactions) of certain types such as data packets, or bits in the case of this chapter, considering only events where there is system change, that is, the elapsed time between state changes of the system is relevant to obtain the results, because the system changes to its lingo, emphasizing that the discretization refers to the occurrence of events over time (Chahal & Eldabi, 2010).

Discrete events have three fundamental concepts, being events, entities and time, having a high degree of complexity, which allows the modeling of any type of system, being classified as an occurrence sequence, each responsible for the change in the state of the system, generating data and consequently the information. The universe of actions that provide events is subjective and depends on the ability of the modeler to abstract the events of this universe in which the system is being modeled. This technique has been used to model concepts with a high level of abstraction, such as people waiting in a queue at a bank, messages transmitted through a communications channel, task or processes executed in a computer system, parts of a manufacturing system, even vehicles on a road network and so forth, ie, the entire extent of a communication system (Brito, Trevisan & Booter, 2011; Chahal & Eldabi, 2010).

In Figure 1, simple logic of a sequence of discrete events is shown, where from e1 to e4 represents the states of a system. From X1 to X5 the events themselves are presented, and from t1 to t4 the times in which these events occurred, seeking to clarify the understanding of the interaction between events and the state of the system over time. The events (e1, e2, e3, e4) depend on the actions that cause the state changes (X1, X2, X3, X4, X5) resulting in the evolution of the states in a certain period of time (t1, t2, t3, t4).

Figure 1. Events chart

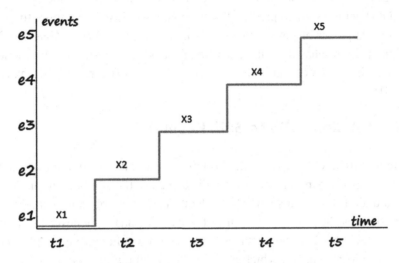

Entities

Discrete Events is seen as a set of entities, that is, they are objects that constitute the model, that move through the system and its behavior is tracked. The entities interact and are part of the system, which determines the sequence of interactions, such as create the events which change the state of the system. Systems are seen primarily from the point of view of entities, each entity can be seen and analyzed individually, depending on the point of view that one wishes to evaluate. Thus, the discrete items of interest in a discrete event simulation are defined, their meaning depends on what is modeled, and the type of system used (Padilha, 2018; Lane, 2000).

It is important to emphasize that the concepts of entities and events are different, whereas events are instantaneous discrete incidents that can change the state variable, an output, and/or an occurrence from another event, in turn, an entity is the object of interest controlled by the system, which is somewhat dependent on what is modeled and the type of system. Thus, the characteristic of a discrete event signal indicates that something (e.g., an accident, an earthquake, a fault, a control, a person, a heartbeat, or any other desirable concept within a system) occurred. So, an event is a conceptual notation that denotes a state change in a system, in this view, the discrete event modeling allows to perform discrete changes within a system (Padilha, 2018; Lane, 2000).

AWGN Channel

The communication channel is the medium responsible for providing the physical connection between transmitters and receivers in a communication system, either a wire or for a logical connection in a multiplexed medium, for example to radio channel in telecommunications networks and computers, it is worth to emphasize the importance of the construction of mathematical models that faithfully reflect the main characteristics of these media and the changes that they introduce in the signals that are transmitted (Tozer, 2012; Rama Krishna, Chakravarthy & Sastry, 2016).

Noise is a term normally used to refer to an unwanted signal, which interferes with the transmission, one of them is the thermal noise by the virtue of the movement of the electrons in the electronic circuit, disturbing the processing of the signal in the communication system, where such noise is generally of a random nature and it is not possible to predict its value at a given instant of future time. A broadly used model applicable to a large set of physical channels is the Additive White Gaussian Noise (AWGN) channel model. This modeling has the characteristic of introducing a statistically modeled noise, such as a white Gaussian additive process, into the transmitted signals (Tozer, 2012; Rama Krishna, Chakravarthy & Sastry, 2016).

DBPSK (Differential Binary Phase Shift Keying)

In DBPSK (Differential Binary Phase Shift Keying) modulation, its modulation format can be differentiated by encoding the data by similarity or by the difference of the symbols in relation to the previous signal, being a modulation scheme responsible for facilitating non-coherent demodulation, a variation of the PSK, where there is the 180 ° inversion in the carrier phase whenever bit 0 occurs. However, PSK (Phase Shift Keying) modulation generally requires only coherent demodulation. This coherent demodulation is related to the carrier, which is modulated to obtain the signal in the passband (Tozer, 2012; Couch II, 2013).

In the DPSK modulation, in turn, there is the modification of the transmissions so that each signal also depends on the previous one, in the demodulation of the current signal is dependent on the signal received in the previous time period, and can be used as the local carrier, where the phase of that modulated signal is shifted relative to the phase element of the previous signal. It is a form of modulation in which the information of the digital signal is embedded in the phase parameters of the carrier. In this modulation system, when there is a transition from a bit 0 to a bit 1 or a bit 1 to a bit 0, the carrier wave undergoes a phase change of 180 degrees Tozer, 2012; Couch II, 2013).

DBPSK, as well as BPSK modulation, are widely used in wireless LAN, RFID and Bluetooth communication applications, as well as are used for long-distance wireless communication, is a modulation technique in most of the adaptive modulation technique adopted in cellular communication. It has great use with CDMA, WiMAX (16d, 16e), WLAN 11a, 11b, 11g, 11n, Satellite, DVB, Cable modem among many others, regarding the difference of 180 degrees between two constellation points, withstand the severe amount of channel conditions. This modulation scheme is used by most of the cellular towers for long distance communication or transmission of the data, its demodulation process requires to make only two decisions in order to recover original binary information, which is very simple compared to other modulation types, in the same way that it requires less power to transmit the carrier with less number of bits, which makes it a power-efficient modulation technique (Padilha, 2018; Tozer, 2012; Couch II, 2013).

METHODOLOGY

The development of this methodology was performed in a computer with hardware configuration being an Intel Core i3 processor, containing two processing cores, Intel Hyper-Threading Technology, and 4GB RAM. To provide enhancements in secure environments, the present study implements a model CBEDE applied to a communication system, and advanced modulation format DBPSK (Differential Binary Phase Shift Keying) in a simulation environment, the Simulink simulation environment of the MATLAB software, improving the transmission of data, through a pre-coding process of bits applying discrete events in the signal before of the modulation process.

Figure 2. Traditional model of a telecommunication system

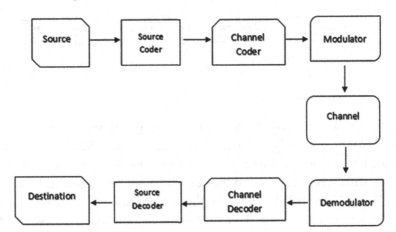

The experiments were conducted through the Simulink tool, from Matlab (2014a). This simulation environment was chosen because it is already consolidated in the scientific medium, having a development and simulation environment already tested and validated. DBPSK and BPSK modulation were chosen in this chapter, because are considered the most robust of modulation schemes in terms of noise immunity, is less immune to the interference, allowing the highest level of distortion in the signal being still successfully demodulated.

Four libraries were used: (1) Communications System ™, which is designed to design, simulate and analyze systems, being able to model dynamic communication systems; (2) the DSP System ™ that is capable of designing and simulating systems with signal processing; (3) Simulink®, which is a block diagram environment for multi-domain simulation, capable of supporting system-level projects for the modeling and simulation of telecommunication systems, and (4) the library SimEvents®, which is classified as a discrete event simulation mechanism and components to develop systems models oriented to specific events In this way, the proposed methodology is based on the development of an AWGN hybrid channel, characterized by the introduction of the discrete event technique in the bit generation process, focusing on bit 1.

In the proposed model, Figure 2, the signals corresponding to bits 0 and 1 will be generated and modulated with the advanced modulation format DQPSK, which will use the phase shift, coming from the modulation format itself. It will then proceed to an AWGN channel according to the parameters shown in Table 01. The signal will then be demodulated to perform the Bit Error Rate (BER) calculation of the channel. The values obtained for BER will be sent to the MATLAB workspace.

The modeling according to the proposal implemented with discrete events is similar to the one presented previously, differentiating that in this model by the addition of discrete events in the pre-coding phase. The proposed bit precoding was implemented through the discrete event methodology. Bit processing is understood as the discrete event methodology in the step of generating signal bits (information) to make it more appropriate for a specific application.

The event-based signal is a signal susceptible to treatment by the SimEvents® library, and posteriorly passed by conversion to the specific format required for manipulation by the Simulink® library. Both time-based signals and event-based signals were in the time domain. This treatment had an emphasis on bits 1 and 0, which were generated as a discrete entity and followed the parameters as presented in

Figure 3. Proposed bit precoding

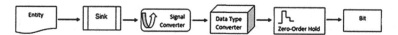

Table 1. Then, Entity Sink® represents the end of the modeling of discrete events by SimEvents library. This tool is responsible for marking the specific point in which Entity Sink will be located, where later the event-based signal conversion will be performed for a time-based signal. This time-based signal was converted to a specific type that followed the desired output data parameter, an integer, the bit. By means of the Real-World Value (RWV) function, the actual value of the input signal was preserved. Then a rounding was performed with the floor function. This function is responsible for rounding the values to the nearest smallest integer.

Also used to a Zero-Order Hold (ZOH) which is responsible for defining sampling in a practical sense, being used for discrete samples at regular intervals (Dragotti, Vetterli & Blu, 2007). The ZOH describe the effect of converting a signal to the time domain, causing its reconstruction and maintaining each sample value for a specific time interval. The treatment logic on bits 1 and 0 is shown in Figure 3.

Subsequently, the signal is modulated with the advanced modulation format DBPSK and is inserted into the AWGN channel. After the signal will pass through the server, it is being converted back to its original format while maintaining its sampling period. The signal modulated in DBPSK and inserted into the AWGN channel, and then demodulated for the purposes of calculating the BER of the signal. The relative values of the BER are sent to the Matlab workspace in the name variable "yout1" to verify equality and generate the BER graph of the signal, as shown in Figure 4.

In the proposed model, Figure 2 and 4, the signals corresponding to bits 0 and 1 will be generated, respecting the rule and mathematical logic shown in Figure 5 below.

This rule and mathematical logic with respect to PSK M-ary numbers generate randomly distributed integers in the interval [0, M-1], where M is the definition for bit representation, following the nomenclature of the MATLAB software. Figure 6 shows the respective generation of the bits by means of this logic.

Figure 4. Model of a telecommunication system with the proposal

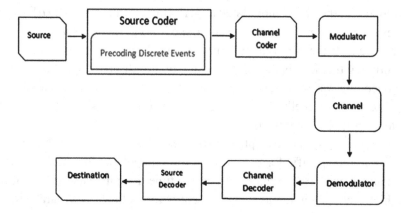

Figure 5. Generation M-ary numbers for bits 0 and 1

$$[0,M-1] \rightarrow [0,2-1] \rightarrow 0,1$$

Figure 6 - Traditional model of a telecommunication system

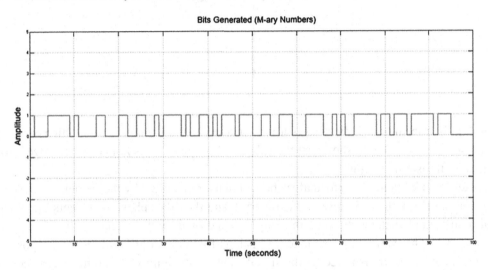

The models are shown in Figures 2 and 4 run with 10000 seconds of simulation and will respect the configuration defined according to Table 1.

The verification of equality of the signals is performed through the "size" and "isequal" functions of the Matlab software, as well as through the bit error rate (BER). These functions are responsible for the mathematical comparison proving that the signals have the same size and the same size. Together with the BER check, it will state that the same amount of information will be transmitted (bits) in both the proposed methodology (hybrid AWGN channel) and the conventional methodology (AWGN channel). Thus, if the signals are of the same size and size, the logical value 1 (true) is returned and the same

Table 1. Parameters channel models DBPSK

AWGN DBPSK	
Sample Time	1 sec
Simulation time	10000 sec
Eb/N0	0 a 14 dB
Symbol period	1 sec
Input signal power	1 watt
Initial seed in the generator	37
Initial seed on the channel	67

Figure 7. Theoretical DBPSK constellation

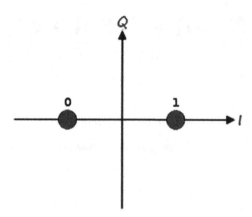

volume of data is transmitted, indicating that the equality of the signals is true. Otherwise, the value will be 0 (false). This check will show that the submitted proposal does not add or remove information to the originally transmitted signal.

The constellation has a function to analyze both signals transmitted by the models. In the case of the DBPSK constellation, a phase represents the binary 1 and the other phase represents the binary 0. As the digital input signal changes its state, the output signal phase will be changed between two angles separated by 180°. This validation methodology has as function to affirm that the proposal will not modify the amount of bits transmitted by the signal, since both signals transmitted in the conventional channel and in the channel containing the proposal of this study, will be of the same size. In Figure 7 the DBPSK constellation diagram.

RESULTS AND DISCUSS

The research presented in this section shows an AWGN transmission channel with DBPSK modulation, being used the Simulink simulation environment of the MATLAB. The model from Figure 8 incorporates the traditional method (left) and the proposed innovation of this chapter (right) is presented, showing the signal transmission flow (corresponding to bits 0 and 1), is generated and then modulated in DBPSK, passing through the channel AWGN. Figures 9 display the constellations for 14 dB for the proposed (left) and the traditional methods (right).

The models developed were investigated from the perspective of memory consumption evaluation. The first simulation of both models in each command is analyzed, since it is in the first simulation that the construction of the model in a virtual environment is performed from scratch, it is in it where all the variables of the model are allocated, the memory of the operating system in which the MATLAB is running is reserved for the execution of the model and the results of this model, according to the evaluation parameters are, in fact, real.

Thus, the experiments considered memory consumption. For memory calculation, the "sldiagnostics" function will be used, where the "TotalMemory" variable will receive the sum of all the memory consumption processes used in the model, by the "ProcessMemUsage" parameter. This parameter counting the amount of memory used in each process, throughout the simulation, returning the total in MB

Figure 8. Transmission flow for DBPSK

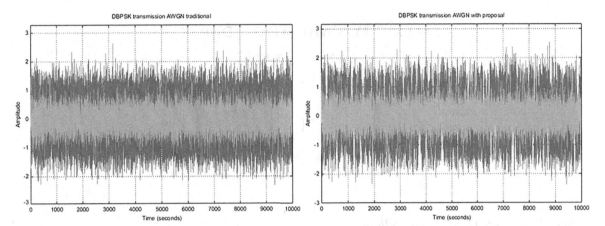

(megabyte). For this was used a computer with hardware configuration being an Intel Core i3 processor, containing two processing cores, Intel Hyper-Threading Technology, and 4GB RAM. This machine relates the proposal to the dynamics of the real world and will affirm its efficiency and applicability.

For this, physical machines with hardware configuration were used, consisting of an Intel Core i3 processor and 4GB RAM, as previously discussed. The experiments were carried out through 4 simulations of each model developed in order to develop the analysis of this chapter, as shown in Figure 10.

The results obtained by the "size" and "isequal" functions, the DQPSK modulation were analyzed through its constellation, by means of the "compass" function, which will display a compass graph with *n* arrows, and how the constellations will be PSKs, their representations of points will be radial. This feature, the graph format has a compass shape, where n is the number of elements in Z. The location of the base of each arrow will be its origin. In turn, the location of the tip of each arrow will be determined by the real and imaginary components of Z, relative to the constellation of the signal. In the same way and with the same intention will be used the diagram of the constellation.

In the Figure 11 is shown the comparison between a traditional methodology and the CBEDE methodology. In this context, the traditional methodology corresponds to a channel without discrete events

Figure 9. Simulated DBPSK constellations

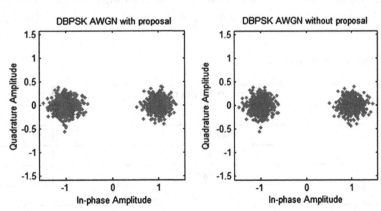

Figure 10. First simulations (memory) model DBPSK

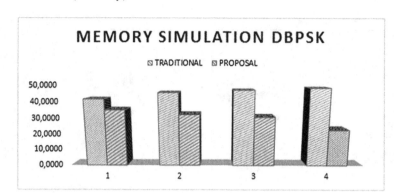

Figure 11. Simulated DBPSK constellation

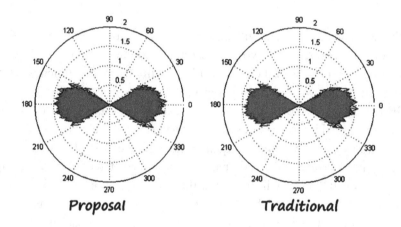

As important as developing the methodology is an improvement of the transmission of a signal that shows better performance, is to make the know-how available to the academic community, as well as to contribute to the area of study of the proposal as well as the theme that this chapter deals with.

The respective amounts of memory consumption shown in Figure 10 are found previously are in Table 2:

To analyze the relationship between the simulation methodology (proposed x traditional method), and the impact on the physical layer of the channel, scripts were made in the MATLAB for processing

Table 2. Amounts of memory consumption

	TRADITIONAL	PROPOSAL
Simulation		
1	41,6211	35,0195
2	45,5703	32,1836
3	47,1836	30,7070
4	48,4805	22,6133

Figure 12. BER between the models DBPSK

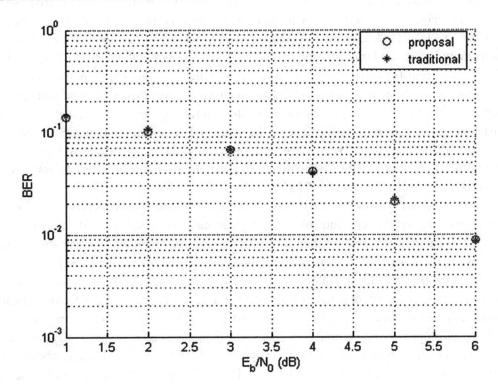

of the graph BER. Figure 12 display the performance of the models during transmission with noise ranging from 0 to 6 dB.

This proposal brings a new approach to signal transmission. In this case, the transmission is performed in the discrete domain with the implementation of discrete entities in the bit generation process.

An undeniable fact is that Cloud Computing technology gains more and more space and notoriety among people, where it differs from the availability of a storage service, a de-bureaucratization of systems used by companies and organizations, which add convenience, ease and optimization in the time of these services.

In this issue, the CBEDE methodology fits in favor of greater effectiveness and efficiency in this environment, which requires a better data transmission and is more fluid. Improving internal and external communication, streamlining services, collaborative work and reducing costs and generating better results by companies that opt for the deployment and use of the most secure cloud computing technology.

Currently, the computer reaches all levels of society, being used in practically all professions, from students, researchers, to professionals who handle budgets, spreadsheets, financial transactions, among other files. Just like any other resource, cloud computing requires attention and care to ensure its best, most efficient, and above all, safe use, and in this scenario to be sure, both individuals and organizations, to use securely solutions such as IDS or IPS, which can certify security and ensure data integrity, in the same way the CBEDE methodology used together in secure IDS-based systems, propitiates and leverages a better interaction between users or security administrators, improving data transmission by ensuring the security and compliance of business-critical applications (Dutta et al., 2018).

And additional basic measures to ensure the security of data availability, such as certification of the use of safe and reliable tools, control over who and when access certain documents, the science of what is being talked about and shared, being of fundamental importance that the cloud provider has an accessibility of communication and transmission of data and agile and light information, subject to CBEDE, that guarantees the security of all its infrastructure, thus offering advantages in supporting applications of different levels of confidence in a same virtual data center, certifying correct segmentation and employing trusted zones in all applications, having visibility and control over network communications between virtual machines, and ensuring scheduling of applications and policies based on IDS or centralized or non-Host-based IPS or not, with a focus on the workloads that will be protected, as well as taking a view of the overall security scope of all secure online infrastructure, even reaching IP addresses or VLANs on the network as a whole (Dutta et al., 2018).

In this way is possible to increase the capacity of information transmission for communication systems. Given the above, the technique of discrete events can be applied in the treatment of bits in its generation stage, being responsible for their conversion into discrete entities. This process is the result of a methodology used in a lower level of application, which acts on the physical layer, than the already used, usually in the transport layer. Able to reduce the consumption of computational resources, such as memory, which is an important parameter to meet the needs of an increasingly technological world.

As previously stated, security is a broadly aborted issue from business to common users. Just as important as protecting your data is notifying your security organ when there are intrusions in a system, since no computer security methodology can be considered 100% secure. Thinking about this, when there is an invasion of a system, be it user data, bank data or business data, it is imperative that there be speed in the transmission of the alert and the data related to a security breach. In this context, CBEDE can be seen as an auxiliary security tool, because through it it is possible to transmit data faster, with lower computational and efficient costs.

In addition, the low memory consumption of the CBEDE methodology is a matter of great importance, since memory consumption is a quantity directly proportional to the rate of crashes in a system. When the subject is security, auxiliary tools should occupy little computational memory in order not to hamper the performance of security programs. In this regard, the CBDE methodology presents lower memory consumption reaching up to 114%, which makes it totally viable in security environments.

FUTURE RESEARCH DIRECTIONS

Future work on the CBEDE methodology includes possible developments in communication systems with discrete events modeling the behavior of the transmitted and received data packets (on normal conditions, possible suspicions or under attack) linked to IDS techniques, since the discrete event technique allows such modeling as a sequence of events, in the same way as performing simulations on a wider variety of hardware, including other types of processors, such as Intel Dual Core, Intel i5 and Intel i7, testing even more the performance of the proposed data transmission, which has already proved positive.

CONCLUSION

Whether it is to monitor and analyze suspicious activity on the network or perform infrastructure auditing, according to existing vulnerabilities, an intrusion detection system becomes essential to optimize the security controls of the organization and better understand the attempts and vectors of attacks that have been emerging and evolving over time. As such, this chapter demonstrates that it has great potential in the improvement of the environments that are employed by IDS or IPS technologies, since it improves the flow of data transmission and consequently the communication services. As well as improving already existing processes can increase the performance of communication response between all the devices in the system and in the protected environment, because the flow of data will consume fewer resources and, therefore, can improve the interactions between all the users.

In this chapter, was shown a methodology for data communication channels that results in a better performance in the transmission of information, making it more fluid from the computational point of view, which directly impacts the data transmission flow between corporate networks, for example, which have an enormous volume of data, being in a protected environment, whether with IDS or IPS, that analyzes, evaluates and guarantees the security of this transmission, not having possible interruptions by bottlenecks, either in sending or receiving.

Thus, the differential of this work of research, was the use of discrete events employed in the physical layer of transmission medium, the lowest level of abstraction possible within a communication system, the bit itself, is done in bit generation, resulting better computational performance with respect to memory utilization related to the compression of the information, showing an improvement of 114.39%, making the protected environment with IDS or IPS more productive, faster and with better performance.

Finally, information compression is a byproduct, since the proposal acts on the bits, that is, the information transmitted, analyzed and evaluated by the IDS / IPS systems, such result have the substantial impact on the compression methods performed in higher layers in the communication system, for example, affecting all the media information (data or information or media of the most varied types) that can be transmitted, resulting in a higher quality of both sending and receiving.

REFERENCES

Amichai-Hamburger, Y. (2017). *Internet psychology: The basics*. Routledge. doi:10.4324/9781315622163

Anwar, S., Mohamad Zain, J., Zolkipli, M. F., Inayat, Z., Khan, S., Anthony, B., & Chang, V. (2017). From intrusion detection to an intrusion response system: Fundamentals, requirements, and future directions. *Algorithms*, *10*(2), 39. doi:10.3390/a10020039

Aziz, A., Amin, M., Ismael, O. A., & Bu, Z. (2017). U.S. Patent No. 9,756,074. Washington, DC: U.S. Patent and Trademark Office.

Brito, T. B., & Trevisan, E. F., E. F. C., & Booter, R. C. (2011). A Conceptual Comparison Between Discrete and Continuous Simulation to Motivate the Hybrid Simulation Technology. In *Proceedings of the 2011 Winter Simulation Conference*, 3915-3927. Academic Press.

Carlin, A., Hammoudeh, M., & Aldabbas, O. (2015). Intrusion detection and countermeasure of virtual cloud systems-state of the art and current challenges. *International Journal of Advanced Computer Science and Applications, 6*(6). doi:10.14569/IJACSA.2015.060601

Chahal, K., & Eldabi, T. (2010). A multi-perspective comparison between system dynamics and discrete event simulation, *Journal of Business Information Systems,* pp. 4-17.

Chawla, A., Lee, B., Fallon, S., & Jacob, P. (2018, September). Host based intrusion detection system with combined cnn/rnn model. In *Proceedings Joint European Conference on Machine Learning and Knowledge Discovery in Databases* (pp. 149-158). Springer, Cham.

Couch, L. W., II. (2013). Digital and Analog Communication Systems, 8th Edition, Prentice Hall, 2013.

Deshpande, P., Sharma, S. C., Peddoju, S. K., & Junaid, S. (2018). HIDS: A host-based intrusion detection system for cloud computing environment. *International Journal of System Assurance Engineering and Management, 9*(3), 567–576. doi:10.100713198-014-0277-7

Dragotti, P. L., Vetterli, M., & Blu, T. (2007). Sampling Moments and Reconstructing Signals of Finite Rate of Innovation: Shannon Meets Strang-Fix. *IEEE Transactions on Signal Processing, 55*(5), 1741–1757. doi:10.1109/TSP.2006.890907

Duhan, S., & Khandnor, P. (2016). Intrusion detection system in wireless sensor networks: A comprehensive review. In *Proceedings 2016 International Conference on Electrical, Electronics, and Optimization Techniques (ICEEOT)* (pp. 2707-2713). IEEE. 10.1109/ICEEOT.2016.7755187

Dutta, U. K., Razzaque, M. A., Al-Wadud, M. A., Islam, M. S., Hossain, M. S., & Gupta, B. B. (2018). Self-adaptive scheduling of base transceiver stations in green 5G networks. *IEEE Access: Practical Innovations, Open Solutions, 6*, 7958–7969. doi:10.1109/ACCESS.2018.2799603

Farhaoui, Y. (2016). How to secure web servers by the intrusion prevention system (IPS)? *International Journal of Advanced Computer Research, 6*(23), 65–71. doi:10.19101/IJACR.2016.623028

Gupta, B., Agrawal, D. P., & Yamaguchi, S. (Eds.). (2016). *Handbook of research on modern cryptographic solutions for computer and cyber security.* IGI Global. doi:10.4018/978-1-5225-0105-3

Gupta, B. B. (Ed.). (2018). Computer and cyber security: principles, algorithm, applications, and perspectives. Boca Raton, FL: CRC Press.

Hossain, M. S., Muhammad, G., Abdul, W., Song, B., & Gupta, B. B. (2018). Cloud-assisted secure video transmission and sharing framework for smart cities. *Future Generation Computer Systems, 83*, 596–606. doi:10.1016/j.future.2017.03.029

Kazanjian, R. K., Drazin, R., & Glynn, M. A. (2017). Implementing strategies for corporate entrepreneurship: a knowledge-based perspective. Strategic entrepreneurship: Creating a new mindset, 173-199.

Kenkre, P. S., Pai, A., & Colaco, L. (2015). Real time intrusion detection and prevention system. In *Proceedings of the 3rd International Conference on Frontiers of Intelligent Computing: Theory and Applications (FICTA) 2014* (pp. 405-411). Springer, Cham. 10.1007/978-3-319-11933-5_44

Lane, D. C. (2000). You Just Don't Understand Me. Working Paper, London School of Economics, Operational Research Group.

Maske, S. A., & Parvat, T. J. (2016, August). Advanced anomaly intrusion detection technique for host based system using system call patterns. In *Proceedings 2016 International Conference on Inventive Computation Technologies (ICICT)* (Vol. 2, pp. 1-4). IEEE. 10.1109/INVENTIVE.2016.7824846

Meng, W., Tischhauser, E. W., Wang, Q., Wang, Y., & Han, J. (2018). When intrusion detection meets blockchain technology: A review. *IEEE Access: Practical Innovations, Open Solutions, 6*, 10179–10188. doi:10.1109/ACCESS.2018.2799854

Mitchell, R., & Chen, R. (2015). Behavior rule specification-based intrusion detection for safety critical medical cyber physical systems. *IEEE Transactions on Dependable and Secure Computing, 12*(1), 16–30. doi:10.1109/TDSC.2014.2312327

Nagasundaram, S., & Aissi, S. (2017). U.S. Patent No. 9,665,722. Washington, DC: U.S. Patent and Trademark Office.

Padilha, R. (2018). Proposta de Um Método Complementar de Compressão de Dados Por Meio da Metodologia de Eventos Discretos Aplicada. In *Um Baixo Nível de Abstração. Dissertação (Mestrado em Engenharia Elétrica)*. Campinas, SP, Brasil: Faculdade de Engenharia Elétrica e de Computação, Universidade Estadual de Campinas.

Peltier, T. R. (2016). *Information Security Policies, Procedures, and Standards: guidelines for effective information security management*. Auerbach Publications. doi:10.1201/9780849390326

Peng, J., Choo, K. K. R., & Ashman, H. (2016). User profiling in intrusion detection: A review. *Journal of Network and Computer Applications, 72*, 14–27. doi:10.1016/j.jnca.2016.06.012

Rama Krishna, A., Chakravarthy, A. S. N., & Sastry, A. S. C. S. (2016). Variable Modulation Schemes for AWGN Channel based Device to Device Communication. *Indian Journal of Science and Technology, 9*(20), DOI: 10.17485 / ijst / 2016 / v9i20 / 89973.

Rathore, M. M., Ahmad, A., & Paul, A. (2016). Real time intrusion detection system for ultra-high-speed big data environments. *The Journal of Supercomputing, 72*(9), 3489–3510. doi:10.100711227-015-1615-5

Saracino, A., Sgandurra, D., Dini, G., & Martinelli, F. (2018). Madam: Effective and efficient behavior-based android malware detection and prevention. *IEEE Transactions on Dependable and Secure Computing, 15*(1), 83–97. doi:10.1109/TDSC.2016.2536605

Snapp, S. R., Brentano, J., Dias, G., Goan, T. L., Heberlein, L. T., Ho, C. L., & Levitt, K. N. (2017). DIDS (distributed intrusion detection system)-motivation, architecture, and an early prototype.

Stergiou, C., Psannis, K. E., Kim, B. G., & Gupta, B. (2018). Secure integration of IoT and cloud computing. *Future Generation Computer Systems, 78*, 964–975. doi:10.1016/j.future.2016.11.031

Subba, B., Biswas, S., & Karmakar, S. (2016, March). A neural network based system for intrusion detection and attack classification. In *Proceedings 2016 Twenty Second National Conference on Communication (NCC)* (pp. 1-6). IEEE. 10.1109/NCC.2016.7561088

Tozer, E. P. (2012). *Broadcast Engineer's Reference Book* (1st ed.). FOCAL PRESS. doi:10.4324/9780080490564

Zaidi, K., Milojevic, M. B., Rakocevic, V., Nallanathan, A., & Rajarajan, M. (2016). Host-based intrusion detection for vanets: A statistical approach to rogue node detection. *IEEE Transactions on Vehicular Technology*, *65*(8), 6703–6714. doi:10.1109/TVT.2015.2480244

Chapter 3
Machine Learning Techniques for Intrusion Detection

Tameem Ahmad

Department of Computer Engineering, Z.H. College of Engineering and Technology, Aligarh Muslim University, Aligarh, India

Mohd Asad Anwar

Department of Computer Engineering, Z.H. College of Engineering and Technology, Aligarh Muslim University, Aligarh, India

Misbahul Haque

Department of Computer Engineering, Z.H. College of Engineering and Technology, Aligarh Muslim University, Aligarh, India

ABSTRACT

This chapter proposes a hybrid classifier technique for network Intrusion Detection System by implementing a method that combines Random Forest classification technique with K-Means and Gaussian Mixture clustering algorithms. Random-forest will build patterns of intrusion over a training data in misuse-detection, while anomaly-detection intrusions will be identiðed by the outlier-detection mechanism. The implementation and simulation of the proposed method for various metrics are carried out under varying threshold values. The effectiveness of the proposed method has been carried out for metrics such as precision, recall, accuracy rate, false alarm rate, and detection rate. The various existing algorithms are analyzed extensively. It is observed experimentally that the proposed method gives superior results compared to the existing simpler classifiers as well as existing hybrid classifier techniques. The proposed hybrid classifier technique outperforms other common existing classifiers with an accuracy of 99.84%, false alarm rate as 0.09% and the detection rate as 99.7%.

DOI: 10.4018/978-1-7998-2242-4.ch003

Copyright © 2020, IGI Global. Copying or distributing in print or electronic forms without written permission of IGI Global is prohibited.

INTRODUCTION

Intrusion detection, a very important aspect from security point of view, can be said to be the process of monitoring the events that occur in an individual computer system or over a computer network and investigating for any intrusions taking into account the confidentiality, integrity and availability of a computer system or other network infrastructure security properties (Chahal & Kaur, 2016). An intrusion causes the confidentiality violation, if it allows intruders to access system information without authorization (password authentication). If an intruder changes the system date or any data residing on or passing through the system, it causes the integrity violation. An availability violation will occur if an intrusion keeps an authorized user from accessing the particular service or system resource when he needs it. The major task of intrusion detection is to gather data that may contain evidences of intrusions, from target system, processing and analyzing the data to identify the potential intrusions thereafter generating the specified responses for every intrusion either manually or automatically.

Intrusion Detection System

Main function of Intrusion Detection System (IDS) is to monitor network traffic for any doubtful activity and if any, then alerts the system or network administrator. In some cases, IDS can take active action (i.e. it may discard the packet incompatible) or passive action (i.e. to alert the system) for malicious traffic by imposing action such as blocking users or source IP addresses from reaching the network. As soon as a new computer searches for a security vulnerability, a crowd of crackers starts knocking on the doors of computers around the world so that they can see whether they can enter their security or not. Many sites employ a combination of boundary router firewalls and host-based packet filters and wrappers to protect themselves, but what is the vulnerability in many systems used to secure the service? How do system administrators know that their machines are being attacked and/or compromised? The best way to catch crackers is to use IDS. Figure 1 shows a Computer Network with Network Intrusion Detection System.

Figure 1. Computer network with network intrusion detection system

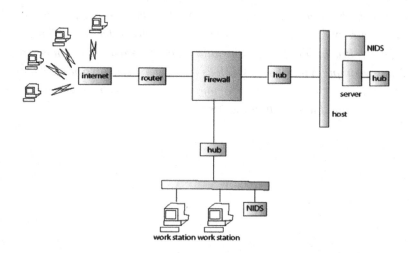

Need for Intrusion Detection System

A computer system should provide confidentiality, integrity and assurance against various types of attacks. However, due to the increasing connectivity especially on the Internet and the huge open spectrum of financial prospects, more and more systems are under attack by intruders. The presence of IDS allows preventing subversion by building a completely secure system. It, for example, requires all users to identify and authenticate themselves. Further, the data can be protected by employing various cryptographic methods and very tight access control mechanisms. However this is not really feasible because:

- Practically, building a completely secure system is not possible (Kumar, Mangathayaru, & Narsimha, 2016).
- Even Cryptographic methods possess certain kind of problems. User passwords can be cracked, users can lose their passwords, and there are ways to break the entire crypto-systems.
- Even a truly secure system is vulnerable to abuse by insiders who misuse their privileges.
- It has been seen that there is an inverse relationship between the levels of access control to the user efficiency, which implies that the stricter the mechanisms are, the lower will be the efficiency.

So, using cryptography method or simply putting a firewall may not be enough to solve problem of vulnerabilities. If there is an attack on the system, they should be identified as soon as possible and appropriate action must be taken.

Types of Intrusion Detection System

The prime goal of IDS is to detect the suspicious traffic coming over the network in various ways. IDS come in a variety of "flavors" and approach. Network based and host based are the two basic categories of IDS.

- **Network Intrusion Detection Systems (NIDS):** Since the traffic from all devices on the network is to be monitored, NIDS is placed on a strategic point or inside the network. Ideally it will scan all inbound and outbound traffic; however, doing this may potentially ruin the network for the overall speed (Elngar, El, Mohamed, & Ghaleb, 2013). In this kind of systems, several hosts can be under scrutiny with single IDS giving a better clarity of threat situation, thus making it more cost effective than Host IDS. Within the network, NIDS work as a separate entity in the network which makes it very tough to compromise its security.
- **Host Intrusion Detection Systems (HIDS):** HIDS runs on individual hosts or devices over the network. A HIDS only monitor the incoming and outgoing packages of the particular device and whenever a suspicious activity is spotted, it alerts the network administrator or the user (Lichodzijewski, Nur Zincir-Heywood, & Heywood, 2003). HIDS typically monitor the log files, resource usage and error messages on a host. The lower false-positive rate makes it more accurate as compared to NIDS in intrusion detection. As HIDS are local to a particular host, having HIDS on every host is not feasible in most cases.

Techniques of Intrusion Detection

Some IDS looks for specific signature of known threats while some compare traffic pattern against a baseline for anomalies for detecting intrusions. The detection methods are normally divided into two categories as signature-based and anomaly-based intrusion detection model.

- **Signature Based:** Also called as misuse detection, a signature-based IDS monitor packets on the network and compare them against signatures or attributes stored in a database from known malicious threats (Duque & Omar, 2015). This is similar to the way the malwares are detected by most of the antivirus software.
- **Anomaly Based:** This kind of IDS monitors network traffic and compare it against an established baseline (Lippmann & Cunningham, 2000). The baseline will identify what is "normal" for that network such as what sort of bandwidth is generally used, the kind of protocols that are being used, which port and device generally gets connected; and alert the administrator or user when traffic is detected as anomalous, or significantly different from the baseline.

In this work, we perform a comparative study of decision tree, Naïve Bayes, and k-mean clustering-based intrusion detection systems and proposes a new hybrid classifier for hybrid Machine learning based intrusion detection technique.

The organization of the rest of the paper is as follows. Section II contains an overview of KDD 99 dataset along with its different components used in our work. Section III presents the earlier research works that have been carried out in similar field of study. Different machine learning techniques have been discussed in Section IV while the proposed hybrid k-mean clustering and random forest-based IDS is discussed along with the idea and steps of implementation in Section V. Section VI presents the result, the evaluation metrics and the estimating methods considered. At last, we conclude our work and discuss some future prospects.

RELATED WORK

This section discusses about existing Techniques for intrusion detection system. Consequently a study of the background of different machine learning techniques, supervised and unsupervised are discussed. Beside that some author used hybrid approach for Intrusion Detection in order to increase the detection rate.

The general notion of Intrusion-detection-system was initially proposed (Kumar et al., 2016). The author contemplated in his report that all the assessment of computer must be distorted and should be able to furnish internal risk and threats for computer safety technicians, and also recommended that in order to examine the behaviour of the user and to identify the masquerades, signiðcant method must be applied. And later Mehmood & Rais (2016) proposed a prototype of IDES (Intrusion Detection System), and the work was considered as a great statistics breakthrough in intrusion detection ðeld.

Using a machine learning technique, Duque & Omar (2015) proposed a framework for security which have low-overhead for a NoC-based custom multicore architecture. This work mainly targets on three attacks, namely, core address spoong attacks, route looping and traffic diversion. In their study, they experimented using SVM with supervised and unsupervised machine learning techniques and found that the most of supervised machine learning methods shows 90 percent accuracy for anomaly while unsupervised techniques are not able to detect Trojans. To test the frame-work, they implemented Attack-Insertion-Module. For the three above mentioned attacks, there proposed framework obtaining 97 percent detection accuracy.

Pan, Morris, & Adhikari (2015) presented an automated and systematic approach to build a hybrid IDS which precisely categorize normal control operations, cyber-attacks and disturbances. This ID was trained by common path mining algorithm. This algorithm improves traditional machine learning algorithms and is appropriate mainly for a power system with large volume of data. At present, the common path mining-based IDS algorithm builds common path from the captured data logs. This paper does not deal with capturing data logs for real systems. The IDS was evaluated only by offline assessment of test datasets and does not concentrate on real time classiôcation.

In order to enhance the accuracy and to minimize the false-alarm rate, proposed an integrated machine algorithms and Nave Bayes (Yassin, Udzir, Muda, & Sulaiman, 2013). The experimental results shows 99.0 per cent of accuracy which is high compared to previous studies using same approach, but the false alarm rate is very high at 2.2 percent. Tahir et al. (Mehmood & Rais, 2016), combined K-means clustering algorithm with support vector machine to obtain the hybrid intelligent system, and were able to obtain accuracy of 96.24 per cent and alarm rate was 3.72 per cent.

Thaseen & Kumar (2014) applied random forest algorithm in the detection of anomaly, hybrid and misuse. They evaluated the proposed methodology over dissimilar datasets gained from KDD'99 datasets and observed that the newly proposed algorithm produces better result over the other best-known KDD'99. In the misuse detection approach, it uses offline phase to build intrusion patterns. For better accuracy, feature selection algorithm is used and to increase the detection rate sampling techniques are used. This misuse detection framework does not detect novel intrusions, so the new method for anomaly detection was proposed. After applying the random forests algorithm the outlier detected each considered to be intrusions. The results are compared with unsupervised anomaly detection approaches and found that this newly proposed approach produces higher detection rate. But the problem noticed in this approach was as the number of attack connection increases the detection of attack reduced drastically. To encounter this, a new framework was proposed by combining the anomaly and misuse detection for random forest algorithm and known as hybrid framework. In this hybrid approach, the detection performance of anomaly approach is improved by ôrst applying the misuse detection approach to ôlter the known intrusions. Though, there may be possibility that new type of intrusion may emerge and may have several connections, which may not be detected by misuse approach. Thus this will lead to the poor performance of anomaly detection approach.

DATA SET DESCRIPTION

We have considered the dataset KDD Cup 99 (Stolfo, 1999) for intrusion detection in our study. The 1999 KDD intrusion detection dataset emerged from DARPA 98 dataset. The MIT Lincoln Labs organized the 1998 DARPA Intrusion Detection Evaluation Program (Laboratory, 1998) with the objective of surveying and evaluating research in intrusion detection. The 1998 DARPA initiative was the base for KDD 99 intrusion detection datasets which provides the developers a benchmark for evaluating different methodologies. A huge amount of raw TCP dump data was acquired by the environment that was set up by the Lincoln Labs for a LAN simulating a typical U.S. Air Force LAN. They operated the LAN assuming it to be a true Air Force environment by peppering it with multiple attacks. From 7 weeks of network traffic it was about four gigabytes of compressed binary TCP dump data collected for training and was processed into about 5 million records.

In 1999, in International Knowledge Discovery and Data Mining Tools Competition, pre-processing of original TCP dump files was carried out to utilize it in the Intrusion Detection System benchmark (Tameem Ahmad, Ahmad, & Jamshed, 2016; Li, 2004). The packet information in dump files was grouped into connections. A connection, labelled as an attack or normal, is a sequence of TCP packets transmitted from a source IP address to a target IP address under the governance of well-defined protocols between a particular time intervals. This process is carried out using the Bro IDS ensuing in 41 features for every connection. This datasets contains 24 attack types.

Different Components of KDD 99 Dataset

The KDD 99 dataset consists of three components as listed in Table 1 namely "WHOLE" dataset that contains all records, the "10% KDD" dataset that contains 10% KDD records and the "Corrected KDD" dataset.

Training Dataset – "80% KDD": Different intrusion detection systems are trained using the 80% KDD dataset, a more concise version of "Whole KDD" dataset having 22 types of attacks (Li, 2004). Most of the connections are kind of attacks rather than normal, Denial of Service being the majority of them (Gupta, Gupta, & Chaudhary, 2017; Kauser, Rahman, Khan, & Ahmad, 2019; Mishra, Gupta, & Joshi, 2011).

Test Dataset – "Corrected KDD": Testing is the sole purpose of using "Corrected KDD" dataset which in comparison to "80% KDD" or "Whole KDD" datasets provides different statistically distributed. During testing, the classification predictions made are verified by the labels against each of the connection records.

MACHINE LEARNING TECHNIQUES

For the purpose of intrusion detection, machine learning, data mining and pattern recognition algorithms can play an important role to differentiate between normal and malicious traffic. To detect an attack, from a sophisticated attacker, a more intelligent intrusion detection system would be required. For this requirement different attempts are made by using machine learning techniques to make better and more secure system.

- **Decision Tree:** Decision Tree is a technique used to find solution to a variety of learning, classification and prediction problems. The basic decision tree deals with two-class problems where

Table 1. Components of the KDD 99 dataset

Dataset	DoS	Probe	U2R	R2L	Normal
10% KDD	391458	4107	52	1126	97277
Corrected KDD	229853	4166	70	16347	60593
Whole KDD	3883370	41102	52	1126	972780

classification of data is done by using decision tree formed during training session of classifier (Belouch, El Hadaj, & Idlianmiad, 2018). It is rule based classifier and rules are formed from moving the leaf node to parent node. The boundary between the two classes is defined by the decision rules. In situations where two classes cannot be separated by decision tree, this problem is solved by mapping input data into high-dimensional feature spaces using a gini-index also called as information function (Dasgupta & Gonzalez, 2001).

- **Random Forest:** Like Decision Tree, Random Forest can also be used for solving different kinds of learning, classification and prediction problems. Random-Forest is a predictive modeling data analysis approach which is mainly used for data exploration, where it generates several trees by recursive partitioning method and then it aggregates its results (Yassin et al., 2013). Each tree will be constructed separately by using the bootstrap sample of data. It is also taken as an amalgamation of tree predictors, where every tree will re-lie on the amount of independently sampled random vectors with equal circulation of the whole trees in the forest.

- **Naive Bayes:** Naive Bayes (NB) classifier is a kind of probabilistic approach to classify the data into different classes. It uses the concept of Bayes theorem. In NB classifier, membership probabilities (probability of a given data or item belonging to a particular class) are calculated for each data set. This is also called as Maximum APosteriori (MAP) (Dash, 2017).

Besides calculating the membership probabilities, NB classifier assumed that selection parameter (features) is unrelated to each other. Presence or absence of any feature does not affect the presence or absence of any other feature. Expression for Bayes theorem is:

$$P(b|a)=(P(a|b) \times P(b))/(P(a)) \tag{1}$$

where,

$P(b|a)$ = Posterior Probability
$P(a|b)$ = Likelihood
$P(b)$ = Class Prior Probability
$P(a)$ = Predictor Prior Probability

K-Mean Clustering: K-Mean is one of the centroid-based method, which is the elementary clustering by partitioning, wherein the objects are arranged into k partitions where $k_i=n$ (Gupta et al., 2017; Somya, Bansal, & Ahmad, 2016). K-means clustering uses a method of outlier detection to identify the outliers, because the mean of the clusters will be distorted when one of the values is far from rest of the data. In this kind of model, normal behavior pattern are more likely to arrive than the anomalous behavior (Thaseen & Kumar, 2014). Expression for K-Mean clustering calculation is:

$$J_c = \sum_{i=1}^{c} \sum_{p \in c_i} \left\| p - M_i \right\|^2 \tag{2}$$

Figure 2. Visualization of clusters of data set

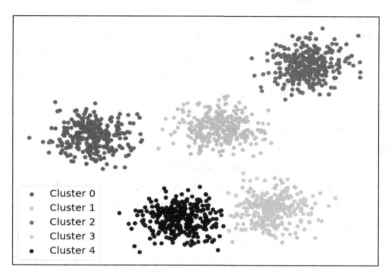

where, M_i is the average number of points in cluster c_i, p is the data point in all the iterating process within the clusters. Comparison of the objective function is made in any of the two iterations and the smallest among them is the best result.

K-Means Clustering Algorithm

For our work, the value of k is set to 5, i.e. we formed 5 clusters of data set.

Cluster 0: Data set which has no intruder i.e. Normal Cluster
Cluster1: Data set which belong to R2L (Remote to local attack)
Cluster2: Data set which belong to DoS (Denial of services)
Cluster3: Data set which belong to U2R (User to root)
Cluster4: Data set which belong to Probe base attack.

Steps

Step-1: The objects in the space are clustered by placing K=5 points. Each point is treated as the initial group centroid.
Step-2: Each object is assigned to the group with closest centroid.
Step-3: Recalculation of the positions of K centroids is done after assigning all the objects to the groups.
Step-4: Repeat step 2 and step 3 until the position of centroid become static.

Gaussian Mixture Clustering: One of the frequently used models for clustering is the Gaussian-mixture models (GMM) (Alheeti, Gruebler, & McDonald-Maier, 2015). Gaussian mixture will produce a different clustering than a k-Means. Thus, the result of both the approaches is combined to obtain better performance. This model will not work well on high dimensional data. PCA algorithm is used for pre-

Figure 3. Visualization of data set using PCA

processing. Normal data set are represented with red color and abnormal data sets are represented with gray color as shown in figure 3.

Hybrid K-Mean Clustering and Random Forest Based IDS

This proposed method applies two clustering techniques namely K-Means clustering and Gaussian-Mixture clustering. The main aspect of clustering is grouping of similar data into one cluster and then the unrelated data into another cluster. Distance will be used to evaluate the similarity of two unique samples. Shorter distance between the two samples indicates that the similarity is higher. In this work we have used KDD data-set, an enhanced version of KDD'99 dataset. Main idea of K-means is to categorize data into clusters and then train different Random Forest classiðers for each of those clusters. As Random Forest returns probabilities, it is possible to improve detection rate for a new types of attacks by adjusting threshold. We have used Weka Tool, Python and Docket Server to implement the proposed algorithm.

System Implementation:

We implement the proposed algorithm in following seven steps:

Step 1: Division of Training Dataset into Subsets

Since the number of records for each of the normal connections and attack connections is very large in the training dataset "10% KDD", so we divide it into five subsets as shown in Table 2. Each subset is named after the category of attack connections it contains.

After the division of training dataset into subsets, the next step is to select the input and output variables.

Step 2: Selection of Input and Output Variables

Table 2. Sub-Datasets for training

Sub-Dataset Name	Type of Connection
Normal	Normal + sample of all attack connections
DoS Attack	Normal + DoS Attack Connections
Probe Attack	Normal + Probe Attack Connections
R2L Attack	Normal + R2L Attack Connections
U2R Attack	Normal + U2R Attack Connections

Here, we select the input and output variables for intrusion detection.

Input Variables: The input variables represent TCP/IP connection records from KDD 99 dataset, with each record consisting of 41 distinct features. For all the intrusion detection systems, we use all the 41 features for each input variable.

Output Variables: Each of the output variables is labelled either as a normal or as an attack of a specific attack type. Attacks may belong to one of the following four categories: Probe, User to Root (U2R), Remote to Local (R2L), and Denial of Service (DoS).

Step 3: Data Preprocessing

Once the selection of most appropriate raw input data has been done, it must go through pre-processing; otherwise, the hybrid classifier will not be able to produce accurate results. The decisions made in this phase of development are critical to the performance of a hybrid classifier based intrusion detection systems. So, we perform following two pre-processing steps namely:

Transformation: It involves the task of manipulating textual data to numeric value. It is important to have the domain knowledge for choosing the appropriate pre-processing method for highlighting the underlying features in the data in order to enhance the network's ability to learn the connotation between input and output (Alheeti et al., 2015).

The textual data of the KDD dataset are protocol type, flag, service, and attack type. These textual data are enumerated to generate the necessary pattern. The KDD 99 dataset contains a lot of redundant records that do not provide useful information, so these are filtered out using "Filters" on MS-EXCEL.

There are 11 distinct flags in training dataset and they are enumerated as shown in Table 3.

Now the next pre-processing step after transformation is normalization of the transformed data.

Normalization: Transformation involves manipulating textual data to numeric value, while normalization is a process of distributing the data evenly and scaling into an acceptable range for the specified neural network (Stein, Chen, Wu, & Hua, 2007). By smoothing the data, the noise entering the network can be reduced. The purpose of data normalization is to ensure uniform statistical distribution of values for each net input and output (T. Ahmad et al., 2017; Tauseef Ahmad, Haque, & Khan, 2018). So, along with the transformations performed on inputs, normalization of the inputs must be done as well.

The data herewith, is normalized by mean and standard deviation technique. All the 42 features of a connection record in the KDD 99 dataset are normalized to have the same means i.e. zero and same variances i.e. one. Table 4 shows the connection records with 42 features in each, before normalization.

Table 3. Enumeration of feature flag

Textual Attribute	Assigned Value	Textual Attribute	Assigned Value
SF	0	S1	1
REJ	2	S2	3
S0	4	S3	5
RSTO	6	RSTR	7
RSTOS0	8	OTH	9
SH	10		

Table 4. Connection records before normalization

```
0,1,3,7,457,356,0,0,0,0,0,1,0,0,0,0,0,0,0,0,0,0,1,1,0,0,0,0,1,0,0,167,255,1,0,0,0,0,0,0,0,0
0,1,3,7,314,1247,0,0,0,0,0,1,0,0,0,0,0,0,0,0,0,0,10,10,0,0,0,0,1,0,0,177,255,1,0,0,0,0,0,0,0,0
0,1,3,7,314,269,0,0,0,0,0,1,0,0,0,0,0,0,0,0,0,0,20,20,0,0,0,0,1,0,0,187,255,1,0,0,0,0,0,0,0,0
```

Step 4: Clustering of data set using K-Mean

K-Mean Clustering is implemented in three parts using Python.

Part-1: We import the K-mean packages from Pyspark which is inbuilt machine learning library present in Python

```
frompyspark.ml.clustering import KMeans
t0 = time()
kmeans_slicer=VectorSlicer(inputCol="indexed_features",outputCol="features",na
mes=list(set(selectFeaturesByAR(ar_dict, 0.1)).intersection(numeric_cols)))
kmeans = KMeans(k=8, initSteps=25, maxIter=100, featuresCol="features",
predictionCol="cluster", seed=seed)
kmeans_pipeline = Pipeline(stages=[kmeans_slicer, kmeans])
kmeans_model=kmeans_pipeline.fit(scaled_train_df)kmeans_train_df=kmeans_model.
transform(scaled_train_df).cache()
kmeans_cv_df=kmeans_model.transform(scaled_cv_df).cache()
kmeans_test_df=kmeans_model.transform(scaled_test_df).cache()
print(time() - t0)
```

Part-2: Function to describe the content of cluster

```
defgetClusterCrosstab(df, clusterCol='cluster'):
return(df.crosstab(clusterCol,'labels2').withColumn('count',col('attack')+c
ol('normal')).withColumn(clusterCol+'_labels2',col(clusterCol+'_labels2').
cast('int')).sort(col(clusterCol+'_labels2').asc()))
```

Part-3: Function for splitting the cluster

```
defsplitClusters(crosstab):
exp = ((col('count') > 25) & (col('attack') > 0) & (col('normal') > 0))
cluster_rf=(crosstab.filter(exp).rdd.map(lambdarow:(int(row['cluster_la-
bels2']), [row['count'], row['attack']/row['count']])) .collectAsMap())
cluster_mapping=(crosstab.filter(~exp).rdd.map(lambdarow:(int(row['cluster_la-
bels2']), 1.0 if (row['count'] <=25)|(row['normal']== 0) else 0.0)).collectAs-
Map())
returncluster_rf, cluster_mapping
kmeans_cluster_rf, kmeans_cluster_mapping = splitClusters(kmeans_crosstab)
print(len(kmeans_cluster_rf),len(kmeans_cluster_mapping))
print(kmeans_cluster_mapping)
```

Step 5: Training of Random Forest Classifier

Random forest classifier is trained on the 5 clusters which are generated after step 4. Following function return the Random forest model for provided cluster.

```
frompyspark.ml.classificationimportRandomForestClassifier
defgetClusterModels(df, cluster_rf):
cluster_models = {}
labels_col = 'labels2_cl_index'
labels2_indexer.setOutputCol(labels_col)
rf_slicer=VectorSlicer(inputCol="indexed_features", outputCol="rf_features",na
mes=selectFeaturesByAR(ar_dict, 0.05))
for cluster in cluster_rf.keys():
t1 = time()
rf_classifier=RandomForestClassifier(labelCol=labels_col,featuresCol='rf_featu
res',seed=seed,numTrees=500,maxDepth=20, featureSubsetStrategy="sqrt")
rf_pipeline=Pipeline(stages=[labels2_indexer,rf_slicer, rf_classifier])
cluster_models[cluster]=rf_pipeline.fit(df.filter(col('cluster') == cluster))
print("Finished %g cluster in %g ms" % (cluster, time() - t1))
returncluster_models
```

Step 6: Testing of test data using trained Classifier

After training the classifier next step is to test the data set, classify the data set in two classes as normal class and abnormal class. Data set is tested by adjusting the threshold of classifier since it returns the probability.

Step 7: Calculation of detection rate and false alarm rate

Depending upon confusion matrix, comparison parameters are calculated.

RESULTS AND DISCUSSION

Various evaluation metrics along with the estimating methods and results of the experiments carried out have been discussed in this section.

Evaluation Metrics

A number of metrics are available for evaluating the performance of the system. Classifying a connection record either as a normal or malicious makes the intrusion detection as a two-class classification problem (Rai, 2014). Its effectiveness is the ability to predict the samples correctly. Confusion matrix, which acts as a baseline for evaluation of performance metrics, is depicted in table 5 for IDS.

When a legitimate action is classified as anomalous (a possible intrusion) by the system, a False-positive is said to have occurred. Although these errors cannot be eliminated completely, but a good system should minimize the FPR.

A False-negative is said to occur if the system treats an actual intrusive action as a non-intrusive behavior. This can be a serious threat as malicious data has not been detected and alerted.

For performance evaluation of Classification and Clustering based intrusion detection systems, following criteria has been taken into account:

- *Accuracy:* The intrusion detection system is said to be more accurate when it detects more attacks while raising fewer false alarm. Accuracy means true-positive or true-negative rate.
- *False Alarm Rate:* False Alarm Rate (FAR) is the error in predicting the connections. A lesser number of false classifications denotes better classification rate of the network and lower FAR (Pappa, Freitas, & Kaestner, 2002).
- *Detection Rate:* Since, we test the data set on different threshold, this parameter is an average of accuracy of classifier at different threshold.

Estimating Methods

Precision: Precision stands for the probability that a normal connection is classified correctly as normal rather than an attack by the IDS.

Precision = TP / (TP+FP)

Table 5. Confusion matrix

Actual		Predicted	
		Negative	Positive
Negative		w	x
Positive		y	z

False-Positive Rate (FPR) = x / (w + x)
False-Negative Rate (FNR) = y / (y + z)

Recall: Recall stands for the probability that an attack is correctly predicted by the IDS from the actual class of attacks.

Recall = TP / (TP+FN)

TESTING RESULTS

Results of Various Classifiers

Table 6 shows results of various classifiers.

Experimental Results of Hybrid Based IDS

Table 7 shows the results of K-Mean and Gaussian Mixture clustering with Random Forest classifier for different threshold values.

Comparison of Results

Tables 8 through 10 show comparison of different classifiers. Whereas Figures 4 and 5 illustrate simple versus hybrid classifiers.

Table 6. Testing results of various classifiers

	Random Forest	**Random Tree**	**Bays Net**	**Naïve Bayes**
Accuracy	93.1	90.12	90.12	85.3
Precision	93.0	91.9	91.0	85.9
Recall	92.98	91.6	91.1	85.8

Table 7. Results of K-Mean and gaussian mixture clustering with random forest classifiers

	Metrics → Threshold ↓	**Accuracy**	**Precision**	**Recall**
K-Means with Random Forest	0.01 0.5	92.76 90.69	93.0 91.0	93.0 91.0
Gaussian Mixture with Random Forest	0.01 0.5	90.69 90.69	91.0 100	91.0 100

Table 8. Comparison of simple classifier

Classifier	TPR	FPR	P	R	CC (%)	IC (%)
Random forest	0.93	0.68	0.93	0.93	92.98	7.12
Random Tree	0.916	0.08	0.92	0.916	91.6	8.4
Bayes-Net	0.91	0.08	0.91	0.911	91	9
Naive-Bays	0.85	0.14	0.86	0.858	85.7	14.3

*TPR = True Positive Rate, FPR = False Positive Rate, P = Precision, R = Recall, CC = Correctly Classified, IC = Incorrectly Classified

Table 9. Comparison of existing hybrid classifier

Author/Year	Techniques	AR (%)	FAR (%)
Muhammed Kabir et al. (2017)	Simple K-means with Random Forest	99.98	0.14
Tahir et al. (2015)	K-means with SVM	96.24	3.715
Yasin et al. (2013)	K-means with Naïve Bayes	99.0	2.2

Table 10: Comparison of proposed hybrid classifier

Techniques	Dataset	AR (%)	FAR (%)	DR (%)
K-means with Random Forest	NSL-KDD	99.84	0.09	99.7
Gaussian Mixture with Random Forest	NSL-KDD	99.83	0.04	99.6

*AR= Accuracy Rate, FAR = False Alarm Rate, DR = Detection Rate

Figure 4. Simple classifier vs. proposed hybrid classifier for accuracy rate

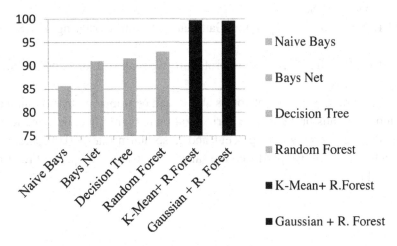

Figure 5. Simple classifier vs. proposed hybrid classifier for false alarm rate

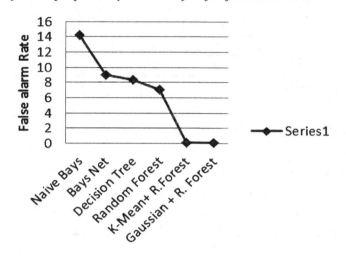

CONCLUSION

In this work, we developed two different intrusion detection systems based on machine learning algorithm and compared their performance on a standard dataset. Important findings of this work may be summarized as follows:

- Accuracy and sensitivity for Naïve Bayes, Decision Tree, Random forest and Bayes Net are compared. We observe that Random forest and Decision Tree are outperforming others for considered parameters.
- For improving the accuracy rate we tried to develop a Hybrid Intrusion detection model and used it for the detection of attack.
- We analyzed KDD data-set by applying Gaussian- Mixture clustering and K-Means clustering methods.
- In order to address the rule-based system problems, we make use of Random-Forest algorithm to build intrusion patterns.
- Experimentally, we observed that network's ability can be improved by choosing appropriate pre-processing steps like transformation and normalization to highlight underlying features in the data.
- For k-means, detection rate is 99.7 percent and false alarm rate is 0.09 percent with threshold value of 0.5, whereas Gaussian produced the same as 99.6 and 0.04 percent respectively for same value of threshold.

FUTURE WORK

Some of the future work possible in the area can be as follows.

In this work, we improved the performance of network intrusion detection systems by using hybrid machine learning algorithm. This work can be extended in future for real time Intrusion Detection by writing a sniffer tool to capture packets on the network, analyze them and extract relevant feature values to classify the record as a normal or an attack connection.

In future, facility of dynamic training of unknown records can be included. This means that for a new incoming connection record that cannot be classified into any of the classes defined on previously trained data, can now be grouped separately and trained on new class labels.

In this work we have focused only on two machine learning techniques i.e. classification and clustering. Other techniques like Genetic Algorithm, Fuzzy Logic, Neural Networks, Rough Set etc. as well as their combinations can also be used to improve the performance in future.

REFERENCES

Ahmad, T., Ahmad, S., & Jamshed, M. (2016). A knowledge based Indian agriculture: With cloud ERP arrangement. In *Proceedings of the 2015 International Conference on Green Computing and Internet of Things, ICGCIoT 2015* (pp. 333–340). 10.1109/ICGCIoT.2015.7380484

Ahmad, T., Haque, M., & Khan, A. M. (2018). An Energy-Efficient Cluster Head Selection Using Artificial Bees Colony Optimization for Wireless Sensor Networks. doi:10.1007/978-3-319-96451-5_8

Ahmad, T., Ahmad, S., Jamshed, M., Sherwani, F. K., Ali, R., & Khan, W. … Qaisar, T. M. (2017). An ISM approach for analyzing the enablers in India's makerspace platforms. In *Proceedings 2017 14th Learning and Technology Conference.* 10.1109/LT.2017.8088121

Alheeti, K. M. A., Gruebler, A., & McDonald-Maier, K. D. (2015). An intrusion detection system against malicious attacks on the communication network of driverless cars. In *Proceedings 2015 12th Annual IEEE Consumer Communications and Networking Conference, CCNC 2015.* 10.1109/CCNC.2015.7158098

Belouch, M., El Hadaj, S., & Idlianmiad, M. (2018). Performance evaluation of intrusion detection based on machine learning using apache spark. In Procedia Computer Science. doi:10.1016/j.procs.2018.01.091

K. Chahal, J., & Kaur, A. (2016). A Hybrid Approach based on Classification and Clustering for Intrusion Detection System. *International Journal of Mathematical Sciences and Computing.* doi:10.5815/ijmsc.2016.04.04

Dasgupta, D., & Gonzalez, F. A. (2001). An Intelligent Decision Support System for Intrusion Detection and Response. doi:10.1007/3-540-45116-1_1

Dash, T. (2017). A study on intrusion detection using neural networks trained with evolutionary algorithms. *Soft Computing, 21*(10), 2687–2700. doi:10.100700500-015-1967-z

Duque, S., & Omar, M. N. Bin. (2015). Using Data Mining Algorithms for Developing a Model for Intrusion Detection System (IDS). In Procedia Computer Science. doi:10.1016/j.procs.2015.09.145

Elngar, A. A., El, D. A., Mohamed, A., & Ghaleb, F. F. M. (2013). *A Real-Time Anomaly Network Intrusion Detection System with High Accuracy.* Inf. Sci. Lett; doi:10.12785/isl/020201

Gupta, B. B., Gupta, S., & Chaudhary, P. (2017). Enhancing the Browser-Side Context-Aware Sanitization of Suspicious HTML5 Code for Halting the DOM-Based XSS Vulnerabilities in Cloud. *International Journal of Cloud Applications and Computing.* doi:10.4018/ijcac.2017010101

Kauser, S., Rahman, A., Khan, A. M., & Ahmad, T. (2019). Attribute-based access control in web applications. In Advances in Intelligent Systems and Computing. doi:10.1007/978-981-13-1819-1_36

Kumar, G. R., Mangathayaru, N., & Narsimha, G. (2016). An approach for intrusion detection using novel gaussian based kernel function. *Journal of Universal Computer Science.*

Laboratory, L. (1998). Darpa intrusion detection data sets (1998). Retrieved from http://Www.Ll.Mit.Edu/Mission/Communications/Ist/Corpora/Ideval/Data/Index.Html

Li, W. (2004). Using genetic algorithm for network intrusion detection. In *Proceedings of the United States Department of Energy Cyber Security Group 2004 Training Conference*, Kansas City, KS. Academic Press.

Lichodzijewski, P., Nur Zincir-Heywood, A., & Heywood, M. I. (2003). Host-based intrusion detection using self-organizing maps. doi:10.1109/ijcnn.2002.1007776

Lippmann, R. P., & Cunningham, R. K. (2000). Improving intrusion detection performance using keyword selection and neural networks. *Computer Networks*, *34*(4), 597–603. doi:10.1016/S1389-1286(00)00140-7

Mehmood, T., & Rais, H. B. M. (2016). Machine learning algorithms in context of intrusion detection. In *2016 3rd International Conference on Computer and Information Sciences, ICCOINS 2016 - Proceedings.* 10.1109/ICCOINS.2016.7783243

Mishra, A., Gupta, B. B., & Joshi, R. C. (2011). A comparative study of distributed denial of service attacks, intrusion tolerance and mitigation techniques. In *Proceedings - 2011 European Intelligence and Security Informatics Conference, EISIC 2011.* 10.1109/EISIC.2011.15

Pan, S., Morris, T., & Adhikari, U. (2015). Developing a Hybrid Intrusion Detection System Using Data Mining for Power Systems. *IEEE Transactions on Smart Grid*, *6*(6), 3104–3113. doi:10.1109/TSG.2015.2409775

Pappa, G. L., Freitas, A. A., & Kaestner, C. A. A. (2002). Attribute Selection with a Multi-objective Genetic Algorithm. doi:10.1007/3-540-36127-8_27

Rai, N. (2014). Genetic Algorithm Based Intrusion Detection System. *International Journal of Computer Science and Information Technologies, 5*(4), 4952-4957.

Somya, B. P., & Ahmad, T. (2016). Methods and techniques of intrusion detection: A review. In Communications in Computer and Information Science. doi:10.1007/978-981-10-3433-6_62

Stein, G., Chen, B., Wu, A. S., & Hua, K. A. (2007). Decision tree classifier for network intrusion detection with GA-based feature selection. doi:10.1145/1167253.1167288

Stolfo, S. J. (1999). KDD cup 1999 dataset. *UCI KDD Repository.* Retrieved from http://kdd.ics.uci.edu/

Thaseen, I. S., & Kumar, C. A. (2014). Intrusion detection model using fusion of PCA and optimized SVM. In *Proceedings of 2014 International Conference on Contemporary Computing and Informatics, IC3I 2014*. 10.1109/IC3I.2014.7019692

Yassin, W., Udzir, N. I., Muda, Z., & Sulaiman, M. N. (2013). Anomaly-Based Intrusion Detection Through K- Means Clustering and Naives Bayes Classification. In *Proceedings of the 4th International Conference on Computing and Informatics, ICOCI 2013*. Academic Press.

Chapter 4
Network Attack Detection With SNMP–MIB Using Deep Neural Network

Mouhammd Sharari Alkasassbeh

Computer Science Department, Princess Sumaya University for Technology, Jordan

Mohannad Zead Khairallah

Computer Science Department, Princess Sumaya University for Technology, Jordan

ABSTRACT

Over the past decades, the Internet and information technologies have elevated security issues due to the huge use of networks. Because of this advance information and communication and sharing information, the threats of cybersecurity have been increasing daily. Intrusion Detection System (IDS) is considered one of the most critical security components which detects network security breaches in organizations. However, a lot of challenges raise while implementing dynamics and effective NIDS for unknown and unpredictable attacks. Consider the machine learning approach to developing an effective and flexible IDS. A deep neural network model is proposed to increase the effectiveness of intrusions detection system. This chapter presents an efficient mechanism for network attacks detection and attack classification using the Management Information Base (MIB) variables with machine learning techniques. During the evaluation test, the proposed model seems highly effective with deep neural network implementation with a precision of 99.6% accuracy rate.

i. INTRODUCTION

The fast development of the internet and network communication have expanded security threats and cybersecurity attacks. A network can be protected against cybersecurity threats using an intrusion detection system. An IDS can protect intrusions and malicious activities by an alert when attacks occur. IDS work as network analyzer for all network traffic. Intrusion detection systems require a lot of maintenance

DOI: 10.4018/978-1-7998-2242-4.ch004

Copyright © 2020, IGI Global. Copying or distributing in print or electronic forms without written permission of IGI Global is prohibited.

to keep its database updated with the latest attacks. Considering this, it shows the importance of. There are two main types of intrusion detection system namely, host-based and network Base.

Host intrusion detection system captures and monitors activities of an individual host or computer device which are installed. The main concern of host-based is on the operating system activity and event logs. Because of Host-based rely on event logs, they become limited by them. Another drawback for host-based can have a huge impact on the performance on the device is installed by parsing every monitored log. Network-based intrusion system monitors multiple connected systems in a network in parallel. Network-based and firewall work together to increase protecting and monitoring the network packet traversing through the network to detect abnormal activities. Network-based also analyze the traffic using different techniques to determine whether normal or abnormal activity (Alom, Bontupalli, & Taha, 2015).

For large enterprise organizations, this considers a difficult task to perform detect classification on an enormous amount of data pass through a network. Standard intrusion system cannot perform such detection. Considering machine learning methodology has been applied widely in IDS. However, applying machine learning while implementing IDS can increase efficiency and higher detection rate against out of the box intrusion detection system.

In the paper, we provided the following contributions:

1. Present MIB for network attacks detection and attacks classification using machine learning.
2. We used a recent dataset provided by SNMP-MIB for classification training.
3. The proposed model shows high accuracy and perfect detection rate.

The rest of the paper is organized as follows. Section 2 includes an overview of some of existing related work in the domain. Section 3 describes the machine learning classifier approach in the deep neural network. Section 4 introduces the proposed architecture model for attacks detection based on SNMP MIB dataset. Finally, section 5 presents the results of the proposed model.

ii. RELATED WORK

Many researchers have applied machine learning on anomaly and attacks detection in computer networks field. Applying different techniques of machine learning classifier were performed on KDD dataset for example in (Obeidat, Hamadneh, Alkasassbeh, Almseidin, & AlZubi, 2019; Siddique, Akhtar, Khan, & Kim, 2019) and others. The approach was focused on two main elements false negative and false positive detection metrics to improve the detection rate of an IDS. After the performance test, it is confirmed the building approach was effective to lower the false negative alerts, on the other hand, random forest classifier has achieved a higher accuracy rate.

DOS or knowns as Denial of service is one of the most popular network attacks currently which requires an effective approach for better detection by implemented Management Information Base (MIB), MIB`s database relates to the Simple Network Management Protocol (SNMP) using machine learning approach. Old and new works in this area have been done to investigate the ability of using MIB data for network faults and security like in (Al-Kasassbeh & Adda, Network fault detection with Wiener filter-based agent, 2009; Yu, Lee, Kim, & Park, 2008) and others as we will see below.

The result of SNMP-MIB data on network anomalies detection using three classifiers types, Random Forest, AdaboostM1 and MLP were required to build the detection model. By implementing machine learning along with the proposed approach, resulted in higher detecting and classifying attack rates. Use of J48, MLP, and Bayes Network classifiers algorithms, it was confirmed that J48 classifier has achieved with the highest accuracy rate for detecting KDD dataset attacks, which categories of DOS, R2L, U2R, and PROBE (Al-Naymat, Al-Kasassbeh, & Al-Hawari, Exploiting SNMP-MIB Data to Detect Network Anomalies using Machine Learning Techniques, 2018).

A proposed NIDS is based on machine learning for handling regression for data and classification tasks with multiple dependent and independent variables.

The Network Intrusion Detection System will detect port scan using Support Vector Machine (SVM), it collects network packets every 4 seconds. With the help of changes in frequency for normal and abnormal packets they train the SVM to identify the differences between these packets.so whenever unknown packets are coming, SVM can classify it whether it is a normal or abnormal packet (Attack). By Applying this method, they could detect 95% of attack packets correctly and warning the administrator (Arjunwadkar Narayan & Parvat, 2015).

Hybrid misuse IDS is implemented to detect attacks on the system and improve intrusion detection. The hybrid approach based on prior feature, attacks or intrusions on the systems can be detected without any previous learning. The model combines both advantages of feature selection approach and machine learning with misuse detection approach. The proposed model is based on a combination of selected network feature which is observing the behavior of attacks and analyze main attribute packets to generate rules over them with a hybrid of two machine learning algorithms, the model is built with no previous learning stage required. J48 and Simple Cart algorithms are required to implement the hybrid IDS model (Al-Naymat, Al-Kasassbeh, & Al-Hawari, Using machine learning methods for detecting network anomalies within SNMP-MIB dataset, 2018).

Machine learning model combining hybrid classifier based on Naive Bayes and C4.5 decision tree for intrusion detection. the hybrid model combined the misuse detection method and anomaly detection method, the proposed model consists of three phases processing, preprocessing phase, the classification phase and finally post-processing stage. C4.5 algorithms used to classify the results after training and testing process are executed over the dataset. Naive Bayes classifier is applied to intrusion detection because of multi types classes in the network. Post-processing phase used to eliminate false alarm rate from the result combines of classification phase by proposing a voting algorithm. which for every 5 consecutive detection result for each pair of Ip addresses to determine the result from the classifier is normal network activity for an intrusion (Tesink, 2007).

In (Al-Kasassbeh M., Network intrusion detection with wiener filter-based agent, 2011) applied statistical methods based on the Wiener filter combined with mobile agent technology to detect anomalies in network traffic using a set of MIB variables from 2 MIB-II groups (interface and IP). The algorithm discussed was evaluated against four types of network attacks (Buffer overflow attack, Decoy port-scan attack, Brute force attack and Null session attack) in order to prove the efficacy of the algorithm in the detection of network intrusion.

In work of (Arjunwadkar, Narayan & Parvat, 2015) proposed another approach based on machine learning and data mining techniques for detecting and classifying attacks using SNMP MIB data. They proposed a system called Protocol Independent Detection and Classification (PIDC) to detect and classify attacks involving a distributed denial of service (DRDoS), such as a DNS attack and a TCP SYN flood attack. They captured 13 MIB variables from the TCP and DNS groups and used a detection algorithm based on correlation to determine the relationship between these variables. The classification algorithm C4.5 was then used to classify the type of attacks considered in this research with MIB variables. Their method achieved a true positive rate of approximately 99 percent and a false positive rate of 1 percent in detecting reflected attacks.

In (Al-Kasasbeh, Al-Naymat, & Al-Hawari, 2016; Al-Naymat, Al-Kasasbeh, & Al-Hawari, Using machine learning methods for detecting network anomalies within SNMP-MIB dataset, 2018) the authors, created a realistic dataset with 34 variables and 4998 records for network anomaly detection. This dataset was actually based on SNMP variables collected from network devices in test-bed real network. The dataset includes 34 variables categorized in 5 groups (Interface, IP, ICMP, TCP, and UDP) and 8 network traffic categories (Normal traffic, TCP-SYN attack, UDP flood attack, ICMP-ECHO attack, HTTP flood attack, Slowloris attack, Slowpost attack, and Brute-Force attack). Many tools were used to generate real attacks like THC-Hydra 5.2, HyenaeFE, DOSHTTP 2.5.1, Slowloris script and Active-Perl language, and HttpDosTool4.0. Then, three machine learning classifiers were used: AdaboostM1, Random Forest, and MLP. Following experiment approach was stepped:

- A new SNMP-MIB dataset was created based on collected network traffic from real test-bed environment.
- Accurate feature selection methods were used to select the most effective variables of the SNMP-MIB variables.
- Machine learning classification methods were applied to classify the attack.
- The MIB variables were classified into 5 groups (Interface, IP, ICMP, TCP, and UDP).
- Each group was classified separately.

As a result, they found that attacks affect most on Interface, and IP groups rather other groups. Other conclusion is that each variables group has a different classifier with high accuracy that may not give the same result with other groups.

In Al-Kasasbeh M., An Empirical Evaluation For The Intrusion Detection Features Based On Machine Learning And Feature Selection Methods (2017) author proposed a method to detect attacks anomaly using three machine learning techniques: BayesNet, Multi-Layer perception (MLP), and Support Vector Machine (SVM). Then, he used feature selection methods to increase his model performance and reduce the computation time. He used two feature selection methods with three attribute evaluators that are: InfoGain, ReleifF for Filter feature selection method, and GeneticSearch for Wrapper feature selection method. He introduced an acceptable detection accuracy model while reducing the complexity with 99.8% accuracy rate in 0.03 second.

The work of Shaheen & Al-kasasbeh (2019) introduced a system that detects the network traffic and varies the DOS attacks from normal traffic based. their results had shown that the adopted algorithms with the ICMP variables achieved a high accuracy percentage with approximately 99.6% in detecting ICMP Echo attack, HTTP Flood Attack, and Slowloris attack. Other work (Manna & Al-kasasbeh, 2019; Al-Kasasbeh M., A Novel Hybrid Method for Network Anomaly Detection Based on Traffic Prediction and Change Point Detection, 2018) using the same dataset but different group variables, in their work they used a REP Tree, J48(Decision Tree) and Random Forest classifiers to detect the anomalies and predict the network attacks that my affect the Internet Protocol(IP) group.

Also the Fazyy system has been used in SNMP variables like in (Almseidin, Al-kasasbeh, & Kovacs, Fuzzy Rule Interpolation and SNMP-MIB for Emerging Network Abnormality, 2019) (Almseidin, Piller,

Al-Kasassbeh, & Kovacs, 2019)to detect the abnormality in the computer network. The work aims to introduce a detection approach for defining abnormality by using the Fuzzy Rule Interpolation (FRI) with Simple Network Management Protocol (SNMP) Management Information Base (MIB) parameters. The proposed approach was tested and evaluated using an open source SNMP-MIB dataset and obtained a 93% detection rate.

iii. MACHINE LEARNING CLASSIFIERS

Machine learning focus tasks associated with classification and recognition, which are related to artificial intelligence science. Generally, these kinds of operations are performed using mathematical and heuristic approaches, in other words, an effective result can be captured from huge space solutions. Machine learning explores mathematical algorithms that can learn from and apply predictions on the provided data. Any machine learning has to learn before it can be used to make a prediction on data. In term of learning which means that the algorithm must be shown samples of data and what are the correct predictions for these samples. The number of samples that must be provided to an algorithm can be within the range of several thousand.

Once the machine learning has learned from the sample data. It can be used to make a prediction on other data. For example, machine learning can be used to monitor the heart rate of patients at a hospital. During the learning stage, machine learning is trained at the heart rate of a patient and the current time. After the training is done, the machine learning can predict what the heart rate of that patient should be based on the current time. By applying machine learning algorithms to determine whether the patient's heart rate is normal by comparing the predicted heart rate and real heart rate.

A. Artificial Neural Network

Neural networks are a set of algorithms designed to recognize a hidden pattern. The pattern they recognize is a numerical value. The neural network helps to cluster and classify problem in our daily lives, they can group unlabeled information from the dataset provided according to similarities. ANN can be considered as a black box model which the nodes are more connected to perform such a task either classification problem or regression problem (Lee, Amaresh, Green, & Engels, 2018). Deep learning is considered of stacked neural networks, in other words, composed of stacked several layers which are connected. Each layer contains nodes. A node is just of computation function. A node combines input from data along with Biases and weights. Fig.1 illustrates what node looks like

B. Deep Neural Network

Deep neural network is structure of several hidden of neurons where the output of a neuron becomes an input to a neuron of the next layer. However, on the last output layer, we can apply different activation functions for hidden layers depending on the type of the problem we have. there are two main problems to work with, regression and classification. Multi-layer architecture is consisting of each neuron (unit) is linked to all the neurons of the next layer but has no link with the neuron of the same layer Fig 2 represents a multilayer basic architecture. The parameter of the architecture is the number of hidden layers and the number of neurons in each layer, also the activation functions are chosen by the user.

Figure 1. Artificial neural network

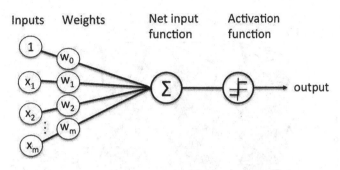

There are more models of deep neural networks which are called recurrent neural network. The idea of these models is to have neurons which trigger for some limited duration of time because of the algorithms for recurrent neural networks are less powerful than the feedforward neural network model.

iv. PROPOSED MODEL

There are well-known approaches in machine learning such as neural network, support vector machine, fuzzy logic, swarm intelligence and more. Despite the number of these approaches and algorithms, there are applications for which a higher degree of accuracy and lower error rate are required. Deep learning networks are acclaimed from the more single hidden layer neural networks by their depth such that, the number of hidden layers data passes through to the process of pattern recognition. In this paper, we applied artificial neural network (ANN) used with the provided dataset SNMP-MIB to be integrated. ANN or deep neural networks can be applied in malware detection or classification, face recognition, fingerprints analysis in which dataset is used for training the model and then predictions of further data are done. However, ANN is fully dependent on the dataset used for training the model, because of that if the data is not accurate and not normalized, the predictive analysis will affect the accuracy rate (Yi, Jung, & Bae, 2017) .

Deep learning is one of the branches of machine learning in which strong base algorithms that have multi-layered processing, higher accuracy rate and a lower error rate with the integrated of deep graph-based learning. Many world-wide applications are used deep learning such as speech recondition, malware detection, natural language processing and many others .

Fig.2 shows a deep neural network with 5 layers. The width of a layer is the number of nodes in that layer, and the width of the net is the number of units of the biggest layer. The depth of the net is equal to the number of layers or the number of hidden layers. The width and the depth of the nets are called hyperparameters, which are values can choose manually when creating the net.

SNMP-MIB Dataset

SNMP is a famous protocol for network management. It can capture network information from several nodes on a network such as routers, switches, and hubs. SNMP provides network information about what is happening under the hood of a network by managing database agent on each device. The captured

Figure 2. Deep neural network

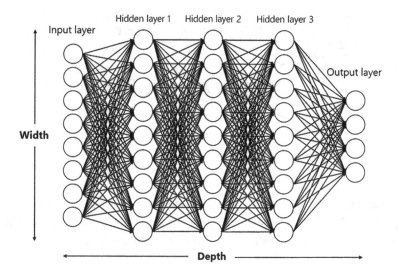

network information from the installed device can be analyzed and categorized network behavior which can be used later for a network intrusion detection system. By appropriate provided data from SNMP-MIB for training and testing model moreover, examine the validity and effectiveness. The SNMP-MIB dataset is used for testing our proposed framework. The MIB dataset contains approximately 4998 records with 34 MIB variables. The data records of attacks fall into 6 types of DoS attacks (TCP-SYN, UDP flood, ICMP-ECHO, HTTP flood, Slowloris, Slowpost) and Brute Force attack. Further description for the MIB dataset and attacks instances can be found in Al-Kasassbeh, Al-Naymat, & Al-Hawari (2016).

Activation Function

Activation functions are needed to break the linearity and represent more complicated relationships. Moreover, activation functions are required in order to stack layers and transform input into outputs of a different kind. Common activation functions are namely, monotonic, continuous and differentiable. (Sharma, 2017) These are important properties needed for optimization. The SoftMax activation function is used to transform a bunch of large numbers into a valid probability distribution. The values that SoftMax outputs are in the range from 0 to 1 and their sum is exactly 1. The property of SoftMax to output probabilities is so useful and intuitive that is often used as the activation function for the final layer.

$$softmax(x) = \frac{e^{xi}}{\sum_{j} e^{xj}}$$

DNN Model Implementation

For the implementation of the ANN, Tensorflow python library was used to develop and train the model. Tensorflow (Google Brain) is an open-source software library used for deep learning. It is based on a set of algorithms for dataflow to achieve multi-layered computation for higher accuracy and lower error rate. TensorFlow was released as open-source in November 2015 by Google and this move has motivated researchers and scientists to work on this powerful library.

As network traffic is captured and normalized from the SNMP-MIB as CSV (Comma separated values) format, the file is ready to be read in Tensorflow for deep learning of the model and further prediction for network traffic which the upcoming traffic can be classified for a probability of being normal traffic or not. For conducting the experiment with the classifier model, the dataset was divided into 70% as training dataset and the rest as testing dataset Both datasets contained normal and the other attack classes. The training of the model was evaluated based on the following parameters

- 10 layers with 20 neurons each.
- Number of classes is 8.
- Batch size is 100.
- Number of epochs is 10000.
- Number of steps required for training the model is 10000.

Experiment Results and Discussion

As above mentioned, we applied machine learning techniques to the MIB dataset using two approaches. This section describes and explains the experimental results of using the first approach. In this approach, the full MIB dataset (both training dataset and testing dataset) was evaluated by Linear neural network classifier. The aim here was to show the differences between linear classifier and deep classifier.

After training and evaluating the process on both models deep neural classifier has improved the detection process by increasing the accuracy rate with multi-layered neural networks. Through the evaluation test of the model was focused on two main elements which are high detection rate and low error and it is confirmed the accuracy rate is 99.6%.

Figure 3. Accuracy result

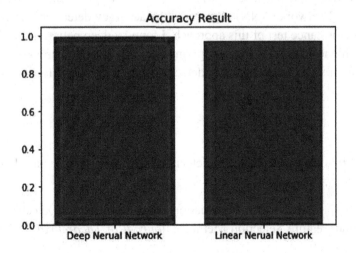

Figure 4. Average loss

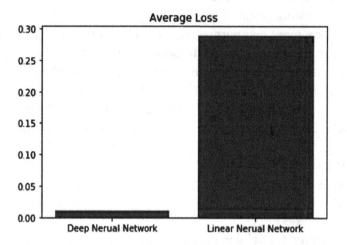

Comparing testing results against linear classifier. I employed neural network learning based on linear classifier to evaluate the same MIB dataset in attacks detection and classification. The result in Fig.3 indicates that linear classifier achieved a lower accuracy rate with a value of 96.8% in identifying the normal traffic.

From the above figure, we can the difference between two approaches towards average loss attribute. Deep neural network approach achieves lower average loss value to minimize the average negative log probability.

v. CONCLUSION

In this paper, I have employed artificial neural network learning approach for network attack detection based on SNMP-MIB data. The purpose of my experiment is to prove the ability and effectiveness of applying artificial neural network (ANN) to increase the accuracy detection rate of intrusion detection systems. From the performance test of this approach, I found a deep neural network or artificial neural network archived the highest accuracy rate comparing against to linear neural network. Overall machine learning techniques improve network anomaly detection with a notable effect on network security.

REFERENCES

Al-Kasassbeh, M. (2011). Network intrusion detection with wiener filter-based agent. *World Applied Sciences Journal, 13*(11), 2372–2384.

Al-Kasassbeh, M. (2017). An Empirical Evaluation For The Intrusion Detection Features Based On Machine Learning And Feature Selection Methods. *Journal of Theoretical and Applied Information Technology, 95*(22).

Al-Kasassbeh, M. (2018). A Novel Hybrid Method for Network Anomaly Detection Based on Traffic Prediction and Change Point Detection. *Journal of Computational Science, 14*(2).

Al-Kasassbeh, M., & Adda, M. (2009). Network fault detection with Wiener filter-based agent. *Journal of Network and Computer Applications, 32*(4), 824–833. doi:10.1016/j.jnca.2009.02.001

Al-Kasassbeh, M., Al-Naymat, G., & Al-Hawari, E. (2016). Towards Generating Realistic SNMP-MIB Dataset for Network Anomaly Detection. *International Journal of Computer Science and Information Security, 14*(9), 1162–1185.

Al-Naymat, G., Al-Kasassbeh, M., & Al-Hawari, E. (2018). Exploiting SNMP-MIB Data to Detect Network Anomalies using Machine Learning Techniques. In *Proceedings of SAI Intelligent Systems Conference*. Academic Press.

Al-Naymat, G., Al-Kasassbeh, M., & Al-Hawari, E. (2018). Using machine learning methods for detecting network anomalies within SNMP-MIB dataset. *Int. J. Wireless and Mobile Computing, 15*(1), 67–76. doi:10.1504/IJWMC.2018.10015860

Almseidin, M., Al-kasassbeh, M., & Kovacs, S. (2019). Fuzzy Rule Interpolation and SNMP-MIB for Emerging Network Abnormality. *International Journal on Advanced Science, Engineering and Information Technology, 9*(3).

Almseidin, M., Piller, I., Al-Kasassbeh, M., & Kovacs, S. (2019). Fuzzy automaton as a detection mechanism for the multi-step attack. *International Journal on Advanced Science, Engineering, and Information Technology, 9*(2).

Alom, Z., Bontupalli, V. R., & Taha, T. M. (2015). Intrusion detection using deep belief network and extreme learning machine. [IJMSTR]. *International Journal of Monitoring and Surveillance Technologies Research, 3*(2), 35–56. doi:10.4018/IJMSTR.2015040103

Arjunwadkar Narayan, M., & Parvat, T. J. (2015). An Intrusion Detection System,(IDS) with Machine Learning (ML) Model Combining Hybrid Classifiers. *connections, 1*(3).

Lee, B., Amaresh, S., Green, C., & Engels, D. (2018). Comparative study of deep learning models for network intrusion detection. *SMU Data Science Review, 1*(1).

Manna, A., & Al-kasassbeh, M. (2019). Detecting network anomalies using machine learning and SNMP-MIB dataset with IP group. *The 2nd International Conference on New Trends in Computing Sciences*. Academic Press.

Obeidat, I., Hamadneh, N., Alkasassbeh, M., Almseidin, M., & AlZubi, M. (2019). Intensive Pre-Processing of KDD Cup 99 for Network Intrusion Classification Using Machine Learning Techniques. *International Journal of Interactive Mobile Technologies, 13*(1).

Shaheen, Y. K., & Al-kasassbeh, M. (2019). A Proactive Design to Detect Denial of Service Attacks Using SNMP-MIB ICMP Variable. *The 2nd International Conference on New Trends in Computing Sciences*. Amman, Jordan.

Sharma, S. (2017). Activation functions: Neural networks. *Towards Data Science*.

Siddique, K., Akhtar, Z., Khan, F. A., & Kim, Y. (2019). KDD Cup 99 Data Sets: A Perspective on the Role of Data Sets in Network Intrusion Detection Research. *Computer*, *52*(2), 41–51. doi:10.1109/MC.2018.2888764

Szegedy, C., *Toshev, A., & Erhan, D.* (2015). Deep Neural Networks for Object Detection.

Tesink, S. (2007). *Improving intrusion detection systems through machine learning.* In Proceedings of ILK Research Group Technical Report Series no. 07--02. Academic Press.

Yi, H., Jung, H., & Bae, S. (2017). Deep Neural Networks for traffic flow prediction. In *Proceedings 2017 IEEE International Conference on Big Data and Smart Computing (BigComp)* (pp. 328-331). IEEE.

Yu, J., Lee, H., Kim, M.-S., & Park, D. (2008). Traffic flooding attack detection with SNMP MIB using SVM. *Computer Communications*, *31*(17), 4212–4219. doi:10.1016/j.comcom.2008.09.018

Chapter 5
A Survey on Detection and Analysis of Cyber Security Threats Through Monitoring Tools

Manjunath Kotari

Alva's Institute of Engineering and Technology, Moodbidri, India

Niranjan N. Chiplunkar

NMAM Institute of Technology, Nitte, India

ABSTRACT

Cyber crime is a serious threat for day-to-day transactions of the digital life. Overexposure of the personal details in social networks will lead to the cyber crime case. Therefore, detection and monitoring of cyber crime are challenging tasks. The cyber criminals are continually flooding the various intrusions all over the network. The cyber safety team should have a noteworthy challenge of filtering various such information. Continuous nonstop cyberattacks or intrusion examinations by security tools will significantly improve the threat alerts. However, cyber security becomes more expensive in the case of the above methods. The chapter provides systematic survey of various cyber security threats, evolution of intrusion detection systems, various monitoring mechanisms, open source cyber security monitoring tools, and various assessment techniques. The chapter also proposes a model of Cyber security detection and monitoring system and its challenges.

1. INTRODUCTION

Cyber security threats are major hurdle for the development activities of the Information Technology (IT) industry. The IT industry is facing severe crisis of cyber-crime activities in their business. A large set of data and assets of organizations are placed in cloud-based platform. The virtual cloud computing is facing various threats which include, Intrusions, Malwares, and Mining of Crypto currency. The

DOI: 10.4018/978-1-7998-2242-4.ch005

Copyright © 2020, IGI Global. Copying or distributing in print or electronic forms without written permission of IGI Global is prohibited.

Virtual Machines faces intrusions and impersonations in the cloud environments. The bitcoin attracts more severe cyber crimes. This can be illustrated in cloud computing by layer wise cyber attacks. Cyber Security (Gupta, Agrawal, & Wang, 2019) is becoming a very important concern for the functioning of web applications. The rising cost of cyber security damages reflects a failure of the security field to offer a solution that is both simple enough to warrant adoption by industry and government and secure enough to protect our valuable assets and data. Most of the organizations are facing shortage of cyber security professionals to monitor the user activities in day to day life. However, IT organizations may use various tools and technologies to maintain privacy of user data. Most of the corporate information security (Quhtani, 2017) is analyzed by data mining applications. In the corporate world, marketing campaign surveys are analyzed according to data mining applications. The objective of this chapter is to provide the comprehensive survey on detection and analysis of various cyber security threats exists in the web applications and network. The chapter also reviews the various open source security monitoring tools with classifications. The challenges faced by cyber-security tools have been included for the purpose of providing future solutions. The architecture of cyber-security threat detection and monitoring system to analyze the working of cyber-security tools has been proposed in this chapter.

1.1 Cyber Security Monitoring

Security monitoring is the collection of data from a range of security systems and the correlation and analysis of this information with threat intelligence to identify signs of compromise. Cyber-Security monitoring is an essential part of cyber risk management systems, which enables the company networks to detect cyber hackers in their early life, and quickly shoot up threats for healing before they cause harm and interference. Baselining is the process of establishing an agreed level of typical network performance. It plays an important role in cyber security monitoring. Any network behavior that falls outside what is considered regular behavior should be analyzed to identify whether or not it could be malicious.

1.2 How Does Cyber Security Monitoring Work?

Cyber security analysts will utilise a range of technologies to achieve visibility of threats. There are two types of monitoring, viz., network security monitoring and endpoint security monitoring. Network security monitoring tools comprise Security Information and Event Management (SIEM) and Intrusion Detection Systems (IDS). SIEM systems collect, manage and correlate log information from a range of sources to provide a holistic view of security posture, and generate alerts for investigation by cyber security analysts. IDS combines network (NIDS) and host (HIDS) based methods to analyse network traffic and identify anomalous behaviour. Endpoint security monitoring technologies provide visibility of activity such as file read, write, executions and registry changes across desktops, laptops, and servers.

1.3 Challenges of In-House Security Monitoring

Basically all the security monitoring tools generates enormous number of alert messages. Filtering of alert messages to identify true threats from false positives is hassle task. In that case, essential alerts may be ignored during the monitoring process. Hence, setting up of new Cyber Security Operations Centre (CSOC) is essential. However, CSOC is more expensive. Instead of recruiting, training and managing in-house experts in latest technologies is a cost prohibitive. Most of the companies use specializing managed device.

1.4 Importance of Security Monitoring

Cyber-security threats are evolving to take advantage of new vulnerabilities that emerge daily. With breaches now an operational reality, proactive detection is essential. While technology alone can block many common signature-based threats, a deeper level of cyber security monitoring is required to identify the latest sophisticated threats, including the latest types of ransomware and memory-resident malware. The continuous monitoring of cyber-security helps the organizations to advanced threat visibility, detect a broader range of threats, reduced response times, performance evaluation of existing security controls and comply with industry and regulatory requirements.

1.5 Proposed Cyber Security Threat Detection and Monitoring System

Cyber security threat detection and monitoring system can be designed for the cloud platform in web services. The architecture can be designed to analyze the traffic, system logs and vulnerably of the network. The analyzed data will be utilized for cyber security threat monitoring system. These results include status information of all the clients and their activities. The security operation is the maintenance activities of security team; it may change the assets and policy databases. The centralized cloud platforms are having more vulnerable to attack by cyber attackers. This monitoring system will reduce the overall maintenance of web services. The proposed architecture is shown in figure 1. The intelligence

Figure 1. Architecture for cyber security threat detection and monitoring system

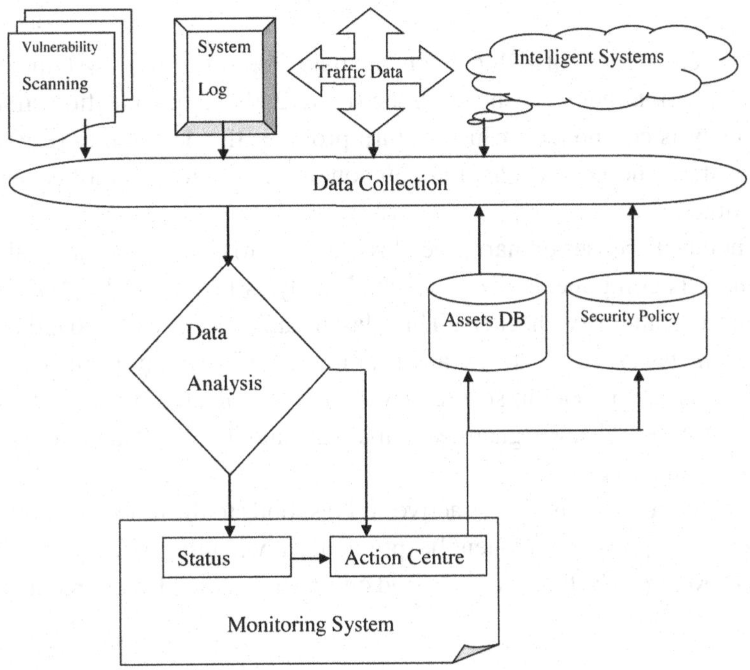

systems, traffic data, system logs and vulnerability scanning are the components of the data collection. The collected data will be used to give the input to data analysis module. The assets databases and security policies should be continuously updated by monitoring system. These two components will be given as input for data collection module. The results of the data analysis module are available in status component of the cyber security monitoring system.

1.6 Chapter Organization

In the Second Section, the chapter discusses the literature reviews of various intrusion detection systems with the types of attacks. The Section Three highlighting about various cyber-security tool for monitoring threats in the user networks. This section also gives comprehensive investigation features of the cyber security tools. The Section Four describes the various special open source cyber-security tools used in corporate systems. Finally Fifth section explains the challenges faced by cyber-security tools during monitoring.

2. BACKGROUND

Intrusion is a one type activity which is more vulnerable for the information protection. It is very difficult to protect the information free from intrusion. However, Intrusion Detection Systems(IDS) (Priyanka &Singh, 2016) are used to protect such vulnerable information in the repository. It is an application applicable for either hardware or software mainly used to monitor the user activities in the distributed network. The monitoring activities should be reported to the network administer time to time. The intrusion detection systems basically used to monitor the suspicious activities of the user network in varieties of methods. The possible intrusions can be avoided and prevented with the help of Intrusion Detection Prevention Systems (IDPS). The majority of the IDPSs are built with a set of components are shown in figure 2.

The data collection component of IDS collects the data from user logs, system calls & system logs and provided to storage component. As shown in the figure 2, the data collection simultaneously sends the information to analysis component, which in turn provides the decision to response component to take preventive measures. The Data Collection component is very important because without it other components are un-functional.

The analysis component focuses on narrative classification to make fewer false alarms. The various methods used by analysis components viz,. statistical analysis (Sung et al., 2005) pattern matching, machine learning and file integrity checkers. This classification reduces the overhead of network administrator and gives the fastest results to get an accurate identification of intrusions.

Storage component saves the data in secure way, which is collected by data collection component. The storage component stores all new signatures of malware and threats. It also stores the updated users' list and system policies time to time.

Finally the response component is always active and responds to the other components quickly as per the needs. The proactive response component beeps an alarm when intrusion exists in the information. Intrusion Detection Prevention Systems not only find out intrusion but also intercept and stop intrusions.

Figure 2. Intrusion detection systems

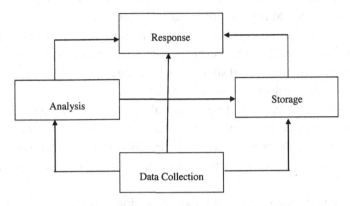

2.1 Intrusion Detection Systems, Vulnerabilities, Attacks and Prevention

There are three types of traditional attacks (DIT, 2006) mainly reported by traditional intrusion detection systems viz., scanning of system network port number, denial of service (DOS), and system breach. All these types of attacks are usually instigated through locally or remotely depending on availability of system and target system respectively. The network admin must able to identify the above attacks through some different set of response messages.

The scanning of the system should happen through the network port scanning attacks by multicasting of packets. The intruder will study the various features and vulnerabilities of the computer system after getting the responses of multicasting messages. These attacks will not go in-depth of the computer systems. Scanning attacks do not infiltrate or else compromise the systems. Varieties tools have been used to carry out these activities like, network mapper, port mapper, network scanners, port scanners, or vulnerability scanners. The scanning attacks may yield the following information such as topology of a target network, types of network traffic allowed through a firewall, active hosts on the network, the operating systems those hosts are running, the server software they are running and the software version numbers for all detected software.

Due to the flooding of packets in to target network by intruder will slow down the services of the network systems. These types of attacks are commonly called as Denial of Service (DOS) attacks. In the present internet services, these types of attacks frequently happen. DoS attacks mainly used to shut down the services of target organizations systems. This leads to huge loss to e-commerce industries, whose customers were unable to access them to make purchases. There are two main types of DOS attacks: fault exploitation DoS and flooding of DoS. It is important for an IDS operator to understand the difference between them.

Fault exploitation attacks usually exploit a fault in the application of remote systems in order to cause a processing failure or to cause it to exhaust system resources such as the 'ping of death' attack. These types of attack usually targeted to Windows Operating Systems by sending a large ping packet. The remote Windows system will crash due to the abnormal activity of the long ping packet. These types of attacks normally targeted to system resources like, CPU Computation time, memory space, disk drive space, Translation Look-a-side Buffer (TLB), and network bandwidth.

Due to flooding of multicasting packets on to target system by intruder, the target and other systems will not able to provide/get the valuable services. Here, attacker will deny the services for the client systems due to overuse of the bandwidth by packets of intruder. Similarly, target system is also not able to handle the type of attacks due to flooding of packets by intruder.

All the modules of an IDSs are susceptible to attacks in multiple ways. For example Data collection component collects various information like user logs, network trails and system calls as an audit trails and tells other component as the distrustful sign for any particular activity is malicious or normal. However, an opponent attacks data collection component, then the IDS become useless. Similarly, analysis component gives the malfunctioned data, if it is attacked by advisory. Storage component also affected by intrusions and it may delete entire database. This data is essential for all kind of profiled activity of IDS. Response component may be compromised by attacker without generating an alarm. An Attacker can make the system in such a way that it denies legitimate activity and accept malicious activity even it is the reactive device.

The analysis of various intrusion detection and prevention systems proved that both the intrusion detection systems and the intrusion prevention systems (Kumar et al., 2013) still require to be improved to make sure an reliable security for a networked computers. They are not consistent and adequate during the alert of false positives and false negatives. So, it is difficult to manage by network administrator. However, it is very important for organizations to make sure their security for entire network. Hence, it is suggested merge several types of malicious intrusion detection systems. The intrusion prevention systems(IPS) tries to balance all the problems raised in intrusion detection systems. However, IPS currently needs to be tested to evaluate its reliability.

2.2 Cyber Attacks Detection Based on Machine Learning and Deep Learning

In the field of Computer Security (Olakanmi et al., 2019), Cyber Security is a detailed, rising field to provide the security to networks. Machine learning algorithm behaviours can be applied to guarantee the security features of the computer networks. There are two types of machine learning tasks can be used to detect the anomalies in the networked computers viz., classification and regression. Also, supervised and unsupervised machine learning technique can be used to categorise the anomalies from the regular data.

Deep learning(Jiang et al., 2018) techniques can be used to recognize the intrusions that present in the network. In that case, authors propose a multi-channel intelligent attack identification method. This method makes use of deep learning technique which is based on long short-term memory recurrent neural networks (LSTM-RNNs). The major features of deep learning technique like, data preprocessing, feature abstraction and multi-channel training and detection are flawlessly incorporated into continuous detection framework. Multi-channel training has been used in this proposed scheme to engender classifiers based on LSTM-RNNs. This helps to identify the intrusions in input vector. The multi-channel processing uses a voting algorithm to infer the attacks in input vector.

2.3 Industrial Internet of Things Threats (IIoTT) and Security

The IoT prototype is relatively new but has an essential evolutionary potential due to the rapid evolution of transmission technologies characterized by ever-increasing speeds and used today for access to the Internet to fly the interconnection of "objects" which will be increasingly independent in the control and exchange of information useful for infrastructure management.

Industrial IoT applications are having highly potential (Chiappetta, 2019), especially for power plant industries, transpiration industries, medical and construction industries. The authors analyzed that, industrial IoT applications are growing exponentially within next decade to enhance the communications. The health and working of various machines in industries can be controlled through IoT applications. However, these industrial IoT are involved with more risks. To provide the protection for data privacy, IoT platform should abide the rules of cyber security properly. It in turn gives the guarantee for security constraints. Most of the industries are using a specific tool to assess the risks in IoT applications. However, these tools will not provide accurate results. Hence, author proposed a new system to analyze the threats in industrial IoT systems.

2.4 Vulnerabilities in Fog and Cloud Computing

Fog computing enhances the advantages of cloud computing and restrain the drawbacks. In addition to the best features of the cloud computing, fog computing improves the overall performance of the system (Paharia & Bhushan, 2019). However, fog computing is having many new limitations. Fog computing is a new kind of services and applications to the end-users by adopting the features of cloud computing. In this regard, providing security and privacy to fog computing is a challenging task than cloud computing. The various types of attacks related to fog computing has been comprehensively discussed by authors.

The cloud based HTML5 applications (Gupta & Chaudhary, 2017) have been infected by Cross Site Scripting (XSS) worms. These worms are harmful for confidential informations present in the cloud platform by injecting the malicious scripts. Also, these intrusions may steal the confidential informations from the authorized users. The sanitization of such suspicious vulnerabilities in cloud-based platform enhances the browser side security for web applications.

B.B. Gupta et al. (2017) proposed a vulnerability sanitation method to remove the suspicious DOM-based XSS vulnerabilities. The key modules of the web pages have been collected by security framework. The framework extracts the doubtful HTML5 strings from the in the beginning. In that case, Initially, the framework collects the key modules of web application, extracts the suspicious HTML5 strings from the hidden injection points. Later, framework performs the clustering of HTML5 strings based on resemblance of such strings. Further, it identifies the injection of malicious HTML5 code in the script nodes of DOM tree by detecting the variation in the HTML5 code embedded in the HTTP response generated. Any variation observed will simply indicate the injection of suspicious script code.

Shashank Gupta et al. (2015) found that modern web applications (Gupta & Gupta, 2015) suffer from XSS attacks and Workflow Violation attacks. The authors propose PHP-Sensor to detect vulnerabilities of web applications. In case of workflow violation attack, authors extract a certain set of axioms by monitoring the sequences of HTTP request/responses. The HTTP request/'response are evaluated by these set of axioms. Suppose, the HTTP request/response bypasses the axioms then it is identified as attack. The XSS attack can be detected by PHP-Sensor by monitoring the outgoing HTTP web request with the scripts that are injected in the currently HTTP response web page.

2.5 Cyber Security and Intelligent Transportation Systems

An Intelligent Transportation Systems (ITS) mainly focus on reducing traffic congestion and environment impacts(USDT, 2019). Also ITS is used to improve the safety and transport efficiency for protecting the mix of technology and systems. Nowadays ransomware encrypts information of target device and demand for ransom to get decryption key.

Figure 3. Hierarchical structure DIDS

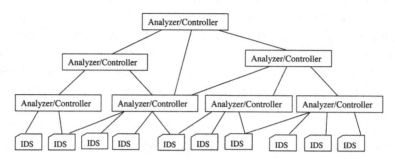

The various types of attack models are available in ITS such as illegal groups, distant services, hackers, within intrusions and terrorists. Firstly, illegal groups focus on financial benefits during attacks. These groups are involved in criminal activities such as phishing and spyware or malware attacks. The illegal groups are always big threat to transportation systems of cyber security systems. The distant services are great threat to military infrastructure of the country. These services are forcefully working towards the information conflicts and theft. The hackers use to hack the network with a great challenge and arrogantly to get the rights into their hackers group. These hackers use the attack scripts to get the rights of the victim sites and they required only basic computer skills for this activity. Most of the hackers seriously spoil the transportation systems during the message passing events. The frustrated employee of an organization is the big threat for computer crimes today. These groups of insiders will have the knowledge of each and every point of computer network of the organization. They need not to struggle to get into the unrestricted access area. These insiders will be injecting intrusions continuously without the knowledge of network administrator. The intrusion detection system has been evolved time to time as per the challenges of Cyber-security threats. There are two types of evolutions in IDS viz,. Distributed IDS (DIDS) and Cyber-security threat control model.

The intelligent cyber security systems are having an intrusion detection system within it. These are called as distributed intrusion detection systems, which is deployed over a large network. This type of DIDS monitors the early detection of intrusions in a large network. The agents are used to communicate each other during the monitoring of large networks. These DIDS helps the network administrators to take preventive measures in the networks (Abraham et al., 2005). The DIDS is used to control the scattering of intrusions, which inturn improves network monitoring and incident analysis in the network. The DIDS also focus on detection of newly generated intimidation from unauthorized users. It stops the attackers who entering from backdoors and hackers to the network across multiple locations, which are geographically separated.

The distributed intrusion detection systems performing with network intrusion detection systems with a special component called Cooperating Security Managers (CSM). Each individual CSM detects malicious activity on the local host and reports it to the host systems. Later, local CSM gives the notification alerts to the all other networked computers if malicious activity is found.

As shown in the figure 3, the hierarchical architecture of the DIDS, the Central Analyzer and Controller (CAC) is the heart and soul of the DIDS. The CAC generally consists of a database server and Web server. These servers help the network administrators to analyze attack information continuously interactive manner. Later, it helps to initiate the preventive measures. The CAC is responsible for following activities such as aggregating the attack scenarios, building statics, and identifying attack patterns

Figure 4. Cyber security threat control model

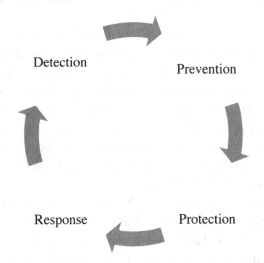

in the network. The CSM is one of the most important components of the DIDS, basically located on separate network segments. The data analysis of host machines will be taken care by agent modules of DIDS. Agent module reports to network administrator automatically in the event of modification. The analyzer / controllers contain the agents module, which in turn is responsible for dispatching, updating, regeneration of agents and maintenance of intrusion signatures.

2.6 Cyber Security Threats and the Risk Control Model

The cloud computing platform is facing several security issues, in which cloud virtual machines (VM) facing a great threat of intruders(Yan et al., 2019). In the current scenario, cloud platform facing following issues viz., intrusion, malware mass scanning, crypto currency mining and ransomware viruses. The virtual machines will be overtaken by the attacker through replay attacks or password guessing attacks. The cyber criminals are attracted by crypto currency mining of Bitcoin. Once the target system affected by ransomware virus then target system need to pay the ransom amount to get back their data. The third-party attackers will take the control of VMs for spreading the attacks in cloud. The WebShell is the type of vulnerability in web services, mainly affected through remote code executions. The identified threats of web services can be controlled through cyber security risk control system.

The system consists of four phases viz., detection phase, prevention phase, protection phase and response phase. As shown in the figure 4, the threat intelligent systems can be used to analyze as well as detect the vulnerabilities in the network traffics. The intrusion can be avoided by giving awareness to the users of the network. The training to the network user also prevents the attacks. The security policy needs to be reviewed time to time and need to conduct the continuous assessment & auditing to avoid the intrusions. By deploying Firewall Systems, Intrusion Protection System (IPS), and Web Application Firewall (WAF) leads the protection of the network information.

2.7 Cyber Security Monitoring Requirements and Standards

While each monitoring methods affords insight into only a inadequate set of prospective attacker strategies such as Source-Load Coordinated Reserve Allocation and Strategy Considering Cyber-Attack Risks. The conventional method of protecting the smart grid is to be updated time to time for the purpose of providing effective services. The vulnerability assessment needs to be considered to improve the security functions at smart-grid services. The control systems of the smart grids are to be prevented from cyber-attacks.

In the present era of internet world and impulsive cyber threats, proactive cyber security monitoring is very important part of day-to-day cyber risk management. Monitoring of any company network is not an easy task today, requires expertise use of resources properly in any network. The latest technology is enough to maximise its benefits.

A Cybersecurity Software is a must for Cyber Security and Privacy of a business or individual. Cybersecurity is the method that is used to protect the network, system, or applications from the cyber attacks. It is used to avoid unauthorized data access, cyber-attacks, and identity theft.

Application security, information security, network security, disaster recovery, operational security, etc. are the different parts of cyber-security. It needs to be maintained for various types of cyber threats like Ransomware, Malware, Social Engineering, and Phishing.

2.8 Network Security Monitoring Strategies with TOMATO

Monitoring systems are used to summarizing and analyzing the malicious behavior of information continuously. These data will be obtained from network flows, system logs and end users. However, there's no perfect methodology to compute the observability and efficiency of a security monitoring strategy. A tool that can be used to evaluate such data sources are called as TOMATO (Threat Observability & Monitoring Assessment Tool)(Halvorsen et al., 2019). TOMATO is a tool to assess the efficacy of a safety monitoring approach by discovering intrusions and false positives. The intrusion can be detected in local network along with examining the number of false positives produced by monitoring tool.

Monitoring systems for suspicious activities progressively more requires cumulatively and examining information from various computer nodes, such as distributed systems, workstation logs, and end-point monitoring platforms. However, there is at present a need of security metrics and techniques to compute the effectiveness of a security monitoring strategy.

2.9 Monitoring Techniques

Each and every monitoring tool provides the insight of intrusions, malwares and suspicious attackers in the network. The monitoring may help the system to improve their efficiency as well as security measures. A system primarily used to keep track of the other systems in a network is, known as monitoring systems. The network monitoring expresses the usage of the system that continuously observes the networked computer in case of slow or failure and gives an alert message to network administrator (Mittal et al., 2013). It usually comprises of the following components such as monitoring module, event identifier, and monitoring hardware, detection of events and processing of events. Specifically, monitoring is, accomplished in two operations, i.e., detection of events that is relevant to program execution and storing or recording the collected data. The failure nodes (Kotari et al., 2016) have been tracked by running monitoring application on network. Most of the time Simple Network Management Protocol(SNMP) agent accesses a monitor of another network to obtain current system status.

Tsai et al.(2012) explained the necessity of distributed monitoring system and anticipated a distributed monitoring architecture. According to author, monitoring system is categorized in to two types, namely internal monitoring system and external monitoring system. In case of an internal monitoring system (Eckhardt et al., 2012), the monitoring system is, integrated with each client. Each client's monitoring system keeps track of program executions of the same system and records the data here. The recorded information is, transmitted to central monitoring system. Whereas, in case of an external monitoring system, the monitoring system resides outside the existing network and monitors the target system. Here the target system is usually present in the distributed system.

Monitoring systems are required for the purpose of adaptation in distributed systems. Hence, the monitoring systems are used in Adaptive Systems to provide the Quality of Service. Monitoring systems(Schwiderski, 1996) provide the rapid change of information about current situations in adaptive distributed systems. This information is utilized to analyze the entire systems and enhance the performance of the system. Monitoring is essential to provide intended functionalities to the distributed system. This could be achieved by allowing the monitoring node to gather different parameters dynamically at run time about the changes in the distributed environment. Every system monitors (Matthew et al., 2004) its neighboring assets and transmits multicast packets which includes monitoring information on a well-known group address whenever some important changes happen. Mobile agents (Chu &Brockmeyer, 2010) are used to perform the monitoring tasks efficiently and effectively, thus reducing the network traffic and carrying the tasks to wherever the required data can be obtained with a good performance".

Kyungkoo et al. (2004) proposed an adaptive fault monitoring distributed system consists of two phases such as detection and dissemination. In the detection phase, distributed nodes are periodically check the neighboring nodes each other and forms a ring topology. The dissemination phase, forwards the results of detection phase to other neighboring nodes. On receiving the faulty or fault free information, nodes update the local database and diagnose the faulty nodes.

In the case of distributed monitoring (Agha et al., 2006), each distributed node contains local monitor. The monitoring node maintains entire view of monitoring system. The monitoring has been propagated through messages among the different nodes. The monitoring system (Novikov et al., 2011) has a level wise function and is distributed over neighboring elements theoretically a complex objects.

2.10 Monitoring Tools

The network monitoring tool helps to monitor utilization of traffic, bandwidth availability and utilization, latency, CPU utilization, responsiveness of CPU and fault identification. These monitored parameters help the network monitoring tool to estimate the performance of distributed systems easily. Normally, network monitoring tool is a combination of software and hardware products. It completely tracks the network activities and raises an alert if required.

In energy manufacturing plant (Wiczer et al., 2015) it is very difficult to decide about how much capacity is required to get desired output. There is a chance of capacity review and capacity measurement techniques, but it should be associated with new machine with many functions. One of the solutions to measure capacity is use of multiple sensors. This solution has been used to quantify variations in power input throughout monitoring. It determines the amount of power input reduction during manufacturing. A monitoring tool has been used to identify and validate energy use reduction system.

2.10.1 Features of Network Monitoring Tools

The network monitoring tool acts as eyes and ears of an organization to solve the problems. These tools monitor the server or system crash, running application, utilization of bandwidth and utilization of CPU as well as memory. Monitoring tool has been included with following features viz., automatic discovery, inventorying devices, warnings and web-based interface. The monitoring tool (Dmitrienko, Blinov & Novikov, 2011) should be able to diagnose both IPv4 and IPv6 traffics of traditional network. Most of the monitoring tool uses sensors to collect information for the purpose of analysis. Some monitoring tools uses agents to collect information, but use of these agents affect the overall performance of the system. Hence, agent less monitoring tool may be considered as a little efficient product. One more important feature of the monitoring tool is that, monitoring tools are able to monitor all applications and services which run across the network. It enables the network administrators to analyse performance issues from either the network or application itself. This feature of monitoring tool lets network administrators to track response time of application such as processing of server request and response of networks. The following list provides the various features of the monitoring tools:

- **Auto Discovery:** It is very awkward for system administrators to insert each healthy device manually. Most of the monitoring tools perform auto discovery of system. It helps system administrators to get a glance of IT infrastructure catalogue.
- **Network Traffic Status:** Apart from monitoring CPU, memory and disk utilization, monitoring tools may be used to monitor network bandwidth usage. It helps the network administrators to get an insight into the ISP's bandwidth utilization.
- **Log Monitoring:** Monitoring tools manage the activity logs created by operating systems. It verifies the file size of activity log and performs configuration actions. This feature helps the system administrator to control the entire network infrastructure.
- **Alert Management:** The monitoring tool provides alert signal alongside mere network monitoring activity. For example, if a firewall system drops more number of packets or if the CPU of a server crosses the 95% of utilization etc. In all these cases, the tool should generate alert message to network administrator.
- **Customisable Web Dashboard:** The monitoring tool must be customisable in such ways that, user can decide about what should be on the dashboard. It helps to decide how much manpower should be utilised to address monitoring activities.
- **Security Monitoring:** Monitoring tool should be secure during monitoring. The possible attack on data link layer, network layer and application layer should be encountered with this tool. The network administrators must decide what needs to be monitored, rather than monitoring all parameters.

2.10.2 How Network Monitoring Works

For observing the issues of network connectivity, ping utility is sufficient for simple network. The Microsoft network monitoring provides analysis of network packets mainly to resolve network issues. Normally open source network monitoring tool provides accuracy of data based on metrics, but these require additional utilities like automatic alert signals. These open source monitoring tools are inexpensive, but these are inefficient.

2.10.3 GEMOM Monitoring Tool

The security related evidences as well as maintaining of the security metrics in the database is the responsibility of GEMOM Monitoring Tool. Each Message Broker contains one Monitoring Tool. The Monitor Core (MC) process normally runs in the background and it offers messaging services to Monitor Modules. The GEMOM adaptive security uses a State of Security (SoS). The SoS helps to estimate appropriate collection of security metrics purely based on security performance level. Basically, the concept of SoS includes five steps, viz., Initial SoS, Current SoS, Compare SoS, Adapted SoS, and Predicted SoS. All the above sets of SoS's are time dependent estimation of security performance level of the Systems. The performance level is, usually based on the collection of security metrics.

2.10.4 Sharpcap Based Data Packet Capturing

Yin Guohui et al. (2010) addressed about information capture with the help of Sharpcap monitoring tool. The Sharpcap is a tool for capturing the high level network layer information. Here, information that passes through data link layer is usually captured. The Sharpcap is also a perfect combination of the Winpcap module and networks API's. Sharpcap captures the packets accurately, efficiently, steadily and rapidly. It also integrates network management activities and Winpcap packet at the same time. That is why it is used as a network monitoring activity. Sharpcap is more accurate and faster than Wireshark tool. The Wireshark captures traffic data in real time environment (Hernandez, Pedraza, & Salgado, 2013). It captures one packet for every ten milliseconds of one time slot. So, very large number of packets has been stored one hour time slot. For every such capture, the Wireshark saves the elapsed time, capture number, protocol used for capturing, size of the packet, source IP address and destination IP addresses have been maintained in capture file.

Florin et al. (2011) presented a solution for limiting the security breaches during monitoring service. An enough security protection against nasty achievement of the monitoring has been provided through the SELinux OS. The security policy has been applied based on new configuration of OS.

2.10.5 Passive Monitoring Framework

Jeswani et al. (2012) proposed a manual as well as automatic based approach for system monitoring. Author's present frameworks with probes for adjusting monitor levels. A typical requirement for any monitoring systems is good quality of monitoring data. This monitoring framework is deployed to capture the activities of communication, computation and storage components. Monitoring metrics needs to be calculated for different collected parameters of nodes. Many of the monitoring tools are able to collect large amounts of metrics as per needs.

The traditional approach of monitoring data leads to collect small amounts of data and modern approach of monitoring leads to a huge amount of information. The second approach is complex and difficult to store. In addition, the analysis of large volumes of information is a difficult task. Authors are focused on, how to merge the two methods to develop proficient solutions for balancing the two techniques.

2.11 Contemporary Cyber Security Social Engineering Solutions

The cyber security can be made official, if and only if all the activities of the user should be consummated. The systems engineering should be reviewed thoroughly and need to establish the fundamentals for cyber security engineering properly(Aldawood & Skinner, 2019). This is the first step towards the incorporation of cyber security into systems engineering. The curriculum of cyber security should be modified to create the incorporation into systems engineering. Finally, cybersecurity specific engineering methods and techniques need to be developed according to the NIST standards. This study offers a critical review of existing protection measures, tools, and policies for organizations to fight the issues of cyber security social engineering. Security measures includes staff understanding programs, awareness and training to non-technical staff members, new security protocols, software application usage, and security protocols to address social engineering threats.

The definition of a socially engineered attack as stated by Atkins et al. (2013) is "a psychological exploitation which scammers use to skillfully manipulate human weaknesses and carry out emotional attacks on innocent people." Social engineering goes away from the technical vulnerability of the users' system. Social Engineering is the act of fraudulence in which target systems are prejudiced into exploring information to a attacker who then carry out tasks pretending to be the target user. The attacked computer system is then used without their information for acts that may be viewed as an exploitation of the authorized use (Twitchell, 2007) & (Diane et al., 2016). The kinds of intrusions that systems are exposed to as a result of social engineering include phishing of private information and targeted attacks based on information gained. Such socially engineered cyber-attacks include the interruption or infection of complex information systems, transfer of unauthorized funds, and stealing of credentials (Lemos, 2017) and (Breda, Barbosa, & Morais, 2017). The techniques used by cyber attackers now days are not through the tools of hardware and software. Cyber threats will not happen through vulnerabilities on information security, instead have focused on operator or vulnerable link of the target organizations (Aldawood, & Skinner, 2018; Lee, Assante, & Conway, 2014).

Setting up controls for socially engineered attacks is necessary in light of the damages these attacks can cause. The attackers used the method of targeted phishing emails that captured a user's credentials to gain access to the back office and production network, causing massive damage to the plant (Applegate, 2009). For detecting malicious email, it is very essential to block the hostname and IP Address continuously. This is the major measure against the attacks in social engineering.

The security tools will be breached by Social engineers to get the informations on various sites of the reputed organizations. The preventive counter measures need to be addressed for such types of attacks. The users data like one time password, username and passwords. The counter measures are designed to overcome such types of psychological stratagems of attackers (Fan, Kevin, & Rong, 2017; Serban, & Serban, 2014). End-users should be very careful with applications that attempt to gain unauthorized access to their operating systems. These types of attacks normally happen during installation of applications without verification. However, staff are unlikely to avoid such attacks without periodically reviewing the newly-used methods of social engineers to attack the human factor. The staffs usually provide the sensitive informations to fake websites without their knowledge. Origination people should educate employees about common tricky methods used by attackers and constantly remind employee of how their vulnerability can cause harm to the organization (Airehrour, Nair, & Madanian, 2018). Their enlightenment through the measure of education has the potential to diminish employees' vulnerability to hacking while performing online activities (Aldawood & Skinner,2018).

Safety measures alertness in any association should be implemented with a official plan. It is very imperative for staffs to be periodically gives awareness and assessed through internal official recognition programs about their familiarity of commonly-used social engineering strategy by attackers. This kind of awareness program gives more information about the suspicious attack detections. Most of the authors (Fan, Kevin, & Rong, 2017; Wang, Li, Tang, & Ni, 2019) prove that it is dangerous to keep employee prepared to perform their duties and behave safely in the workplace. However, social engineers use to revealing sensitive information time to time, even though a rigid use of technical security tools like intrusion detection systems. The awareness program gives the more confidence in employees about their vulnerability point of issue (Applegate, 2009).

2.12 Cyber Extortion Tools

All the smart devices which is connected through the internet of things (IoT) is facing lot of problems related to Ransom viruses. The cybercriminals now a days misuse the internet facility and making cyber threats constantly. The people also tacked by these cyber criminals time to time. Ransomware(Zhang et al., 2010) is the one such weapon for cyber extortion path to newer technology trends such as IoT and smart mobile devices. Ransomware highlight the evaluation of the malware known as ransomware and how it has become a global threat, additionally to recommend on how to stay protected against such threat.

A user - centric cyber security system, collects agents' data to analyze the threats continuously. The analysis and load control schemes (Aldawood & Skinner, 2018) consists of components like Data Acquisition Agents and Online Service Providers to identify the threats and resolve the same. The tool works based on user feedback and develops the analysis process continuously.

The cyber security framework developed for IoT based intrusion detection systems. A security model is built for the plurality of IoT devices based at least in part on the IoT device data, wherein the security model comprises one or more IoT device data ranges . The plurality of IoT devices are monitored to identify a potential intrusion in any of the plurality of IoT devices based at least in part on the IoT device data exceeding any of the one or more IoT device data ranges .

Modern Cyber Security Social Engineering Solutions, Measures, Policies, Tools and Applications: A Critical Appraisal Social engineering is a major threat to organizations as more and more companies digitize operations and increase connectivity through the internet. After defining social engineering and the problems it presents, this study offers a critical review of existing protection measures, tools, and policies for organizations to combat cyber security social engineering. Through a systematic review of recent studies published on the subject, our analysis identifies the need to provide training for employees to ensure they understand the risks of social engineering and how best to avoid becoming a victim. Protection measures include awareness programs, training of nontechnical staff members, new security networks, software usage, and security protocols to address social engineering threats.

A method for assessing effectiveness of one or more cyber security technologies in a computer network includes testing each of two or more component stages of an attack model at a first computer network element twice.

3. CYBER SECURITY TOOLS FOR MONITORING THREATS

Cyber security tools are very important for protecting an IT environment. Irrespective of the size of the network, safeguarding the network is important (Vijay,2019). Security measures need to be in place for the user network. Cyber Security Software can be categorized into different types as per the following functionalities mentioned below:

- Network Security Monitoring Tools.
- Encryption Tools.
- Web Vulnerability Scanning Tools.
- Network Defence Wireless Tools.
- Packet Sniffers.
- Antivirus Software.
- Firewall.
- PKI Services.
- Managed Detection Services.
- Penetration Testing.

3.1 Mimecast, CIS and Snort

Mimecast is most commonly used trendy Cyber Security tools (Vijay, 2019) for providing a security to users email systems. It provides its services in cloud platform. Also it provides the cyber flexibility for the users of the network. It provides multiple products and services like Email security with threat protection, Information protection, Web security, Cloud Archiving, etc. The Mimecast is best suitable for small scale to large scale organizations cyber protections. It is available for reasonable prices. The following are various features of Mimecast.

1. Email Security with risk management protects from phishing attacks, spam emails, ransomware virus attacks, masquerade and some other types of embattled attacks by hackers.
2. Mimecast has features for computerized Content Control and information loss prevention.
3. It provides web security by blocking improper business websites and protecting against user-initiated malevolent web activity & malware.
4. Mimecast provides a Cloud Archiving facility to securely store images files, documents, email messages, and other valuable information.

Centre for Internet Security (CIS) provides various cyber security tools, security services, and membership options for users of the networked organization. CIS provides membership options to Cloud users, Managed Service Providers, product vendors, IT consultants and hosting. CIS Secure Suite is used for commercial purposes. CIS Security suite contains CIS controls and CIS Benchmarks components to analyze and detect the intrusions. CIS is suitable for small scale to large scale business organizations. Users of the network need to pay only for CIS Secure Suite commercial versions. All the other components like CIS CAT Lite, CIS RAM, CIS CSAT, CIS Controls, CIS Benchmarks are available for free of cost for the users. CIS Hardened Images and CIS Services are available for Pay peruse. The CIS is used to identify specific threats in specific platforms. The following are the best features of the CIS tool viz,..

1. For securing your organization, it offers a variety of products like CIS Controls, CIS-CAT Lite, CIS RAM, CIS CSAT, etc.
2. CIS-CAT Lite performs an automated assessment.
3. It provides 24/7 Security Operations Center and Incident Response Services.
4. It provides tools like CIS-CAT Lite, CIS-CAT Pro, CIS Workbench, CIS RAM, and CIS CSAT.

Snort is an open-source platform freely available for users to install it in their networks. Snort is an application used for network intrusion prevention. It is suitable for small scale to medium scale business organizations. Since it is available in open source platform, snort supports FreeBSD, Fedora, Centos, and Windows platform. It can carry out the task of monitoring network packets and streaming data to your screen. Snort protection can be deployed behind the firewall, hence it is considered as a second level defense to network. The snort should have the following features in it viz., real-time packet analysis, packet logging and Open-source platform.

3.2 Wireshark Monitoring Tool

Wireshark is one more network packet analyzer tool, which has been used to capture the network packets(Sharpe, Warnicke, & Lamping,2015). The Wireshark is an open source tool currently used to capture the network packets. The Wireshark tool could be used to monitor the online computers by using IP Address of the nodes. The Software developers, Network engineers, Network system administrators and Researchers use Wireshark tool for various purposes which include the following (Sharpe, Warnicke, & Lamping, 2015):

- Network System Administrators use this tool for troubleshooting the network problems.
- Network engineers use this tool for observing the security problems.
- Software developers are using it for debugging the protocol implementations.
- Researchers have been using this tool for studying the network protocol internals.

3.2.1 Characteristics of Wireshark

The following are the Characteristics of the Wireshark tool:

- By using the network interface, Wireshark tool captures live network packets.
- The complete protocol information can be displayed in each and every captured network packet.
- The captured packets could be saved and opened later. Also these captured packets could be filtered based on some specific criteria and protocol.
- Wireshark tool colorizes the captured packets based on filtrations of packets.

3.2.2 Limitations of Wireshark

The following are some of the limitations of the Wireshark tool when it is used in monitoring networked systems:

1. Wireshark tool never detects any intrusions during monitoring. Hence it does not act as an Intrusion Detection System. For example, Wireshark tool does not provide any vigilant message if some other user changes the network bustle or performs unauthorized modifications in the network.
2. By using Wireshark tool it is very difficult to detect any kind of manipulation over the network.
3. Wireshark tool gives the dump of information at a time. It is difficult to do the customization of data by using this tool.
4. By using Wireshark tool, any user who resides within the network can view the contents of the packets which flow through the network.
5. It is very difficult to implement and integrate with users connections, because Wireshark tool is an open source.
6. It is very hard to keep track of the network activity of individuals, since it is not user-friendly.

3.3 Webroot, SolarWinds Threat Monitor and GnuPG

Webroot(Vijay, 2019) is a one more cloud-based protection application used by all the users. Webroot can protect Personal Computers, Apple Mac Systems, and various mobile devices. It is best suitable for small scale business organizations to large scale business organizations along with individual users. Webroot is best suitable for individual use, small start-ups offices and small business organizations. The following are the features of the webroot application. Webroot provides Domain Name System (DNS) security, End user security and threat intelligence security. It provides security attentiveness preparation for business organizations. It provides a good protection to the network. However, it slows down the other web applications. The Webroot application has advanced features, which includes instantaneous protection against intrusions, end-users sheltered with multi-layer protection, cloud-based threat intelligence services and provides a predictive intrusion detection services.

Solarwinds Threat Monitor tool is a kind of network-based IDS and host-based intrusion detection system. It performs concurrent watching, counter measures, and reporting of security warnings. It has highly indexed log search capabilities. SolarWind is also a cloud-based tool to perform scalable solution. Solarwinds threat monitor is developed for managed service providers. It is suitable for small scale to large scale business organizations. Solarwinds threat monitor is more expensive. However, it is availed for 14 days trial version for the users. The following are the list of features available in SolarWinds threat monitor application:

- The continuous update of Threat intelligence systems.
- SolarWinds Monitor has functions for Safety Information and Incident Response.
- It provides features of Log relationship and Log occurrence records.
- It offers a absolute set of integrated reporting techniques.

GnuPG is a security tool for encipherment and digitally signed information with secure communications. It supports for Apple ioS, Apple Mac, Windows Systems and all Linux platforms. It is freely available for all users in the network. GnUPG is suitable for small scale to large scale business organizations. The features available in GnuPG are listed below. It is used for file and email encryption. This tool is feasible open source alternative for Pretty Good Privacy (PGP) of the user e-mail security.

- Flexible key administration system.

- GnUPG has access components for all categories of public key infrastructures.
- Ease of integration with all other modules or tools.
- It supports both S/MIME and Secure Shell mechanisms.

3.4 Bitdefender Total Security, Nortan Security and BluVector

Bitdefender Total Security (Vijay, 2019) provides an online-based information security tool for the individual user PCs. It is having a feature of file shredder, social network protection, privacy firewall, susceptibility assessment, secure online banking, etc. It offers non-stop widespread support to the users. It has features for Anti-Phishing and Anti-Theft. Bitdefender is an anti-malware software to provide the cyber security solutions for home appliances, business organizations, service providers and service partners. It also supports Apple Mac, iOS devices, Windows systems and Android devices. It is suitable small scale to large scale organizations. The application is available for pay per basis. However, it is also available for 30 days trail version. The security features included in the Bitdefender Total Security are 1)multilayer ransomware security along with ransomware therapy, 2) provides Network Intrusion Protection, 3)It has features for comprehensive instantaneous information security and advanced intrusion defense and 4)It has features for Web-based attack Prevention, Anti-Fraud, and Rescue Mode.

Norton Security provides an all in one service through Norton Security 360 with Life Lock. This security offers a cybersecurity software solution such as Antivirus, Virus elimination, Malware security, Cloud-based platform backing, Password Manager, and Secure Virtual Private Network (VPN). Norton security not available for free. However, it is available for 30-day free trial version. The following are the features of Norton Security application:

1. Norton Security will defend against ransomware, worms. trosions, intrusions, malware, and online threats.
2. Norton Security offers a five-layer defence for identifying and blocking intrusions.
3. Norton Security provides cloud-based backup systems which can accumulate and protect documents.
4. Norton Password Manager maintains user passwords in simple and secure way.
5. Norton Security offers a secure Norton Virtual Private Network.

BluVector offers an instantaneous sophisticated threat identification mechanism to the users. This kind of Network-based Intrusion Detection Systems (NIDS) are based on Artificial Intelligence, Machine Learning, and speculative code execution. It is suitable for medium scale to large scale business organizations. It is used for commercial purpose. It has flexible deployment options and used for large sized network. The following are the best features of BluVector:

- BluVector Cortex can respond to all types of intrusions on networks.
- Intrusions such as Zero-day malware and Ransomware can also be monitored, identified, investigated, and controlled instantaneously.
- BluVector Cortex contains three modules i.e. Artificial Intelligence based Detection Engines, Intelligent Decision Support, and Connectors Framework.

3.5 NMap and Truecrypt

NMap is a port scanning tool used for large networks and individual host systems. NMap can be applied for network detection and security auditing. It is available for free and open source. It can be used for upgrading the various networking components like switch, router, hub, bridge etc. NMap can be used to maintain the various networking components. It will also helps to monitor the host or service uptime. It is a powerful, flexible and easy tool for port scanning techniques. NMap has working both in a command-line interface as well as Graphical User Interface. It supports for all platforms, so it can able to monitor large networks at a time. The NMap offers a support to a variety of sophisticated techniques.

Most of the open source applications are available at disk level encryption (Garbade, 2019) Truecrypt is a one such disk level encryption application used in networks. It is used for plug and play option by disk level encryption. It encrypts automatically before information is saved on the disk and decrypts.

3.6 Open Web Application Security

Open Web Application is used for against the web vulnerabilities. It is a critical security application because as the usage of web application is increasing day to day life rather than desktop applications. This application provides most excellent practices and code check measures among other strategy.

3.6.1 ClamAV

ClamAV is an virus detection tool at individual PC level security. It provides security for particular systems like router servers and individual PCs. ClamAV is the ideal virus detection systems to examine information deriving from different computers. This is an open-source virus detection tool designed for grab hold of intrusions, viruses and malwares which tries to filch data from server.

3.6.2 Open Source SECcurity (OSSEC)

OSSEC is an open source integrated intrusion detection tool that provides SIM and SEM clarification as well as log monitoring. It is an open source host-based intrusion detection system (HIDS) used to detect viruses. The best features of the OSSEC including File Integrity Checking, Monitoring Logs, Detecting Rootlets, Active Response and Providing seamless network security. It helps the customers to assemble standards and incorporate security occurrence organization and protection incident supervision.

3.6.3 Open VulnerAbility Scanning(OpenVAS)

OpenVAS provides a comprehensive vulnerability scanning tool freely available for the users. It is a formulation of framework of services. This tool offers a rigorous vulnerability scanning and management systems. It is similar to Nessus intrusion detection system, which is freely available for users. Vulnerability administration can be incorporated to patch and configuration management plus virus detection tool for eliminating intrusions or malware.

3.6.4 BackTrack, OSSIM, IPCop

BackTrack is a popular open source security tool for testing viruses in the network. It comprises of highest number Operation Support (OSS) Tools that classified into various areas. It provides continuous solutions as per security requirements. It helps to track the entire networked systems to provide essential security.

Open Source Security Information Management (OSSIM) provides an all in one security solution for a security data and event administration. It is best suitable for monitoring the healthiness of networked nodes. It is available at low cost, compare to other tools.

IPCop is the linux-based firewall tool configured to protect the host network. It provides the security till sphere of perimeter, which is the last border where the network ends and internet security begins. IPCop can be operated on Personal Computer machines or at the back of the Internet Service Provider (ISP) network. IPCop provides the features such as Domain Name System Server, Application Gateway and Dynamic Host Configuration Protocol server.

4. SPECIAL CYBER SECURITY TOOLS

Some of the special cyber security tools can be used to avoid the cyber attacks in networked computers of the organizations has been demonstrated by Nubera eBusiness S.L. (2010). These cyber security tools help to monitor the network continuously for improving the efficiency of the network. The following are the some of the popular cyber security tools.

4.1 Manage-Engine Firewall Analyzer

Manage-Engine Firewall Analyzer monitors the user firewall system, VPN and Server functionality. This analyzer provides the most excellent utility of networking security devices with widespread log details, auditing, and reporting. Manage-Engine maintains a network firewalls such as Cyberome, Fortinet, SonicWall and so on. It analyzes incoming and outgoing packets of the firewall systems. It also provides the notifications during dynamic changes in the networks. It controls probable network attacks. The Manage-Engine helps the user to get information about possible malwares or intrusions, there by stops the breaches.

4.2 Splunk Enterprise Security

Splunk Enterprise Security provides a service through threat intelligence and malware detection. Users can puddle several intrusion sources and can regulate the activities related to intrusions. Splunk provides the statistical analysis and anomaly detections. It also monitors the user activities for detecting threats and provides enterprise security systems. Splunk Enterprise Security system analyzes user email, monitoring irregular activities, reply to sql injections and SSL protocol.

4.3 Websense Triton and Nexpose

Websense Triton is a one more open source intrusion detection system that provides complete network security elucidation to find the complicated security breaches. This application also helps to detect and prevent the identified network risks. Trion Application Gateway is a proxy server that classifies the suspected websites of the present internet world. All kinds of website-based intrusions can be blocked by Websense Triton application software. It constantly monitors the activities of user dynamically as and when it is accessed.

Nexpose is intrusion detection software that manages the vulnerabilities in the network and provides more security to the systems was demonstrated by EDUCBA (2019). By using the threat intelligence systems, Nexpose reduces the risky activities there by helps the network administrator. It can be deployed very easily and provides a scalability and flexibility. It determines the security measures properly and certifies that an assessment of security follows the regulations of security system. Nexpose automatically scans and monitors all types of suspicious viruses, policy breaches and malware intrusions. It also monitors the wrong configurations of the networked computers.

4.4 IBM Security QRADAR, Solar Winds Firewall Security Manager and NCHRONOS

IBM Security QRadar is an one more complete intrusion detection software utilized in IT infrastructure today. It instantly analyzes the normal threats with false positive intrusions. It correlates the current data with real intrusions in the network, there by helps to identify the false positives. The threat intelligence can be incorporated with IBM QRadar for identifying the IP spoofing activities in the network. The IP spoofing activities are based on malicious IP addresses that include malicious nodes, spam nodes and other intrusions. The architecture of QRadar analyze the logs, vulnerabilities and flooding activities. It works based on the priority of data.

SolarWinds Firewall Security Manager provides a absolute and simplified firewall functions in network layer. It provides a customized risk management system and performs quickly with users. SolarWinds automatically performs the security audits and sends the reports quickly to network administrator. The policy check to making auidit trails includes NIST, SNAs and NSA. The analysis provides a detailed report containing transportation of packets in adaptive networks. It offers a regulation, legalization of access control lists and management of security breaches.

nChronos is a complete security solution to identify, defend and avoid cyber attacks or cybercrimes. It is not limited to SNMP network. The nChronos economically examine all incoming and outgoing traffic activity of the network. It engenders the alerts and notices in case of abnormal activities of the network. The alerts and notifications will be based on email and discussion sessions. nChronos a network application that is suitable for both medium and large networks. This tool constantly sniffs the packet to monitor the abnormal activities of the network. nChronos helps the network administrator to replay the recorded data packets to find the cyber attacks.

4.5 Cyber Security Penetration Testing Tools

With the present propagation of intrusions on computer nodes, need to protect the critical information systems safely. Penetration testing is the one of the best methods utilized by organizations and personal computers to protect the data from attacks. Penetration testing is also called as pen testing, used to determine the vulnerabilities present in the networks. This discovery should happen before hackers get into them. There are four types penetration testing tools are used by various organizations at present. Penetration Testing was demonstrated by Nubera eBusiness S.L. (2010).

Metasploit is one of the very fashionable online based applications installed on server systems to discover the vulnerabilities. This tool is widely used by Cyber security professionals for evaluating the security management. It formulates protection techniques to accomplish goals of the IT experts, there by identifies the vulnerabilities before it identified by attackers.

Aircrack-ng is a complete collection of functions for analyzing the vulnerabilities of the wireless network. This tool facilitates the network admin to examine the security of the network by packet sniffing techniques. Further, sniffed packet will be analyzed for enhancing the security of the network. This tool helps to verify the routine works of the wireless network cards by capture packets and SQL injection techniques. Aircrack-ng tool can be used to ensure the reliability of the Wireless Encryption Protocol (WEP) and WPA-PSK.

Most of the cyber security attack happens due to use of simple conventional passwords multiple times. Hackers generally negotiate users' passwords and cause substantial damages to the networks. So, penetration test can examine such types of attacks. John the Ripper is one such tool used for discovering vulnerabilities of the networks. John the Ripper is available for freely and combine various password crackers into single package. This tool is used to launch attacks with the intention of finding password vulnerabilities in a networked system or a database.

Burp Suite is a popular tool for inspecting the security of one line based applications. It contains different collections of tools used for carrying out various safety testing. Burpsuite is a tool that analyses the requests and replies take place between client and server system. It also maps the attack surface of the software application and works automatically. This tool is available in two different versios viz., free version and professional version.

5. CHALLENGES OF CYBER SECURITY

More than 3.5 million cybersecurity job offers will be available by year 2021 due to huge number of cyber attacks by cyber criminals. The major duty of cyber security professional is to avoiding ransomware attempts to provide privacy to customers of the networked systems. The following are the major challenges of the cyber security professionals explained by John Mason, (2018, Jan 10).

5.1. Ransomware Evolution

Ransomware is one of the irritations for cyber security professionals, Information Technology industry, data professionals, and other organizations. The cyber criminals demand millions of dollars to unlock the information of the users from ransomware viruses. This kind of cybercrime viruses are increasing fastest now days. One of the surveys finds that, almost 36 percent of attacks have been increased every year. The sad part of Ransomware is that, attacks are not vanishing with time. Almost, 20 percent of the existing organizations still not installed their failure recovery solutions. In such cases, Ransomware viruses are more vulnerable to attack. The Disaster Recovery Solutions (DRSs) are the best protection against ransomware attacks. DRSs automatically backing up your data during data processing itself and it launch fail-over data as and when it required.

5.2. Artificial Intelligence(AI) Expansion

The AI Robots may be used to protect against inbound cyber attacks. Most the organizations spend more than 2.5 billion dollars on AI robotics to avoid cyber attacks in the network. The AI Expansion development gives major benefits compare to all other types of solutions. Also, AI Robots performs its works 24/7 without any break. Sometimes recovery is very difficult fact, once damage was done. This AI Robot stops the malware and other intrusions while downloading the data itself.

5.3. IoT Threats

Nowadays most of the individual devices are always connected each other with internet world. A survey says that, almost 80 percent of the handhold devices are plugged in, this is the beginning for threats in Internet of Things (IoT). The IoT helps user to control all the household devices of the home. For example, refrigerator may give the information when the vegetables runs out or Alexa may order you a ice-cream. However, beyond the benefits of IoT, user devices are more vulnerable to cyber attacks by hackers. Almost 70 percent of the Internet of Things appliances have susceptible to intrusion attacks. The types of vulnerabilities that can be open to attacks are:

- Insecure websites.
- Insecure data transfers.
- Deficiency in authentication techniques.
- Lack of customer safety measures.

This kind of risks can be avoided by making use of time-out sessions, two-layer authentication, username checking, integrated passphrases and complicated security protocols.

5.4. Blockchain Revolution

Blockchain is the one of the new technology that can be used to provide the security to user data effectively. The cryptocurrencies built upon blockchains ensures the decentralized secure transactions. Blockchain helps the organizations to manage the medical records securely. Also, this technology helps the cyber security professionals to decentralized access control and uniqueness administrations. The blockchain revolution enables the complementary integrations with conventional cyber security approaches.

5.5. Serverless Applications Vulnerability

Consumer data is more vulnerable to attack, when it is accessed through Serverless applications. This kind of access invites more risks for cyber attacks. When the information is available in server, user can provide more security precautions than serverless applications. In serverless applications, user needs to overcome activities of cyber criminals. However, serverless apps are usually utilized by most of the organizations.

CONCLUSION

This chapter is a systematic review of various cyber security threats and attacks in the present internet world. In this survey, possible cyber security threats and attacks were discussed along with detection and analysis of intrusions, malware as well as viruses by using Intrusion Detection Systems. Vulnerabilities of IDS, monitoring tools also have been discussed.

Finally, this chapter provides the various cyber security tools, its advantages; usage, cost and vulnerabilities were discussed. Various categories of cyber security tools and its deployment challenges are also discussed in detail.

REFERENCES

Abraham, A., Grosan, C., & Chen, Y. (2005). *Cyber Security And The Evolution Of Intrusion Detection Systems*. Information Management & Computer Security - IMCS. 1. . doi:10.26634/jfet.1.1.968

Airehrour, D., Vasudevan Nair, N., & Madanian, S. (2018). Social Engineering Attacks and Countermeasures in the New Zealand Banking System: Advancing a User-Reflective Mitigation Model. *Information*, *9*(5), 110. doi:10.3390/info9050110

Al Quhtani, M. (2017). Data Mining Usage in Corporate Information Security: Intrusion Detection Applications, *Business Systems Research*, *8*(1), 51–59.

Aldawood, H., & Skinner, G. (2019). Contemporary Cyber Security Social Engineering Solutions, Measures, Policies, Tools, and Applications: A Critical Appraisal, *International Journal of Security (IJS)*, *10*(1), p. 15.

Aldawood, H., & Skinner, G. (2018). Educating and Raising Awareness on Cyber Security Social Engineering: A Literature Review. In the *Proceedings of IEEE International Conference on Teaching, Assessment, and Learning for Engineering (TALE)*. Australia: IEEE.

Aldawood, H., & Skinner, G. (2018). Challenges of Implementing Training and Awareness Programs Targeting Cyber Security Social Engineering. In *International Conferences on Cyber Security and Communication Systems,* Melbourne, Australia. Academic Press.

Applegate, S. D. (2009). Social engineering: Hacking the wetware! *Information Security Journal. Article*, *18*(1), 40–46.

Atkins, B., & Huang, W. (2013). A study of social engineering in online frauds. *Open Journal of Social Sciences*, *1*(3), 23–32. doi:10.4236/jss.2013.13004

Bhumika, P., & Bhushan, K. (2019). Fog Computing: Concepts, Applications, and Countermeasures Against Security Attacks, *Handbook of Research on Cloud Computing and Big Data Applications in IoT,* pp. 302-329, IGI Global.

Breda, F., Barbosa, H., & Morais, T. (2017). Social engineering and cyber security. In the *Proceedings of International Technology, Education, and Development Conference*, 4204-4211. Valencia, Spain, 10.21125/inted.2017.1008

Chiappetta, A. (2019). *Survey on Industrial Internet of Things (IoT) Threats and Security. In Handbook of Research on Cloud Computing and Big Data Applications in IoT* (pp. 330–366). IGI Global.

Chu, C., & Brockmeyer, M. (2010). Mobile Agents and Eventually Perfect Predicate Detection: An Intelligent General Approach to Monitoring Distributed Systems. In A. Hākansson, R. Hartung, & N. T. Nguyen (Eds.), *Agent and Multi-agent Technology for Internet and Enterprise Systems. Studies in Computational Intelligence* (Vol. 289). Berlin, Germany: Springer. doi:10.1007/978-3-642-13526-2_12

Department of Information Technology-Government of India. (2006). *Indian Computer Emergency Response Team Handling Computer Security Incidents Intrusion Detection System* (CERT). In *Security Guideline CISG 2003-06*. India: Ministry of Electronics & Information Technology.

Dmitrienko, A., Blinov, A., & Novikov, V. (2011). Distributed smart system for monitoring the state of complex technical objects. *Measurement Techniques*. pp. 235-239. . doi:10.100711018-011-9713-0

Jiang, F., Fu, Y., Gupta, B. B., Lou, F., Rho, S., Meng, F., & Tian, Z. (2018). *Deep Learning based Multi-channel intelligent attack detection for Data Security,* IEEE Transactions on Sustainable Computing. DOI:. doi:10.1109/TSUSC.2018.2793284

Donkervoet, B., & Agha, G. (2006). Reflecting on Aspect-Oriented Programming, Metaprogramming, and Adaptive Distributed Monitoring. In *Proceedings 5*[th] *International Symposium FMCO 2006*, (pp. 246-265). Berlin, Germany: Springer.

Eckhardt, J., & Miouhlbauer, T. (2012, Feb 15). Enhancing Safety and Security of Distributed Systems through Formal Patterns. Retrieved from http://ceur-ws.org/Vol-834/paper6_essosds2012.pdf

EDUCBA. (2019). Top 32 most important cyber security tools you must aware, Retrieved August 21, 2019 from https://www.educba.com/32-most-important-cyber-security-tools/

Fan, W., Kevin, L., & Rong, R. (2017). Social engineering: IE based model of human weakness for attack and defense investigations. *IJ Computer Network and Information Security*, 9(1), 1–11. doi:10.5815/ijcnis.2017.01.01

Garbade, M. J. (2019). Seven best cyber security tools, Retrieved from https://www.cybrary.it/0p3n/7-cyber-security-pentesting-tools/

Greavu-Serban, V., & Serban, O. (2014). Social engineering a general approach. *Informatica Economica*, 18(2), 5.

Gupta, B., Gupta, S., & Chaudhary, P. (2017). Enhancing the Browser-Side Context-Aware Sanitization of Suspicious HTML5 Code for Halting the DOM-Based XSS Vulnerabilities in Cloud. [IJCAC]. *International Journal of Cloud Applications and Computing*, 7(1), 1–31. doi:10.4018/IJCAC.2017010101

Gupta, B. B., Agrawal, D. P., & Wang, H. (2019). *Computer and Cyber Security: Principles, Algorithm, Applications, and Perspectives*. Boca Raton, FL: CRC Press, Taylor & Francis Group.

Gupta, S., & Gupta, B. B. (2015). PHP-sensor: a prototype method to discover workflow violation and XSS vulnerabilities in PHP web applications, *Proceedings of the 12th ACM International Conference on Computing Frontiers*, pp. 1-8, Italy: ACM NY. 10.1145/2742854.2745719

Halvorsen, J., Waite, J., & Hahn, A. (2019). Evaluating the Observability of Network Security Monitoring Strategies With TOMATO. *IEEE Access: Practical Innovations, Open Solutions*, 7, 108304–108315. doi:10.1109/ACCESS.2019.2933415

Heartfield, R., & Gan, D. (2016). Social Engineering in the Internet of Everything. Cutter IT Journal, 29(7), 20-29.

Hernandez, C., Pedraza, L. F., & Salgado, C. (2013). A proposal of traffic model that allows estimating Throughput mean values, *Proceedings of 27th International Conference on Advanced Information Networking and Applications Workshops*, Washington, DC: IEEE Computer Society. 10.1109/WAINA.2013.216

Kumar, B. S., Ch, T., Raju, R. S. P., Ratnakar, M., Baba, S. D., & Sudhakar, N. (2013). Intrusion Detection System- Types and Prevention. *International Journal of Computer Science and Information Technologies*, 4(1), 77–82.

Jeswani, D., Natu, M., & Ghosh, R. K. (2012). Adaptive Monitoring: A Framework to AdaptPassive Monitoring using Probing, In *Proceedings of 8th International Conference on Network and Service Management (CNSM 2012)*, Las Vegas, NV. Academic Press.

Jun, K., & Kang, S. (2004). Adaptive and Distributed Fault Monitoring of Grid by Mobile Agents, In *Third International Conference on Grid and Cooperative Computing(GCC 2004)*. (pp. 975-978). China: Springer-Verlag Heidelberg.

Lee, R. M., Assante, M. J., & Conway, T. (2014). German steel mill cyber attack. *Industrial Control Systems*, 30, 62.

R. Lemos. (2017,Nov). Expect a New Battle in Cyber Security: AI versus AI. Symantec Publications.

Manjunath, K., Chiplunkar, N. N., & Nagesh, H. R. (2016). Framework of Security Mechanisms for Monitoring AdaptiveDistributed Systems, *IOSR Journal of Computer Engineering (IOSR-JCE)e-, 18*(4), Ver. I, pp. 25-36.

Mason, J. (2018, Jan. 10). Cyber Security trends and challenges, Retrieved from https://www.globalsign.com/en-in/blog/cybersecurity-trends-and-challenges-2018/

Massie, M. L., Chun, B. N., & Culler, D. E. (2004). *The ganglia distributed monitoring system: design, implementation, and experience, Parallel Computing* (pp. 817–840). Elsevier; doi:10.1016/j.parco.2004.04.001

Mittal, H., Jain, M., & Banda, L. (2013). Monitoring Local Area Network using Remote Method Invocation. *International Journal of Computer Science and Mobile Computing*, 2(Issue. 5), 50–55.

Nubera eBusiness S. L. (2010). *Top 10 Network Cybersecurity tools for Enterprises*, Retrieved Sept 27, 2019 from https://www.coranet.com/top-10-network-cybersecurity-tools/

Olakanmi, O. O., & Dada, A. (2019). An Efficient Privacy-preserving Approach for Secure Verifiable Outsourced Computing on Untrusted Platforms. *International Journal of Cloud Applications and Computing*, 9(2), 79–98. doi:10.4018/IJCAC.2019040105

Pop, F., Arcalianu, A., Dobre, C., & Cristea, V. (2011). Enhanced Security for Monitoring Services in Large Scale Distributed Systems, *IEEE International Conference on Computer Communication and Processing (ICCP 2011)*, pp. 549-556. Cluj-Napoca, Romania, 10.1109/ICCP.2011.6047929

Priyanka, S., & Singh, K. R. (2016). Cyber Attacks On Intrusion Detection System, *International Journal of Information Sciences and Techniques (IJIST), 6*(1/2).

Schwiderski, S. (1996, April). *Monitoring the Behaviour of Distributed Systems* (Doctoral Thesis). Retrieved from https://www.microsoft.com/en-us/research/wp-content/uploads/2016/02/scarlets-scarletschwiderskiphd.pdf

Sharpe, R., Warnicke, E., & Lamping, U. (2015). Wireshark User's Guide, Retrieved from http://www.wireshark.org/docs/wsug_html_chunked/

Sung, A., Abraham, A., & Mukkamala, S. (2005). *Cyber-Security Challenges: Designing Efficient Intrusion Detection Systems and Anti-Virus Tools*. Enhancing Computer Security with Smart Technology.

Twitchell, D. P. (2007). Social engineering in information assurance curricula. In *Proceedings of the 2006 Information Security Curriculum Development Conference, InfoSecCD '06*. Academic Press.

U.S. Department of Transportation. (2019). *Cybersecurity and Intelligent Transportation Systems, A Best Practice Guide* (Publication Number- FHWA-JPO-19-763). USA: Office of the Assistant Secretary for Research and Technology.(www.its.dot.gov/index.htm)

Vijay. (2019). Most Powerful Cyber Security Software Tools. Software Testing Help, Retrieved from https://www.softwaretestinghelp.com/cybersecurity-software-tools/

Wang, Q., Li, M., Tang, Y., & Ni, M. (2019). Source-Load Coordinated Reserve Allocation Strategy Considering Cyber-Attack Risks. *IEEE Access, 7*, 111332–111340. doi:10.1109/ACCESS.2019.2934646

Wiczer, J., Wiczer, M. B., & Hills, V. (2015). Improving Energy Efficiency Using Customized Monitoring Tools, In *Proceedings of 17th Metalcasting Congress, Modern Casting*, pp. 36-39. Academic Press.

Yan, T., Zeng, S., Qi, M., Hu, Q., & Qi, F. (2019). *Cyber security detection and monitoring at IHEP private cloud for web services*. EPJ Web of Conferences. 214. 07016. 10.1051/epjconf/201921407016

Yi, H., & Zhang, Y. (2010). Research of campus network security system based on intrusion detection, In *the Proceedings of International Conference on Computer Design and Applications*, Qinhuangdao, China. Academic Press.

Yin, G., & Wei, G. (2010).Application Design of Data Packet Capturing Based on Sharpcap, In *Proceedings of Fourth IEEE International Joint Conference on Computational Sciences and Optimization*, Washington, DC: IEEE Computer Society.

Chapter 6
Identification and Classification of Cyber Threats Through SSH Honeypot Systems

José María Jorquera Valero

Department of Information and Communications Engineering, University of Murcia, Spain

Manuel Gil Pérez

Department of Information and Communications Engineering, University of Murcia, Spain

Alberto Huertas Celdrán

https://orcid.org/0000-0001-7125-1710

Telecommunications Software and Systems Group, Waterford Institute of Technology, Ireland

Gregorio Martínez Pérez

Department of Information and Communications Engineering, University of Murcia, Spain

ABSTRACT

As the number and sophistication of cyber threats increases year after year, security systems such as antivirus, firewalls, or Intrusion Detection Systems based on misuse detection techniques are improved in detection capabilities. However, these traditional systems are usually limited to detect potential threats, since they are inadequate to spot zero-day attacks or mutations in behaviour. Authors propose using honeypot systems as a further security layer able to provide an intelligence holistic level in detecting unknown threats, or well-known attacks with new behaviour patterns. Since brute-force attacks are increasing in recent years, authors opted for an SSH medium-interaction honeypot to acquire a log set from attacker's interactions. The proposed system is able to acquire behaviour patterns of each attacker and link them with future sessions for early detection. Authors also generate a feature set to feed Machine Learning algorithms with the main goal of identifying and classifying attacker's sessions, and thus be able to learn malicious intentions in executing cyber threats.

DOI: 10.4018/978-1-7998-2242-4.ch006

Copyright © 2020, IGI Global. Copying or distributing in print or electronic forms without written permission of IGI Global is prohibited.

1. INTRODUCTION

Traditional security systems based on signatures, such as firewalls, antivirus systems or Intrusion Detection Systems (IDS) based on *misuse detection* techniques (Depren, Topallar, Anarim & Ciliz, 2005), are generally not quite effective against unknown threats or new attack patterns not previously registered. However, IDSs based on *anomaly detection* techniques are able to recognise unknown threats, but they are prone to generate false positives –alerts generated when identifying the possible existence of a real threat, when they are actually false alerts because the threat is not true. To cover this need and try to get information of novel threats or attacks, honeypots (Spitzner, 2003) arise, which consist of lure or trap systems whose main goal is to simulate a real system that can be attacked. Through gathered information, it is possible to adapt the IDSs with new detection signatures (those based on misuse detection) or label datasets used by those based on anomaly detection (Jorquera et al., 2018) to retrain their search engine, and, therefore, to increase their precision and recall by reducing the number of false alerts. In addition, one of the main objectives of honeypots is to complement the different traditional techniques in threats detection with a system capable of detecting previously unknown threats, thereby providing a higher level of security (Olakanmi & Dada, 2019).

Honeypots, as the name suggests, are designed to attract the attention of attackers or hackers, so that their efforts to attack and cause serious damage to real systems will be diminished because they are running in a virtual environment. These systems simulate networks and application services such as Report Desktop Protocol (RDP), Secure Shell (SSH), File Transfer Protocol (FTP) and Telnet, amongst others. From the attacker's standpoint, the honeypot system is perceived as a vulnerable execution server that can be used to enter in servers that are currently operational and execute any kind of malicious action.

One of the primary advantages of honeypot systems over traditional systems is that honeypots are able to detect zero-day attacks (Zhang, Wang, Jajodia, Singhal & Albanese, 2016), that is, attacks on vulnerabilities that have not been patched or made public. Another benefit of using honeypots is that they only gather data in case an attack is being generated. Therefore, these systems are able to register a reduced dataset, which involves a lower cost in the system and a lower resource consumption by producing a lower number of alerts that will avoid, in some cases, that administrators can ignore alerts due to the existence of a higher alerts amount and a higher rate of false alerts. In the case of honeypots, whatever access to the system is not normally authorised, therefore, through its use enterprises and organisations can decrease the number of false alerts registered. Finally, another benefit supplied by these systems is to help Information Technology (IT) teams identify vulnerabilities in active servers.

Since there are many honeypot systems that simulate different network and application services, this chapter is focused on Medium-Interaction Honeypots (MIH) (Fraunholz, Krohmer, Anton & Schotten, 2017), that is, honeypots that allow capturing and registering logs about activities and executions from attackers without compromising production systems, based on the SSH (Barrett, Silverman & Byrnes, 2005) network service, being this one the most used by attackers to compromise systems exposed on the Internet. In this subcategory, there are several honeypots that provide similar functionalities amongst others. Since many devices exposed to the Internet are based on Unix systems, one of the most popular honeypot systems is Cowrie (Oosterhof, 2019), which records attacker's commands execution on the system. Another of the main reasons so that this software has been selected is due to its capability to monitor activities and executions carried out by attackers. Furthermore, Cowrie is a honeypot based on SSH, being the brute-force attack the most repeated one when a system is threatened (eSentire, 2017). One more determinant reason so that Cowrie is selected is because amongst all available honeypots of the same family, such as Kippo (Valli, Rabadia & Woodward, 2013) or Kojoney2 (Keane, 2019), Cowrie is currently the most up-to-date SSH-based MIH.

In spite of benefits provided by honeypot systems, these also have a set of challenges that should be tackled to supply an effective system for detecting previously unregistered threats, as well as discovering new patterns of known threat attacks. Some of the challenges to address are an appropriate configuration of the trap system, the risk determination under which our real production system is being exposed, according to the interaction level of the honeypot system, and a suitable features selection to identify threats from the logs generated by honeypots.

With the aim of generating a system that meets the most relevant challenges considered above, this chapter consists of researching, designing and implementing a system capable of classifying the attacker's behaviour on the basis of actions taken (for example, execution of commands) during the duration of their sessions in a protected and simulated environment, such as the one provided by the Cowrie SSH honeypot. Since a honeypot is not capable of carrying out the threat detection phases based on the information that will be gathered in its logs, this work extracts the most relevant features of each session, providing a layer of intelligence (Jiang, Fu, Gupta, Lou, Rho, Meng & Tian, 2018) to Cowrie through various Machine Learning (ML) techniques (Gupta & Sheng, 2019). For this purpose, different ML techniques based on supervised and unsupervised learning have been used with the main objective of classifying similar behaviours between different sessions. In addition, the system allows storing, analysing and visualising the data provided by each attacker during his/her interaction, through tools such as the ElasticSearch search engine (Rosenberg, Coronel, Meiring, Gray & Brown, 2019) or the Kibana data viewer (Sharma, 2017). Likewise, the presented work can be used as a future basis for the subsequent generation of detection signatures with which to update systems based on misuse detection, or the labelling of datasets for detection engines retraining of systems based on anomaly detection.

The rest of this chapter is structured as follows. Section 2 reviews previous works in the same field, focusing attention on proposals based on SSH-based MIHs, as well as solutions that present relevant results from logs generated. Section 3 explains the methodology and the main objectives of the proposed solution. Next, the different experiments performed to improve the final solution are explained in Section 4, while in Section 5 we compare the proposed system with others of the literature and then discuss its possible limitations. Finally, Section 6 summarizes the work carried out and proposes different future steps to continue with the development of the system.

2. LITERATURE REVIEW

In this section, we provide a detailed analysis of the current state-of-the-art for SSH-based MIH systems, as well as several experiments carried out by previous researchers that have been published in different scientific articles and are based on the detection of threats using different honeypots.

In Sadasivam, Hota & Anand (2018), the authors carried out an investigation to differentiate the SSH attacks received in Kippo, a honeypot that was taken as a base for the development of Cowrie with new characteristics, allowing to classify the cyber threats (Gupta, 2018) in two categories (see Figure 1). The first category, also known as *severe attacks*, identifies any session type that logs one or more commands into the system, using a compromised SSH server. The second category includes attacks related to SSH port scans, SSH brute-force attacks and brute-force attacks that are successful but are not subsequently performed on the system. The second category is called *not-so-severe attacks*. Some of the features that

Figure 1. Phases for features acquisition and determination of attacks with Kippo

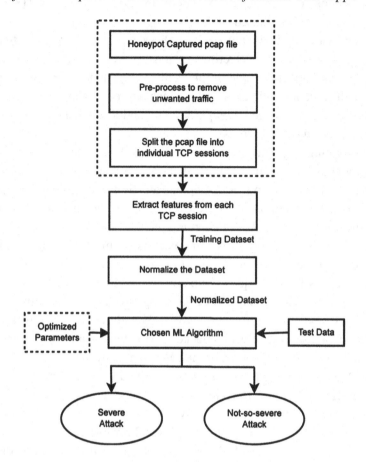

they selected to classify sessions are based on TCP streams, such as the total number of packets received or sent, or the sum of all bytes containing the received payloads. From these features, and using ML algorithms such as k-NN, J48 or PART, the authors obtained in the best case (using J48 and PART) a precision of 1.0, an accuracy of 0.99 and an F2-score of 0.942. Despite obtaining remarkable performance measures to classify SSH attacks according to the nature of the attack, the research provided by authors is not able to determine what type of attack it was.

In a subsequent publication, malicious traffic captured on the network from brute-force attacks on the Kippo honeypot was analysed in (Sadasivam, Hota & Anand, 2018b). Its main purpose was to propose a methodology to segregate individual botnets from network traffic, allowing a more detailed understanding of distributed brute-force attacks that provided a way to detect these attacks. For this purpose, authors analysed the captured TCP flow and determined relevant features that allow linking different traffics to the same botnet. For example, in distributed brute-force attacks, most programs that use a bot are written in the same programming language, SSH client and cryptographic algorithm, and it is possible to use these features to select a set of hots infected by the same botmaster, or even if each of the login credentials are different it is highly likely that this set of IPs forms a botnet.

On the other hand, the research tackled by (Dowling, Schukat & Melvin, 2017) has as its main objective to attract as much malicious traffic as possible and to observe whether the attacker is interested

Figure 2. Network architecture built by the Canadian Institute for Cybersecurity

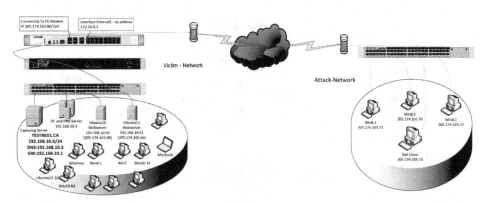

in ZigBee networks. For this, the authors made use of the Kippo SSH honeypot. With this honeypot, attackers can find fictitious ZigBee medical traffic on Wireless Sensor Networks and honeytokens (Padayachee, 2014) pointing to another server, where the researchers had deployed a honeynet. In their testing environment, authors claimed that about 94% of the attacks recorded are dictionary-based attacks. In addition, they claimed that each brute-force detected attack triggered a system reconnaissance attack. It worth mentioning that amongst the attacks that can be detected based on logs we can highlight dictionary-based attacks, brute-force attacks, launched attacks or individual attacks, where the latter shows certain interest in honeytokens and trying to manipulate them, recognition scripts and botnets.

Another study based on attacks on honeypots is the one presented by Sharafaldin, Lashkari & Ghorbani (2018). The authors, who conducted the research in conjunction with the Cybersecurity Institute of Canada, analysed TCP traffic entering their honeypots to obtain a feature set that can detect attacks categories. The test environment consists of a machine set that make up the victim network and a set of 4 computers with different IPs that make up the attackers (see Figure 2). In the case of the attackers, they used both Linux and Windows systems, while in the case of the victims the main operating systems were macOS, Linux and Windows. These authors carried out all the necessary tests in their own controlled environment for 5 days. Each day, specific attacks were performed which were afterwards used to analyse and label the data flows. After testing, they managed to generate a classification for 5 types of attacks: brute-force attacks, Denial of Service (DoS) attacks and Distributed Denial of Service (DDoS) attacks, web attacks, infiltration attacks and botnets. Finally, through the use of classification algorithms such as k-NN and Random Forest, they were able to obtain an accuracy of 0.96 and 0.98, a recall of 0.96 and 0.97, and an F1-score of 0.96 and 0.97, respectively. A limitation of this approach is to face changes in the attack patterns of already known threats such as botnets, which periodically change their activity and their Command & Control (C&C) location mechanisms so that they are not easily detected.

The study carried out by Pauna & Bica (2014) presents a novel implementation of an adaptive honeypot system, which follows the approach used by the Heliza adaptive honeypot, improving several of its disadvantages. The proposed solution, also known as Reinforced Adaptive SSH Honeypot (RASSH), uses the Kippo honeypot code as a base, simulating an SSH server that improves functionalities, in particular providing greater learning capabilities and scalability. This solution improved the Kippo honeypot through the implementation of several new commands, this being one of main reasons why Cowrie was developed later. RASSH is able to interact with attackers through reinforcement learning,

Figure 3. Reinforced learning scheme and available RASSH actions

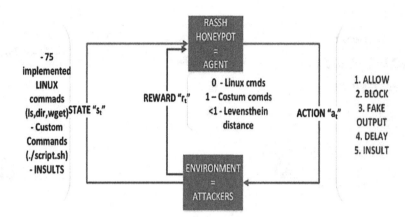

that is, trying to solve the problem faced by an agent when it must learn the behaviour when interacting with a dynamic environment through a test and error mechanism. In addition, the system proposed by Pauna & Bica (2014) develops an intermediate module between a honeypot and the learning layer by reinforcement that allows offering to attackers a wide set of actions (see Figure 3) that will be activated based on the type of commands that the attacker typed. This idea is another improvement to highlight, since one of the main reasons why Kippo was easily detected as a honeypot by attackers was due to it only had two possible actions when a command was typed: accepted or denied. The main disadvantage of this proposal is that the proposed system is not fully operational, so there are no performance measures to prove its effectiveness.

On the other hand, the research undertaken by Kheirkhah, Mehdi, Jahanshahi & Acharya (2013) is based on the study of brute-force SSH attacks received by six different servers from a university network using the Kojoney honeypot. This is a Low-Interaction Honeypot (LIH) that simulates an SSH server. After carefully studying data retrieved from honeypots, the authors reflected in their research some similarities between recorded traffic. The researchers were able to differentiate three categories based on the entered commands. The first category consists of all successful session attempts, without the execution of subsequent commands. The purpose of this category could be the generation of new dictionaries that will be used in later brute-force attacks. The second category is composed by sessions in which attackers make use of commands only to obtain system information, such as *uname -a, proc, cpuinfo, uptime*, etc. Finally, the third category is formed by the rest of the sessions where introduced commands have a higher threat level to the system; for example, the download and execution of malware. In addition, amongst all commands registered in various honeypots, the authors stated that the 20 most repeated commands from attackers intend to provide information about the system.

An interesting study is the one presented by Fraunholz, Krohmer, Anton & Schotten (2017), where an SSH-based MIH (Kippo in this case) was configured, offering Telnet and SSH services. With this honeypot, data of attack sessions were captured to use them for statistical and behavioural analysis, such as the attacks distribution and different IPs of attackers, origin countries, anonymisation used services or skill levels of an adversary. In addition, this paper presents various automatic learning techniques that are capable of identifying unique types of sessions. Specifically, the authors proposed three different approaches to classify each session of attacks. First, the authors attempted to classify sessions according

Figure 4. Metrics to classify attacker's skills

Feature	Example
Delete Commands	history -c
Check Presence	w, who, last, whoami
Delete Malware	rm (-rf) /tmp, rm (-rf) ./
Check System	ifconfig, netstat, cat /proc/ /etc/, lsmod, ps
Edit Config. File	nano/pico/vi/vim/> /etc/
Change System	nano/pico/vi/vim/> /usr/
Change Password	passwd
Manipulate Users	adduser, useradd, deluser, userdel
Manipulate Firewall	iptables, nfttables
Check Env. Variables	echo $

to the length and number of commands. However, due to the small variation in these values, no valid classification could be derived. The second approach was to classify attacks based on the attacker's skill levels, i.e., from a predefined metric the attacker received one point for each of the commands executed that belonged to the list (see Figure 4). Therefore, the higher the total number of points attackers gets, the more expert attackers were. As with the previous approach, this proposal did not obtain optimal results because most of the traffic captured by the honeypot belonged to bots, being the skill level quite uniform. Finally, the third approach was based on generating clusters from two different sets of features. On the one hand, the authors proposed to cluster from the credentials used at the beginning of each session. On the other hand, clustering was proposed based on the commands introduced by attackers. After conducting the appropriate tests, the authors stated that clustering-based approaches worked quite well in terms of generating different groups, while the skills-based approach failed due to honeypot configuration. Note that the authors did not provide graphs where to observe the represented clusters or any measure of performance, beyond indicating the similarity of each cluster with the rest.

On the other hand, in Melese & Avadhani (2016), the authors implemented in their research a Kippo honeypot to analyse SSH attacks. The main objective of this study is the statistics compiled from generated logs during sessions, as well as the conclusions that the authors contributed after studying these results. After carefully analysing the results, the authors described a sequence of common steps that most attacks carry out. First, attackers guess the credentials using automated dictionary-based attacks. Note that all login attempts with username and password were stored by Kippo, allowing through this research that future users avoid using such pairs. Amongst the most repeated credentials were default passwords such as admin, root, 123456, etc. After logging into the simulated SSH server, almost all attackers began their intrusion downloading tools from external servers. Next, attackers began their software installation and configuration tasks, and the most repeated shell commands were recorded. In addition, the authors tracked the location of attackers based on their IP addresses, as well as the SSH client used during each session. In the case of IP addresses, most attacks were originated from China and U.S., while the main used SSH client was SSH-2.0-libssh2. Finally, the authors used the Dionea honeypot (Sochor & Zuzcak, 2014) to capture and analyse possible malware that attackers tried to download. The final results achieved by the authors could be improved in the case of using High-Interaction Honeypots (HIH), which allow

Figure 5. Iterative and incremental cycle

gathering more sophisticated information that is not possible to collect with MIHs. The main disadvantage is that there is currently no SSH-based HIHs that continue to be updated on a regular basis.

3. METHODOLOGY

The work addressed in this chapter has been carried out following an iterative and incremental methodology divided into several blocks (see Figure 5). First, the analysis process on the current state-of-the-art about SSH honeypots. Second, the investigation of the most used techniques to classify attacks or threats. Third, the design and implement of a system that covers the main disadvantages of the current state-of-the-art, and finally, the system evaluation through several public datasets and a pool of specific ML classification techniques. Each block has been reiterated throughout the investigation duration, as a sample of this can be seen three experiments performed (see Section 5), addressing in each of them a new iteration in the iterative and incremental cycle.

In the first stage, an initial planning was carried out, where early steps of the research were established. Amongst them, it was the selection of an SSH-based MIH, specifically Cowrie. Also, to identify the threats registered by the honeypot and to visualise graphs where the most peculiar features about registered attacks are shown. After knowing the initial planning, the next step was the in-depth analysis of the state-of-the-art related to the classification of attacks and SSH honeypots. At the same time, an investigation of public datasets (Zkik, Orhanou & El Hajji, 2017) Cowrie available on the Internet was initiated. Next, the design and implementation of the system was undertaken. To this end, it was necessary to determine the features of the dataset and the most appropriate ML classification algorithms to obtain and analyse the results. Once the ML algorithms were determined, the next step was to verify whether the developed system was capable of identifying and classifying attacks from the selected feature set. After carrying out the first experiment, the obtained results did not reach the expected objectives, therefore we carried out a new iteration cycle with the main purpose of improving the system precision.

Prior to the analysis and redesign phase of the first proposed system, it was necessary to carefully plan the steps to be executed in this second iteration, in order to reduce the shortcomings presented in previous phase. Subsequently, it was derived for second time to the analysis and design phase, as well as to the implementation and evaluation. The obtained results in this second iteration improved satisfactorily the ones gathered during the first iteration, however, after reading new state-of-the-art researches we were aware that these results could be improved with a new iteration. For this reason, it was decided to start a new iteration of the cycle with the new objectives to fulfil. Among them, the insertion of a new set of features or the selection of the Scriptzteam dataset. Note that the rest phases of the iterative and incremental cycle were carried out without any novel changes to highlight.

The main reason for using this type methodology lies in the fact that, unlike other fields of research, projects in this type of engineering undergo constant changes throughout their stages, from new requirements to necessary modifications during the development or evaluation phase. A clear example of this are the three experiments carried out to refine the proposed system.

The accomplishment of the previous iterations was defined to achieve the primary objective of this work, the design and implementation of an intelligent system capable of detecting and classifying the attacks received in an SSH-based MIH, specifically Cowrie. This main objective is composed of the following sub-objectives:

§   Study of the current research on SSH honeypots, as well as the search and analysis of public datasets with logs registered by Cowrie.
§   Visualisation and subsequent analysis in Kibana (Sharma, 2017) of the obtained features from the results generated by attackers, through their interaction in the registered sessions.
§   Determination of relevant features to generate a dataset capable of identifying and classifying each stored session.
§   Study of the most suitable ML techniques to maximise the expected results.
§   Use of ML techniques and dimensionality reduction that allow to link and classify similar behaviours amongst all registered sessions.
§   Careful analysis and discussion of the obtained results in each of the experiments undertaken.

4. RESULTS

This section explains the design and implementation decisions of the threat classification system proposed. Steps taken to acquire features that will make up the dataset, the decisions made regarding to ML algorithm and, finally, different experiments that have been carried out with the different sets of features and datasets.

a.   **Data Visualisation in Kibana**

Before showing and analysing statistics and data about the registered sessions, it is necessary to store each session in ElasticSearch. Through this search engine, Kibana will allow us to make a large number of requests to the stored data, thus allowing to visualise sessions characteristics. To carry out the deployment of ElasticSearch and Kibana applications, it was determined to use the Docker tool that automates the applications deployment, packaged in software units, called *containers*, that will provide greater speed, simplicity and low consumption of resources.

Once all data are recorded in ElasticSearch, Kibana is used to display certain relevant data graphically. Note that the statistics shown below are related to the Scriptzteam dataset (Scriptzteam, 2019) by way

Figure 6. Combination of most used credentials in Scriptzteam dataset

username.keyword: Descending ⇕	password.keyword: Descending ⇕	Count ⌄
admin	admin	6,263
root	support	5,333
1111	1111	5,065
admin	1111	4,900
root	root	4,666
user	1234	4,438
root	admin	3,445
root	system	2,979
root	123456	2,639
admin	1234	2,375

of example, given that it will be the last dataset on which the validation tests of the system presented will be carried out.

Next, we show some graphics that provide the most outstanding information in the Scriptzteam dataset logs. First, the user/password pairs most commonly used to access the SSH honeypot are shown in Figure 6. As shown, default passwords such as *root/admin*, *admin/password*, *admin/admin* or *root/123456* are in the top 10 most used credentials, because nowadays many users do not yet change the default passwords that devices bring from factory, so the probability of accessing a system with such credentials remains high. For this reason, attackers try to access routers or firewalls with established default credentials. In addition, on the basis of this information, an in-depth search could be performed on user/password dictionaries most commonly used by attackers. For example, in the case of brute-force attacks generated by botnets, possible relationships could be established between the credentials, their relationship with the used dictionaries and possible links with IP addresses that use those credentials.

Figure 7. Most used SSH clients in the Scriptzteam dataset

version.keyword: Descending ⇕	Count ⌄
SSH-2.0-PUTTY	219,670
SSH-2.0-libssh2_1.6.0	43,180
SSH-2.0-libssh2_1.4.3	18,276
SSH-2.0-libssh-0.2	18,051
SSH-2.0-OpenSSH_7.3	16,848
SSH-2.0-Granados-1.0	12,380
SSH-2.0-libssh-0.6.0	6,740
SSH-2.0-libssh-0.1	6,696
SSH-2.0-sshlib-0.1	6,649
SSH-2.0-libssh2_1.7.0	5,334

Figure 8. Heat map with different IPs origin of proxies in Scriptzteam dataset

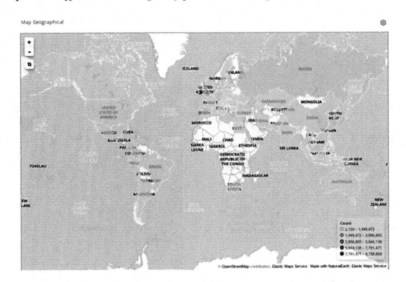

On the other hand, in Figure 7, it can be seen the SSH clients most used by attackers when they try to access the honeypot deployed in the Scriptzteam environment. The results obtained on the most used SSH clients have certain relations with the results published by ElevenPaths in a 2018 white paper (ElevenPaths, 2019), about the most relevant characteristics of different honeypots. Therefore, the SSH client might be considered as a significant feature when linking possible sessions so that repeated threats can be identified.

As a third initial test, Figure 8 depicts a heat map generated by Kibana in which the coordinates associated with each IP of a given session are represented and displayed. In a first glance, we can see that Ireland and United Kingdom are the two states from which the greatest number of attacks come. These results are certainly unusual as the countries with the highest number of generated attacks are usually U.S., China and Russia. This fact is often stated in several state-of-the-art proposals such as the one presented by Melese & Avadhani (2016) or the report published by ElevenPaths (ElevenPaths, 2019), where the authors show that countries such as the U.S. or China are amongst the countries that generate the most attacks. Therefore, we can assume the existence of proxies operating in Ireland and the United Kingdom, which act as intermediaries between the attacker origin and the destination, so the IP addresses logged by the honeypot does not correspond to real IP addresses.

Since the above map of Figure 8 does not show consistent results with the state-of-the-art and general statistics, we decided to filter out the most repeated IP addresses coming from Ireland and United Kingdom. Figure 9a shows how intermediate proxies actually exist in both countries, and which are origin countries with most of sessions recorded. In this new heat map, it is can be seen that China is positioned as one of the countries from which the greatest number of attacks are carried out, in addition to other countries such as the south of North America which begins to show itself as more malicious in terms of actions taken by attackers.

Finally, with the main objective of providing a heat map as realistic as possible, we decided to apply a new filter that only counts all attacks carried out under the same IP address as a single attack, avoiding increasing the attacks number per country if we find ourselves in a situation of the same IP address

Figure 9. Heat map with IPs over Scriptzteam dataset; (a) Real source IPs per session, (b) Real and unique source IPs

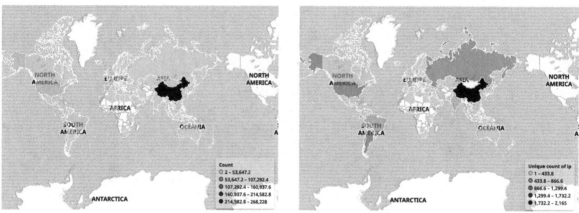

launching repeated attacks. Figure 9b illustrates this new heat map, in which it can be seen with more intense colours (i.e., higher number of attacks) other countries such as Russia, Alaska and much of South America as countries of origin of the attacks.

b. First Experiment

Through the different experiments, we are intended to achieve a system capable of evaluating sessions generated in the Cowrie SSH honeypot and identify and classify, as far as possible, the attacks types recorded in sessions. The aim of this first experiment is to obtain a set of features to determine which ML technique provides the best (optimal) results, i.e., algorithms based on supervised or unsupervised techniques. It is worth noting that the public dataset used for this first experiment was Rapid 7 (Rapid 7, 2019) that establishes a default setting in their honeypots.

After carefully observing each of the logs generated when an attacker establishes a connection, we can conclude that some displayed messages were shared by all sessions, because they are part of the configuration parameters that must be established during Cowrie's configuration. Therefore, despite containing a large amount of information in session-generated logs, not all logs can be used as discriminating features between sessions. In the case of encryption algorithms, for example, Cowrie determines the enabled algorithms in its configuration, and it is not possible to use an algorithm not previously configured. Thus, attackers will not be able to choose an encryption algorithm considered as in case it is not amongst the set of predefined algorithms. Consequently, after analysing possible actions that any attacker could perform without depending on Cowrie's configuration, we concluded that the command set introduced in each session would be the most relevant and discriminating features when classifying threats generated in each session.

As a consequence of the wide variety of commands that can be introduced by attackers, we decided to shorten the generated commands so as to reduce the set of different dimensions. Some examples of how the commands was shortened are the following. In the case of commands with a multitude of arguments, e.g., *echo -e -n 'bin/cowrie stop'*, they were reduced to *echo -e*. In the case of commands with paths to directories or files, e.g., *cd /var/tmp/* or *wget* http://86.101.34.88/Sbin.sh, they were reduced to *cd /var/* and *wget* http://86.101.34.88/, respectively. It is true that this decision entails a loss of the information provided by the attacker, however, the amount of information that is discarded would only be essential in the case of wanting to detect very specific attacks of a particular type of malware, and not by identifying attacks generically that it is our target.

Given that the dataset was not labelled beforehand, as a first test, and in order to analyse whether there was a high relationship between all recorded sessions, it was thought to apply a clustering algorithm, in particular k-means (Hartigan & Wong, 1979), in order to visualise whether data could be partitioned into *k* groups from features that commands originated in each session could provide. K-media is a grouping method, which aims at partitioning a set of *n* observations into k-groups in which each observation belongs to the group whose mean value is closer.

A first obstacle we had with this approach was the visualising of the data provided by the k-means algorithm, given that it had a high number of dimensions (each of the possible recorded commands) and it was not possible to graphically represent the points assigned to each session. After investigating how to visualise this data, it was found out the possibility of applying dimensionality reduction techniques, which aim to maintain the distances between represented points in space and densities between different groups. In ML-based solutions, the dimensionality reduction techniques attempt to project a set of high-dimension vectors into a much lower dimensionality space, while preserving relevant information from the overall data structure. In addition to the obvious advantages of data compression, one of its main objectives is to provide an easy way to visualise the intrinsic structure of projected samples. Likewise, through reduction of the dimensions number it is possible to contribute a minor overfitting to the ML algorithm.

In a first instance, the dimensionality reduction algorithm called t-Distributed Stochastic Neighbor Embedding (t-SNE) was used (van der Maaten, 2014). This algorithm is a non-linear technique for dimensional reduction that is particularly suitable for visualisation of high-dimensional datasets. Although, t-SNE can be used as a technique to visualise data when there are a large number of dimensions, however, it should not be used as a dimensional reduction technique, since different characteristics of clusters can vary between different executions, including distance between points represented or clusters density. For this reason, an investigation into new dimensionality reduction techniques was carried out, which would allow both data visualisation in circumstances of multiple dimensions and enable the dimensions reduction. Finally, a novel multiple learning technique for dimensional reduction called Uniform Manifold Approximation and Projection (UMAP) was selected (McInnes, Healy & Melville, 2018). The UMAP algorithm is as competitive as t-SNE in visualisation quality, which can retain larger data structures providing superior runtime performance. In addition, UMAP has no computational constraints on embedded dimensions, so it is feasible as a general-purpose dimensional reduction technique for automatic learning.

After determining a dimensionality reduction technique according to data needs, the next step was to execute different instances of the clustering algorithm to confirm whether grouping was possible. To this end, it was necessary to apply One Hot Encoding (Rodríguez, Bautista, González & Escalera, 2018) to the selected features, which corresponds to a pre-processing step that is applied to categorical data in order to convert them into a non-orderly numerical representation, so that they can be properly interpreted by the ML algorithms. Then it was necessary to calculate the optimal number of clusters that are grouped (clustered) within the dataset. The elbow method was used for this purpose. This method was applied to a set of raw logs of more than 75 GBs, generating a total set of 80 features. Next, we can observe the output of this method in Figure 10.

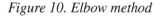

Figure 10. Elbow method

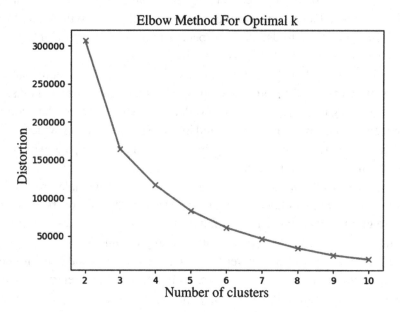

As can be seen in Figure 10, the optimal *k* for the dataset is determined between 6 and 7 clusters. To verify the optimal number of clusters, along with the rest of parameters that make up the k-means algorithm, a tuned hyperparameter technique was applied. This technique consists in appropriate parameters selection of the ML algorithm for the dataset provided. Once the optimal parameters configuration was selected, both for dimensionality reduction technique (UMAP) and clustering algorithm (k-means), the following groupings were obtained as shown in Figure 11.

Figure 11 shows how data that make up the dataset generated from the Cowrie instances, deployed in the Rapid 7 environment, cannot be precisely partitioned into *k* groups, since there is overlapping of vectors between different clusters. Given that a correct pre-processing of data was done, this being one of main reasons why clustering algorithms can produce erroneous solutions, the impossibility of grouping the dataset into properly separated clusters may be due to other factors. One of them is the inadequate selection of relevant features to determine the clusters and differentiate between attacks. Another possible cause is the nature of log set, since the Cowrie honeypot used by Rapid 7 was incorrectly configured, which might affect the generation of a limited dataset. As a consequence of the inability to apply clustering, and to determine whether the reason was due to an inappropriate selection of the ML technique, we decided to make use of classification algorithms, keeping as features the same ones that were selected for k-means algorithm.

Since data that make up the dataset are not pre-tagged, it was necessary to generate a vector label according to a predefined criterion. Before tagging vectors, it was necessary to carefully analyse the variety of commands that were executed by attackers. Once all the introduced commands had been observed, as well as the reiteration of each one of them, we decided to define a labelled set based on threat levels represented by the execution of commands in each session. To do this, three threat levels were defined based on severity to which the system could be subjected in case certain commands were executed:

Figure 11. Representation of the sessions stored in the Rapid 7 SSH honeypot through clustering

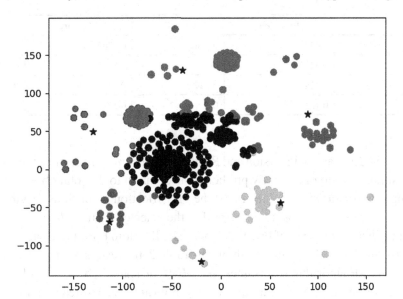

- **Level 1**: It refers to the most critical level. This is made up of sessions that attempt to both the download and execution of suspicious software, the removal of critical files from system and the suspension or shutdown of relevant system processes.
- **Level 2**: It is composed of commands that are intended to install packages on the system, compile and grant new permissions to unknown files. This level is considered an intermediate threat.
- **Level 3**: It denotes the level with the lowest threat and is composed of all commands that aim to acquire information about the current system, in order to find possible vulnerabilities in the system.

Next, a search was conducted on the most specific classification algorithms for stored data characteristics. Among the different algorithms found, it was decided to make use of k-Nearest Neighbors (k-NN), Decision Tree (DT), Random Forest (RF) and Support Vector Machines (SVM), these being some algorithms with the best results for classification. Other classification algorithms such as Logistic Regression or Naive Bayes (NB) were not selected since both classifiers assign each vector to evaluate a probability of belonging to a class instead of a deterministic assignment. Moreover, in the case of the NB algorithm is not able to provide adequate results when the dataset is composed of a large number of features as occurs in this experiment.

Once the classification algorithms had been determined, the dataset, where all SSH honeypot sessions were located, was divided into a training dataset (80%) and an evaluation dataset (20%). Besides, a stratified sampling technique was used to divide the dataset in proportion to the number of vectors contained in each class. After adjusting the algorithms, each of them was trained with its training dataset and proceeded to analyse the evaluation dataset, obtaining the results shown in Table 1. Note that *Precision* is the ratio of correctly predicted positive observations to the total predicted positive observations; *Recall* is the ratio of correctly predicted positive observations to the all observations in the actual class;

Table 1. Performance measurements of the Rapid 7 dataset (experiment 1)

	Precision	Recall	F1-Score	Accuracy
k-NN	**0.4991**	**0.4662**	**0.4709**	**0.4698**
Decision Tree	0.3287	0.3298	0.3276	0.3312
Random Forest	0.3285	0.3299	0.3275	0.3309
SVM	0.3286	0.3298	0.3276	0.3311

F1-Score is the weighted average of Precision and Recall; and *Accuracy* is the most intuitive performance measure and it is simply a ratio of correctly predicted observation to the total observations.

After obtaining low performance values in all the classification algorithms, having previously adjusted each of them, the next step was to confirm that the selected features had a relevant weight and were determinant to characterise the different sessions. The Random Forest (RF) algorithm was used to show the weight assigned to each feature. As shown in Table 2, the results returned (denoted as feature's weight ϵ [0,1]) by the RF algorithm determines that ~65% of features were not relevant to determine to which class a vector belongs, as well as which were relevant selected features from the commands introduced by attackers.

Therefore, the next experiment was to perform a new investigation of possible characteristics of each session and determine which feature set may be significant to classify the threats.

c. **Second Experiment**

In this second experiment, several features of the previous dataset were removed and others that are considered to be of interest were added. The aim of this experiment is to select more relevant features to identify and classify cyber threats through SSH honeypot systems. In addition, a new public dataset was selected, specifically the one provided by Scriptzteam (Scriptzteam, 2019), in order to contrast the results between a correctly configured set of logs and the ones obtained when using the default configuration (Rapid 7).

Table 2. Top 10 most relevant commands for the Rapid 7 dataset

Command	Feature's Weight
cat /proc/cpuinfo	0.1019
chmod 777	0.0793
wget	0.0771
grep name	0.0568
uname –a	0.0551
cd /tmp	0.0508
cat //.nippon	0.0476
sh tftp1.sh	0.0457
rm -rf *	0.0402
w	0.0388

Table 3. Performance measurements of the Rapid 7 dataset (experiment 2)

	Precision	Recall	F1-Score	Accuracy
k-NN	0.7674	0.8103	0.7526	0.7515
Decision Tree	0.8297	**0.8392**	**0.8205**	**0.8609**
Random Forest	0.8297	**0.8392**	**0.8205**	**0.8609**
SVM	**0.8298**	0.8391	0.8204	0.8607

First, a new research was conducted on which new features could be selected to find an association between the introduced commands and the threat levels defined above. To do this, a rule generation algorithm called A-priori (Gupta, Kochhar, Jain & Nagrath, 2019) was used. The purpose of this algorithm is to find a set of rules that comply with the characteristics and weights indicated as parameters. The use of A-priori allows us to observe which sequence of commands is commonly used, thus being able to observe the purpose of attackers. Based on the rules obtained on the total dataset, we decided to create a new set of features in relation to the consequence that has execution of each command introduced in that session, registering a value of 1 in the case of complying with this feature and 0 in the case of not complying. Specifically, the following features were defined:

- Disk reading.
- Writing to disk.
- Obtaining system information.
- Internet connections and downloads.
- Compilation or installation of programs.
- Execution of programs.
- Suspension or elimination of processes in the system.

It should be noted that the process of vector tagging remained the same as in the previous experiment. As in the previous experiment, in this new one was also necessary to apply the tuned hyperparameter technique to adjust each classification algorithm again, since the structure of the vectors was modified between experiments. After adjusting the classification algorithms, each of them was instantiated with optimal configuration parameters, the performance measurements shown in Table 3 were obtained, which belong to the same dataset used in the previous experiment, the Rapid 7 set of logs. Note that the dataset formed from the data obtained from the Rapid 7 repository is composed of the 7 features listed above.

As can be seen in Table 3, precision, recall, F1-score and accuracy have improved significantly between experiment 1 and the current one. This is mainly due to the elimination of irrelevant features from the dataset. As suspected during the beginning of the previous experiment, the very low performance measurements of the Rapid 7 dataset could be linked to a set of inappropriate features to determine the threats produced during each session, not allowing the possible link between several attacks with similar characteristics.

Once confirmed that the new proposed set of features was able to determine precisely the generated threat type in each session, from the impact triggered by the execution of the introduced commands, the next objective of this experiment is to determine how an appropriate configuration of the system affects to the Cowrie SSH honeypot. To this end, it was decided to select public logs provided by Scriptzteam

Table 4. Performance measurements of the Scriptzteam dataset (experiment 2)

	Precision	Recall	F1-Score	Accuracy
k-NN	0.9859	0.9573	0.9708	0.9765
Decision Tree	**0.9874**	**0.9574**	**0.9714**	**0.9767**
Random Forest	0.9859	0.9573	0.9708	0.9765
SVM	**0.9874**	0.9573	**0.9714**	0.9765

(Scriptzteam, 2019), since it was configured with the purpose of obstructing an early detection of decoy system by attackers, as well as to originate a set of logs whose recorded sessions are as heterogeneous as possible. In addition, this public dataset was collected more recently (until the end of 2017) than the previous set of logs, which entails the registration of newer threats.

As in the previous experiment, it was necessary to apply a tuned hyperparameter technique to adjust each classification algorithm again, since the set of vectors was modified between experiments. Once the classification algorithms were adjusted, each of them was instantiated with the optimal configuration parameters, obtaining the performance measures shown in Table 4.

Contrasting the results provided by the performance tests carried out by the two different datasets, one with a default honeypot Cowrie configuration (Rapid 7) and another with a specific configuration (Scriptzteam), it was possible to demonstrate how the correct configuration of the decoy system is a determining factor when classifying attacks stored in the sessions. In the case of both datasets, the generated balance at each level from the labelling rules used, which were not modified since the first experiment, demonstrates that the recorded sessions play an important role in threats classification. Thus, we can conclude that not only features are decisive when it comes to obtaining classification algorithms able to detect attacks accurately, but also that an inadequate configuration of a honeypot can reduce the precision of the system considerably.

d.   **Third Experiment**

After results obtained in the previous experiment, we decided to carry out a new research to obtain new ideas that would allow adding some differentiating features between sessions, given that the set of logs provided by Scriptzteam had a heterogeneous nature and so increasing the success level of the system presented. Although this dataset is not equally balanced between the three predefined threat levels (see Figure 12), which is an unusual situation in most scenarios, a stratified sampling technique was used to divide the dataset between training and testing. In addition, within the stratified sampling techniques, the proportional allocation has been selected, that is, the size of each stratum in the sample is proportional to its size in the population. Therefore, after the division of the general dataset between training and testing datasets, the threat levels with fewer recorded vectors are not greatly impaired. The total balance of the Scriptzteam dataset by the predefined threat levels is 5017 vectors at Level 1, 723 at Level 2 and 1003 at Level 3.

Once analysing different scientific articles related to SSH honeypots, we decided to add the following features, being some of them related to the researchers analysed in Section 2. It should be noted that these new set of features, together with the ones presented in Experiment 2, was the final set used to identify and classify cyber threats by using the Cowrie SSH honeypot.

Figure 12. Balanced dataset of Scriptzteam

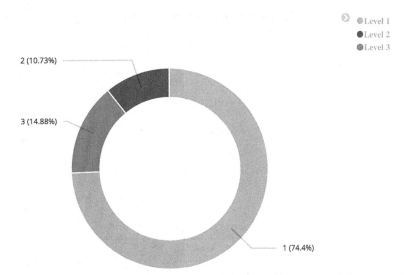

§ Total time of the session.
§ Country to which the session belongs.
§ Version of the SSH client used.

As in the rest of the tests approached, it was necessary again to apply the tuned hyperparameter technique to adjust each classification algorithm, being in this last experiment only affected the set of selected characteristics, since the set of logs continued being the one provided by Scriptzteam. The performance measures obtained for the third experiment are shown in Table 5.

Through the obtained results, it has been possible to reduce the number of incorrectly classified attacks through the introduction of a new set of features in the dataset, thus improving performance measures provided by the classification algorithms. Specifically, the Random Forest algorithm was selected as the best algorithm to use in the proposed system given its precision and recall capability of 0.99.

Finally, a graph is depicted in Figure 13 where the precision-recall curves of the final dataset for each class are shown. This graph allows us to see from what recall we have a degradation of precision, and vice versa. The ideal solution would be a curve that gets as close as possible to the upper-right corner (high precision and high recall), being this objective achieved by means of features that have been proposed. The reason for showing a curve based on precision-recall, as opposed to the usual ROC curve (Receiver Operating Characteristic), is due to the unbalance presented by the different levels of the

Table 5. Performance measurements of the Scriptzteam dataset (experiment 3)

	Precision	Recall	F1-Score	Accuracy
k-NN	0.9666	0.9642	0.9652	0.9775
Decision Tree	0.9968	0.9968	0.9968	0.9979
Random Forest	**0.9982**	**0.9973**	**0.9977**	**0.9989**
SVM	0.9917	0.9883	0.9900	0.9948

Figure 13. Precision-recall curve for final dataset on Scriptzteam data

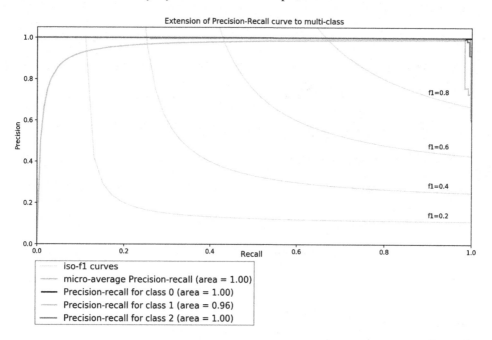

established threats. In addition, as the dataset is characterised for being multi-class, it will be necessary to binarize each of them to be able to be visualised in the following graph (see Figure 13). Therefore, the precision-recall assigned to class 0 belongs to threat level 1, the precision-recall assigned to class 1 belongs to threat level 2 and, finally, the precision-recall assigned to class 2 belongs to level 3. As shown in Figure 13, the final set of the defined features, which is composed of features introduced in Experiment 2 together with those of Experiment 3, are able to determine exactly to which class each of the evaluated vectors belongs, providing an almost perfect ROC curve.

Through the three experiments approached, it has been possible to identify and classify cyber threats by using an SSH honeypot system (Cowrie). For this purpose, the actions that involve the execution of commands in the system, the origin country, and, finally the SSH client and the total time of a session have been selected as features. Finally, four classification algorithms have been used that have been providing similar performance measures, however, the Random Forest algorithm obtains the best performance when detecting and classifying attacks, generating an accuracy of 0.998 and a recall of 0.997.

5. DISCUSSION

The proposed system in this chapter is a novelty in the state-of-the-art since there is no other work that combines the same set of features, uses the most current SSH-based MIH (Cowrie) and provides the performance measures we obtained. As shown in Table 6, despite the advances achieved by the previous solutions, a series of shortcomings are presented. For example, the most state-of-the-art solutions make use of Kippo, which is the honeypot predecessor to Cowrie. Kippo has a set of limitations, such as a reduced number of commands that attackers can use, which were extended in its new version (Cowrie).

Table 6. Comparison of the most current solutions

Proposal	Considered Features	Honeypot's Type	ML techniques	Results
(Sharafaldin, Lashkari & Ghorbani, 2018)	Data flows	Own deployed environments	k-NN and Random Forest	Accuracy: 0.96 and 0.98 Recall: 0.96 and 0.97 F1-score: 0.96 and 0.97
(Sadasivam, Hota & Anand, 2018)	Features based on TCP streams	Kippo	J48 and PART	Precision: 1.0 Accuracy: 0.99 F2-Score: 0.9420
(Sadasivam, Hota & Anand, 2018b)	TCP flows	Kippo	-	-
(Dowling, Schukat & Melvin, 2017)	-	Kippo	-	-
(Fraunholz, Krohmer, Anton & Schotten, 2017)	Length and number of commands, attacker's skill level	Kippo	K-means	5 clusters were generated.
(Melese & Avadhani, 2016)	Shell commands	Kippo	-	-
(Pauna & Bica, 2014)	Attacker's command	Heliza	Reinforcement learning algorithms	-
(Kheirkhah, Mehdi, Jahanshahi & Acharya, 2013)	Attacker's command	Kippo	-	-
Our proposed system	Consequences of executing commands, total session time, SSH client, country.	Cowrie	Random Forest	Precision: 0.9982 Recall: 0.9973 Accuracy: 0.9977 F1-Score: 0.9989

Therefore, Kippo provides less accurate detection than Cowrie when identifying attackers based on the commands entered in their sessions.

In this sense, the proposed solution in this work seeks to improve existing solutions. To do this, we use Cowrie as an MIH, which is the today's most mature honeypot, and we analyse the logs generated by it to determine which features would be most relevant ones for identifying and classifying cyber threats. In addition, we utilise different supervised and unsupervised learning techniques to compare and analyse the results obtained. As a novelty with respect to other state-of-the-art research, this investigation consists of the research, design and implementation of a system capable of classifying attackers' behaviour from actions carried out during their sessions in a protected and emulated environment (Cowrie). In addition, this work makes use of a set of public datasets, which were recently published and is composed of a set of current threats. Finally, the proposed system extracts the most relevant characteristics of each session, contributing a layer of intelligence to Cowrie. It should be noted that this research does verify (through three experiments) that the characteristics obtained from the visualisation of the logs can be used to determine what type of threats are registered in the honeypot.

As shown in Table 6, the work presented by (Sharafaldin, Lashkari & Ghorbani, 2018) is able to obtain a relevant performance measurement through data flows, however, the authors have the vectors tagged because they generated each attack beforehand. However, a honeypot only generates records without tags and users are who need to determine a feature set within which honeypot provides.

On the other hand, both Sadasivam, Hota & Anand (2018b), Dowling, Schukat & Melvin (2017), Kheirkhah, Mehdi, Jahanshahi & Acharya (2013) and (Melese & Avadhani, 2016) do not provide an intelligence layer using logs recorded by honeypots. The authors only research and show statistics about which are the main attacker's behaviours, however, that information is not contrasted with real experiments. In some cases, the authors use IP addresses as a possible feature to identify attackers, but do not consider that an IP address might not be real as our proposal does, that is, an IP address used through a proxy to mask real addresses of attackers.

As system limitations, Cowrie continues to be an MIH, which has a delimited command set, though larger than its predecessor honeypots. Therefore, the classification of attacks cannot be very precise since there is not a large set of features to differentiate, for example, amongst different types of malware. In addition, the available SSH-based HIHs are outdated, which could provide a risk to our real systems if we deployed them, so opting for an MIH is the best choice for safety reasons.

6. CONCLUSION AND FUTURE WORK

This work proposes a system for the identification and classification of cyber threats through SSH-based honeypot systems. With the ideas presented, it has been possible to address the relevant information extraction from logs generated by the Cowrie honeypot. Through this information, three threat levels were generated to classify attacker's session based on a set of features. The presented system complements the different traditional threat detection techniques (IDSs, antivirus, etc.) with a novel system capable of detecting previously unknown threats, while providing a higher security level. In order to provide an intelligence layer to the proposed system, several supervised ML algorithms based on classification have been used to evaluate each session registered by the Cowrie honeypot. The visualisation of characteristics belonging to sessions through the Kibana data viewer, as well as different experiments conducted through several ML algorithms, dimensionality reduction techniques and the use of a rule generation algorithm, have allowed to obtain and validate an optimal solution capable of identifying and classifying cyber threats.

As future work, we plan to examine new High-Interaction Honeypots (HIH), both SSH and other families oriented to services or applications in order to obtain greater user interaction. In addition, the undertaken study will be used as a basis for the subsequent generation of detection signatures, with which to update IDSs based on misuse detection or the labelling of datasets for detection engines re-training of systems based on anomaly detection. Finally, we plan to generate a new set of features from MIH and HIH honeypots, as well as using additional Machine Learning o Deep Learning algorithms to test the efficiency classification of attacks with new improvements added. It should be noted that in order to obtain a new set of features with MIHs, it is intended to generate a specific parser that allows new information to be obtained from logs generated by the MIHs and that information is not available through the basic information they provide.

REFERENCES

Barrett, D. J., Silverman, R. E., & Byrnes, R. G. (2005). *SSH, the Secure Shell: The definitive guide.* O'Reilly Media.

Depren, O., Topallar, M., Anarim, E., & Ciliz, M. K. (2005). An intelligent intrusion detection system (IDS) for anomaly and misuse detection in computer networks. *Expert Systems with Applications*, *29*(4), 713–722. doi:10.1016/j.eswa.2005.05.002

Dowling, S., Schukat, M., & Melvin, H. (2017). A ZigBee honeypot to assess IoT cyberattack behaviour. In *Proceedings 28th Irish Signals and Systems Conference*, 1-6. 10.1109/ISSC.2017.7983603

ElevenPaths. (2019). Honeypotting, un oído en Internet. Retrieved October 9, 2019, from https://empresas.blogthinkbig.com/informe-ciberseguridad-honeypotting-un-oido-en-interne/

Fraunholz, D., Krohmer, D., Anton, S. D., & Schotten, H. D. (2017). Investigation of cyber-crime conducted by abusing weak or default passwords with a medium interaction honeypot. In *2017 International Conference on Cyber Security and Protection of Digital Services (Cyber Security)*, 1-7. 10.1109/CyberSecPODS.2017.8074855

Gupta, B. B. (2018). Computer and cyber security: principles, algorithm, applications, and perspectives. Boca Raton, FL: CRC Press, Taylor & Francis.

Gupta, B. B., & Sheng, Q. Z. (2019). *Machine Learning for Computer and Cyber Security: Principle, Algorithms, and Practices*. CRC Press. doi:10.1201/9780429504044

Gupta, M., Kochhar, S., Jain, P., & Nagrath, P. (2019). Hybrid recommender system using A-priori algorithm. In *Proceedings International Conference on Sustainable Computing in Science, Technology and Management*, 26-28. Academic Press.

Hartigan, J. A., & Wong, M. A. (1979). Algorithm AS 136: A k-means clustering algorithm. *Journal of the Royal Statistical Society. Series A (General)*, *28*(1), 100–108.

Jiang, F., Fu, Y., Gupta, B. B., Lou, F., Rho, S., Meng, F., & Tian, Z. (2018). Deep learning based multi-channel intelligent attack detection for data security. *IEEE transactions on Sustainable Computing*.

Jorquera, J. M., Sánchez, P. M., Fernández, L., Huertas, A., Arjona, M., De Los Santos, S., & Martínez, G. (2018). Improving the security and QoE in mobile devices through an intelligent and adaptive continuous authentication system. *Sensors (Basel)*, *18*(11), 3769. doi:10.339018113769 PMID:30400377

Keane, J. K. (2019). Kojoney2 SSH medium-interaction honeypot. Retrieved October 5, 2019, from https://github.com/madirish/kojoney2

Kheirkhah, E., Mehdi, S., Jahanshahi, H. A., & Acharya, H. (2013). An experimental study of SSH attacks by using honeypot decoys. *Indian Journal of Science and Technology*, *6*(12), 5567–5578.

McInnes, L., Healy, J., & Melville, J. (2018). UMAP: Uniform manifold approximation and projection for dimension reduction. *The Journal of Open Source Software*, *3*(29), 861. doi:10.21105/joss.00861

Melese, S. Z., & Avadhani, P. S. (2016). Honeypot system for attacks on SSH protocol. *International Journal of Computer Network and Information Security*, *8*(9), 19. doi:10.5815/ijcnis.2016.09.03

Melese, S. Z., & Avadhani, P. S. (2016). Honeypot system for attacks on SSH protocol. *International Journal of Computer Network and Information Security*, *8*(9), 19. doi:10.5815/ijcnis.2016.09.03

Olakanmi, O. O., & Dada, A. (2019). An Efficient Privacy-preserving Approach for Secure Verifiable Outsourced Computing on Untrusted Platforms. [IJCAC]. *International Journal of Cloud Applications and Computing*, 9(2), 79–98. doi:10.4018/IJCAC.2019040105

Oosterhof, M. (2019). Cowrie SSH honeypot (based on Kippo). Retrieved October 5, 2019, from https://github.com/cowrie/cowrie

Padayachee, K. (2014). Aspectising honeytokens to contain the insider threat. *IETF Information Security*, 9(4), 240–247. doi:10.1049/iet-ifs.2014.0063

Pauna, A., & Bica, I. (2014). RASSH-Reinforced adaptive SSH honeypot. In *Proceedings 10th International Conference on Communications*, 1-6.

Rapid 7. (2019). Public data of the honeynet deployed by the company Rapid 7 in Heisenberg. Retrieved October 7, 2019, from https://opendata.rapid7.com/heisenberg.cowrie/

Rodríguez, P., Bautista, M. A., González, J., & Escalera, S. (2018). Beyond one-hotencoding: Lower dimensional target embedding, *Image and Vision Computing*, 75, 21-31.

Rosenberg, J., Coronel, J. B., Meiring, J., Gray, S., & Brown, T. (2019). Leveraging ElasticSearch to improve data discoverability in science gateways. In Practice and Experience in Advanced Research Computing on Rise of the Machines Learning, 19. doi:10.1145/3332186.3332230

Sadasivam, G. K., Hota, C., & Anand, B. (2018). Detection of severe SSH attacks using honeypot servers and machine learning techniques. *Software Networking*, 2017(1), 79–100. doi:10.13052/jsn2445-9739.2017.005

Sadasivam, G. K., Hota, C., & Anand, B. (2018). Honeynet data analysis and distributed SSH brute-force attacks. In Towards Extensible and Adaptable Methods in Computing, 107-118. doi:10.1007/978-981-13-2348-5_9

Scriptzteam. (2019). Public repository in GitHub. Retrieved October 8, 2019, from https://github.com/scriptzteam/REALTiME-SSH-HoneyPot_v1.1

Sharafaldin, I., Lashkari, A. H., & Ghorbani, A. A. (2018). Toward generating a new intrusion detection dataset and intrusion traffic characterization. In *Proceedings 4th International Conference on Information Systems Security and Privacy*, 108-116. 10.5220/0006639801080116

Sharma, V. (2017). Cap. getting started with Kibana. *Beginning Elastic Stack, Apress*, 29-44.

SOC eSentire. (2017). Annual threat report. Retrieved October 5, 2019, from https://www.esentire.com/resource-library/2017-annual-threat-report

Sochor, T., & Zuzcak, M. (2014). Study of internet threats and attack methods using honeypots and honeynets. In *Proceedings International Conference on Computer Networks*, 118-127. 10.1007/978-3-319-07941-7_12

Spitzner, L. (2003). *Honeypots: Tracking hackers* (p. 1). Reading: Addison-Wesley.

Valli, C., Rabadia, P., & Woodward, A. (2013). Patterns and patter - An investigation into SSH activity using Kippo honeypots. In *Australian Digital Forensics Conference*, 141-149.

Van der Maaten, L. (2014). Accelerating t-SNE using tree-based algorithms. *Journal of Machine Learning Research, 15*(1), 3221–3245.

Zhang, M., Wang, L., Jajodia, S., Singhal, A., & Albanese, M. (2016). Network diversity: A security metric for evaluating the resilience of networks against zero-day attacks. *IEEE Transactions on Information Forensics and Security, 11*(5), 1071–1086. doi:10.1109/TIFS.2016.2516916

Zkik, K., Orhanou, G., & El Hajji, S. (2017). Secure mobile multi cloud architecture for authentication and data storage. [IJCAC]. *International Journal of Cloud Applications and Computing, 7*(2), 62–76. doi:10.4018/IJCAC.2017040105

Chapter 7
Data Access Management System in Azure Blob Storage and AWS S3 Multi-Cloud Storage Environments

Yaser Mansouri
Adelaide University, Australia

Rajkumar Buyya
The University of Melbourne, Australia

ABSTRACT

Multi-cloud storage offers better Quality of Service (QoS) such as availability, durability, and users' perceived latency. The exploitation of price differences across cloud-based storage services is a motivate example of storing data in different Geo-graphically data stores, where data migration is also a choice to achieve more cost optimization. However, this requires migrating data in tolerable time from the perspective of users. This chapter first proposes a comprehensive review on different classes of data stores inspiring data migration within and across data stores. Then, it presents the design of a system prototype spanned across storage services of Amazon Web Services (AWS) and Microsoft Azure employing their RESTful APIs to store, retrieve, delete, and migrate data. Finally, the experimental results show that the data migration can be conducted in a few seconds for data with a magnitude of Megabytes.

INTRODUCTION

Cloud computing has gained significant attention form the academic and industry communities in recent years. It provides the vision that encompasses the movement of computing elements, storage and software delivery away from personal computer and local servers into the next generation computing infrastructure hosted by large companies such as Amazon Web Service (AWS), Microsoft Azure, and Google. Cloud computing has three distinct characteristics that differentiate it from its traditional counterparts: pay-as-

DOI: 10.4018/978-1-7998-2242-4.ch007

Copyright © 2020, IGI Global. Copying or distributing in print or electronic forms without written permission of IGI Global is prohibited.

you-go model, on-demand provisioning of infinite resources, and elasticity (Buyya, Shin, Venugopal, Broberg & Brandic, 2009).

Cloud computing offers three types of resources delivery models to users: (i) Infrastructure as a Service (IaaS) which offers computing, network, and storage resources, (ii) Platform as a Service (PaaS) which provides users tools that facilitate the deployment of cloud applications, and (iii) Software as a Service (SaaS) which enables users to run the provider's software on the cloud infrastructure.

One of the main components of IaaS offering by cloud computing is Storage as Services (StaaS) that provides an elastic, scalable, available, and pay-as-you-go model, which renders it attractive for data outsourcing, both for the users to manipulate data independent of the location and time and for firms to avoid expensive upfront investments of infrastructures. The well-known Cloud Storage Providers (CSPs)–AWS, Microsoft Azure, and Google– offer StaaS for several storage classes which differ in price and performance metrics such as availability, durability, the latency required to retrieve the first byte of data, the minimum time needed to store data in the storage.

The data generated by online social networks, e-commerce, and other data sources is doubling every two years and is expected to augment to a 10-fold increase between 2013 and 2020-from 4.4 ZB to 44 ZB[1]. The network traffic, generated from these data, from datacenters (DCs) to users and between DCs was 0.7 ZB in 2013 and is predicated to reach 3.48 ZB by 2020[2]. The management of such data in the size of several exabytes or zettabytes requires capital-intensive investment; the deployment of cloud-based data stores (data stores for short) is a promising solution.

Moving the data generated by data-intensive applications into the data stores guarantees users the required performance Service Level Agreement (SLA) to some extent, but it causes concern for monetary cost spent in the storage services. Several factors substantially contribute to the monetary cost. First, monetary cost depends on the size of the data volume that is stored, retrieved, updated, and potentially migrated from one storage class to another one in the same/different data stores. Second, it is subject to the required performance SLA (e.g., availability[3], durability, the latency needed to retrieve the first byte of data) as the main distinguishing feature of storage classes. As the performance guarantee is higher, the price of storage classes is more. Third, monetary cost can be affected by the need of data stores to be in a specific geographical location in order to deliver data to users within their specified latency. To alleviate this concern (i.e., monetary cost spending on storage services) from the perspective of application providers/users, it is required to replicate data in an appropriate selection of storage classes offered by different CSPs during the lifetime of the object regarding to the satisfaction of latency for Put (write), Get(read), and data migration from the perspective of users.

The use of multiple CSPs offering several storage classes with different prices and performance metrics respecting their Quality of Service (QoS) in terms of availability and network latency. In this direction, we designed algorithms that take advantage of price differences across CSPs with several storage classes to reduce monetary cost on storage services for time varying workloads (Mnasouri, Y.; Buyya, R., 2016). This mandates data migration across data stores. As a concern for users, it is important to migrate data in tolerable time. This chapter sheds a light on this gap through the following contribution:

- We provide a taxonomy of cloud-based data stores offered by the well-known cloud providers to bring the attention of researchers for future research directions.
- We provide modules using RESTful API of AWS and Microsoft Azure to store, retrieve, delete, and migrate data for AWS' and Microsoft Azure' data stores.

- We profile data migration time between a pair of data stores within and across regions. We also show that this time is reasonable for transferring users' data, which reaches to a magnitude of Megabytes (MBs).

BACKGROUND

Well-known cloud providers such as AWS, Azure, and Google offer resources, where Storage as a Service (StaaS) is one of its main components. StaaS supports several classes of storage, which are differentiated in price and performance metrics[4]. These metrics are (i) durability, (ii) availability SLA, (iii) minimum object size: an object smaller than s kilobytes in size is charged for s kilobytes of storage, (iv) minimum storage duration: an object deleted less than d days after storing in storage incurs a minimum $d-$day charge, (v) retrieval first byte latency: the time taken to retrieve the first byte of an object. The storage classes supported by AWS, Azure, and Google are as follows.

AWS provides four classes of storage[5]: (i) Simple Storage Service (S3) is a highly reliable, available, and secure storage service for data frequently accessed; (ii) Reduced Redundancy Storage (RRS) offers users storage resources with lower cost at the expense of lower levels of redundancy as compared to S3. RSS is suitable for data which require less durability as compared to those stored in S3; (iii) Standard-Infrequent Access (S-IA) is optimized for data accessed less frequently, but needs a low retrieval time (e.g., backup data); (iv) Glacier storage is the cheapest AWS storage which is suited to data with very low access rates and without the need for rapid access.

Microsoft Azure supports four classes of storage services[6], which are mainly distinguished based on the number of replicas of an object that are stored in a single or multiple DCs. These classes are: (i) Locally Redundant Storage (LRS) stores three synchronous replicas within a single DC; (ii) Zone Redundant Storage (ZRS) stores three asynchronous replicas across multiple DCs within or across regions; (iii) Geographical Redundant Storage (GRS) is the same as LRS, in addition to storing three asynchronous replicas in a secondary DC that is far away from the primary DC; (iv) Read-access GRS (RA-GRS) is the same as GRS with the added functionality of allowing users to access data in the secondary DC. All classes of Azure storage support five types of storage: Blob, Table, Queue, File, and Disk. Each type of storage is used for a specific purpose. Blob storage is specialized for unstructured object data, Table storage for structured data, Queue storage for reliable messaging between different components of cloud services, File storage for sharing data across the components of an application, and Disk (premium) storage for supporting data intensive workload running on Azure virtual machines (VMs). Besides these classes and types of storage, Azure also provides Blob storage with two access tiers. These are hot and cold access tiers which are supported in three classes of storage: LRS, GRS, and RA-GRS. Hot (resp. cold) access tier is used for data that are frequently (resp. rarely) accessed. Hot tier access is more expensive than the cold one, and this allows users to save cost when they switch between these access tiers based on a change in the usage pattern of the object. This switch incurs additional charges, and thus users are required to select each access tier in the appropriate time during the lifetime of the object.

Google supports five storage classes[7]: (i) Multi-regional storage is appropriate for frequently accessed data. This class is Geo-redundant storage service that maintains an object in at least two regions; (ii) Regional storage enables users to store data within a single region. This class is suitable for Google Compute Engine (GCE) instances; (iii) Durable Reduced Availability (DRA) has a lower availability SLA with the same cost (apart from the cost of operations) compared to Regional storage; (iv) Nearline storage is suitable for data that are accessed on average once a month or less. Thus, this class is a good choice for data backup, archival storage, and disaster recovery; (v) Coldline storage is the cheapest Google storage, and it is a suitable option for data accessed at most once a year.

Based on the offered storage classes, we classify them into five tiers. (i) Very hot tier provides the highest levels of redundancy across multiple regions and allows users to access the data in the secondary DC as the primary DC faces faults. (ii) Hot tier stores data in multiple regions, the redundancy level is lower than the first tier. (iii) Warm tier is the same as hot tier in redundancy level, but less durable. (iv) Cold tier provides lower availability and durability as compared to the first three tiers and imposes restriction on metrics like minimum object size and minimum storage duration. (v) Very cold tier has the same durability and availability levels compared to the cold tier, but it has more minimum storage duration. The last two tiers impose retrieval cost and they are more expensive than the first three tiers (i.e., very hot, hot, and warm) in operations cost. Table 1 summarizes the characteristics of the storage tiers offered storage services by AWS, Azure, and Google based on the discussed tiers.

A crucial concern in respect to cloud-based storage services is security and privacy. All discussed cloud storage services provide a comprehensive set of security mechanisms to enable users to build and deploy secure applications. This set includes encryption of data at rest and transit, access control, authentication, etc. Although these mechanisms help users to store and access data in secure way, there is still the challenge of defending resources against Denial-of-Service (DoS) and Distributed DoS (DDoS) attack.

An overview of DoS and DDoS attacks as well current solutions addressing these attacks were provided in (Gupta, Badve, & Omkar, 2017). Accurate detection of these attacks within legitimate traffic is an essential issue and demands intelligent and novel frameworks (Gupta, Gupta & Chaudhary, 2017). Obviously, analysis of different security issues in the context of cloud is necessary to provide a comprehensive solution of securing data in computing, storage and network resources (Gupta B. B., 2016; 2018). In our work, we rely on the security mechanisms offered by Microsoft Azure and AWS as described later.

Another imperative concern about these storage services is performance metrics and these metrics are directly proportional to price. For example, AWS offers S3 (belongs to hot tier) and RRS (belongs to warm tier) as online storage services, but RRS compromises redundancy for lower cost. Moreover, the price of storage resources across cloud providers is different. Thus, given these differences, many cost-based decisions can be made. These decisions will become complicated especially for applications with time-varying workloads and different QoS requirements such as availability, durability, response time, and consistency level. To make satisfactory decisions for application providers, a joint optimization problem of resources cost and the required QoS should be characterized. Resources cost consists of: (i) storage cost calculated based on the duration and size of storage the application provider uses, (ii) network cost computed according to the size of data the application provider transfers out (reads) and in (writes) to data stores (typically data transfer into data stores is free), and (iii) computing cost calculated according to duration of renting a VM by the application provider. The first two costs relate to the cost of data storage management.

With respect to the above discussion, we can define many optimization problems in conjunction with QoS such as availability, latency, and consistency. One of these is monetary cost reduction by exploiting price differences among CSPs, which mandates data migration across data stores. Although data migration may reduce the monetary cost of data management across data stores, this is a concern about the migration time of data between data stores within and across regions. We measure this time and show the feasibility of data transfer required a reasonable time. It is worth to mention that this time is only

Table 1. The characteristics of different storage classes for the well-known cloud providers: Amazon Web Service (AWS), Azure (AZ), and Google (GO)

Storage Class	Durability Availability MOS/MSD Retrieval Fee FBL	Examples		
		AWS	Azure	Google
Very Hot	NA 6 Replicas NA/NA NA ms	NA GRS NA RA-GRS		
Hot	11 nines 3-3.5 nines NA.NA NA ms	S3 ZRS Regional Multi-Regional		
Warm	NA 4 nines (AWS) NA/NA NA ms 2 nines (GO)	RRS LRS DRA		
Cold	11 nines 2 nines 128KB(AZ) Per GB ms NA (GO)/30 days	Standard Cool-tier Nearline IA GRS		
Very Cold	NA NA(AWS) NA/90 days Per GB hours(AWS) 2 nines (GO) ms(GO)	Glacier Cool-tier Coldline LRS		

measured between a pair of data stores without relaying to DCs as a mediator. This is because that we do not make any optimization on the time of data migration across data stores.

RELATED WORKS AND MOTIVATION

Migrating data into a single data store facilitates user's performance SLA/QoS to some extent but faces them with several limitations. Data store unavailability can confront users with inaccessible data if the data is stored in a single data store. This is counted as one of the top ten obstacles for cloud adoption (Armbrust et al., 2009). Reliance on a single data store makes it difficult to migrate data from a data store to another in the face of price increment by the cloud provider, the emergence of a new data store with lower price, the mobility of users, and changes in workload that demands data migration. This is recognized as data lock-in and is listed as another main obstacle regarding cloud services. Storing data in a single data store faces the fact that the read (Get) and write (Put[8]) requests are not served with adequate responsiveness. This is because the requests are issued by users who are located worldwide and, consequently users experience more network latency to retrieve/store data from/into a data store. Furthermore, the use of a single data store deprives users from the opportunity to exploit the pricing differences across CSPs. Therefore, storing data within a single data store can be inefficient in both performance SLA and monetary cost.

Abbreviations:

MOS: Minimum Object Size; **MSD**: Minimum Storage Duration; **GRS**: Geographically Redundant Storage;

ZRS: Zone Redundant Storage; **LRS**: Locally Redundant Storage; **S3**: Simple Storage Service; **RRS**: Reduced

Redundant Storage; **Standard-IA**: Standard Infrequent Access; **DRD**: Durable Reduced Available

These factors make inevitable the use of multiple CPSs which improve availability, durability, and data mobility. The deployment of multiple CSPs also brings another benefit to users. (i) If the outage of a data store happens then the requests issued by users are directed to another data store. (ii) Users can have a wider selection of data stores, which results in reducing user-perceived latency as experimentally confirmed (Wu & Madhyastha, 2013). (iii) This deployment also allows application providers to select storage classes across CSPs based on the workload on data and the QoS specified by users to reduce monetary cost of storage and network resources.

The workload on data can be a determining factor for the selection of a storage class. Some data-intensive applications generate a time-varying workload in which as the time passes the rate of read and write requests on the data changes. In fact, there is a strong correlation between the age of data stored in a data store and data workload. For example, in Online Social Network (OSN) data initially receive many read and write requests and gradually these requests reduce (Muralidhar et al., 2014). Based on this change of requests rate, we define two statuses for data: hot-spot and cold-spot. Hot-spot data receives many read and write requests, while cold-spot data receives a few.

This demands for a suitable selection of storage classes throughout the lifetime of an object. Each storage class provided by the well-known CSPs can be suited for data with specific requirements. For instance, one class may be suitable for data that is frequently accessed. Another class may be designed to host data that is rarely accessed and required for a lower availability and durability.

Therefore, CSPs with a variety of storage classes with different prices and performance SLAs and data-intensive applications with time-varying workloads give us an incentive to design novel algorithms to optimize monetary cost (Mnasouri & Buyya, 2016; Mansouri, Nadjaran Toosi & Buyya, 2017). These algorithms work for any data to which workload transits from hot-spot to cold-spot and vice versa, as observed in OSN applications (Muralidhar et al., 2014). Significant studies have been done in the area of cost optimization of OSN applications across CPSs, as conducted in SPANStore (Wu, Butkiewicz, Perkins, Katz-Bassett & Madhyastha, 2013) and Cosplay (Jiao, Li, Xu, Du & Fu, 2016). Neither leverage different storage classes owned by different CSPs nor consider the object with hot- and cold-spot status, which results in migration of data across different data stores or movement of data between storage classes within a data store (Mansouri, 2017).

Fig. 1 illustrates a simple data placement across data stores (owned by different providers) to clarify data placemen across data stores. Among all available data stores, application providers, for example OSNs, select a subset of data stores to replicate data to serve their users. OSN users are typically assigned to the closest DCs and have a set of friends and followers who make network connections with them. These connections are between users who are assigned to the same DC as represented by a graph in rectangles (see Fig. 1) or different DCs (e.g., user connections UC1 and UC2). In this model, for example, a user in user group UG1 puts data in AWS DC named replica R1. To make this data available to his/her friends and followers, the data is also replicated in Azure DC as replica R2. These replicas stay in DCs until they receive many read and write requests. As time passes, one replica probably migrates to another DC or moves between storage classes (e.g., Simple Service Storage (S3) and Reduced Redundancy Storage (RRS) in AWS) within a DC as backup data. This data migration reduces the monetary cost though it arises a concern about the of data migration for users. We demonstrate this is not of concern because the data migrated between data stores locating within and across regions within several seconds for a magnitude of Megabytes (MBs).

SYSTEM DESIGN

In this section, we introduce a modular architecture for object placement across cloud-based data stores. It enables users/application providers to store, retrieve, delete, list, and migrate objects across data stores based on the desired user's QoS (i.e., latency), the specification of objects and DCs. As shown in Fig. 2, the architecture contains several main components:

1. **Users/Application Provider**: This component is the entry point to the system and allows users to store, retrieve, delete, list, migrate objects across data stores.
2. **Object Information:** This component includes objects' metadata like object ID/name and size.
3. **Datacenters (DC) Information**: This is available to the system and consists of DC region/ID, and the price of storage and bandwidth.
4. **Object Placement Decision**: This component is the core of the system and is responsible to find appropriate locations for objects based on the objective function (i.e., cost optimization) and the users perceived latency (i.e, migration, read, and write latency). It consists of three modules: (i) Cost Calculation acts based on the proposed algorithms in (Mansouri, Y., 2017) and calculates the management cost of objects based on the price of storage and bandwidth, and the size of objects. (ii) Location Determination: this decides based on the previous module to store objects in the corresponding data store. (iii) Storing Objects's Metadata: metadata can be stored in VMs deployed across DCs or in Replica Placement Migration (RPM) Manager discussed in the next section.
5. **Cloud Provider API**: Amazon S3 and Microsoft Azure Storage provide REST (Representational State Transfer) APIs to Get(read), Put(write), delete, and monitor data in data stores around the world. We use these APIs offering for Java programming to manage data across these two cloud providers.

(1) **Cloud Resources**: This includes two classes of AWS storage services (i.e., S3 and RSS) and two Azure storage services (LRS and ZRS). More details on these storage services discussed in Section 2.

Data Access Management Modules

To implement the architecture depicted in Fig. 2, we implemented two packages using Java programming language:

1. **Data Placement**: As depicted in Fig. 3, this is an extension of CloudSim (Calheiros, Ranjan, Beloglazov, De R., Cesar & Buyya, 2011) in which we extended Datacenter and File classes according to the properties and methods required for data placement across data stores. Moreover, we implemented MigrationObject class for objects migrated within or across data stores.
2. **DC Connection**: As shown in Fig. 4, this consists of two classes for each cloud provider. One class is related to the securing information and makes secure connections to the desired DC, and another class represents methods to manage data across and within data stores. To provide these methods, we implemented a prototype system across Amazon Web Service (AWS) and Microsoft Azure cloud providers. For this purpose, we use JAVA-based AWS S3[9] and Microsoft Azure[10] storage REST APIs. With this prototype, an individual end-user can (i) manage data across two

Figure 1. A simple system model

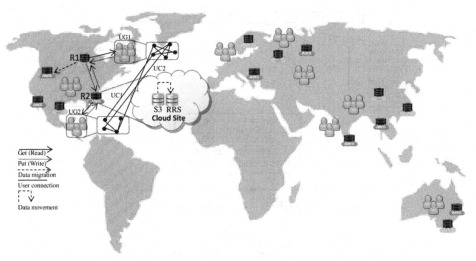

well-known cloud providers, and (measure) the perceived latency for operations conducted on the data.

Our prototype system provides a set of modules that facilities users to store, retrieve, delete, migrate, list data across AWS and Microsoft Azure data stores. Tables 2 - 5 show the list of main web services that is used in the prototype system for data access across AWS and Microsoft Azure clouds. All these services are RESTful web services that utilize AWS S3 and Microsoft Azure storage APIs in Java. They produce response in the JavaScript Object Notations (JSON) format in successful cases and error message in the error cases. We use JSON format because it is a lightweight data-interchange format and easy to understand. In the following we discuss the provided web services in more details.

Table 2 shows the following modules that are provided by the prototype system for data management in AWS data stores.

- **amazonCreateS3Client**: This module provides users to create a client with the type of AmazonS3client for accessing the Amazon S3 web services. It also allows user to set a region for the created AmazonS3 client account.
- **createBucket**: This module creates a bucket in the AmazonS3 client specified by users. It also allows users to determine the Access Control List (ACL) in terms of private, publicRead, and PublicReadWrite.
- **amazonCreateFolder**: This module creates a folder in a bucket and allows users to determine the storage class of objects stored in a folder.
- **amazonUploadObject**: This module facilitates users to store objects in the specified directory which has a scheme like /AmazonS3 client/bucket/folder/.
- **amazonDownloadObject**: This module allows users to retrieve objects from AWS data stores in the specified directory with a scheme like /AamzonS3 client/bucket/folder/.
- **amazonDeleteFolder/Objeject**: As its name implies, it deletes folders or objects.
- **amazonListObjects**: This module lists folders in a bucket as well as the objects stored in a folder.

Figure 2. Key architectural components of object placement across cloud-based data stores

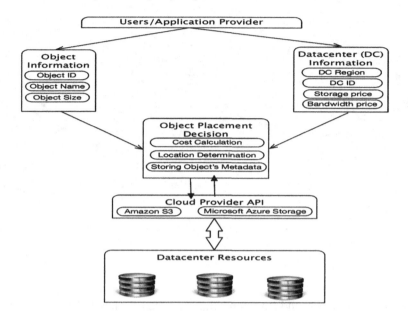

- **amazonChangeClassStorageFolder**: This module changes the storage class for objects stored in a folder.
- **amazonTransferFolder**: This module allows users to transfer objects (stored in a folder) from an AWS data store to another one.
- **amazonToAzureTransferFolder**: This module facilitates users to migrate objects from an AWS data store to Azure data store.

Table 3 summarizes the type and description of the main input parameters used in the above modules. It is worth nothing that the storageClass parameter can be one of the four constant values: STANDARD, REDUCED REDUNDANCY, STANDARD IA (IA for infrequent access), and GLACIER. In our prototype, we use the first two storage classes as discussed in Section 2. Some input parameters used in the above modules are the same in the type and description while they are different in the name. We excluded these param-eters in Table 3 and give their details here. All (src/des)Client, (src/des)BucketName, and (src/des)FolderNmae parameters are respectively the same with the client, bucketName, and folderName parameters in the type and descriptions. The srcClient, srcBucketName, and srcFolderNmae parameters represent that from which client, bucket and folder data are transferred. The desClient, desBucketName, and desFolderNmae parameters indicate the location to that data are transferred.

Similarly, we provide a set of modules to manage data across Microsoft Azure data stores. As listed in Table 4, these modules are mostly like the discussed ones in the functionality.

- **azureCreateCloudBlobClient**: This module creates an Azure cloud storage account in a region to access Azure cloud storage web services.
- **createContainer**: It creates a container in the the Azure storage account specified by users. This module can determine the type of ACL in the forms of Container, Blob, and OFF (i.e., nor blob

Figure 3. Data placement package

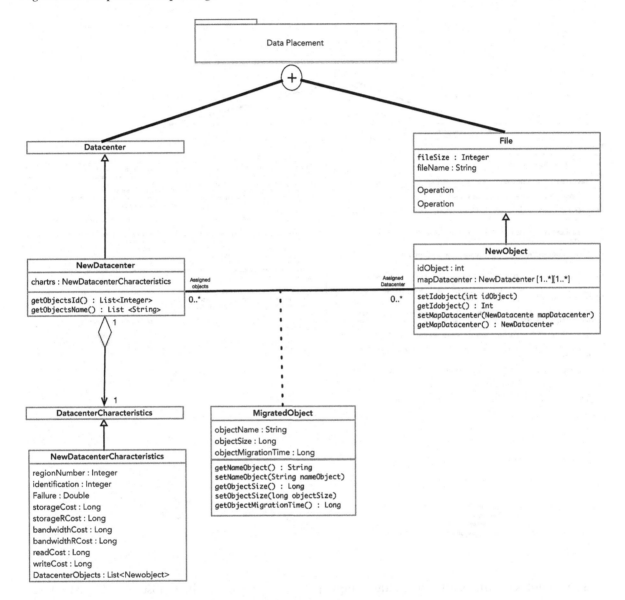

neither container). It is worth noting that container in Azure data stores and bucket in AWS data stores are the same in the concept.

- **azureTransferFolder**: It facilitates users to transfer objects (stored in a folder) from an Azure data store to another one.
- **azureToAmazonTrasnferFolder**: This allows users to transfer object from Azure data stores to Amazon data stores.
- **azureCreateFolder, azureUploadObject, azureDownloadObject, azureDeleteFolder/ Objeject, azureListObjects** modules respectively allow users to create folder, store objects, download object, and list objects in Azure data stores.

Figure 4. DC connection package for connecting to AWS and Azure datacenters

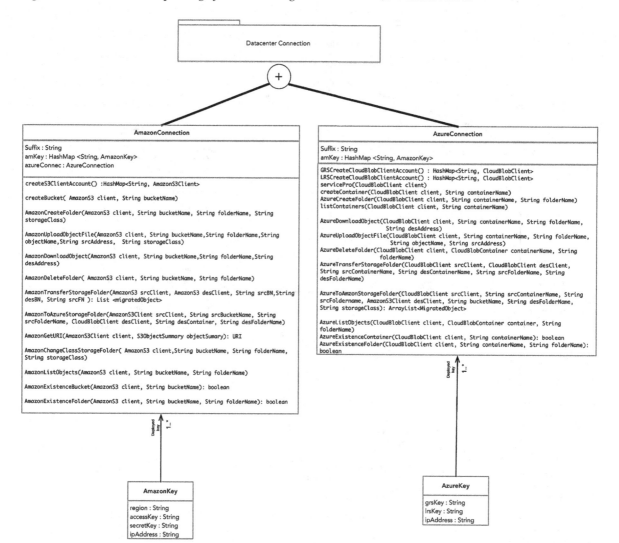

The modules of Microsoft Azure require input parameters which are like those of AWS data stores to the large extent. Table 5 gives a list of those that are only used in Microsoft Azure Modules. The accessKey parameter is a 512-bit storage access key which is generated when users create their storage accounts. The client parameter allows users to create containers in different Azure regions. The containerName parameter is an instance of the "CloudBlobContainer" class and its name is a string value used in Microsoft Azure modules. Note that the desClient parameter in the amazonToAzureTransferFolder module is an instance of the "cloudBlobClient" class; likewise, this parameter in the azureToAmazonTransferFolder module is a reference variable of the "AmazonS3Client" class.

Table 2. The modules used for data access management in AWS

Input Parameters Input Parameters Output
amazonCreateS3Client accessKey,secretKey AmazonS3Client createBucket client,bucketName Bucket
amazonCreateFolder client,bucketName,folderName,storageClass Folder amazonUploadObject client,bucketName,folderName,objectname, path,storageClass Put object amazonDownloadObject client,bucketName,folderName,desPath Get objects amazonDeleteFolder/Objects client,bucketName,folderName,desPath Delete folder/objects amazonListObjects client,bucketName,folderName Object list
amazonChangeClassStorageFolder client,bucketName,folderName,storageClass Change storage class amazonTransferFile srcClient, srcBucketName,srcFolderName,desClient,desBucketName Transfer objects amazonToazureTrannsferFolder srcClient, bucketName,srcFolderName,desClient,desBucketName azureToAmazonTransferFolder srcClient,srcContainerName,srcFolderName,desClient,containerName,desFolderName Transfer objecs

Table 3. The input parameters used in modules of AWS

Input Parameters Type Description
accessKey String This key is uniquely assigned to the owner of AWSaccount.secretKey CloudBlobClient String This key is the password for the owner of AWS S3 account. Client AmazonS3Client This parameter allows users to invoke the service methods on AWS S3. bucketName String This refers to the name of the bucket that contains folders. folderNmae String This refers to the name of the folder containing objects. storageClass String This specifies constants that include four storage classes of AWS S3. objectName String This parameter specifies the name of object generated by users. srcPath String This represents the path from which the data can be transferred. desPath String This indicates the path to which the data can be transferred.

Table 4. The modules used for data access management in Microsoft Azure

Input Parameters Input Parameters Output
azureCreateCloudBlobClient accessKey CloudBlobClient createContainer client,containerName Container
azureCreateFolder client,containerName,folderName Folder azureUploadObject client,containerName,folderName,objectname, path Put object azureDownloadObject client,containerName,folderName,desPath Get objects azureDeleteFolder/Objects client,containerName,folderName,desPath Delete folder/objects azureListObjects client,containerName Object list
azureTransferFlder srcClient,srcContainerName,srcFolderName,desClient, Transfer objects desContainerName, desFolderName azureToAmazonTransferFolder srcClient,srcContainerName,srcFolderName,desClient, Transfer objects BucketName,desFolderName

Table 5. The modules used for data access management in Microsoft Azure

Input Parameters Type Description
accessKey String This key is used to authenticate when the storage account is accessed. client CloudBlobClient This parameter allows users to invoke the service methods on blob storage. containerName String This refers to the name of the container that contains the folders.

PERFORMANCE EVALUATION

We design a simple prototype as shown in Fig. 5. The way in which the deployed virtual machines (VMs) should serve Puts and Gets for each object is dictated by a central replica placement and migration (RPM) manager. The RPM manager makes decision on replica placement across data stores

based on the proposed heuristic solution (Mansouri, Y., 2017). The RPM issues Http requests (REST call) to the VMs deployed in cloud sites and receives Http responses (JSON objects). The VMs process the received requests via the deployed web services that are implemented based on Spring Model-View-Controller (MVC) framework (Johnson, R.; Hoeller, J.; Arendsen, A.; Risberg, T.; Kopylenko, D., 2005) as illustrated in Fig. 6.

We measured the latency for Gets across 18 data stores spanned around the world. The object size is between 1 KB and 10 KB for 100 users (in the Twitter traces) (Mnasouri & Buyya, 2016) who tweeted on their Feed. As shown in Tables 6 and 7, a subset of data stores is appropriate to store users' data according to the required QoS, i.e., latency. To measure the time spent on data migration across DCs, we utilized the federation of cloud sites from Microsoft Azure and Amazon in our prototype. We spanned our prototype across 3 Microsoft Azure cloud sites in Japan West, North Europe, and South Central US regions and 3 Amazon cloud sites in US East (North Virginia), US West(Oregon), and US West (North California) regions. In each Azure cloud site, we created a Container and deploy a DS3 V2 Standard VM instance. In each Amazon cloud site, we created a Bucket and deployed a t2.medium VM instance. All VM instances used in the prototype run Ubuntu 16.04 LTS as operating system. After the set-up,

Figure 5. An overview of prototype

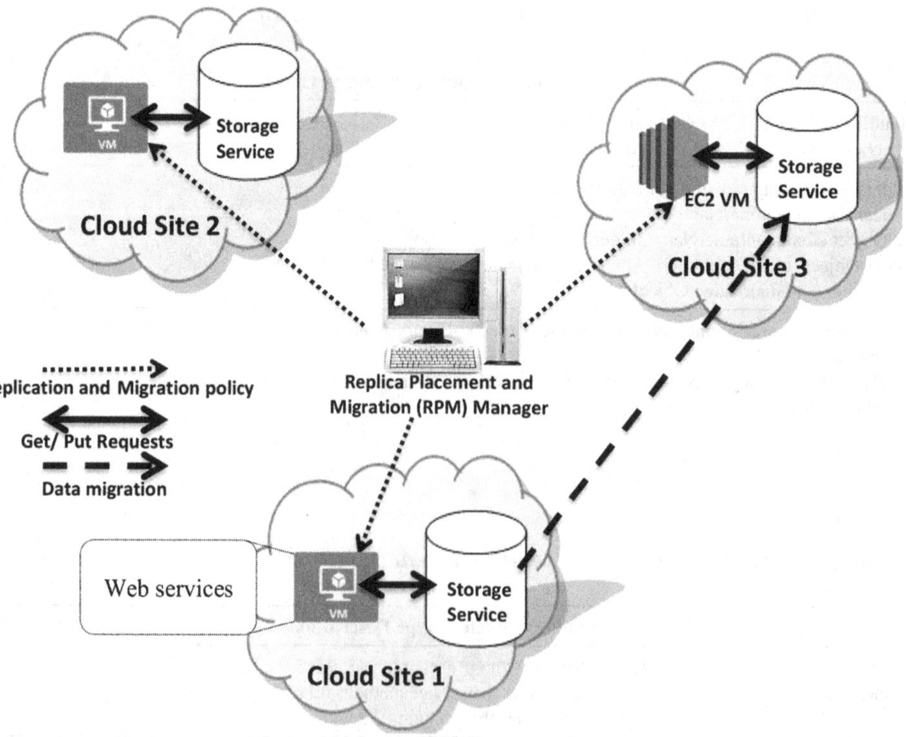

Figure 6. Web services components used in the prototype

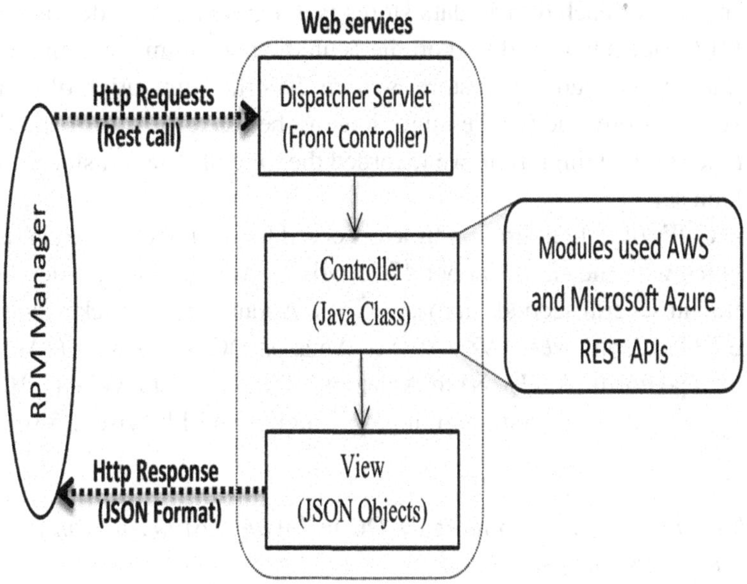

Table 6. Latency (in milliseconds) between Amazon' and Azure's data stores to Azure' data stores (Abbreviations: AZ: azure, AM: Amazon, SUS: South USA, CUS: Central USA, EA: East Asia, JW:

Datacenter Location	AZ-SUS	AZ-CU	AZ-Sao	AZ-Dub	AZ-Ams	AZ-EA	AZ-JW	AZ-Sin	AZ-AUE
AZ-SUS	1	25	146	115	127	176	135	210	190
AZ-CU	25	1	156	105	117	185	135	212	210
AZ-Sao	146	156	1	196	195	322	280	341	313
AZ-Dub	115	105	196	1	24	292	241	313	305
AZ-Ams	127	117	195	24	1	290	250	302	281
AZ-EA	176	185	322	290	292	1	60	38	118
AZ-JW	135	135	280	241	250	60	1	85	13
AZ-Sin	210	212	341	313	302	38	85	1	150
AZ-AUE	190	210	313	305	281	118	113	150	1
AM-Oregon	56	48	209	146	158	187	184	185	177
AM-Virginia	38	40	130	87	86	231	237	253	214
AM-California	37	42	176	153	156	179	182	178	152
AM-Sao	146	155	5	218	216	394	368	384	408
AM-Dub	123	106	207	3	24	259	252	254	305
AM-Frankfurt	121	123	213	29	10	262	254	243	299
AM-Tokyo	159	169	270	268	256	54	11	70	173
AM-Sin	216	212	348	337	316	38	140	3	130
AM-Sydney	169	317	317	330	325	149	158	159	5

Japan West, AUE: Australia East, Ams: Amsterdam, Sin: Singapore) we run the heuristic algorithm (Mansouri, 2017) for 100 users (in the Twitter traces) who are assigned to the cloud sites. The data of each user in data stores is integrated in a folder (analogous to bucket in Spanner (Corbett, 2013) for each user. Based on the heuristic algorithm, data migration happens when the cost of storing data in the source data store is more than the summation of (i) the cost of storing data in the destination data store, and (ii) the migration cost between the source and the destination data stores. In the occurrence of data migration, we recorded the time of data transfer from source cloud site to the destination cloud site.

Fig. 7. Shows the CDFs of data migration time observed for 100 buckets (each user is associated to a bucket), each of which with the size of about 47.35 MB in average. Fig. 7.a depicts that data migration can be transmitted in several seconds across regions. About 60% of buckets are transmitted in 2.5 seconds from Azure DC in Japan west (AZ-JAW) to Amazon DC in US west (AWS-USW) as well as from Azure DC in Europe north (AZ-EUN) to Amazon DC in US east (AWS-USE). Also, all buckets are transmitted in 3.5 seconds from Asia region to US region and likewise 4.5 seconds from Europe

Figure 7. CDF of data migration time from Azure DC in Japan west to Amazon DC US west and from Azure DC in Europe north to Amazon US east

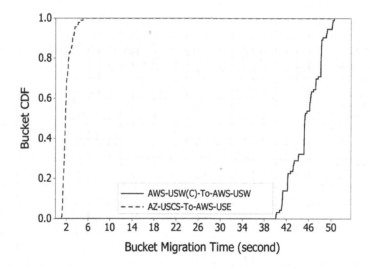

Table 7. Latency between different Amazon's datacenters

Datacenter Location	Oregon	Virginia	California	Sao Paulo	Dublin	Frankfurt	Tokyo	Singapore	Sydney
Oregon	1	72.4	212	181.2	133.6	146.2	90.7	162.3	177
Virginia	73.6	1	80.4	120.9	11776.3	88.9	157.2	231.4	238.2
California	21.3	74.8	1	194.6	195153.2	169.2	107.2	177	159.5
Sao Paulo	181.2	120.6	194.6	1	192.4	199.6	275.9	349.6	313.6
Dublin	144.7	76.4	150.1	192.5	1	20	226.4	267.4	312.4
Frankfurt	146.3	88.9	169.2	199.6	19.9	1	240.2	250.7	325.5
Tokyo	91.5	160.6	107.7	281.7	215.8	242.2	1	76.6	106
Singapore	170.7	229.4	177	349.7	267.1	250.7	76.6	1	177.1
Sydney	177	235.4	156.4	313.5	331.1	325.5	106	177	1

Figure 8. CDF of data migration time from Amazon DC in US west (California) to Amazon DC in US west and Azure DC in US Center south to Amazon US east

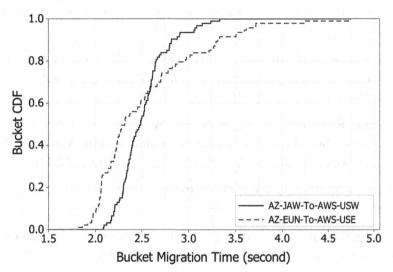

region to US region. Fig. 8. Illustrates the data migration time within US region. About 80% of buckets are migrated from Azure DC in US center south (AZ-USCS) to Amazon US east (AWS-USE) below 2 seconds. In contrast, bucket migration time between Amazon DC in US west (North California) (AWS-USWC) to another DC in US west (Oregon) (AWS-USW) is between 40-48 seconds for about 80% of buckets. From the results, we conclude that the duration of buckets migration is considerably low. In the case of many buckets, we can transfer data in bulk across DCs with the help of services such as AWS Snowball[11] and Microsoft Migration Accelerator[12].

CONCLUSION

This chapter presented a comprehensive review of the well-known and commercial cloud-based storage resources and compared them in the main QoS criteria such as availability, durability, first byte latency, etc. Then, it discussed the motivation of using the cloud-based storage resources owned by different Cloud providers and indicated the latency for Get (read), Put (write), and data migration with respect of replicating data across Geo-graphically distributed data stores. We presented the design of a system prototype spanned across storage services of Amazon Web Services (AWS) and Microsoft Azure. We deployed the RESTful APIs to store, retrieve, delete, migrate and list objects across data stores. We also measured the latency of data migration within and across regions, which shows that it is tolerable to migrate a data bucket (the integration of objects belonging to the specific user) as its size is a magnitude OF MEGABYTES (MBS).

REFERENCES

Armbrust, M., & et al. (2009). *Above the clouds: a berkeley view of cloud computing.* Berkeley: University of California.

Buyya, R., Shin, Y., Venugopal, S., Broberg, J., & Brandic, I. (2009). Cloud computing and emerging it platforms: vision, hype, and reality for delivering computing as the 5th utility, 25, 599–616, 2009. *Future generation computing system*, 599-616.

Calheiros, R. N., Ranjan, R., Beloglazov, A., De Rose, C. A., & Buyya, R. (2011). Cloudsim: A Toolkit For Modeling And Simulation Of Cloud Computing Environments And Evaluation Of Resource Provisioning Algorithms. *Software, Practice, & Experience, 41*(1), 23–50. doi:10.1002pe.995

Corbett, J. C. (2013). Spanner: Google's Globally Distributed Database. *ACM Transactions on Computer Systems*, 31.

Gupta, B., Gupta, S., & Chaudhary, P. (2017). Enhancing the browser-side context-aware sanitization of suspicious html5 code for halting the dom-based xss vulnerabilities in cloud. *International Journal of Cloud Applications and Computing*, 1–31.

Gupta, B. B. (2016). Analysis Of Various Security Issues And Challenges In Cloud Computing Environment. *Survey (London, England).*

Gupta, B. B. (2018). *Computer and cyber security: principles, algorithm, applications, and perspectives. Boston*, MA: Auerbach Publications.

Gupta, B. B., & Badve, O. P. (2017). Taxonomy Of Dos And Ddos Attacks And Desirable Defense Mechanism In A Cloud Computing Environment. *Neural Computing & Applications, 28*(12), 3655–3682. doi:10.100700521-016-2317-5

Jiang, F., Fu, Y., Gupta, B. B., Lou, F., Rho, S., Meng, F., & Tian, Z. (2018). Deep learning based multi-channel intelligent attack detection for data security. *IEEE transactions on sustainable computing*, 1-1.

Jiao, L., Li, J., Xu, T., Du, W., & Fu, X. (2016). Optimizing Cost For Online Social Networks On Geo-Distributed Clouds. *IEEE/ACM Transactions on Networking, 24*(1), 99–112. doi:10.1109/TNET.2014.2359365

Johnson, R., Hoeller, J., Arendsen, A., Risberg, T., & Kopylenko, D. (2005). *Professional java development with the spring framework.*: John Wiley & Sons.

Mansouri, Y. (2017). *Brokering algorithms for data replication and migration across cloud-based data stores.* Melbourne: The University Of Melbourne.

Mansouri, Y., Nadjaran Toosi, A., & Buyya, R. (2017). Cost optimization for dynamic replication and migration of data in cloud data centers. *IEEE Transactions On Cloud Computing*, 705-718.

Mansouri, Y., Nadjaran Toosi, A., & Buyya, R. (2017). Data storage management in cloud environments: taxonomy, survey, and future directions. *Acm computing survey (ACM CSUR)*, 50.

Mnasouri, Y., & Buyya, R. (2016). To Move Or Not To Move: Cost Optimization In A Dual Cloudbased Storage Architecture. *Journal of Network and Computer Applications*, *75*, 223–235. doi:10.1016/j. jnca.2016.08.029

Muralidhar, S., Lloyd, W., Roy, S., Hill, C., Lin, E., Liu, W., ... & Kumar, S. (2014). F4: Facebook's warm blob storage system. *Usenix symposium on operating systems design and implementation (OSDI 14)* (pp. 383–398). Broomfield: USENIX.

Rodrigo,, N., & CALHEIROS, R. R. (2011). CLOUDSIM: A toolkit for modeling and simulation of cloud computing environments and evaluation of resource provisioning algorithms. *Software, Practice, & Experience*, 23–50.

Wu, Z., Butkiewicz, M., Perkins, D., Katz-Bassett, E., & Madhyastha, H. V. (2013). Spanstore: cost-effective geo-replicated storage spanning multiple cloud services. Acm sigcomm (pp. 292-308). Farminton, PA: ACM.

Wu, Z., & Madhyastha, H. (2013). Understanding The Latency Benefits Of Multi-Cloud Webservice Deployments. *Computer Communication Review*, *43*(1), 13–20. doi:10.1145/2479957.2479960

ENDNOTES

[1] International Data Corporation (IDC). https://www.emc.com/leadership/digital-universe/2014iview/index.htm.

[2] The Zettabyte Era—Trends and analysis. http://www.cisco.com/c/en/us/solutions/collateral/service-provider/visual-networking-index-vni/vni-hyperconnectivity-wp.html

[3] Availability and durability are described in terms of *nines*.

[4] Key features of storage classes. https://aws.amazon.com/s3/storage-classes/

[5] AWS storage classes. https://aws.amazon.com/s3/storage-classes/

[6] Microsoft Azure storage classes. https://azure.microsoft.com/en-us/pricing/details/storage/blobs/

[7] Google storage classes. https://cloud.google.com/storage/

[8] Read and Write are respectively interchangeable with Get and Put in this chapter.

[9] Amazon S3 REST API http://docs.aws.amazon.com/AmazonS3/latest/API/Welcome.html

[10] Azure storage REST API https://docs.microsoft.com/en-us/rest/api/storageservices/fileservices/azure-storage-services-rest-api-reference

[11] AWS Snowball. https://aws.amazon.com/snowball/.

[12] Microsoft Migration Accelerator. https://azure.microsoft.com/en-au/blog/introducing-microsoft-migration-accelerator/.

Chapter 8
Intrusion Detection Systems for Internet of Things

Gayathri K. S.
https://orcid.org/0000-0002-4029-3165
Mar Baselios College of Engineering and Technology, India

Tony Thomas
Indian Institute of Information Technology and Management, Kerala, India

ABSTRACT

Internet of things (IoT) is revolutionizing this world with its evolving applications in various aspects of life such as sensing, healthcare, remote monitoring, and so on. These systems improve the comfort and efficiency of human life, but the inherent vulnerabilities in these IoT devices create a backdoor for intruders to enter and attack the entire system. Hence, there is a need for intrusion detection systems (IDSs) designed for IoT environments to mitigate IoT-related security attacks that exploit some of these security vulnerabilities. Due to the limited computing and storage capabilities of IoT devices and the specific protocols used, conventional IDSs may not be an option for IoT environments. Since the security of IoT systems is critical, this chapter presents recent research in intrusion detection systems in IoT systems.

1. INTRODUCTION

Today the whole world is digitized. Internet has revolutionized the life of people around the world. Just as how human-to-human communication happened from remote location, we are entering into an era of device-to-device communication. The Internet of Things (IoT) is an interconnection of computing devices that can communicate with each other requiring minimum human-to-human or human-to-computer interaction. IoT market is growing at a breathtaking pace, starting with two billion objects in the year 2006 to a projected 200 billion by 2020; a rise of 200% is observed (Chaabouni, 2018). Owing to the intelligent nature of IoT devices, they are used in almost all fields like finance, health care, education, energy distribution, smart cities etc., The Padova Smart City in Italy is an example of IoT based smart city.

DOI: 10.4018/978-1-7998-2242-4.ch008

Copyright © 2020, IGI Global. Copying or distributing in print or electronic forms without written permission of IGI Global is prohibited.

High access to Internet makes network security a necessity in IoT networks. Internet usage has given rise to cyber critical threats ranging from a malware to a network intrusion, thereby causing business losses. An intrusion is any unauthorized activity on a device or a network with some malicious intention. The aim of intruder ranges from modifying system logs, making resources engaged; to threaten the security of data and resources in the network. The security loopholes of IoT systems create various security threats to the different IoT layers. Attacks on critical applications like medical and power plants may cause severe consequences in controlling a person or bringing down power supply. Attacks on household appliances cause loss of properties or can be threatening to the security and privacy of families.

IoT networks are vulnerable to a variety of different attacks towards disrupting the network. There are several built-in vulnerabilities of IoT devices through which a hacker can invade the system. Some of these vulnerabilities published by OWASP are weak or guessable passwords, insecure network services, insecure cloud, mobile or backend API services, lack of secure updates, use of insecure or outdated components, insufficient privacy protection, insecure data transfer and storage, insecure default settings etc., Also millions of services are using obsolete protocols like FTP and Telnet, through which majority of attackers invade the system. Moreover, the protocols used for communication lacks security as neither they check the data they transport nor they encrypt the data. So attackers try to use any of these loopholes to evade the system and cause various attacks of their choice. Mostly, malwares focus on low-level vulnerabilities to infect the system. The need for an Intrusion Detection System (IDS) is critical for IoT applications.

IoT devices are restricted with computation, memory, bandwidth and energy and hence cannot execute computationally intensive and latency-sensitive security solutions. This makes most of the existing security solutions involving heavy computation, communication overhead inapplicable to IoT networks. Many companies are investing in research using intelligent techniques to design lightweight IDS for IoT networks. This chapter is organized as follows: Section 2 covers the IoT networks and Architectures. Section 3 focuses on the Intrusion Detection System in IoT. Section 4 discusses the intrusion attacks in IoT. Section 5 focuses on some of the existing research works on IDS in IoT. Finally, the Section 6 provides the future research directions and challenges of implementing IDS in IoT.

2. IOT NETWORK AND ARCHITECTURE

IoT is not a single technology, rather a collection of various technologies that work together in a collaborative manner. IoT devices are embedded with sensors, actuators, processors and transceivers. Sensors are devices that collect data from the physical environment. Common sensors are temperature, camera, pressure, UV etc., Data from sensors are stored and processed either on the edge of the network or in remote servers. Actuators are devices used to effect a change in the environment based on the processed information. IoT devices are installed at geographically dispersed location and so uses wireless communication medium. Devices, local network (gateway), Internet and back-end services form the core infrastructure of IoT architecture.

The most basic architecture of IoT is a three-layered architecture. The three layers are perception layer, network layer and application layer as shown in Fig 1.

The perception layer resembles the physical layer equipped with sensors. Perception layer is responsible for the data coming from the physical environment. The network layer is responsible for connecting other devices, network devices and servers for processing and transmitting data. The application layer is

Figure 1. 3-layered architecture of IoT

Application Layer

Network Layer

Perception Layer

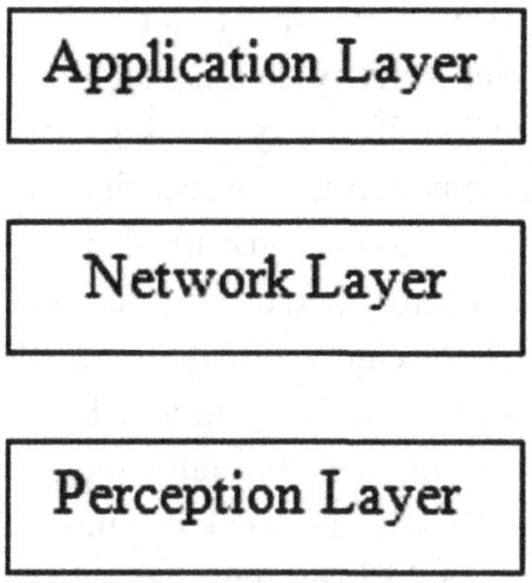

responsible for providing application specific services to the users. More detailed finer-level architecture of IoT includes five layers, namely perception, transport, processing, application and business layers as shown in Fig. 2. The transport layer is responsible for transferring data from the perception layer to the processing layer and vice-versa. Protocols like RFID, 3G, NFC, Bluetooth etc., works in the transport layer. The processing layer or middleware layer is responsible storing and processing large amount of data coming from the transport layer. This layer employs technologies like database, cloud computing and big data processing. The business layer manages the entire IoT system. In some architectures, the storage and the processing of the data is carried at a centralized cloud server.

All the heavy computation algorithms can be processed at the cloud which provides large amount of storage and processing resources. However, the cloud architecture is not suitable for the mobile IoT

Figure 2. 5-layered architecture of IoT

Business Layer

Application Layer

Processing Layer

Transport Layer

Perception Layer

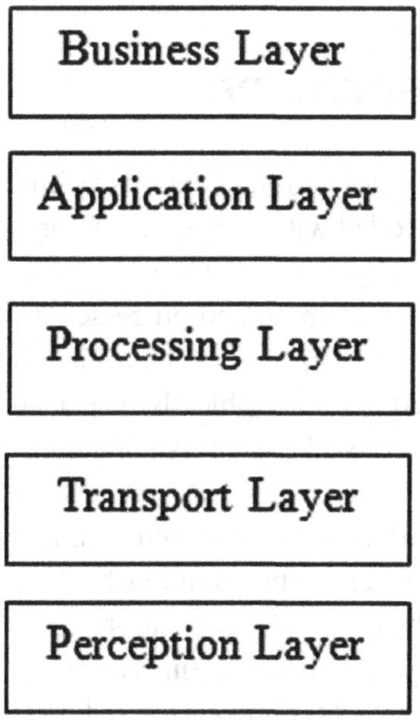

nodes. Also, lot of communication is involved in transferring data from border router to cloud which in turn increases the bandwidth usage.

Another architecture that was framed as a solution to the cloud architecture is the fog computing. In fog computing, the network gateway does part of data processing. Fog architecture shown in Fig. 3 involves physical, monitoring, preprocessing, storage, security and transport layers. The physical layer has sensors for collecting data from the environment, the monitoring layer monitors the resources, the preprocessing layer performs analytics of collected data, storage layer provides storage of data, and security layer ensures data integrity. The tasks of monitoring and preprocessing layers are done on the edge of the network.

3. INTRUSION DETECTION IN IOT

Intrusion detection can be a software or hardware solution, the primary function of which is to detect unauthorized malicious attacker. IDS works in 3 stages namely, data collection stage (monitoring), detection stage and alarming stage. In the monitoring stage, data from host-based or network based sensors are collected. These are the raw data. The raw data is processed to extract the necessary features. For example, features like CPU usage, RAM usage, packet payload, packet count, source address, protocol usage, destination address, number of processes running etc., are considered for intrusion detection. The extracted features are fed to the detection stage which analyzes the features for the presence of any intruders. If the detection stage encountered any intrusion, an alarm message will be raised indicating the presence of an intruder in the system as shown in Fig 4.

IDS is broadly categorized into two based on its placement: Host based IDS (HIDS) and Network based IDS (NIDS). HIDS examines activities centered on a host. These activities can be like application usage, file access, RAM usage, CPU usage etc., HIDS captures the current view of existing files and compares it with the pre-captured view of the files, any mismatch is reported to the administrator for further investigation.

NIDS monitors traffic at the network level (routers, gateways etc.,). They analyze the network for anomalous behavior based on features like packet data, protocol use, source/destination IP, port usage, incoming and outgoing time of packets etc., NIDS helps to detect an intruder before it enters the network whereas HIDS will not detect the presence of intruder till it breaches the system. Intrusion detection techniques are broadly classified into four based on detection mechanism used as: static analysis, dynamic analysis, specification-based analysis, and hybrid analysis. In dynamic analysis, a controlled environment such as a virtual machine or sandbox is used to execute the program. The approach collects the behavioral attributes of executing the program like resources used, execution path, privilege requested etc., to classify the program as

either benign or malicious. The dynamic approach is also called anomaly based detection. On the other hand, the static analysis examines the program statically for detecting anomalous behavior. This approach uses static features like byte sequence, opcode sequence, API calls, n-gram analysis, control flow graph etc., for detecting malicious functionalities. The static approach is popularly called as signature- based approach. In specification-based intrusion detection, manually specified program behavioral specifications are used as a basis to detect attacks. Hybrid analysis uses both static dynamic features for intrusion detection.

Figure 4. Working of IDS

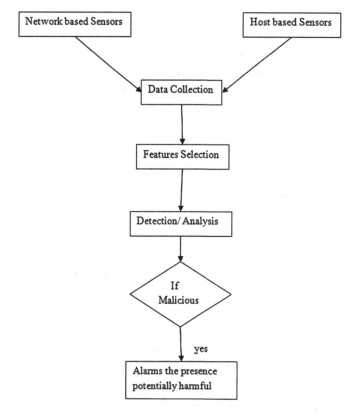

Fig. 4 Working of IDS

3.1 Signature-Based Approaches

Signature-based IDS use a static database of known malware and intrusion patterns to detect attacks. If any situation matching the stored pattern happens, then an alert will be triggered. Signatures can be anything from a port number in the packet header to a byte sequence in packet payload. Signature-based IDSs are accurate and very effective in detecting known attacks. However, this approach is ineffective in detecting zero day attacks or new attacks since a matching signature for these attacks is still unknown. Also, there can be a time lag between the discovery of a new threat and updating of signature in the database. By this time, the system can be compromised by the new threat.

3.2 Anomaly-Based Approaches

Anomaly-based IDS works by observing the way a program executes. This IDS creates the profile of normal working behavior of the system. It then compares the activities of new system at any instant against this profile and generates an alert if any deviation is found. This approach is efficient to detect new attacks. But learning the entire range of the normal behavior of a system is not easy as each new application may show different behavior. Hence, this method usually has high false positive rates. Also,

Figure 5. Classification of IDS

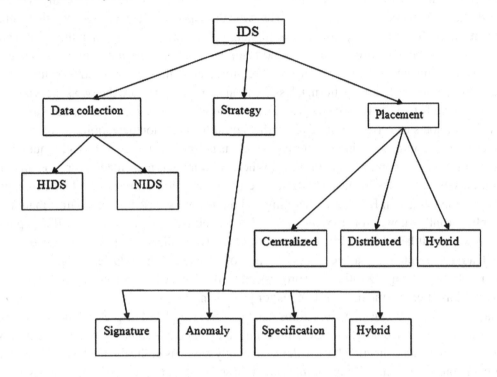

to construct the normal behavior profile, researchers usually employ statistical techniques or machine learning algorithms that can be too heavy for light weight IoT nodes.

Anomaly-based detection is further classified based on the approach used as data mining based, statistical model based, rule based, protocol based, machine learning based, reputation based, payload based, voting based, game theory based and so on.

3.2.1 Data Mining Based Detection

Data Mining is the process of automatically analyzing large volumes of data for patterns using association rules. It is used for extracting useful features from huge amount of data. Some of the data mining techniques are data summarization with statistics, visualization, clustering, association rule discovery and classification. Data mining techniques like principal component analysis (PCA) helps in dimensionality reduction of heterogeneous data. Data mining techniques can be used for both preprocessing data and methods like visualization and clustering aid in intrusion detection. However, due to the high computations in the data mining methods, they cannot be employed in resource-constrained IoT devices. Data mining-based IDS can be implemented in fog devices or in cloud platforms, but node level implementation is difficult.

3.2.2 Machine Learning

Machine learning techniques help the system to learn from patterns and make a decision based on the learning. It involves two steps – training and testing. In the training phase, the system will be trained based on different input patterns. For example, to classify an application into malware, the system will be trained with the different possible features such as API call, Opcodes, RAM usage etc., that can be used to detect a malware. In the testing phase, a new application will be provided which the system classifies as either malware or benign based on the learned features. Machine learning approaches are classified as supervised learning, unsupervised learning and reinforced learning. Supervised learning has an input and the exact target for each input pattern. Classification and regression are the two supervised learning approaches. Methods like SVM, naïve bayes, k-nearest neighbor, decision tree, random forest etc., are some of the common supervised learning algorithms used for intrusion detection.

Unsupervised learning has an input pattern but there is no specific target. Such techniques group patterns into a cluster having common functionality. When a new input is presented, it is placed in the cluster to which it closely resembles. K-means, DB-scan, c-means etc., are some of the clustering algorithms used for intrusion detection. Reinforced learning techniques work based on critic information i.e., the target is only partially known. It makes the system learn itself based on experiences. If a step is correct a positive reward will be given and a negative reward is given otherwise. Based on these rewards the system will adjust itself to reach at the goal. Examples of such learning are Q-learning, Dyna-Q etc., but almost all machine learning algorithms are process intensive. Hence they can be applied to IoT networks if the network has atleast some powerful nodes for processing.

The dataset needed for learning algorithms can be either simulated or pre-existing data sets. Some researchers have generated dataset by executing benign and malicious samples in their test environment. Generally, real-time data collection for IoT devices mainly happens at the device level. The sensors collect heterogeneous data from IoT environments and these are send to the cloud for analysis.

In Dehghantanha (2018), the authors used a dataset of 1078 benign and 128 malware samples from ARM based IoT systems. The malware samples were collected from the VirusTotal platform for a period of about 2 years. Benign samples were taken from different official IoT application stores such as Pi Store. They extracted OpCode sequence as features from these applications using Class-Wise Information Gain feature selection approach to train the machine learning algorithm.

In Allan (2018), the authors noted that the existing malware detection techniques such as signature based, heuristic based and behavior-based yield high false positive rates (FPR). Hence, they used data mining techniques to reduce the FPR in the existing methods. They found that malwares could be best identified using their behavior rather than signature. To capture the behavior, the authors used API system calls made by PE files. Malware PEs were collected from online repositories which had malware classes such as virus, worm, trojan and backdoor. Benign samples were collected from fresh Windows 7 OS systems. The PE files were labeled based on the results given by Cuckoo and VirusTotal. The dataset had 552 samples with 452 malwares and 100 benign samples. N-gram API call was used as the feature and this was extracted from the dataset using Term Frequency Inverse Document Frequency technique (TF-IDF).

In Modiri (2018), the authors used a dataset which has ARM-based malware and benign samples, Vx-Heaven having 22000 Microsoft Windows samples with malware and benign data, Kaggle with nine classes of Microsoft Windows malware and Ransomware having OpCodes of six different ransomware families. Class-Wise Information Gain feature selection approach was used to extract OpCode features from the datasets.

In Xiao (2019), the authors used a dataset containing 1760 samples with 880 malwares and 880 benign samples. Malware samples were collected from VxHeaven. From the dataset, 11164 features of API were extracted. These features were further reduced to 500 features using stack based autoencoders.

In Shi (2019), the authors considered the energy consumption data for monitoring the system security. For experimenting, the authors used four Raspberry Pi 3 Model with Raspbian OS. It had a background program installed to emulate the normal behavior of IoT devices. These background programs collect data from sensors periodically and store them locally and then send the data to cloud as a batch. Here, the authors used energy meters as sensors. Six types of attacks, each with a length of 2 minutes were launched. For simulating virus attacks, a program that consume computational resource was created, for intrusion attack, ssh commands were used to create a login, for trojans a program was created to send trained model to server every 2 minutes. Other physical attacks for heating and power-line cuts were also created to collect malicious data. The collected data were preprocessed to remove noise using Savitzky-Golay filter. This dataset was further reduced using PCA. The dataset had data from 4 IoT devices. Each data recording was of 2 hours length. Three recordings were collected from each device. So, a total of 85666 samples from 12 recordings were collected of which half were benign and other half were attack samples.

In Hussain (2019), the authors used 20 different sensors connected with Intel ATLASEDGE board having ARM processor. At each device Perf tool was used in order to collect HPC traces. HPC information was captured by running applications in Linux Container (LXC). A total of 3000 malware and benign applications were executed to collect HPC information. Benign applications include MiBench, SPEC2006, Linux system programs, browsers, text editors and word processor. Malware applications were collected from VirusTotal which included Linux ELFs, python scripts, perl scripts and bash scripts containing 452 backdoors, 350 rootkits, 650 viruses and 1169 trojans. 44 CPU events were extracted using the Perf tool.

In Souri (2018), the authors used a dataset consisting of 6192 benign and 5560 malware applications collected from Google Play Store and Chinese App. Store.

In Takase (2019), the authors extracted processor information by emulating a CPU using QEMU. They used 10 selected programs installed by default in Raspbian as benign programs. They used Cowrie honeypot emulating ARM architecture for detecting malwares.

In Raza (2013) and Cervantes (2015), the authors used Cooja simulator to simulate RPL attacks such as sinkhole and selective forwarding attacks.

In Wallgren (2013), the authors simulated selective forwarding and sinkhole attacks using Cooja simulator of the Contiki OS. The OS has a support for RPL through ContikiRPL. It provides IP communication with the help of μIP. For selective forwarding attack, the malicious node was made to drop all packets except RPL packets. This made the application to lose the data, while the RPL functions normally. This attack simulation was executed for 24 hours, in order to make the RPL perform self-healing to correct it. However, the results showed that the attack still persisted. Sinkhole attack was simulated by changing the advertised rank of nodes while sending RPL messages. This simulation was also executed for 24 hours for RPL to perform self-healing. However, the result showed that RPL could not correct the attack.

Raw data collected from simulations cannot be used for training machine learning algorithms as they are very large and make the learning process time consuming. Hence to obtain useful features from IoT data, data mining techniques need to be employed. Data mining involves 2 steps: data preprocessing and data analysis. In the preprocessing phase, the essential features from the entire dataset are extracted. Further, the quality of real-time data can be poor. Hence data cleaning methods can be adopted to improve the quality of the data. Data transformation is another preprocessing step, where the data in different formats are harmonized. In the analysis phase, suitable techniques are used to train the preprocessed data. In IoT environments, sensors are responsible for collecting the data. The collected data is preprocessed to extract the features needed for detecting intrusion attacks. The features can be API calls, opcodes, energy consumption etc., This step is called feature selection. Another method used for reducing the number of features is the dimensionality reduction, which transforms the dataset to a lower dimensional set. Dimensionality reduction can be achieved using techniques such as principal component analysis (PCA), auto encoders, random forests, high correlation filter etc.

3.2.3 Deep Learning

Deep learning is a class of machine learning algorithms that closely resembles to the working of human brain. In deep learning, number of layers will be dense compared to other machine learning approaches. It gives more accurate results than other approaches. Algorithms such as autoencoders, deep belief networks (DBN), convolutional neural networks (CNN) etc., have been used for intrusion detection. Deep learning techniques are highly efficient in performing intrusion detection compared to all other methods, but their highly complex computations make their direct usage inapplicable to IoT nodes having a memory less than 2 KB.

3.2.4 Statistical Model Based

Statistical model profiles the normal network activities. Any traffic that falls beyond normal is classified as anomalous. This approach captures network traffic and process information with statistical algorithms. The observed information is represented using a statistical measure. The measure is a random variable representing a quantitative measure taken over a period of time. Each packet is given an anomaly score. When anomaly score goes beyond a predefined threshold value, the IDS will generate an alarm. But the effectiveness of this IDS lies on the ability of the system to learn the regular working pattern of the traffic and also on the threshold. If the threshold is very high then the system may not generate alert and if it is very low then system may lead to too many false positives. Also, the diverse nature and mobility of nodes makes it difficult for the implementation of statistical models. Some examples of statistical models used for IDS are operational model, mean and standard deviation model, multivariate model, Markov process, time series model etc.

The computations involved in this approach are highly processor intensive. However, this approach is recommended if the IDS is placed centrally with some powerful components like a border router.

3.2.5 Rule Based

Rule based model works by creating rules for data traffic. Any violation from these defined rules is categorized as anomalous. The system has to be monitored for a long time inorder to define the the rules. Rules can be framed on the basis of packet header information, payload or both. The rules used are:

- Integrity rule specifies that the message payload must be the same from its origin to destination. Attacks based on modifying the contents of received messages can be detected using this rule.
- Jamming rule specifies that the number of collisions with a message must be lower than the expected number. If a node introduces a noise into the network for disturbing the communication channel, it can be detected using this rule.

- Interval rule specifies the interval between the receptions of two consecutive messages. If the interval is longer or shorter than the allowed limits, then an alarm is triggered.
- Repetition rule specifies that a node can retransmit same message only for a limited number of times. Wormhole attacks can be detected using this rule.
- Retransmission rule is used to detect black hole and selective forwarding attacks. In both these attacks, the intruder suppresses either some or all messages that were supposed to be retransmitted, preventing them from reaching their destination.
- Delay rule specifies that retransmission of a message must occur before a defined timeout period, failing which is triggered as an alarm.

3.2.6 Payload Based

Payload based approach focuses on analyzing payload information for detecting intrusion. A common method for payload analysis is the ngram approach. ngrams from one packet is compared with predefined ngrams. On the basis of the number of ngrams, the packet is labeled as benign or malware. The maximum and minimum occurrence frequencies of a particular ngram are used and any deviation from this range is detected as an anomaly. This approach reduces the number of false alarms significantly. New attacks can be detected as the payload is fully analyzed. However, this approach fails if data obfuscation techniques like encryption are used. Also, in the training phase the approach expects a traffic that is intrusion free as the approach assumes analyzed payload to be of normal and builds the model accordingly.

3.2.7 Protocol Based

The protocol approach is used for monitoring and analyzing protocol usage in a system. It works by monitoring protocols in different layers of the system. An IDS based on this approach detects anomalies associated with a specific protocol or a protocol that is not available in benign application.

3.2.8 Game Theory Based

Game theory-based IDS models attackers and IDS as players in a game. This approach aims to guide the IDS towards an optimal sampling strategy. The optimal strategy assigns sampling rates to each link, thereby maximizing the probability of detection. The effectiveness of applying game theory for IDS in IoT is difficult to predict as the resource usage will depend heavily on the games used. If one can chose a game that only strains few resources, then it can be applied to IoT. Another difficulty with game theory-based model is that they are highly interactive and it requires administrators to adjust the detection rate from time to time, thereby making the approach expensive.

3.2.9 Trust Based

Trust based IDS calculate the trust of each neighboring node. Based on these trust values, neighboring nodes are declared as trustworthy or malicious. Packets will be forwarded only to trustworthy nodes. Trust calculation involves simple computation and they also occupy less storage. These advantages make the approach suitable for IoT networks. To calculate the trust of each node, a node has to listen to not only its own traffic but also to the traffic other nodes as well. Such long channel listening time can drain the battery of these devices faster.

3.2.10 Voting Based

In voting based IDS, the border router sends requests to all nodes in the network. Each node responds by sending the node ID and their rank. The ranks should be increasing form root to nodes. Using this information, a mapping of all nodes in the network will be created. Each edge of the network is iterated to check if the nodes agree with their rank. A node is classified as faulty if the number of disagreements a node has with respect to other nodes is larger than a fixed threshold. The decision for evaluating the current system as malware is made collaboratively on the basis of vote collected from the different nodes in the network. This method is lightweight in its working as it does not involve much computing making it suitable for the resource-constrained IoT network. However, due to its unsophisticated nature, the rate of false negatives can be high.

3.3 Specification-Based Approaches

Specification-based detection aims at detecting attacks by examining suspicious characteristics. Rather than looking at specific patterns, the IDS look for certain commands or instructions within the program which are not normal in benign applications. Specification is a set of rules and thresholds that define the expected behavior of network components like nodes, protocols, routing tables etc., This IDS alarms an intrusion when network behavior deviates from the defined specifications. This approach is more or less similar to anomaly-based detection. Specification-based approaches requires human expert to set the specifications whereas anomaly-based approaches use machine learning techniques to extract the feature. Manually defined specifications usually provide lower false positive rates than anomaly-based detection. Specification-based detection system does not require a training phase. The limitation with this approach is that manually defined specifications may not adapt to different environments and can lead to errors. It is suitable for IoT as it is lightweight, however the cost for defining the specifications will be high.

3.4. Hybrid Approaches

Hybrid approaches utilize the advantages of the other three methods - signature-based, specification-based and anomaly-based detection thereby minimizing the impact of their downside.

Depending on the location where IDS is placed, it is categorized into central, distributed and hierarchical. In the centralized placement strategy, an IDS mechanism will be implemented at the host level or at the network level (either HIDS or NIDS). The limitation with this approach is that if the central node fails or if the central node is compromised then the entire network will be at risk. Also it will be a burden for the central IDS node to monitor the entire network.

In distributed strategy, the IDS will be distributed over all the nodes in the network. Each node can then monitor itself against intrusions. But these are very costlier to implement. Also maintaining of IDS over all nodes is practically infeasible in IoT networks. In the hierarchical approach, the network is partitioned into clusters. Nodes that are close located are grouped into a cluster. Each cluster has a cluster head (CH) assigned to it. The CH monitors other nodes in the cluster and will communicate with other CHs to detect intrusions. But cluster formation requires lots of communication between the nodes and is therefore energy-intensive. The placement of IDS is very critical for the effectiveness of intrusion detection.

The effectiveness of IDS can be measured using the four metrics, namely true positive rate, true negative rate, false positive rate and false negative rate. True positive (TP) is defined as the ability of IDS in correctly detecting and alerting an attack. True negative (TN) focuses on correctly detecting the system as normal in the event of no attack. False positive (FP) is the measure of IDS in detecting an attack under normal behavior of the system. Finally, false negative (FN) is defined as the event of IDS not detecting and alerting the presence of an attack. Accuracy is defined as the number samples correctly detected by the IDS divided by the total number of samples. It is given by,

$$Accuracy = \frac{TP + TN}{TP + TN + FP + FN}$$

Another measure called precision is the ratio of intrusions that are correctly labeled as intrusions. It is given by:

$$Precision = \frac{TP}{TP + FP}$$

4. INTRUSION ATTACKS IN IOT NETWORKS

An intrusion is any unauthorized activity on a device or a network with some malicious intention. Causes of intrusion vary from a simple malware to more complex intrusion attack. The aim of an intruder ranges from modifying system logs, making resources engaged to threatening the security of data and resources in the network. The security loopholes in IoT systems create various security threats to the different IoT layers. The perception layer faces attacks like physical damage, hardware failure, and power limitations. DoS attacks, sniffing, gateway attack and unauthorized access are challenges relevant to the network layer.

Malicious code attacks, application vulnerabilities, and software bugs are the attacks targeted at the application layer. Enabling security solutions in IoT must consider the different technologies, services, standards, security requirements etc., of each device. Some typical malware types are:

1. Virus: Virus is malicious software attached to a file to execute its code and spreads from host to host. Once downloaded, the virus remains inactive till the particular file is opened.
2. Worms: Worms are self-replicating malicious software that can spread to any device within the network. Worms do not require a host to replicate. It infects a device via a downloaded file.
3. Trojan Horse: Trojan horse disguises themselves as helpful applications or add-ons in stealth mode. But once the user downloads it, the Trojan can gain access to sensitive data in the system.
4. Spyware: Spyware is malicious software runs secretly on a computer and reports back to a remote user. Spyware can grant remote access to attackers. Keylogger is a special form of spyware that captures the keystrokes of legitimate user and reports to the attacker.

Figure 3. Fog architecture

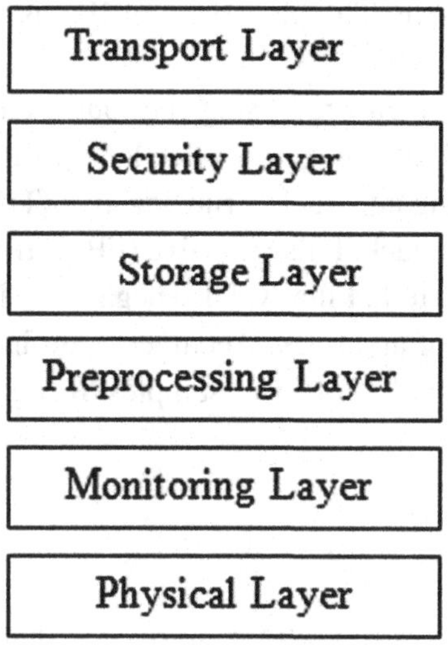

Transport Layer
Security Layer
Storage Layer
Preprocessing Layer
Monitoring Layer
Physical Layer

5. Adware: Adware is malicious software that collects data usage from one's computer and provides them with advertisements. They can divert the browser to unsafe sites.

6. Ransomware: Ransomware is malicious software that gains access to sensitive information within a system, encrypts that information so that the user cannot access it, and then demands a financial payment for the data to be released. By clicking a disguised link, the user downloads the ransomware.

7. Fileless Malware: Fileless malware is a memory-resident malware. This malware operates from the victim's memory and not from files. These are difficult to detect as they will disappear when the system is rebooted.

8. Bot: Bots are software programs that are created to perform certain operation automatically. Collections of bots form a botnet which are capable of performing DDoS attacks.

9. Rootkit: A rootkit is a type of malicious software that can remotely control a computer without the knowledge of the users. Once a rootkit has been installed it is possible for the attacker to remotely execute files, access information, modify system configurations, alter software etc., install concealed malware, or control the computer as part of a botnet. Rootkit detection is difficult as it hides its presence. Organizations can protect themselves from rootkits by regularly patching vulnerabilities.

Some common intrusion attacks are Denial of service attack, Sinkhole attack, Selective forwarding attack, Sybil attack etc., which are discussed below:

1. Sinkhole Attack: IoT network uses RPL (Routing Protocol for Low Power and Lossy Networks) as the routing protocol with 6LoWPAN. In RPL, a node chooses a neighbor that provides minimum hops to destination. In sinkhole attacks, an attacker advertises a beneficial routing path and thus makes many nodes in the network route traffic through it.

2. Wormhole Attack: In wormhole attack, the attacker uses two or more malicious nodes linked by a tunnel. In this way, the attacker creates a fake route shorter than the original one. The tunnel is called the wormhole.

3.   Selective Forwarding Attack: In this attack, the malicious node behaves like a normal node, selectively dropping some packets. Packets normally travel through some intermediate nodes so as to reach the destination. If the attacker is able to compromise the intermediary node, then he can block the forwarding of some packets, allowing only the packets that will benefit the attacker. Black hole attack is the selective forwarding attack in which all packets are dropped by the malicious node.

4.   Sybil Attack: Attackers create fake identities to compromise the system. These attacks threaten the reputation of the system. Such attacks can be easily employed on IoT networks where the nodes are deployed in an unstructured manner. Some Sybil attacks are target routing, distribution storage, data aggregation, and resource allocation.

5.   Denial of Service Attack: Denial of Service or DoS attacks aims to degrade the availability of computational resources like bandwidth, processing time etc., to legitimate users. If this type of attack is organized by an army of devices, then the attack is called a Distributed Denial of Service or DDoS attack. Such attacks are critical for IoT as these IoT devices will be prone to resource depletion attacks.

6.   Jamming: A variant of DoS attack, the jamming attack disturbs communication by intentionally transmitting interferences on the links, thereby preventing the nodes from cooperating with each other.

An intrusion detection system monitors the operations of hosts or networks for possible intrusions and triggers an alert if one such is found. An IDS for IoT analyzes packets in different layers of IoT with different protocol stacks and generates real time response. The main aim of IDS is to observer the individual nodes as well as the network to detect various intrusions and alert the administrators of the network, thereby avoiding any damage to the network. Attacks can be either internal or external. Internal attacks are launched by malicious nodes within the network. External attacks are launched by malicious nodes outside the network.

4.1. Case Studies of Intrusion Attacks

In this section, we discuss some cases of intrusion attacks in IoT networks.

Smart plug is an IoT device widely used in home automations. With the help of these plugs, users can control their homes remotely. For example, users can turn on air conditioner before they return home to make the environment cool during sunny days. With the increasing dependence on these plugs, there is a corresponding increase in the security attacks. If these smart plugs are compromised, then it can even risk the life of human beings. In Ling (2017), the authors investigated the security issues of the Edimax SP-210W smart plug. The authors identified vulnerabilities in the device's communication protocols that could lead to attacks such as device scanning attack, brute force attack, spoofing attack, and firmware attack. By launching these attacks, an attacker can capture the victim's authentication credentials. The communication protocols used in smart plugs are not secured with cryptographic algorithms, giving the attacker the ability to capture network traffic by reverse engineering approaches. This gives room for the attacker to perform eavesdropping attack. The plug uses MAC address as its identity, thereby allowing an attacker to perform device scanning which reveals details such as password change of the device. Most of the time, the users will not change the default password of the device. Even if the password has been changed, through brute force attack an attacker can infer the password of the device in most of the cases. Another attack that can happen in smart plugs is via firmware updates. Through these updates, the attacker can inject a malware. The malicious firmware can do any task as commanded by its master. Such attacks leave the complete control of the device to the attacker whereby an intruder is allowed access to our home. Some of these attacks can be mitigated using cryptographic techniques by encrypting the communications. Secure protocols like DTLS, TLS/SSL etc., can be adopted to encrypt the contents transmitted between the plug and the server. A good intrusion detection system can mitigate brute force attacks, eavesdropping attacks, scanning attacks etc.

Security issues in IoT can occur due to the vulnerabilities in wireless sensor devices, Ipv6 protocol, integrated cloud platfrom and sensing devices. In Bhattasali (2013), the authors consider the example of a healthcare system to illustrate the security vulnerabilities that exist in IoT. Healthcare system records health data in an electronic format (EPR). EPR is accessible from anywhere as it is placed in a network. This can lead to security risks to health data such as unauthorized access, tampering of EPR data etc. One major attack that can occur in healthcare system is the alteration of EPR data of specific patients. This can lead to incorrect diagnosis and treatment. These healthcare systems use wireless communication medium between the sensors and the server. These days' different types of wearable healthcare devices are used for monitoring patients for a long time. Any intrusion into these devices can endanger the life of the people. The security issues of these devices have not been much explored yet.

DDoS attacks are normally launched by botnets. A family of malwares namely, Bashlite (also known as Lizkebab, Garfyt and Torlus) carried out large-scale DDoS attacks in 2014. It infected over 1 million IoT devices. The targeted IoT devices were cameras and video recorders.

Intrusion detection in IoT gained focus with the Mirai malware attack in 2016 which has its root in Bashlite malware. Mirai created an army of bots by compromising the IP cameras and DVR recorders and attacked the Dyn DNS server of US. Mirai launched a DDoS attack by hindering the sevices of Amazon, Twitter and Netflix to legitimate users. Mirai made a scanning of vulnerable IP devices via port 23 and 2323 of Telnet. Mirai was able to create a botnet by using the weak credentials of these devices. Mirai had a Command & Control (C&C) server, a collector module which logs information about active bots, and a loader for propagating the malware to a new victim. To identify a new victim, every bot performs a random scan on the IP address space. For each of the IP addresses, it probes the ports 23 and 2323 of TELNET protocol. This is done to detect the target machine's application that requests user credentials. After this, the bot performs a brute force attack to guess the password. If all the above steps are successful, the bot reports the characteristics of the victim such as IP address, port, and login credentials to the C&C server through the collector. The victim then becomes a part of the botnet army and performs the commands instructed by the C&C server. These kinds of attacks can be detected using an IDS at the host or network level. The IDS can monitor the traffic on ports 22, 23 and 2323. If an attack is planned, these ports will be loaded with lot of authorization attempts to gain access to the IoT device which can be detected. Apart from this, frequent communications with the loader can also be identified. A properly designed IDS can monitor the traffic of IoT devices to identify such attacks.

5. EXISTING RESEARCH WORKS

In section, we briefly discuss some of the existing research works on intrusion detection in IoT.

Raza et al. (2013) implemented SVELTE, the first IoT IDS. It is a real time hybrid network (signature and anomaly) intrusion detection system which is distributed among the nodes. This work focused on routing attacks like sinkhole and selective-forwarding attacks. SVELTE uses lightweight IDS modules for the resource-constrained IoT devices. It incorporates centralized network-based IDS at the border router. It creates a Destination-Oriented-Directed-Acyclic-Graph (DODAG). Each node has a rank that determines their position with respect to the root node. There are three modules placed in the 6BR - 6Mapper, IDS component and a mini firewall. 6Mapper gathers information about RPL network and reconstructs the network in 6BR. The IDS module analyzes mapped data for intrusion detection and the mini firewall filters unwanted traffic before it enters the resource-constrained network. SVELTE detected sinkhole attacks with 90% true positive rate in a small lossy network and almost 100% in a lossless network. This method failed to consider the mobility of nodes. Also, DoS attacks are not detected with this approach.

Kasinathan et al. (2013) developed a DoS detection mechanism for 6LoWPAN. This is an example for centralized signature-based method. IDS probes are used to sniff the network in promiscuous mode and then send data to the main NIDS via wired connection. When the latter matches traffic with an attack signature, an alert is launched to the DoS protection manager. The protection manager analyzes the attempt with additional data collected from other ebbits managers, and reduce the false alarm rate. This solution overcomes the limitations of SVELTE since the IDS mechanism does not depend on the network architecture and thus it cannot be affected by DoS attacks against the IoT network. Ebbits does not consider node mobility and results in high resource consumption.

Cervantes et al. (2015) used distributed hybrid approach to detect sinkhole attack on the routing services in IoT. They proposed an intrusion detection of sinkhole attacks on 6LoWPAN for Internet of Things (INTI). The approach combined watchdog, reputation and trust strategies for the detection of attackers. The nodes are first classified as leaders. Then, the nodes can change role over the time based on network requirements. Each node monitors a number of transmissions performed by a superior node. If an attack is detected, an alert message is broadcasted and a cooperative isolation of the malicious node is performed. Cervantes et al. gave importance for node mobility and network self-repair, which were the limitations with Raza et al. approach. Their simulation results show sinkhole detection rate of 92% on 50 fixed nodes scenario and of 75% for 50 mobile nodes. Also, authors reported low false positives and false negatives compared to SVELTE.

Fei Xiao et al. (2019) proposed a deep learning-based approach to protect IoT devices from being attacked by local computers. They proposed a novel behavior-based deep learning framework (BDLF) which is built in cloud platform for detecting malwares in IoT environment. The proposed BDLF consists of two modules: behavior graph construction and SAE-based malware detection. This approach is implemented in cloud platform's detectors. Here, each program is represented by a behavior graph which consists of many API call graphs. After the behavior graphs are constructed, CP transforms the behavior features into binary vectors and then uses these vectors as input to the neural network-Stacked Auto Encoders (SAEs) for extracting high-level features from behavior graphs. Sending data from IoT devices to cloud each time is very arduous and involves increased latency and communication overhead. Also, the paper does not give any details on how the actual implementation in IoT is carried out.

Shi et al. (2019) proposed a machine learning based attack detection framework in the Internet of Things (IoT) devices. The framework is implemented in real hardware. Due to the characteristic of the energy data, not only cyber attacks but also physical attacks such as heating can also be emulated and tested. The authors have used Raspberry Pi 3 Model B and INA 219 energy meter for capturing energy data. Preprocessing of signals is done to smoothen signals and remove noise. Statistical and spectral features are extracted from the preprocessed data. PCA is used to further reduce the dimensionality of data. The features are then trained with k-NN and multilayer perceptron algorithm. They obtained an accuracy of 99% and 97% respectively. However, the approach considered data from only homogeneous devices. Its effectiveness in handling the big heterogeneous data is not tested.

Dinakarrao et al. (2019) proposed a lightweight machine learning approach for runtime malware detector (*HaRM*). HaRM employed Hardware Performance Counter (HPC) values to detect the malware and benign applications. It is implemented in the nodes. The authors used OneR classifier to train the network based on processor data. The classifier uses a single rule based on the features chosen to make the classification. It is lightweight as the computations are less. However, using a single rule classifier for intrusion detection in IoT will be inefficient with the huge heterogeneous data coming from the diverse IoT networks. Also, the number of HPC counters used (four) cannot be increased due to additional overhead that will be incurred.

Rajesh Kumar et al. (2019) presented a novel framework that combines the advantages of both machine learning techniques and blockchain technology to improve the malware detection for Android IoT devices. The proposed technique is implemented using a sequential approach, which includes clustering, classification, and blockchain. The implementation of the clustering technique includes calculation of weights for each feature set. The classification algorithm is implemented to extract the various features of Android malware using naive Bayes classifier. Finally, the framework used permissioned blockchain to store extracted features to increase run-time detection of malware with more speed and accuracy and to announce malware information to all users. However, this approach is not able to handle some obfuscation techniques. Blockchain implementation is not clear in the paper.

Azmoodeh et al. (2017) presented a deep learning based method to detect Internet Of Battlefield Things (IoBT) malware via the device's Operational Code (OpCode) sequence. An OpCode graph is constructed which is then transmuted into a vector space using eigenvectors and eigenvalues. Then convolution neural network (CNN) is used to classify malicious and benign application. The proposed approach gives an accuracy of 99.68% and a precision of 98.59%. Experimental setup is not defined and the approach is not tested for IoT or IoBT. Also, CNN involves lot of computational overheads.

Hayate Takase et al. (2019) proposed a malware detection mechanism using values extracted from the processor which includes the obtained program counter, opcode, and register number when each instruction is executed. The authors used random forest algorithm to classify malwares. However, the algorithm takes longer training time compared to other learning algorithms.

Anton Prokofiev et al. (2018) proposed a method for detecting botnets using packet level features employing logistic regression techniques. The method showed an accuracy of 97%. However, it is not applicable to detect botnets performing attacks on TELNET or SSH servers. Further the implementation details are not provided.

Christian Dietz et al. (2018) proposed a method for botnet detection using isolation of access routers. IDS is placed centrally on the access router. The approach scans for connected IoT devices. For each IoT device found, a scan for common vulnerabilities is performed. Firewall rules are written to automatically block any communication to vulnerable services of IoT devices. For IP scanning, DHCP tables are used to identify all IPs connected in the network. However, this approach depends on DHCP and ARP cache for scanning which are themselves vulnerable to attacks. Further, the scanning process is time consuming.

Table 1. Comparison of various intrusion systems for IoT

S.No	References	IDS Deployment	Detection Method	Treated Threats	Advantages	Disadvantages
1.	Raza et al.	Centralized	Hybrid (Signature and Anomaly)	Routing attacks like Spoofing, Sinkhole, Selective forwarding	• Lightweight • Distributed mini firewall to protect 6LoWPAN networks from attacks due to Internet usage • Flexible – model can be extended to find more attacks	Mobility of nodes is not considered
2.	Kasinathan et al.	Centralized	Signature	DoS attack	Scalable and real world applicable	• Node mobility is not considered • High resource consumption • Low system performance
3.	Cervantes et al.	Distributed	Hybrid	Sinkhole attack	• Node mobility and network self-organization and self-repair are considered. • Less false positive and false negative than SVELTE	Placement of IDS changes over time thereby consuming more resources
4.	Xiao et al.	Centralized (at cloud)	Deep Learning	Malware	• Accuracy achieved is 98.6% • Auto-encoders are used for dimensionality reduction	• Implementation in IoT is not clear. • Involves computational overhead
5.	Shi et al.	Distributed	Machine learning	Malware	• Cyber attacks and physical attacks are detected. • Accuracy of 98% achieved.	• Model considers data from only Raspberry Pi (homogeneous data) • The method showed a misclassification for Trojans and Virus.
6.	Dinakarrao et al.	Distributed	Machine learning	Malware	• Lightweight in having less computations • Classifier has less power consumption and latency • Achieved 94.7% accuracy with 8 HPCs	• Detection rate is only 92% with 4 HPCs • Counters cannot be increased due to additional overhead • Algorithm is robust for detecting malwares with data from heterogeneous architecture
7.	Kumar et al.	Distributed (at Blockchain)	Machine learning	Malware	• Achieved accuracy of 98% • Increased runtime malware detection with more speed and accuracy	• Not able to handle some obfuscation techniques • Blockchain framework is not clearly explained
8.	Azmoodeh et al.	Centralized (at cloud)	Deep learning	Malware	• First opcode based deep learning method for malware detection • Accuracy of 98.37% achieved	• Experimental setup is not clear in the paper. • High computational overhead from CNN • Evaluations are done in MATLAB on Windows 10 system
9.	Takase et al.		Machine learning	Malware	• Malwares including packed ones of same family are detected correctly	• Not tested in IoT environment • Random forest takes longer training time compared to SVM and naïve Bayes
10.	Prokofiev et al.	Centralized	Machine learning	Botnets	• Accuracy of 97% achieved	• Applicable to detect botnets performing attacks on TELNET or SSH servers • Implementation not clear
11.	Dietz et al.	centralized	Signature (IP scanning with CVE vulnerabilities)	Botnets	• Tested for IoT applications	• Depends on DHCP and ARP cache for scanning which are vulnerable • Scanning is time consuming

6. RESEARCH ISSUES AND CHALLENGES

With the rapid growth of IoT applications, need for data security and privacy increases exponentially. Though there are many solutions available for securing IoT networks, none of them prove to be good for real IoT applications. The reasons like resource-constrained devices, heterogeneous data from different applications (healthcare, industrial sector, education etc.,), different technologies and protocol usage, mobility, unavailability of IoT data for learning etc., contribute to this. Research works are ongoing in developing novel lightweight intrusion detection systems for IoT networks.

The question here is, as IoT closely resembles the traditional IT domain in terms of software, hardware, network and applications, is it possible to port the existing security solutions of traditional IT domain to IoT networks? Unfortunately, the traditional Internet is equipped with high computing devices that can process large volumes of data. On the other hand, IoT devices are resource constrained which can only gather data from the environment. They do not have enough capability to process large data. The second reason pertains to the heterogeneous nature of data from IoT devices. A single IoT application is equipped with different sensors capable of capturing different data with varying formats. Future research can be concentrated on handling the heterogeneous big data generated by IoT networks at regular intervals. Lastly, the different protocols of IoT networks like ZigBee, BLE, 6LoWPAN, Zwave, COAP, MQTT etc., hinders the adaptation of the available sophisticated security solutions in the conventional IT domain to the IoT environments.

Due to the resource constrained nature of IoT devices, they are not capable of processing the data collected by these devices. Hence, in IoT, mostly data analytics and preprocessing are done at various cloud data centers which facilitate high power computing resources. However, cloud has shown several limitations such as security and privacy issues of data stored in remote data centers, communication overhead of transferring data from border router to cloud periodically which increases the latency and bandwidth, non-support to geographic distribution and mobility of devices etc., So, future research can focus on bringing the processing of data closer to the devices. These can be achieved through technologies like Edge and Fog computing, which are equipped with devices like smart router, smart gateways etc. These devices provide facilities for temporary storage and processing of data nearer to the devices, thereby reducing the processing delay. Also the geographic distribution and mobility of nodes can be achieved with fog computing.

Machine learning techniques are a hot topic these days for intrusion detection. Since these learning techniques provide more accurate results than other methods, many research works are going on in utilizing machine learning techniques for IDS. In particular deep learning, a type of learning technique similar to the working of a human brain provides more accurate results in detecting zero day attacks. However, these learning techniques involve a lot of computations during the training phase, which in turn requires lot of powerful resources. Hence, direct application of such high computing learning methods to IoT environments is not feasible. Future research can focus on designing lightweight machine learning techniques for intrusion detection in IoT networks.

CONCLUSION

IoT has diversified applications like smart home, smart cities, smart parking, smart metering etc., for making the human life smoother and comfortable. There are also critical applications related to military, healthcare, nuclear reactor etc., where a security attack can lead to disastrous effects. Most of the IoT devices are manufactured without much security considerations. These security vulnerabilities can act as a backdoor for attackers. Intrusion detection mechanisms provide a means to ensure security in IoT. To enhance the efficiency of detecting zero day attacks, recent research works focus on incorporating machine learning techniques with the IoT environment. However, most of the machine learning techniques requires high computational power for their processing. Hence there is a need to develop lightweight machine learning algorithms for the resource-constrained IoT networks.

This chapter focused on various research works on intrusion detection in Internet-of-Things. We discussed the various types of IDS, intrusion detection mechanisms, placement strategy, IDS research in IoT and the challenges of implementing IDS in IoT networks. From the existing literature on IDS, we can conclude that at present there are not much efficient intrusion detection mechanism suitable for the resource constrained IoT networks.

REFERENCES

Abusnaina, A., Khormali, A., Alasmary, H., Park, J., Anwar, A., Meteriz, U., & Mohaisen, A. (2019). Examining Adversarial Learning against Graph-based IoT Malware Detection Systems. *Cornell University – Computer Science – Cryptography and Security, 2019.*

Alhajri, R., Zagrouba, R., & Al-Haidari, F. (2019). Survey for Anomaly Detection of IoT Botnets Using Machine Learning Auto-Encoders. *International Journal of Applied Engineering Research, 14*(10), 2417-2421.

Allan, N. (2018). *Behavioral Malware Detection by Data Mining.* Lambert Academic Publishing.

Alsaadi, T. (2015). *Internet of Things: Features, Challenges, and Vulnerabilities. International Journal of Advanced Computer Science and Information Technology.* IJACSIT.

Azmoodeh, A., Dehghantanha, A., & Choo, K. K. R. (2018). Robust malware detection for internet of (battlefield) things devices using deep eigenspace learning. *IEEE Transactions on Sustainable Computing, 4*(1), 88-95.

Azmoodeh, A., Dehghantanha, A., Conti, M., & Choo, K. K. R. (2018). Detecting crypto-ransomware in IoT networks based on energy consumption footprint. *Journal of Ambient Intelligence and Humanized Computing, 9*(4), 1141-1152.

Bazrafshan, H., & Fard, H. (2013). A Survey on Heuristic Malware Detection Techniques. In *Proceedings of the 5th Conference on Information and Knowledge Technology (IKT).* 10.1109/IKT.2013.6620049

Bernardi, C. (2017). A fuzzy-based process mining approach for dynamic malware detection. In *Proceedings of the IEEE International Conference on Fuzzy Systems.* 10.1109/FUZZ-IEEE.2017.8015490

Bhattasali, C. R., & Chaki, N. (2013). Study of Security Issues in Pervasive Environment of Next Generation Internet of Things. In *Proceedings of the 12th International Conference on Information Systems and Industrial Management (CISIM)*. 10.1007/978-3-642-40925-7_20

Breitenbacher, D., Homoliak, I., Aung, Y. L., Tippenhauer, N. O., & Elovici, Y. (2019). HADES-IoT: A Practical Host-Based Anomaly Detection System for IoT Devices. In *Proceedings of the ACM Asia Conference on Computer and Communications Security (AsiaCCS '19)*. 10.1145/3321705.3329847

Cervantes, P., & Nogueira, S. (2015). Detection of Sinkhole Attacks for Supporting Secure Routing on 6LoWPAN for Internet of Things. In *Proceedings IFIP/IEEE International Symposium on Integrated Network Management (IM)*. 606 – 611. 10.1109/INM.2015.7140344

Chiang, Z. (2016). *Fog and IoT: An Overview of Research Opportunities*. IEEE Internet of Things Journal.

da Costa, K. A., Papa, J. P., Lisboa, C. O., Munoz, R., & de Albuquerque, V. H. C. (2019). Internet of Things: A survey on machine learning-based intrusion detection approaches. Computer Networks, 151, 147-157. Elsevier.

De Donno, M., Dragoni, N., Giaretta, A., & Spognardi, A. (2017, September). Analysis of DDoS-capable IoT malwares. In 2017 Federated Conference on Computer Science and Information Systems (FedCSIS) (pp. 807-816). IEEE.

Dietz, C., Steinberger, W., & Antzek, A., Pras. (2018). IoT-Botnet Detection and Isolation by Access Routers. *Proceedings of the 9th International Conference on the Network of the Future*. 10.1109/NOF.2018.8598138

Dinakarrao, S. M. P., Sayadi, H., Makrani, H. M., Nowzari, C., Rafatirad, S., & Homayoun, H. (2019, March). Lightweight Node-level Malware Detection and Network-level Malware Confinement in IoT Networks. In *Proceedings 2019 Design, Automation, & Test in Europe Conference & Exhibition* (pp. 776-781). IEEE.

Elrawy, M. F., Awad, A. I., & Hamed, H. F. (2018). Intrusion detection systems for IoT-based smart environments: a survey. *Journal of Cloud Computing, 7*(1), 21.

Gupta, B. B., Agrawal, D. P., & Yamaguchi, S. (2016). Handbook of Research on Modern Cryptographic Solutions for Computer and Cyber Security. IGI Global.

Gupta, B. B., Agrawal, D. P., & Wang, H. (2019). Computer and Cyber Security: Principles, Algorithm, Applications, and Perspectives. Boca Raton, FL: CRC Press.

Hu, D., & Ning, Q. (2017). Survey on Fog Computing: Architecture, Key technologies, Applications and Open Issues. *Journal of Network and Computer Applications, 98*, 27–42. doi:10.1016/j.jnca.2017.09.002

Hussain, F., Hussain, R., Hassan, S. A., & Hossain, E. (2019). Machine Learning in IoT Security: Current Solutions and Future Challenges. *Cornell University – Cryptography and Security*.

Xiao, L., Wan, X., Lu, X., Zhang, Y., & Wu, D. (2018). IoT security techniques based on machine learning. *IEEE Signal Processing Magazine*.

Jiang, L., Tan, R., Lou, X., & Lin, G. (2019, April). On Lightweight Privacy-Preserving Collaborative Learning for Internet-of-Things Objects. In *Proceedings of the 19th International Conference on Internet of Things Design and Implementation.* (pp. 70-81). ACM. 10.1145/3302505.3310070

Kambourakis, G., Kolias, C., & Stavrou, A. (2017, October). The mirai botnet and the IoT zombie armies. In MILCOM 2017-2017 IEEE Military Communications Conference (MILCOM) (pp. 267-272). IEEE.

Kasinathan, P., & Spirito, V. (2013). Denial-of-Service Detection in 6LoWPAN-based Internet of Things. In *Proceedings of the International Conference on Wireless and Mobile Computing, Networking and Communications.* Academic Press.

Kasinathan, P., Costamagna, G., Khaleel, H., Pastrone, C., & Spirito, M. A. (2013, November). DEMO: An IDS Framework for Internet of Things Empowered by 6lowpan. In *Proceedings of the 2013 ACM SIGSAC Conference on Computer & Communications Security.* 1337 – 1340. 10.1145/2508859.2512494

Khan, H. (2019). *Recent Advancements in Intrusion Detection Systems for the Internet of Things.* Hindawi Security and Communication Networks. doi:10.1155/2019/4301409

Kumar, Z., Wang, K., & Kumar, J. (2019). A Multimodal Malware Detection Technique for Android IoT Devices Using Various Features. *IEEE Access: Practical Innovations, Open Solutions, 7,* 64411–64430. doi:10.1109/ACCESS.2019.2916886

Ling, L., Xu, G., & Wu, F. (2017). *Security Vulnerabilities of Internet of Things: A Case Study of the Smart Plug System.* IEEE Internet of Things Journal.

Lu, W., Hu, X., Li, X., & Wei, Y. (2016). A new method of QoS prediction based on probabilistic latent feature analysis and cloud similarity. *International Journal of High Performance Computing and Networking, 9*(1-2), 52-60.

Mahdavinejad, R., Barekatain, A., & Barnaghi, S. (2018). *Machine learning for internet of things data analysis: a survey.* Digital Communications and Networks. doi:10.1016/j.dcan.2017.10.002

Min, V. (2015). Design and Evaluation of Feature Distributed Malware Attacks against the Internet of Things (IoT). In *Proceedings of the 20th International Conference on Engineering of Complex Computer Systems.* 10.1109/ICECCS.2015.19

Modiri, A., Dehghantanha, N., & Parizi, K. (2018). *Fuzzy Pattern Tree for Edge Malware Detection and Categorization in IoT.* Journal Of System Architecture.

Najari, L. (2014). Malware detection using data mining techniques. *International Journal of Intelligent Information Systems.*

Chaabouni, N., Mosbah, M., Zemmari, A., Sauvignac, C., & Faruki, P. (2019). Network Intrusion Detection for IoT Security based on Learning Techniques. *IEEE Communications Surveys and Tutorials.*

OConnor, T. J., Enck, W., & Reaves, B. (2019, May). Blinded and confused: uncovering systemic flaws in device telemetry for smart-home internet of things. In *Proceedings of the 12th Conference on Security and Privacy in Wireless and Mobile Networks* (pp. 140-150). ACM.

Pecorella, T., Brilli, L., & Mucchi, L. (2016). The role of physical layer security in IoT: A novel perspective. Information, 7(3), 49.

Plageras, P., & Stergiou, W. (2018). Efficient IoT-based Sensor BIG Data Collection-Processing and Analysis in Smart buildings. *Future Generation Computer Systems*, *82*, 349–357. doi:10.1016/j.future.2017.09.082

Prokofiev, A. O., Smirnova, Y. S., & Surov, V. A. (2018, January). A method to detect Internet of Things botnets. In *Proceedings 2018 IEEE Conference of Russian Young Researchers in Electrical and Electronic Engineering (EIConRus)* (pp. 105-108). IEEE 10.1109/EIConRus.2018.8317041

Raza, W., Wallgren, L., & Voigt, T. (2013). Svelte: Real – time Intrusion Detection in the Internet of Things. *Ad Hoc Networks*, *11*(8), 2661–2674. doi:10.1016/j.adhoc.2013.04.014

Sethi, S., & Sarangi, S. R. (2017). Internet of Things – Architectures, Protocols and Applications. *Hindawi – Journal of Electrical and Computer Engineering*, *2017*, 1–25. doi:10.1155/2017/9324035

Shi, L., & Song, L., Ye. (2019). Energy Audition based Cyber-Physical Attack Detection System in IoT. *Proceedings of the ACM Turing Celebration Conference*. 10.1145/3321408.3321588

Singla, B., & Bertino, E. (2019). How Deep Learning Is Making Information Security More Intelligent. *IEEE Security and Privacy*, *17*(3), 56–65. doi:10.1109/MSEC.2019.2902347

Souri, H. (2018). *A state-of-the-art survey of malware detection approaches using data mining techniques*. Human-Centric Computing and Information Sciences. doi:10.118613673-018-0125-x

Stergiou, C., Psannis, K. E., Kim, B. G., & Gupta, B. (n.d.). Secure integration of IoT and cloud computing. *Future Generation Computer Systems*. 964 - 975.

Su, J., Vasconcellos, V. D., Prasad, S., Daniele, S., Feng, Y., & Sakurai, K. (2018, July). Lightweight classification of IoT malware based on image recognition. In *Proceedings 2018 IEEE 42nd Annual Computer Software and Applications Conference (COMPSAC)* (Vol. 2, pp. 664-669). IEEE. 10.1109/COMPSAC.2018.10315

Sun, A., Ji, T., & Wang, J. (2016). Cloud platform scheduling strategy based on virtual machine resource behaviour analysis. *International Journal of High Performance Computing and Networking*, *9*(1-2), 61-69.

Takase, K., & Kato, O. (2019). A prototype implementation and evaluation of the malware detection mechanism for IoT devices using the processor information. *International Journal of Information Security*. doi:10.100710207-019-00437-y

Tang, C., & Hefferman, W. (2015). A Hierarchial Distributed Fog Computing Architecture for Big data Analysis in Smart Cities. In *Proceedings of the ASE BigData & Social Informatics. Academic Press.*

Wallgren, R., Raza, S., & Voigt, T. (2013). Routing Attacks and Countermeasures in the RPL-Based Internet of Things. *International Journal of Distributed Sensor Networks*, *9*(8). doi:10.1155/2013/794326

Wang, X., Cao, J., & Wang, J. (2016). A dynamic cloud service selection strategy using adaptive learning agents. *International Journal of High Performance Computing and Networking, 9*(1-2), 70-81.

Xiao, L., & Sun, M. (2019). *Malware Detection based on Deep Learning of Behavioural Graphs.* Hindawi – Mathematical Problems in Engineering.

Zhang, M., Duan, Z., Li, Q., & Chu, H. (2016). Transformation from business process models to BPEL with overlapped patterns involved. *International Journal of High Performance Computing and Networking, 9*(1-2), 82-92.

Chapter 9
Internal and External Threat Analysis of Anonymized Dataset

Saurav Jindal
Punjab Engineering College, India

Poonam Saini
Punjab Engineering College, India

ABSTRACT

In recent years, data collection and data mining have emerged as fast-paced computational processes as the amount of data from different sources has increased manifold. With the advent of such technologies, major concern is exposure of an individual's self-contained information. To confront the unusual situation, anonymization of dataset is performed before being released into public for further usage. The chapter discusses various existing techniques of anonymization. Thereafter, a novel redaction technique is proposed for generalization to minimize the overall cost (penalty) of the process being inversely proportional to utility of generated dataset. To validate the proposed work, authors assume a pre-processed dataset and further compare our algorithm with existing techniques. Lastly, the proposed technique is made scalable thus ensuring further minimization of generalization cost and improving overall utility of information gain.

INTRODUCTION

Over the last decade, data has increased substantially on a large scale in almost every field. In 2011, according to a record from IDC (International Data Corporation), overall stored and created data volume was almost 2 ZB (nearly 10^{21} B) that is expected to double every two years (Laney, 2001). The rapid expansion is due to social networking applications, such as Twitter, Facebook, Snapchat etc., which allows a user to create content freely, hence adding more data in already existing web data volume. Other than social media, mobile phone generates a lot of data through sensors like GPS, health-tracking applications, Call Data Records (CDR) and other. Moreover, technologies like cloud computing and Internet of Things (IoT) promotes the sharp growth of data. Currently, big data analytics (Gantz & Reinsel, 2011)

DOI: 10.4018/978-1-7998-2242-4.ch009

Copyright © 2020, IGI Global. Copying or distributing in print or electronic forms without written permission of IGI Global is prohibited.

has come as a computational process to provide better solution in order to understand and analyse such huge volume of data and thus ensure improvements in healthcare, law enforcement, financial trading and many other real-time applications. The use of big data poses major challenges like data representation (aims to make data more meaningful for analysis), redundancy (high level of duplicate datasets), expandability and scalability (analytical algorithms must be able to process expanding and more complex datasets), information sharing and data privacy (security of sensitive information). Although, most of the challenges have been addressed and overcome to a larger extent with the use of improved data analytic techniques, *privacy* is still a major concern. The privacy of data can be maintained in following two ways:

1. Restrict access to the data, thereby, providing limited access to sensitive information.
2. Anonymize data fields such that sensitive information cannot be identified by anyone and trustworthiness.

As the first approach has limitation in terms of data accessibility, anonymization may result in better utilization of data while maintaining data privacy.

Basic Terminology in Data Privacy

The data anonymization process comprises of three essential entities, namely, *participants*, *operations* and *attributes*. The entities are responsible for data collection during initial stages to data anonymization and final release of data into public with preserved privacy. There are following four participants in big data process with different roles (Yu, 2016):

1. **Data Generator**: Individuals and organizations who generate the original raw data.
2. **Data Curator**: Organizations that collect, store and release the data.
3. **Data User**: People who require the released data for some purposes.
4. **Data Attacker**: Person who try to use the data for malicious purposes.

Further, there are three main operations on dataset in privacy establishing models (Figure 1):

1. **Collection**: Data curators collect data (raw data) from various sources.
2. **Anonymization**: Data curators anonymize the collected data in order to be released in public.
3. **Communication**: Data users retrieve information from the released data (anonymized data).

Furthermore, there are three types of attributes in privacy study:

1. **Explicit Identifiers**: Attributes which uniquely represents an individual or an organization, for example, social security number, email id etc.
2. **Quasi Identifiers**: Attributes which alone cannot represent an individual, however, when combined with other quasi attributes or any other external information may identify an individual.
3. **Sensitive Attributes**: Attributes which are private to an individual like disease, salary etc.

Figure 1. Operations and participants in big data model

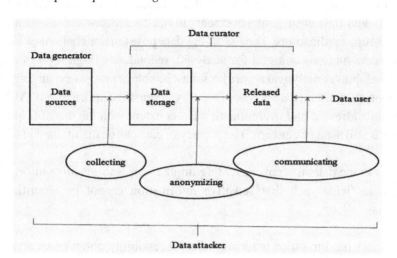

RELATED WORK

Before 2000, it was believed that to make data anonymized, just remove the attributes that directly depict an specific individual, like mobile number, name, email id, social security number etc., these attributes are known as explicit attributes. In Massachusetts, the Group Insurance Commission (GIC) is responsible for purchasing health insurance for state employees. For approximately 135,000 state employees and their families, patient related data was collected. GIC gave a copy of the data by removing all the explicit attributes to researchers, believing it to be anonymous. For twenty dollars, L. Sweeney purchased the voter registration list for Cambridge Massachusetts. This data included the name, address, zip code, birth date and gender of each voter. This information can be linked using birth date, zip code and gender (known as quasi-identifiers), to the medical information released by GIC, thereby breaking the privacy of an individual. The data is divided into:

- **Structured Data:** The data that is well organized either in the form of tables or in some other way, that can be easily operated is known as structured data. For example, data stored in the relational databases in the form of tables, having multiple rows and columns.
- **Semi-structured Data:** It is basically a structured data that is unorganized. Web data such as JSON (JavaScript Object Notation) files, .csv files, XML and other markup languages are the examples of semi-structured data. Due to unorganized information, it is difficult to retrieve, analyze and store as compared to structured data.
- **Unstructured Data:** The data that is unstructured or unorganized, operating such type of data becomes difficult and requires advance tools and softwares to access information. For example, images, graphics, pdf files, audio, video, emails, etc.

Background

The related work has been divided based on anonymization of structured and unstructured data.

Figure 2. Attacks on k-anonymity

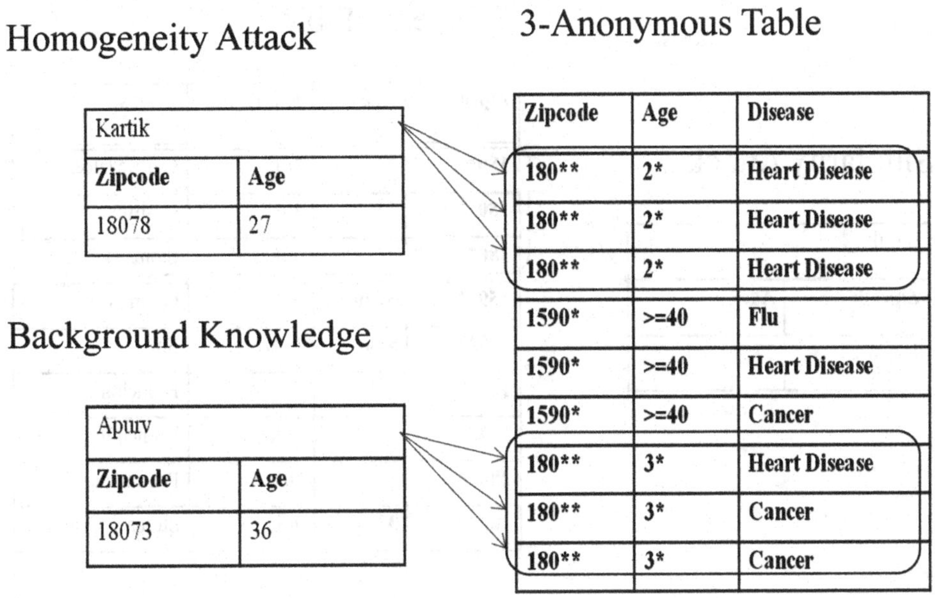

Homogeneity Attack   3-Anonymous Table

Kartik	
Zipcode	**Age**
18078	27

Background Knowledge

Apurv	
Zipcode	**Age**
18073	36

Zipcode	**Age**	**Disease**
180**	2*	Heart Disease
180**	2*	Heart Disease
180**	2*	Heart Disease
1590*	>=40	Flu
1590*	>=40	Heart Disease
1590*	>=40	Cancer
180**	3*	Heart Disease
180**	3*	Cancer
180**	3*	Cancer

- **Anonymization of Structured Data**

Sweeney (2002) proposed solution to the problem, how data holder could release the data to the public for research work without affecting or violating the privacy of individuals whose data it is. The solution for the problem is *k*-anonymity protection which means the information for each person contain in the released data cannot be distinguished from at least *k*-1 individuals in the same released data. All the explicit identifiers are needed to be removed and quasi identifiers of at least *k* tuples or individuals need to be same irrespective of the sensitive attributes.

Bayardo et al. (2005) proposed the new approach that tames the combinatorics of the np-hard problem and developed data management strategies to reduce the need of again and again sorting with the help of framework given by Iyengar. Used valued ordering and graphical representation made pruning very easy and efficient. The problem was that the dataset output was too generalized.

Machanavajjhala et al. (2006) showed that *k*-anonymity was not free from attacks like homogeneity attack (if all the sensitive attribute in an equivalence class are same) and background knowledge attack, shown in figure 2. Solution to these problems were given, that there should be minimum number of different sensitive attributes in each equivalence class. Homogeneity attack is itself vanished as "*l*" different attributes and background knowledge attack also, as adversary has to eliminate *l*-1 cases. This is too restrictive in some cases like when there is a Boolean value to sensitive attribute and the probability of occurrence or not, is near to 1%. Then *l*-diversity gives the more knowledge than the raw data that the given person has 50% chance rather than 1% called skewness attack. Also suffers from similarity attack as shown in figure 3.

Li et al. (2007), for the first time in the privacy history, addressed the semantics of sensitive attribute. Principle of *t*-closeness is "An equivalence class is said to have *t*-closeness if the distance between the distribution of a sensitive attribute in this class and the distribution of the attribute in the whole table is no more than a threshold *t*. A table is said to have *t*-closeness if all equivalence

Figure 3. Attack on l-diversity

3-Diverse Table

Zipcode	Age	Salary	Disease
180**	2*	20K	Gastric Ulcer
180**	2*	30K	Gastritis
180**	2*	40K	Stomach Cancer
1590*	>=40	50K	Gastritis
1590*	>=40	100K	Flu
1590*	>=40	70K	Bronchitis
180**	3*	60K	Bronchitis
180**	3*	80K	Pneumonia
180**	3*	90K	Stomach Cancer

Similarity Attack

Kartik	
Zipcode	Age
18078	27

classes have *t*-closeness". The problem in the given solution was that there were limitations of assuming only one sensitive attribute and the problem was np-hard and moreover, it is not fit for dynamic dataset.

O'Keefe et al. (2016) proposed a two-step approach to anonymizing analysis outputs from online data centres. First, a data preparation stage that requires data custodians to apply some basic treatments to the dataset before making it available, like identifiers are removed, datasets differ by a sufficient number of records, adding noise, data swapping etc. A subsequent output anonymization stage requires researchers to use a checklist at the point of downloading analysis output like individual values, threshold n, dominance(n, k) etc. Limitation of the paper is, lack of practical advice or guidelines assisting researchers.

(Kayem & Meinel (2017), used generalization hierarchy for numerical valued and categorical attributes, first separately then combined the results in order to determine loss of information. To determine the loss of privacy level, severity weighting is introduced, for instance, on a scale of 1-10, for cancer=9, while for allergy=3. Algorithm use jacard-coefficient for calculating inter tuple distance between categorical attributes. Results, kullback-leibler distance between the severity weightings both within the clusters and the dataset are relatively low which indicates high level of privacy.

- **Anonymization of Unstructured Data**
  Motwani & Nabar (2008), for the first time, performed anonymity on unstructured data. The data set taken were market-basket data and queries searched by various users. Used clustering technique and tried to minimize the sum of the hamming distances of points to their cluster centers. Basically used *k*-anonymity by changing the data set into traditional relational data set by creating a binary attribute for every item and a tuple for every set, then 0's and 1's are flipped, as few as possible, so that every tuple is identical to at least *k*-1 other tuples. Instead of anonymizing entire session,

anonymized threads only. However, there is no proof that a user's threads could not somehow be stitched together to reconstruct his session, which would no longer be k-anonymized.

Wang et al. (2010) discuss the solution to problem where dataset is updated in short intervals of time, which means data cannot be regarded as static data but dynamic. To maintain privacy in such cases is difficult because of skewed distribution on sensitive values. Thus, the classical methods cannot be applied directly on such dataset. A "reposition model" is proposed in which some records are withheld to be released next time, so that *l*-diversity can be applied efficiently. Drawback of proposed model is that many queries become useless because of crossing of time-stamp.

Zhang et al. (2015) propose a novel technique for anonymization of categorical information and dataset used is candidate voting. The proposed technique involves two-phase anonymization. In first phase the candidate encoding sequences are sent from data publisher to data receiver and second phase the anonymized votes are sent from data publisher to data receiver. The proposed technique can identify if a valid vote is changed to a dummy vote and if a dummy vote is changed to another dummy vote. However, cannot identify if a dummy vote is changed to a valid vote or if vote cast to one candidate is changed to vote for another.

Maeda et al. (2016) proposed a system that identifies the substrings which should be redacted to satisfy the conditions, such as, any terms in the quasi-identifier list satisfies *k*-anonymity by redacting characters and the number of redacted characters is minimized. Quasi-identifier directory is maintained in which number of characters that are redacted and the number of similar words is mentioned. Limitation is that, it is for very limited data input.

Ye et al. (2016) discuss the problem caused by Location-Based Services, as these may reveal the location privacy of clients. The proposed solution involves the integration of cliquecloak theorem and modified top location algorithm. The points missed in *k*-anonymity are reprocessed, known as personalized *k*-anonymity, thus increasing the density of users at a place. The benefits of proposed technique are, less burden to the mobile clients and maintenance is easy. Further, (Liu et al, 2013) and (Niu et al, 2014) also discussed solution for privacy in Location Based Services, however till now, quality of services was ignored. Later, the issue was addressed by minimizing query latency and server workload (Li et al, 2016).

Khan et al. (2018) proposed an algorithm for adaptive anonymity problem in shared as well as distributed memory. The proposed algorithm weights on the edges of a dissimilarity matrix iteratively and then computes, in the graph, the minimum weighted b-Edge cover at each iteration. However, the proposed algorithm is not tested on the systems or processes that require very high storage and during testing, the results for utility of the data produced is lesser than the previous existing algorithms.

The observations have been summarized in table 1

THE PROPOSED ALGORITHM

The section describes the proposed algorithm. We consider an example to firstly present the major limitations in existing redaction technique followed by the proposed method. Further, the proposed algorithm is extended and made scalable in order to minimize the overall generalization cost of anonymization process and maximize the utility of generated datasets.

Table 1. Observations from literature on anonymization

S.No.	Title and Authors	Source	Observations
1.	k-anonymity: A model for protecting privacy (Sweeney, 2002)	International Journal of Uncertainty, Fuzziness and Knowledge-Based Systems	• A formal protection model named k-anonymity and asset of accompanying policies for deployment. • Also examines re-identification attacks unless accompanying policies are respected. • One limitation is, homogeneity attack due to lack of diversity in sensitive attributes. • Other limitation is, background knowledge attack based on adversary's knowledge.
2.	Data privacy through optimal k-anonymization (Bayardo, 2005)	International Conference on Data Engineering, IEEE	• Identifies provably optimal anonymization of real census data under a flexible and highly combinatorial model of attribute value generalization. • No automatic stopping condition and could be too generalized.
3.	l-diversity: Privacy beyond k-anonymity (Machanavajjhala et al., 2006)	International Conference on Data Engineering, IEEE	• No homogeneity attack and background attack also minimized. • Offers more information gain to attackers in some specific cases and cannot handle multiple sensitive attributes.
4.	t-closeness: Privacy beyond k-anonymity and l-diversity (Li et al., 2007)	International Conference on Data Engineering, IEEE	• Discusses the problem with l-diversity's limitation of assumption of adversarial knowledge. • Considers semantics of sensitive attributes. • Not fit for dynamic dataset, cannot handle more than one sensitive attributes and limitation of using EMD.
5.	Anonymizing unstructured data (Motwani & Nabar, 2008)	arXiv preprint	• Considered dataset in which each individual is associated with set of items constituting private data. • Used limited dataset and cannot be applied on data on fly.
6.	Anonymizing temporal data (Wang et al., 2010)	International Conference on Data Mining, IEEE	• Works for data on fly and used classical methods of anonymity. • Not fast enough since many queries are to be ignored due to timestamp and not efficient.
7.	Fast text anonymization using k-anonymity (Maeda et al., 2016)	International Conference on Information Integration and Web-based Applications and Services, ACM	• Preserve original texts as much as possible and could be used for both structured and unstructured data. • Not properly experimented on large dataset.
8.	An improved Location-Based Service authentication algorithm with personalized k-anonymity (Ye et al., 2016)	China Satellite Navigation Conference (CSNC), Springer	• Less burden to mobile clients and easy to maintain and update. • Totally dependent on third party server, if it fails whole system is ruined.
9.	Anonymization for outputs of population health and health services research conducted via on online data center (Keefe et al., 2016)	Journal of the American Medical Informatics Association	• A method for anonymizing analysis outputs from ODCs for publication in academic literature. • Limitations are, for less outcomes analysis and kind of a manual method.
10.	Clustering heuristics for efficient t-closeness Anonymization (Kayem et al., 2017)	International Conference on Database and Expert Systems Applications, Springer	• Minimized risk of privacy disclosure of tuples containing high severity weight sensitive attributes. • Too greedy technique, as in different cases severity weight may differ and only for single sensitive attribute.
11.	On efficient and robust anonymization for privacy protection on massive streamin categorical information (Zhang et al., 2017)	IEEE Transactions on Dependable and Secure Computing, vol. 14, no. 5, pp: 507-520, IEEE	• Proposed technique gave fast speed performance and low communication overhead. • Very effective to protect the privacy of data against possible tampering by adversaries. • Limitations are, number of dummy votes should be optimized and technique does not distinguish between actual votes and dummy votes.
12.	Adaptive Anonymity of Data using b-Edge Cover (Khan et al., 2018)	International Conference for High Performance Computing, Networking, Storage and Analysis, IEEE	• The algorithm provides a great scalable approach that can be used in the systems requiring environment of shared as well as distributed memory. • The proposed algorithm is noy tested on the systems or processes that require high storage. • During the comparison with existing algorithms, the results for utility of generated anonymized data were not good in some cases.

Proposed Modification in Existing Technique: The main drawback of anonymization is loss of information because of generalization and suppression. Generalization means changing the value of attribute to higher level value in hierarchy. On the other hand, suppression is special case of generalization, meaning to 'null' the attribute value or remove the whole tuple. In order to lessen the information loss, the above-mentioned parameters should be as low as possible while maintaining data privacy. This can be achieved by changing the redaction technique being used during generalization process. The term 'redaction' means to change original characters to "*" or any pre-specified character to specify that numerous values are possible. For different types of data, different techniques are required in order to implement it efficiently.

The Existing Redaction Approach: In case, the attribute is a numeric value, first level of generalization is created by redacting the unit place digit followed by redaction of tens place to create next level. The process is continued in the left side in order to suppress the whole digits. In order to fit into an equivalence class, wherever we find different values for the first time, redaction is initiated from that place to unit place.

Example: Levels of generalization for zip-code = 180101 are:

Suppose the number of cities in a state is 25 with zip-codes from 180101 to 180125. Two rows have zip-code attribute with value 180102 and 180122. To fit these two rows into an equivalence class, the generalized value according to existing approach of redaction would be 1801**. The penalty for this generalization would be 25 since all zip-codes from 180101 to 180125 can be assumed while analysis. Such higher cost of generalization is a major drawback of the existing approach.

The Proposed Redaction Approach: The drawback of previous approach can be diminished by changing the redaction technique, such that the penalty is minimal. The proposed redaction technique focuses on redaction of distinguished digits only rather than all digits. This technique can be applied by comparing all digits of an attribute in order to fall in same equivalence class and wherever the digits are found different, redaction is performed.

Example: Taking the same scenario as in previous case, the generalized value of zip-code would be 1801*2 with the proposed redaction technique. Now, the penalty of generalization would be 3 since only zip-codes satisfying the generalized value are 180102, 180112 and 180122. Here, the generalization cost i.e., 3 is much lesser than generalization cost of existing method i.e., 25. Hence, with new redaction technique, utility of anonymized dataset is substantially higher in comparison to previous techniques. Figure 4 presents a schematic view of the proposed technique.

Description: In the proposed approach, we made equivalence classes satisfying all three parameters i.e., k, l and t to ensure data privacy. The attributes are segregated based on priority and generalization is performed accordingly. To speed up the computation, following process of generalization is executed:
a)   The total generalization penalty is saved in a global variable at the completion of first iteration.
b)   In any iteration, if generalization penalty is less than the value of global variable, the previously stored value is swapped with new value and corresponding tuples are updated.
c)   However, for any iteration, if generalization penalty is more or equal to the stored value, current iteration is terminated and new iteration begins.
d)   Lastly, to select the output combination, least generalization penalty set is selected whose total penalty is saved in the global variable.

The Extended Approach: Big data suffers from dimensionality issues i.e., more the number of attributes, more complex is the processing. The similar problem occurs while data anonymization and makes it difficult to achieve perfect anonymity. Another major concern in anonymity is subsequent release of subsets of same dataset with different attributes or number of tuples. Some tuples or attributes are common to previous releases due to which chances of privacy loss increases by many folds. If data is alphabetic e.g., name of a city, the existing generalization process at the first level writes the name of its state (or country, if further generalization applied) with penalty calculated as total

Figure 4. Process flow of proposed approach

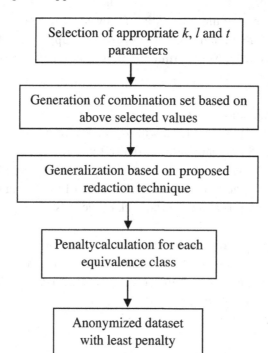

number of cities in that state. For example, the cost of generalization for 25 cities in a state would be 25. The extended approach use pre-processing and attribute unification as described below:

To reduce the cost, pre-processing is used where data in words (alphabets) is changed into numeric data like changing name of city with its zip code (pin code). In case, values are not directly convertible to numerical value, the proposed method assign some ordered range of numerical values to that attribute like assigning number to course names in a university. For example, the name of 25 cities can be converted to their respective zip-codes prior to generalization which clearly reduces the overall cost as observed in previous cases.

Another solution is attribute unification which means to combine two or more attributes in order to form a single attribute. This can be achieved either by combining numerical valued attributes or converting word elements into numerical values as discussed above. If any attribute has higher priority, it is generalized separately and not with lesser priority attributes. For example, in a university dataset, year, branch and course attributes can be combined to form one attribute by changing the course and branch into numerical data and new element is designated as 'id' (Figure 5).

In a nutshell, it is worth mentioning here that combining pre-processing and attribute unification with the previously proposed redaction approach will minimize the threat to privacy which is due to subsequent release of subsets from same dataset. Instead, the whole dataset can be released in a single version since generalization penalty is reduced to a larger extent.

Figure 5. Attribute unification

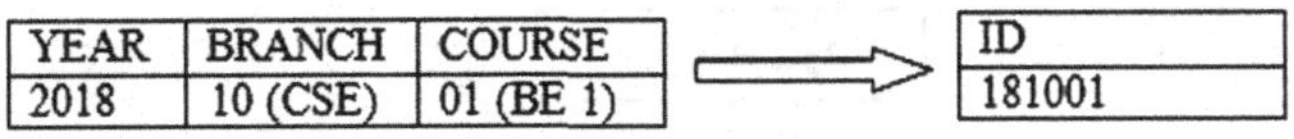

YEAR	BRANCH	COURSE
2018	10 (CSE)	01 (BE 1)

→

ID
181001

THE IMPLEMENTATION METHODOLOGY

The implementation of proposed technique is described stepwise according to the performed task (Figure 6) with example.

Step 1: Take raw dataset and select the attributes to be released in public. Next, segregate attributes based on explicit identifiers, quasi identifiers and sensitive attributes. In our case, adult dataset is chosen and hence corresponding attributes are age, gender, zip-code (instead of country names) and salary. Here, sensitive attribute is salary while other are quasi-identifiers.

Step 2: Check for least priority attributes *e.g.*, in our case, "gender" is one. If such attribute exists, suppress their value by redacting to "*".

Step 3: Select high priority attribute with highest generalization penalty, *e.g.*, age. Make some criteria for generalization of such attributes while maintaining utility. As we assume age in intervals of 5 years, hence the value being generalized is 30 for age group 30-34. Further, create groups of tuples having same attribute same age group.

Step 4: Furthermore, groups on the basis of sensitive attribute are formed. In case, the sensitive attribute is two-valued (binary) *e.g.*, salary has two values only: $<= 50K$ and $> 50K$, this step is executed, otherwise, avoidable.

Step 5: Now select values of k, l and t depending on given dataset. Our dataset select l as 2 since sensitive attribute is two-valued and k to be 8. For t distribution of $<= 50K$ and $> 50K$, the proportion is 75% and 25% respectively. If sensitive attribute is not binary, metric like EMD, decision tree etc. may be used according to the property of attribute.

Step 6: Now make combinations satisfying above selected values. The rows are taken 8 in an equivalence class with same age group, out of which six rows are with salary $<= 50K$ and two with $> 50K$ to maintain the 75% and 25% proportion.

Step 7: Find generalization penalty for each equivalence class by counting the number of zip-codes satisfying generalized value from set of all possible zip-codes in the dataset.

Step 8: Add generalization penalty for all combinations. To fasten the computation, pruning is done in this step (as discussed in proposed redaction approach). Lastly, the set with minimum generalized penalty becomes the output and corresponding records are made public.

RESULTS AND DISCUSSION

From following figure 7, it is obvious that there is a substantial reduction in generalization cost using proposed redaction approach i.e., 284 in comparison to the generalization cost in existing method being

Figure 6. Proposed implementation for anonymization of dataset with binary sensitive attribute

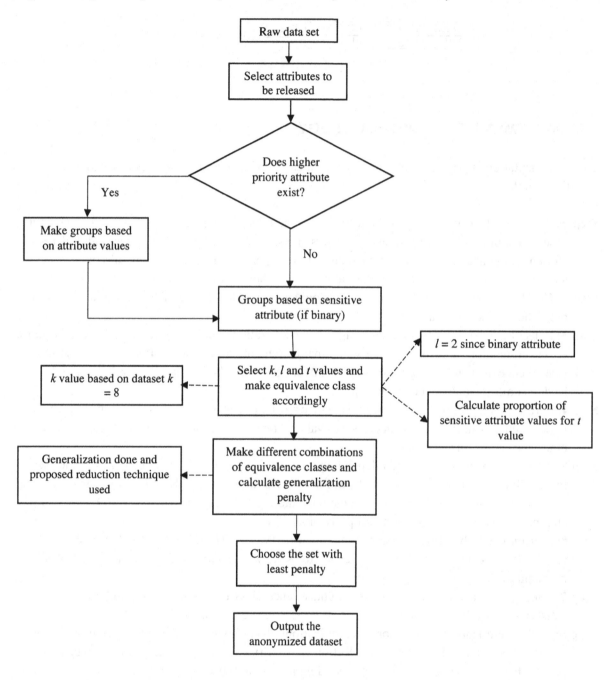

Figure 7. Comparison of generalization cost

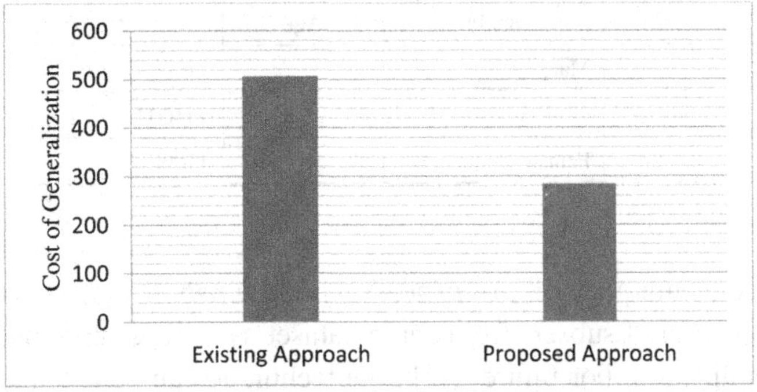

500. Further, when tested on more sub-sets of adult dataset, we found that on an average generalization penalty comes between 53-65% of the previous generalization penalty.

Lesser penalty means increase in utility of generated dataset. In order to further validate the efficiency of the proposed method, we conducted a query test (Table 2). The corresponding graph is shown in figure 8 where for query 1, for example, the actual value is 2 according to raw dataset. With existing approach, the value was 12, however, the proposed method reduces the value to 6, thus, maximizing the utility of generated dataset.

CONCLUSION AND FUTURE WORK

Data anonymity is a big challenge nowadays with large amount of data emerging from various social media platforms around us. This, in turn, violates the privacy of an individual. In the chapter, existing techniques of anonymization in order to preserve privacy of individuals have been discussed. Further, we proposed a novel method of redaction and reduce generalization overhead, thus, ensuring maximum utility of datasets. We have used brute-force technique with pruning to find perfect generalization with minimal penalty. The proposed technique is validated and compared with existing techniques. Also, a query test is performed to further validate the utility factor of generated datasets. Lastly, we presented

Figure 8. Result of query set

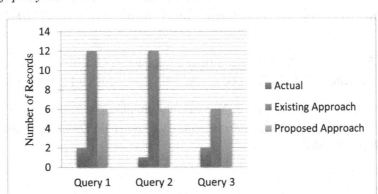

Table 2. Query set

Query	Gender	Age	Zip-code	Salary
1	Male	24	110004	<= 50K
2	Male	37	151007	<= 50K
3	Female	47	110001	<= 50K

an extension of proposed technique with *pre-processing* and *attribute unification* to minimize privacy loss due to subsequent release of subsets from same dataset as well as more number of attributes that necessitates more generalization. For future work, the technique can be extended for more number of attributes and clustering algorithms may be included in proposed methodology.

REFERENCES

Bayardo, R. J., & Agrawal, R. (2005). Data privacy through optimal k-anonymization. *IEEE 23rd International Conference on Data Engineering, ICDE,* 217-228. doi: 10.1109/ICDE.2005.42

Gantz, J., & Reinsel, D. (2011). Extracting value from chaos. *IDC iview*, 1-12.

Kayem, A. V., & Meinel, C. (2017). Clustering Heuristics for Efficient t-closeness Anonymisation. In *Proceedings International Conference on Database and Expert Systems Applications*.pp. 27-34. Cham, Switzerland: Springer. 10.1007/978-3-319-64471-4_3

Khan, A., Choromanski, K., Pothen, A., Ferdous, S. M., & Halappanavar, T. A. (2018). Adaptive Anonymization of Data using b-Edge Cover. In *Proceedings SC18: International Conference for High Performance Computing, Networking, Storage and Analysis*, Dallas, TX. IEEE. doi: 10.1109/SC.2018.00062

Laney, D. (2001) 3D data management: Controlling data volume, velocity and variety. *META Group Research Note,* 1-6.

Li, N., Li, T., & Venkatasubramanian, S. (2007). t-closeness: Privacy beyond k-anonymity and l-diversity. In *Proceedings IEEE 23rd International Conference on Data Engineering, ICDE*, 106-115. doi: 10.1109/ICDE.2007.367856

Li, X., Wang, E., Yang, W., & Ma, J. (2016). DALP: A demand-aware location privacy protection scheme in continuous location-based services. *Concurrency and Computation*, *28*(4), 1219–1236. doi:10.1002/cpe.3613

Liu X, Liu K, Guo L, Li X, Fang Y. (2013). A game-theoretic approach for achieving k-anonymity in location-based services. In *Proceedings 2013 INFOCOM IEEE*, 2985-2993. doi:10.1109/INFCOM.2013.6567110

Machanavajjhala, A., Gehrke, J., Kifer, D., & Venkitasubramaniam, M. (2006). l-diversity: Privacy beyond k-anonymity. In *Proceedings 22nd International Conference on Data Engineering, ICDE*, 24-24. doi: 10.1145/1217299.1217300

Maeda, W., Suzuki, Y., & Nakamura, S. (2016). Fast text anonymization using k-anonyminity. *Proceedings of the 18th International Conference on Information Integration and Web-based Applications and Services*, *ACM*, 340-344. doi: 10.1145/3011141.3011217

Motwani, R., & Nabar, S. U. (2008). Anonymizing unstructured data. *arXiv preprint arXiv:08* doi:10.5582.2008

Niu B, Li Q, Zhu X, Cao G, Li H. (2014). Achieving k-anonymity in privacy-aware location-based services. In *Proceedings 2014 INFOCO IEEE*, 754-762. doi:10.1109/INFOCOM.2014.6848002

O'Keefe, C. M., Westcott, M., O'Sullivan, M., Ickowicz, A., & Churches, T. (2016). Anonymization for outputs of population health and health services research conducted via an online data center. *Journal of the American Medical Informatics Association*, *24*(3), 544–549. doi:10.1093/jamia/ocw152 PMID:28011594

Sweeney, L. (2002). k-anonymity: A model for protecting privacy. *International Journal of Uncertainty, Fuzziness, and Knowledge-based Systems*, *10*(5), 557–570. doi:10.1142/S0218488502001648

Wang, K., Xu, Y., Wong, R. C. W., & Fu, A. W. C. (2010). Anonymizing temporal data. In *Proceedings International Conference on Data Mining, ICDM, IEEE*, 1109-1114. doi: 10.1109/ICDM.2010.96

Wu, X., Zhu, X., Wu, G. Q., & Ding, W. (2014). Data mining with big data. *IEEE Transactions on Knowledge and Data Engineering*, *26*(1), 97–107. doi:10.1109/TKDE.2013.109

Ye, Y. M., Pan, C. C., & Yang, G. K. (2016). An Improved Location-Based Service Authentication Algorithm with Personalized K-Anonymity. In *Proceedings China Satellite Navigation Conference, 2016 CSNC*. pp. 257-266. Singapore, Springer. doi: 10.1007/978-981-10-0934-1_23

Yin, C., Zhang, S., Xi, J., & Wang, J. (2017). An improved anonymity model for big data security based on clustering algorithm. *Concurrency and Computation*, *29*(7). doi:10.1002/cpe.3902

Yu, S. (2016). Big privacy: Challenges and opportunities of privacy study in the age of big data. *IEEE Access: Practical Innovations, Open Solutions*, *4*, 2751–2763. doi:10.1109/ACCESS.2016.2577036

Zhang, J., Li, H., Liu, X., Luo, Y., Chen, F., Wang, H., & Chang, L. (2015). On efficient and robust anonymization for privacy protection on massive streaming categorical information. *IEEE Transactions on Dependable and Secure Computing*, 507–520. doi:10.1109/TDSC.2015.2483503

Chapter 10
A Comprehensive Survey on DDoS Attacks and Recent Defense Mechanisms

Brij B. Gupta

National Institute of Technology, Kurukshetra, India

Amrita Dahiya

National Institute of Technology, Kurukshetra, India

Chivesh Upneja

National Institute of Technology, Kurukshetra, India

Aditi Garg

National Institute of Technology, Kurukshetra, India

Ruby Choudhary

National Institute of Technology, Kurukshetra, India

ABSTRACT

DDoS attack always takes advantage of structure of Internet and imbalance of resources between defender and attacker. DDoS attacks are driven by factors like interdependency of Internet's security, limited resources, fewer incentives for home users and local ISPs, flexibility of handlers to control multiple compromised systems at the same time, untraceable nature of malicious packets and unfair distribution of resources all over the Internet. This survey chapter gives a comprehensive view on DDoS attacks and its defense mechanisms. Defense mechanisms are categorized according to the deployment position and nature of defense. Comprehensive study of DDoS attacks will definitely help researchers to understand the important issues related to cyber security.

DOI: 10.4018/978-1-7998-2242-4.ch010

Copyright © 2020, IGI Global. Copying or distributing in print or electronic forms without written permission of IGI Global is prohibited.

Figure 1. DDoS attack architecure

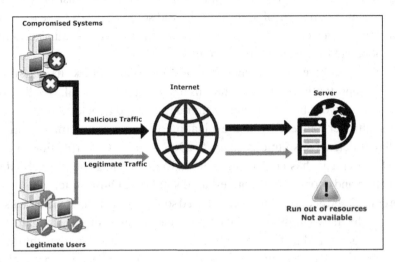

1. INTRODUCTION

Distributed denial of service attack is a brute force attempt by several attacker hosts to completely crash or slowdown one or more victim hosts. DDoS attack overwhelms victim and intermediate network by sending voluminous traffic so as to make target run short of resources (Bhuyan et al., 2014; Gupta et al., 2009). It aims to prevent service providers from being available with resources to legitimate users. A vulnerable service protocol or a network device is exploited to generate traffic or requests are amplified via server for consuming all resources (Gupta, 2011). Figure: 1 illustrates DDoS attack. A DoS attack involves single attacker host and victim while DDoS attack relies on the huge network of compromised systems (Botnet) to attack multiple targets. Unfamiliarity of defenders with multi vector DDoS attacks, for example attackers are using NTP rather than traditional amplification technique to proliferate scale; have resulted in making this problem more complex and unsolved (Incapsula, 2019). Moreover, absolute technical knowledge is not needed as there are so many "on demand" DDoS tools present on Internet to assist naive users for carrying out attack. This attack becomes more hazardous than any other possible attack as it is difficult to detect and easy to carry out. Moreover, predicting the victim host is very difficult as attackers send voluminous legitimate looking packets to exhaust the resources. Problem space of exploring and addressing various types of DDoS attacks is very vast. Further, we are lacking benchmarks for assessing efficiency, robustness and cost to compare various defensive solutions. For example, Software Defined Networking (SDN) is evolving as a new networking platform and this technology has proven very beneficial to detect and filter DDoS attacks. But SDN technology combined with Cloud has open up numerous vulnerabilities for the attackers (Bhushan & Gupta, 2019).

Now a days, companies and big firms rely on automation and virtualization (cloud computing) to make their business operations and services more efficient and available. But the security evolution could not keep its pace with this giant transformation of technologies. Vulnerable devices like IoT (Internet of Things) and networking devices are increasing faster than the efforts for securing these devices, making easier for attackers to perform any kind of cyber-attack. All these aspects make us think more about the severity and seriousness of the problem.

Right now, we are no near to robust and comprehensive solution against DDoS attack. We need to think different from mainstream ideas of security. A hybrid solution needs to be developed that can address unpredictable attacks, that can be deployed widely and in which every Internet entity has incentives to participate and cooperate for making Internet a more safer place.

In this chapter, we try to give a comprehensive view on DDoS attack, its classification, attacker's motivations and most importantly defensive solutions against it (Gupta et al., 2018). We classify DDoS attacks into volumetric, network based and application layer-based attacks. Apart from it, we discussed various attack tools, attacker's incentives and evaluating measures. Most importantly, we categorized and discussed different defensive solutions against DDoS attacks. Classification of existing defensive solutions against DDoS attacks has been categorized into three categories namely; deployment point, type of defensive action and economic incentive-based solutions. Our chapter is different from existing surveys as we have considered economic incentive-based solutions against DDoS attacks. We have laid the importance of the fact that how liabilities and incentives can act as strong tools against DDoS attackers.

Rest of the paper is organized as follows. In section 2, we discuss some recent trends and statistics related to DDoS attack and Internet security followed by section 3 which describes architecture of DDoS attack. In section 4, taxonomy of DDoS attack is presented in which motivations of attackers, attack types and various DDoS attacking tools are discussed. In section 5, classification of defensive mechanisms is discussed followed by section 6 in which we enumerate various performance evaluation parameters used to measure the accuracy of a defensive mechanism. Section 7 finally concludes the paper.

2. STATISTICS AND RECENT TRENDS IN DDOS ATTACKS

DDoS attack landscape is becoming complex day by day and attackers are constantly driven by great incentives. Attackers have always higher incentives than defenders or legitimate users. Attackers are continuously exploiting well known vulnerabilities, well established botnets and attack techniques to come up with new innovative ideas of carrying out attack. There does not exist any domain that remained untouched by DDoS attack i.e. online social networking (Sahoo & Gupta, 2019), Software Defined Networking (SDN) (Bhushan & Gupta, 2019), IoT (Tewari & Gupta, 2018), mobile environment (Sharma & Gupta, 2018) and cloud environment (Chaudhary et al., 2018) etc. As soon as a new vulnerability is marked, it gets rapidly exploited by attackers to launch a new series of DDoS attacks. Figure 2, illustrates maximum recorded sized DDoS attack from last 12 years. Mirai botnet (Josh Fruhlinger, 2018); an IoT based botnet; initially created just for making little money, grew like a giant than its creators ever dreamed possible. In (Adat & Gupta, 2018), authors have surveyed various issues, challenges and architecture of various security mechanisms for IoT environment. Various authentication mechanisms for IoT devices have been proposed in literature (Tewari & Gupta, 2017; Tewari & Gupta, 2018; Mamta & Gupta, 2019; mamta et al., 2019; Gupta et al., 2016). Authentication mechanisms can secure IoT devices and prevent them from being getting compromised. Poorly secured Internet devices that haven't changed their factory's default username and password are exploited by using telnet. On October 2016, a large DDoS attack was carried out against Dyn Company by using Mirai. 2016 is seen as the revolutionary year for malware as Mirai's source code was published. Mirai's source code was extended by attackers to create Mirai's variants like OMG, Satori (ASERT Team, 2018) etc. (Stephanie Weagle, 2018). For example, OMG is a Mirai's variant which facilitates bot author to have more scans than normal to find new vulnerabilities or to launch new types of DDoS attacks without updating the original source code.

Figure 2. Maximum SIZED DDoS attack recorded (Source: Arbour Network Inc.)

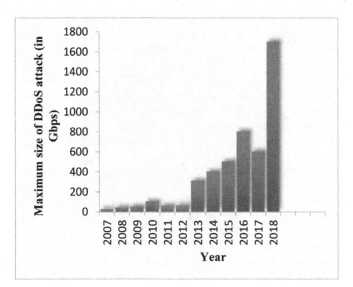

In 2018, 1.3 TBPS sized DDoS attack was carried out against Github Company which is a record in itself. Later, in an interval of just five days, DDoS attack of size 1. 7 TBPS was again carried out against Github Company (Skottler, 2018). This was the largest DDoS attack till date. It was a Memcached attack. A memcache DDoS attack is an attack on memcache servers. Memcache server is a database caching server for increasing speed of websites and networks. It is an amplification attack where attacker sends spoofed data requests to vulnerable UDP memcache server. Internet of Things (IoT), zero day attacks increase the potency of DDoS attacks and make it more disastrous. There exist application layer attacks against encrypted service. Figure 3, shows the targets of application layer attacks. There exists another high trend in 2017, ransom based DDoS attack. According "Visual Networking Index Complete Forecast Update, 2015-2020" published by CISCO (LOIC, 2019), there was 25 per cent growth in DDoS attack in 2015 which will rise 2.6-fold to 17 million by 2020.

2.1 Open Research Issues and Challenges in DDoS Attack

Now, we will discuss open research issues and challenges in DDoS attacks.

1. Internet is composed of various heterogeneous networks owned by different domains. Every IP network has different MTU (Maximum Transmissible Unit), different bandwidth links and various service providers. So, it is very difficult for researchers and security professionals to develop a solution that can be deployed globally irrespective of above-mentioned constraints.
2. Every Internet entity has positive or negative externality on other entities. An organization cannot ensure its security unless all Internet devices ensure their securities. Internet has highly dependent structure where security of one entity depends on other entities.
3. Every device connected to Internet has limited resources. Attacker takes advantage of this fact. Attacker can exhaust the limited resources sooner or later.

Figure 3. Targets of application layer attack (Source: Arbour Network Inc.)

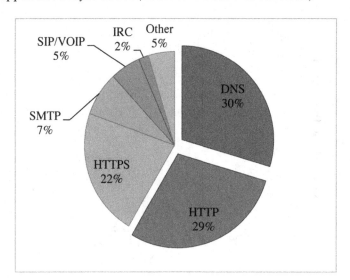

4. There is no denying the fact that a botnet consists of large number of compromised machines. They need to attack only a few specified targets. There exist many to one relationship between bot machines and victim machine.

5. There exists very uneven distribution of resources all over the Internet. Computing resources are located at end server while bandwidth resource is located at intermediate network. This distribution of resources is exploited by attacker as he needs high bandwidth links to transmit his dummy data requests while computing resources at end server are exploited to process dummy data requests. If the location of resources is considered computing resources must be located at intermediate network so that data packets are monitored.

6. Hierarchical architecture of botnet is a major issue because it facilitates attacker to remain anonymous. Till now, there has not been any solution that can trace back the actual attacker. This is the main reason why DDoS attack is very easy to carry out. Moreover, a single attacker can control numerous bot machines at the same time.

7. Incentives play a major driving force to motivate users to send traffic data wisely to the network (pricing Internet traffic) or to keep their systems secure. But there is no denying the fact that there exists a huge misalignment of incentives between attackers and defenders. There has been a tremendous research present in technical aspects of DDoS attacks but a very few present in economical domain. Now, its high time for researchers to give equal importance to economical solutions too while dealing with DDoS attacks.

3. ARCHITECTURE OF DDOS ATTACK

There are two types of attack network architectures present namely master slave architecture and Internet Relay Chat (IRC) based architecture. Master slave architecture usually has a hierarchical structure where an attacker is at the top, handlers or slaves in the middle and finally the huge network of compromised systems. Attacker first creates slaves or handlers and then instructs the same to create botnet by infecting them with malware (Bhuyan et al., 2013; Esraa et al., 2016). Strategy of DDoS attack includes selection of agents, compromising selected agents through malicious code, communication with compromised agents to give them instructions and finally performing attack (Bhuyan et al., 2013; Mishra et al., 2011). Victim node falls short of resources while handling huge amounts of dummy requests sent by botnet. While handling malicious packets, legitimate nodes get deprived of resources. Figure 4, shows the architecture of master slave based botnet.

An IRC communication channel is used between vulnerable systems and agents in IRC based DDoS network architecture. After setting a channel between client and agent, IRC ports are used to send commands to the clients to direct their traffic towards a specific target. IRC based network architecture gives attacker benefit of hiding his identity as, IRC channel contains large volume of data. Attackers use IRC based attack network because it provides anonymity to attacker as well as guarantees delivery of attack to the specified victim (Chen et al., 2006).

It is a matter of fact that compromised systems should not necessarily be present in the same network. Malwared systems of a botnet are scattered in different networks which makes attacker undetectable. Traffic from individual system is not huge enough to be detected by local ISPs which facilitates attacker in accumulating small traffic from different networks to a huge traffic against a specific target. Attackers takeover legitimate systems by infecting them with different types of viruses, worms, malwares, Trojan horses and backdoors (Puri & Ramneek, 2003; Bailey et. al., 2009). After infecting the systems with malicious codes, their resources are exploited against a specific server. Moreover, IP spoofing makes more difficult for defenders to detect source of attack. With the advancement in technology and tools, great incentives and hierarchical structure of botnet which maintains anonymity of attacker; attackers become so much innovative in launching complex DDoS attacks at large scale.

4. TAXONOMY OF DDOS ATTACKS

4.1 Attacker's Motivations

Attackers have different incentives or motivations to carry out an attack. They have different background as well knowledge which affects their incentives for performing an attack.

a) **Capital Gain**: This is the main reason behind almost every attack now a days and the main concern for every organization. Attackers having capital gain as the main motive are the experienced ones and have good technical knowledge. Since the attackers have good technical knowledge, hence it is difficult to defend these attacks.

b) **Espionage**: Espionage can also be the main reason behind carrying out DDoS attack. Attackers want to steal trade secrets and important credentials while keeping defenders busy in stopping DDoS attack from a particular source while actual harm is done from other source.

c) **Cyber Warfare:** Attackers having cyber warfare as a primary motive usually belongs to some terrorist group or some political party which is ideologically affected by some extremist thought. Attackers belong to this group target a particular organization to spread fear and their own beliefs.

Figure 4. Master-slave architecture of botnet

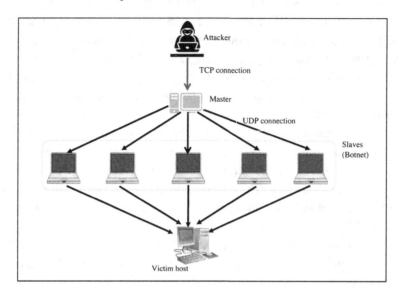

d) **Causing Annoyance**: Some attackers carry out attacks just to create nuisance and temporary fun or for seeking attention or to show off their skills to other hacking groups.

e) **Showing Disagreement:** Sometimes attacker creates fuss just to show disagreement on a point and let others know his demands or his thoughts on a certain issue. It is just a way of protesting against an issue.

4.2 Types of DDoS Attacks

Attackers have launched numerous types of DDoS attacks till date and categorization of these attacks can be done mainly into three categories as mentioned below (Incapsula, 2019; Chaudhary et. al., 2018). Figure 5, shows classification of DDoS attacks and their respective examples.

4.2.1 Volumetric DDoS Attacks

In a volumetric DDoS attack, attacker attempts to send large amount of data traffic or dummy request to a specified target to overwhelm its bandwidth. Ease with which attackers generate large amount of data is due to low technical restrictions in Internet infrastructure. Amplification techniques assist attackers in scaling the launched DDoS attacks. Reflective DDoS attack is a type of volumetric DDoS attack. In reflective DDoS attack, attacker usually sends a small request to server which will demand large response from server. Service request also seems like to be appearing from a legitimate source. As a result, server sends large response to a small request which will definitely exhaust intermediate bandwidth. Some volumetric DDoS attacks are discussed below.

a) **Smurf Attack** (Lau et al., 2000)**:** Smurf attack takes advantage of IP broadcast network and ICMP's features. Network administrators use ICMP to exchange information regarding Internet's management and it is used to ping other networking devices to check whether they are operational or not.

In a normal scenario, in an IP broadcast network a ping request is send to every host in a network to check their operational status. Attackers take advantage of this fact and use this as a trick for amplifying the DDoS attack. A spoofed (containing Victim server's IP address) echo request is send to intermediate IP broadcast network. Every host in the IP broadcast network responds to the echo request resulting into huge number of echo responses congesting the victim's network and makes it run out of bandwidth and resources.

b) **UDP Storm Attack** (Lau et al., 2000): UDP is a connectionless protocol and unlike TCP it does not require three-way handshake process to set up a connection with server. UDP has least overhead in network and thus attackers use UDP packets to flood a victim. Attackers use "best effort" data traffic through UDP channels to flood a victim server. UDP does not have any provision for checking the traffic hence UDP flooding attack can be performed with so much of ease and few resources.

c) **DNS Amplification Attack** (Rossow & Christian, 2014): Attackers send DNS requests with target's spoofed IP address to open DNS server which will direct all the responses from DNS servers to the target. This is how attacker turns a small request in to a much larger payload capable of exhausting all bandwidth and resources at server side.

d) **Peer to Peer Attack** (Lau et al., 2000): Unlike traditional client server architecture, P2P is a distributed network where every node can behave as client as well as server. Nowadays P2P technology is trending for file sharing, downloading and distributed computing. P2P based botnet is different than normal botnet because in former, attacker need not to communicate with every client for malwaring it and secondly, automated feature of P2P based botnet facilitates attackers for amplifying the DDoS attack. Attackers can easily direct all client's traffic present in a peer to peer network towards a specific node without using many resources.

4.2.2 Protocol Based Attacks

Attackers perform protocol-based DDoS attacks by exploiting some vulnerability present in layer 3 or layer 4's protocol stack. Attackers attack directly on computing or processing ability or memory of the server. Now we discuss some protocol-based DDoS attacks.

a) **Neptune Attack (SYN Flood)** Cert Advisory, 2014): Normally, a TCP connection requires three-way handshake procedure. First a client sends a connection request using SYN flag and then server sends a SYN-ACK flag for acknowledgment. To SYN-ACK packet, client responds with an ACK flag. Attackers take advantage of this whole procedure and exploit it against a server. Attacker sends large number of SYN packets to every port of TCP server. To every SYN packet, TCP server responds with ACK flag. But at the same time, client does not respond with ACK which leaves large number of half open connections resulting into exhaustion of TCP server's memory and other resources. TCP server is not able to respond to legitimate users.

Ping of Death: In PoD attack, attacker uses ping command to destabilize the target by sending oversized malformed packets. PoD attack exploits traditional vulnerabilities present in the TCP/IP structure of Internet. We discuss this vulnerability in this section. Generally, size of legitimate IP packet is 65,535 bytes including IP header and maximum payload size of 84 bytes (Ping of Death, 2019). Many systems would easily get crashed after receiving these huge size IP packets. Now, sending a packet larger than

Figure 5. Types of DDoS attack

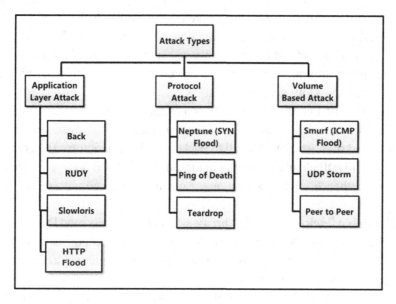

maximum allowed size is not allowed in IP channels. Attackers have come up with a trick where they can send malformed large sized packets into fragments. Malicious fragments when reassembled at server side, it results into oversized packets which will make server's memory full and make server run out of memory. However, these vulnerabilities have been patched in the protocols but still there are some systems where these vulnerabilities are still open and PoD attack is still very dangerous to them.

b) **Tear Drop Attack:** Tear drop attack exploits the reassembly algorithm present at server side. This attack also exploits fragment offset field of IP packet. A server might crash after finding any flaw in reassembling packets (CERT Advisory CA-1997-28, 2014). Fragment offset field of an IP packet shows the address of first byte of packet and sum of first byte and length of the packet gives the value of fragment offset field of second fragmented packet. All fragmented packets which have been gone through different networking paths are reassembled by server after checking fragment offset field of IP header. Attacker creates discrepancy in the fragment offset field resulting into overlapping of packets at server side which can crash the server. For example, if fragment offset field of a packet is 930 and size of the packet is 1000 bytes then the value of offset field for next packet becomes 1931. But the attacker makes it 960 bytes which will make the server paralyze.

4.2.3 Application Layer Attack

Application layer-based DDoS attack target 7th layer of OSI model by making deliberate changes in web applications. Application layer DDoS attacks are more dangerous than protocol-based DDoS attacks because it consumes network and server resources at the same time. HTTP attacks are the most frequent attacks now days. We will discuss some of the important application layer attack.

a) **HTTP Flood**: A sophisticated HTTP Flood attack does not require tampering, IP spoofing, reflection or amplification technique to make a server unavailable (Enrico C et al., 2013). A HTTP client basically sends HTTP GET or POST commands for communicating with the server. GET command is used to retrieve static content like images, while POST command is used to retrieve dynamic content. HTTP POST is more resource-effective than GET because a single POST command can force the target to invest more number of resources. HTTP POST command start a complex processing at server side. HTTP flood basically use botnet-based method to carry out an attack. Moreover, HTTP attack traffic is difficult to be distinguished against legitimate traffic as attackers use standard URL requests. It is difficult for flow rate-based detection techniques to detect HTTP flood traffic as it is always a slow rate attack and always under threshold of these techniques.

b) **RUDY Attack:** (R-Y- Dead Yet) RUDY is an application layer attack in which slow and low volume of attack traffic is generated. This attack tends to attack a web server by submitting long form fields. This attacks hunts for vulnerable embedded forms in websites. In this attack, attacker tries to send a legitimate HTTP POST request by sending a full-length header containing only one byte of data. Attacker sends multiple data packets with full size header with less data. Generally, legitimate user sends this data in one or two data packets.

c) **BACK Attack**: In this attack, attacker sends data request with URL containing 6000-8000 backslashes which ultimately crashes web server. This attack only slows down the server for some time. This attack can be detected by employing threshold value.

d) **Slowloris attack** (Enrico C et al., 2013): It is a slow rate attack which sends incomplete information to the server which leaves server to wait indefinitely for the rest of the information to complete the request. It eventually exhausts the connection capacity of server. Attacker sends HTTP Get request without termination code.

5. CLASSIFICATION OF DDOS ATTACKS DEFENSE MECHANISMS

DDoS attacks can be carried out in numerous ways; therefore one type of solution is not sufficient to fight against DDoS attacks. With the advancements in tools, techniques and methods, attackers having naive knowledge with mere resources can bypass any security measure and appear to be legitimate user to victim. There are a lot of defensive mechanisms proposed to combat DDoS attacks in past. Some solutions are statistical (Chen et. al., 2006; Mirkoviac et. al., 2002; Saifullah, 2009; Chen, 2009), knowledge (Gil & Poletto, 2001; Thomas, 2003; Limwiwatkul & Rungsawang, 2004), soft computing (Jalili et al., 2005; Karimazad & Faraahi, 2011; Gavrilis & Dermatas, 2005) and machine learning (Hwang et al., 2003; Lee et al., 2008; Rahmani et al., 2009; Gupta & Sheng, 2019) based approaches. In this paper, classification of DDoS attacks has been done on the basis of deployment location, when the defense mechanism takes action against DDoS attacks and economic incentive based solutions. Defense mechanisms against Network/Transport layer on the basis of deployment location is classified into categories namely; near to source, near to destination, at network routers and hybrid. Defense mechanisms against application layer DDoS attacks are classified into near to destination and distributed (hybrid) on the basis of point of deployment.

Based on the second criterion i.e. when the defense solution takes action against DDoS attack, we classify defense mechanisms into before the attack, during the attack and after the attack.

5.1 Classification Based on Deployment Location

In this section, we will discuss defensive solutions against network/transport level DDoS attacks in the categories namely; near to source, near to destination, intermediate networking routers and hybrid.

5.1.1 Near to Source

In this category, we will discuss defensive mechanisms which are deployed near to source of attacks. Defensive mechanisms of this kind are centralized in nature. Centralized refers to the fact that defensive action taken by mechanism takes place only at a single point in a network. There is no communication or cooperation from other Internet entities. There are certain advantages and disadvantages of these kinds of solutions against DDoS attacks. Advantage is that it is best possible way to protect victim network as well as intermediate network to get flooded from data traffic. By doing this, we can stop the attack traffic at the source itself. Disadvantages are much serious and real than advantages, as attack traffic towards a victim network is not coming from a single source. Sources of attack traffic are dispersed (distributed) throughout the network and traffic from a single source is not huge enough to be detected by local ISPs or local defensive mechanisms. Motivation behind deployment near to source of attack is very obscure as question "Who will pay the expenses for deployment or maintenance of defensive mechanism (customers or service providers)?" arises. So, these are the some challenges in deploying solutions for DDoS attacks near to source of attack. But, the defense mechanisms near to source of attack can effectively filter malicious packets based on IP spoofing and ingress/egress filtering. Now, we will discuss the solutions proposed by researchers.

a) **Filtering at the Edge Routers:** Though it is difficult to stop DDoS attacks at source of attack but filtering of malicious packets from the legitimate data traffic can be done by local ISPs. Current IP structure enables user to change IP address in IP packets. This process of alteration of IP address is called IP spoofing. IP spoofing makes DDoS attack detection a bit difficult. In (Atkinson & Kent; 1998; Kent & Atkinson; 1998), IPSec protocol was proposed to handle IP spoofing problem in IPV4 and IPV6 packets. The problem with this solution is its increased complexity and overhead. Ingress/egress filtering is used to check incoming and outgoing traffic from a local network respectively on the basis of valid IP address range known to local network. Ingress/egress filters are basically deployed at edge routers of a local network. In (Lee et al., 2015) a mechanism has been proposed to detect and prevent spoofed packets. In (Ferguson & Senie, 2000) authors had proposed ingress filtering mechanism to defeat DoS attacks. Ingress filtering at edge routers effectively reduces the impact of IP address spoofing. Main disadvantage of this scheme is if the spoofed IP address is also in the valid IP address range then spoofed IP packet can easily pass the ingress/egress filtering mechanisms.

b) **D-WARD** (Mirkoviac et al., 2002): (DDoS Network Attack Recognition and Defense): This scheme believes that DDoS attack can be effectively stopped at the source before attack traffic enters into rest of the Internet and blends with other legitimate traffic flows. This scheme aims to defend DDoS attack by monitoring and analysing incoming and outgoing traffic from source and by comparing observed statistics with predefined normal traffic profile. Identification and rejection of attack traffic takes place at the edge of source network if it does not match with normal profile. Main disadvantage of this scheme is that it consumes large memory and processing power. Moreover, there is no strong motivation for service provider to deploy D-WARD for protection against DDoS attacks because as it protects the source network but not provider's network from flooding DDoS attacks.

c) **Flow Rate Based Mechanisms**: MULTOPS (Gil & Poletto, 2001) is a tree based data structure that router uses to detect and filter malicious data packets at the edge of a source network. This approach has assumption that rate of incoming and outgoing traffic is directly proportional to each other in an ideal situation. A significant difference between outgoing and incoming rate is detected by the proposed mechanism and it confirms that either of the two end nodes is source of malicious attack traffic. Flow information of outbound and inbound traffic is stored on different interfaces separately. Flow information of inbound traffic is stored on the basis of source addresses while information of outbound traffic is stored on the basis of receiving IP addresses. Main drawback of this scheme is that it is prone to memory exhaustion attack because it uses dynamic tree structure for recording packet rate for each IP address of the local network.

Another method TOPS (Abdelsayed et al., 2003) uses hash tables and probability distribution functions for monitoring packet rate in a network. It is more efficient and accurate as it reduces false alarm rate of the network by taking flow rate as the random variable. This scheme is also based on the same assumption discussed above which proves to be its main drawback. As multimedia request has high data rate from server side, so this assumption completely fails in this case. If the attackers increase the proportion of incoming and outgoing traffic rate by downloading the large data from different servers through legitimate sources in a non-attack scenario; then the attack traffic goes undetected because it matches the rate that has been increased legitimately by the attackers.

d) **Reverse Firewall** (Mananet): Firewall protects a network by shielding it from rest of the Internet i.e. incoming traffic from Internet. Reverse firewall works opposite to the traditional firewall because it protects rest of Internet from a local network i.e. checks outgoing traffic from a local network. A reverse firewall basically intercepts the flow rate of packets that are not asked for by any other host on Internet. For example, packets for starting a new conversation or a request to start a new online game can be delayed or forwarded with a low data rate. Drawback of this mechanism is that it requires manual intervention for its process. Moreover, it's configuration cannot be changed dynamically at run time.

5.1.2 Near to Destination

Detection and response based defensive mechanisms are placed near to destination of attack. These defense mechanisms are deployed at the edge routers of the victim network. Likely, near to source based defensive mechanisms, these defensive mechanisms cannot filter out attack traffic properly as attack traffic is very much concentrated at the boundary of victim network. Despite, being so in defensive mode or in filtering mode there always some malicious traffic which entered in victim's network. Now, we will discuss some of the near to destination based solutions against DDoS attacks.

a) **IP Traceback Mechanisms**: Traceback (John & Sivakumar, 2009) is the mechanism used by victim network to find the true IP address (source) of malicious attack packets used to carry out attack rather than finding their spoofed IP address. Various solutions have been proposed to defend

DDoS attack using traceback mechanism. Packet marking schemes (Chen et al., 2006; Al-Duwairi & Govindarasu, 2006; Savage et al., 2000) use traceback concept by marking every data packet intended for a victim network. Routers in the path between source and victim network mark every data packet with a unique specifier which helps victim network later to trace back the path of identified malicious packets to their actual sources. Traceback schemes have high false positive rate because it is very difficult to generate unique path identifier for every packet every time. Methods in (Yu et al., 2016; Kalkan & Alagöz, 2016) are some of the packet marking schemes proposed in recent years. In Yu et al. (2016), MoD (Marking on Demand) scheme is proposed to detect DDoS attack. This scheme is based on deterministic multiple packets marking scheme and addresses scalability issue of existing DPM schemes. In Kalkan & Alagöz (2016) a mechanism has been proposed to detect and prevent packets having spoofed IP address. Link testing (Burch & Cheswick, 2000; Glave, 1998) is another method used by victim network to traceback illegitimate data packets. Link testing is a recursive method where test itself starts from the closest router to the victim network and test its upstream routers to find the link used by attacker to send the malicious data packets. There are certain disadvantages of these mechanisms because of high network management overhead.

b) **Management Information Base (MIB):** MIB (Cabrera et al., 2001) is a repository of statistics related to data packets and routers in a network. By continuously monitoring the MIB information, it can be easily concluded that network is under DDoS attack or not. This method is efficient as it can easily analyze oddity in ICMP, UDP and TCP packets by identifying statistical patterns and find out the specific type of DDoS attack. It also helps in betterment of network.

c) **Packet Marking and Filtering Mechanisms:** Packet marking mechanisms aim to mark the legitimate packets with the path from source to destination which help routers in between to differentiate malicious data packets. These mechanisms have provision for dynamic filtering by letting intermediate routers to filter out malicious packets. There is one mechanism named hop count filtering (Wang et al., 2007) which aims to aims filter the attack packets on the basis of hop count. Destination used to store the source's IP address and its neighbouring hops when there is no attack. Once the DDoS attack seems to happen, victim network monitors incoming packets and neighbouring hops to filter out malicious packets. This algorithm is a light weight and its space complexity is also very less. But, what if the attacker gets legitimate IP address and hop count of a legitimate user. Packet score (Kim et al., 2004), a score-based packet dropping mechanism has been proposed where legitimacy of data packets is checked using scores of given attribute values. Score is calculated using Bayesian-theoretic metric which prioritize data packets. It is ineffective against low rate DDoS attacks. Probabilistic filter scheduling (Seo et al., 2011) is a cooperative filtering mechanism where filter is propagated through a network to an optimal location closer to attack. It has high effectiveness as it chooses best k filters throughout the network according to frequency. Problem with this mechanism is that it used fixed scheduling. Same authors have solved the problem of fixed scheduling by proposing adaptive scheduling (Seo et al., 2013). But this mechanism has high overhead of marking and filter relocation.

5.1.3 At Intermediate Routers

These mechanisms are usually deployed at intermediate routers of a network between source and destination. Deploying a defensive solution at intermediate routers overcome drawbacks of source based and destination-based defense solutions. Intermediate router is the ideal location to locate any defensive mechanism against DDoS attack.

a) **Route Based Packet Filtering** (Park & Lee, 2001): It is similar to ingress filtering as it uses the concept of ingress filtering at core routers of a network. It requires information about network topology for the proper functioning. This mechanism worked on the principle that core router has incoming traffic from only a specific set of source addresses. Any data packet having spoofed IP address cannot escape through intermediate routers. A main drawback of this mechanism is that if the attacker uses non-IP spoofed packets for carrying out attacks than this mechanism cannot filter out malicious packets. This mechanism cannot cope up with constantly changing network topology. It requires modification in BGP protocol for smooth running.

b) **Malicious Routers Detection and Filtration**: Attackers can even leverage intermediate routers to amplify DDoS attack. Several solutions also have been proposed to protect intermediate routers from getting compromised. In (Mizrak et al., 2008) routers that deviate from normal behaviour i.e. by discarding or misrouting packets are detected by mechanism called Watchers. There could be misidentification of a good router as a bad one if the attackers send spoofed packets. Intermediate routers require high processing power for detecting and fighting against DDoS attacks but redundant detection and response by every router on the path completely waste crucial resources of intermediate routers. Moreover, it is not necessary that DDoS attack is always caused due to heavy malicious traffic. Sometimes, it is due to voluminous legitimate traffic (flash crowd) that causes DDoS attack. In (Bhushan & Gupta, 2018), authors have presented a scheme for defending multimedia flash crowd where general statistical analysis has been performed to detect malicious traffic from flash crowd.

5.1.4 Hybrid Approaches

Defensive mechanisms against DDoS attack that are deployed either at source or destination or at intermediate router don't have cooperation among different Internet entities i.e. they are centralized in nature. They function in isolation without cooperation from rest of the Internet which is the main drawback of all of the above discussed defensive solutions. Unlikely centralized solutions, hybrid approaches have distributed architecture where there is cooperation among different deployment points. Distributed defensive solutions are deployed at multiple locations all over the Internet and every entity work as per its capability and cooperate with other entities to compensate for weaker traits. For example, in distributed solution detection is performed at victim side and then victim network informed all of the upstream core routers to stop attack traffic i.e. response and filtering performed at source and core routers.

a) **Packet Marking and Filtering Based Cooperative Solutions:** Distributed packet marking and filtering based cooperative solutions perform attack detection near to the victim end and filtering at source end by exchanging commands. These mechanisms do not harm legitimate traffic flows instead just limit the flow rate of malicious traffic. In Mahajan et al. (2002) proposed a cooperative pushback mechanism against aggregation of multiple traffic flows. An aggregate can be a subset of flow of packets having similar characteristic like particular source IP address or packets destined to a particular port or similar kind of packets containing HTTP packets or TCP SYN packets or ICMP ECHO packets. In order to control congestion by these multiple flows, two ACC (Aggregate based congestion control) mechanisms have been proposed. In first mechanism, local ACC is deployed consisting of identification algorithm that identifies aggregate causing congestion in a network and a control algorithm that lessens the throughput of the aggregate to a certain level. In second mechanism, pushback is performed where a router requests its nearby routers to rate limit the traffic flow of an aggregate. A threshold rate limit is set and if the aggregate is under the limit set by threshold then the aggregate is allowed to pass otherwise it is dropped to match the threshold value. Pushback mechanism is also used in Yau et al. (2005) to notify the upstream routers about limiting rate of traffic. But these methods are not effective if the attack is evenly distributed. In (Chen & Park, 2005) proposed a cooperative approach named attack diagnosis (AD) that combines packet marking and pushback schemes to mitigate DDoS attacks. In this scheme, once attack is detected near victim end, it triggers AD by sending commands to upstream routers. Upon receiving commands by victim, routers start marking packets with the information given by interface. Interface processes packets entering into a network. After receiving and analyzing marked packets, victim node comes to know about the attack source. Attack traffic is then filtered by routers validated by AD. Authentication of AD commands is confirmed by TTL field of IP header. One disadvantage of this mechanism is that it is not meant for large scale attacks. Extension to this work is PAD i.e. parallel AD that has been proposed to cover the shortcomings of AD. PAD is able to diagnose and filter attack traffic from multiple routers at the same time. PAD is efficient against large scale DDoS attacks. In Chen et al. (2006) authors proposed a comprehensive DDoS defensive scheme based on router port marking and packet filtering. Router port marking module marks all IP packets with router's interface port number which is a 6 digit unique number. After collecting the marked packets along attacking path, victim tried to find out the attack source using information appended in packets. Upstream routers are then commanded to filter the malicious packets. Advantages of this scheme are low computation overhead. This scheme has two major limitations. First is attacker can make changes in marking field of IP packets and thus easily can avoid being tracked. Second is this scheme is good for IP traceback for zombie machines not for identifying the IP address of actual master that ordered zombie machines to carry out DDoS attack. Next, in Gupta & Badve (2017), authors have proposed a DDoS attack detection and filtering mechanism using Chaos theory. Non-linear time series model i.e. GARCH has been used to predict the network traffic state. GARCH model is used for detection of DDoS attacks while back propagation ANN model is used for filtering malicious traffic. In (Gupta et. al., 2012), authors have proposed a scheme where DDoS attack is detected through statistical analysis of network traffic and dynamic threshold identification algorithm.

b) **Signature Based Cooperative Defense Mechanism:** COSSACK (Papadopoulos et al., 2003) (coordinated suppression of simultaneous attacks) mechanism based on attack signatures is proposed. COSSACK uses a software system called watchdog consisting of all border routers of edge networks. COSSACK is built on the usage of attack signatures, edge router's capability to filter out malicious attack using attack signatures and continuous connection between watchdogs. Functions of watchdog are to perform ingress and egress filtering at border routers to counter DDoS attacks and it also multicast notifications from victim node to source node. Disadvantage of this solution is that it cannot mitigate DDoS attacks in legacy networks that do not use COSSACK mechanism.

c) **Capability-based Cooperative Defense Solutions:** In capability-based systems, senders have to obtain short term authorizations from receiver in order to send packets to receiver. This short-term authorization is called capability. Sender has to make their packets eligible by putting these authorizations as a stamp. After verification of the traffic as legitimate by certain verifying points on the route between sender and receiver, receiver is allowed to process the packets. In Anderson et al. (2004), receiver gives "permission to send" to the users whose traffic receiver agrees to accept. Permission to send is like tokens which sender has to append to their packets before sending. Distributed verification centres all over the network check credibility of the packets before forwarding them to next node and these tokenized packets get priority during attack time. Many capability-based solutions have been proposed in history by researchers (Yang et al., 2005; Parno et al., 2007; Yaar et al., 2004). Disadvantages of capability-based system are high computational costs and memory overheads. One more issue of authentication in CBS is resolved by Yang et al. (2008) and Liu et al. (2008). In Liu et al. (2017), authors have proposed capability-based overlay solution named MiddlePolice. It is a destination driven defensive strategy where traffic is filtered according to destination-based services.

d) **Datagram Based Cooperative Solution:** In filtering based cooperative solution against DDoS attacks, there is a need to provide ISPs some incentives so that so they reserve some portion of their credible resources for filtering purpose. In Dahiya & Gupta (2018), authors have discussed the importance of incentives and liabilities in Internet structure. In (Argyraki & Cheriton, 2009) a filter-based scheme named AITF (Active Internet Traffic Filtering) is proposed. In AITF, receiver is allowed to contact attacking sources and warn them to stop sending malicious traffic. Here, attacking source's local ISP is hired to monitor his traffic. For this, incentive must be given to this local ISP. Here local ISP has two options, either it has to support AITF for policing its malicious nodes or it has to lose its access to server's resources. This is the incentive that AITF model provides local ISPs to cooperate with each other. There are various issues associated with this technique. Firstly, three-way handshake is used to check the legitimacy of the packets but if the traffic comes from outside AITF's network then request packets come along with attack traffic and hence could not be processed by server. Secondly, there are major deployment issues with this technique.

e) **Anomaly Based Cooperative Solution:** In Liu et al. (2008) authors have proposed a hybrid cooperative defensive mechanism named StopIt where each receiver in a network is allowed to install a network filter that stops the malicious traffic. This mechanism uses passport (Yang et. al., 2008) to authenticate the source nodes. Results in this paper show the supremacy of StopIt over AITF and StopIt also provides undisturbed communication under a wide range of DDoS attacks. But, it cannot perform better than capability based systems.

f) **DEFensive Cooperative Overlay Mesh (DEFCOM):** DEFCOM (Mirkovic et al., 2003) is a distributed defensive mechanism that incorporates heterogeneous nodes and made them exchange information in order to achieve effective defense against DDoS attacks. In this defense mechanism devices present in the current Internet infrastructure are programmed to perform specialized functions. There is no need for extra infrastructure to deploy DEFCOM. Every node in the network must perform one of the three functions i.e. first is alert generator, second is rate limiters and third is distinguishing nodes. Alert generator nodes detect DDoS attack and alert its peer network. Rate limiters (core routers) after getting alert (signatures) start rate limit traffic traversing through them. Distinguishing nodes communicate with downstream neighbours so that legitimate traffic could not suffer. Disadvantage of DEFCOM is if most of the networks in Internet do not deploy DEFCOM then the traffic from these networks could be DoS attack to legitimate users of the network having DEFCOM. This is a deployment issue.

g) **SENSS:** In Ramanathan et al. (2018), a collaborative mechanism named SENSS has been proposed to mitigate volumetric DDoS attacks. SENSS enables a victim to ask for monitoring and filtering traffic intended for him by paying for the service. In this solution, remote and immediate ISPs can be involved by just sending a secure request message. Moreover, the most important thing which previous solutions lack is incentives. SENSS provides incentives not only to attack victims but also to ISPs. It also provides protection in sparse deployment also.

h) **SPIFFY:** SPIFFY's (Kang et al., 2016) working is complementary to SENSS. In this mechanism, short term collaboration is developed between bottleneck of a network and traffic sources. It temporarily expands bottleneck to identify malicious sources as legitimate sources do not increase their rate of data transfer.

5.2 Classification on When Defensive Mechanism Gets Active

In this category, we classify DDoS defensive solutions into before the attack, during the attack and after the attack categories.

5.2.1 Before the Attack

These mechanisms include attack prevention techniques. Prevention techniques aim to stop DDoS attack at its launching stage. Prevention mechanisms can be deployed at source or destination or at intermediate routers. Following are some techniques.

a) **Fix Network/ Protocol Vulnerabilities**: It is the first step towards any kind of cyber-security. First remove any kind of vulnerability or loophole to lessen the possibility of exploitation of present vulnerability by attacker. Updating current protocols, removing bugs and illegitimate access to the machines are some of the initial steps that could be taken to stop DDoS attacks.

b) **Reservation of Resources**: Having extra resources and admission control by monitoring user's behavior and history (Saini & Somani, 2014; Baig & Binbeshr, 2013; Andersen, 2003; Mankins et al., 2001). In (Bhushan & Gupta, 2019), authors have designed a defensive mechanism to detect fraudulent resource consumption attacks. Detection of fraudulent resource consumption attack at a very initial stage can mitigate DDoS attack effectively to a great extent.

c) **Local Solutions**: Local ISPs can play a very important role in preventing DDoS attacks. Not only local ISPs but local solutions proposed by researchers like (Ferguson, 2007; Wang et al., 2007; Park & Lee, 2001; Mahajan et al., 2002; Chen et al., 2006) are some of the solutions that can prevent DDoS attack before it gets launched. Local ISPs can employ dynamic pricing strategies to impose cost on users for sending service requests to the service provider. Honeypot is one of the local solutions that is easy to deploy and can be used to discover new types of attack signatures. Honeypot is a technique used to lure attackers by pretending to be legitimate systems. In (Gupta & Gupta, 2018), authors have surveyed various issues, challenges and defensive mechanisms related to honeypot technology. In (Chhabra & Gupta, 2014) a novel DDoS prevention scheme has been proposed.

d) **Load Balancing and Flow Rate**: A single server cannot handle all service requests of users. There is need to have multiple server ports so that during attack period legitimate users can have their desired QoS. For this we need to have load balancing techniques so that one server does not have to bear the entire load. Secondly, controlling flow rate at intermediate routers/core routers can contribute much in preventing DDoS attacks.

5.2.2 During Attack

Defensive mechanisms that need to take action during DDoS attack period are basically detecting mechanisms. These defensive solutions also can be deployed at any location of a network. Detecting flow rate of packets i.e. whether the flow rate is reached to a certain threshold value or not is one of the class of these solutions.

Risk transfer can also be the option to defend DDoS attack during attack period. Third parties are hired in return of monetary payments so that resources of these willing third parties can be utilized during attack period by transferring all the attack traffic towards them. In Adat et al. (2018) and Gupta & S.A. (2019) authors have designed risk transfer mechanisms to mitigate DDoS attacks.

Anomaly detection, normal patterns and signatures are traced during non-attack period. Normal patterns or profile are identified from web access logs, established connections, packet traces and packet headers. During attack period, traffic is compared with these normal patterns and signatures while entering into the network. Data mining and artificial techniques are employed to improve the detection rate of malicious packets. Anomaly detection techniques are further classified on the statistical technique used or granularity level or analyzed parameters. D-WARD, MIB, MULTOPS, TOPS are some detection techniques. Other than these, (Feinstein etv al., 2003; Shamsolmoali & Zareapoor, 2014; Vissers et al., 2014; Kim et al., 2004; Jiang et al., 2018) are some of the anomaly detection-based techniques for DDoS attacks. Main drawbacks of anomaly based detection method are overhead of training of traffic features and scalability issue. There are two main issues associated with all detecting mechanisms; first, there is no wide deployment of any defense mechanism and second, there is no cooperation between deployed points. In (Tripathi et al., 2013; Chhabra et al., 2013) novel detection schemes have been proposed. In (Tripathi et al., 2013) a Hadoop-based DDoS detection mechanism has been proposed while in (Chhabra et al., 2013) a DDoS prevention scheme has been proposed in MANET.

Resource allocation is a new perspective from researchers to defend DDoS attacks. Distributing resources judiciously and economically among users can prove to be a very good solution against DDoS attacks. There exist many resource allocation schemes that have used auction mechanism to allocate resources fairly among users. In (Samimi et al., 2016) authors have proposed CDARA model where resources are allocated greedily. A greedy based algorithm is approximated by $\sqrt{M}$ factor where M denoted the number of requested number of resources by users. Similarly, in (Zaman & Grosu, 2013), authors have designed two approaches other than fixed price mechanism to distribute resources through auction mechanism i.e. linear programming-based method and greedy based approach. In both the mechanisms critical value-based payment schemes have been used. Many schemes (Baranwal & Vidyarthi, 2015; Zaman & Grosu, 2013; Li et al., 2009; AuYoung et al., 2004) have been designed in the same domain of resource allocation judiciously among users.

5.2.3 After the Attack

After the attack mechanisms include techniques which can mitigate DDoS attacks and lessen the damage caused by it. Once a DDoS attack has been detected, victim network has to respond it with the mechanisms used to traceback the source of attack. Solutions proposed so far for mitigating DDoS attack cannot provide protection from all types of DDoS attacks. Mitigating solutions aim to reduce DDoS attack's impact and make the resources available to legitimate users. Since, with the evolution in technology and Internet, attackers have numerous ways to perform DDoS attacks. Every time, it is not possible for established solutions to detect new types of attacks. But one thing we can ensure that, a particular type of attack should not repeat in future. One way to deal with this is to identify the attack source. Honeypot technology can be used to analyse captured attack packets after the DDoS attack has been carried out. Traceback mechanisms help in this direction. Another way to deal with is to generate an appropriate response towards attack. Some victim network applies throttling, filtering at core routers, migrate victim server to other servers, employ resource management methods or transfer attack traffic towards third party (cyber insurance).

5.3 Economic Incentive Based Solution Against DDoS Attacks

There exists very few research in this domain. But this is a completely a new domain where attackers are imposed with some computational work to prove their legitimacy. These solutions work cooperatively and distributively against DDoS attacks. Design of various payment schemes, fair distribution of resources, imposition of penalty, dynamic pricing of resources, dynamic negotiation between cost and types of resources are some aspects of economic incentive based solution.

5.3.1 Resource Allocation Schemes

In (Dahiya & Gupta, 2018; Gulihar & Gupta, 2018) authors have used auction mechanism to mitigate DDoS attacks. Auction is a type of dynamic pricing scheme where users can participate with service provider equally in deciding the prices of the services and resources. In Dahiya & Gupta (2018), authors have designed a VCG-based economical approach to mitigate DDoS attacks by allocating resources among users judiciously. In Gulihar & Gupta (2018), authors have used auction mechanism for cache servers. Cache server can give their resources to service provider as they have much underutilized resources. Moreover, there exist many schemes (Samimi et al., 2016; Zaman & Grosu, 2013; Baranwal & Vidyarthi, 2015) which deal with resource allocation in cloud computing. Resource allocation schemes for mitigating DDoS attacks are greatly inspired from these schemes.

5.3.2 Pricing and Usage Based Schemes

In Geng & Whinston (2000), authors have proposed e-postal mechanism where user has to purchase e-stamps and store them onto nearest router. Edge router consumes one e-stamp for allowing one data request to enter into a specified network. This whole process will definitely incentivise users to use e-stamps judiciously. This approach is inspired from usage based schemes.

In Huang et al. (2007), authors have analysed broken incentive chain in two very efficient technological solutions namely cooperative filtering and cooperative caching. Authors have proposed usage-based pricing and capacity provisioning networking as solutions to deal with broken incentives in these two technical solutions.

In Geng et al. (2002), a framework for mitigating DDoS attacks has been proposed where cooperative solutions are incorporated with economic solutions. Device security, user based traffic management, coordinated filters and trace back mechanisms are included in the technological solution while usage based pricing scheme is included in economic solution. This solution is proposed for wireless environment.

In Gupta et al. (2009), authors have laid the importance of pricing Internet traffic for fair allocation of resources and to provide acceptable level of QoS to legitimate users. A comprehensive survey of various Internet pricing schemes have been presented in Gupta et al. (1996) and Shenker et al. (1996). In Shenker et al. (1996), authors have presented dynamic adaptive pricing strategy based on different levels of QoS.

5.3.3 Game Theory and Analytical Based Solutions

In this section we will discuss some of the significant papers which provide game theory or analytical based solution against DDoS attacks.

In Wang et al. (2016), authors have presented a trustworthy crowdsourcing model in Social Internet of Things (SIoT) environment. In this model, storage and computational services have been proposed by the social cloud to end users and sensing entities. On the basis of accuracy of reported values or data, sensing entities receive rewards or penalty from service provider. Moreover, a reputation-based auction mechanism has been incorporated for winner and payment determination to address issues like DDoS attacks. Reputation of a sensing entity is checked on the basis of reliability of crowdsourcing participants.

In Wang et al. (2014), authors have proposed an incentive compatible alleviate malicious behaviour of rational or irrational of intelligent bots or users in spectrum sharing environment. Dealing with malicious behaviour of users in an economic way can help us a lot in mitigating DDoS attacks. We can track or analyse malicious behaviour of rational attackers and irrational bot machines. In this paper, as per the monitoring of malicious behaviour, joint spectrum access mechanism has been proposed to stop malicious users from sending false data.

In Zhu et al. (2012), authors have proposed a scheme named GUIDEX where game theory and trust management has been utilized to design an incentive compatible mechanism for intrusion detection mechanism. This scheme can be explored for detection of DDoS attacks.

6. PERFORMANCE EVALUATION PARAMETERS

Evaluation of a defensive mechanism in the form of some mathematical expression is very important as it gives a clear idea how good a defensive mechanism can be if deployed in a network. Evaluating parameters help us in comparing different solutions proposed against DDoS attacks. In table 1 we have listed some important evaluation parameters commonly used by researchers (Zargar et al., 2013; Gupta & Badve, 2017).

7. ATTACK TOOLS

There are so many freely available DDoS attacking tools on Internet. Attacker just has to put specifications in the fields to carry out an attack. Even a naive user can user these tools with so much ease. In table 2, we have listed some of the major DDoS attack tools.

Table 1. Performance evaluation parameters

Evaluating Measure	Description
Accuracy	• True Positive: When a malicious packet is identified as malicious then it is true positive. Let's say w be the number of true positives of a defensive solution • True Negative: When a legitimate packet is identified as legitimate then it is true negative. Suppose x be the number of true negatives. • False Positive: When legitimate packet is identified as malicious then it is false positive. Let's assume y be the number of false positives. • False Negative: When malicious packet is identified as legitimate one then it is false negative. Let's say z be the number of false negatives. $$Accuracy = \frac{(w+x)}{w+x+y+z}$$
Sensitivity	• True Positive Rate is known as sensitivity. • Ratio of malicious packets identified as malicious to the total number of malicious packets. $$TPR = \frac{w}{w+z}$$
Specificity	• True negative rate is known as specificity. • Ratio of legitimate packets identified as legitimate ones to the total number of legitimate packets. $$TNR = \frac{x}{x+y}$$
Precision	• Ratio of malicious packets identified as malicious to the total positives of the system $$Precision = \frac{w}{w+y}$$
Reliability	• Ratio of legitimate packets identified as malicious one to the total number of legitimate packets. $$Reliability(FPR) = \frac{y}{y+x}$$
FNR	$$FNR = \frac{z}{z+w}$$
ROC	• Used to measure the accuracy of the system • Every point on a ROC curve represents (sensitivity/specificity pair). • It represents how well a defensive solution distinguishes between legitimate and malicious packets.
Confusion Matrix	• It a 2×2 matrix generated by a binary classifier. • Used to describe the performance of the classification model on dataset. • It compares actual and predicted values of classification • It is mainly used when machine learning concepts are used in classification.
Performance	• Depends on factors like configuration of the server it is running and network traffic being monitored. • Certain measures like processing time, memory consumed and numbers of packets processed per unit time are some of the measures used to calculate performance.
Scalability	• A DDoS defensive solution must be scalable as attack scale can reach to a very high limit in a small duration. • A DDoS defensive must be able to handle voluminous amount of traffic.
Usability	• User Interface provided by a defensive solution must be user friendly.
Comprehensive	• A DDoS defensive system is said to be comprehensible if it able to protect a system from all types of known DDoS attacks.
Implementation Ease	• A defensive mechanism is said to be good in this category if its implementation complexity in the network is less i.e. can be implemented easily in a network.
Deployment Point	• As we mentioned the merits and demerits of a source or destination or intermediate router based solutions. • A defensive mechanism can be easily evaluated on the basis of deployment location in a network.

Table 2. DDoS attack tools

Attack Tool	Description	Attack
Trin00 (Dittrich, 1999)	• Make victim run out of bandwidth. • Use master/slave architecture of botnet to carry out attack against many hosts. • Cannot spoof IP address.	UDP Flooding
Mstream (Dittrich, 2000)	• Forged TCP packets are used with ACK flag set to carry out attack. • Master/slave architecture is used • It sends spoofed TCP SYN packet to different servers, proxies or a broadcasting network. In response to TCP SYN packets, these servers, proxies and broadcasting network generate ACK packets directed towards victim network. • Bandwidth depletion attack tool	TCP ACK
LOIC (LOIC, Sourceforge.net, 2019)	• It can perform URL and IP address based attack. • It does not hide attacker's IP address. • It enables other users to join DDoS attack via IRC.	UDP,TCP,HTTP flooding attack
XOIC (XOIC, Sourceforge.net, 2019)	• More powerful than LOIC. • Attacker has to specify IP address, port number or type of protocol to carry out the attack • Easy tool for beginners. • Attacker can easily be traced back.	TCP, UDP, HTTP and ICMP flooding attack.
HOIC (HOIC, Sourceforge.net, 2019)	• Successor of LOIC capable of attacking 256 targets at the same time. • Generates voluminous amount of dummy HTTP GET and POST requests to overwhelm the application server. • Manual coordination is required among attackers to perform a DDoS attack. • Attacker can easily be traced out.	HTTP Flooding attack
HULK	• Generates obfuscated and unique traffic to bypass a caching engine. • It can avoid attack detection. • It can forge different fields of a web request. • Traffic from HULK can be blocked.	HTTP flooding attack.
Stacheldraht (Dittrich, 1999)	• Features of Trinoo and Tribe flood Network are combined with encryption as the added feature. • Uses agent handler architecture. TCP is used between client and handler while ICMP is used to connect agent and handler. • Blowfish algorithm is used to secure TCP connection which makes intrusion detector to decode the TCP connection.	UDP and ICMP flooding attack, TCP SYN attack, Smurf Attack
Tribe Flood Network (TFN) (Dittrich, 1999)	• No encryption between handler and attacker or agent and handler. • Handlers are instructed using command line argument. • Can attack bandwidth and other resources at target.	ICMP, TCP SYN, UDP flooding attack. Smurf attack
PyLoris	• Testing tool for servers. • Use SOCKS proxies and SSL connections to perform DoS attack. • It can attack a wide range of protocols namely FTP, SMTP, HTTP, Telnet and IMPAP. • Written in Python • Open TCP connections for as much long as possible.	TCP SYN attack, HTTP flooding attack.
DDoSim	• It can generate many zombie hosts to perform a DDoS attack. • All zombie hosts create full TCP connection with the victim server. • It can create legitimate HTTP requests to carry out DDoS attack. • Application layer DDoS attack is also possible with this tool. •	TCP and HTTP flooding attack possible with valid and invalid requests.
Knight (King & Morda, 2001)	• IRC based, a strong attacking tool. • Back Orifice, a Trojan Horse program is used to compromise a system. • It has a checksum generator,	UDP and TCP Flooding attack. TCP SYN attack.

8. CASE STUDIES ON DDOS ATTACKS

In, 2018, a major DDoS attack of size 1.7 TBPS was carried out against one of the most reputable websites for coders i.e. Github (Kottler, 2018). It was a memcached attack where DDoS attack was carried out against memcached database server used for speeding up websites. Attacker has exploit memcached instances that are available on UDP enabled public Internet. Attackers have used 51000 as amplification factor i.e. for one byte sent by attacker, 51KB data has been sent towards Github. Here along with memcached attack, IP spoofing is used to hide identity of attacker. Attack traffic is generated from numerous autonomous systems. After this attack, Github has tried to make its edge infrastructure more resilient and fully automated against DDoS attack. Company has made some serious investment in analysing and monitoring technologies and tried to reduce their response time and recovery time i.e. MTTR (Mean time to recovery).

In 2014, Boston's children hospital was attacked by an anonymous hactivist group (ERT case studies, 2019). It was all began with threat followed by three major DDoS attacks. This was the first healthcare organization to be attacked by DDoS attackers. On March, 2014 this hospital got a twitter message related to a custody case of a 15 year old girl. Massachusetts protective services have taken the custody of this girl who has to gone through a complex diagnosis. Attackers have warned the hospital authority and instructed it to take disciplinary actions against some clinician and returned girl to her parents. During the first phase, attackers have launched slow rate DDoS attacks and attacked hospital's external website. First phase continued for almost one week which results into slow movement of legitimate inbound and out bound traffic. In phase 2, attackers have raised the seriousness by launching various DDoS flooding attacks like TCP fragmented flood, DNS reflection. Various mitigation schemes had been deployed by hospital security system to protect critical services from DDoS attack. In third phase, attackers have tried to infiltrate hospital's network through direct DDoS attacks on vulnerable open ports and services. Spear phishing has been used by attacker to lure various users to click on malicious links to gain access to the network behind firewall. Hospital's security system has used multidisciplinary incident response team as soon as it became aware of DDoS attack. This team has quickly assessed three major impacts of DDoS attack and tried to protect hospital accordingly. If the hospital were to suffer major DDoS attack, then it might be possible that it is impossible to send prescriptions to pharmacies electronically. Secondly, there was a need to protect those departments where critical processes are handled by email systems. Thirdly, it will be difficult for hospital authority to access remotely located health care records. There is no denying in the fact that DDoS attack has not spared any sector and can cause disastrous effects.

9. CONCLUSION

In this paper, we addressed the seriousness of DDoS attacks on global economy. Apart from it, a comprehensive classification of DDoS attacks is presented. Further, classification of defensive solutions is presented along with their advantages and disadvantages. We discussed the importance of a solution which is distributed, widely deployable, cooperative and incentive provider to users and local ISPs. Moreover, various evaluating parameters are discussed used to measure accuracy, completeness and efficiency of s defensive solution.

Liabilities and incentives can play a very important role in handing DDoS attacks. We need to think differently from conventional DDoS attack approaches. More emphasize must be given on economic aspect of any solution. In our future, we will try to frame solutions that can incentivise legitimate users to send data wisely and making attacker deprived of the same.

ACKNOWLEDGMENT

This research work is being supported by (i) sponsored project grant (SB/FTP/ETA-131/2014) from SERB, DST, Government of India, and (ii) YFRF grant under the project Visvesvaraya PhD Scheme of Ministry of Electronics & Information Technology, Government of India and being implemented by Digital India Corporation..

REFERENCES

Yu, S., Zhou, W., Guo, S., & Guo, M. (2016). A feasible IP traceback framework through dynamic deterministic packet marking. *IEEE Transactions on Computers*, *65*(5), 1418–1427.

Alomari, E., Manickam, S., Gupta, B. B., Anbar, M., Saad, R. M., & Alsaleem, S. (2016). A survey of botnet-based ddos flooding attacks of application layer: Detection and mitigation approaches. In Handbook of Research on Modern Cryptographic Solutions for Computer and Cyber Security (pp. 52–79). IGI Global.

Abdelsayed, S., Glimsholt, D., Leckie, C., Ryan, S., & Shami, S. (2003, December). An efficient filter for denial-of-service bandwidth attacks. In GLOBECOM'03. IEEE Global Telecommunications Conference (IEEE Cat. No. 03CH37489) (Vol. 3, pp. 1353-1357). IEEE.

Adat, V., Dahiya, A., & Gupta, B. B. (2018, January). Economic incentive-based solution against distributed denial of service attacks for IoT customers. In *Proceedings 2018 IEEE International Conference on Consumer Electronics (ICCE)* (pp. 1-5). IEEE.

Adat, V., Dahiya, A., & Gupta, B. B. (n.d.). *Economic Incentive Based Solution Against Distributed Denial of Service.*

Adat, V., & Gupta, B. B. (2018). Security in Internet of Things: Issues, challenges, taxonomy, and architecture. *Telecommunication Systems*, *67*(3), 423–441.

Advisory, C. E. R. T. CA-1996-21, Carnegie Mellon University. (2014). Retrieved from https://www uxsup.csx.cam.ac.uk/pub/webmirrors/www.cert.org/advisories/CA-1996-21.html

Advisory, C. E. R. T. CA-1997-28, Carnegie Mellon University. (2014). Retrieved from https://resources. sei.cmu.edu/asset_files/whitepaper/1997_019_001_496176.pdf

Al-Duwairi, B., & Govindarasu, M. (2006). Novel hybrid schemes employing packet marking and logging for IP traceback. *IEEE Transactions on Parallel and Distributed Systems*, *17*(5), 403–418.

Andersen, D. G. (2003, March). Mayday: Distributed Filtering for Internet Services. In *USENIX Symposium on Internet Technologies and Systems* (Vol. 4).

Anderson, T., Roscoe, T., & Wetherall, D. (2004). Preventing Internet denial-of-service with capabilities. *Computer Communication Review, 34*(1), 39–44.

Argyraki, K., & Cheriton, D. R. (2009). Scalable network-layer defense against internet bandwidth-flooding attacks. [ToN]. *IEEE/ACM Transactions on Networking, 17*(4), 1284–1297.

ASERT Team. NETSCOUT "OMG - Mirai Minions are Wicked". Link available at https://www.netscout.com/blog/asert/omg-mirai-minions-are-wicked

Atkinson, R., & Kent, S. (1998). Security architecture for the internet protocol.

AuYoung, A., Chun, B., Snoeren, A., & Vahdat, A. (2004, October). Resource allocation in federated distributed computing infrastructures. In *Proceedings of the 1st Workshop on Operating System and Architectural Support for the On-demand IT InfraStructure* (Vol. 9).

Baig, Z. A., & Binbeshr, F. (2013). Controlled Virtual Resource Access to Mitigate Economic Denial of Sustainability (EDoS) Attacks Against Cloud Infrastructures, in *Proceedings of the 2013 International Conference on Cloud Computing and Big Data, CLOUDCOM-ASIA '13*, pp. 346–353. IEEE Computer Society, Washington, DC. doi:10.1109/CLOUDCOM-ASIA.2013.51

Bailey, M., Cooke, E., Jahanian, F., Xu, Y., & Karir, M. (2009, March). A survey of botnet technology and defenses. In Proceedings 2009 Cybersecurity Applications & Technology Conference for Homeland Security (pp. 299-304). IEEE.

Baranwal, G., & Vidyarthi, D. P. (2015). A fair multi-attribute combinatorial double auction model for resource allocation in cloud computing. *Journal of Systems and Software, 108*, 60–76.

Bhushan, K., & Gupta, B. B. (2018). A novel approach to defend multimedia flash crowd in cloud environment. *Multimedia Tools and Applications, 77*(4), 4609–4639.

Bhushan, K., & Gupta, B. B. (2019). Distributed denial of service (DDoS) attack mitigation in software defined network (SDN)-based cloud computing environment. *Journal of Ambient Intelligence and Humanized Computing, 10*(5), 1985–1997.

Bhushan, K., & Gupta, B. B. (2019). Network flow analysis for detection and mitigation of Fraudulent Resource Consumption (FRC) attacks in multimedia cloud computing. *Multimedia Tools and Applications, 78*(4), 4267–4298.

Bhuyan, M. H., Bhattacharyya, D. K., & Kalita, J. K. (2013). Network anomaly detection: Methods, systems and tools. *IEEE Communications Surveys and Tutorials, 16*(1), 303–336.

Bhuyan, M. H., Kashyap, H. J., Bhattacharyya, D. K., & Kalita, J. K. (2013). Detecting distributed denial of service attacks: Methods, tools and future directions. *The Computer Journal, 57*(4), 537–556.

Burch, H., & Cheswick, B. (2000, December). Tracing Anonymous Packets to Their Approximate Source. In LISA (pp. 319-327).

Cabrera, J. B., Lewis, L., Qin, X., Lee, W., Prasanth, R. K., Ravichandran, B., & Mehra, R. K. (2001, May). Proactive detection of distributed denial of service attacks using mib traffic variables-a feasibility study. In *2001 IEEE/IFIP International Symposium on Integrated Network Management Proceedings*. Integrated Network Management VII. Integrated Management Strategies for the New Millennium (pp. 609-622). IEEE.

Case Studies, E. R. T. (n.d.). DDoS Case Study: DDoS Attack Mitigation Boston Children's Hospital. Available at https://security.radware.com/ddos-experts-insider/ert-case-studies/boston-childrens-hospital-ddos-mitigation-case-study/

Chaudhary, D., Bhushan, K., & Gupta, B. B. (2018). Survey on DDoS attacks and defense mechanisms in cloud and fog computing. [IJESMA]. *International Journal of E-Services and Mobile Applications*, *10*(3), 61–83.

Chen, C. L. (2009). A new detection method for distributed denial of-service attack traffic based on statistical test. *Journal of Universal Computer Science*, *15*, 488–504.

Chen, R., & Park, J. M. (2005, October). Attack Diagnosis: Throttling distributed denial-of-service attacks close to the attack sources. In *Proceedings 14th International Conference on Computer Communications and Networks, 2005. ICCCN 2005.* (pp. 275-280). IEEE.

Chen, R., Park, J. M., & Marchany, R. (2006). TRACK: A novel approach for defending against distributed denial-of-service attacks. Technical P~ eport TR ECE—O6-02. Dept. of Electrical and Computer Engineering, Virginia Tech.

Chen, R., Park, J. M., & Marchany, R. (2006). NISp1-05: RIM: Router interface marking for IP traceback. In Proceedings IEEE Globecom 2006 (pp. 1-5). IEEE.

Chen, Y., Hwang, K., & Ku, W. S. (2006). Distributed Change-Point Detection of DDoS Attacks Over Multiple Network Domains. Proc. IEEE Int. Symp. Collaborative Technologies and Systems, pp. 543–550. Las Vegas, NV, May 14–17, IEEE CS.

Chhabra, M., Gupta, B., & Almomani, A. (2013). A novel solution to handle DDOS attack in MANET. *Journal of Information Security*, *4*(3), 165.

Chhabra, M., & Gupta, B. B. (2014). Research Article An Efficient Scheme to Prevent DDoS Flooding Attacks in Mobile Ad-Hoc Network (MANET). *Research Journal of Applied Sciences, Engineering and Technology*, *7*(10), 2033–2039.

Dahiya, A., & Gupta, B. B. (2018). Importance of Providing Incentives and Economic Solutions in IT Security. In Machine Learning for Computer and Cyber Security: Principle, Algorithms, and Practices. (p. 320). MLCCS.

DDoS Attack Types and Mitigation Methods, Incapsula Inc. (2019). Retrieved from http://www.incapsula.com/ddos/ddos-attacks/. Accessed on Jan 2019.

Dittrich, D. (1999). The DoS project's "trinoo" distributed denial of service attack tool, Retrieved from https://staff.washington.edu/dittrich/misc/trinoo.analysis. Accessed on January, 2019.

Dittrich, D. (1999). The 'Stacheldraht' Distributed Denial of Service Attack Tool. Technical Report. University of Washington, Seattle, WA. Retrieved from https://staff.washington.edu/dittrich/misc/stacheldraht.analysis.txt

Dittrich, D. (1999). The Tribe Flood Network Distributed Denial of Service Attack Tool. Technical Report. University of Washington, Seattle, WA. Retrieved from https://staff.washington.edu/dittrich/misc/tfn.analysis.txt

Dittrich, D., Weaver, G., Dietrich, S., & Long, N. (2000). The 'mstream' distributed Denial of Service Attack Tool. Technical Report. University of Washington, Seattle, WA. Retrieved from https://staff.washington.edu/dittrich/misc/mstream.analysis.txt

Feinstein, L., Schnackenberg, D., Balupari, R., & Kindred, D. (2003, April). Statistical approaches to DDoS attack detection and response. In *Proceedings DARPA information survivability conference and exposition* (Vol. 1, pp. 303-314). IEEE.

Ferguson, P. (2000). Network ingress filtering: Defeating denial of service attacks which employ IP source address spoofing.

Fruhlinger, J. (2018). The Mirai botnet explained: How teen scammers and CCTV cameras almost brought down the internet, CSO Blog [Online]. Available at https://www.csoonline.com/article/3258748/security/the-mirai-botnet-explained-how-teen-scammers-and-cctv-cameras-almost-brought-down-the-internet.html. Accessed on Jan, 2019.

Gavrilis, D., & Dermatas, E. (2005). Real-time detection of distributed denial-of-service attacks using RBF networks and statistical features. *Computer Networks and ISDN Systems*, *48*, 235–245.

Geng, X., Huang, Y., & Whinston, A. B. (2002). Defending wireless infrastructure against the challenge of DDoS attacks. *Mobile Networks and Applications*, *7*(3), 213–223.

Geng, X., & Whinston, A. B. (2000). Defeating distributed denial of service attacks. *IT Professional*, *2*(4), 36–42.

Gil, T. M., & Poletto, M. (2001). MULTOPS: A Data-Structure for Bandwidth Attack Detection. *In Proc. 10th Conf. USENIX Security Symp.*, *Vol. 10*, Berkeley, CA, August 13–17. 3. USENIX.

Glave, J. (1998). Smurfing cripples ISPs, in Wired Technology News [online]. Retrieved from http://www.wired.com/news/news/technology/story/9506.html

Gulihar, P., & Gupta, B. B. (2018, July). Cooperative Mitigation of DDoS Attacks Using an Optimized Auction Scheme on Cache Servers. In *Proceedings International Conference on Advanced Informatics for Computing Research* (pp. 401-412). Springer, Singapore.

Gupta, A., Stahl, D. O., & Whinston, A. B. (1996). Economic issues in electronic commerce. In R. Kalakota, & A. B. Whinston (Eds.), *Readings in Electronic Commerce* (pp. 197–227). MA: Addison Wesley.

Gupta, A., Stahl, D. O., & Whinston, A. B. (1999). The economics of network management. *Communications of the ACM*, *42*(9), 57–57.

Gupta, B. B. (2011). *An Introduction to DDoS Attacks and Defense Mechanisms: An Analyst's Handbook*. Lap Lambert Academic Pub.

Gupta, B. B. (Ed.). (2018). Computer and cyber security: principles, algorithm, applications, and perspectives. Boca Raton, FL: CRC Press.

Gupta, B. B., Joshi, R. C., & Misra, M. (2009). Defending against distributed denial of service attacks: issues and challenges. *Information Security Journal: A Global Perspective 18*(5), 224-247.

Gupta, B. B. (n.d.). An efficient KP design framework of attribute-based searchable encryption for user level revocation in cloud. Concurrency and Computation: Practice and Experience, e5291.

Gupta, B. B., & Ali, S. T. (2019). Dynamic Policy Attribute Based Encryption and its Application in Generic Construction of Multi-Keyword Search. [IJESMA]. *International Journal of E-Services and Mobile Applications*, *11*(4), 16–38.

Gupta, B. B., & Badve, O. P. (2017). Taxonomy of DoS and DDoS attacks and desirable defense mechanism in a cloud computing environment. *Neural Computing & Applications*, *28*(12), 3655–3682.

Gupta, B. B., & Badve, O. P. (2017). GARCH and ANN-based DDoS detection and filtering in cloud computing environment. *International Journal of Embedded Systems*, *9*(5), 391–400.

Gupta, B. B., & Dahiya, A. (n.d.). An Auction Based Incentivized Scheme for DDoS Attacks, *Journal of Information Technology Research (JITR),* IGI Global, (Accepted, In press),

Gupta, B. B., Dharma, P. A., & Yamaguchi, S. (Eds.). (2016). Handbook of Research on Modern Cryptographic Solutions for Computer and Cyber Security. IGI Global.

Gupta, B. B., & Gupta, A. (2018). Assessment of Honeypots: Issues, Challenges and Future Directions. [IJCAC]. *International Journal of Cloud Applications and Computing*, *8*(1), 21–54.

Gupta, B. B., & Harish, S. A. (2019). A Risk-Transfer based DDoS Mitigation Framework for Cloud Environment, *4th International Conference Information, Communication & Computing Technology (ICICCT-2019), Scopus Indexed Springer CCIS Conference Proceeding,* JIMS Rohini, Delhi (Accepted, In Press).

Gupta, B. B., Misra, M., & Joshi, R. C. (2012). An ISP level solution to combat DDoS attacks using combined statistical based approach. *arXiv preprint arXiv:1203.2400*.

Gupta, B. B., & Sheng, Q. Z. (Eds.). (2019). Machine Learning for Computer and Cyber Security: Principle, Algorithms, and Practices. Boca Raton, FL: CRC Press.

HOIC. Sourceforge.net. (2019). Retrieved from http://sourceforge.net/projects/hoic/

Huang, Y., Geng, X., & Whinston, A. B. (2007). Defeating DDoS attacks by fixing the incentive chain. *ACM Transactions on Internet Technology*, *7*(1), 5.

Hwang, K., Dave, P., & Tanachaiwiwat, S. (2003). NetShield: Protocol Anomaly Detection with Datamining Against DDoS Attacks. *Proc. 6th Int. Symp. Recent Advances in Intrusion Detection*, pp. 8–10. Pittsburgh, PA, September 8–10, Springer.

Jalili, R., Imani-Mehr, F., Amini, M., & Shahriari, H. R. (2005). Detection of Distributed Denial of Service Attacks Using Statistical Pre-Processor and Unsupervised Neural Networks. *Proc. Int. Conf. Information Security Practice and Experience*, pp. 192–203. Singapore, April 11–14, Springer.

Jiang, F., Fu, Y., Gupta, B. B., Lou, F., Rho, S., Meng, F., & Tian, Z. (2018). Deep learning based multi-channel intelligent attack detection for data security. *IEEE Transactions on Sustainable Computing*.

John, A., & Sivakumar, T. (2009). Ddos: Survey of traceback methods. *International Journal of Recent Trends in Engineering*, *1*(2), 241.

Kalkan, K., & Alagöz, F. (2016). A distributed filtering mechanism against DDoS attacks: ScoreForCore. *Computer Networks*, *108*, 199–209.

Kang, M. S., Gligor, V. D., & Sekar, V. (2016, February). SPIFFY: Inducing Cost-Detectability Tradeoffs for Persistent Link-Flooding Attacks. In NDSS.

Karimazad, R., & Faraahi, A. (2011). An Anomaly-Based Method for DDoS Attacks Detection Using RBF Neural Networks. *Proc. Int. Conf. Network and Electronics Engineering*, Singapore, pp. 44–48. IACSIT Press.

Kent, S., & Atkinson, R. (1998). RFC 2402: IP authentication header.

Kim, M. S., Kong, H. J., Hong, S. C., Chung, S. H., & Hong, J. W. (2004, April). A flow-based method for abnormal network traffic detection. In *Proceedings 2004 IEEE/IFIP network operations and management symposium* (Vol. 1, pp. 599-612). IEEE.

Kim, Y., Lau, W. C., Chuah, M. C., & Chao, H. J. (2004, March). PacketScore: Statistics-based overload control against distributed denial-of-service attacks. In Proceedings IEEE INFOCOM 2004 (Vol. 4, pp. 2594-2604). IEEE.

King, B. B., & Morda, D. (2001). *CERT Coordination Center, CERT Advisory CA-2001-20 Continuing Threats to Home Users. Technical Report CA-2001-20*. Pittsburgh, PA: Carnegie Mellon Software Engineering Institute; Retrieved from https://seclists.org/cert/2001/14

Kottler, S. (2018). "February 28th DDoS Incident Report" an official report by Github. Link available at https://github.blog/2018-03-01-ddos-incident-report/

Lau, F., Rubin, S. H., Smith, M. H., & Trajkovic, L. (2000). Distributed denial of service attacks. In IEEE International Conference on Systems, Man, and Cybernetics, 2000, vol. 3. pp. 2275–2280. Nashville, TN.

Lee, K., Kim, J., Kwon, K. H., Han, Y., & Kim, S. (2008). DDoS attack detection method using cluster analysis. *Expert Systems with Applications*, *34*, 1659–1665.

Lee, S.-W., & Seo, D. I. (2015). Authentication method and apparatus for detecting and preventing source address spoofing packets. U.S. Patent No. 8,966,609. Feb. 24, 2015.

Li, L., Liu, Y. A., Liu, K. M., & Ming, Y. A. N. G. (2009). Pricing in combinatorial double auction-based grid allocation model. *Journal of China Universities of Posts and Telecommunications*, *16*(3), 59–65.

Limwiwatkul, L., & Rungsawang, A. (2004) Distributed Denial of Service Detection Using TCP/IP Header and Traffic Measurement Analysis. In *Proc. IEEE Int. Symp. Communications and Information Technology*, pp. 605–610. Sapporo, Japan, October 26–29. IEEE CS.

Liu, X., Yang, X., & Lu, Y. (2008, August). To filter or to authorize: Network-layer DoS defense against multimillion-node botnets. ACM. *Computer Communication Review, 38*(4), 195–206.

Liu, Z., Jin, H., Hu, Y. C., & Bailey, M. (2017). Fine-Grained Endpoint-Driven In-Network Traffic Control for Proactive DDoS Attack Mitigation. *arXiv preprint arXiv:1709.05710.*

LOIC. Sourceforge.net. (2019). Retrieved from http://sourceforge.net/projects/loic/

Mahajan, R., Bellovin, S. M., Floyd, S., Ioannidis, J., Paxson, V., & Shenker, S. (2002). Controlling high bandwidth aggregates in the network. *Computer Communication Review, 32*(3), 62–73.

Mananet, Reverse Firewall, Retrieved from http://www.cs3–inc.com/pubs/Reverse FireWall.eps.

Mankins, D., Krishnan, R., Boyd, C., Zao, J., & Frentz, M. (2001, December). Mitigating distributed denial of service attacks with dynamic resource pricing. In *Proceedings Seventeenth Annual Computer Security Applications Conference* (pp. 411-421). IEEE.

Mirkoviac, J., Prier, G., & Reiher, P. (2002) Attacking DDoS at the Source. In *Proc. 10th IEEE Int. Conf. Network Protocols*, pp. 1092–1648. Paris, France, November 12–15, IEEE CS.

Mirkovic, J., Reiher, P., & Robinson, M. (2003, August). Forming alliance for DDoS defense. In *New Security Paradigms Workshop* (pp. 18-21).

Mishra, A., Gupta, B. B., & Joshi, R. C. (2011). A comparative study of distributed denial of service attacks, intrusion tolerance and mitigation techniques. In *Proceedings 2011 European Intelligence and Security Informatics Conference.* (pp. 286-289). IEEE.

Mizrak, A. T., Savage, S., & Marzullo, K. (2008). Detecting compromised routers via packet forwarding behavior. *IEEE Network, 22*(2), 34–39.

Papadopoulos, C., Lindell, R., Mehringer, J., Hussain, A., & Govindan, R. (2003, April). Cossack: Coordinated suppression of simultaneous attacks. In *Proceedings DARPA Information Survivability Conference and Exposition* (Vol. 1, pp. 2-13). IEEE.

Park, K., & Lee, H. (2001, August). On the effectiveness of route-based packet filtering for distributed DoS attack prevention in power-law internets. ACM. *Computer Communication Review, 31*(4), 15–26.

Parno, B., Wendlandt, D., Shi, E., Perrig, A., Maggs, B., & Hu, Y. C. (2007, August). Portcullis: Protecting sconnection setup from denial-of-capability attacks. ACM. *Computer Communication Review, 37*(4), 289–300.

Ping of Death. (2019). Cloudflare blog. Available at https://www.cloudflare.com/learning/ddos/ping-of-death-ddos-attack/. Accessed on Jan 2019.

Puri, R. (2003). Bots & botnet: An overview. *SANS Institute, 3,* 58.

Rahmani, H., Sahli, N., & Kammoun, F. (2009) Joint Entropy Analysis Model for DDoS Attack Detection. In *Proc. 5th Int. Conf. Information Assurance and Security*, Vol. 02, pp. 267–271. Xian, China, August 18–20. IEEE CS.

Ramanathan, S., Mirkovic, J., Yu, M., & Zhang, Y. (2018, December). SENSS Against Volumetric DDoS Attacks. In *Proceedings of the 34th Annual Computer Security Applications Conference* (pp. 266-277). ACM.

Rossow, C. (2014). *Amplification Hell: Revisiting Network Protocols for DDoS Abuse*. NDSS.

Sahoo, S. R., & Gupta, B. B. (2019). Classification of various attacks and their defence mechanism in online social networks: A survey. *Enterprise Information Systems*, *13*(6), 832–864.

Saifullah, A. M. (2009). Defending Against Distributed Denial-of-Service Attacks with Weight-Fair Router Throttling. Technical Report 2009-7. Computer Science and Engineering, Washington University, St. Louis, MO.

Saini, B., & Somani, G. (2014, March). Index page based EDoS attacks in infrastructure cloud. In *International Conference on Security in Computer Networks and Distributed Systems* (pp. 382-395). Berlin, Germany: Springer.

Samimi, P., Teimouri, Y., & Mukhtar, M. (2016). A combinatorial double auction resource allocation model in cloud computing. *Information Sciences*, *357*, 201–216.

Savage, S., Wetherall, D., Karlin, A., & Anderson, T. (2000, August). Practical network support for IP traceback. ACM. *Computer Communication Review*, *30*(4), 295–306.

Seo, D., Lee, H., & Perrig, A. (2011, October). PFS: Probabilistic filter scheduling against distributed denial-of-service attacks. In *Proceedings 2011 IEEE 36th Conference on Local Computer Networks* (pp. 9-17). IEEE.

Seo, D., Lee, H., & Perrig, A. (2013). APFS: Adaptive probabilistic filter scheduling against distributed denial-of-service attacks. *Computers & Security*, *39*, 366–385.

Shamsolmoali, P., & Zareapoor, M. (2014, September). Statistical-based filtering system against DDOS attacks in cloud computing. In *Proceedings 2014 International Conference on Advances in Computing, Communications and Informatics (ICACCI)* (pp. 1234-1239). IEEE.

Sharma, K., & Gupta, B. B. (2018). Taxonomy of distributed denial of service (ddos) attacks and defense mechanisms in present era of smartphone devices. [IJESMA]. *International Journal of E-Services and Mobile Applications*, *10*(2), 58–74.

Shenker, S., Clark, D., Estrin, D., & Herzog, S. (1996). Pricing in computer networks: Reshaping the research agenda. *J. Telecommunications Policy*, *20*(3), 183–201.

Skottler. (2018). February 28 DDoS Incident Report, Github Report. Available at https://githubengineering.com/ddos-incident-report/

Cambiaso, E., Papaleo, G., Chiola, G., & Aiello, M. (2013). Slow DoS attacks: Definition and categorisation. *International Journal Trust Management Computer Communication*, *1(3-4)*, 300–319.

Tewari, A., & Gupta, B. B. (2017). A lightweight mutual authentication protocol based on elliptic curve cryptography for IoT devices. *International Journal of Advanced Intelligence Paradigms*, *9*(2-3), 111–121.

Tewari, A., & Gupta, B. B. (2018). A lightweight mutual authentication approach for RFID tags in IoT devices. *International Journal of Networking and Virtual Organisations*, *18*(2), 97–111.

Thomas, R., Mark, B., Johnson, T., & Croall, J. (2003). NetBouncer: Client-Legitimacy-Based High-Performance DDoS Filtering. Proc. 3rd DARPA Information Survivability Conf. and Exposition, pp. 111–113, Washington, DC, USA, April 22-24. IEEE CS.

Tripathi, S., Gupta, B., Almomani, A., Mishra, A., & Veluru, S. (2013). Hadoop based defense solution to handle distributed denial of service (ddos) attacks. *Journal of Information Security*, *4*(3), 150.

Vissers, T., Somasundaram, T. S., Pieters, L., Govindarajan, K., & Hellinckx, P. (2014). DDoS defense system for web services in a cloud environment. *Future Generation Computer Systems*, *37*, 37–45.

Wang, H., Jin, C., & Shin, K. G. (2007). Defense against spoofed IP traffic using hop-count filtering. *IEEE/ACM Transactions on Networking (ToN)*, *15*(1), 40-53.

Wang, K., Qi, X., Shu, L., Deng, D. J., & Rodrigues, J. J. (2016). Toward trustworthy crowdsourcing in the social internet of things. *IEEE Wireless Communications*, *23*(5), 30–36.

Wang, W., Chen, L., Shin, K. G., & Duan, L. (2014, April). Secure cooperative spectrum sensing and access against intelligent malicious behaviors. In *Proceedings IEEE INFOCOM 2014-IEEE Conference on Computer Communications* (pp. 1267-1275). IEEE.

Weagle, S. (n.d.). New Report Points to Alarming DDoS Attack Statistics and Projections. Available at https://www.corero.com/blog/736-new-report-points-to-alarming-ddos-attack-statistics-and-projections. html. Accessed on Jan, 2019.

XOIC. Sourceforge.net. (2019). Retrieved from http://sourceforge.net/projects/xoic/

Yaar, A., Perrig, A., & Song, D. (2004, May). SIFF: A stateless Internet flow filter to mitigate DDoS flooding attacks. In Proceedings IEEE Symposium on Security and Privacy, 2004. 130–143. IEEE.

Yang, X., Wetherall, D., & Anderson, T. (2005, August). A DoS-limiting network architecture. ACM. *Computer Communication Review*, *35*(4), 241–252.

Yang, X. L. A. L. X., & Wetherall, D. (2008). Passport: Secure and adoptable source authentication.

Yau, D. K., Lui, J. C., Liang, F., & Yam, Y. (2005). Defending against distributed denial-of-service attacks with max-min fair server-centric router throttles. *IEEE/ACM Transactions on Networking*, *13*(1), 29–42.

Zaman, S., & Grosu, D. (2012, June). An online mechanism for dynamic vm provisioning and allocation in clouds. In *Proceedings 2012 IEEE Fifth International Conference on Cloud Computing* (pp. 253-260). IEEE.

Zaman, S., & Grosu, D. (2013). Combinatorial auction-based allocation of virtual machine instances in clouds. *Journal of Parallel and Distributed Computing*, *73*(4), 495–508.

Zargar, S. T., Joshi, J., & Tipper, D. (2013). A survey of defense mechanisms against distributed denial of service (DDoS) flooding attacks. *IEEE Communications Surveys and Tutorials*, *15*(4), 2046–2069.

Zhu, Q., Fung, C., Boutaba, R., & Basar, T. (2012). GUIDEX: A game-theoretic incentive-based mechanism for intrusion detection networks. *IEEE Journal on Selected Areas in Communications*, *30*(11), 2220–2230.

Chapter 11
A Legal Framework for Healthcare:
Personal Data Protection for Health Law in Turkey

Veli Durmuş

https://orcid.org/0000-0001-6124-6109

Marmara University, Turkey

Mert Uydaci

Marmara University, Turkey

ABSTRACT

This chapter provides a holistic general overview of the data protection regime in Turkey. Authors present the principal rights of data protection and transmission in health law and latent ethical concerns by specifying decisions of the Supreme Court in Turkey and the European Court of Human Rights on using personal data. The research describes data protection law for health care setting in Turkey. Primary and secondary data have been used for the study. The primary data includes the information collected with current national and international regulations or law. Secondary data include publications, books, journals, and empirical legal studies. Privacy and data protection regimes in health law show there are some obligations, principles, and procedures which shall be binding upon natural or legal persons who process health-related personal data.

INTRODUCTION

Every patient who needs to get a medical treatment should share health-related personal data with healthcare providers. Therefore, personal health data plays an important role to make health decisions and identify health threats during every encounter between patient and caregivers. In other words, health data can be defined as privacy and sensitive information which is protected by various health laws and

DOI: 10.4018/978-1-7998-2242-4.ch011

Copyright © 2020, IGI Global. Copying or distributing in print or electronic forms without written permission of IGI Global is prohibited.

regulations. In many cases, the data are an outcome of the confidential relationship between patients and their healthcare providers.

Health data usually consist of individual, personal health and other related information. The European Group on Ethics in Science and New Technologies (EGE), in the Opinion No 13 Ethical Issues of Health Care in Information Society defines "health data" as including "a wide range of information about an individual, which all touch upon an individual's private life (OECD, 2015).

Globally, almost all nations have own laws, regulations or rules in order to protect personal health data. Several countries state that difficulties negotiating data sharing arrangements among public authorities. Especially, legal regulations and a lack of interagency co-operation limit data sharing among public authorities in Turkey. In the same way, Norway, which has the strongest health information system with the greatest data availability, do not permit the Ministry of Health to share data with any other legal entity. On the other hand, in Singapore, there are a variety of challenges to negotiating data sharing arrangements with public agencies because of separate legal entities. In the same way, the different authorising legislation of Japan applying at the national level. However, at regional levels and for public corporations set barriers to data sharing arrangements among national authorities and limit data linkages. (OECD, 2015).

BACKGROUND

There is a variety of instruments that allow authorities to use the health data or to set the barriers data sharing across international borders. In Turkey, for example, the protection of personal data depends primarily on the Law on Personal Data Protection (LPDP). This legislation numbered 6698 published at the Official Gazette dated 7 April 2016 has entered into force at the date of its publication. On the other hand, the General Data Protection Regulation (GDPR) was passed in the European Parliament and the European Council on 27 April 2016 as a Regulation on "the Protection of Natural Persons with Regard to the Processing of Personal Data and on the Free Movement of Such Data" (Regulation, 2016/679), after 6698 numbered law in Turkey. Law on Personal Data in Turkey, hence, is largely based on the European Union Data Protection Directive (also known as Directive 95/46/EC) instead of GDPR (Akıncı, 2017, p. 2). GDPR whose provisions became directly applicable in all EU addresses the protection of fundamental rights and freedoms of natural persons and in particular their right to the protection of personal data. Similarly, the LPDP presents set forth obligations, principles, and procedures for the privacy of personal data such as health-related data.

Until very recently, Turkey did not have specific legislation governing the protection of personal data. The situation has changed upon the enactment of the LPDP in 2016. This law has introduced solid principles of data protection in Turkey that are in line with compatible principles of European Union regulations (Republic of Turkey Prime Ministry Investment Support, 2017). In fact, a law on the protection of personal data was a step taken towards harmonizing the Turkish legislation with EU legislation. The LPDP was prepared based on Directive 95/46/EC on data protection. It is very similar to this Directive, however, it is not entirely the same and the differences in this law are deficiencies rather than improvements.

This chapter deals with general aspects of the Personal Data Protection for Health Law in terms of the principal rights of data protection in health law and latent ethical concerns by specifying decisions of Supreme Court in Turkey and the European Court of Human Rights (ECHR). Turkey has been linked to the ECHR by Association Agreement since 1990. And the precedents of the ECHR are also persuasive legal resources in domestic law since the Republic of Turkey duly ratified the Convention for the Protection of Human Rights and Fundamental Freedoms. This study, therefore, not only focus mainly on data protection regulations for health care setting at the national and international level, but it also provides how the protection of personal data for health care is implemented and experienced by health employees in the light of Supreme Court Decisions in Turkey and the ECHR decisions.

The central research question of this literature review is: *What is the position of Turkey's data protection and legal functions for health data privacy with court decisions?* In addition to practical implications, the present study also contributed to existing literature by identifying important characteristics of health data privacy that should be considered in early stages of the lawmaking process. Moreover, this study added to existing holistic view of data protection scheme by highlighting the ECHR decisions.

LEGAL FRAMEWORK FOR HEALTHCARE IN TURKEY

The Ministry of Health (MOH) is the largest provider of healthcare and the only public provider of preventive services in Turkey. At a national level, MOH is responsible for the country's health policy and health services. MOH has been implementing its Health Transformation Program (HTP) with the goal of realizing universal health coverage since 2003 through the General Health Insurance (GHI) program, which is now administered by the Social Security Institution (SSI) (Atun et al., 2013, pp.65-99). Before the introduction of the HTP, five health insurance schemes existed in Turkey (the Social Insurance Organization, the Government Employees Retirement Fund, Bağ-Kur, the Active Civil Servants Insurance Fund, and the Green Card scheme). In 2006, the Grand Assembly ratified the Social Insurance and the GHI to bring the five existing health insurance schemes under one frame (Tatar et al., 2011). Finally, all social security and health insurance schemes transferred to the newly established SSI. Now, the GHI provides a comprehensive benefits package in healthcare with reimbursement for a range of preventive, diagnostic, and curative services (Atun et al., 2013, pp.65-99). All these developments in the Turkish health system contribute to the progress of legalization in the health law in order to improve the governance of health service delivery and to create an effective legal framework.

The legal framework for healthcare offers a legal protection in achieving the objectives of the health and safety policy such as establishing service access rights, regulating service quality and safety and giving legal recognition to patient health rights. Law and regulation are crucial implementation tools for translating health plans and strategy into action through the setting of standards, requirements and the use of sanctions. Many countries, hence, have health and safety regulations to improve the community health and provide additional protections on fundamental rights for health care. However, health law and policy are constantly changing.

The Supreme Court in Turkey is one of the policy-making body for health legislation as well as Ministry of Health, The Turkish Grand National Assembly that is the highest policy-making authority for all sectors, including health field. The MOH is the most significant actor in health care policy-making, both as the leader of the majority of policy initiatives and as the major agency involved in implementation (Tatar et al., 2011). On the other hand, the Supreme Court has an important role in health policy-making because the court has the power to cancel many health-based regulations, hindering the implementation of policies. In the Turkish legal system, the Supreme Court is authorized to suspend any law that is considered to infringe legal and constitutional rights related to health.

As the highest legislative authority in Turkey, article 56 of the 1982 Constitution established a legal framework to guarantee that everyone leads a healthy life physically and mentally. The third para of article 56 explicitly states that *"The State shall regulate central planning and functioning of the health services to ensure that everyone leads a healthy life physically and mentally, and provide cooperation by saving and increasing productivity in human and material resources."* And, the Constitutional Amendments of 2010, which introduced individual applications to the Constitutional Court in cases of violation of the fundamental rights and freedoms under the Constitution or the ECHR, provides fundamental personal data protection rights, including health data, and legal requirements. Article 148/3 of the Constitution set forth that: *"Everyone may apply to the Constitutional Court on the grounds that one of the fundamental rights and freedoms within the scope of the European Convention on Human Rights which are guaranteed by the Constitution has been violated by public authorities. In order to make an application, ordinary legal remedies must be exhausted"*. In addition, Turkish Constitution contains a right to data privacy in para 3 of Article 20, which added by amendment of 2010, stating that *"Everyone has the right to request the protection of his/her personal data. This right includes being informed of, having access to and requesting the correction and deletion of his/her personal data, and to be informed whether these are used in consistency with envisaged objectives. Personal data can be processed only in cases envisaged by law or by the person's explicit consent. The principles and procedures regarding the protection of personal data shall be laid down in law."*

Health Data: Benefits, Risks, And Barriers

Healthcare is a very complex, knowledge-driven industry that created massive amounts of clinical and financial data. Hence, the health sector experiencing great transformations with the effort to reduce costs and improve the care quality and efficiency of healthcare services (Wu et al., 2016). This health industry produces enormous variety in the type of the collected data. Over time, as the delivery of health care has changed and technology has advanced, the number of individuals and organizations accessing health data has greatly expanded.

The term of health-related data is defined as "health-related data, including health history, symptoms, biometric data, treatment history, lifestyle choices, and other information, created, recorded, gathered, or inferred by or from patients or their designees to help address a health concern." (Shapiro et al., 2012). The continuous growth of health data includes not only regular examinations, medical tests, hospitalizations, and traditional interviews in a hospital, but it involves data that people collect using a wide variety of health and wellbeing apps (Roesems-Kerremans, 2016). Processing and analysis of this health data can help to identify cure and prevention of diseases, besides improving patient safety and quality of life.

Health data allows researchers to get a more complete picture of the disparate factors that contribute to the physical and mental health of a population. Moreover, by enabling researchers to access larger samples, population-wide health and health-related data enable the study of rare events such as rare diseases or rare adverse reactions to treatments (Jutte et al., 2013). Literature also highlights wider potential benefits span contributions to: health policy, health systems planning and strategy for resource allocation; drug payment and reimbursement mechanisms (Sonja et al., 2018; Couillard et al. 2015).

During the digitalization of critical health data, electronic health records became one of the hot topics in medical informatics. In addition, the proliferation of new monitoring and health-care instruments have led to dramatic growth in individual-level data on factors that affect individual health, social well-being, and the provision of health care.

Although routinely collected health data has been used for health research and system innovation for decades, the rapidly expanding scope of electronic data provides new opportunities. These data enable the study of serious diseases, comparison of incidence rate or measure of overall potential factors on well-being. Research using these data can improve health outcomes and patient safety, better inform a range of health and social policies, enable beneficial innovations, reduce health-care practices of little or no benefit, and slow the growth in health-care costs (Ross et al., 2008; Lewis, 2011). Health data can also enhance the quality of research and innovation processes. Real-world data from pragmatic trials, for example, can increase confidence in study results given that sample populations may be more representative of actual practice (Sonja et al., 2018).

Beside benefits of accessing health data, in allowing the use of these data, one risk is that private information will be revealed. Although the health data benefits both the patient and the physician in providing advanced and well-analyzed treatment, there are four main risks of using health data (Council of Europe, 2015, pp. 4-27), First, it is a possibility that the data accidentally release if data handling procedures are not appropriate. Health data, for example, can be stolen by mobile devices such as laptops and USB (Universal Serial Bus) keys. Second, illegal access to databases leads to misuse by intruders such as the hacking of healthcare database. Third, inadvertent access can cause to recognize someone's private data. For example, an employee of the data custodian doing statistical analysis on a data set could inadvertently recognize a neighbor or relative in the database. Finally, anonymized data (de-identification) that prevents individual identities from being revealed in the information provided to the external researcher. If anonymization is done poorly, the data could still contain sufficient information that individuals could be identified and their sensitive information revealed.

Governance mechanisms require continual and periodically reviewed at international and national level to maximise benefits (beter care, greater value, more knowledge) and minimise privacy risks. Otherwise, a wide variety of health data such as images, biometric data, structured financial and administrative reports in health can create a dynamic environment where risks and benefits continuously evolve.

Turkey restricts non-profit and university-based researchers from access to the majority of national de-identified health micro datasets (OECD, 2015). In addition, duly processed data must be deleted or anonymized if and when the processing is no longer needed. Anonymization is the process of taking out all personally identifiable data so that the data cannot be associated with any specific or identifiable person. Data is deleted or anonymized by the data controller *ex officio* or upon request by the data subject. The LPDP does not provide the details of the request process.

Barriers to accessing health data is another factor to get into account during health data process. Many potential and real barriers to accessing of health data have been recognized such as privacy issues or legal constraints. A study identified and classified these barriers in six categories: technical, motivational, economic, political, legal and ethical (Panhuis et al., 2014). The most common technical barriers include problems with failure to collect data, poor data preservation, incompatible data format with modern software systems, lack of technical solutions to share complex and heterogeneous data. Motivational barriers, on the other hand, consider personal or institutional motivations and beliefs that limit data sharing. Economic barriers concern the cost of data accessing and sharing mechanisms. Because all these require human and technical resources under economic pressure or in low income settings. Political barriers are absence of non-restrictive policy guidelines, resulting from various possible underlying factors such as a general sense of distrust, negative prior experiences (Keller et al., 2009). Legal instruments are often responsible for the restrictive policies on all types of health data due to privacy concerns. Finally, ethical

Table 1. Benefits, risks, and barriers of health data

Benefits	Risks	Barriers
More knowledge and larger samples for researchers.	Possibility for leak of personal health data	Technically, dealing with a difficult situation can be insufficent.
Enable the big picture for studying of rare events and serious diseases in health care.	Insufficcent security for data leads to misuse.	Technically, dealing with a difficult situation can be insufficent.
Contribute to health planning and policy.	Accidental access to health information can reveal someone's private data.	Strict regulations may discourage the using of health data.
Monitorize to individual health and social well-being.	Poor anonymization can lead to sensitive information revealed.	Absence of effective policy guideliness.
Improve the quality of research and innovation processes.	Bigger health data, greater responsibilities, technically, socially and structurally.	Ethical values are considered as a sensitive item to debate for some time.

barriers which are normative barriers include moral principles and values, with vast amounts of personal health data widely accessible electronically by employers, insurers, and the government.

While some barriers can affect timely access to available data, others can limit potential or interest to use data to generate research and innovation. Cost, for example, is a factor in enabling access to data. Adequate and stable funding is needed to set up a sound infrastructure, attract and retain skilled staff members, and support the continued success of an organization (Marchessault, 2011). In addition, The access process may be unclear for researchers, and they may lack the skills or time to determine how they should proceed (Academy of Medical Sciences, 2006). Benefits, risks, and barriers to personal health data are outlined briefly in Table 1.

According to the OECD (Organization for Economic Cooperation and Development) report regarding data assets and how they are governed, a set of key data accessibility factors that are directly linked to legislative frameworks and their interpretation in practice were asked to Turkey. These factors include whether or not identifiable national personal health data are ever shared among data custodians or government entities and whether personal health data, after de-identification, can be approved for access by applicants from different sectors of society and by foreign applicants. Findings show that Turkey is one of the countries which with the lowest sharing and accessibility of health data (OECD, 2015).

The Value and Importance of Personal Health Data Privacy

Although there are a variety of definitions of the term "privacy" (Terry & Francis, 2007; Moore, 2005; Nissenbaum, 2004) it addresses the ability of an individual to prevent certain disclosures of personal health information to any other person or entity in the context of personal health data (Rothstein, 2007). In the field of health information, the concept of privacy often encompasses not only confidentially but also the security of information, thus safeguarding informational autonomy. Furthermore, it is generally concerned with the collection, storage, and usage of personal health information that identifies a particular individual who receiving health care services. Even though security is essential for protecting personal health data, it's a lack of addressing privacy issues. As a result, health data privacy actually aims to protect an organization's or individual's health-related personal data from critical risk resulting from the processing of their data. Table 2 focuses on additional difference between security and privacy.

Table 2. Differentation between security and privacy in terms of health data

Security	Privacy
Security is the "confidentiality, integrity and availability" of data	Privacy is the appropriate use of user's information
Various techniques like Encryption, Firewall, etc. are used in order to prevent data compromise from technology or vulnerabilities in the network of an organization	The organization can't sell its patient/user's information to a third party without prior consent of the user
It may provide for confidentiality or protect an enterprise or agency	It concerns with patient's right to safeguard their information from any other parties
Security offers the ability to be confident that decisions are respected	Privacy is the ability to decide what information of an individual goes and where to

Source: Abouelmehdi et al., 2018.

There are many significant reasons for placing a high value on protecting the privacy of health data. While some authors believe that privacy is valuable and essential in terms of human well-being and moral values (Moore, 2005; Terry & Francis, 2007), the common view is that it encourages some fundamental values such as individuality, respect to personality, dignity (Solove, 2006; Post, 2001) and autonomy. Protecting the privacy of this health information is important because every health data requires storage after the collection, and use of large amounts of personally identifiable health information, which may be sensitive. Furthermore, the collection and use of personal health data present a number of important risks to the privacy of patients. These risks relate to the potential harms (e.g. stigmatization in case of HIV/AIDS or discrimination due to the ethnicity of patients or medical finance status when accessing to personal data) to patients that could result from the misuses of their personal health information. Another one is also the risk of loss of public confidence in government and its public institutions that could result from misuses of patients' health records and a loss of confidence in the national health care system (OECD, 2013).

The increased use of computerized documentation results in faster and wider distribution of information with an increased risk of unauthorized access (Blightman et al., 2013). Medical records, for example, can contain some exclusive details about a person's life, the most sensitive information that people want protected. In addition, medical documents can include some details on a patient's social status, personal relationship, and financial revenues (Klosek, 2011). All these information create responsibilities for health providers and healthcare institutions when respecting patients' privacy and autonomy are inappropriately ignored. In fact, the degree to which a physician has an ethical and legal responsibility to address inappropriate disclosure depends in part on his or her awareness of the breach, relationship to the patient affected, the administrative authority in respect of the medical documentation, and authority to act on behalf of the practice or institution.

One of the importance of health data privacy is to promote more effective communication between physician and patient, which is necessary for the quality of health care. Because confidentiality is central to the preservation of trust between doctors and their patients, failure to maintain this obligation may result in suboptimal treatment (Blightman et al., 2013). Ensuring privacy can promote more effective communication between physician and patient, which is necessary for quality of care. Without privacy, patients may be reluctant to candidly and completely disclose sensitive information about their medical status. It can also help to support social-based health research activities, that is clinical trials and epidemiological studies evaluating diseases of public health importance including malaria, HIV and global emerging infectious diseases. People are more likely to participate in and support research if they believe their privacy is being protected (Institute of Medicine, 2009). Ensuring privacy, hence, is also seen as enhancing data quality for research and quality improvement initiatives (Goldman, 1998).

Advances in health information technology today are changing rapidly and becoming more complex. This is enabling each country has its own data protection rules that prohibit the disclosure or misuse of information. Hence, no single legislative framework concerning the protection of privacy can ensure the safety of data across the world. In Turkey, for example, patient privacy issues are addressed with a patient right under the regulations such as statutes, directives, rules. On the other hand, Medical Statute of Deontology includes patient rights, clarification of diagnosis and treatment, confidentiality, withdrawal of the doctor from patient treatment as well as the privacy of patients' issues. Another legal framework for patient rights is The Patient Rights Directive (1998), covers utilizing health services according to the principles of justice and equity, right to request information, right to choose and change the medical facility, right to know, choose and change the personnel, right to request determination of priority, right to request being diagnosed, treated and cared appropriate to medical reasons, refuse interventions that are not related to medical necessities, right to receive medical attention, right to receive general information, right to examine records, right to request record correction, right of privacy.

The advancements in medical technology have resulted in an enormous increase in the amount and complexity of medical data that are being collected. These technologies, however, are offering a wide variety of opportunities to collect, use and share health data more efficiently in order to empower patients in managing their diseases and to improve the quality, safety, and efficiency of healthcare systems. Medical images and biomedical signals, for example, allow the collection of large amounts of complex data. All these types of data contain confidential or sensitive information about patients and need to be privacy-protected.

Besides medical technology, clinical information systems in hospitals, such as web-based electronic health record systems, tools for personal health monitoring, and physician order entry systems, have already adopted in many aspects of the healthcare industry. These systems also contain sensitive information that must be managed in a privacy-preserving way. In order to achieve this, specific legal regulations for health data privacy, such as the RPHD (Regulation on Processing and Ensuring Privacy of Personal Health Data) and the LPDP, are an important step in relation to efforts aimed at further improving the implementation of health data privacy and protection procedures in Turkey. In fact, these legal frameworks set the privacy rules and specify the responsibilities of organizations regarding the protection of personal health data.

Legal Instruments for Health Data Privacy

Although the Turkish Constitution of 1982 included one privacy-related para of article 20 on the right to request the protection of personal data in 2010, some other nations in the European Union met data privacy laws have been enacted in 1990's since 1970 of the global diffusion of data privacy laws (Custers et al., 2019; Greenleaf, 2018). In 1999, for example, the protection of personal data is laid out in a constitutional provision in the Finnish Constitution (Ojenan, 2017). On the other hand, a general privacy right was included in the revised Belgian Constitution of 1994 with article 22 (De Hert, 2017). In 1990, a new Federal Data Protection Act incorporated into the German Constitution (Custers et al., 2019; Eichenhofer & Gusy, 2017).

Unlike the Turkish Constitution of 1982, the LPDP represents the most comprehensive and influential legislative framework regarding the protection of personal data. In other words, the LPDP is the key legislation in Turkey. However, the RPHD, which is a secondary legislation of the LPDP, has been enacted by the Ministry of Health on 20 October 2016 by introducing substantial liabilities upon sector-specific entities such as those engaged in commercial activities in health, insurance, and health tourism sectors. This regulation is not only applicable to the health institutions and the data subjects whose personal data is processed but also covers natural persons and legal entities who process health data within the scope of a legislation. Therefore, institutions and organizations processing of personal health data for some reasons such as employment procedures, periodic inspection or due to obligations arising from social security legislation will be subject to the provisions of the RPHD. As a result, the provisions of this regulation shall apply to natural persons whose personal health data are processed as well as to natural or legal persons who process such data in order to provide the health service.

According to the Circular of Ministry of Health in Turkey (2016), based on field research shows that maintaining compliance with privacy principles is not enough to keep patient privacy especially in intensive care unit, clinical examination, and medical treatment, surgical procedures. In this regard, it is essential to have certain health data protection that inspects compliance with the LPDP. The main purpose of the RPHD is to set out the procedures and principles to protect personal health data and to ensure its privacy, to regulate the provisions regarding the system which will be established to collect, process, transfer the personal health data and to access to such data and regarding the security and supervision of the systems (Article 1).

Unlike the LPDP, the RPHD primarily concerns the health service providers and health data processors that operate in the health sector in general, rather than the institutions and organizations that have access to any type of personal data due to their operations. On the other hand, the sanctions of the RPHD refer to provisions of the LPDP such as imprisonment, administrative fine. For example, article 17 states that Turkish Penal Code No. 5237 shall apply in terms of the crimes concerning personal data. Those who fail to erase or anonymize personal data shall be punished under the Turkish Penal Code. The article 18, on the other hand, says those who fail to comply with an obligation to inform, obligations related to data security, the decisions issued by the Board shall be required to pay an administrative fine. Furthermore, the LPDP and the Turkish Penal Code impose custodial sentences for the unlawful processing of data. The Turkish Civil Law grants the right to claim compensation for the unjust use of data and a number of other sector specific laws impose administrative fines. The LPDP, for example, clearly introduces administrative fines up to TRY (Turkish Liras) 1.000.000 (approximately €155.000, according to the exchange rate on October 2018 in Turkey) for those who fail to comply with an obligation to inform, obligations related to data security, the decisions issued by the Personal Data Protection Board.

The RPHD, the Personal Data Protection Board and the Turkish Medical Association (TMA) provide both legal framework and ethical guidance about medical confidentiality for health professionals who are actively involved in the health services. The TMA, which is the professional association and registered trade union for doctors in Turkey, might also initiate disciplinary action against the physicians in case of medical privacy breach (Law on The Turkish Medical Association, 1953). Although civil claims in medical negligence have occurred and damages awarded when confidence has been breached by revealing medical information concerning the patients' treatment without explicit consent (Individual Application to the Constitutional Court of the Republic of Turkey, Decision number 2014/14189), there has been no criminal conviction of a doctor for breach of confidence until now in Turkey. However, there is a supreme court decision of the General Board of Penalty concerning illegal accessing and obtaining patients' health data (E.2012/12-1584, K:2014/312). According to this court decision, a health employee who has violated a Turkish Penal Code of article 136 (Any person who illegally obtains, disseminates or gives to another person someone's personal data shall be sentenced to a penalty of imprisonment for a term of two to four years), in the hospital illegally obtains another person's medical report to give an evidence in court.

Court Decisions on Health Data

The protection of personal data, including medical information, is a fundamental feature of the right to respect for private life. Health data are considered sensitive by both the GDPR and the RPHD for Turkey, are subject to stricter rules of processing. Respecting the confidentiality of health data is crucial not only for the protection of a patient's privacy but also for the maintenance of that person's confidence in the medical profession and in the health services in general. Without such protection, those in need of medical assistance may be deterred from seeking appropriate treatment, thereby endangering their own health (Council of Canadian Academies, 2015, pp. 55-65). The actual protection, on the other hand, does not only depend on the legal implementation but also the ways in which it is enforced by courts.

There is a decision about particular health data collection in the ECHR. The main subject of judgment is the applicant alleged in particular that the collection of her personal medical data by a state agency in Latvia without her consent. The court emphasized that the importance of the protection of medical data to a person's enjoyment of the right to respect for private life. As a result, the court held in 2014 that there had been a violation of Article 8 of the Convention in the applicant's case (Case No. 52019/07 – L.H. v. Latvia, Judgment of 29 April 2014).

In Finland, once a decision has been taken, the applicant's HIV infection data was shared with the national court during the proceeding of ex-husband convicted of manslaughter as an evidence despite her disapproval. The applicant's medical data had become part of the criminal proceedings against her ex-husband without her consent. As a result, the European Court of Human Rights found that a violation of Article 8 of the Convention (Case-law No.22009/93, Z. v. Finland, 25 February 1997). In an Australian High Court case (Case-law No. 186 CLR 71, Breen v. Williams, 6 September 1996), on the other hand, it was held that medical records remain the property of the healthcare professionals (Case-law No. 2 SCR 138., McInerney v. MacDonald, 11 June 1992), and patients have no right of access to their medical records. In some jurisdictions such as New Zealand, United Kingdom, United States, legislations have been enacted to allow patients the right of access to their medical records under certain conditions.

Under the Directive 95/46/EC principles, according to the European Court of Justice (Case C-101/01 – Bodil Lindqvist, 6 November 2003), the notion of "data concerning health" must be considered a broad interpretation to include information concerning all aspects (both physical and mental) of an individual's health (Costa et al., 2017).

General Assembly of the Supreme Court in Turkey has held that personal data is not required to be confidential (Decision dated, 17.06.2014, E.2012/12-510, K.2014/331). With this decision, the Supreme Court distinguishes between the concepts of privacy and confidentially. Because confidentially refers to the duties and practices of people and organizations to ensure that individuals' personal information. However, privacy broadly encompasses the protection of one's physical self, protection of one's private physical space, and protection of information about oneself and one's activities. Therefore, privacy law to determine whether privacy is respected.

The LPDP numbered 6698 authorizes the Personal Data Protection Board to make the necessary examination in the matters falling within its scope of work upon complaint or ex officio, where it learned about the alleged violation. The primary duties and powers of the Board are to ensure that the personal data are processed in compliance with fundamental rights and freedoms and to determine the adequate measures which are necessary for the processing of the data of special nature. In addition, the board can examine whether the personal data are processed in compliance with the laws, upon complaint, or *ex officio* where it learned about the alleged violation, and to take temporary measures, if necessary (Article 20-22).

The Board announced a decision (dated 21.12.2017 and numbered 2017/62) at the beginning of 2018 that healthcare service providers must ensure that they have taken all technical and administrative measures to prevent presence of unauthorized persons at the tables, gates or benches and to prevent the recipients of services hearing, seeing, learning or reaching out each other's data. In Turkey, however, vast majority private and public health organizations provide a service that ensures personal data (i.e. patient's name and ID number) to call the patient. During a routine medical examination, for example, the patient's full name/ID number is displayed on the overhead patient call screen in the waiting room in most healthcare institutions. Apparently, this practice does not protect a patient's privacy. In this respect, according to the Board's decision, hospital or other healthcare institutions are obliged to take all necessary technical and administrative measures to provide a sufficient level of patient privacy. This practice, however, does not effectively and efficiently performing in most health services. The Board held that those who do not comply with the decision will be subject to administrative fines as per the Law.

The Implementation of National Electronic Health Record System

Electronic Health Record (EHR) systems in a country enable patients to have an electronic record of their key characteristics and health concerns, as well as their history of encounters with the health care system and the treatments that they received from a variety of healthcare providers. The goals of such systems include not only improving the quality and safety of care for patients but also facilitating optimal care pathways and promoting efficiency in the use of health system resources (OECD, 2013). Furthermore, these systems are also considered as a tool for reducing the rate of medical error, improving quality, preventing adverse health outcomes from inappropriate treatment combinations, managing the huge volume of clinical, administrative, and regulatory information in contemporary health care (Farsi & West, 2006; Koontz, 2017).

Turkey's National Health Information System (NHIS) initiative has started with the launch of the Health Transformation Programme (HTP) in 2003 in order to provide a nation-wide infrastructure for easy and efficient sharing of electronic health records. EHR is primarily aimed at improving the safety and quality of care, enhancing the accuracy of data, and reducing the huge cost of healthcare services in Turkey. Since 2003, Ministry of Health of Turkey has established some health data information systems such as national health digital dictionary, decision support systems, Health-NET, health insurance integration, electronic health records and also digital security systems e-signature (Ministry of Health Turkey, Department of Health Informatics, 2016). Health-NET, for example, is an integrated and expandable information system which aims to improve the efficiency and quality of healthcare services. Health-NET uses patient data collected from various healthcare system stakeholders, and MOH determines policies related to public health (Country Case Study, 2016).

To be useful for the assessment of the quality of care, health and medical data collections need to be organized in a systematic and efficient way (OECD, 2013). At the same time, the confidentiality of the data needs to be protected and privacy rights addressed. In order to use of data to monitor and describe pathways of care and health care outcomes to enable health care quality and health system performance monitoring and research, the circular of " E-Pulse" enacted by the Ministry of Health of Turkey in 2015. Regarding with processing of personal health data, MOH put into practice a new information system that called "E-Pulse", which is a personal health record system that Turkish Ministry of Health integrated all the information systems of all health institutions. Thanks to e-Pulse, people can access their lab results, medical images, prescription and medication details, emergency information, diagnosis details, reports and health records that contain all the details concerning the examinations via desktop and mobile platforms. People can also share their medical records with their doctor(s) and relatives within specific regulations. Furthermore, this online system provides the opportunity for the national citizens to reach their personal health data with their own e-signature. This personal health record system, however, has been criticized by decision and policy makers in many ways such as protection of privacy, ensuring the safety of health data, the consent with respect to the processing of personal health data issues. All these criticism subjects needed to be discussed under the national and international regulations. On the other hand, the OECD has been surveying some countries, including Turkey, about their health information assets and the use of these assets for statistics and research since 2011. As a result, Turkey was found one of the most limited health information systems in the OECD Report of 2015.

CONCLUSION

Some suggest that the right to control future use of health information is part of privacy protection, while others believe it is part of personal autonomy (Pritts, 2008). Regardless of the nature of the interest, approaches to this right to control vary from more restrictive to more flexible. A very restrictive view is that people should provide consent for every specific future use of data for which they did not originally give their explicit informed consent. A more flexible view is that autonomy is respected when data are used for research related purposes in line with the type of research for which people originally provided consent.

The personal health data protection has become crucial, especially in the context of patient confidentiality and the privacy of information. Medical information is one of the most sensitive personal data. Patients share information related to their disease to receive a better treatment. Because there is a large amount of health data flowing through the health care systems, the issues of privacy and data protection are not trivial nor easy to implement or enforce.

The protection of personal data, particularly health data, is of fundamental importance to a person's enjoyment of his or her right to respect for private and family life as well as patient confidentiality and the privacy of information. Respecting the confidentiality of health data is a vital principle in the Turkish legal system. However, the implementation of the data protection legislation, especially health data privacy, into national regulations are very new and transparency on personal data processing practices is low. Although the protection of personal health data is harmonized within the EU by Directive 95/46/EC, many differences still exist in the actual protection of personal data in practice.

It is very important to regularly review the relevant policy to make sure it is still compatible with the practices of the workplace and the data it maintains and processes in Turkey. The research results in this chapter offer a legal framework for health data privacy and protection for policymakers, legislators, and data protection authorities in Turkey to learn from experiences, practices, court decisions. It shows that although the protection of personal data law is fairly new, the data protection board practices systematically give shape the form of data protection including health data privacy in Turkey. Hence, the introduction of the LPDP and RPHD is an important step for Turkey as a starting point for future improvement and experiences in the health data practices.

FUTURE RESEARCH DIRECTIONS

Data are essential to improving health care and health system performance. As a primary legislation, the LPDP predominantly determine the legal framework for the obligations of individuals whose health data are collected and processed. Furthermore, implementation and interpretation of the legislation and court decisions provide a framework for the actual protection of health data. Therefore, legal implementation of the data protection regime in Turkey should be compared with different developed countries, especially EU member states, for future study. Because this comparative approach can show some remarkable findings for Turkey to strengthen and improve health data privacy and protection practices.

This research received no specific grant from any funding agency in the public, commercial, or not-for-profit sectors.

REFERENCES

Abouelmehdi, K., Beni-Hassane, A., & Khaloufi, H. (2018). Big healthcare data: Preserving security and privacy. *Journal of Big Data*, 5(1), 1–18. doi:10.118640537-017-0110-7

Academy of Medical Sciences (AMS). (2006). *Personal Data for Public Good: Using Health Information in Medical Research*. London, UK: AMS.

Akıncı, A. N. (2017). Avrupa Birliği Genel Veri Koruma Tüzüğü'nün Getirdiği Yenilikler ve Türk Hukuku Bakımından Değerlendirilmesi [*Evaluation of General Data Protection Regulation in the aspect of Turkish Law and Regulations*]. Paperwork Number-6, Kalkınma Bakanlığı, Yayın No: 2968.

Atun, R., Aydin, S., Chakraborty, S., Sümer, S., Aran, M., Gürol, I., ... Akdağ, R. (2013). Universal Health Coverage in Turkey: Enhancement of Equity. *Lancet*, 382(9886), 65–99. doi:10.1016/S0140-6736(13)61051-X PMID:23810020

Blightman, K., Griffiths, S. E., & Danbury, C. (2013). Patient confidentially: When can a breach be justified? *Continuing Education in Anaesthesia, Critical Care & Pain*, 14(2), 52–55. doi:10.1093/bjaceaccp/mkt032

Costa, A., Yelshyna, A., Moriera, T. C., Andrade, F., Julian, V., & Novais, P. (2017). A legal framework for an elderly healthcare platform: A privacy and data protection overview. *Computer Law & Security Review*, 33(5), 647–658. doi:10.1016/j.clsr.2017.03.021

Couillard, G., Denefle, P., Gissot, C., Grossin, B., Guépratte, C., Hilali, I., Lamarsalle, L., London, T., Manaud, N., Olivier, P., Prados, P., Sclison, S., Szwarcensztein, K., & Umhoefer, C. (2015, November). *Unlocking the Full Potential of Data Analytics for the Benefit of All*. Paris, France: Healthcare Data Institute.

Council of Canadian Academies. (2015, May). *Accessing health and health-related data in Canada. The expert panel on timely access to health and social data for health research and health system innovation*. IHE Innovation Forum, Edmonton, Canada.

Council of Europe. (2015, June). *Health-related issues in the case-law of the European Court of Human Rights*. Thematic Report. Retrieved from https://www.echr.coe.int/Documents/Research_report_health.pdf

Country Case Study: Turkey. (2016). *Top Markets Report Health IT Country Case Study*. International Trade Administration, United States of America. Retrieved from https://www.trade.gov/topmarkets/pdf/Health_IT_Turkey.pdf

Custer, B., Sears, A., Dechesne, F., Georgieva, I., Tani, T., & Hof, S. (2019). *EU Personal Data Protection in Policy and Practice*. Springer, Asser Press. doi:10.1007/978-94-6265-282-8

De Hert, P. (2017). Courts, privacy and data protection in Belgium: Fundamental rights that might as well be struck from the Constitution. In M. Brkan, & E. Psychogiopoulou (Eds.), Courts, Privacy and Data Protection in the Digital Environment. Edward Elgar Publishing. doi:10.4337/9781784718718.00011

Eichhenhofer, J., & Gusy, C. (2017). Courts, privacy and data protection in Germany: Informational self-determination in the digital environment. In M. Brkan, & E. Psychogiopoulou (Eds.), Courts, Privacy and Data Protection in the Digital Environment. Edward Elgar Publishing. doi:10.4337/9781784718718.00013

European Court of Human Rights. (1997). The Court's case-law No.22009/93, Z. v. Finland, February 25, 1997, Available at https://hudoc.echr.coe.int/eng#%22itemid%22:[%22002-9432%22]

European Court of Justice. (2003). Judgment of November 6, 2003, Case C-101/01 – Bodil Lindqvist, 50 and 51.

European Court of Justice. (2014), Judgment of April 29, 2014, Case No. 52019/07 – L.H. v. Latvia.

European Union. (2016). Regulation (EU) 2016/679 of the European Parliament and of the Council of 27 April 2016 on the Protection of Natural Persons with Regard to the Processing of Personal Data and on the Free Movement of Such Data, and Repealing Directive 95/46, *Official Journal of the European Union*. Retrieved from http://eurlex.europa.eu/legal-content/EN/TXT/PDF/?uri=CELEX:32016R0679

Farsi, A. L., & West, D. J. Jr. (2006). Use of electronic medical records in Oman and physician satisfaction. *Journal of Medical Systems, 30*(1), 17–22. doi:10.100710916-006-7399-7 PMID:16548410

Goldman, J. (1998). Protecting privacy to improve health care. *Journal of Health Affairs, 17*(6), 47–60.

Greenleaf, G. (2018, May). *Global Convergence of Data Privacy Standards and Laws: Speaking Notes for the European Commission Events on the Launch of the General Data Protection Regulation (GDPR)*. Brussels & New Delhi, May 25, 2018. University of New South Wales Law Research Paper No. 18-56.

High Court of Australia. (1992). The Court's case-law No. 2 SCR 138., Mclnerney v. MacDonald, June 11, 1992, Available at https://scc-csc.lexum.com/scc-csc/scc-csc/en/item/884/index.do

High Court of Australia. (1996). The Court's case-law No. 186 CLR 71, Breen v. Williams, September 6, 1996, Available at http://www.julieclarke.info/publications/1998breen.pdf

Institute of Medicine. (2009). *Beyond the HIPAA Privacy Rule: Enhancing Privacy, Improving Health Through Research*. Washington, DC: The National Academies Press.

Jutte, D. P., Roos, L. L., & Brownell, M. D. (2011). Administrative record linkage as a tool for public health research. *Annual Review of Public Health, 32*(1), 91–108. doi:10.1146/annurev-publhealth-031210-100700 PMID:21219160

Keller, M., Blench, M., Tolentino, H., Freifeld, C. C., Mandl, K. D., Mawudeku, A., ... Brownstein, J. S. (2009). Use of unstructured event-based reports for global infectious disease surveillance. *Emerging Infectious Diseases, 15*(5), 689–695. doi:10.3201/eid1505.081114 PMID:19402953

Klosek, J. (2011). *Protecting your health privacy: A citizen's guide to safeguarding the security of your medical information*. Santa Barbara, CA: Praeger.

Koontz, L. (2017). What is Privacy? In Information Privacy in the Evolving Healthcare Environment (Second Edition). Boca Raton, FL: CRC Press.

Law on Ratification of the Convention for the Protection of Human Rights and Fundamental Freedoms and the Additional Protocol. (1950), (ECHR), adopted by law [6366, 10 March 1954] OJ 8662, 19 March 1954. Retrieved from http://www.coe.int/en/web/conventions/search-on-treaties/-/conventions/chartSignature/3

Law on The Turkish Medical Association of 1953. Retrieved from http://www.mevzuat.gov.tr/Mevzuat-Metin/1.3.6023.pdf (Turkish).

Lewis, S. (2011). How has health services research made a difference? *Healthcare Policy, 6*(Special Issue), 74–79. PMID:24933375

Marchessault, G. (2011). The Manitoba Centre for Health Policy: A case study. *Health Policy (Amsterdam), 6*(Special Issue), 29–43. PMID:24933371

Medical Statute of Deontology of 1960. Retrieved from http://www.mevzuat.gov.tr/MevzuatMe-tin/2.3.412578.pdf (Turkish).

Ministry of Health Turkey, Department of Health Informatics. (2016). Ministry of Health Turkey, Department of Health Informatics. Retrieved from https://sbsgm.saglik.gov.tr (Turkish).

Moore, A. (2005). Intangible property: Privacy, power, and information control. In M. Adam (Ed.), Information Ethics: Privacy, property, and power. Seattle, WA: University of Washington Press.

Nissenbaum, H. (2004). Privacy as Contextual Integrity. *Washington Law Review (Seattle, Wash.), 79*, 101–139.

OECD. (2013). *Strengthening Health Information Infrastructure for Health Care Quality Governance: Good Practices, New Opportunities, and Data Privacy Protection Challenges. OECD Health Policy Studies*. Paris, France: OECD Publishing.

OECD. (2015). *Health Data Governance: Privacy, Monitoring, and Research, OECD Health Policy Studies*. Paris, France: OECD Publishing.

Ojenan, T. (2017). Courts, privacy and data protection in Finland: Making privacy and data protection real with a little help from the courts. In M. Brkan, & E. Psychogiopoulou (Eds.), Courts, Privacy and Data Protection in the Digital Environment. Edward Elgar Publishing. doi:10.4337/9781784718718.00012

Panhuis, W. G., Paul, P., Emerson, C., Grefenstette, J., Wilder, R., Herbst, A. J., ... Burke, D. S. (2014). A Systematic Review of Barriers to Data Sharing in Public Health. *BMC Public Health, 14*(1), 144. doi:10.1186/1471-2458-14-1144 PMID:25377061

Post, R. (2001). Three concepts of privacy. *The Georgetown Law Journal, 89*(6), 2087–2089.

Pritts, J. (2008). *The Importance and Value of Protecting the Privacy of Health Information: Roles of HIPAA Privacy Rule and the Common Rule in Health Research*. Washington, DC: Institute of Medicine.

Republic of Turkey Prime Ministry Investment Support. Promotion Agency. (2017). *Legal Guide to Investing in Turkey*, CMS, p. 113. Retrieved from http://www.invest.gov.tr/en-US/infocenter/publications/Documents/Legal-Guide-to-Investing-in-Turkey.pdf

Roos, L. L., Brownell, M., Lix, L., Roos, N. P., Walld, R., & MacWilliam, L. (2008). From health research to social research: Privacy, methods, approaches. *Social Science & Medicine, 66*(1), 117–129. doi:10.1016/j.socscimed.2007.08.017 PMID:17919795

Rothstein, M. A. (2007). Health Privacy in Electronic Age, *The Journal of Legal Medicine, Oct-Dec; 28*(4), 487–501.

Shapiro, M., Johnston, D., Wald, J., & Mon, D. (2012). *Patient-Generated Health Data. White Paper* (Prepared for Office of Policy and Planning, Office of the National Coordinator for Health Information Technology), RTI International, Research Triangle Park, NC.

Social Insurance and Universal Health Insurance Law of 2006, (GHI). Retrieved from http://turkish-laborlaw.com/images/turkish-social-security-law/social-security-law-5510.pdf

Solove, D. J. (2006). A taxonomy of privacy. *University of Pennsylvania Law Review, 154*(3), 516–518. doi:10.2307/40041279

Sonja, M., Ioana, G., Miaoging, Y., & Anna, K. (2018). Understanding value in health data ecosystems: A review of current evidence and ways forward. *Rand Health Quarterly, 7*(2), 3. PMID:29416943

Tatar, M., Mollahaliloglu, S., Sahin, B., Aydın, S., Maresso, A., & Hernandez-Quevedo, C. (2011). Turkey: Health System Review. *Health Systems in Transition, 13*(6), 21. Retrieved from http://www.euro.who.int/__data/assets/pdf_file/0006/158883/e96441.pdf PMID:22455830

Terry, N. P., & Francis, L. P. (2007). Ensuring the privacy and confidentiality of electronic health records. *University of Illinois Law Review, 2*, 681–736.

The Circular of Ministry of Health. (2016, July 15). Number: 2016/10. Retrieved from https://dosy-amerkez.saglik.gov.tr/Eklenti/4283,hasta-mahremiyetine-saygi-gosterilmesi-2016-10pdf.pdf?0 (Turkish).

The Circular of Ministry of Health. (2015, February). Number: 2015/5. Retrieved from https://dosyaism.saglik.gov.tr/Eklenti/23257,enabizgenelge20155pdf.pdf?0 (Turkish).

The Constitution of the Republic of Turkey (Turkiye Cumhuriyeti Anayasası) [2709, October 18, 1981] OJ repeated, November 9, 1982. Retrieved from https://global.tbmm.gov.tr/docs/constitution_en.pdf (English).

The Constitutional Court of the Republic of Turkey, Individual Application, Decision number 2014/14189, Date: 25.10.2017.

The General Board of Penalty, Supreme Court, E.2012/12-1584, K:2014/312.

The Patient Rights Directive of 1998, Retrieved from http://mevzuat.basbakanlik.gov.tr/Metin.Aspx?MevzuatKod=7.5.4847&MevzuatIliski=0&# (Turkish)

Turkey's National Health Information System Portal (Saglik-Net). Retrieved from http://www.sagliknet.saglik.gov.tr/giris.htm (Turkish)

Wu, J. H., Kao, H. Y., & Sambamurthy, V. (2016). The integration effort and E-health compatibility effect and the mediating role of E-health synergy on hospital performance. *International Journal of Information Management*, *36*(6), 1288–1300. doi:10.1016/j.ijinfomgt.2016.09.002

ADDITIONAL READING

Custer, B., Sears, A., Dechesne, F., Georgieva, I., Tani, T., & Hof, S. (2019). *EU Personal Data Protection in Policy and Practice*. Springer, Asser Press. doi:10.1007/978-94-6265-282-8

(2012). European Data Protection. InGutwirth, S., Leenes, R., De Hert, P., & Poullet, Y. (Eds.), *Good Health?* Springer Publishing.

Gkoulalas-Divanis, A., & Loukides, G. (2015). *Medical Data Privacy Handbook*. Springer Publishing. doi:10.1007/978-3-319-23633-9

Herzig, T. W. (Ed.). (2010). *Information Security in Healthcare Managing Risk*. HIMMS Press.

Hoffman, S. (2016). Electronic Health Records and Medical Big Data – Law and Policy. Cambridge University Press. Emam, K.(Ed.), (2013). Risky Business: Sharing Health Data While Protecting Privacy, Trafford Publishing.

Munns, C., & Basu, S. (2016). *Privacy and Healthcare Data 'Choice of Control' to 'Choice' and 'Control*. Routledge Publishing.

Robichau, B. P. (2014). *Healthcare Information Privacy and Security: Regulatory Compliance and Data Security in the Age of Electronic Health Records*. Apress Publishing. doi:10.1007/978-1-4302-6677-8

KEY TERMS AND DEFINITIONS

Data Protection: It is an implementation that controls how information can be used or disclosed. In other words, data protection is a practice that safeguards some important data from corruption and loss.

Electronic Health Record System: EHR is the digital form of recording, processing, and accessing to patient's medical history such as diagnosis, laboratory reports, medications, clinical decisions.

Health Data: Health data is every type of data related to health status, personal choice about selecting a treatment, health security or policy number, all kind of treatment reports, causes of death, socio-economic parameters regarding health and wellness, historical healthcare background such as diseases in past years, and this kind of information.

Health Data Management: It is a comprehensive process that includes managing, storing, collecting, sharing, protecting required health information in order to ensure managers to create holistic views of patients and enhance health outcomes.

Health Privacy: As a conceptual definition, it is to restrict or limit to access the individual's protected health information or any status regarding health activities.

Chapter 12
Auto Fill Security Solution Using Biometric Authentication for Fake Profile Detection in OSNs

Brij B. Gupta
National Institute of Technology, Kurukshetra, India

Somya Ranjan Sahoo
National Institute of Technology, Kurukshetra, India

Vaibhav Bhatia
National Institute of Technology, Kurukshetra, India

Adil Arafat
iD https://orcid.org/0000-0002-2192-5868
National Institute of Technology, Kurukshetra, India

Abhik Setia
National Institute of Technology, Kurukshetra, India

ABSTRACT

This chapter discusses a model that allows the user to access social networking sites through login using smart phone-based biometric authentication. Currently, social networking websites permit the user to access their page through login and some sites provide auto fill system to login into users account through browser by permit. The browser saves the password in password protected space and automatically auto fills the password to access the account by user. This facility is not highly reliable due to the auto fill system for laptop users. When someone uses the laptop of others and visits any website, the auto fill system opens the content with saved password. Secondly, elderly people have problems logging into today's websites. To remember the password for every account is very difficult for elderly people. This chapter describes a model for security and authenticity. Authors used a hybrid model with android as the application with fingerprint authentication and chrome extension as the auto fill process for user access.

DOI: 10.4018/978-1-7998-2242-4.ch012

Copyright © 2020, IGI Global. Copying or distributing in print or electronic forms without written permission of IGI Global is prohibited.

1. INTRODUCTION

Online Social Network (OSN) (Fire et al., 2014) is an online social platform for communication between the people having same interest, friend, friends of friends and other belongings. It also allows users to create a profile with certain public content for identification. Currently, the social network platforms are the easiest way for communication and content sharing among others like photos, video and current status of the user. OSN platform connects old friends, other personality of the same interest and bring them into a new platform. The daily activity of the users shared to update the current status of individuals in this platform. Due to the advancement of the technologies as OSN, it becomes a suitable way of transformation of content in the web. OSN's are becoming the most convenient way for users to keep in touch with belongings, share personal information, daily activities, travel plans, photos, friends, and family. The structure and the nature of behavior describe the overall architecture of the profile holder. The various popular social networking sites for communication are, Google+ (Vic Gundotra, 2011), Facebook (Mark Zuckerberg, 2004), Twitter (Jack Dorsey, 2006), and LinkedIn (Reid Hoffman, 2002), have a billions of users across the globe.

As the uses of the social network increases and it becomes growingly more struck in users' everyday life, the private information of the user becomes easily revealed and perverted. With valuable information user shared among others that lead to huge damage for the society and individuals (Gupta & Gupta, 2015; Almomani, 2013; Sahoo & Gupta, 2018; Zheng et al., 2017). Presently, many threats have been detected and reported that feat private information of the user or exposures of OSN's. Regrettably, many social network users are unaware of the different circumstances related to the various threats and security risk factors present in the network that use for personal communication. The various security risk associated with OSN's are, privacy risks (Sahoo & Gupta, 2020), identity theft attack (Kiruthiga & Kannan, 2014), malware attack, fake profiles (Ersahin et al., 2017; Conti et al., 2012; David et al., 2016) (also known as Sybil attack (Alsaleh et al., 2014) or socialbots), and cyber bullying in the form of sexual harassment among others. The information shared in the OSN can be harvested by OSN operators or any third-party service with the help of commercial companies. The elicited entropy can be misused in various ways for the different purpose and exploit user's personal information. For example, companies can use user's personal information for sharing of the advertisement or even to share the users' personal and private content with the government organizations (Jain & Gupta, 2017; Gupta et al., 2017; Zhang et al., 2017; Gupta et al., 2015). The different categories of threat that hamper user's personal information over the web are describes below.

When the internet becomes popular, specific threats are addressed called classical threats. Though these threats are very popular and old, that can spread their network over the network and still personal information of the user. Take advantage of profile holders own content to compromise his privacy as well as his/her friends just by adapting' the threat to conciliate the users' personal information. The various threats related to classic threats are Malware, Phishing Attacks (Shafahi et al., 2016), Spammers (Mateen et al., 2017; Alam & Faris, 2017), XSS attack (Cross-Site Scripting) (Chaudhry et al., 2016) and fraudulent activity on internet (Nandini & Das, 2016; Gupta, 2018). Other types of threats called modern threats, those threats are unparalleled to OSN platforms. These types of threats targeted to theft private profile content of the user and the community of users those are associated with that account. For example, the attacker gets the private content of the user, which is available publicly at their friend's profile by creating a fake account of the same name. After creating a fake account, the account holder sends a friend request to other users those are associated with that account. If the user accepts his/her friend request, then the profile content visible publicly can appear on that account and doing some malicious activity by using that content. The different threats that are coming under modern threats category are De-anonymization Attacks, Click jacking (Faghani et al., 2014; Rehman et al., 2013), fake Profiles (Sahoo & Gupta, 2019; Sahoo & Gupta, 2019) (social bots), Face Recognition, Identity Clone Attack (Devmane & Rana, 2014), Information Leakage, Inference Attack (Praveen et al., 2017), Socware and Location Leakage. The combination of the modern and classic threats together called Combination threats. For example, an attacker gathers the password of a user in any social network and uses this password for sending the malicious link to others in the network. Day by day, thousands of new accounts are created over the web in the different social network. For unique identification, every account needs user id and password on different OSN's. In 2007, the limited web users have 25 online accounts had an average that requires a password, and they are motivated about eight times per day to verify that password 9Florencio & Herley, 2007). Sometimes, it can be assured well that a user faced certain problem due to set a long password in different accounts. The service provider regulation must follow by the user for establishing a strong and unique password for the account (Bafna & Kumar, 2012). In addition to the above concern, the user has to change the password multiple times by following the instruction of the service provider. By this process the strength of the password weaker time to time and guessing the same is easier by the attacker (Ahmed et al., 2017). Some of the authentication schemes like, insider attack (Alomar et al., 2017), automatic face recognition attacks, statistical guessing attacks, image comparison attacks, and identity impersonation attacks used by the user. The above issues solved by using biometric authentication, these are not easy for break to do clone attacks and cannot be easily hacked. However, the methods used to protect user information have certain problem due to unavailability of biometric system on any desktop system. So we need some external hardware devices for the implementation. But nowadays, that can be avoided with the help of fingerprint-based Smartphone device and face recognition system to autofill the security content into the user account (Michelin et al., 2016). All the threats cited above awaits dissimilar but the activities of all these threads to steal personal information of the user. To slim down these variousattacks, users have to carefully handle the OSN sites at the time of logedin. The manual prediction of these sophistication attacks cannot predict previously. The attacker tries to attack other profiles by generating fake accounts. Thus a hybrid method required to protect the user personal information and to avoid these attacks. With the motive of cutting down these attacks based on fake profiles and conventional authentication strategies, we are delivering a hybrid impendent model based on biometric authentication system with autofill security solution for detection of fake profiles in OSN's for protective and assure access to the OSN's utilizing Smartphone base android system with internet connectivity. The suggested method will help the social network users to forbid themselves from various attacks.

The rest of the paper is organized as follows. In section 2, we describe history, background and motivation related to the topic. In section 3, we elaborate on the usage of biometric authentication for security solutions. In section 4 and section 5, we describe the taxonomy of threats and various existing security solutions. The various problem statements are defined in section 6. In section 7, we describe details of android fingerprint authentication. Finally, we conclude our work in section 8 and some future research direction in section 9.

2. HISTORY, BACKGROUND AND MOTIVATION

Fake Profiles are semi-automated or automated profiles that look like the original profile of any users and that mimic the behaviour of others in different OSNs. Sometimes the fake accounts also called Sybil account or social bot. These accounts are usually doing a certain malicious activity that causes the problem in accessing the information of the user and chance of data theft. That undesired activity leads to hampering the social connection in the same as well as in different network also. The basic idea behind such an approach is that every bot account followed other accounts in the network to steal personal information of the user.

The common abuse of OSNs profile content through defamation of account holders is commonly referred as trolling of accounts. To defame a person in social network, sometimes people create fake accounts and spreading malicious and fraudulent content in the network. By this process, the community and friends of the original account holder affected with that content and it creates a wrong impression about the profile holder. If a company launched a new product and advertised through social network, many individuals on the OSN likes and shared those product according their interest. But, if someone creates a profile similar to the original profile and spread some malicious content through those profiles, the reputation of the company degrades. This is how false advertising is propagating over the network on social media. It is better and intelligent exercise if the genuine user posted the review time, but, at the same time fake profile user generates deceptive impression about that specific product. By creating Fake profiles, attackers steal users' confidential information and gaining the credential of the system which he/she can't collect by using their technical skills. Sometimes, fake profiles are created for click jacking attack. By this process, the user redirects to a different site without knowingly. In this type of attack, the malicious contents are stored in the form of a link. The malicious code plated inside an attractive spam post to attract the user to click on that link. The detection of the malicious code or link (Alghamdi et al., 2016) very hard to detect manually and take advantage of this, malicious user spread malicious content over the network. Technology advancement is an excellent problem for elder people due to lack of awareness and usability. To habituate with the technology-specific, elder people have to know the pros and cons of each activity running on the social network through the internet. To enhance the security related to their account in day to day life, protection of user account through password is required. For the above concern, Password manager and autofill is a solution for password protector to protect user account and their information by a stored password for every login attempt. The operation of the autofill security will work by using the following. Firstly, they encrypt these passwords provided by the user and stored in a database and decrypts the same by using a master password to autofill the content. But, the security factor related to autofill manager on a different browser is not authentic decent, so we proposed a model using biometric based autofill security system. Biometrics uses its physical features to recognize users and provides authenticity.

Similarly, various other problems related to authenticity come into picture. When spammers create fake accounts in the same network as well as in different network, and try to scam users to turning their password to them due to the unawareness of technology related pros and cons. So, providing them with a suitable fake detector framework and the environment with the help of biometric authentication based autofill solution with the help of android phone and as a complete solution towards increasing the overall security of user's data.

3. USAGE OF BIOMETRICS AUTHENTICATION

This paper emphasized on using biometric not in place of password but in place of enhanced security for autofill manager for browsers. There are some questions which are needed to be answered to understand our approach more clearly.

1. What is biometry and why we are using biometrics?
2. Why use biometrics from mobile phones?
3. Why use web-based access using a password or pin?

Answer for the above scenario by briefing

Biometry and why we are using biometrics? The identification of human characteristics uniquely is biometry. Broadly the biometrics can be categorized into two different principles based upon the certain features they are using. These are: physiological, which is based on measurements of a portion of the human being body parts, iris, fingerprint, face, hand shape, etc. Secondly, behavioral which based on measurements of information retrieved from an action performed by the user and, thus, circuitously appraising some characteristics of the human body like, voice, keystroke dynamics, signature-handwriting, gait. The Biometric-recognition system divided into two different groups called identification and authentication. Identification describes the owner of biometrics and authentication shows original authenticity of the user i.e. (Am I the person I claim to be?). In the case of a large data set, the identification requires more time and large amount of processing capability. It is often used to identify and determine the suspect from crime. In case of verification, it requires less load as the user content sample match with extracted guide and it is used to access information as well as placed that information. The basic method used for authentication is via PIN/password but its impuissance's are almost distinctly documented. It is usually easy to guess and hack, if it is easy to remember, but if it is difficult, it is usually unmanageable to attack. Hence, a lot of people write them down and never change them. Worrying canvass on the trouble of passwords from a commercial point of view can be found. The problem with tokens is that, they attest their bearing, but not the bearer; they can be easily forgotten, lost, or stolen. As a result, the solution like biometry appears as a good mechanism, which is generally used with previous mechanism in addition with current solution to enhance the security levels one step ahead. Some cases fingerprints and DNA are the most-commonly used authentication principle to detect fraudulent activity.

Biometric for mobile devices: With the advancement in technology, nowadays mobile phones come with powerful computing and networking capabilities to furnish users with a various compass of possibilities. Now mobile devices also support fingerprint and facial based authentication, which is also seemingly faster and more secure. With the recent technological improvement in biometric based authentication is mobile phones, it makes it easier for users to use it and makes it more portable as a device which includes fingerprint or facial recognition sensor. In this paper, we have enclosed modern way to autofill passwords using biometrics on mobile phones.

The main characteristics of using biometrics from mobile phones depicted below:

1) **Simplicity:** Nowadays, mobile phones have taken over every generation. Children, students, adults and elders everyone uses it. It has become a daily part of our life. It is easy to use and user-friendly.

Developing an application such as an Android application is easier and it doesn't need a complex application for biometrics purpose. A simple app will be enough.

2) **Low Cost:** Biometrics is mostly used in fingerprint authentication nowadays in mobile phones. So the need to make it low cost is necessary. Due to the latest developments in technology, it is now cheaper and now every Smartphone is mandate to come with at least fingerprint or facial recognition sensor. Therefore, for our purpose the mobile phone fits best for end users to opt for biometrics use.

3) **Portable:** Before fingerprints were present in mobile phones, people used to carry an external hardware device for fingerprint authentication which is not portable enough. But this is not a case with mobile phones, they are easy to carry and use. Hence, they are more portable.

4) **Multiplatform:** Mobile phones can be used to access almost any service nowadays which can be accessed via a PC. Therefore, it also supports multiple platforms.

5) **Multi-biometrics:** Multiple people registered their biometrics in mobile devices and hence it supports multi-biometrics which enables users to extend their reach to various different websites with different account under different account holders.

6) **Secure:** In current scenario, biometric is the mandatory requirement for the devices to protect user content. However, our method overcomes the issues in communication layer with HTTPS platform. In all the systems developed this has been used.

Why used web based access using password or pin? Almost every website uses different way of password or pin-based architecture for authentication. These methods of authentication have deepened its root and therefore we need a model which works on the top. The hybrid model in this paper uses biometrics with autofill manager leaving the password or pin architecture intact. Therefore, there is no need for website developers to change their method of authentication instead only users will be required to authenticate from mobile phones using biometric. There is no need to store biometric data in any database and then compared it later. Everything related to biometrics is done on user end and not on database. We have used real-time database to support faster transactions between different stages.

4. TAXONOMY OF THREATS

There are much security emerges that be in online social network authentication strategies as well as biometric authentication. The person exists in the social group having used social authentication scheme for their protection toward data loss. For instance, even if a user fixes his/her user account in an OSN as private, the adversaries take advantages of social group to capture the data content through different users those are associated with those user account. Unfortunately, biometric authentication in various devices is not a proper authentication to protect the system as well as user content. Many researchers have proven that the biometric is easier to hack rather than normal passwords. Since, to protect the user content from all these attacks was never been designed to be secret. There are a lot of automated attacks against social authentication schemes. These attacks totally rely on advanced algorithms, sophisticated mechanisms and various machine learning approaches for collecting social information from users shown in figure 1. Now in the following sections, various attack classes related with social authentication schemes.

Figure 1. Taxonomy of threats and solutions

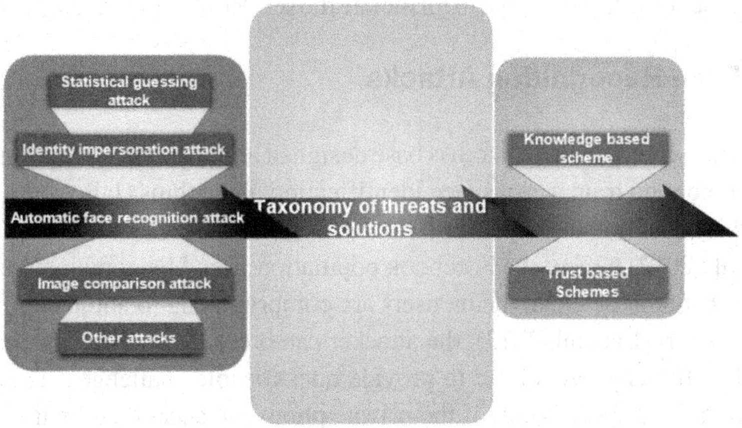

4.1 Statistical Guessing Attacks

Passwords of any user can be guessed if it is common or related to user's personal information that is not private. On shared arcane, such as passwords and the answers to security questions in case user forget his password, that are used to authenticate a user, may be applied as main or secondary factor of authentication, alarms a need for making the guessing of passwords more difficult. The difficulty of passwords can be increased either by have quantitatively evaluated attackers' ability for guessing the correct answer of the security question or preventing users from choosing common passwords.

Users' released message and interactions with others in online contexts may enhance the chance of an attacker to guess the solutions to gainsay questions and that expect about knowledge related to social networking items known to the users. For instance, profile photo of users, biographies and comments, may assist close attackers to estimate the proper answers to security questions (Chaudhry et al., 2016). Therefore, questions in knowledge-based social authentication systems it is highly essential to contract the chance that an attacker can conjecture the replies to challenge.

4.2 Identity Impersonation Attacks

To exert the believability and trustiness of social authentication, it is important to ascertain that the process of appointing trustees exclude suspicious user accounts and preparation of the challenge questions. It is very crucial to identifying the fake identities before they build up social associations with the victims' friends. The author in (Javad et al., 2014) introduced the Trusted Friend Attack and elaborate the capturing details the user. When the user accepts the fake friend request by which the attackers may gain access to users' accounts and steal the personal information of the user. OSN user can't assert the personal identity of other user accounts earlier making connection with him. The attackers take advantage of this lacking feature of OSN and clone the other user's identity in order to access the personal information of their victims' friends circle and build devised faith relationship. These attacks are referred to as Identity Cloning Attacks, if the victim profile is same as the other OSN user profile and the cloned attacks are maliciously designed. And called fake profile attacks, if the user's information in other social network are used to make an account in any other social network to communicate with others for collecting user content of the user. Thus, the security based authentication schemes failed due to the social knowledge published by fake account holder were used to formulate the secrete question related to user authentication.

4.3 Automatic Face Recognition Attacks

In social authentication schemes where photo is base design of authentication, attackers can collect users' publically profile photos and train various face identification algorithms (Jain et al., 2015). Facebook is the leading photo-sharing online social platform for the users and since, according to the survey (Dantone et al., 2011; Dey et al., 2012) 67% of the Facebook population friend list remain unprotected by default. Also, it was proved that 88% of social media users are compromising to automatic face recognition attacks. According to report (Lancini, 2013), the attacker can break 22% of the Facebook photos that are available publicly by efficient way related to provide questionable challenges. They also claimed that the attacker success rate can rise to 100% if the private photo can accessible by the attacker.

In the case of protected Facebook accounts, if the user shares their contents or tag with others whose accounts are publicly available, then the accessibility of the profile content based on the photo is 38% accessible. According to Danton et al.'s study, the accuracy of face recognition scheme increases if the user available content in the profile significantly increased and leads to public profile information day by day then achieve a true positive rate of at least 79% (Dantone et al., 2011). Becker et al. applied various machine learning approaches to identified faces in a big dataset of Facebook images and analyse that the detection rate in the form of accuracy of 65% was accomplished using the SVM (Support vector machine) approach. Jin et al. analysed attacker uses mutual friend features provided by the OSNs helps to discover public profile content of victims by 60%. When these interactions become approachable to adversaries, information can be collected about the targeted user by easily accessing publicly information of that user in the social circle. For example, using the properties of the nodes to which he/she has connected they can infer the interests of a user. For the above concern it is not so easy to protect users social structure in online platform and the information also extracted from others profiles by publicly available content.

4.4 Comparison Attacks Based on Image

Comparison techniques based on image were proved to be more effective than face detection technique algorithms for solving challenge questions related to photo (Polakis et al., 2014). In order to successful these attacks, photos collected by the attacker from victim's social network and apply image based comparison techniques to recognize the subject concern that appear in their collections (Jain et al., 2015; Polakis et al., 2014). Using supplied tagging information and collected photos an adversary could use the concept of similarity index in photo matching algorithms to identify the user faces presented in security questions. The detection mechanism for accuracy of these frameworks by showing that 98% of the pictures used in the questions challenge included in their dataset were identified by their image based comparison approach. The success of image comparison attack totally depends upon quality of supplied tag information as well as coverage of collected information. Therefore, the attacker tries to get more photos of victim because it increases the chances of successfully detecting subjects in equating challenge based on analysis.

4.5 Other Classes of Attacks

Some researchers describe in their research about the vulnerability of knowledge based social authentication systems to deal with denial of service attacks, in this attack the attacker attempt to upload malicious photo that contain some subject matter unknown to the other users and supply the content with wrong tagging. By this the information decrease the possibility of answering the question related to the challenge. Further, investigators have aroused fears related to the vulnerability of trustee-based information systems that leads to DOS (denial of service attacks) (Alieyan et al, 2019; El-Latif et al., 2018; Gupta & Gulihar, 2020; Dahiya & Gupta, 2019). The different authentication schemes deployed in various Social network authentications in online platform such as in Facebook and Twitter, are vulnerable to various social engineering attacks due to high level of social trust that govern user communication in social network platform that leads to disclose the personal information of the user or befriends malicious the other users in the same group (Mitnick, 2013). Some of the advanced level attacks on OSNs are depicted below.

- **Fake Profile Attack:** By collecting information about the user from different OSN, adversary creates a new account like the original user account in any social network to collect information from another user. The fake profile attack (Aggrawal et al., 2012) is also similar to Sybil or social bots attack (Koll et al., 2017). By originating friend request to other users who frequently receive the requests, social bots assemble user's personal data.
- **DDoS Attack:** DDoS (Distributed Denial-of-Service) attack is an attack coming from many locations which overtakes user's resources and prevents users from serving legitimate customers. Attacker uses OSN, which could be exploited by anyone to conduct powerful DDoS attack. As an example, Facebook notes allow users to include <img> tags. Whenever this tag is used, Facebook crawls image from the external server and caches it. The Facebook user includes any image multiple times with dynamic parameters and some text also. Later, Facebook servers are forced to download the same file multiple times in one-page view.
- **Graph Based Attack:** Graph-based attack: OSN is the geographical representation of the users. When the user increases their contacts by appending other users, the size of the user's graph is also enhanced. To search the subject matter in OSN, the user uses graph-based searching on the OSN. The searching approaches have increased the privacy and security issues (Zhang et al., 2014) for the users and the stored data.
- **Speculation Attack:** OSN user uses anonymization technique to defend and conceal sensitive information and protect their identity from unauthorized access. Speculation attack uses machine-learning techniques to distil information that is available publicly to anticipate the user's secret information like religious association and sexual preference.
- **Online Chat Risk:** Most of the OSNs provide the facility to communicate with other users through online chat. Apart from this, the other free chat rooms like Internet Relay Chat, ICQ and Microsoft MSN were used by teenagers for direct communication (Fire et al., 2012). During this action, they share their personal information like contact number, name, location and much more without the fear of information abuse. Any hacker or attacker can easily access their information and use these messages for malicious purpose in MySpace account.
- **Vicinity Attack:** Sharing of information is the main factor for using OSN. The information may contain some credential data like bank account number, sensitive personal information of any indi-

viduals. To protect the data, anonymization technique is required before making the data available publicly. If attacker has certain victim information, the attacker can easily collect the information from neighbors; the victim may be re-identified from the social network even if anonymization technique is used by the victim to protect their personal information.

- **De-anonymization Attack:** Anonymization is the process of hiding personal information by using certain techniques from unauthorized access. In de-anonymization technique (Ding et al., 2010), attacker tracks the network topology, user group membership and cookies to expose user information.
- **Sybil attack:** Sybil attack was described by (Alrubaian et al., 2015) that mainly work on peer-to-peer systems and distributed environments. In this attack, adversary creates many fake profiles to gather the user's personal information. The main reason is one online entity can manage several fake profile entities to reduce the reputation values of the user on the OSN. By this attack, the adversary can promote popularity and reputation of his account by voting for it.
- **Illation Attacks:** The author in (Mislove et al., 2015)] described illation attack, in which the adversary tries to guess the information about the user that is not available in the user's profile by prediction using available data. This type of attack can be implemented by using network analysis and from friends of those users.
- **Plug-in Attack:** Some of the online social networking sites permit certain plug-ins such as Flash and Silver light in the browser environment. Due to the installation of such plug-ins, it can spread or get directed to another site with some malicious content and invite other attacks on the social network.

5. TAXONOMY OF EXISTING SOLUTION BASED ON THREATS

By deliberating the dimensions that may tone up or sabotage the security of trust based and knowledge based authentication principles based on social trust (discussed in Section III and Section IV), this section manifests the potential schemes that could help against defend from attacks and may degrade the security of these proposed scheme.

5.1 Scheme Based on Knowledge

In order to gain the validity of the security questions based on knowledge-based social authentication schemes, an elite result have been aimed for reducing the probability of guessing the answers for insiders or outsiders. For image based matching schemes, various remedies have been proposed, which applied some image translation processes to the images delivered by social authentication schemes, excluding the social knowledge based posted by close friends or friends of friends whose user profile pages are not secured under authentication scheme, and also provide the option for the user to customize his/her challenge questions. While it could be argued that for better security to formulate the challenge for their own questions would be the better alternative that furnishes greater security, and researcher investigated that the selection of own questions furnishes deficient security levels and have some shortcomings for usability.

Another method of fighting versus these types of attacks is to restrict the flow of information of social knowledge disclosed to individuals and adversaries who resist within users' community. OSNs could add certain features that can measure the effectiveness of social interactions or the in-degree and out-degree nodes of separation between a user and each of his/her friends associated directly and indirectly and determine on the percentage of a user's account contents that could be presented for the individual users in the network. It has been observed that minimizing the number of guessing attempts allowed for each user, adding features enabling users to monitor all failed and correct guessing attempts associated with their accounts can reduce the guessing attempts associated with their account. Former researchers have aimed developing challenge questions based on the private communication of the users with others they know. For instance, it is observed that edge questionnaires are more prominent than node questionnaires, because they ask about the private information that is shared between two users (Jain et al., 2015; Yang et al., 2019). However, it should be noted that, where the social authentication schemes are used at that point the interaction of the user is limited. Thus, for guessing the question, it is easier to guess the edge questions as compared to guess than node or pseudo-edge questions, the implementation of this scheme would not be relevant to all user those are associated to that classes.

5.2 Trust-Based Schemes

Trustees: To reduce the degree of generation of fire attacks in forest systems that utilize authentication scheme based on vouching-based, it has been advised that the specific person selection as a trustee by a hues count of others should be kept by, for example, fixing the out-degree position of every account in the equating trustee networks (Gong et al., 2014). For the best of our knowledge to identify the optimal number of appointments is the lack of experimental evidence that should be linked to a trustee in order to assure the safety of someone in a particular online and offline community. In (Rubinsten et al., 2017; Cho et al., 2018), was proposed an approach that leads the selection process of trustee and determines the determinate of forest fire attacks by assuring that the trustees selected by each profile user belong to disjoint social interaction. Thus, a greater security guarantee would be achieved by selecting the trustees of a given user increases as per number of clusters employed. Still there is insufficient research evidence that choose best technique to form clusters that could be applied for better security and robustness of trustee-based social authentication schemes.

It was also proposed in (Rubinsten et al., 2017) that the choice of regents should be limited, and the researcher advised scores based technique to each node in social network and selecting the nodes with the highest scores as trustees for the representing user. This could be explicitly achieved by augmenting the community and implicitly calculated based on certain graph properties and some moderation features that told the users to rate the level of trustworthiness of each associated. However, we still argue that the trust between two individual nodes in a community should be identified that accurately reflect the level of trust. For instance, mutual friends of two individuals shared in the network cannot be considered a good indicator of the level of trust in OSN. This is due to more users that shared the content in the network and they are tightly coupled although they do not have much trust in that account on the network.

1) **Social relationships Trustworthiness:** Identifications of various degree of trust of each connection in the social network belonging to a specific node in their community, for example, by examining the user's behaviour and analysing the graph structure of the social network, helps to analyse the suspicious behaviour of the users and the users account also. This mechanism also prevents other users from selecting that account in the form of trustees. The patented method presented in (Lunt, 2012), defines the concept of a black list, a white list and a grey list for each user according to the

trustworthiness of nodes is examined at user's side in the social network. Thus the authenticity for the communication between the node A and T in a specific community, examines that the path starts from A and goes up to node T through various node in between. But the mechanism ensures that the intermediated nodes are not included in destination node T's grey list, and are already added in T's white list.

According to the report (Rubinsten et al., 2017), the authors analysed social network knowledge communicated by two given profile holders accounts in order to determine the probability that the identification of both the account holder should know each other owners in the real world identity and it simplifies the communication process by generating trust worthiness over the platform. For instance, the objective of communication decides whether there is any hierarchical relationship between the user exists in the social network or not. Underwood et al. proposed one comparison properties associated both the account holders those are in communication and the level of interaction between users over the network in order to collect the information of the user, what they are sharing in the conversation. For example, common addresses, common friends, or the involvement of the user in common social activities. The authors of (ye et al., 2015) also proposed one framework that increases the reliability of a friend request sent from user A to user B in the social platform and the link associated with that account in the community and calculating the calculating the degree of familiarity of every account in the network those are associated with B. Also modify the content by using authentication principle or by sending request to the profile holder that include information about the whole communication between the belongings. The amount of relationship between the different account and the flow of information between the accounts can be calculated by the degree of familiarity between the accounts in online social network mentioned in. In (Dom et al., 2004), the author measures the additional metric related to the quality of social interaction in a specific context like private conversation between the individuals and the mutual interaction among the community in a network for sharing of information and thought.

2) **Vouch codes:** The author describes the concept of vouch code in (Gong et al., 2014). In this approach the constraints should be imposed for the generated vouch codes and can be imposed within the given time period. However, the effect of such constraints on the generation speed of forest fire attacks has not yet been explored. In (Rubinsten et al., 2017), authors proposed a scheme that determining on the number of vouch codes that should be allowed for retrieving each user profile in social network community according to the analysis of the actions of every account and the degree of suspicion should measure.

3) **Verification of Social Interactions:** Verification of users' communication in social platform and the identification of troll profiles in OSNs would positively determine the social authentication schemes based on the security of knowledge-based and trust-based mechanism. Various schemes have been imposed for detecting fake accounts in social communities, which concentrate mainly by analysing social graph, studied user communication, participation in other actions and by building other actions that rank the users by authentic way. For protecting the account against fake profile attack that does not need prior presence of the attacker on the same platform to attack the victims in a community structure. Conti et al., proposed one solution that identifying the development growth rate and the behavioural properties of graph structure for identifying suspicious user activity and behaviour. Thus, the profile treated as fake behaves differently as compared to the other profiles.

For example, social networks profiles that are associated with fake profiles have more involvement in the community and grow faster as compared to others.

As this approach mentioned in (Goga et al., 2014) require the availability of the user communication and the involvement in the community to detect the fake profiles. Xiao et al. enforced a framework based on machine learning model for classifying newly logged in profiles as fake or not before they associated with other users in any community related to friends or belongings. In (Boshmaf et al., 2015), introduced another method for detecting fake profiles in social network platform was proposed that uses the concept of rank based on their likelihood and the behavioural prospect being fake or legitimate. Also, the author predicts the leverages by applying feature-based analysis extracted from victim accounts in social network and assign some weight to user's accounts and analyse the level of legitimacy. Wang et al. proposed one approach from different prospective, the effectiveness of different analysis of the profile related to the user behaviour while surfing the internet and social media for finding the fake activities of the user.

6. PROBLEM STATEMENT

In today's world, for securing websites and the content shared in the web by the user, authentication is considered as crucial solution. The greatest challenge is to provide authenticity to user's profile and the personal content of the user. To prevent the intrusion of non-legitimate users as well as detection of fake profiles on OSN's, this paper provides the hybrid solution to solve this problem. The problems that are incurred to OSN's and users are discussed below.

- To protect the content, the better mechanism like figure print authentication based on biometric mechanisms, more hardware cost is increased. But the authentication of the user for securing the content is enhanced due to adoption of new technology, nowadays more or less every smart phones comes with new feature called fingerprint authentication sensors which can be used for better protecting the websites as well.
- When the existing protection system i.e. autofill system is used the user content stored in the computer memory become unsafe. If biometric authentication system is used, it will provide additional security solution to the user as well as user contents. to user's data.
- Fake profiles created on OSN's lure users to fall into scam's and thus users lose their credibility to login on websites but by providing both fingerprint authentication as well as detection of fake profiles, the overall security of user's data can be increased.
- Fake profiles are made for many purposes such as identity clone attack, to spread malicious URL's, publish spam messages, Sybil attacks, click jacking.
- OTP (One Time Password) are used for online payments, sometimes this facility misused by children's where as providing figure print authentication can help to reduce the mishandling of accounts without prior knowledge of parents.
- If someone belongings and friend use other personals computer and the autofill system can lead to data theft by that user i.e. non- legitimate user can access and use the legitimate user's personal information.

To solve the entire above problem, we can enable a hybrid solution which solves these problems and also provides additional security and authenticity to users and user's data.

7. ANDROID FINGERPRINT AUTHENTICATION

Fingerprint authentication is the principle of impression left by human fingers friction ridge. That principle used in forensic science to collect the information through recovery process in a crime scene. Fingerprints are easily captured through glass surface, metal and polished stone by the natural process through the secretion of sweat from eccrine glands that are present in epidermal ridge. Human fingerprints are unique in nature, detailed, durable and difficult to alter over the life on human being and treated as long term human identities without any similarities with others. If someone conceal their identity, then the fingerprint is used by the police man for identify the individual. The Biometric characteristics have good extent of uniqueness, availability, collectability. If we use these characteristics in our daily authentication system, the system gives good performance and throughput. In all biometric techniques, fingerprint recognition is considered the most prominent and reliable one.

Fingerprint has some prominent properties:

1) **Universality:** Every person has a unique set of characteristics of his/her own fingerprint.
2) **Distinctiveness:** No two persons can have same fingerprint. It is distinct and unique.
3) **Permanence:** The best part of fingerprint is it doesn't change with time and place. Making it useful for a prolonged period.
4) **Performance:** Acuracy factor of fingerprint authentication is more in comparison to other security factor in terms of recognition time and it also reduce the operational and environmental factors that affect the accuracy and speed for detection and recognition.
5) **Circumvention:** It reflects how easily the system can be trapped by fraudulent person.

7.1 Finger Print Analysis

For successfully implemented of image processing techniques, it is essential to know the properties and structure of human skin.

The various patterns of fingerprints are:

1. **Arch**: It creates a wave-like pattern related with plain arches and tented arches. In case of Tented arches, it rises a sharper point rather than plain arches. It covers at least 5% of all pattern types.
2. **Whorls**: It forms spiral and circular patterns, like tiny whirlpools. Basically the whorls group divided into four categories. These are: concentric circles, central pocket loop, double loop and accidental loop. It covers up to 35 percent of pattern types.
3. **Loops**: It forms a loop shape by re-curve back on them. It categorizes into o radial pointing toward the radius bone, or thumb (loops) and pointing toward the ulna bone, or pinky (ulnar loops), and it covers approximately 60 percent of pattern types.

7.2 Types of Fingerprint Sensor

There are mainly two types of fingerprint sensors:

1. Optical sensor.
2. Capacitance sensor.

The Optical Sensor uses LED lights to illuminate the finger for fingerprint scanning. By determining the light and dark areas the sensor creates and detects fingerprints image with the help of fingerprint long narrow natural elevation. When the device users place his/her finger on the glass surface or plate, the scanning process starts.

Capacitance Sensor, Capacitive sensor scan the fingerprint by using electrical current to sense the image instead of light used in optical sensor. It is another common way to capture fingerprint of the device user. It uses an array of capacitor plates to capture the fingerprint image. Compare to optical sensor the capacitance sensor generates an image of the long narrow natural elevation and valleys that fingerprint. The skin of Human is conductive enough and it provide capacitive coupling in combination with an individual.

7.3 Comparison Between Optical and Capacitance Sensor

In optical scanners, there is no need for any special maintenance and treatment for sensor surface due to very durable in nature. The glass plate is made of an unbreakable material as hard as quartz and they are scratch-resistant in nature. These scanners are also immune to extreme weather, shock and electrostatic discharge in nature. They are manufactured to execute well in high traffic and as well as durable for rough and or outdoor environment. The operational application of this content is having large emerging area due to its larger and high-resolution images. The production cost of optical scanner lower as compared to others and it has long life with zero maintenance.

On the other hand, capacitive scanner uses the concept of semiconductor or chip type of sensor. The upper layer or coated layer of this scanner is wearing out over the time and the sensor is uneven in nature. This results in a degraded performance and also shortens the lifetime of the product. These types of e sensors usually need a coated layer over the material and like ESD and other protective coated over the glass plate. These sensors have lower durable capability and affected by electrostatic discharge. Repeated dealing and casual exposure can lead to corrode and damage the surface easily. Moreover, the material like silicon chips inherently fragile in nature and damaged by rough use from external entities due to external impact and scratches. As compared to optical scanner, capacitive scanner usually has smaller sensing area which captures smaller image size having lower resolution. It is very difficult to maintain due to expensive for surface coatings. The other expenses are replacement cost, maintenance costs and downtime.

7.4 Different Stages of Fingerprint Sensing

There are mainly three stages of fingerprint sensing:

1. Capture Fingerprint image.

2. Comparison with store data in the database and with stored templates.
3. Process image and extract features.

In current fingerprint system matching is the key component and operation for identification. The objective of this fingerprint system is to by comparing the input to achieve the high reliability with respect to the stored data in the database pattern. Constantly matching fingerprint images is an enormously very difficult job, due to the large unevenness in unlike effects of the same finger or large intra-class variations. The various factors responsible for the mismatching and intra-class variations are: feature extraction errors, non-linear distortion, changing of skin condition, partial overlap, rotation, displacement, variable pressure, and noise etc. Therefore, the same fingerprint behaves differently in different circumstances and the different finger behaves similar result. In this approach the minutiae-based matching was used for sensing the fingerprint and match the content with stored data. This approach matching the alignment between different temples and the input sets for the pairing of maximum number of minutiae.

7.5 Factors Affecting the Scan

Darkness due to average pixel: It rejects the scanning process if the overall complexion of image is too dark or too light.

1. **Image Definition (Sharpness):** This process looks at various directed lines acting vertically and horizontally throughout the entire image.
2. Distortion
3. **Resolution**: Higher the resolution is better for sensing. If it is too low, then it is very difficult to detect.
4. **Sensing Area**: The average fingerprint sensing area is about 0.5" x 0.7". Large area i.e. 1.0" x 1.0", ascertains that the overlap effects are reduced (leading to false rejections).

7.6 Fooling of Devices

According to Japanese cryptographer, using a combination of low cunning, cheap kitchen supplies and a digital camera the fingerprint recognition system can be fooled. At very First, Tsutomu Matsumoto used gelatin and a plastic mold to make a fake finger and that can be used to fool the fingerprints four times out of five attempts. Flushed with his success, he used possible fingerprints from a glass plate with the enhanced feature like using super-glue fumes (cyanoacrylate adhesive) and digital camera-based photograph. To enhance the contrast of the image, he used Photoshop and a transparency sheet. Matsumoto took a photo-sensitive printed-circuit board that can be found in many electronic hobby shops and used the transparency method of fingerprint to engrave the fingerprint into the copper plate. From this method he made a gelatin finger by using the print on the PCB. The device attached with Finger prints or biometric devices that attempt to identify the user or person on the basis of their fingerprint, are boasted as extremely assure and nearly impossible to fool the device but Matsumoto's work cracks the concept of others. The equipment used to break the security is neither hi-tech nor expensive.

Figure 2. Cloud based storing encrypted data

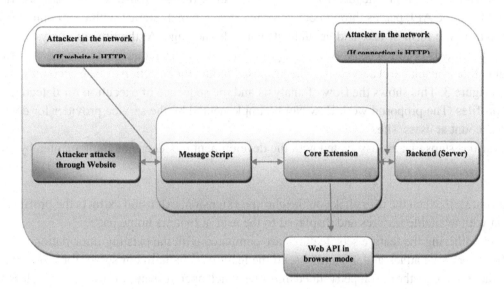

7.7 Browser Extension and Their Security

Nowadays extensions are supported by most of the browsers and they provide an extension to the overall usability of browsers by providing new functionalities. They enable users to tailor browser functionality and behavior according to the needs of users or preferences. Vulnerabilities that exist in extensions put user's data at risk; there is no way to store private data such as passwords in extensions. In our hybrid model we stored data on server in cloud in encrypted format, saving it from the risks of being hacked or misused shown in figure 2.

This paper elaborates a hybrid method to protect the user content in OSN environment by providing security to the content and autofill security of login process. First section elaborates the concept of Autonomous Detection of Fake Profile model on social network platform and very next section consists of Biometric Authentication based Autofill Security model to protect the user from unauthorized access of device and the personal information.

7.8 Proposed Model for Detection of Fake Profile Autonomously on OSN

To detect the fake profiles on OSN autonomously, we analyze the different features that are associated with every twitter profiles such as user name, profile name, date of birth, like, following, followers, date of creation, tweets and other profile related contents etc. the collected information's are categorized in to two category called personal information as well as public information. We use both the information to detect the fake profile at user site. The collected information's are gathered and process through various machine learning approach in WEKA environment to analyze the accuracy factor for detection method. The various classifiers classify the content into two groups called benign profile and fake profile based on the collected information. The accuracy factor of the classification is the input parameter for our extension to detect the fake profile. For the backend service, we create an API and deploy our API at server site that contain the datasets and API for the performance analysis. The developed API can gather information related to the profile for analysis and it can handle request from user site. The classifier result generated from the API, passes through our chrome extension that interact with user content and show the resultant in the form of fake and genuine at twitter home page. At the time of analysis by chrome extension the crawls profile when it activates by the user and send a request to the server for processing the content that is available at server site. The proposed model for detection of fake account workflow is shown in figure 3. This shows the flow of analysis and the sequence of execution for detection method of fake profiles. The proposed work flow can be implemented by the service provider for detection of the fake account at users' site.

The various steps that are associated with the development model can be implemented by following steps:

1. At first step, when the user clicks on the chrome extension, extension extracts the profile information with available features and displayed to the user at twitters home page.
2. After gathering the feature sets, features are compared with the existing information available on server for clone attack and in parallel send the features content to our server for processing.
3. At the server end, the developed trained machine which operate using various suitable classification methods trained again by using updated information that extracted from the user's profile. Every moment the server updates the data content and approved by the verifier for detection method.
4. The classifier classifies the user content and shows the output as per the user content available on that page. Also, it identifies if the profile having some misleading contents or not. If found, displayed as fake otherwise it's a benign profile.
5. To optimize the classification and the detection system, user's feedback is necessary for the further updating at server end and that leads to better detection method.
6. This process goes on repeatedly and collects user feedback for the betterment purpose.

7.9 Biometric Authentication Based Autofill Security Model

Presently most of the systems come with high authentication mechanism like fingerprint sensor. But without using the advancement of the technology people uses computer and laptops to log into the system. Therefore, in order to provide high security for social network users, we proposed fingerprint authentication for auto filling credentials by the user using fingerprint sensor inbuilt in a smart phone shown in figure 4. The proposed model categorized into 3 different parts:

1. Browser based Extension.
2. Own real time server with database.
3. Mobile devices with certain application.

First of all, user will have to registered under the same account for both extension and the mobile application. Then user will have to save the login credentials for each website he/she want to provide fingerprint authenticated autofill for logging in.

The working model of the process is as follows:

1. When the social network user opens the website, then the extension automatically read the web address and update the status of authentication in the stored database for that the website pending.

Figure 3. Workflow of fake detection with feedback by the user

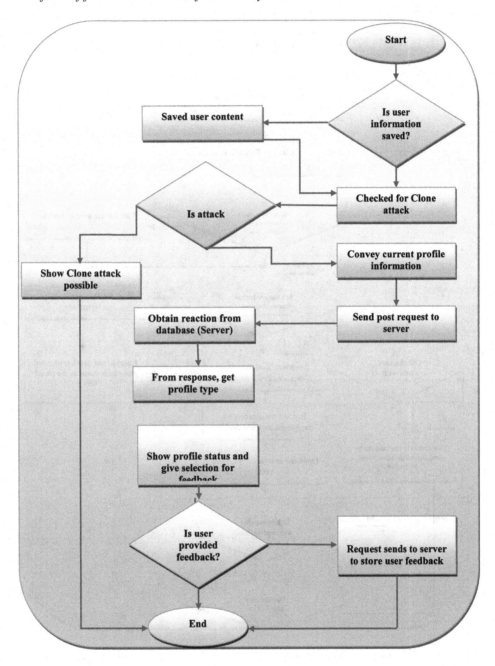

Figure 4. Workflow of fingerprint authentication and autofill security

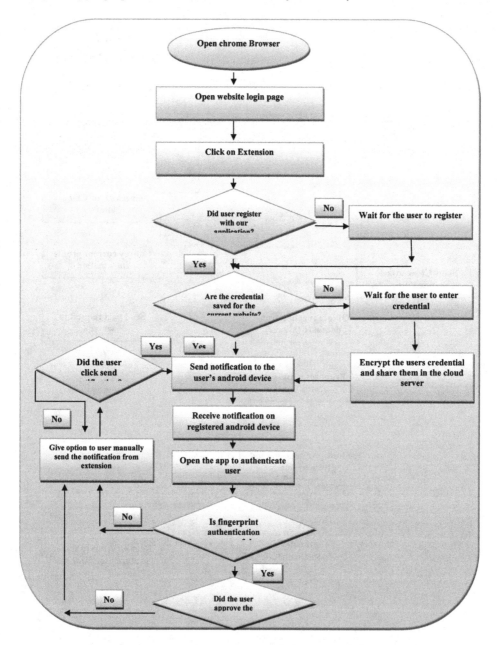

2. At the next step, the server will send a notification to the user's mobile using notification server.
3. Then the user authenticates and approves the autofill system with certain credential.
4. The status of the mobile application will update from pending to approval after getting approval from the authenticated user.
5. After the status is update and listing from the user the extension autofill the content/credential, so that the user can easily and safely log into the required website.

8. CONCLUSION

Fake accounts are germinating with time and technology; they evolve to evade their presence in the network. Therefore, it is very crucial to develop new applications and techniques to handle and filter these fake accounts from others. Taking into consideration, we have proposed a model that takes some features and analyzes the behavior of profile and that also helps to detect fake accounts by filtering the malicious accounts. The whole process of our detection method is automated and avoids the process of manual work of separation by using biometric authentication. Thus we can conclude that the auto-detection system for fake profile detection increased the overall security of user information and the network performance. In OSN the authenticity and the security of user content and their account is most crucial. Therefore, we developed a hybrid framework that consisting of both automated fake profile detection and biometric authentication-based autofill system for better protection. We used modern technology with smart phone fingerprints with autofill management system to enhance the security feature for the social network users. This hybrid approach framework provides the users to use their fingerprints with encrypted format, save the user password in cloud environment and let them use without any limitation to log into any website. By this process, guessing the password is very difficult as compared to other defense mechanisms. The feedback facility provided by the user also improve the detection rate for detecting fake accounts as well as the malicious content spreading in the network. The experimental framework revealed that the proposed framework can be successfully deployed at user site on Chrome environment to detect the fake account in real-time. Also, the mail disadvantage of the proposed framework is, it needed fingerprint based password protection handset for proper operation.

9. FUTURE WORK

In future, for first section of our research i.e. fake profile detection at real-time, we intend the functionality by using different genetic algorithm based feature extraction and selection model for better decision making and imposed the same in different social media platforms like Facebook and LinkedIn, which are quite promising area of the user for content sharing and advertising. We will also work to improve the detection of fake account and profile by gathering the current dataset time to time with new feature extraction strategy. For the remaining part of our model i.e. second section of our hybrid model we plan to impose the same technique for the android environment and application. The extension will also be built for other r popular browsers such as Google Chrome and Mozilla Firefox. We also intend to extend our work for the implementation of biometric verification such as iphone-X, which uses special facial recognition technique for the security feature.

REFERENCES

Aggarwal, A., Rajadesingan, A., & Kumaraguru, P. (2012). PhishAri: Automatic realtimephishing detection on twitter, eCrime Res. Summit, eCrime, pp. 1–12.

Ahmed, E., DeLuca, B., Hirowski, E., Magee, C., Tang, I., & Coppola, J. F. (2017, May). Biometrics: Password replacement for elderly? In *Proceedings 2017 IEEE Long Island Systems, Applications, and Technology Conference (LISAT)*, (pp. 1-6). IEEE.

Ala'M, A. Z., & Faris, H. (2017, April). Spam profile detection in social networks based on public features. In *Proceedings 2017 8th International Conference on Information and Communication Systems (ICICS)*, (pp. 130-135). IEEE.

Alghamdi, B., Watson, J., & Xu, Y. (2016, October). Toward detecting malicious links in online social networks through user behavior. In *Proceedings IEEE/WIC/ACM International Conference on Web Intelligence Workshops (WIW)*, (pp. 5-8). IEEE. 10.1109/WIW.2016.014

Alieyan, K., Almomani, A., Anbar, M., Alauthman, M., Abdullah, R., & Gupta, B. B. (2019). DNS rule-based schema to botnet detection. *Enterprise Information Systems*, 1–20. doi:10.1080/17517575.2019.1644673

Almomani, A., Gupta, B. B., Wan, T. C., Altaher, A., & Manickam, S. (2013). Phishing dynamic evolving neural fuzzy framework for online detection zero-day phishing email. *arXiv preprint arXiv:1302.0629*.

Alomar, N., Alsaleh, M., & Alarifi, A. (2017). Social authentication applications, attacks, defense strategies and future research directions: A systematic review. *IEEE Communications Surveys and Tutorials*, 99.

Alrubaian, M., Al-Qurishi, M., Rahman, S. M. M., & Alamri, A. (2015). A novel prevention mechanism for Sybil attack in online social network, *Proceedings 2015 2nd World Symp. Web Appl. Networking, WSWAN 2015*, pp. 1–6. 10.1109/WSWAN.2015.7210347

Alsaleh, M., Alarifi, A., Al-Salman, A. M., Alfayez, M., & Almuhaysin, A. (2014, December). Tsd: Detecting sybil accounts in Twitter. In *Proceedings 2014 13th International Conference on Machine Learning and Applications (ICMLA)*, (pp. 463-469). IEEE.

Bafna, A., & Kumar, S. (2012). ProActive Approach for Generating Random Passwords for Information Protection. *Procedia Technology*, 4, 129–133. doi:10.1016/j.protcy.2012.05.018

Boshmaf, Y., Logothetis, D., Siganos, G., Lería, J., Lorenzo, J., Ripeanu, M., & Beznosov, K. (2015, February). Integro: Leveraging Victim Prediction for Robust Fake Account Detection in OSNs. In NDSS (Vol. 15, pp. 8-11).

Chaudhary, P., Gupta, B. B., & Yamaguchi, S. (2016, October). XSS detection with automatic view isolation on online social network. In *Proceedings 2016 IEEE 5th Global Conference on Consumer Electronics*, (pp. 1-5). IEEE. 10.1109/GCCE.2016.7800354

Cho, V., & Ip, W. H. (2018). A Study of BYOD adoption from the lens of threat and coping appraisal of its security policy. *Enterprise Information Systems*, 12(6), 659–673. doi:10.1080/17517575.2017.1404132

Conti, M., Poovendran, R., & Secchiero, M. (2012, August). Fakebook: Detecting fake profiles in on-line social networks. In *Proceedings of the 2012 International Conference on Advances in Social Networks Analysis and Mining (ASONAM 2012)* (pp. 1071-1078). IEEE Computer Society. 10.1109/ASONAM.2012.185

Dahiya, A., & Gupta, B. B. (2019). A PBNM and economic incentive-based defensive mechanism against DDoS attacks. *Enterprise Information Systems*, 1–21. doi:10.1080/17517575.2019.1700553

Dantone, M., Bossard, L., Quack, T., & Van Gool, L. (2011, November). Augmented faces. In *Proceedings 2011 IEEE International Conference on Computer Vision Workshops (ICCV Workshops)*, (pp. 24-31). IEEE. 10.1109/ICCVW.2011.6130218

David, I., Siordia, O. S., & Moctezuma, D. (2016, November). Features combination for the detection of malicious Twitter accounts. In *Proceedings of the 2016 IEEE International Autumn Meeting on Power, Electronics, and Computing (ROPEC)*, (pp. 1-6). IEEE. 10.1109/ROPEC.2016.7830626

Devmane, M. A., & Rana, N. K. (2014, May). Detection and prevention of profile cloning in online social networks. In Proceedings Recent Advances and Innovations in Engineering (ICRAIE), 2014 (pp. 1-5). IEEE. doi:10.1109/ICRAIE.2014.6909237

Dey, R., Jelveh, Z., & Ross, K. (2012, March). Facebook users have become much more private: A large-scale study. In *Proceedings 2012 IEEE International Conference on Pervasive Computing and Communications Workshops (PERCOM Workshops)*, (pp. 346-352). IEEE. 10.1109/PerComW.2012.6197508

Ding, X., Zhang, L., Wan, Z., & Gu, M. (2010). A brief survey on de-anonymization attacks in online social networks, *Proc. - Int. Conf. Comput. Asp. Soc. Networks, CASoN'10*, pp. 611–615. 10.1109/CASoN.2010.139

Dom, B., Ruvolo, J., & Tewari, G. (2004). U.S. Patent Application No. 10/323,568.

Egele, M., Stringhini, G., Kruegel, C., & Vigna, G. (2017). Towards detecting compromised accounts on social networks. *IEEE Transactions on Dependable and Secure Computing*, (1), 1–1.

El-Latif, A. A. A., Abd-El-Atty, B., Hossain, M. S., Rahman, M. A., Alamri, A., & Gupta, B. B. (2018). Efficient quantum information hiding for remote medical image sharing. *IEEE Access: Practical Innovations, Open Solutions*, 6, 21075–21083. doi:10.1109/ACCESS.2018.2820603

Erşahin, B., Aktaş, Ö., Kılınç, D., & Akyol, C. (2017, October). Twitter fake account detection. In *Proceedings of the 2017 International Conference on Computer Science and Engineering (UBMK)*, (pp. 388-392). IEEE. 10.1109/UBMK.2017.8093420

Essentials of Machine Learning Algorithms. Analytics Vidhya, accessed 2017. [Online]. Available:https://www.analyticsvidhya.com/blog/2017/09/common-machine-learning-algorithms

Facebook, accessed 2017. [Online]. Available: http://www.facebook.com/

Faghani, M. R., & Nguyen, U. T. (2014, August). A study of clickjacking worm propagation in online social networks. In *Proceedings 2014 IEEE 15th International Conference on Information Reuse and Integration (IRI)*, (pp. 68-73). IEEE. 10.1109/IRI.2014.7051873

Fire, M. (2012). Strangers Intrusion Detection - Detecting Spammers and Fake Profiles in Social Networks Based on Topology Anomalies, pp. 26–39.

Fire, M., Goldschmidt, R., & Elovici, Y. (2014). Online social networks: Threats and solutions. *IEEE Communications Surveys and Tutorials*, 16(4), 2019–2036. doi:10.1109/COMST.2014.2321628

Florencio, D., & Herley, C. (2007, May). A large-scale study of web password habits. In *Proceedings of the 16th international conference on World Wide Web* (pp. 657-666). ACM. 10.1145/1242572.1242661

Galán-García, P., Puerta, J. G. D. L., Gómez, C. L., Santos, I., & Bringas, P. G. (2016). Supervised machine learning for the detection of troll profiles in twitter social network: Application to a real case of cyberbullying. *Logic Journal of the IGPL, 24*(1), 42–53.

Goga, O., Venkatadri, G., & Gummadi, K. P. (2014). Exposing impersonation attacks in online social networks.

Gong, N. Z., & Wang, D. (2014). On the security of trustee-based social authentications. *arXiv preprint arXiv:1402.2699.*

Google. +, accessed 2017. [Online]. Available: https://plus.google.com/

Gupta, B., Gupta, S., & Chaudhary, P. (2017). Enhancing the browser-side context-aware sanitization of suspicious HTML5 code for halting the DOM-based XSS vulnerabilities in cloud. [IJCAC]. *International Journal of Cloud Applications and Computing, 7*(1), 1–31. doi:10.4018/IJCAC.2017010101

Gupta, B. B. (Ed.). (2018). Computer and cyber security: principles, algorithm, applications, and perspectives. Boca Raton, FL: CRC Press.

Gupta, B. B., & Gulihar, P. (2020). Taxonomy of Payment Structures and Economic Incentive Schemes in Internet. [JITR]. *Journal of Information Technology Research, 13*(1), 150–166. doi:10.4018/JITR.2020010110

Gupta, S., & Gupta, B. B. (2015). BDS: browser dependent XSS sanitizer. In *Handbook of Research on Securing Cloud-Based Databases with Biometric Applications* (pp. 174–191). IGI Global. doi:10.4018/978-1-4666-6559-0.ch008

Gupta, S., & Gupta, B. B. (2015, May). PHP-sensor: a prototype method to discover workflow violation and XSS vulnerabilities in PHP web applications. *Proceedings of the 12th ACM International Conference on Computing Frontiers.* ACM, 2015. 10.1145/2742854.2745719

Jain, S., Lang, J., Gong, N. Z., Song, D., Basuroy, S., & Mittal, P. (2015). New directions in social authentication. *Proc. USEC.*

Jain, A. K., & Gupta, B. B. (2017). Phishing detection: Analysis of visual similarity-based approaches. *Security and Communication Networks.*

Javed, A., Bletgen, D., Kohlar, F., Durmuth, M., & Schwenk, J. (2014, June). Secure fallback authentication and the trusted friend attack. In *Proceedings 2014 IEEE 34th International Conference on Distributed Computing Systems Workshops (ICDCSW)* (pp. 22-28). IEEE. 10.1109/ICDCSW.2014.30

Jiang, F., Fu, Y., Gupta, B. B., Lou, F., Rho, S., Meng, F., & Tian, Z. (2018). Deep learning based multi-channel intelligent attack detection for data security. *IEEE Transactions on Sustainable Computing.*

Kiruthiga, S., & Kannan, A. (2014, April). Detecting cloning attack in Social Networks using classification and clustering techniques. In *Proceedings of the 2014 International Conference on Recent Trends in Information Technology (ICRTIT),* (pp. 1-6). IEEE. 10.1109/ICRTIT.2014.6996166

Koll, D., Schwarzmaier, M., Li, J., Li, X. Y., & Fu, X. (2017). Thank You for Being A Friend: An Attacker View on Online-Social-Network-Based Sybil Defenses, *Proc. - IEEE 37th Int. Conf. Distrib. Comput. Syst. Work. ICDCSW 2017*, no. i, pp. 157–162. 10.1109/ICDCSW.2017.67

Lancini, M. (2013, April). Social authentication: Vulnerabilities, mitigations, and redesign. In *Proc. DeepSec Conf.* (pp. 476-492).

LinkedIn. accessed 2017. [Online]. Available: http://www.linkedin.com

Lunt, C. (2012). U.S. Patent No. 8,302,164. Washington, DC: U.S. Patent and Trademark Office.

Mateen, M., Iqbal, M. A., Aleem, M., & Islam, M. A. (2017, January). A hybrid approach for spam detection for Twitter. In *Proceedings 2017 14th International Bhurban Conference on Applied Sciences and Technology (IBCAST)*, (pp. 466-471). IEEE. 10.1109/IBCAST.2017.7868095

Michelin, R. A., Zorzo, A. F., Campos, M. B., Neu, C. V., & Orozco, A. M. (2016, December). Smartphone as a biometric service for web authentication. In *Proceedings 2016 11th International Conference for Internet Technology and Secured Transactions (ICITST)*, (pp. 405-408). IEEE. 10.1109/ICITST.2016.7856740

Mislove, A., Viswanath, B., Gummadi, K. P., & Druschel, P. (2010). *You are who you know: inferring user profiles in online social networks* (pp. 251–260). Wsdm. doi:10.1145/1718487.1718519

Mitnick, K. D., & Simon, W. L. (2011). *The art of deception: Controlling the human element of security.* John Wiley & Sons.

Nandhini, M., & Das, B. B. (2016, March). An assessment and methodology for fraud detection in online social network. In *Proceedings Second International Conference on Science Technology Engineering and Management (ICONSTEM)*, (pp. 104-108). IEEE. 10.1109/ICONSTEM.2016.7560932

Polakis, I., Ilia, P., Maggi, F., Lancini, M., Kontaxis, G., Zanero, S., ... Keromytis, A. D. (2014, November). Faces in the distorting mirror: Revisiting photo-based social authentication. In *Proceedings of the 2014 ACM SIGSAC Conference on Computer and Communications Security* (pp. 501-512). ACM. 10.1145/2660267.2660317

Praveena, A., & Smys, S. (2017, January). Prevention of inference attacks for private information in social networking sites. In *Proceedings 2017 International Conference on Inventive Systems and Control (ICISC)*, (pp. 1-7). IEEE. 10.1109/ICISC.2017.8068648

Rehman, U. U., Khan, W. A., Saqib, N. A., & Kaleem, M. (2013, December). On detection and prevention of clickjacking attack for osns. In *Proceedings 2013 11th International Conference on Frontiers of Information Technology (FIT)*, (pp. 160-165). IEEE. 10.1109/FIT.2013.37

Rubinstein, Y. D., Brill, J. A., Bejar, A., Frank, J. H., & Breger, D. (2017). U.S. Patent No. 9,626,725. Washington, DC: U.S. Patent and Trademark Office.

Sahoo, S. R., & Gupta, B. B. (2019). Classification of various attacks and their defence mechanism in online social networks: A survey. *Enterprise Information Systems*, *13*(6), 832–864. doi:10.1080/17517 575.2019.1605542

Sahoo, S. R., & Gupta, B. B. (2019). Hybrid approach for detection of malicious profiles in twitter. *Computers & Electrical Engineering*, *76*, 65–81. doi:10.1016/j.compeleceng.2019.03.003

Shafahi, M., Kempers, L., & Afsarmanesh, H. (2016, December). Phishing through social bots on Twitter. In *Proceedings 2016 IEEE International Conference on Big Data (Big Data)*, (pp. 3703-3712). IEEE. 10.1109/BigData.2016.7841038

Sugandhi, R., Pande, A., Chawla, S., Agrawal, A., & Bhagat, H. (2015, December). Methods for detection of cyberbullying: A survey. In *Proceedings 2015 15th International Conference on Intelligent Systems Design and Applications (ISDA)*, (pp. 173-177). IEEE. 10.1109/ISDA.2015.7489220

Twitter, accessed 2017. [Online]. Available: http://www.twitter

"WEKA," accessed 2017. [Online]. Available: https://www.cs.waikato.ac.nz/ml/weka/

Yang, M., Yu, Y., Bandara, A. K., & Nuseibeh, B. (2014, September). Adaptive sharing for online social networks: A trade-off between privacy risk and social benefit. In *Proceedings of the 2014 IEEE 13th International Conference on Trust, Security, and Privacy in Computing and Communications (TrustCom)*, (pp. 45-52). IEEE. 10.1109/TrustCom.2014.10

Yang, Y., Chen, F., Chen, J., Zhang, Y., & Yung, K. L. (2019). A secure hash function based on feedback iterative structure. *Enterprise Information Systems*, *13*(3), 281–302. doi:10.1080/17517575.2018.1564942

Ye, J., & Mo, J. (2015). U.S. Patent No. 9,009,232. Washington, DC: U.S. Patent and Trademark Office.

Zhang, X., Zheng, H., Li, X., Du, S., & Zhu, H. (2014). You are where you have been: Sybil detection via geo-location analysis in OSNs, *Proceedings 2014 IEEE Glob. Commun. Conf. GLOBECOM*, *2014*, 698–703.

Zhang, Z., Sun, R., Zhao, C., Wang, J., Chang, C. K., & Gupta, B. B. (2017). CyVOD: A novel trinity multimedia social network scheme. *Multimedia Tools and Applications*, *76*(18), 18513–18529. doi:10.100711042-016-4162-z

Zheng, Q., Wang, X., Khurram Khan, M., Zhang, W., Gupta, B. B., & Guo, W. (2017). A lightweight authenticated encryption scheme based on chaotic scml for railway cloud service. *IEEE Access: Practical Innovations, Open Solutions*, *6*, 711–722. doi:10.1109/ACCESS.2017.2775038

Chapter 13

An Attribute–Based Searchable Encryption Scheme for Non–Monotonic Access Structure

Mamta

National Institute of Technology, Kurukshetra, India

Brij B. Gupta

National Institute of Technology, Kurukshetra, India

ABSTRACT

Attribute based encryption (ABE) is a widely used technique with tremendous application in cloud computing because it provides fine-grained access control capability. Owing to this property, it is emerging as a popular technique in the area of searchable encryption where the fine-grained access control is used to determine the search capabilities of a user. But, in the searchable encryption schemes developed using ABE it is assumed that the access structure is monotonic which contains AND, OR and threshold gates. Many ABE schemes have been developed for non-monotonic access structure which supports NOT gate, but this is the first attempt to develop a searchable encryption scheme for the same. The proposed scheme results in fast search and generates secret key and search token of constant size and also the ciphertext components are quite fewer than the number of attributes involved. The proposed scheme is proven secure against chosen keyword attack (CKA) in selective security model under Decisional Bilinear Diffie-Hellman (DBDH) assumption.

INTRODUCTION

Recently, cloud computing has become a technology trend. Considering its flexibility, affordability and availability more and more organizations are shifting to cloud paradigm as it also unburdens them from the cumbersome task of data management. Although, cloud computing provides some innovative benefits yet this concept has also raised some privacy concerns as the data stored over third party cloud server cloud be misused. To address such concerns the concept of searchable encryption is introduced which

DOI: 10.4018/978-1-7998-2242-4.ch013

Copyright © 2020, IGI Global. Copying or distributing in print or electronic forms without written permission of IGI Global is prohibited.

not only provides data security by encrypting data but also facilitate seamless search over encrypted data (Zheng, et. al, 2017; Yu et al., 2018; Premkamal et al., 2020; Olakanmi et al., 2019;).

To develop a searchable encryption scheme using public key cryptographic primitives, there are several options like identity-based encryption (IBE), attribute-based encryption (ABE), homomorphic encryption (HE) and function encryption (FE) etc. In this paper, we have used attribute-based encryption scheme and particularly its ciphertext policy (CP) framework to build a searchable encryption scheme (CP-ABSE) for non-monotonic access structure. All the searchable encryption schemes based on ABE which have developed so far considers the access structure to be monotonic which does not support negative attributes. To support non-monotonic access structure, we have used a reduced ordered binary decision diagram (ROBDD) which efficiently supports all the Boolean operations (AND, OR, NOT) over attributes. The first attempt of using ordered binary decision diagram for the construction of ABE was done by Li et al. (2017). But the access structure represented by OBDD contains many redundant nodes which leads to increased computation cost. Hence, to reduce this cost we have used ROBDD which does not contain any redundant node and developed a CP-ABSE scheme which is efficient in terms of computational and storage cost.

Contributions

The major contributions of this chapter are as follows:

- In attribute-based searchable encryption scheme the access policy is assumed to be monotonic which does not support negative attributes. If an access policy can handle the negative attributes in addition to AND, OR gates; then it is known to have more expressiveness. Most of the attribute-based searchable encryption schemes do not possess this feature. The proposed scheme in this chapter is an attempt to increase the expressiveness of the access policy in terms of the support for the negative attributes.
- To achieve the primary goal stated above, the authors have used reduced ordered binary decision diagrams which can represent any Boolean formula with great efficiency. In the literature OBDD have been used to develop the ABE scheme but this is the first attempt where authors have further applied reduction methods to minimize the redundant nodes in an OBDD.
- The size of the ciphertext is independent of the number of attributes in the access policy, thus a reduction in storage cost is observed. Further, the number of pairing operations in the search operation are again independent of the number of attributes which results in fast search.

Importance of the Proposed Scheme in an Intrusion Detection System (IDS)

Typically, an IDS is used to analyze the network traffic for the suspicious activities. The traditional IDS works well in the scenario where the network traffic is not in an encrypted form. However, in the current scenario, due to the raised concern about privacy the percentage of encrypted network traffic is rapidly increasing. Therefore, there is need to develop techniques that can work well for the encrypted traffic. To analyze the encrypted traffic and to retrieve the relevant information without decryption one can use searchable encryption. Because the searchable encryption has the same fundamental property i.e. one can get the desired information without decryption if he/she possess the correct credentials. To develop an IDS for encrypted traffic one can embed the searchable encryption technique to encrypt the traffic and later on the searching functionalities can be used to retrieve the desired information without disclosing any other information about underlying network traffic (Jiang et al., 2018; Gupta et al., 2016; Gou et al., 2017; El-Latif et al., 2018; Almomani et al., 2018). The proposed scheme in this chapter is a searchable encryption scheme based on the ABE technique which enables fine-grained search capabilities. Further, the proposed scheme supports non-monotonic access structure and thereby further enhancing the fine-graininess by constructing the more expressive and powerful access policies. In terms of efficiency, the proposed schemes offer fast search and low storage cost as compared to the existing schemes of similar type.

RELATED WORK

The first searchable encryption scheme using public key cryptographic primitive was proposed by Boneh et al. (2004). However, it does not support multi-user scenario where the data owner wants to share their data in a differential manner with multiple users. To address this issue, several ABE based keyword search schemes have been proposed in the literature from time to time (Zheng et al., 2014; Sun et al., 2016; Li et al., 2016; Hu et al., 2017; Wang et al., 2017; Qiu et al., 2017; Cui et al., 2018; Chaudhari & Das, 2019; Mamta & Gupta, 2019a; Mamta et al., 2019b). The basic construction for attribute-based keyword search (ABKS) was given by Zheng et al. (2014) and Sun et al. (2016) in which they have used the access policy to determine who can perform search operation over encrypted data. But on the downside, in both schemes the secret key size, the trapdoor size and the number of pairing operations in search are proportional to the number of attributes associated with them. Li et al. (2016) tried to resolve the issue by outsourcing heavy computational tasks to the cloud server, although it reduces the computational burden but results in an increased communication cost. Chaudhari and Das (2019) introduced a searchable encryption scheme where the concept of anonymity was introduced but all the three parameters mentioned above were proportional to the number of attributes.

A DABKS scheme was proposed by Hu et al. (2017) where the main focus was to support an update operation on access policy, which was delegated to the cloud server. Wang et al. (2017) proposed an ABKS scheme which supported fast keyword search for which they had used an aggregate search key. In this scheme, the size of secret key was proportional to the number of attributes while the trapdoor had the constant size. In a paper by Qiu et al. (2017) the main focus was on improving the security of the ABKS scheme against keyword guessing attack (KGA) in addition with security against chosen keyword attack (CKA). Recently, Cui et al. (2018) proposed an ABKS scheme where the accuracy of search result can be verified and also supported user revocation. Recently, Mamta & Gupta (2019) proposed a scheme which provides constant secret key size, trapdoor size and number of pairing operations together. Thus reduces computational cost, saves the bandwidth and also supports fast search. However, none of the schemes proposed so far have been developed which supports non-monotonic access structure. In this regard, the authors have proposed an attribute based searchable encryption scheme using the ciphertext policy design known as CP-ABSE which can handle any Boolean operation over attributes. Furthermore, the proposed CP-ABSE achieve other remarkable features like constant size for secret key, search token and supports fast search. A detailed comparison of our scheme with existing schemes in literature is given in Table 1. The exact number of group elements involved in the secret key, the keyword ciphertext and the trapdoor will be shown later after the construction of the proposed scheme.

Table 1. Comparative analysis of the key features of the proposed scheme with the existing schemes

Features	Access Structure	Non-Monotonic	Operations Supported in the Access Structure	Policy Embedded in	Secret Key Size	Trapdoor Size	Cipher Text Size Depends Upon	# of Pairing Operations Depends Upon
Zheng et al. (2014)	General	X	AND, OR and Threshold	User secret key and keyword ciphertext	Variable	Variable	# of attributes	# of attributes
Sun et al. (2016)	AND	X	AND	Keyword ciphertext	Variable	Variable	# of attributes	# of attributes
Li et al. (2016)	General	X	AND, OR and Threshold	User secret key	Variable	Variable	# of attributes	# of attributes
Hu et al. (2017)	General	X	AND, OR and Threshold		Variable	Variable	# of attributes	# of attributes
Wang et al. (2017)	AND	X	AND	Keyword ciphertext	Variable	Variable	# of attributes	independent
Qiu et al. (2017)	AND	X	AND	Keyword ciphertext	Variable	Variable	# of attributes	# of attributes
Cui et al. (2018)	General	X	AND, OR and Threshold	Keyword ciphertext	Variable	Variable	# of attributes	independent
Chaudhari and Das (2019)	AND	X	AND	Keyword ciphertext	Variable	Variable	# of attributes	# of attributes
Mamta & Gupta (2019a)	General	X	AND, OR and Threshold	User secret key	Constant	Constant	# of attributes	independent
Mamta et al. (2019b)	General	X	AND, OR and Threshold	User secret key	Constant	Constant	# of attributes	independent
Proposed Scheme	General	X	AND, OR NOT and Threshold	Keyword ciphertext	Constant	Constant	# of valid paths	# of valid paths

As it can be seen from Table 1, the proposed scheme supports general tree structure access policy and further it supports NOT gate in addition to AND, OR and threshold gates which results in more expressive access policy. Moreover, the size of the secret key and trapdoor is constant which results in reduced computational cost and the size of ciphertext does not depend upon the number of attributes like in exiting scheme while it depends upon the number of valid paths which contains comparatively lesser number of attributes as compared to the total number of attributes in access policy in case of the CP-ABE based searchable encryption. The number of pairing operations are again depending upon the number of valid paths which makes the search faster as compared to other existing schemes except the schemes where the number of pairing operations are independent of the number of attributes.

BACKGROUND

This section discusses the essential mathematical and structural background required to properly understand the proposed scheme.

Bilinear Map and Complexity Assumption

This section provides the basic definition of the building blocks used in the construction of the proposed scheme.

Bilinear Map

Let G, G_T be the source and target cyclic groups of the prime order p and g be the generator of the source group G. Let $e: G \times G \to G_T$ be the symmetric bilinear map between G and G_T which satisfies the following properties:

- **Bilinearity**: $\forall x, y \in G = e\left(x^a, y^b\right) = e(x, y)^{ab}$, where $a, b \in Z_p$.
- **Non-Degeneracy**: If g is the generator of source group G, then $e(g, g) \neq 1$
- **Computability**: $\forall l, m \in G; e(l, m)$ is efficiently computable.

Decisional Bilinear Diffie-Hellman Assumption

It is hard to distinguish the tuples of the form $\left(g^a, g^b, g^c, e(g, g)^{abc}\right)$ from the tuple of the form $\left(g^a, g^b, g^c, e(g, g)^z\right)$ where $a, b, c, z \in Z_p$ and $g \in G$.

Reduced Ordered Binary Decision Diagram

Binary Decision Tree (BDT) is a data structure that can represent any digital circuit but due to the exponential growth of the number of nodes with respect to inputs, it is not feasible to generate it in polynomial time. So, the concept of Ordered Binary Decision Diagram (OBDD) was introduced (Li et al. (2017)) to cater the high complexity of BDT. OBDD is a binary decision diagram (BDD) which has the ordering for variables of a Boolean function. Basically, BDD is a directed acyclic graph which can represent any Boolean function and has no redundant node therefore it has much lower number of nodes as compared to BDT. But BDD does not restrict the reoccurrence of a variable in the diagram which can lead to redundant decisions. For e.g. – a same variable may take two different values simultaneously along the same path. Thus to solve this issue, a restriction should be imposed upon the order of occurrence of variables from root to leaves such that each variable will occur only once along any path from root to leaf node. Hence, there would be no redundant decisions and such a diagram is known as OBDD. The size of OBDD is greatly influenced by the variable ordering, so to keep the size minimal an optimal variable ordering must be determined. To find an optimal ordering is a NP-complete problem but there are some heuristics which can be used to get a good variable ordering. In the proposed scheme we have used static variable ordering where the order of variables is fixed before the construction of the variables. To further reduce the number of nodes in OBDD the reduction techniques can be applied to eliminate the redundant nodes which results in a reduced OBDD (ROBDD).

Definition- ROBDD

It is a rooted directed acyclic graph with no redundant nodes and a fixed ordering, O, of variables. The ROBDD for a Boolean function f with variables $(x_1, x_2, \cdots, x_n)$ with fixed ordering $O = x_1 < x_2 < \cdots < x_n$ has the following properties:

- There are two types of nodes: terminal and non-terminal.
- A terminal node, u, corresponds to a value either 0 or 1 i.e. $value(u) = 0/1$ and a non-terminal node, u, corresponds to an attribute which can be represented by the tuple $(index, low, high)$ where $index(u) \in \{1, 2, ..., n\}$ and $low(u), high(u)$ are the children of node u.
- Each non-terminal node has exactly two children and the two arcs from parent to child nodes are labelled by a dashed line and a solid line. The dashed line denotes that the value assigned to the variable is 0 (returned by function $low(u)$) and the solid line denotes the value assigned to the variable is 1 (returned by function $high(u)$).
- Each variable appears only once on any path from root to leaf and $index(u) < index(low(u))$ and $index(u) < index(high(u))$ if $low(u)$ and $high(u)$ are also non-terminals. It denotes that the non-terminal nodes along any path must have strictly increasing *index*.

Access Structure

In the proposed scheme we will use non-monotonic access structure which allows AND, OR and NOT operation between attributes. An access structure represented by a Boolean function can be efficiently expressed using ROBDD data structure where the attributes are represented by the variables of the function.

Any access policy can be converted to a Boolean function $f(x_1, x_2, \cdots, x_n)$. To convert AND, OR and NOT gates to Boolean operation is trivial but to transform a threshold gate is a bit complex task. A threshold gate $T(t, n)$ outputs 1 if t out of n attributes are present where n is the total number of attributes contained in a set N. Following steps are used to transform a threshold gate $T(t, n)$ to a Boolean function (Li et al., 2017):

- Compute all subsets of *N* which contains *t* different attributes.
- For each subset with size *t*, apply conjunction operation between these *t* attributes.
- To get the final Boolean expression for $T(t,n)$, apply disjunction operation between each subset.

PROPOSED SCHEME BASED ON ROBDD ACCESS STRUCTURE

This section discusses the system model, system definition and security model of the proposed scheme.

System Model

The system is composed of the following four parties as shown in Figure 1:

- **Data Owner**: Who wants to outsource their data in an encrypted form for the purpose of sharing it with multiple users in a differential manner
- **Data Users**: Who wants to retrieve the data stored by the data owner at the cloud server
- **Trusted Authority (TA)**: Who grants essential credentials to the data owners and data users

Figure 1. System model

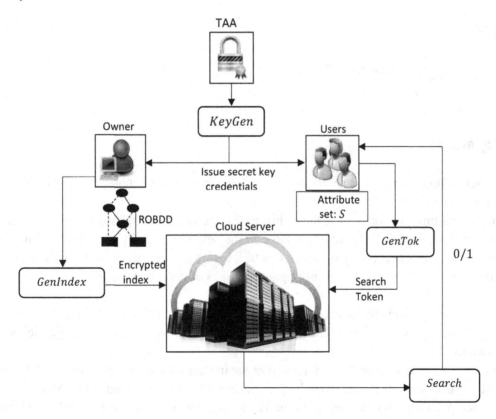

- **Cloud Server**: Which stores the encrypted data and performs search operation on the behalf of data user. In order to search a particular keyword, the user will generate a trapdoor for that keyword and gives it to the cloud server. The cloud server will perform the search over encrypted data using that trapdoor and returns the corresponding result to the user.

System Definition

The system is composed of the following polynomial time algorithms:

- **Setup**: This algorithm is executed by trusted authority and it generates the public parameters (*param*) and master secret key (*MSK*).
- **KeyGen**: This algorithm is again executed by trusted authority and it generates the secret key credentials for each user by using the MSK.
- **GenIndex**: This algorithm is executed by the data owner who wants to share his data with other users. For this purpose, the data owner encrypts the keywords under his access policy to generate the corresponding index.
- **GenTok**: This algorithm is executed by the data user to generate the search token for a given keyword.
- **Search**: This algorithm is executed by the cloud server. It takes the encrypted index and the trapdoor as input and perform search over encrypted index for the keyword specified in the trapdoor.

Correctness

$$\left\{ Search\left(T_i, C_i\right) = 1 \middle| \begin{array}{c} C_i \leftarrow GenIndex\left(K_{pub}, w_i\right) \\ T_i \leftarrow GenTok\left(K_{pri}, w_i\right) \end{array} \right\}$$

Security Model

Security Definition: Indistinguishability of keywords against selective chosen keyword attack (sCKA): Canetti et al. (2003)

A polynomial time adversary $\mathcal{A}$ cannot distinguish the ciphertext of two keywords of her choice unless the trapdoor for that keyword is available in the selective security model where the adversary have to commit to the access policy it intends to attack before the security game between the challenger $\mathcal{C}$ and an adversary $\mathcal{A}$ begins. The security game consists of the following phases:

- **Init**: $\mathcal{A}$ selects the challenge access structure, $ROBDD^*$, and gives it to the challenger $\mathcal{C}$.
- *Setup Phase:* $\mathcal{C}$ runs the *Setup* algorithm of the proposed scheme and gives the public parameters, *param*, to $\mathcal{A}$.
- **Phase 1:** $\mathcal{A}$ can query secret key for any user having attribute set SS provided $S \nvDash ROBDD^*$. In addition, the challenger $\mathcal{C}$ can answer the query for trapdoor of any keyword, COMMENTS"w"w by generating the secret key credentials and add that keyword to the list L_t for which the adversary has asked the trapdoor.

- **Challenge Phase:** $\mathcal{A}$ chooses two keywords w_0, w_1 of equal length for which $\mathcal{A}$ has not queried the trapdoor in Phase 1, i.e. $w_0, w_1 \notin L_t$. The challenger, $\mathcal{C}$ selects a bit $b \xleftarrow{\$} \{0,1\}$ $\mu \in \{0,1\}$ and runs the $GenIndex\left(PP, w_\mu, \xi^*\right) \to C^*$. The challenge ciphertext C^* corresponding to the keyword w_μ which is then sent to the adversary $\mathcal{A}$.

- **Phase 2:** $\mathcal{A}$ can continuously query like in Phase 1 with the additional restriction that $\mathcal{A}$ cannot query for search token corresponding to w_μ.

- **Guess Phase:** Given the challenge ciphertext, C^*, $\mathcal{A}$ outputs a guess μ' of μ and wins the game if $\mu' = \mu$ with the following advantage:

$$Adv_{\mathcal{A}}^{sCKA}\left(k\right) = \left| Pr\left(\mu = \mu'\right) - \frac{1}{2} \right| = \varepsilon \tag{1}$$

CONSTRUCTION OF THE PROPOSED SCHEME

Core Idea: For the construction of the proposed scheme first of all an ordered binary decision diagram (OBDD) for a fixed ordering is built and then we will apply the reduction techniques (Bryant, 1986) to get the compact size OBDD which is more accurately known as ROBDD. The resulting ROBDD which represent the access structure of the data owner is then embedded in the ciphertext to generate the encrypted index. The benefit of using ROBDD is that it not only efficiently represents any Boolean function but we can also check the satisfiability for the given attribute set with quite less complexity which is independent of the number of attributes. To check if a given attribute set satisfies ROBDD, we just need to traverse it and check if the path ends at constant 1. If the attribute is contained in the set, then we need to move to the solid arc otherwise we will move to the dashed arc and this process is repeated till the terminal node is reached. So, it results in fast search and also provides the flexibility to efficiently represent any non-monotonic access structure.

Build ROBDD for the Given Boolean Function

The concept of OBDD was first used by Li et al. (2017) for the construction of ciphertext-policy attribute-based encryption. In their construction they have efficiently used OBDD to represent any non-monotonic access structure. However, the size of OBDD was not compact since it contains many redundant nodes. Hence, it results in more computation in the search as well as it increases the number of ciphertext components. To represent OBDD in compact size, there is a need to identify and eliminate any redundant node in OBDD and for this purpose we will use the reduction technique given by Bryant (1986). We will use the same example as used in (Li et al., 2017) and construct the corresponding ROBDD which does not possess any redundancy.

To construct the ROBDD for a given access policy we will use the algorithms given in Table 2, 3 and 4.

Table 2. Algorithm for the construction of ROBDD corresponding to a given Boolean function

	BUILD_ROBDD(*f*)
1.	Initialize *n* = # of variables in *f*
2.	int *i*=1
3.	node u
3.	Initialize table *T* to be empty
4.	*U=BUILD_OBDD(f,i)*
5.	*REDUCE(v: nodes inOBDD)*

To construct OBDD the algorithm *BUILD_OBDD(f,i)* given in Table 3 uses Shannon's expansion (R. E. Bryant (1986)) where any Boolean function, *f*, can be represented by the sum of two sub-functions of the original function.

$$f(x) = x \cdot f[1/x] + \bar{x}f[0/x]$$

where $\bar{x}$ - complement of x, $f[0/x]$ and $f[1/x]$ are the function obtained on replacing the variable x with 0 and 1 respectively.

Table 4 describes the algorithm for eliminating redundant nodes from OBDD by assigning a label, *id*, to each node and merging all the nodes which have same id. This algorithm uses two functions on non-terminal nodes: *low(x)* and *high(x)*. *low(x)* returns the node pointed to via dashed arc and *high(x)*

Table 3. Algorithm for the construction of OBDD

	BUILD_OBDD(*f,i*)
1.	node u, v_0, v_1
2.	if *i*>*n*
3.	if *f* is false return 0 else return 1
4.	else
5.	$v_0 = BUILD\_OBDD\left(f[0/x_i], i+1\right)$
6.	$v_1 = BUILD\_OBDD\left(f[1/x_i], i+1\right)$
7.	if entry $\left(v_0, v_1, u\right)$ exists return *u*
8.	else *index(u)=i* *low(u)=v_0* *high(u)=v_1*
9.	Store $\left(v_0, v_1, u\right)$ in T
10.	return *u*

Table 4. Algorithm for the reduction in OBDD

REDUCE(*v: nodes in OBDD*)	
1.	node $vlist[n+1]$ //array of indexes of nodes in OBDD graph G
2.	node x
3.	Put each node x on the list $wlist[x(index)]$
4.	int $nextid = 1$
5.	for $i=n+1$ downto 1
6.	if $index(x) = n+1$
7.	set $id(x) = value(x)$
8.	else if $id(low(x)) = id(high(x))$ then set $id(x) = id(low(x))$
9.	else if $\exists$ a node *y:* $(index(x) = index(y)) \wedge (id(low(x)) = id(low(y))) \wedge (id(high(x)) = id(high(y)))$ then set $id(x) = id(y)$
10.	else $nextid = nextid + 1$ and set $id(x) = nextid$
11.	Merge all nodes having same id and redirect edges accordingly
12.	return the resultant subgraph of G

returns the node pointed to via solid arc. Here the index value for terminal node is assumed to be $n+1$, where n is the number of variables in the Boolean function.

To demonstrate the construction of ROBDD, we have used the same access policy as used in (Li et al., 2017). Let $\{x_1, x_2, x_3, x_4\}$ be the attributes contained in access policy which states that any user who possesses attribute x_1 or any two attributes among $\{x_2, x_3, x_4\}$ can perform the search over encrypted data. The second part of the access policy contains a threshold gate $T(2,3)$. The access policy defined above can be expressed by the following Boolean function:

$$f(x_1, x_2, x_3, x_4) = x_1 + x_2 x_3 + x_2 x_4 + x_3 x_4$$

Let $O = x_1 < x_2 < x_3 < x_4$ be the variable ordering for f and it is assumed that the terminal nodes has the *index*= # of variables in f+1.

Apply Shannon's expansion to get the corresponding OBDD:

$$f[0/x_1] = x_2 x_3 + x_2 x_4 + x_3 x_4 = g(x_2, x_3, x_4)$$

$$f\left[1/x_1\right]=1$$

$$g\left[0/x_2\right]=x_3x_4=h\left(x_3,x_4\right)$$

$$g\left[1/x_2\right]=x_3+x_4=i\left(x_3,x_4\right)$$

$$h\left[0/x_3\right]=0$$

$$h\left[1/x_3\right]=x_4=j\left(x_4\right)$$

$$i\left[0/x_3\right]=x_4=j\left(x_4\right)$$

$$i\left[1/x_3\right]=1$$

$$j\left[0/x_4\right]=0$$

$$j\left[1/x_4\right]=1$$

Now, to eliminate redundant nodes apply *REDUCE* given in Table 4 and get the corresponding ROBDD as shown in Figure 2.

The label marked with # sign represents the *id* assigned to each node. The number of nodes in ROBDD are significantly less as compared to the number of nodes in the OBDD given by Li et al. (2017). The final ROBDD access structure is described as: $ROBDD=\left\{node_i^{id}\mid i\in I\right\}$, here I is the set formed by attributes appearing in the access structure and *id* is the label assigned to each node in the reduction process.

Construction of ROBDD-Based CP-ABSE

The proposed CP-ABSE scheme uses both positive and negative attributes using the same notation as used by Sun et al. (2016). An attribute index is represented by $\underline{i}:\underline{i}=i$ if $\underline{i}$ is a positive attribute, otherwise $\underline{i}=\neg i$. Let $Att=\left\{x_1,x_2,...,x_n\right\}$ be the attribute universe and $W=\left\{w_1,w_2,...,w_{|W|}\right\}$ be the keyword space where each keyword $w\in\left\{0,1\right\}^*$. The proposed CP-ABSE scheme consists of the following algorithms:

- ***Setup*** $\left(»,Att\right)$**:** Let $e:G\times G\to G_T$ be a bilinear map between source and the target group of prime order p and g be the generator of source group. Let $H:\left\{0,1\right\}^*\to Z_p$ be a collision resistant hash function. Randomly select $\alpha,\left\{t_i,t_i'\right\}_{1\le i\le n}$ from Z_P. Compute $Y=e\left(g,g\right)^\alpha$, $T_i=g^{t_i}$, $T_i'=g^{t_i'}$

Figure 2. ROBDD for the Boolean function

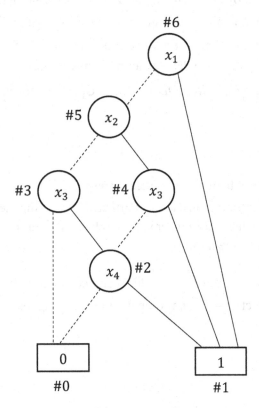

and generate the public parameters, $param = \left(e, g, Y, \underline{T_i} = \{T_i, T_i'\}_{1 \leq i \leq n}, H \right)$, and master secret key,

$MSK = \left(\alpha, \{t_i, t_i'\}_{1 \leq i \leq n} \right)$.

Here, T_i corresponds to positive attributes and T_i' corresponds to negative attributes.

- ***KeyGen(MSK, S)***: This algorithm generates the secret key credentials for a user as per the attribute set, $S = \{x_1, x_2, ..., x_m\} : S \subseteq Att$, assigned to him/her. If an attribute does not belong to set S, it is assumed that it is a negative attribute with a default value $\neg i$. When a new user wants to register to the system, first of all TA selects a random number $u \leftarrow Z_p$ and computes $Y_u = Y^u$ and publish it with *param*. Now, TA selects another random number $r \leftarrow Z_p$ and computes the following secret key $\left(SK = [u, K_1, K_2] \right)$ components:

$$K_1 = g^{\alpha+r}, K_2 = g^{r / \sum\limits_{1 \leq i \leq m} t_i}$$

Where the value of $\underline{t_i}$ is defined as follows:

If $(i \in S) \wedge (\underline{i} = i)$ then $t_i = t_i$ else $\underline{t_i} = t_i'$.

275

- **GenIndex(*param*, w_l, *ROBDD*):** This algorithm generates the index for the keyword $w_l \in W$ encrypted under non-monotonic access structure $ROBDD = \{node_i^{id} \mid i \in I\}$. First of all, find all the paths from *root* to terminal node 1 and are called as valid paths. Let $V = \{V_1, V_2, ..., V_T\}$ represents the set of all valid paths. The data owner randomly selects a number $s \leftarrow Z_p$ and computes the following ciphertext, $\left(C_l = \left[ROBDD, C_1, C_{2,V_{Path}}, C_3 \right] \right)$ components:

$$C_1 = g^{s/H(w_l)}, C_{2,V_{Path}} = \prod_{i \in I} T_i^{\,s}, C_3 = Y^s$$

Here, $C_{2,V_{Path}}$ represents the ciphertext component corresponding to each valid path and hence contains the information related to the attributes in each V_i. Furthermore, a component, C_u, is computed for every newly registered user, u, with whom data owner wants to share his data, $C_u = Y_u^{-s}$ and is sent to the cloud server along with the identity of the user.

- **GenTok(*param*, *SK*, w_m):** Data user uses his secret key to generate the search token for the keyword, w_m. Randomly select $t \leftarrow Z_p$ and computes the following search token $\left(Tok_m = [D_1, D_2, D_3] \right)$ components:

$$D_1 = K_1^{H(w_m)t}, D_2 = K_2^{t}, D_3 = t + u$$

- **Search(*param*, C_l, Tok_m):** The cloud server executes this algorithm to perform search for a keyword w_m over encrypted index C_l. This algorithm outputs 1 if the keyword being searched is found else returns 0. The search process is performed by the following recursive algorithm starting from the root of ROBDD:

Correctness Proof

From L.H.S. of eq. (2):

$$C_3^{D_3} \cdot C_u = e(g,g)^{\alpha s(t+u)} \cdot e(g,g)^{-\alpha su} = e(g,g)^{\alpha st} \tag{3}$$

From R.H.S. of eq. (2):

$$\frac{e(C_1, D_1)}{e(C_{2,V_{Path}}, D_2)} = \frac{e\left(g^{s/H(w_l)}, g^{(\alpha+r)H(w_m)t}\right)}{e\left(\prod_{i \in I} T_i^{\,s}, g^{rt/\sum_{1 \le i \le m} t_i}\right)} = \frac{e(g,g)^{\alpha st} e(g,g)^{\alpha rt}}{e\left(g^{s\sum_{1 \le i \le m} t_i}, g^{rt/\sum_{1 \le i \le m} t_i}\right)} = e(g,g)^{\alpha st} \tag{4}$$

From eq. (3) and (4): If $w_l = w_m$, *L.H.S. of eq.(2) = R.H.S. of eq.(2)*.

Table 5. Recursive algorithm for search process

	$Search(param, C, Tok_m)$
1.	Starting from the root node, set root node as the current node, *current=root*
2.	Extract each current node information from $node_i^{id}$ for attribute *i*, if $(i \in S) \wedge (\underline{i} = i)$ go to step 3 otherwise go to step 4.
3.	Follow the solid arc: • If the node appearing on solid arc is a terminal node having value 0, terminate and return $\perp$. • If the node appearing on solid arc is a terminal node having value 1, go to step 5. • If the node appearing on solid arc is a non-terminal node, set it as *current* and go to step 2
4.	Follow the dashed arc: • If the node appearing on dashed arc is a terminal node having value 0, terminate and return $\perp$. • If the node appearing on dashed arc is a terminal node having value 1, go to step 5. • If the node appearing on dashed arc is a non-terminal node, set it as *current* and go to step 2
5.	Store the resulting valid path $(root \rightarrow 1)$ in the set V_{path} and returns 1 if the following condition holds, else returns $0. C_3^{D_3} \cdot C_u = \dfrac{e(C_1, D_1)}{e(C_{2,V_{Path}}, D_2)}(2)$

Security Analysis

The following theorem guarantees the security of the proposed CP-ABSE scheme:

Theorem 1: The proposed scheme is IND-sCKA secure under DBDH assumption if $\forall \mathcal{A}$ (probabilistic polynomial time adversary), the advantage, ε of winning the security game is negligible.

Proof: Let there exists an adversary $\mathcal{A}$ who can win the IND-sCKA game with advantage ε then there exists a challenger $\mathcal{C}$ who can break the DBDH assumption with advantage $\dfrac{\varepsilon}{2}$, given an instance (g^a, g^b, g^c, Z) of DBDH assumption. Challenger simulates the IND-sCKA game defined in security model as follows:

- *Init:* $\mathcal{A}$ selects the challenge access structure, $ROBDD^* = \{node_i^{id} \mid i \in I\}$, and gives it to the challenger $\mathcal{C}$.

- *Setup Phase:* $\mathcal{C}$ sets $Y = e(g^a, g^b) = e(g,g)^{ab}$ which implicitly sets $\alpha = ab$ and selects $\{t_i, t_i'\}_{i \in I} \leftarrow Z_p$ for each attribute. Randomly choose $\theta \leftarrow Z_p$ and set $Y_u = Y^\theta$.

- *Phase 1:* $\mathcal{A}$ can query for secret key for attribute set *S* provided $S \not\models ROBDD^*$ such that $\exists j \in I : ((j \in S) \wedge (\underline{j} = \neg j)) \vee ((j \notin S) \wedge (\underline{j} = j))$. For such an attribute, $t_{\underline{j}} = b \cdot t_j'$. For $i \neq j$, $t_{\underline{i}}$ is defined as:

If $(i \in S) \wedge (\underline{i} = i)$, set $t_{\underline{i}} = t_i$

If $(i \in S) \wedge (\underline{i} = \neg i)$, set $t_{\underline{i}} = b \cdot t_i$

If $(i \notin S) \wedge (\underline{i} = \neg i)$, set $t_{\underline{i}} = t_i'$

If $(i \notin S) \wedge (\underline{i} = i)$, set $t_{\underline{i}} = b \cdot t_i'$

Now, set the secret key components as: $K_1 = g^{ab+r}, K_2 = g^{r/\sum_{1 \le i \le m} t_i}$ and using these credentials C can answer search token query for any keyword and stores that keyword in a list L_t.

- **Challenge Phase:** A submits two keywords w_0, w_1 of equal length for which A has not queried the trapdoor in Phase 1, i.e. $w_0, w_1 \notin L_t$COMMENTS"$w\_0, w\_1 \notin L\_t$". The challenger generates $C_1 = g^{c/H(w_\mu)}$, $C_{2,V_{Path}} = g^{c\sum_{i \in I} t_i}$, $C_3 = Z$ and send the challenge ciphertext, C_μ^*, to A.
- **Phase 2:** A can continuously query like in Phase 1 with the additional restriction that A cannot query for the trapdoor corresponding to w_μ.
- **Guess Phase:** Given the challenge ciphertext, C^*, A outputs a guess μ' of μ and wins the game if $\mu' = \mu$.

Challenger selects a binary number, $v \leftarrow \{0,1\}$ and if $v=1$, then $Z = e(g,g)^{abc}$ otherwise Z. is a random element from G_T. If $Z = e(g,g)^{abc}$, then C_μ^* represents a valid ciphertext and $Pr(\mu' = \mu | v = 1) = \varepsilon + \frac{1}{2}$. If $v=0$, C_μ^* contains no information about the keyword and $Pr(\mu' = \mu | v = 0) = \frac{1}{2}$. Hence, the total probability of correctly guessing the keyword is $\frac{1}{2}\left(\varepsilon + \frac{1}{2} + \frac{1}{2}\right)$. The advantage with which C can solve the DBDH sumption is $\frac{1}{2}\left(\varepsilon + \frac{1}{2} + \frac{1}{2}\right) - \frac{1}{2} = \frac{\varepsilon}{2}$. Since DBDH is a known hard problem, which makes $\frac{\varepsilon}{2}$ negligible and hence ε is negligible. Thus the proposed scheme is secure against IND-sCKA.

Comparative Analysis

This section covers the analysis of the proposed scheme in a comparative manner where the storage and computational cost of the proposed scheme is compared with the existing attribute based keyword search schemes as shown below in Table 6:

Notations used in the above defined Table 6 are given below in Table 7:

As it can be observed from Table 6, the storage as well as computational cost for secret key and search token generation does not depend upon the number of attributes and is therefore . In the ciphertext generation algorithm, the storage cost and computational cost depends on the number of valid paths which are quite less as compared to the number of attributes. Similarly, in search process the number of pairing operations also depends upon the set of valid paths, hence results in faster search as compared to the schemes where the number of pairing operations varies linearly with the number of attributes.

Table 6. Comparative analysis of the storage and the computational cost

Scheme	Algorithm	Storage Cost	Computational Cost
Zheng et al. (2004)	KeyGen	$(2N)|G|$	$(2\xi+2)E+\xi H$
	GenIndex	$(\xi+3)|G|$	$(2N+4)E+NH$
	GenTok	$(2N+2)|G|$	$(2\xi+4)E$
	Search		$(2N+3)P+NE_T$
Sun et al. (2016)	KeyGen	$1|Z_p|+(2\xi+1)|G|$	$(2\xi+2)E$
	GenIndex	$(N+2)|G|$	$(3N+2)E+1H$
	GenTok	$(2\xi+2)|G|$	$(2\xi+1)E+2H$
	Search		$(N+1)P+NE_T$
Li et al. (2016)	KeyGen	$(2N+4)|G|+1|Z_p|$	$(2N+6)E$
	GenIndex	$k|G_T|+(\xi+2)|G|$	$(\xi+2)E+2kE_T+KH$
	GenTok	$(2N+2)|G|$	$2E+1H$
	Search		$(2\xi+2)P+\xi E_T+1H$
Hu et al. (2017)	KeyGen	$(2\xi+1)|G|$	$(2\xi+1)E+\xi H$
	GenIndex	$(2N+3)|G|$	$(2N+4)E+(N+1)H$
	GenTok	$(2\xi+3)|G|$	$(2\xi+4)E$
	Search		$(2N+3)P+NE_T$
Wang et al. (2017)	KeyGen	$(\xi+3)|G|$	$(3\xi+2)E+\xi H$
	GenIndex	$1|G_T|+(N+2)|G|$	$(N+2)E+NH+1E_T$
	GenTok	$1|G_T|+1|G|$	$1E+1E_T+1P'$
	Search		$3P'$

continues on following page

Table 6. Continued

Scheme	Algorithm	Storage Cost	Computational Cost
Qiu et al. (2017)	KeyGen	$(2\xi+1)|G_2|+1|Z_p|$	$(2\xi+2)E$
	GenIndex	$1|G_T|+(N(m+1)+1)|G_1|$	$(N(m+1)+2)E+1H$
	GenTok	$1|Z_p|+(2\xi+1)|G_2|$	$(2\xi+1)E$
	Search		$(2N+1)P+1E_T$
Cui et al. (2018)	KeyGen	$(\xi+1)|G|+1|Z_p|$	$(\xi+1)E$
	GenIndex	$(2N+4)|G|+1|G_T|+1|Z_p|$	$(2N+5)E+1E_T$
	GenTok	$4|G|+2|Z_p|$	$2\xi P+(\xi+5)E+\xi E_T+2H$
	Search		$3P+2E_T$
Mamta & Gupta (2019a)	KeyGen	$1|Z_p|+3|G|$	$3E+1H$
	GenIndex	$(\xi+3+2|U|)|G|$	$(\xi+6)E+(k+1)H$
	GenTok	$6|G|$	$7E+1P+1H$
	Search		$(\xi+2)E+6P$
Chaudhari and Das (2019)	KeyGen	$(m\xi+2)|G|$	$(m\xi+1)E+m\xi H$
	GenIndex	$(mN+2)|G|$	$(3Nm+2)E+2NmH$
	GenTok	$(m\xi+2)|G|$	$(m\xi+2)E$
	Search		$(mN+1)P$
Proposed Scheme	KeyGen	$2|G|$	$2E$
	GenIndex	$(T+1)|G|+2|G_T|$	$(T+1)E+1H+2E_T$
	GenTok	$2|G|+1|Z_p|$	$2E+1H$
	Search		$(T+1)P+1E_T$

Table 7. Description of the notations

Notation	Description
$|G|, |G_T|$	Length of source (G) and target group (G_T) elements respectively in case of symmetric bilinear pairing
$|G_1|, |G_2|, |G_T|$	Length of source (G_1, G_2) and target group (G_T) elements respectively in case of asymmetric bilinear pairing
$|Z_p|$	Length of an element of a group of integers of prime order, p
P	Bilinear pairing operation
P'	Pairing operation in multi-linear map
E, E_T	Exponent operation in source and target group respectively
H	Collision resistant one-way hash function
ξ	# of attributes associated with users
N	# of attributes associated with access policy
U	# of authorized users in the system
m	# of possible values an attribute can take
k	# of keywords in case of a multi-keyword search scheme

CONCLUSION

This chapter proposes a ciphertext policy attribute based searchable encryption scheme (CP-ABSE) for non-monotonic access structure based on ROBDD. The resulting scheme is quite efficient in terms of computational and storage cost and flexible in terms of access structure. By making use of ROBDD the data owner can create high complexity access structures which can efficiently implement all kind of Boolean operations. Further, the proposed scheme is proved secure under DBDH assumption against IND-sCKA attack. In future the authors aim to add more features like support for user revocation and verifiability of the search result.

ACKNOWLEDGMENT

This publication is an outcome of the R&D work undertaken under (i) YFRF Award grant and (ii) Visvesvaraya PhD Scheme of Ministry of Electronics & Information Technology, Government of India and being implemented by Digital India Corporation.

REFERENCES

Almomani, A., Alauthman, M., Albalas, F., Dorgham, O., & Obeidat, A. (2018). An online intrusion detection system to cloud computing based on NeuCube algorithms. [IJCAC]. *International Journal of Cloud Applications and Computing*, 8(2), 96–112. doi:10.4018/IJCAC.2018040105

Boneh, D., Di Crescenzo, G., Ostrovsky, R., & Persiano, G. (2004, May). Public key encryption with keyword search. In *Proceedings International conference on the theory and applications of cryptographic techniques* (pp. 506-522). Berlin, Germany: Springer.

Bryant, R. E. (1986). Graph-based algorithms for boolean function manipulation. *IEEE Transactions on Computers*, *100*(8), 677–691.

Canetti, R., Halevi, S., & Katz, J. (2003, May). A forward-secure public-key encryption scheme. In *International Conference on the Theory and Applications of Cryptographic Techniques* (pp. 255-271). Berlin, Germany: Springer.

Chaudhari, P., & Das, M. L. (2019). *Privacy Preserving Searchable Encryption with Fine-grained Access Control*. IEEE Transactions on Cloud Computing. doi:10.1109/TCC.2019.2892116

Cui, J., Zhou, H., Zhong, H., & Xu, Y. (2018). AKSER: Attribute-based keyword search with efficient revocation in cloud computing. *Information Sciences*, *423*, 343–352. doi:10.1016/j.ins.2017.09.029

El-Latif, A. A. A., Abd-El-Atty, B., Hossain, M. S., Rahman, M. A., Alamri, A., & Gupta, B. B. (2018). Efficient quantum information hiding for remote medical image sharing. *IEEE Access: Practical Innovations, Open Solutions*, *6*, 21075–21083. doi:10.1109/ACCESS.2018.2820603

Gou, Z., Yamaguchi, S., & Gupta, B. B. (2017). Analysis of various security issues and challenges in cloud computing environment: a survey. In Identity Theft: Breakthroughs in Research and Practice (pp. 221-247). IGI Global. doi:10.4018/978-1-5225-0808-3.ch011

Gupta, B., Agrawal, D. P., & Yamaguchi, S. (Eds.). (2016). *Handbook of research on modern cryptographic solutions for computer and cyber security*. IGI Global. doi:10.4018/978-1-5225-0105-3

Hu, B., Liu, Q., Liu, X., Peng, T., Wang, G., & Wu, J. (2017, May). DABKS: Dynamic attribute-based keyword search in cloud computing. In *2017 IEEE International Conference on Communications (ICC)* (pp. 1-6). IEEE. 10.1109/ICC.2017.7997108

Jiang, F., Fu, Y., Gupta, B. B., Lou, F., Rho, S., Meng, F., & Tian, Z. (2018). Deep learning based multi-channel intelligent attack detection for data security. IEEE Transactions on Sustainable Computing.

Li, J., Lin, X., Zhang, Y., & Han, J. (2016). KSF-OABE: Outsourced attribute-based encryption with keyword search function for cloud storage. *IEEE Transactions on Services Computing*, *10*(5), 715–725. doi:10.1109/TSC.2016.2542813

Li, L., Gu, T., Chang, L., Xu, Z., Liu, Y., & Qian, J. (2017). A ciphertext-policy attribute-based encryption based on an ordered binary decision diagram. *IEEE Access: Practical Innovations, Open Solutions*, *5*, 1137–1145. doi:10.1109/ACCESS.2017.2651904

Mamta, G., & Gupta, B. B. (2019a). An efficient KP design framework of attribute-based searchable encryption for user level revocation in cloud. *Concurrency and Computation*, e5291. doi:10.1002/cpe.5291

Mamta, G., Gupta, B. B., & Ali, S. T. (2019). Dynamic Policy Attribute Based Encryption and its Application in Generic Construction of Multi-Keyword Search. [IJESMA]. *International Journal of E-Services and Mobile Applications*, *11*(4), 16–38. doi:10.4018/IJESMA.2019100102

Olakanmi, O. O., & Dada, A. (2019). An Efficient Privacy-preserving Approach for Secure Verifiable Outsourced Computing on Untrusted Platforms. [IJCAC]. *International Journal of Cloud Applications and Computing*, *9*(2), 79–98. doi:10.4018/IJCAC.2019040105

Premkamal, P. K., Pasupuleti, S. K., & Alphonse, P. J. A. (2020). Efficient Escrow-free CP-ABE with Constant Size Ciphertext and Secret Key for Big Data Storage in Cloud. [IJCAC]. *International Journal of Cloud Applications and Computing*, *10*(1), 28–45. doi:10.4018/IJCAC.2020010103

Qiu, S., Liu, J., Shi, Y., & Zhang, R. (2017). Hidden policy ciphertext-policy attribute-based encryption with keyword search against keyword guessing attack. *Science China. Information Sciences*, *60*(5), 052105. doi:10.100711432-015-5449-9

Sun, W., Yu, S., Lou, W., Hou, Y. T., & Li, H. (2014, April). Protecting your right: Attribute-based keyword search with fine-grained owner-enforced search authorization in the cloud. In *Proceedings IEEE INFOCOM 2014-IEEE Conference on Computer Communications* (pp. 226-234). IEEE.

Wang, H., Dong, X., & Cao, Z. (2017). Multi-value-independent ciphertext-policy attribute-based encryption with fast keyword search. *IEEE Transactions on Services Computing*, 1. doi:10.1109/TSC.2017.2753231

Yu, Z., Gao, C. Z., Jing, Z., Gupta, B. B., & Cai, Q. (2018). A practical public key encryption scheme based on learning parity with noise. *IEEE Access: Practical Innovations, Open Solutions*, *6*, 31918–31923. doi:10.1109/ACCESS.2018.2840119

Zheng, Q., Wang, X., Khan, M. K., Zhang, W., Gupta, B. B., & Guo, W. (2017). A lightweight authenticated encryption scheme based on chaotic scml for railway cloud service. *IEEE Access: Practical Innovations, Open Solutions*, *6*, 711–722. doi:10.1109/ACCESS.2017.2775038

Zheng, Q., Xu, S., & Ateniese, G. (2014, April). VABKS: verifiable attribute-based keyword search over outsourced encrypted data. In *Proceedings IEEE INFOCOM 2014-IEEE Conference on Computer Communications* (pp. 522-530). IEEE. 10.1109/INFOCOM.2014.6847976

Chapter 14
The State–of–the–Art Cryptography Techniques for Secure Data Transmission

Bhanu Chander

iD https://orcid.org/0000-0003-0057-7662

Pondicherry University, India

ABSTRACT

Cryptography is a progression where message correspondences are intelligently sent from one abuser to an additional abuser which endows with frequent defense services like privacy, data truthfulness, or verification to the wireless transportation structure. An encryption method keeps exceptional crucial contribution to communication safety measures. Here we mentioned characteristics of various Symmetric and Asymmetric encryption techniques along with inclusion of optimization techniques in cryptography for decrease computation difficulty. Moreover, advanced encryption techniques such as Zero-knowledge, Multi-party, Homomorphism encryptions, and Cognitive cryptography, Blockchain with their associated protocols are described. The present day's extensive research practices on quantum computer machines explain mathematical tribulations which are complicated or stubborn for classical computers. Quantum cryptography, challenges, Goal of Quantum resistant cryptography with associated literature work is described.

INTRODUCTION

The advancements in expansions of communication and electronic technologies, one steadfast barrier need to be proven as one of the major challenges which called as Data security. Present days the entire world depends on the internet and its applications for our everyday digitalized part work. Internet-based applications are steadily improved and emergent at a fast rate. Noticeable and continuous progress in digital communication is a bystander for internet application enlargement. Moreover, the increasing growth in machinery principally in digital communications is one of the methodological establishments for modern society. Considering the outstanding development in the view of technological progress,

DOI: 10.4018/978-1-7998-2242-4.ch014

Copyright © 2020, IGI Global. Copying or distributing in print or electronic forms without written permission of IGI Global is prohibited.

made the safe way of data diffusion over the internet turns to be an interested assignment. Information security grown-up as a foremost issue in our daily digitalized life. Moreover, the importance of network security increases day by day as the size of the information being transformed across the internet. The advancements of new broadcast technologies force a definite stratagem of security mechanism principally in the circumstances of data communication (Omar et al., 2018; Eminam et al., 2018; Ramesh et al., 2016; Feng et al., 2018).

Information security can be in the form of summed information, procedures, protocols, strategies and a group of steps, instructions that are exploited to prevent and deeply examine illegitimate issues, perturbation, troubleshoot and adjustment of computer network resources. Otherwise, intruder/adversaries may hack/steal the data and use it for some other favorable purpose. As a result, while data transmission secure communication sessions must be added, it turns to a key feature in order to evaluate network performances. For enhance, the security, privacy, and reliability involve a lot of work to reinforce the existing methods from constant trails to break them and develop up-to-the-minute methods that are dead set against the majority kinds of attacks. To get connected securely, quickly in the course of electronic information broadcast via the web, that information should be encoded (Omar et al., 2018; Mateusz Zych et al., 2018; Valileias et al., 2018; M.Guru et al., 2016).

BACKGROUND

Digital communication backed continuous improvement in many appliances of the internet world. Internet-based applications growing at the fast face, however, information security is one of the crucial concerns in our digital world. The progress in the novel, inventive transmission technologies enforces a specific stratagem of security structures particularly in the circumstances of data communication. More importantly, as much as data broadcasted over the wireless internet communication the consequence of network security increases more and more. Cryptography and stenography are the two most important techniques afford various procedures for information security. At present most of the network system utilizes cryptography, which is the leading method in defending sensible secret, undisclosed information in a variety of applications. The appliances like medical databases, e-mail, e-banking, social media, financial documents transactions, e-commerce every part of them have need of the transaction of confidential information. Both of the stenography and cryptography somehow allied concepts – stenography is hidden writing, cryptography is secret writing. Cognitive as well as crypto-optimization techniques produces best results in protecting private information with limited energy constraints.

CRYPTOGRAPHY

Cryptography is a mathematical production which plays the most important responsibility in information security through secret writing. Cryptography produces numerous security objectives toward make-sure of security, privacy, and on-alteration of data. Cryptography also referred to as the procedure of protecting data which is in transmission, stored more importantly in opposition to the third-party adversaries who are interested to steal data. Cryptography has been known and used from thousands of years for securing a message from illegitimate third parties. The word cryptography is linguistically derivative from two popular Greek words "Kryptos" and "Graphein" which represents "Hidden" and "Writing". It has two important properties namely encryption and decryption. Encryption is the procedure of convert any plaintext to ciphertext where decryption is exactly reverse procedure like encryption transforming cipher text to plain text. Both encryption and decryption procedures execute under control of keys. The scheme of encryption by which we can program/encode our data in secret code and not be capable to understandable by hackers or unconstitutional even it is hacked/captured.

Fundamental Concepts

Cryptography has some fundamental concepts which are commonly used while discussing cryptography procedures (Omar et al., 2018; Mateusz Zych et al., 2018; M. Guru et al., 2016; Eminam et al., 2018; Shivendra Singh et al., 2015; Alfred et al., 2016).

1. **Cryptography**: Cryptography is the method to transform decipherable and readable text to another complicated form which is not able to understand and decipherable in order to secure data.
2. **Cryptanalyst**: It refers to a person who as good knowledge to understand as well as an expert in analyzing and breaking codes.
3. **Cryptology**: Cryptography and cryptanalysis combined term called as cryptology.
4. **Network security**: Network security refers to the design of network with some specified goals such as integrity, authentication, access control, confidentiality and protecting data or information at the time of transmission on that network.
5. **Computer Security**: Computer security refers to a set of tools which secure any data from adversaries, stealing, tampering while allowing these data to the available authenticated abuser.
6. **Information Security**: Generally information concept exploits to be as an unstated quantity. Information security noticeable itself in numerous behavior according to the state of affairs with necessity. It mainly describes how to detect and prevent attacks on information-based systems.
7. **Plain Text**: The original, natural message that is in a comprehensible, understandable arrangement for humans. It is given as input to encryption technique.
8. **Ciphertext**: It is a jumbled message which is in indecipherable form and not able to read by humans. Normally it considers as the output of encryption technique furthermore utilize as input to the decryption algorithm whereas recreating the original plain text.
9. **Encryption Algorithm**: The algorithm which performs various methods, concepts, mathematical equations, and various operations to convert plain text to cipher text. It takes plain text along with secret key as input and fabricates ciphertext as output.
10. **Decryption Algorithm**: Decryption algorithm is the same as the encryption method but programmed in reverse order. The algorithm takes ciphertext along with secret-key just as input and constructs plain text like the output.
11. **Secret-key**: Secret-key is important information for both encryption and decryption. Stability of any cryptography algorithm leans on key value - how well it is designed, length of the key, etc.
12. **Public Key**: The key which is used toward encrypt the data, information is acknowledged as a public key.
13. **Private KEY**: The key which is used toward decrypt the encrypted message is acknowledged as Privet key.
14. **Keyspace**: Keyspace indicates the size or quantity of encryption as well as decryption key pairs accessible in a cipher system.

15. **Encryption Time**: It is the time period taken for transferring or processing the original ordinary text to encrypted one.
16. **Decryption time**: The period of time taken for decoding the decrypted message into human-readable text.
17. **Throughput**: The amount of time taken for enciphering measured in megabytes.
18. **Stream Cipher**: Stream cipher is nothing but converting one bit or symbol of plain text directly into one bit or symbol ciphertext.
19. **Block Cipher**: Block cipher which converts a group of bits of pain texts as cipher block.

Security Goals

Cryptography ensures some goals which can achieve altogether at one time in one single application. Otherwise some of them individually achievable in one or dissimilar applications. Security in computer science is an extensive research field, where it consists of numerous services, principles, concepts and mechanisms along with methodologies. It has no single definition, security hardly depends on security objectives, which point of security services can fulfill the required security mechanism. CIA is the fundamental principle when designing and describing the security of any system. CIA stands for Confidentiality, Integrity, and Availability. Nonetheless, the CIA cannot able to cover all the security aspects of the system, where need more concepts like authentication, Non-repudiation, access control and others addition grant more security (Omar et al., 2018; Mateusz Zych et al., 2018; M. Guru et al., 2016; Eminam et al., 2018; Shivendra Singh et al., 2015; Alfred et al., 2016).

Those are explained briefly below:

1. **Confidentiality**: Confidentiality ensures that message should be in-secure and can access by legitimate authorities only. It refers to indication for privacy and secrecy, where privacy indicates protection of personal/individuals information/data, coming to secrecy indicates protection of data belonging to an organization.
2. **Unlinkability**: Unlinkability means two or more items of interest cannot sufficiently distinguish whether they related or not.
3. **Anonymity**: Anonymity indicates a guarantee that a subject cannot be identified within a set of subjects.
4. **Integrity**: Integrity ensures that the receiver receives the message as it is, it is not modified or changed or altered from its original form. Integrity prevents unauthorized modification and destruction of data while it's under broadcast. There are two kinds of integrities - data integrity – which produces integrity of all digital information, System integrity - refers to a position of a system where it performing its intended functionalities without being degraded by distributions in its environment.
5. **Availability**: Availability grantees that services and recourses must be available whenever required by the legitimate entities all the times.
6. **Accountability**: Accountability ensures all the actions of a thing can be traced outstandingly to that entity. Simply all the proceedings affecting are traceable back to the responsible party, it depends upon authentication, access control and identification of abuser.
7. **Authentication**: Entities must be proved and verify their identification before exchange messages. It is done through, entities must forward some credential information to the system, then system

Figure 1. Symmetric/Single key encryption technique

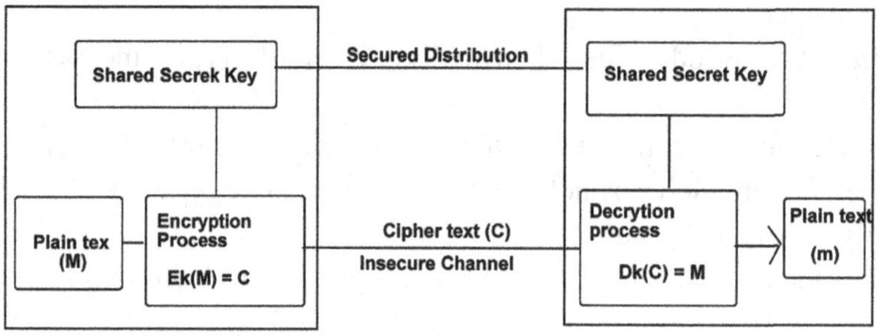

verify received credential detail with its database stored credential if they match then the only entity can be authenticated. Sender, as well as the receiver, must authenticate each other before transmitting the original message.

8. **Nonrepudiation**: Non-repudiation indicates confidence by providing undeniable evidence that an action has done. An entity cannot deny having sent a message and an entity cannot deny receiving a message.

9. **Identification**: Identification is an allegation of whom and what. Identification is very much needed thing in cryptography which was utilized to recognize an individual abuser.

10. **Receipt**: Indicates acknowledgment on behalf of information have been received.

11. **Conformation**: Acknowledgment with the intention of requested services is afforded.

12. **Access Control**: Access control specifies policies for which information and computing services can able to access, by whom under what conditions, actions are allowed to do. Simply it prevents illegitimate entities to access or use available resources.

13. **Ownership**: Ownership provides an entity can able to transfer a resource to other entities with appropriate legal rights.

14. **Time-stamping**: It ensures recording and exact time of creation, execution, and existence of information.

15. **Signature**: Is a mathematical induction that binds information to an entity.

16. **Validation**: Validation affords appropriateness authorization to use or manipulate the available resources.

17. **Certification**: Certification is digitalized formation of authentication that provides all information in order to gain the endorsement of the information by a trusted entity.

18. **Authorization**: Authorization provides conveyance to another entity or as like an official sanction to do or be something.

ENCRYPTION AND DECRYPTION PROCESS

Encryption is the technique that transforms plain text into cipher-text or cryptogram with the help of a key, which cannot readable, understandable and modified easily by undesirable people. If that key is same for ends like sender as well as the receiver, then that acknowledged as symmetric-key or secret-key encryption technique Figure 1. Instead of one key, a pair of keys (Public, Private) used on behalf of encryption where sender utilizes receiver's public key to encrypting the message as well as receivers

Figure 2. Asymmetric/Two key encryption technique

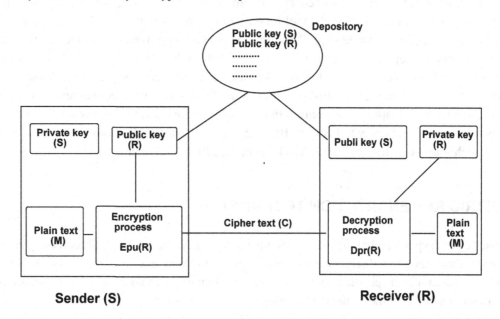

utilizes its own private key directed toward decrypt the encrypted message Figure 2. This procedure is acknowledged as asymmetric-key or public key cryptosystem. It was proven that encoding is one of the most reliable strategies used to secure information since the ancient days of the Romans who used similar methods to enable security on their valued information, documents (Chadi riman et al., 2015; Nidi et al., 2011; Pratap et al., 2012; Omar et al., 2018; Eminam et al., 2018; Ramesh et al., 2016).

Stream Cipher

Stream cipher is one kind of encryption scheme where plaintext message is encrypted bitwise generally an XOR operation with a random key stream. In this, each bit of plain text is transformed into equal length bit cipher texts. The great advantage with stream ciphers is that both encryptions as well as decryption perform the same operations which are easy for fast computation. But there is a small drawback, each bit plaintext consumes one bit from key stream means that selected key streams have to be as long as the plain text. And that key stream must be in random formation which is composite as well as exclusive in large quantities; in addition, key communication is another impediment. (Pratap et al., 2012; Srinivas., 2014; Vasileios., 2018; Mansoor et al., 2013).

Block Cipher

Stream cipher is best against small message transmission in a secure manner but it is not so useful against large quantity of data moreover secure key size must equal to plaintext. Block cipher method acts as a substitute to stream cipher; it handles a large amount of data. Block cipher secure communication procedure looks alike as stream cipher; it uses smaller secret key sizes typically 64-128 bit blocks. If a sender or initiator wants to send block cipher encrypted message to the appropriate receiver. For this sender have to show some procedural work – sender have to choose one secure cryptographic algorithm which slices the message into blocks and encrypt it with the secret key, and generates a secure ciphertext. At this time ciphertext over insecure channel forwarded to the receiver, then the receiver by applying known secret key which was shared securely before the network deployment can decrypt the ciphertext using the same cryptographic algorithm which was used at senders end to encrypt the message. There are only two possible choices for an adversary, knowledge of the secret key and break the encryption algorithm to decipher the ciphertext. But present standardized symmetric techniques are hard to break so an adversary trying to capture information that is encrypted and search for any useful knowledge of secret key which is the only way to decrypt. Block ciphers size of key determines the security level of encryption technique (Chadi et al., 2015; Vasileios et al., 2018; Nidi et al., 2011).

SYMMETRIC KEY ENCRYPTION TECHNIQUE

Symmetric key encryption technique is also known as single-key, shared-key and secret-key encryption. As discussed above the same distinct key utilized in support of both encryptions, decryption processes. The sender or initiator encrypts the original message or plaintext with a key which was shared between sender and receiver at the time of network deployment. A receiver who has the same shared secret key can only decrypt the message and obtain the original plaintext message. If the key is stolen or captured, entire data and network security are compromised. Moreover, there is impenetrability in the secure key distribution process and for n number of users there is a need of more than n-1 keys, storage of these keys in a secure manner is another level of impenetrability (Omar et al., 2018; Mateusz Zych et al., 2018; M. Guru et al., 2016; Eminam et al., 2018; Shivendra Singh et al., 2015; Alfred et al., 2016; Pratap et al., 2012; Srinivas et al., 2014; Vasileios et al., 2018; Mansoor et al., 2013).

Data Encryption Standard (DES)

Currently, in the view of symmetric-key encryption technique DES, 3DES, and AES are standardized block ciphers. The main function of the DES algorithm is to protect crucial financial transactions. Data encryption standard considered as an older version which was developed by IBM in the year of 1977 by Horst Feistel. Later it was adopted by US governments National Institute of standards and technology (NIST). The fundamental concept of DES algorithm taken from Feistel cipher formation with 16 rounds of transformation. DES is also famous as 64-bit block cipher algorithm where it accepts 64-bit original message, each block of 64-bit original messages converts into a 64-bit block of ciphertext. DES comes with the 64-bit key but uses the only 56-bit secret key for encryption and decryption process. Remaining similar 8-bits removed from the 64-bit key through exposing them to their key permutations, which are used for parity check or error correction in data. DES in its first round performs initial permutations of 64-bit plain text which was independent on a secret key. In the second round 64-bit plain text block divided into two halves with equal 32-bit length left and right. Right 32-bit part added to a function, before that it expands (expansion/permutation table) in terms of permutation to raise the size of bits to 48-bits. Then XOR with 48-bit key length and produces the same 48-bit size data. In the next step, it passes through the S-box (Substitution box) that replaces the key length and reduces 48-bits block to 32-bit. Then permutation is performed on the outcome of 32-bit S-box and finally XOR with the left side 32-bit block to produces the right 32-bit cipher block which will again do the same process starting from expansion function to XOR with left side 32-bit block, this all will be done in single DES round. Except for initial permutation (First stage) at starting point all the above-stated operation will run 16 rounds and the outcome of the 17 stages (DES 16 rounds + 1 initial permutation) performs 32-bit swap function (18th stage) and at finally it will perform inverse initial permutation (19 stages) to produce 64-bit ciphertext. Hence overall DES has 19 distinct stage performances to produce plain text to cipher text. Here the 48-bit secret key which was applied on function is different for 16 rounds process which was produced by DES key distribution process (Guru et al., 2016; Ramesh et al., 2016; Chadi et al., 2015; Srinivas et al., 2014; Vasileios et al., 2018). DES encrypts plaintext blocks of 64-bit with 56-bit keys, which provide the security level of 56-bit key that is not so secure. DES suffers from avalanche effect, where a single bit or one bit of key change produces modifications in many bits of the ciphertext. A small change in the plain text or secret key will produce momentous changes in the ciphertext. Moreover, there is a possibility for exploiting the distinctiveness of the DES algorithms. The main focus on the construction of Substitution boxes (S-box) which plays the main role in each iteration was not made public, there are possible chances to attack by the opponent who has good knowledge of S-boxes. To access more secure form DES, a variant of DES was designed which called as 3DES pronounced as triple DES. 3DES goes from end to end 3 iteration of DES efficiently encrypting data from beginning to end by 168-bit (56-bit * 3 = 168-bit) key that is awfully well-built on behalf of protecting the trackable message.

Blowfish Algorithm

Blowfish is one of the uttermost frequent public domain symmetric-key block cipher algorithm formulated by Bruce schneier in the year 1993. It is designed to endeavor four aspects fast, simple, variably secure and compact. Blowfish algorithm consists of two parts: - *Data encryption part* - variable key space starting 32 to 448 bits, *key expansion part* - expansion translates key space from 448-bits to numerous sub-key arrays totalize 4168-bytes. It has 16 round iterations of Feistel network with 64-bit block size as well as variable key space from 32 to 448 bits. Each round encloses a key-dependent permutation and data dependent substitution. Still, blowfish has several classes of unsteady keys, to avert these isolated rounds end up with the same round-keys (Gurjeevan Singh et al., 2012, Eminam et al., 2018 Pratap et al., 2012).

Advanced Encryption Standard (AES)

On 26 November 2001 NIST - National Institute of standards and technology comes up with a new technology acknowledged as Advanced Encryption Standard (AES). Same year AES becomes as Federal Information Processing Standards (FIPS) publication which is US government computer security standard used to grant, agree on cryptographic modules. DES with 64-bit block size is not sufficient and when it comes to security it will questionable in many of drawbacks. Triple DES twisted to slow for efficiency for a reason it consists three times as many rounds as DES so it is correspondingly lethargic. Moreover, it does not have sufficient hardware and software code. The previous encryption techniques, for example, consider DES can be able to destruct with advanced or modern computation systems and that has been proving in the year 1998, a group of people broke DES security with ease on modern computational systems with the cost of less than 250.000 US dollars. As a result, there is a need for one new brand encryption algorithm that capable to restrict all the known attacks. NIST takes responsible for design new algorithm and makes announcement worldwide to take part in that work, moreover makes clear requirements in what kinds of security levels that cipher has to reach like resistance not favor of branded attacks, speed with code firmness on a broad range of platforms, blueprint must be simple all kinds of attacks and entire design must be in documentary formation not like S-boxes where no one knows how these S-boxes working procedures. After lots of screenings and verifications procedures, five techniques namely MARS, RIJNDAEL, SERPENT, TWOFISH, RC6 are recommended for the final round. These five techniques deeply tested for security and efficiency by top-most cryptographers and NIST professionals. After all these testes RIJNDAEL selected by NIST which was also known as advanced encryption standard (AES). Previously it called as RIJNDAEL because it develops and submitted by two famous cryptographers Dr. Joan Daeman and Dr. Vincent Rijmen. In a couple of ways, AES was different and better than DES. The block and key sizes preferred independently from 128, 160, 192, 224, 256-bits, however, AES can only choose 128-bit block size with choices of 128, 192, 256-bit key sizes. The numbers of AES parameters lean on key length for instance chosen key size as 128 bits, in that case, the number of rounds is 10 while it will be 12, 14 for 192, 256 bits. But 128-bit key size is most preferably used at present times (Nidi et al., 2011; Mansoor et al., 2013; Eminam et al., 2018; Alfred J et al., 2016; Omar et al., 2018; Vasileios et al., 2018).

AES allocate 128-bit information length divides into four active blocks, transmits into the line of bytes moreover combined into a matrix of 4*4 named "state". "State" is nothing but breaks the plain text into matrix formation to create (4*4) matrix. In support of encryption and decryption process, the cipher or encryption procedure starts with an "Add round key" then "sub bytes", shit rows", and "mix-columns" transformation takes place 10 basic rounds. But at the last tenth round mix columns transformation is not taking place.

1. **Add Round Key:** XOR between 128-bits of the existing state along with 128-bits of the round key.
2. **Sub-byte Operation**: AES has 128-bit plain text block means it consists of data items of 16 bytes. This stage is purely a tale look up; every bit of data item is replaced with another piece by implementing 8-bit sequences with the help of 16*16 matrix or S-box. Here S-box is just random permutation of input block and designers of AES defined method for creating S-boxes.
3. **Shift Rows**: The bytes in the rest three lines of the state depending on their line up positions, shifted in a cycleway. Here first row bits will not change anymore, in second line 1-byte left-circular-shift done, in third line two bytes and finally in the last line three byte left-circular-shifts takes place successively.
4. **Mix Columns**: The formed mix columns transformation is described as mix-columns, which function on each column separately. Every byte of a column generalized into a new-fangled value that is meaning of entire four bytes in that column.

International Data Encryption Algorithm

International Data Encryption Algorithm generated by miniature variation, modifications regarding former cipher named proposed encryption standard (PSE). For that reason IDEA is acknowledged as Improved PES (IPES). It was proposed and premeditated by Xuejia, James of ETH-Zurich. IDES encrypt a 64-bit block plaintext into 64-bit block ciphertext as a result of applying a 128-bit key block. Key generation method which was employed in IDEA receive 128-bit block key that generates 52 subkeys each one has 16-bits long. Compare with other DES algorithms IDEA has 17 rounds, among these 9 rounds be add number rounds which takes 4 subkeys, remaining 8 rounds are even which takes 2 subkeys. But the first three rounds extremely defenseless to related-key attacks like key-schedule, timing attacks. IDEA can easily insert into any encryption software (Ramesh et al., 2016; Vlad Dragoi et al., 2018; Riman et al., 2015).

Tiny Encryption Algorithm (TEA)

TEA is a special kind of symmetric key encryption algorithm, input data with 64-bit along with 64 iterations coming to key length 218-bit through non-uniform 32 sequences. TEA produces better-improved security.

Serpent

Serpent encryption technique based on a hierarchical collection of Substitution-box (S-Box) as well as permutation-box (P-box). It contains 128-bit text in the company of 32 sequences furthermore variable key length of 128/192/256 bits. Compare to other traditional crypto techniques serpent with 16 iterations produces equal secure of 3-DES moreover provides sufficient security adjacent to all branded attacks. To protect from future potential discoveries it extended to 32 iterations.

MARS

It is heterogeneous formation, exercises 128-bit text with 32 iterations along with key length 128-448 bits. The difference is it contains solitary substitution-box (S-box). Compare with DES, MARS has faster and superior security. MARS security in mid iterations reaches to better-quality; it's somehow hard to visualize cryptanalysis because its security depends on data-rotations, Boolean complexity functions.

CAST 128

CAST design based on Feistel network introduced by two well-known cryptographers Carlisle Adams, Stafford Traverses in the year of 1977. It constrains sixteen rounds that operate on 64-bit block plaintext to formulate 64-bit ciphertext. CAST 128 performs 3 dissimilar kind functions among the above-mentioned 16 known rounds. Here rounds 1, 4, 7, 10, 13 and 16 uses some function and Rounds 2, 5, 8, 11, 14 uses another function which differs from the previous function, finally the rounds 3, 6, 9, 12, 15 uses another function which is completely dissimilar from previous two functions. The key size differs starting 40-bits to 128-bits with 8-bit advancements such as 40, 48 …. 120, 128-bits. For key size, fewer than 80-bits means 40, 48 …… 64, 72-bits instead of 16 rounds algorithms apply 12 rounds operations only. On behalf of key size more than 80-bits mean 88 to 128-bits algorithm implemented in 16 rounds of operation. However, the 64-bit key to CAST some ways helpless to special cryptanalysis attacks (Ramesh et al., 2016; Guru et al., 2016).

Rivest Cipher (RC) Algorithms

The main intention of any encryption algorithm is in the direction of data security if it not called an insecure algorithm. An encryption technique cannot easily break, then it is said to be perfectly secure. Rivest cipher techniques fit into the family symmetric key encryptions. They are designed and developed renowned MIT institutes professor "Ron Rivest". RC stands for Rivest Ciphers; they are extensively employed in numerous networking appliances for the reason of their constructive speed and variable key-length capabilities (Shetal et al., 2014; Rashmi et al., 2015; Milind et al., 2014; Gary et al., 2015; Ronals L et al., 1998).

1. **RC-1**: Rivest Cipher-1 (RC-1) was the initial project which Rivest designed in order to advance with designing a series of symmetric key algorithms which are traditionally known as "Rivest cipher algorithms". The intention of rivest research was focused on to design symmetric key techniques that could shield data as it passed throughout the network. However, the RC-1 algorithm is not published. Afterward, dissimilar designs and nonstop research is carried out.
2. **RC-2**: RC-2 industrialized in the year of 1987. It is a secret key block cipher encryption procedure which uses unpredictable key sizes from 1 byte to 128 bytes. It receives 64-bit block plain text as input and generates the 64-bit ciphertext. This was treated as a replacement for the existing DES algorithm.
3. **RC-3**: When RC-3 algorithm developed in the existence of the RSA technique was broken even before it used. Hence it was not used in any techniques and not published anywhere.
4. **RC-4**: RC-4 is stream cipher based symmetric key algorithm both encryption and decryption use the same unchanged algorithm. Plain text XOR with randomly generated keys which are outcome result of the key scheduling algorithm. The keystream selection is independent of used or applied plaintext. A variable key space starts 1 to 256-bit used to program a 256-bit circumstances table, vernam be an example on behalf of stream cipher based with variable key size which is mostly utilized in SSL due to its simplicity. But it is vulnerable to BEAST attack.
5. **RC-5**: RC-5 initiated and designed for the RSA algorithm in 1994 by rivest. It consists of key sizes 32, 64, 128-bit blocks along with a variable number of rounds, word sizes. It is a simple algorithm suitable for hardware and software, it provides great security if parameters choose correctly. The key size which is utilized makes it as strong as possible, if the selected key size is small then the algorithm is weak.
6. **RC-6**: RC-6 is a block cipher-based algorithm, which uses 128-bit block size plain text and key sizes vary from 128, 192, 256 bits. RC-6 is one of the final list algorithms in AES development in 1978. It is considered an improvement for RC-5 algorithm by use of 4 registers each contains 32 bit and provides better security against attacks those are possible in the RC-5 algorithm. RC-6 has fewer rounds but produces higher security from various attacks with higher throughput.
7. **RC-7**: RC-7 is extensive work for RC-6 to improve efficiency and effectiveness. It takes moderately less time to encrypt data moreover reasonably more adaptable. On behalf of functioning with four registers in RC-6, RC-7 construct six such registers which formulate it a superior choice to RC-6.

Mandal et al. (2012) Examined DES, Blowfish, AES and 3DES presentations based on evolution parameters, rounds, key sizes, and block sizes, power consumption. Among the four algorithms Blowfish somehow presents better results. (Srinivas et al., 2014) Investigate DES along with Blowfish on ECB mode operations in the view of key size, data type, cipher block modes. Based on the outcomes encryption moment increases with increase in key size. Blowfish computes faster than DES against entire analyzed ciphers. Mansoor et al. (2013) briefly examined symmetric techniques DES, IDEA, AES, MARS, Blowfish, TEA, 3DES, CAST, RC6, and RC7 on numerous characteristics such as security, authentication, privacy, integrity, reliability, scalability and flexibility furthermore authors mentioned each techniques strengths, weaknesses. Finally they noted AES is best performer in the view of memory usage, security and encryption presentation.

ASYMMETRIC KEY ENCRYPTION TECHNIQUE

Asymmetric encryption algorithms which also famous as Public-key encryption system, where pair of keys specifically public key and private key utilized and the relationship among keys plays a major role in encryption as well as decryption procedure. There is no need to kept public key securely in truth to be told made it as broadly accessible but merely its legitimacy is essential to promise that entity (initiator) be undeniably the lone party that make-outs subsequent private key. This type of procedure has an advantage than symmetric key systems for a reason that contributing authentic public keys is usually effortless than allocating secret keys securely. The central intention of public key-based encryption techniques is headed for present confidentiality and privacy through additional techniques consists of digital signatures, hash functions, digital certificates, and message authentication. These algorithms security depends on the strength of mathematical problems which measured as hard for conventional computers to decipher. These algorithms use factorization problem and discrete logarithmic problem. These algorithms also called as "One-way" functions since they are simple to compute in one direction, but the inversions are not easy (Alfred et al., 2016; Vlad Dragoi et al., 2018; Omar et al., 2018; Riman et al., 2015; Kim et al., 2012; Rams et al., 2013; Vasileios et al., 2018).

RSA

RSA was designed and published by three recognized scientists namely Ronald Rivest, Adi Shamir and Leonard Adelman (RSA) in the year of 1977. It is considered a standard technique for the public key encryption scheme. RSAs security most probably supports on fractiousness of integer factorization complication. Every participating entity generates its RSA public (n, e) as well as private key (d) pairs. Here integer's (e, d) called as encryption promoter and decryption promoter, (n) is entitling as the modulus. Entities A and B want to communicate with each other with the help of RSA algorithm. Entity A has to do the following things:

1. Chose two massive, specific prime numbers namely p, q each one roughly the same size and nowadays they should be at least 1024 bits.
2. Calculate n = p*q which is nearly superior to 2018 bit along with ϕ (n) = (p - 1) * (q - 1).
3. Go for random integer e by using Eulers Phi function $\phi(n) = (p - 1) \cdot (q - 1)$ to decide on a public exponent e Î {1, 2, ..., $\phi(n) - 1$} corresponding that gcd(e, $\phi(n)$) = 1.
4. Make utilize of extended Euclidean algorithm in-order calculate exclusive integer d, 1 < d < $\phi(n)$, corresponding that ed ° 1 (mod $\phi(n)$). Here d is considered as Private Key.
5. Entity A's public key be (n, e) and the private key is (d).

Entity B has to perform following steps to encrypt message m for A.

6. Obtain As authentic public key (n, e).

7. Select a plain text message X in the course (0, n-1) and uses Public key and private key to creating ciphertext Y and send it to A.

$$Y = X^e \,(\text{mod } n)$$

8. After receiving ciphertext from Entity B, A uses Private Key d and has to the following procedure to recover plain text X from ciphertext Y.

$$X = Y^d \,(\text{mod } n)$$

Problems

1. There are many issues like how to compute the big numbers multiplications.
2. There are no unique algorithms which gives this much length of prime numbers (512 and 1024 bits) because RSA security is to depend on factorization.

The Diffie-Hellman Key Exchange Encryption Technique

This protocol designed and published by Diffie and Hellman particularly for the purpose of Key exchange, subsequent to that it called as Diffie-Hellman key exchange protocol. Here sender, as well as the receiver, agrees on familiar secret in-order to securely interchange a key that can be adapted for successive encryption of messages with no need of meeting each other. The technique itself limited to swapping secret values. Diffie-Hellman algorithm security strength builds upon complicatedness from calculating discrete logarithms. In the algorithm, there are two publicly available parameters entitled domain parameters. Those are p which is the big prime number along with α that is a primitive root or generator in the multiplicative group modulo p. Suppose two entities called A and B wants to interchange a key, sender A generates random number X, as well as receiver B, generates a random number Y. After that both take the generator g and raise it to their respective generated number and send it to each other. Principally, the sender entity A calculates $X_A < p$ and computes $Y_A = \pm^{X_A} \bmod q$. entity B calculates $Y_A < p$ and computes $Y_B = \pm^{X_B} \bmod q$. Both entities keep X values with them securely and publish Y values to each other over insecure channel. The sender raises the value received from the receiver with her generated number and the receiver does the same, the answer which will become their secret key. Mathematically it look like this, entity A calculate $K = \left(Y_B\right)^{X_A} \bmod p$ and entity B calculate $K = \left(Y_A\right)^B \bmod p$. A probable adversary has only p, α, Y_A, Y_B and thus from this information the adversary not proficient to obtain shared secret key of sender and receiver. Adversary mandatory to acquire a discrete logarithm to find out the key.

Digital Signature Algorithm

Compared with handwritten signatures digital signature provides more authentication and security measurements. Coming to clear definition – "Digital signature is a number dependent on some secret is known only to the signer and additionally being signed on the content of the message". A digital signature mainly provides authentication, integrity, and Non-repudiation. The sender can able to sign on document digitally by hashing the document and encrypt it with his own private key. For verifying signature receiver has to decrypt received document with sender's public key where it completes authentication and Non-repudiation security measures and hashes the original document. If these two hash values match integrity will be satisfied hence the signature is to trust. Digital Signature Algorithm is a well-known algorithm which performs digital signature scheme in three phases those are key generation, signing, and verification. *Key generation* – It receives a security parameter n as input, create both secret key (Sk) plus public key (Pk). *Signing* – Provided with a private key along with a message (Sk, m) produces a signature ($\neg$) of a given message. *Verification* - Verification process involves signature, message and public key ($\neg$, m, Pk) as input and returns 1/0 in a Boolean value.

Nguyen et al. (2011) described extension work on Digital signature standards with the employment of Belarusian stands which act as elastic and fabricates opportunity of expected extension of their roles. Campbell et al. (2003) explained utilization of digital signatures in mobile networks. Zhang et al. (2011) presented improved work of Digital signatures base on Elliptic curve cryptography headed for improvement in original digital signatures. Geric et al. (2012) proposed for XML signatures which helps on XML transactions.

Digital Certificate

In the era of increasing internet usage, use of present protocols as well as creating new protocols grows continuously. Numerous protocols may have to provide authentication as well as secure. At present digital signatures and digital certificates are handy to provide the above-mentioned security requirements. Hence, it is important to know the overview and roles of digital certificates. X.509 describes a framework for verification services with the X.500 directory to its entities. This directory restrains public key-based certificates which contains public key of an entity with dully sign with private key of an authentic certification authority. X.509 originally published in 1988, complete revised edition published in 1993. The final version was released in 2003. X.509 is entirely depended on public key cryptography, moreover it does not indicate any specific algorithm but mostly recommends RSA.

The main function of the X.509 proposal is to connect public key certificate (PKC) with each one user. Here abuser certificates generated through some authentic third party named Certification Authority (CA) where an abuser makes available all its information with trust on it. CA stores all certificates in a respective directory which purely endow with an easily reachable position for abusers in order to acquire certificates.

Hashing Techniques

Hash functions essential in designing strong cryptography techniques utilize most of the broad appliances such as digital signature, message authentication as well as integrity and timestamp. Hash functionality takes input as arbitrary length message (M) along with key length (K) finally produce a fixed-length output (D) which documented as Message Digest. Above mentioned definition simplified as H (M.K) = D. Message Digest-5 (MD5): it is a 128-bit hash value function, process as variable size message into fixed size output length of 128-bit. Here input divided into 512-bit chunks, after that message padded for making to make its length divisible by 512. Message Digest-6 (MD6): MD6 significantly viewed in a tree-based structure that consent to superior parallelism along with 4-t0-1 compression base function that reduces the overall length of the message at each level. SHA-1: Secure hash function nearly and most widely used in various appliances like PGP, TLS, SSH, and SSL. It outputs a fixed length 160-bit digest message for any sized input file. SHA-256 which is also known as successor of SHA-1 fabricates unique 256-bit; this creates it as appropriate for anti-tamper, digital signature, password justification, etc.

ADVANCED ENCRYPTION TECHNIQUES

Homomorphic Encryption Schemes

Secure levels of encryption techniques depend on a shared key, it may be the public or private key between the associates concerned in swapping an encrypted message. However, this kind of techniques causes privacy distresses. Then the word homomorphism was created and used in special areas, especially in cryptography field it used as the encryption type. Homomorphic Encryption (HE) method permits the third party to execute definite computable operations on the encrypted data whereas defending the features of the function and format of the encrypted data. Rivest et al first employed homomorphism as a promising resolution for computing with no decrypting difficulty. Forgetting an idea about HE, consider Client- Server homomorphism scenario here primarily client encrypts his own data and forwards to the server, in case of client wants to perform a function on his own data client need to forward the function to the server. Then the server performs homomorphic function over the client forwarded encrypted data by employing Eval function and returns the results to the client. At last, the client gets the data with his own secret key. Here if Eval function at the server side does not require the private key of the client and allows various operations on the encrypted client data. All HE base encryption methods categorized into three categories, *Partially Homomorphic Encryption (PHE)* – no bounded stages means permits one type of function by an unrestricted number of times. RSA, Goldwasser- Micali, Elgamal, Benaloh Paillier are some well-dressed examples for PHE. *Somewhat Homomorphic Encryption (SWHE)* – Permits a few type operations in a restricted number of times Boneh-Goh-Nissim (BGN), Polly cracker format, SYY and IP are examples for SWHE. *Fully Homomorphic Encryption (FHE)* – Unrestricted number of operations for unrestricted number of times. Ideal lattice base, Over integers, LWE base, and NTRU like come under FHE (Abbas et al., 2018; Armknecht et al., 2015; Hrestak & Picek et al., 2014).

Armknecht et al. (2015) afford efficient enlightenment of the innovative terminology associated with FHE. Furthermore, while the survey in (Aguilar-Melchor et al., 2013) only coated the signal dispensation appliances, that in (Hrestak & Picek et al., 2014) wrap a small number of FHEs and that only cloud appliance. (Armknecht et al., 2013) present defense and categorization of every obtainable group homomorphism encryption proposals.

Zero Knowledge

Zero-knowledge proofs (ZKP) most abstract and fascinating concepts of modern applied cryptography. Providing secure transaction for public blockchain, applied to nuclear disarmament talks are some of the ground-breaking cryptography techniques for ZKPs. ZKPs idea was first introduced by well-known researcher Shafi Goldwasser, Charles Rackoff in the year 1985. Here they mentioned a metric for the number of facts that is desirable to transmit from a prover to a verifier for it to be measured as valid. In the end, authors want to show that, with a quantity of interface between a prover and a verifier they may possibly, effectively reduce the quantity of information that desired to be conveyed among them to zero. Their main concentration on information leakage means what quantity of information a verifier study over the course of will confirm a claim is legal. However, the construction of Zero-knowledge proofs (ZKPs) on internet protocols was the challengeable task and moreover, it requires improvement of witness-indistinguishable testimony procedures. Non-interactive ZKPs finally fabricated where the interface among the prover and verifier is disinterested. As a replacement common reference string shared among the prover and verifier to achieve computational zero-knowledge (Andre 2018).

ZKPs are where a prover can prove to a verifier that some information known to him devoid-of communicate any supplementary information to Bob other than the information which was well-known to him. A perfect ZKPs must satisfy the following things *Completeness* - is the high probabilistic chance that if prover telling the truth, the verifier will eventually be convinced that she is telling the truth. *Soundness* - is the reality that prover can purely prove to Verifier is he saying the truth. *Zero-knowledgeness* - is that Verifier does not find out anything regarding prover top secret facts. ZKPs correctly take attention as one of the most complicated and unique technologies used in blockchain technology. The appliance of ZKPs in crypto-currencies will prolong to escort the way in enlightening one of the most electrifying and unidentified equipment today. Zero-knowledge proofs endlessly apply on where they are helpful as they prolong to enlarge. The underlying technology may be tremendously compound, but they probably for confidentiality, validity, and protection cannot be overstated (Andre, 2018).

Multi-Party Computation (MPC)

It also acknowledged as Multi-party computation, secure computation or Privacy-preserving computation which is a subfield of cryptography. MPC established by famous researcher Yao in the year 1982 but the foundation placed in 1970 with work on mental poker. Unlike classical cryptography methods, the main intention of MPC is generating procedures for various parties to mutually work out a function over their inputs at the same time as remain those inputs confidential and shield participant's confidentiality, integrity from each other. Security inside MPC indicates with the intention of the participant's inputs remain secret and outcomes of the computation are guaranteed to be correct. The working procedure of MPC as follows – First the condition to be computed must be specified through a course of the finite field consisting of addition, multiplication of gates. Every input value along with the intermediate result is shared appropriately to all participants so there is no cheat and learns anything. The course examined gate by gate, perform sub-protocol for each gate moreover the outcomes mutually recreated. Input privacy and accuracy are the two assets that MPC plans to guarantee. In input privacy, any kind of information regarding private data detained by the parties could be secondary from the messages sent throughout the implementation of the protocol. Inaccuracy suitable compartment of opposition parties enthusiastic to distribute information or diverge from the commands throughout the protocol, an implementation must be capable of strength truthful parties to harvest a mistaken consequence.

COGNITIVE CRYPTOGRAPHY

Convolution cryptography associate with secured encryption methods by utilizing mathematical functions those conceded to complete better confidentiality and privacy of broadcasting data. Most of these mathematical base crypto-techniques entirely same or else not at all depend on encrypted input data or selected representative protocols. This line of statement advises regarding involvement of personal parameters, characteristic of trusted participants even make use of some extracted high dependable features which demonstrate encrypted data. Means cryptographic solutions look like to be morphological importance of encrypted data or special characteristic features of participants for cryptographic methods. Cognitive sciences have a vast impact on modern computer information processing infrastructures. Cognitive science mostly interlinked with linguistics, psychology, robotics, and neurobiology. Based on the current research proofs show that cognitive technologies can also have a huge weight in providing security moreover it allocates to describe an innovative branch of contemporary cryptography acknowledged as "Cognitive cryptography". Which merge procedures that applied to promise data protection, privacy, more importantly, formulate encryption procedure to be personalized; dependent on individual features related to a definite person or else encrypted data. With the help of selected exceptional information or behavioral features, those can apply in security protocols. Individual features can obtain biometric services, advanced vision systems or more multifaceted sensor nodes and that permit to analyze visual pattern representing particular persons (Ahmed et al., 2017; Ogiela et al., 2019; Ogiela et al., 2017).

The main features of cognitive cryptography are – It provides simplicity to utilize special individual innate for the purpose of strong security, allow involvement of human expert knowledge for better security procedures, agree to engage semantic information insecurity, allows to make use of cognitive capabilities or perceptual skills for individual security purposes (Ogiela et al., 2019; 2017; 2016).

Cognitive cryptography protocols:

1. **Secret Content Sharing:** In this, methods of information sharing with the involvement of cryptographic techniques. Proposals like Biometric patterns or biological computational procedures are the extensive applications come under this category.
2. **Visual Cryptography with Individual Threshold Value**: Here probability moments employ cognitive cryptography that may be expressed by individually generated visual perception thresholds values. Those allow visual information to be reconstructed in a variety of ways for dissimilar individuals.
3. **Cognitive CAPTCHA Codes:** Build upon perception skills of a distinct person and produce solutions for multi user's cognitive authentication. With users moving attention, the confirmation could be done in numerous authentication phases. Multi question CAPTCHA- More than a few dissimilar questions or else objects associated with the presented pattern, for the purpose of quick verification.

As mentioned above cognitive cryptography also endeavors in view of encryption techniques reflect on the importance of encrypted or collective information, and make use of it into encryption dealings. Expansion of such safety code of behavior must permit to expand conventional encryption practice with innovative vital points and allocate to spotlight them to be assigned for the exact consumer.

CRYPTOGRAPHY WITH OPTIMIZATION TECHNIQUES

In Cryptographic techniques some may utilize the same key for both encryption and decryption process some other crypto techniques utilize a pair of keys (public, private). In modern cryptography key management is one of the major issues because of the distribution environment and organization. In recent times this kind of problems answered through optimization methods. From a general point of view, the optimization process is nothing but find out the best explanation of the operation within system constraints. The outcome of the particular operation involves minimized or maximized scalar quantitative process based on system or set-up expenditure, earnings and capitulate. More importantly, optimization alters the problem into a group of equations and variations in the order of constraints which utilized to cooperate an achievable area which defines the limits in the progression of the system. In basic words, the optimization technique encloses a set of maximum or else minimum real tasks from which prefer an input assessment from acceptable values and calculate the worth of operation. Genetic algorithms, Cuckoo search, particle swarm optimization, Ant colony optimization some of the frequently applicable optimization algorithms (Shanker et al., 2016; Durga et al., 2012).

Shankar et al. (2015) presented an ECC base image encryption technique with the Differential Evolution (DE) optimization algorithm. In order to progress the image encryption, DE applied on private key generation phase. Authors employed swarm based key generation algorithm for text encryption. And methods show that algorithm encrypting a unique message of unreliable sizes. (Saveetha et al., 2011) described genetic algorithm-based encryption which declines the computational complication of cryptosystem. (Arti soni et al., 2013) describe AES based image encryption and Generic algorithm utilized for key generation procedure.

CONCLUSION AND FUTURE WORK

Most of the innovations starting Symmetric cryptosystem to public key cryptosystems could be brittle to susceptible molests apart from quantum cipher along with the one-time pad. Even though both innovations are almost indestructible but the accomplishment of those two is computationally tough. Not even one public key cryptosystem has been verified to be safe, throughput rates of well-liked public key techniques are more than a few levels of degree slow than finest symmetric key techniques. The safety measures of public key cryptosystems found on the difficulty of unfathomable mathematical dilemmas. But this change with the invention of quantum computers which works on the physical quantum basic principles that unquestionably pose a threat to the current cryptosystems. On the other hand, every part of possible algorithms defenseless by cyclic search through every possible key and brute force attacks. In reply broad investigate has been performed that resulted in quantum resistant. Lattice-based primitives which is one of the quantum resistant cryptosystem so far established flexibility, elasticity, not even support of quantum molest, but their accomplishment on existing services such as assembled hardware will be prone to physical molests. However, latest lattice-based schemes emerged and quantity of their employment enlarge, this will maintain to be an imperative region follow a line of investigation, research going further.

REFERENCES

Memos, V. A., Psannis, K. E., Ishibashi, Y., Kim, B. G., & Gupta, B. B. (2018). An Efficient Algorithm for Media-based Surveillance System(EAMSuS) in IoT Smart City Framework. *Future Generation Computer Systems*, *83*, 619–628. doi:10.1016/j.future.2017.04.039

Abdel-Karim, A. (n.d.). Performance Analysis of Data Encryption Algorithms.

Acar, A., Aksu, H., & Selcuk Uluagac, A. A. (2018). A Survey on Homomorphic Encryption Schemes: Theory and Implementation. *ACM Computing Surveys*, *51*(4), 79. doi:10.1145/3214303

Aguilar-Melchor, C., Fau, S., Fontaine, C., Gogniat, G., & Sirdey, R. (2013). Recent advances in homomorphic encryption: A possible future for signal processing in the encrypted domain. *IEEE Signal Processing Magazine*, *30*(2), 108–117. doi:10.1109/MSP.2012.2230219

Armknecht, F., Katzenbeisser, S., & Peter, A. (2013). Group homomorphic encryption: Characterizations, impossibility results, and applications. *Designs, Codes, and Cryptography*, *67*(2), 209–232. doi:10.100710623-011-9601-2

Armknecht, F., Boyd, C., Carr, C., Gjøsteen, K., Jäschke, A., Reuter, C. A., & Strand, M. (2015). A guide to fully homomorphic encryption. *IACR* 1192.

Chadi, R. I. M. A. N., & Pierre, E. (2015). Comparative Analysis of Block Cipher-Based Encryption Algorithms: A Survey. Information Security and Computer Fraud, 3(1).

Chailloux, A. (2018). *Relativistic commitment and zero-knowledge proofs. Seventeenth Bellairs CryptoWorkshop 2018, Mar 2018*. Barbados: Holetown.

Charbathia, S., & Sharma, S. (2014). A Comparative Study of Rivest Cipher Algorithms, *International Journal of Information & Computation Technology*, *4*(17). pp. 1831-1838.

Chawla, V., & Nagpal, R. S. R. (2015). The RC7 Encryption Algorithm, *International Journal of Security and Its Applications 9*(5), pp. 55-60.

Dragoi, V., Richmond, T., Bucerzan, D., & Legay, A. (2018). Survey on Cryptanalysis of Code-Based Cryptography: from Theoretical to Physical Attacks. In *Proceedings 2018 7th International Conference on Computers Communications and Control (ICCCC)*.

Durga Bhavani, A., & Soundarya P. M. (2012). Optimized Elliptic Curve Cryptography, *International Journal of Engineering Research and Applications (IJERA)*, *2*(5), pp. 412–419.

Dworkin, M., Barker, E., & Nechvatal, J. (2001). Advanced encryption standard (AES). *Federal Inf. Process. Stds.(NIST FIPS)-197*.

Ebrahim, M., Khan, S., & Khalid, U. B. (2013). Symmetric Algorithm Survey: A Comparative Analysis, *International Journal of Computer Applications, 61*(20).

Elmisery, A. M., Sertovic, M., & Gupta, B. B. (2017). Cognitive Privacy Middleware for Deep Learning Mashup in Environmental IoT, 2169-3536 (c) 2017 *IEEE Transactions*.

Geric, S., & Vidacic, T. (2012). XML Digital Signature and its Role in Information System Security, *MIPRO* 2012, May 21-25, 2012, Opatija, Croatia.

Hrestak, D., & Picek, S. (2014). Homomorphic encryption in the cloud. In *2014 37th International Convention on Information and Communication Technology, Electronics, and Microelectronics (MIPRO'14)*. pp. 1400–1404. IEEE.

Jiang, F., Fu, Y., Gupta, B. B., Lou, F., Rho, S., Meng, F., & Tian, Z. (2018). Deep Learning based Multi-channel intelligent attack detection for Data Security, 2377-3782 (c) 2018 *IEEE transactions*.

Kessler, G. (2014). An Overview of Cryptography.

Khan, N., & Gorde, K. S. (2015). Data security by video steganography and cryptography techniques.

Kim, C. H. (2012). Improved Differential Fault Analysis on AES Key Schedule. *IEEE Transactions on Information Forensics and Security, 7*(1), 41–50. doi:10.1109/TIFS.2011.2161289

Kumar, M. G. V., & Ragupathy, U. S. (2016). A Survey on Current Key Issues and Status in Cryptography, *IEEE WiSPNET 2016 conference.*

Mandal, A. K., Parakash, C., & Tiwari, A. (2012). Performance evaluation of cryptographicalgorithms: DES and AES, *in IEEE Students Conference on Electrical, Electronics, and Computer Science,* pp. 1–5.

Mandal, P. C. (2012). Evaluation of performance of the Symmetric Key Algorithms: DES, 3DES, AES and Blowfish. *Journal of Global Research in Computer Science Department of Computer Application, 3,* 67–70.

Mathur, M., & Kesarwani, A. (2013). Comparison Between Des, 3DES, RC2, RC6, Blowfish And AES, *Proceedings of National Conference on New Horizons in IT – NCNHIT.*

Menezes, A. J., van Oorschot, P. C., & Vanstone, S. A. (2016). A Handbook of Applied cryptography, Taylor and Francis Inc. Boca Raton, FL: CRC Press.

Nguyen, M. H., Ho, D. N., Luu, D. H., Moldovyan, A. A., & Moldovyan, N. A. (2011, August). On functionality extension of the digital signature standards. In *Proceedings The 2011 International Conference on Advanced Technologies for Communications (ATC 2011)* (pp. 6-9). IEEE.

Ogiela, L. (2017). *Cognitive information systems in management sciences.* Elsevier, Academic Press.

Ogiela, M. R. (2019). Cognitive Solutions for Security and Cryptography, Cognitive Systems Research, 55, 258-261.

Ogiela, M. R., & Ogiela, L. (2016). On using Cognitive Models in Cryptography. In *Proceedings IEEE AINA 2016 - The IEEE 30th International Conference on Advanced Information Networking and Applications,* pp. 1055-1058.

Omar, G. A., & Guirguis, S. K. (2018). A Survey on Cryptography Algorithms. *International Journal of Scientific and Research Publications, 8*(7).

Patila, P., & Narayankarb, P., Narayan, D. G. C., & Meena, S. M. (2015). A Comprehensive Evaluation of Cryptographic Algorithms: DES, 3DES, AES, RSA and Blowfish, *International Conference on Information Security & Privacy (ICISP2015),* December 11-12, 2015, Nagpur, India. Academic Press.

Pillai, B., Mounika, M., Rao, P. J., & Sriram, P. (2016). Image steganography method using k-means clustering and encryption techniques. In *Proceedings 2016 International Conference on Advances in Computing, Communications, and Informatics (ICACCI).* pp. 1206-1211. IEEE.

Rams, T., & Pacyna, P. (2013). A Survey of Group Key Distribution Schemes With Self-Healing Property. *IEEE Communications Surveys and Tutorials, 15*(2), 820–842. doi:10.1109/SURV.2012.081712.00144

Riman, C., & Abi-Char, P. E. (2015). Comparative Analysis of Block Cipher-Based Encryption Algorithms: A Survey. *Information Security and Computer Fraud, 3*(1), 1–7.

Riman, C., & Pierre, E. (2015). Comparative Analysis of Block Cipher-Based Encryption Algorithms: A Survey. Information Security and Computer Fraud, 3(1).

Rivest, R. L. S., & Adleman, L. (1978). A Method for Obtaining Digital Signatures and Public Key Cryptosystems. Comm. ACM, 21, 120-26.

Rivest, R. L., & Robshaw, M. J. B. (1998). The Security of the RC6 Block Cipher. *Version 1.0* – August.

Saveetha, P., Arumugam, S., & Kiruthikadevi, K. (2014). Cryptography and the Optimization Heuristics Techniques, *International Journal of Advanced Research in Computer Science and Software Engineering, 4*(10), 408–413.

Shankar, K., & Eswaran, P. (2015). ECC Based Image Encryption Scheme with aid of Optimization Technique using Differential Evolution Algorithm. *International Journal of Applied Engineering Research, 10*(5), 1841–1845.

Shankar, K., & Eswaran, P. (2016). *An Efficient Image Encryption Technique Based onOptimized Key Generation in ECC Using Genetic Algorithm, Artificial Intelligence and Evolutionary Computations in Engineering Systems* (pp. 705–714). India: Springer.

Shankar Sriram, V. S., Dinesh, S., & Sahoo, G. (2010). Multiplication Based Elliptic Curve Encryption Scheme with Optimized Scalar Multiplication (MECES), International Journal of Computer Applications, 1(11), pp. 65–70.

Singh, G., Singla, A. K., & Sandha, K. S. (2012). Superiority of Blowfish Algorithm in Wireless Networks. *International Journal Computer Applications, 44*(11), pp. 23-26.

Singh, S., Iqbal, M. S., & Jaiswal, A. (2015). Survey on Techniques Developed using Digital Signature: Public key Cryptography, *International Journal of Computer Applications, 117*(16), pp. 0975 – 8887.

Singhal, N., & Raina, J. P. S. (2011). Comparative Analysis of AES and RC4 Algorithms for Better Utilization. *International Journal of Computer Trends and Technology*, 177–181.

Soni, A., & Agrawal, S. (2013). Key Generation Using Genetic Algorithm for Image Encryption, *International Journal of Computer Science and Mobile Computing (IJCSMC), 2*(6), pp. 376– 383.

Sreelaja1, N. K., & Vijayalakshmi Pai, G. A. (2011). Swarm intelligence based key generation for stream cipher, *Security and Communication Networks, 4*(2), 181–194.

Srinivas, B. L., Shanbhag, A., & D'Souza, A. S. (2014). A Comparative Performance Analysis of DES and BLOWFISH Symmetric Algorithm. *IJIRCCE*.

Wood, G., & Ethereum. (2014). A secure decentralised generalised transaction ledger. *Ethereum Project Yellow Paper.*

Yegireddi, R., & Kumar, R. K. (2016, November). A survey on conventional encryption algorithms of cryptography. In *Proceedings 2016 International Conference on ICT in Business Industry & Government (ICTBIG)* (pp. 1-4). IEEE.

Zhang, Q., Li, Z., & Song, C. (2011). The Improvement of digital signature algorithm based on elliptic curve cryptography. *IEEE Transactions.*

Zyskind, G., Nathan, O., & Pentland, A. (2015). Enigma: Decentralized computation platform with guaranteed privacy, *arXiv preprint arXiv:1506.03471.*

Chapter 15

Cloud Computing Security:
Taxonomy of Issues, Challenges, Case Studies, and Solutions

Chhavi Chaturvedi
National Institute of Technology, Kurukshetra, India

Brij B. Gupta
National Institute of Technology, Kurukshetra, India

ABSTRACT

The applications and software using cloud computing as a base have significantly increased, and cloud computing is nowadays developed as a scalable and cost-effective technique. It facilitates many features in the computing environment like resource pooling, multi-tenancy, virtualization, etc. The cloud environment has led to the proliferation of various attacks that affect the security of applications and software developed by using cloud services and also cloud user's data. Data security is the main concern in cloud computing because it is stored in data centers provided by service providers. The chapter presents the background history of cloud computing and different challenges faced by the cloud environment, especially in terms of providing security for customer data stored in data centers. Authors also discuss the case studies on Microsoft Azure (i.e. a cloud platform) and Aneka (i.e. a cloud development and management platform).

1. CLOUD COMPUTING

Cloud computing is defined as *"a model for enabling convenient, on-demand network access to a shared pool of configurable computing resources (e.g., networks, servers, storage, applications and services) that can be rapidly provisioned and released with minimal management effort or service provider interaction"*, according to National Institute of Standards and Technology (NIST) (Mell & Grance, 2011). On the other hand, cloud computing provides services without the installation of software and infrastructure on the user's own system, eliminating maintenance overhead that automatically reduces overall costs and improves system performance. Entities using cloud services are known as 'cloud users'; Including

DOI: 10.4018/978-1-7998-2242-4.ch015

Copyright © 2020, IGI Global. Copying or distributing in print or electronic forms without written permission of IGI Global is prohibited.

Figure 1. Cloud Computing Architecture

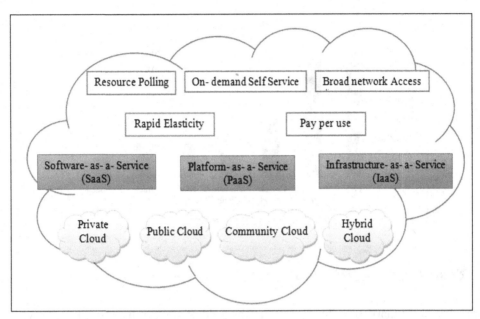

mobile devices, tablets, thin and thick clients such as computers, servers, web browsers, etc., and organizations that provide cloud-related services and provide solutions on demand to consumers, are known as cloud service providers (CSPs) (Hayes, 2008; Zhu et al., 2011; Furht, & Escalante, 2010; Rimal, Choi & Lumb, 2010; Gou, Yamaguchi & Gupta, 2017; Gupta, Agrawal & Yamaguchi, 2016; Gupta, 2019; Joshi & Gupta, 2019). Figure 1 depicts architecture of cloud computing environment.

2. MOTIVATION

Nowadays cloud computing has become popular and its domain has expanded. Figure 2 shows the trend of adopting the cloud services world-wide in year 2019 and the estimated statistics for the year 2020. It clearly shows that cloud adoption is rapidly growing and it has many advantages for both customers and providers, but it also faces many security challenges. The public cloud computing market grows rapidly, including infrastructure, platform, software and business processes delivered in the form of a service. The public cloud market was $ 146 billion in 2017 and $ 178 billion in 2018. It's estimated worth is $ 208 billion for year 2019 and $ 236 billion for year 2020. Global market growth of cloud computing is shown in figure 3.

Cloud computing is actively evolving and, therefore, has many vulnerabilities that can be exploited by malicious insiders or cyber criminals. Some of them are shared technology, weak cryptography, provider lock-in, vulnerable cloud services, malicious insiders etc. The primary purpose of cyber attackers is to prevent access to cloud services for legitimate users and to gain access to user data. This causes cloud users to lose confidence in cloud services and cloud users suffer heavy losses (Stergiou, Psannis, Gupta & Ishibashi, 2018; B. B. Gupta., S. Gupta & Chaudhary, 2017; Gupta (Ed.), 2018; Li, Z. Zhang & L. Zhang, 2018; Gupta & Badve, 2017).

Figure 2. World-wide usages of cloud services

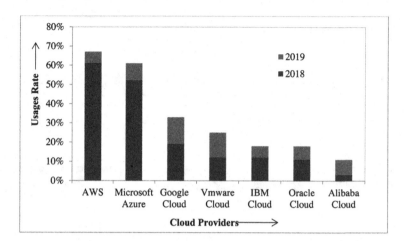

3. HISTORY AND BACKGROUND

Cloud computing is a remarkable phenomenon in the field of computing and it has evolved from most computing technologies like parallel computing, virtualization, grid computing and web based utility computing (Rimal, Choi & Lumb, 2009). In year 1950, IBM designed mainframe timesharing computers, which were mainly used for transaction processing, volumetric data processing and important applications. It was accessible through thin users. IBM developed the first hypervisor in the 1960s, which allowed multiple operating systems to run concurrently as a VM and provided full virtualization. In this hypervisor, the guest operating system can be run on every VM with its own memory and other infrastructure, making it possible to share these resources. It evolved into the concept of virtualization which became popular. In 1969, ARPANET was developed by the U.S. Advanced Research Project Agency (ARPA). It was capable to communicate and share resources between connected devices in the network. Trends towards cloud computing began in 1980 with the development of grid computing. A grid is a group of computers and servers that are connected in parallel. Grid size can vary from small network to wide area

Figure 3. Global market growth of cloud computing

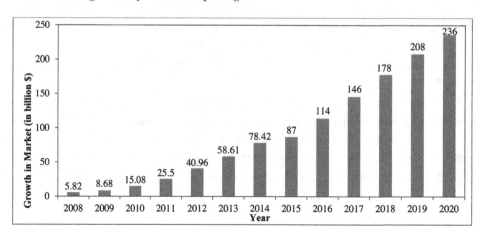

Figure 4. Evolution phases of cloud computing

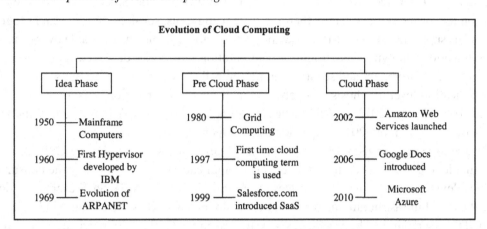

network and is implemented through a number of computing resources with a variety of applications like educational, scientific, or mathematical functions.

In the 1990s, the virtualization concept was extended beyond virtual servers - including virtual applications, network resources and storage. In 1997, for the first time, cloud computing term was used by R. Chalappa. After this the cloud attracted the attention of the companies and major companies made their own cloud according to their needs. In the year 1999, salesforce.com provided CRM software as a service on the Internet. In 2002, Amazon launched Amazon Web Services (AWS), which enables businesses to create their own applications on Amazon's infrastructure. The concept of Simple Storage Service (S3) and Elastic Compute Cloud (EC2) was later added to it in 2006. Google also launched its cloud service, Google Docs in 2006 which was based on Google Spreadsheets and Writely. In 2008, Microsoft announced its cloud, which included five main components; Microsoft Azure for networking, computing and storage; Microsoft .Net services for developers; Live sharing services for file sharing; Microsoft sharing services; and Microsoft SQL Services for databases. The Microsoft cloud services are eventually launched in 2010. Figure 4 depicts the evolution phases of cloud computing.

4. CLOUD SERVICES

Following are the basic services offered by cloud:

- **Infrastructure as a Service (IaaS):** CSP delivers services like hardware, storage, network, and computational power to cloud users as IaaS. Users can run or deploy their software such as operating system or application. The key aspect of the IaaS model is virtualization. CSP builds multiple virtual machines on one host, and the customer can control the services hosted on its infrastructure, operating systems, and some parts of the network. Customers have better control over security in the IaaS cloud, unless there are no security holes in Virtualization Manager. Example: - Google Compute Engine (GCE) (Google Inc., 2018), Digital Ocean, Rackspace, Microsoft Azure (Microsoft Corporation, 2018), Cisco Metapod, Amazon Web Services (AWS) (Amazon, 2018), etc.

- **Platform as a Service (PaaS):** It provides a framework for consumers to deploy their applications on it. Consumers can deploy their software using tools, services, libraries and programming languages supported by the CSP. These applications are scalable and available over time. In PaaS, the application deployment environment configuration settings for deployed applications, application-hosting environment and security can be controlled by the consumer; but security other than the application level like hosts and networks is in the provider's scope. Example: - Google App Engine (Google Inc., 2018), AWS Elastic Beanstalk (Amazon, 2018), Force.com, Windows Azure (Microsoft Corporation, 2018), Apache Stratos, OpenShift etc.

- **Software as a Service (SaaS):** Services or application software running on CSPs infrastructure is available to consumers on the Internet. These applications are accessed by the consumer using various devices through the web services or program interface (API). SaaS users have no control over the cloud infrastructure including network, storage as well as the execution platform that are beyond the user's limit. The SaaS users have to rely on the CSP for appropriate security measures. Example: - Salesforce (Salesforce Inc., 2018), Google Apps, Concur, Dropbox, Cisco WebEx (Cisco, 2018), GoToMeeting, etc.

5. CLOUD DEPLOYMENT MODELS

The cloud is classified into four deployment models based on user suitability and requirement by NIST (Mell & Grance, 2011):

- **Public Cloud:** Services of cloud are accessible to common users, and are maintained by a government organization, academia, business, or some combination of them. The Cloud resides on the premises of the CSP. Public cloud ensures scalability and reliability but there are many security issues such as the location of data, the type of storage used by the provider, and certain issues of multi-tenancy. When an organization migrates to the public cloud, it has to compromise on some security issues. Examples are Windows Azure Services Platform, Google App Engine, Sun cloud, IBM's Blue Cloud, and Amazon Elastic Compute Cloud (EC2).

- **Private Cloud:** Services of cloud are exclusively provisioned for a single organization comprising multiple consumers (business unit). The cloud is maintained by the third party or organization itself and is located inside or outside the organization's premises. It has fewer security concerns but also has maintenance overhead of resources. Examples are Microsoft ECI data center, VMware Cloud Infrastructure Suite, Amazon VPC (Virtual Private Cloud) etc.

- **Community Cloud:** Cloud infrastructure is shared by a limited individual who belongs to a particular community with common concerns. The cloud services are accessible by the users of that particular community. The cloud is owned and managed by the third party or by the one or more of the organization in the community, located inside or outside premises.

- **Hybrid Cloud:** It provides cloud solutions for combination of one or more distinct private cloud or public cloud infrastructures that remains unique entities but integrated together. Hybrid cloud provides cost benefit like a public cloud and also takes care of security issues such as private cloud. A major concern is the data flow from the private to the public cloud or vice-versa since access control varies significantly.

6. CLOUD VIRTUALIZATION MODELS

According to the cloud's virtual infrastructure, all the deployment models outlined so far have been classified. The essential requirement of cloud computing is virtualization as it provides services by creating virtual machines, which are accessible to end users. In each type of virtualization technique, a unique method is used to match the physical server to customers' virtual servers (Subashini & Kavitha, 2011). Virtualization Models have been classified as follows:

- **Full Virtualization:** Full virtualization is a cost-effective way in which the virtual machine (VM) uses the hypervisor and allows the OS to run in the isolation from the hardware. Software and OS (whose information cannot be modified) are run on top of VMs hardware and hardware and OS are completely separate from each other. There are two types: - Hardware Assisted and Software Assisted.
- **Para Virtualization:** In Para-virtualization, the hardware is not emulated for VMs and the operating system is aware of other OS in the environment. Without the use of a hypervisor, the system load is balanced between all operating systems. The information of the OS can be modified with the key information to communicate with the host and communication has been done with the help of drivers.
- **OS Level Virtualization:** OS level virtualization is a type of server virtualization that provides transparency among applications belongs to different users. The underlying host OS works as a hypervisor and is also capable to transfer applications from one OS to other to increase performance. Applications are isolated in OS virtualized environment and their communication with the host OS is monitored.

7. CLOUD CHARACTERISTICS

Cloud computing has five essential features such as pay per use, on-demand self-service, rapid elasticity, broad network access and resource pooling (Mell & Grance, 2011).

- **Pay Per Use:** Cloud computing provides services based on metering, which mean that resource usage can be monitored, and services can be billed on the basis of usage. This is done by providing transparency between the service provider and the consumer via SLA.
- **On-demand Self-service:** A customer can enable the provision of computing resources like storage, bandwidth and server time as per their requirement. Self-service means that the consumer can enable the services themselves without human interaction with the service provider.
- **Rapid Elasticity:** Computing resources are dynamically provisioned and released according to user request to provide scalability in services on-demand. For the consumer, the resources are unlimited and available at any time.
- **Broad Network Access:** Computing resources are hosted over the network and accessed through Internet using standard methods from anywhere-anytime with multiple thin and thick devices (mobile phone, pc, tablets etc.).
- **Resource Pooling:** It allows the CSP to pool large-scale computing resources (storage, server, application, bandwidth and network) to serve many consumers of the cloud. By sharing the com-

puting capabilities of resources, the rate of resource utilization increases and the cost is reduced. These are the virtual and physical resources which are location independent and provisioned dynamically to the consumer on demand.

8. TAXONOMY OF SECURITY CHALLENGES IN CLOUD COMPUTING

Cloud capabilities are accessed through the network or the Internet. Although cloud computing provides many facilities for the IT industry; It faces many security threats that degrade the Quality of Service (QoS). Figure 5 shows the taxonomy of security challenges present in cloud.

8.1 Data Related Security Threats

A huge amount of data is processed by cloud computing. Using websites or APIs, data can be stored in the cloud and information can be retrieved from previously stored data. Stored data may contain sensitive information like government files, medical files and financial information and the exposure to such information can lead to disaster. The security of data can be considered as a security of confidentiality, integrity, and availability (CIA) of data (Ouaguid, Abghour & Ouzzif, 2018; Kaushik & Gandhi, 2019;

Figure 5.Taxonomy of security challenges in cloud

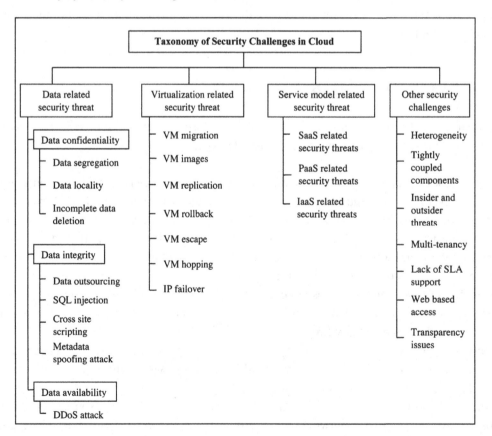

Gupta & Sheng, pp. 352, 2019; Gupta & Gugulothu, 2018; Zhang et al., 2017; Chhabra, Gupta & Al-momani, 2013). Cloud computing has many security threats that breach the CIA of data (Modi et al., 2013; Fernandes, 2014; Beloglazov & Buyya, 2010).

8.1.1 Data Confidentiality

It refers to the protection of data from revelation to unauthorized user, entity or program. In Cloud environment, the unauthorized users may be consumers or providers themselves. The consumer can access other consumer data that is stored in the same table or available as shared access. The provider can view or tamper the consumer's data. Some Cloud providers do not allow data to be stored in the encrypted form and the data at the provider's side processed in plaintext. The cloud provider is responsible for the confidentiality of a consumer's data if the service is used by the consumer is SaaS.

- **Data Segregation:** Some Cloud providers allows the shared access to storage capacity that contains data from multiple consumers. This can lead to loss of data confidentiality. The other users who have the right to access shared storage may alter the data of other users. So the user data partitioning is needed to prevent unauthorized access by other users and it is managed by the service provider. Encryption of data is another way to prevent unauthorized access of data.
- **Data Locality:** Data is stored by the user is transferred between one data centers to other data center by the service provider. This can be an issue. The compliance or data privacy laws of the different countries are different, so localization of data is important. For example, if user processed data in India, store it on servers in the UK and send it via the US, then there's a question of whose law will apply on data if an investigation occurs. Due to the sensitivity of information, many countries do not allow certain types of data to leave the country.
- **Incomplete Data Deletion:** Improper alteration/ deletion of data by the service provider is risky for the user who requests the deletion of the data. This data may contain sensitive information whose exposure cause disaster.

8.1.2 Data Integrity

Integrity is the property of information security which ensures that the accuracy and completeness of data is protected throughout the lifecycle of the data. Integrity maintains protection of data from origination, evaluation, storage, and transfer. Accuracy and consistency of data can be broken if an update or delete operation is performed by the unauthorized user.

- **Data Outsourcing:** Private and hybrid Clouds are managed by third- party and public Clouds are managed by a Cloud provider that will perform operations to manage the Cloud. This third- party or Cloud provider may alter the user's data or send an incomplete data set. That will breach the integrity of data.
- **SQL Injection:** Attack mostly performed on data centric applications to retrieve data from unauthorized access. A malicious code will be injected into the database by exploiting the vulnerabilities of the web server. A huge amount of data is processed by mostly Cloud services. SQL injection attacks enable malicious actors to become administrators of the database server.

- **Cross Site Scripting:** Is a web application vulnerability that will use to inject malicious scripts into vulnerable web pages (JavaScript, VBScript, ActiveX, and HTML etc.) to get unauthorized access in the database of application and comprise the integrity of data. Cloud applications are hosted over the internet and access by web browsers so there is a high chance to perform this attack.
- **Metadata Spoofing Attack:** Is an attack which modifies the content of the web service description document (WSDL) files in order to perform an operation for which he is unauthorized. The WSDL file contains data such as required parameters or security requirements, message format, and web service address. The alteration of these parameters is done by an attacker to perform unauthorized operations. To prevent such attack, check authenticity of the metadata document prior to using them, but there is no standard method to check the authenticity of the metadata file till now.

8.1.3 Data Availability

This ensures that data and security ecosystem mention in the SLA is fully available every time for the authorized user. Availability of resources or data, maintained by multi-tier architecture or replication of data and replicas stored at different places. If a disaster occurs, then at the same time a disaster recovery or business continuity plan is executed to maintain the availability of data. An organization must ensure high availability and minimum downtime. Distributed Denial of Service (DDoS) attacks are one of the major causes for unavailability of data or service (Kaufman, 2009; Sharma & Saxena, 2012; Idziorek, Tannian & Jacobson, pp. 99-106, 2012; Modi et al., 2013; Adat & Gupta, 2017; Schuba et al., 1997; Hwang & Li, 2010; Gupta, Joshi & Mishra, 2012; Gupta, S., & Gupta, B. B., 2015; Dahiya & Gupta, B. B., 2019; Gupta, B. B. & Gulihar et al., 2020; Alieyan et al., 2019).

8.2 Virtualization Related Security Threats

The basis of Cloud computing architecture is virtualization. Using the virtualization concept, the resources of the Cloud will be shared among multiple users. This is the concept of multi-tenancy. A hypervisor or virtual machine monitor (VMM) is hardware or software that allows multiple VMs to be created and runs on the single host OS and is the main unit of virtualization. If at any instance of time the hypervisor is compromised and breached, then the entire guest OS can be controlled. An attacker can exploit the weaknesses of the hypervisor or virtualization and perform attacks like DDoS attack or cross-VM side channel attack.

- *VM migration* is an aspect of Cloud computing, in which for fault tolerance, scalability and load balancing the VM is moved to another host operating system. During the migration of the VM, the confidentiality and integrity of the VM instance and metadata needs to be preserved.
- *Virtual Machine Images (VMI),* can be created with different configurations by the user or provider. Some intruders upload malicious VMI to compromise the services assigned to other legitimate users and to obtain unauthorized access to the data. Virtual machine manager (VMM) is controls or monitors its virtual machine. Flaws in VMM are also leading to compromises with user's data. Some of the VMMs do not offer perfect isolation for virtual machines running on the single host.

- *VM Replication* is a factor of unwanted data leakage. For protecting the data of VM a replica is created but it leaks information about the VM if not handled properly.

VM rollback, VM escapes, VM hopping, and IP failover is other vulnerability issues in virtualization

8.3 Service Model Related Security Threats

As discussed above cloud computing architecture have three service delivery models shown in figure 6. The capabilities of these service delivery models are inherited from each other because the IaaS model provides basic infrastructure for setting up a platform for all cloud services and deployed services on it, and it is the backbone of cloud. PaaS services builds on the infrastructure provided by IaaS and SaaS Services builds on the platform provided by PaaS. With the capabilities, security risks are also inherited. The attacks will affect directly or indirectly to the CIA of data and the services provided by different service models such as networking, storage, hardware, virtualization etc. The security of these service models varies from CSP to customer. Cloud capabilities / resources are accessed through web browser or APIs, therefore, vulnerability or potential attack on web browser or API is also a security risk for cloud services. There are many security threats in different service delivery models (Shahzad, 2014; Tsai, Sun & Balasooriya, 2010; Basu et al., 2018; Modi, Patel, Borisaniya, Patel & Rajarajan, 2013; Fernandes, 2014; El-Latif et al., 2018; Jiang et al., 2018):

- **SaaS Related Security Threats:** In SaaS model the services/ applications are already available on the Cloud and that is remotely hosted by the service provider. There are several advantages such as cost and maintenance but the entire control is in the hands of the service provider. The client will have to depend on the service provider for all security measures. The service provider provides security to consumer's data to gain trust. There are many security threats such as insider intruders, vulnerability in web browsers, application/software vulnerability, network layer attacks, virtualization vulnerability, data security, data locality, availability, data integrity, sign-on process, identity management, authentication and authorization, data access, data breaches, data confidentiality, data segregation and backup.
- **PaaS Related Security Threats**: The PaaS model provides a platform for developing the applications on it but does not have any information about the infrastructure of the system. A user can build application according to him on the platform hence the security of application depends on the user itself. Even now, security below the application level fully depends on the service provider this will gives an open invitation to hackers or attackers. Hackers can attack the PaaS services from behind the IaaS and perform extensive black box testing. PaaS is more flexible, scalable and reliable than SaaS, but also requires more security, which increases the cost of security. There are some security threats such as tolerance of fault, continuity of service, access control, host vulnerability, interoperability and object vulnerability.
- **IaaS Related Security Threats:** The IaaS model has completely changed the frame of the IT industry. Companies use IaaS services instead of building their own data centers or infrastructures. Due to this, they have no overload of maintaining infrastructure and the scalability is also provided by the service provider. In the IaaS model, virtualization plays an important role. Security of the IaaS model mainly depends on the security of virtualization. Reliability of data is another factor because the data of an organization is stored in the service provider's data centers.

Figure 6. Service models of cloud computing

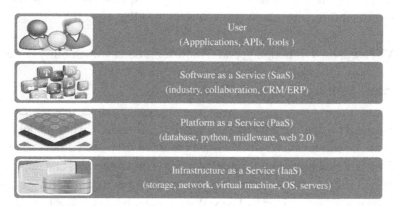

8.4 Other Security Challenges

Despite the deployment of several security solutions against cloud attacks, cloud computing has many challenges in which the CSP may face problems.

- **Heterogeneity**: Cloud services are provided by different service providers and every service provider has its unique way of application deployment and management. If a user wants to switch from one Cloud to other, then its simple meaning is a redevelopment of application. Also, the security is provided in different ways by different providers thus generating integration is a challenge.
- **Tightly Coupled Components:** When a consumer uses a Cloud service then he also bounded to use those services which are related to that service provided by a service provider. Rather than this if the service is provided according to user's requirement such as the service is constructed according to users need, hence it will provide more flexibility and fewer security issues. Advantages of building service according to a user are there is a wider selection of components, and service is available at cheaper cost.
- **Insider and Outsider Threats:** Attacks outside the company premises on cloud services are more common and dangerous. Because the motive of the attacker cannot be predictable and sometimes the origins of the attack cannot be ascertained. There are various attacks and methods to perform an attack from outside the company. Attacks from inside the company are also the possible and such type of attacks considered most dangerous. Insiders know all the workflow of the company and also have access to confidential data. Such attacks are hard to detect because the insiders know about all the security measures used by the company to prevent the attacks (Sahoo, & Gupta, 2019, pp. 832-864; 2019, pp. 65-81; 2018, pp. 591-606).
- **Multi-tenancy**: The key aspect of cloud computing is virtualization. Many VMs are run on a system and use by the different Cloud service users. These users may be rivals of each other or maybe an intruder who wants to attack the system. Some Cloud providers are providing single shared storage for multiple users. Customer penetration testing may cause unavailability of data for other users to run on the same host. Due to lack of proper isolation in services running on VMs, resource sharing and customization system is a challenge in security.

- **Lack of SLA Support:** The resources available on the Cloud are dynamically provisioned and provide on- demand to Cloud user. SLA is used to establish trust between service provider and user; it is a document that is created at the time of service opted by the user. SLA is a static document, so the contract between the service provider and the user for dynamic services requires some negotiation mechanism.

- **Network or Web based Access:** Cloud environment is affected by the web or network vulnerabilities. Many web-based attacks are possible on Cloud services to gain access to data. Such attacks are SQL injection, XSS, URL- guessing or phishing. There needs to vulnerability free or secure web browsers. Some attacks like ARP spoofing, DNS poisoning, flooding are possible using vulnerabilities of internet protocol. There are some solutions and prevention mechanisms that are used to develop intrusion detection, anti-spyware, anti-virus, anti-phishing, anti-spam etc.

- **Transparency Issues:** Cloud service providers do not offer customers with visibility into their operating environments. The customer does not know where the data resides physically or virtually and what operations are performed on the data. The absence of transparency can break the trust and customers have to move to their own data centers.

9 CASE STUDY

9.1 Microsoft Azure

There are many cloud computing platforms offered by different organizations. Windows Azure is one of them, which is provided by Microsoft. Azure can be described as the managed data centers that are used to build, deploy, manage and provide services through a global network. The services provided by Microsoft Azure are PaaS and IaaS. Many programming languages and frameworks are supported by it (Wilder, 2012).

Azure as PaaS (Platform as a Service): As the name suggests, a platform is provided to clients to develop and deploy software. The clients can focus on the application development rather than having to worry about hardware and infrastructure. It also takes care of most of the operating systems, servers and networking issues.

Pros:
- The overall cost is low as the resources are allocated on demand and servers are automatically updated.
- It is less vulnerable as servers are automatically updated and being checked for all known security issues. The whole process is not visible to developer and thus does not pose a risk of data breach.
- Since new versions of development tools are tested by the Azure team, it becomes easy for developers to move on to new tools. This also helps the developers to meet the customer's demand by quickly adapting to new versions.

Cons:
- There are portability issues with using PaaS. There can be a different environment at Azure, thus the application might have to be adapted accordingly.

Azure as IaaS (Infrastructure as a Service): It is a managed compute service that gives complete control of the operating systems and the application platform stack to the application developers. It lets the user to access, manage and monitor the data centers by themselves.

Pros:
- This is ideal for the application where complete control is required. The virtual machine can be completely adapted to the requirements of the organization or business.
- IaaS facilitates very efficient design time portability. This means application can be migrated to Windows Azure without rework. All the application dependencies such as database can also be migrated to Azure.
- IaaS allows quick transition of services to clouds, which helps the vendors to offer services to their clients easily. This also helps the vendors to expand their business by selling the existing software or services in new markets.

Cons:
- Since users are given complete control they are tempted to stick to a particular version for the dependencies of applications. It might become difficult for them to migrate the application to future versions.
- There are many factors which increases the cost of its operation. For example- higher server maintenance for patching and upgrading software.
- There are lots of security risks from un-patched servers. Some companies have well-defined processes for testing and updating on premise servers for security vulnerabilities. These processes need to be extended to the cloud-hosted IaaS VMs to mitigate hacking risks.
- The unpatched servers pose a great security risk. Unlike PaaS, there is no provision of automatic server patching in IaaS. An unpatched server with sensitive information can be very vulnerable affecting the entire business of an organization.
- It is difficult to maintain legacy apps in IaaS. It can be stuck with the older version of the operating systems and application stacks. Thus, resulting in applications that are difficult to maintain and add new functionality over the period of time (Luo, Jin, Song & Dong, 2011).

It becomes necessary to understand the pros and cons of both services in order to choose the right one according your requirements. In conclusion it can be said that, PaaS has definite economic advantages for operations over IaaS for commodity applications. In PaaS, the cost of operations breaks the business model. Whereas, IaaS gives complete control of the OS and application platform stack.

9.2 Aneka

Aneka is a market-oriented Cloud development and management platform with rapid application development and workload distribution capabilities. Aneka is an integrated middleware package which allows you to seamlessly build and manage an interconnected network in addition to accelerating development, deployment and management of distributed applications using Microsoft .NET frameworks on these networks. It is market oriented since it allows you to build, schedule, provision and monitor results using pricing, accounting, QoS/SLA services in private and/or public (leased) network environments.

Aneka is a workload distribution and management platform that accelerates applications in Microsoft .NET framework environments. Some of the key advantages of Aneka over other GRID or Cluster based workload distribution solutions include:

- Rapid deployment tools and framework.
- Ability to harness multiple virtual and/or physical machines for accelerating application result.
- Provisioning based on QoS/SLA ·support of multiple programming and application environments.
- Simultaneous support of multiple run-time environments built on-top of Microsoft .NET framework, with support for Linux environments through Mono.

Aneka Architecture

Aneka is a platform and a framework for developing distributed applications on the Cloud. The architecture of Aneka is shown in Figure 7. It harnesses the spare CPU cycles of a heterogeneous network of desktop PCs and servers or data centers on demand. Aneka provides developers with a rich set of APIs for transparently exploiting such resources and expressing the business logic of applications by using the preferred programming abstractions. System administrators can leverage on a collection of tools to monitor and control the deployed infrastructure.

This can be a public cloud available to anyone through the Internet, or a private cloud constituted by a set of nodes with restricted access. The Aneka based computing cloud is a collection of physical and virtualized resources connected through a network, which are either the Internet or a private intranet. Each of these resources hosts an instance of the Aneka Container representing the runtime environment where the distributed applications are executed. The container provides the basic management features of the single node and leverages all the other operations on the services that it is hosting. The services are broken up into fabric, foundation, and execution services. Fabric services directly interact with the node through the Platform Abstraction Layer (PAL) and perform hardware profiling and dynamic resource provisioning. Foundation services identify the core system of the Aneka middleware, providing a set of basic features to enable Aneka containers to perform specialized and specific sets of tasks. Execution services directly deal with the scheduling and execution of applications in the Cloud. One of the key features of Aneka is the ability of providing different ways for expressing distributed applications by offering different programming models; execution services are mostly concerned with providing the middleware with an implementation for these models. Additional services such as persistence and security are transversal to the entire stack of services that are hosted by the Container. At the application level, a set of different components and tools are provided to: 1) simplify the development of applications (SDK); 2) porting existing applications to the Cloud; and 3) monitoring and managing the Aneka Cloud.

A common deployment of Aneka is presented in Figure 8. An Aneka based Cloud is constituted by a set of interconnected resources that are dynamically modified according to the user needs by using resource virtualization or by harnessing the spare CPU cycles of desktop machines. If the deployment identifies a private Cloud all the resources are in house, for example within the enterprise. This deployment is extended by adding publicly available resources on demand or by interacting with other Aneka public clouds providing computing resources connected over the Internet.

Figure 7. Overview of Aneka Framework

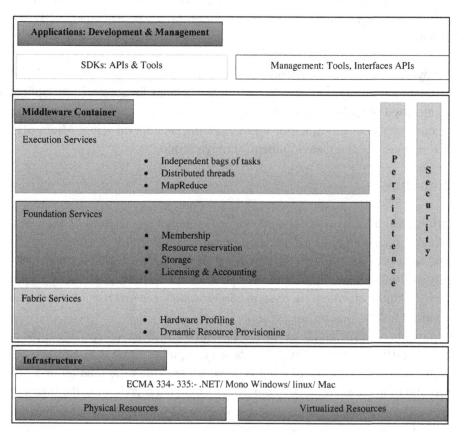

Figure 8. A Typical Aneka Cloud Deployment

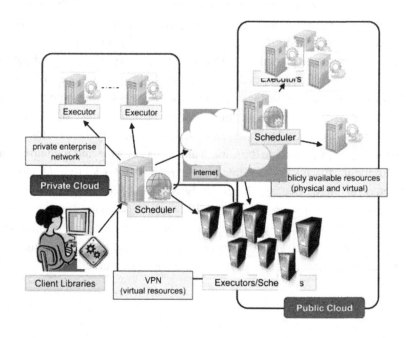

10 CONCLUSION AND FUTURE WORK

Cloud Computing has a considerable impact on the IT industry. It provides various business benefits; however, there are several security challenges and threats in the Cloud computing environment that impair the service quality. In this chapter, we illuminate the background of cloud computing since the evolution of the idea of cloud computing and number of possible types of attack scenarios that affect the confidentiality, integrity and availability of data. We have also discussed various applications running by using cloud computing environment such as Google Compute Engine, AWS Elastic Beanstalk, Cisco WebEx, Google Apps etc. as an example. In this Chapter, we also discussed about Microsoft Azure; a cloud provider and Aneka; a cloud platform to develop cloud applications and build PaaS Cloud.

In the future we focus on formation and implementation of the solutions to detect and mitigate various types of attack that cause the services to be unavailable for cloud users. We will focus on the use of smart networking or software based networking tools bypassing the traditional networking architecture to provide scalability and programmability in real time environment. A large number of applications are present in the cloud environment and a dedicated apparatus is required for a particular application. We will detect various faults in cloud environments and also detect various attacks performed by using them. We will develop a security mechanism to prevent and detect those attacks so that cloud users' data is protected.

ACKNOWLEDGMENT

This publication is an outcome of the R&D works undertaken under YFRF grant of the Visvesvaraya Ph.D. Scheme of Ministry of Electronics & Information Technology, Government of India and being implemented by Digital India Corporation.

REFERENCES

Adat, V., & Gupta, B. B. (2017, April). A DDoS attack mitigation framework for internet of things. In *Proceedings 2017 International Conference on Communication and Signal Processing (ICCSP),* (pp. 2036-2041). IEEE. 10.1109/ICCSP.2017.8286761

Alieyan, K., Almomani, A., Anbar, M., Alauthman, M., Abdullah, R., & Gupta, B. B. (2019). DNS rule-based schema to botnet detection. *Enterprise Information Systems*, 1–20. doi:10.1080/17517575. 2019.1644673

Amazon Elastic Compute Cloud (Amazon EC2), Amazon. (n.d.). Available from https://aws.amazon. com/ec2/. Accessed on Sept 2018.

AWS Elastic Beanstalk, Amazon Web Services, Amazon. (n.d.). Available from https://aws.amazon. com/elasticbeanstalk/. Accessed on Sept 2018.

Azure: Microsoft's Cloud Platform, Microsoft Corporation. (n.d.). Available from https://azure.microsoft. com/en-in/. Accessed on Sept 2018.

Basu, S., Bardhan, A., Gupta, K., Saha, P., Pal, M., Bose, M., . . . Sarkar, P. (2018, January). Cloud computing security challenges & solutions-A survey. In *Proceedings 2018 IEEE 8th Annual Computing and Communication Workshop and Conference (CCWC),* (pp. 347-356). IEEE. 10.1109/CCWC.2018.8301700

Behl, A. (2011, December). Emerging security challenges in Cloud computing: An insight to Cloud security challenges and their mitigation. In Proceedings 2011 World Congress on Information and Communication Technologies (WICT), (pp. 217-222). IEEE.

Beloglazov, A., & Buyya, R. (2010, May). Energy efficient resource management in virtualized cloud data centers. In *Proceedings of the 2010 10th IEEE/ACM international conference on cluster, cloud and grid computing* (pp. 826-831). IEEE Computer Society. 10.1109/CCGRID.2010.46

Brij, B. (2019). *Gupta, Quan Z. Sheng, Machine Learning for Computer and Cyber Security: Principle, Algorithms, and Practices* (p. 352). CRC Press, Taylor & Francis.

Chhabra, M., Gupta, B., & Almomani, A. (2013). A novel solution to handle DDOS attack in MANET. *Journal of Information Security, 4*(3), 165–179. doi:10.4236/jis.2013.43019

Cisco WebEx, Cisco. (n.d.). Available from https://www.webex.co.in/. Accessed on Sept 2018

CRM Salesforce Cloud, Salesforce Inc. (n.d.). Available from https://www.salesforce.com/in/?ir=1. Accessed on Sept 2018

El-Latif, A. A. A., Abd-El-Atty, B., Hossain, M. S., Rahman, M. A., Alamri, A., & Gupta, B. B. (2018). Efficient quantum information hiding for remote medical image sharing. *IEEE Access: Practical Innovations, Open Solutions, 6*, 21075–21083. doi:10.1109/ACCESS.2018.2820603

Fernandes, D. A., Soares, L. F., Gomes, J. V., Freire, M. M., & Inácio, P. R. (2014). Security issues in cloud environments: A survey. *International Journal of Information Security, 13*(2), 113–170. doi:10.100710207-013-0208-7

Fernandes, D. A., Soares, L. F., Gomes, J. V., Freire, M. M., & Inácio, P. R. (2014). Security issues in Cloud environments: A survey. *International Journal of Information Security, 13*(2), 113–170. doi:10.100710207-013-0208-7

Furht, B., & Escalante, A. (2010). *Handbook of cloud computing* (Vol. 3). New York: Springer. doi:10.1007/978-1-4419-6524-0

Google App Engine, Google Inc. (n.d.). Available from http://Cloud.google.com/appengine. Accessed on Sept. 2018.

Google Compute Engine, Google Inc. (n.d.). Available from https://Cloud.google.com/compute/. Accessed on Sept 2018.

Gou, Z., Yamaguchi, S., & Gupta, B. B. (2017). Analysis of various security issues and challenges in cloud computing environment: a survey. In Identity Theft: Breakthroughs in Research and Practice (pp. 221-247). IGI Global. doi:10.4018/978-1-5225-0808-3.ch011

Gupta, B., Agrawal, D. P., & Yamaguchi, S. (Eds.). (2016). *Handbook of research on modern cryptographic solutions for computer and cyber security*. IGI global. doi:10.4018/978-1-5225-0105-3

Gupta, B. B. (Ed.). (2018). *Computer and cyber security: principles, algorithm, applications, and perspectives*. UK: CRC Press, Taylor & Francis.

Gupta, B. B. (2019). *Modern Principles, Practices, and Algorithms for Cloud Security* (p. 344). Hershey, PA: IGI Global.

Gupta, B. B., & Badve, O. P. (2017). Taxonomy of DoS and DDoS attacks and desirable defense mechanism in a cloud computing environment. *Neural Computing & Applications*, *28*(12), 3655–3682. doi:10.100700521-016-2317-5

Gupta, B. B., & Gulihar, P. (2020). Taxonomy of Payment Structures and Economic Incentive Schemes in Internet. [JITR]. *Journal of Information Technology Research*, *13*(1), 150–166. doi:10.4018/JITR.2020010110

Gupta, B. B., Gupta, S., & Chaudhary, P. (2017). Enhancing the browser-side context-aware sanitization of suspicious HTML5 code for halting the DOM-based XSS vulnerabilities in cloud. [IJCAC]. *International Journal of Cloud Applications and Computing*, *7*(1), 1–31. doi:10.4018/IJCAC.2017010101

Gupta, B. B., Joshi, R. C., & Misra, M. (2012). Distributed denial of service prevention techniques. *arXiv preprint arXiv:1208.3557*.

Gupta, S., & Gugulothu, N. (2018). Secure nosql for the social networking and e-commerce based bigdata applications deployed in cloud. [IJCAC]. *International Journal of Cloud Applications and Computing*, *8*(2), 113–129. doi:10.4018/IJCAC.2018040106

Gupta, S., & Gupta, B. B. (2015, May). PHP-sensor: a prototype method to discover workflow violation and XSS vulnerabilities in PHP web applications. In *Proceedings of the 12th ACM International Conference on Computing Frontiers* (p. 59). ACM. 10.1145/2742854.2745719

Hayes, B. (2008). Cloud computing. *Communications of the ACM*, *51*(7), 9–11. doi:10.1145/1364782.1364786

Hwang, K., & Li, D. (2010). Trusted Cloud computing with secure resources and data coloring. *IEEE Internet Computing*, *14*(5), 14–22. doi:10.1109/MIC.2010.86

Idziorek, J., Tannian, M., & Jacobson, D. (2012, June). Attribution of fraudulent resource consumption in the Cloud. In *Proceedings 2012 IEEE 5th International Conference on Cloud Computing (CLOUD)*, (pp. 99-106). IEEE. 10.1109/CLOUD.2012.23

Jiang, F., Fu, Y., Gupta, B. B., Lou, F., Rho, S., Meng, F., & Tian, Z. (2018). Deep learning based multi-channel intelligent attack detection for data security. IEEE Transactions on Sustainable Computing.

Joshi, R. C., & Gupta, B. B. (2019). *Security, Privacy, and Forensics Issues in Big Data* (p. 452). Hershey, PA: IGI Global.

Kaufman, L. M. (2009). Data security in the world of Cloud computing. *IEEE Security and Privacy*, *7*(4), 61–64. doi:10.1109/MSP.2009.87

Kaushik, S., & Gandhi, C. (2019). Ensure Hierarchal Identity Based Data Security in Cloud Environment. [IJCAC]. *International Journal of Cloud Applications and Computing*, *9*(4), 21–36. doi:10.4018/IJCAC.2019100102

Li, C., Zhang, Z., & Zhang, L. (2018). A Novel Authorization Scheme for Multimedia Social Networks Under Cloud Storage Method by Using MA-CP-ABE. [IJCAC]. *International Journal of Cloud Applications and Computing*, *8*(3), 32–47. doi:10.4018/IJCAC.2018070103

Luo, J. Z., Jin, J. H., Song, A. B., & Dong, F. (2011). Cloud computing: Architecture and key technologies. *Journal of Communication*, *7*(7), 3–21.

Mell, P., & Grance, T. (2011). The NIST definition of Cloud computing.

Modi, C., Patel, D., Borisaniya, B., Patel, A., & Rajarajan, M. (2013). A survey on security issues and solutions at different layers of Cloud computing. *The Journal of Supercomputing*, *63*(2), 561–592. doi:10.100711227-012-0831-5

Modi, C., Patel, D., Borisaniya, B., Patel, A., & Rajarajan, M. (2013). A survey on security issues and solutions at different layers of Cloud computing. *The Journal of Supercomputing*, *63*(2), 561–592. doi:10.100711227-012-0831-5

Modi, C., Patel, D., Borisaniya, B., Patel, H., Patel, A., & Rajarajan, M. (2013). A survey of intrusion detection techniques in Cloud. *Journal of Network and Computer Applications*, *36*(1), 42–57. doi:10.1016/j.jnca.2012.05.003

Ouaguid, A., Abghour, N., & Ouzzif, M. (2018). A novel security framework for managing Android permissions using blockchain technology. [IJCAC]. *International Journal of Cloud Applications and Computing*, *8*(1), 55–79. doi:10.4018/IJCAC.2018010103

Rimal, B. P., Choi, E., & Lumb, I. (2009, August). A taxonomy and survey of cloud computing systems. In *2009 Fifth International Joint Conference on INC, IMS and IDC* (pp. 44-51). IEEE. 10.1109/NCM.2009.218

Sahoo, S. R., & Gupta, B. B. (2018). Security Issues and Challenges in Online Social Networks (OSNs) Based on User Perspective. In Computer and Cyber Security (pp. 591-606). Auerbach Publications.

Sahoo, S. R., & Gupta, B. B. (2019). Classification of various attacks and their defence mechanism in online social networks: A survey. *Enterprise Information Systems*, *13*(6), 832–864. doi:10.1080/17517575.2019.1605542

Sahoo, S. R., & Gupta, B. B. (2019). Hybrid approach for detection of malicious profiles in twitter. *Computers & Electrical Engineering*, *76*, 65–81. doi:10.1016/j.compeleceng.2019.03.003

Schuba, C. L., Krsul, I. V., Kuhn, M. G., Spafford, E. H., Sundaram, A., & Zamboni, D. (1997, May). Analysis of a denial of service attack on TCP. In *Proceedings, 1997 IEEE Symposium on Security and Privacy, 1997.* (pp. 208-223). IEEE. 10.1109/SECPRI.1997.601338

Shahzad, F. (2014). State-of-the-art survey on cloud computing security Challenges, approaches and solutions. *Procedia Computer Science*, *37*, 357–362. doi:10.1016/j.procs.2014.08.053

Sharma, J., & Saxena, K. (2012). Cloud security challenges. *International Journal Computer Science and Information Technologies*, *3*(3).

Stergiou, C., Psannis, K. E., Gupta, B. B., & Ishibashi, Y. (2018). Security, privacy, & efficiency of sustainable cloud computing for big data & IoT. *Sustainable Computing: Informatics and Systems*, *19*, 174–184.

Subashini, S., & Kavitha, V. (2011). A survey on security issues in service delivery models of cloud computing. *Journal of Network and Computer Applications*, *34*(1), 1–11. doi:10.1016/j.jnca.2010.07.006

Tsai, W. T., Sun, X., & Balasooriya, J. (2010, April). Service-oriented Cloud computing architecture. In *Proceedings 2010 Seventh International Conference on Information Technology: New Generations (ITNG)*, (pp. 684-689). IEEE. 10.1109/ITNG.2010.214

Verisign, Distributed Denial of Service Trends Report, Retrieved from https://www.verisign.com/en_IN/security-services/ddos-protection/ddos-report/index.xhtml

Wilder, B. (2012). *Cloud architecture patterns: Using Microsoft Azure*. O'Reilly Media, Inc.

Wu, L., Garg, S. K., & Buyya, R. (2011, May). SLA-based resource allocation for software as a service provider (SaaS) in cloud computing environments. In *Proceedings of the 2011 11th IEEE/ACM International Symposium on Cluster, Cloud, and Grid Computing* (pp. 195-204). IEEE Computer Society.

Xiao, Z., Song, W., & Chen, Q. (2012). Dynamic resource allocation using virtual machines for cloud computing environment. *IEEE Transactions on Parallel and Distributed Systems*, *24*(6), 1107–1117. doi:10.1109/TPDS.2012.283

Zhang, Z., Sun, R., Zhao, C., Wang, J., Chang, C. K., & Gupta, B. B. (2017). CyVOD: A novel trinity multimedia social network scheme. *Multimedia Tools and Applications*, *76*(18), 18513–18529. doi:10.100711042-016-4162-z

Zhu, W., Luo, C., Wang, J., & Li, S. (2011). Multimedia cloud computing. *IEEE Signal Processing Magazine*, *28*(3), 59–69. doi:10.1109/MSP.2011.940269

Zissis, D., & Lekkas, D. (2012). Addressing Cloud computing security issues. *Future Generation Computer Systems*, *28*(3), 583–592. doi:10.1016/j.future.2010.12.006

Chapter 16
Cybersecurity:
An Emerging ICS Challenge

Selem Charfi
ⓘ https://orcid.org/0000-0002-1701-7306
AUSY, France

Marko Mladenovic
ⓘ https://orcid.org/0000-0002-8452-851X
UPHF LAMIH UMR 8201 CNRS, France

ABSTRACT

Cybersecurity is generally considered as an information security topic, often associated with personal data and information databases: collecting, exposing, corrupting, or deleting these data. However, it is a more global problem, and related to broader aspects, such as controlling cyber-systems. In ICS, the topic of cybersecurity is considered at the operational and responsible level as a secondary threat, and much more as an IT problem. This premise has proven to lead to substantial losses. For example, dangerous aspects in some installation can stress the cybersecurity in ICS, for instance, plants dealing with hazardous materials, as the attackers can take over control of the production lines. This chapter encapsulates points in common on the topic of cybersecurity in IT and ICS. IT has already devoted significant resources into cyber-threats. ICS has yet to do so. To do so, authors review a number of papers dealing with the same topic.

1. INTRODUCTION

The manufacturing sector is currently undergoing its fourth industrial revolution. The first industrial revolution was based on the use of mechanical production to boost production performance. The second one was based on electrical power and mass production. The third revolution occurred by introducing automation advances, based on IT. The fourth revolution, also known as Industry 4.0, and Smart Manufacturing, is established on interconnecting production systems. Then, the manufacturing systems and engines are endowed with communication abilities (i.e. sensors) for better exchange, operation, support

DOI: 10.4018/978-1-7998-2242-4.ch016

Copyright © 2020, IGI Global. Copying or distributing in print or electronic forms without written permission of IGI Global is prohibited.

and agile manufacturing. This enables reactive and effective steering from raw material reception to end use and recovery. Moreover, the manufacturing devices are controlled through computers.

According to (Hermann et al., 2016), the Industry 4.0 design principles are:

1. **Interconnection**: Machines, devices, and human operators are interconnected in order to share real-time information and support fluctuating market demands. The IoT[1] and new communication technology play an important role to promote this interconnection.
2. **Information Transparency**: Through linked sensors and information system (e.g. SCADA[2], MES[3]), a form of information transparency is provided to operators. Then, context-aware systems are indispensable to operators to make appropriate decisions.
3. **Decentralized Decisions:** As human operators and devices are interconnected; the decision is not centralized, but rather decentralized, for better decision-making and increasing overall productivity. In fact, operators are as autonomous as possible.
4. **Technical Assistance:** As manufacturing plants are becoming more and more complex by: the increasing number of devices, the complexity of production, the complexity of networks, the users need to be assisted. More precisely, the factory should be equipped with information system providing comprehensive visualization of the system, so that the human can solve problems efficiently. Mobile devices are generally used to provide real time alarms (SMS messages) and provide real-time information, e.g. Dashboard, KPIs – Key Performance Indicator.

Furthermore, Industry 4.0 offers a concrete contribution to Agile Manufacturing. (Yusuf et al., 1999) define Agile Manufacturing as "with respect to the agile enterprise, products, workforce, capabilities and the environment that gives impetus to the development of agile paradigm''. Moreover, Industry 4.0, through its interconnected system, provides a high level of configurability to support manufacturing agility.

Despite of the advantages of Industry 4.0, some drawbacks can be highlighted. The major one being the cybersecurity concern. In fact, the IoT and CPS[4] interconnection present potential security breaches related to data and plants security.

This chapter is structured as follows. Section 2 provides a comparative overview between ICS[5] and IT perceptions about cybersecurity. Section 3 presents the main cybersecurity threats which highlight the cybersecurity concerns, and ways it differs from IT. In the following section, recommended practices are offered to tackle the cybersecurity threats. Finally, the last section concludes the chapter.

2. ICS / IT: A COMPARATIVE OVERVIEW

Inspired by the definition of industrial control network of (Galloway & Hancke, 2013), we define ICS *as an interconnection of equipment and systems used to monitor and control physical equipment in an industrial environment*. It is able to collect accurate real time data, to aggregate them, and to monitor the industrial process.

According to (Stouffer et al., 2011), classical IT failed to address cybersecurity for ICS. This is due to the differences between IT and ICS:

- ICS main concerns are revolving around the integrity of the process.

Figure 1. IT and ICS priorities

- ICS processes are continuous and require high availability. System stoppage are generally scheduled for maintenance purpose.
- The interactions with the processes are central and generally complex.
- Industrial devices are generally limited to support security mechanisms such is encryption / decryption algorithms.
- The response time is critical in ICS cf. **Figure 1**.
- There are several communication protocols used in ICS (proprietary protocols and standard ones) cf. **Table 1**.
- Unlike in IT, ICS components are infrequently replaced. The average time period for changing the components in ICS is about 15 year, and higher.
- The ICS components are generally distributed and isolated, which makes accessing them difficult and upgrading them equally troubling.

The table below depicts other differences between IT and ICS.

2.1. Communication protocols

As an example, the table below depicts some industrial protocols according to security aspects.

2.2. Ransomware

To further illustrate the ICS / IT disparity, this subsection takes as example *Ransomware*. In 2017 Ransomware was an emerging phenomenon of cybercrime. Researchers from Georgia Institute of Technology demonstrated through a POC that ICS can be threatened by the ransomware (Formby et al., 2017). They developed a worm for Programmable Logic Controllers (PLC) named LogicLocker. It uses a native socket API to scan the network for known vulnerable targets. It is intended to (1) bypass the weak authentication, (2) to lock user's access to the PLC, which make it impossible to recover the PLC, and (3) to replace the original program with a logic bomb.

Table 1. Differences between ICS and IT (Stouffer et al., 2011)

Topic	IT	ICS
Antivirus and mobile code	Common and easily deployed	Can affect the PLC performance, as the memory is limited.
Patch	Commonly defined and deployed	Complicated to be established automatically.
Technology exploitation cycle	Average 2-3 years	Average 10-20 years
Test and audit methods	Modern and standard methods	Test to adapt according to the system
Change management	Regular and frequent change	Planned according to a strategic issue
Asset classification	Regular	Done when compulsory
Incident response	Easily developed and deployed	Focused on system recovery
Physical Environment Security	Variant	Excellent for critical zones
Test environment security	Commonly integrated into the development cycle	Excluded from development cycle

Table 2. Protocols communication comparison between IT and ICS, extracted from (Galloway & Hancke, 2013).

Factor	ICS	IT
Primary Function	Control of physical equipment	Data processing and transfer
Applicable Domain	Manufacturing, processing and utility distribution	Corporate, and home environments
Hierarchy	Deep, functionally separated hierarchies with many protocols and physical standards	Shallow, integrated hierarchies with uniform protocol and physical standards utilization
Failure Severity	High	Low
Reliability Required	High	Moderate
Round Trip Times	250 µs – 10 ms	50+ ms
Determinism	High	Low
Data Composition	Small packets of periodic and aperiodic traffic	Large, aperiodic packets
Temporal Consistency	Required	Not required
Operating Environment	Hostile conditions, often featuring high levels of dust, heat and vibration	Clean environments, often specifically intended for sensitive equipment

Table 3. Example of industrial communication protocols

Protocols	Protocol	Authentication	Encryption	Communication
Modbus TCP	TCP - 502	Not supported	Not supported	- Master slave communication - Communication fame (slave address – code functionality – data – CRC) - Enable to control the industrial process
IEC 104	TCP 2404	Not supported	Not supported	- Master slave communication
S7	TCP 102	Not supported	Not supported	- Read / Write
Ethernet IP	TCP - UDP	Not supported	Not supported	- Send commands
DNP3	TCP	Supported	Supported	- Master-slave communication

Table 4. Ransomware difference between IT and ICS (Formby et al., 2017)

Ransomware	IT – Traditional	ICS
Target	Data	Safety (equipment health and personnel safety) – Operation (downtime)
Method	Encryption	Logic Bomber, Downtime
Restoration	Data backup	Program BackUp, Repairs

Table 4 highlights the differences between classical ransomware and LogicLocker. The main difference with classical ransomware is that attackers cause system downtime and physical damages on the installation, by dangerously operating outputs to reclaim ransom.

Note that, within the ICS context, it can be far more hazardous, as it can impact human safety by operating hazardous equipment manipulation.

3. ICS CYBERSECURTITY THREATS

Modern ICS exploits IT to provide real time information and reliable plant control in order to optimize industrial performances, both in terms of execution time and production cost. ICS plays an important role to interconnect, monitor and control different devices in a variety of industries, such as chemistry, food and drugs, logistics, energy, etc. (McLaughlin et al., 2016). The cybersecurity threats can emerge as a security leak from one of the following reasons:

1. the connections to Internet are increasing.
2. the adoption of standards communication protocols.
3. the adoption of complex network architecture.
4. the adoption of distributed architecture.

To highlight in more detail the cybersecurity threats, the following subsection illustrates some examples of cyberattacks.

3.1. Cyberattacks examples

The gravity cybersecurity in ICS is being emphasized since 2010. In fact, that year the Stuxnet malware was operated into a nuclear plant by the control of an equipment used in a critical phase (Langner, 2001), (Chen & Abu-Nimeh, 2011). Another example is the attack on the Ukrainian power grid in 2015. These attacks can lead to significant consequences.

The potential attack scenario starts off with a spear phishing mail campaign which later infects the network. The attackers then get access to the VPN credentials. They proceed by damaging the installations, by disabling backup power, opening the grid beaker. They even delete the master boot record of the system. The ICS cyberattack threat is further highlighted by the ISA report (ISA, 2016) which mentions that 750 cyberattacks have led to death and/or severe outages.

In 2008, cyber attackers introduced a wireless camera communication software to get in an internal network. They then comprised a PLC at a valve station to cause a hazardous explosion that spilled more than 30 000 oil barrels.

The Stuxnet cyberattacks, in 2010, targeted a Siemens PLM through an USB intrusion. Then, it was propagated onto the whole network.

In 2015, Ukrainian electrical grid was attacked, as the power grid was compromised to temporarily disrupt electrical supply. The cyberattacks comprised the network using spear-phishing mail using a BlackEnergy malware. Then it took over control of SCADA to switch substations off. Next, IT infrastructure components were disabled and file servers were deleted using the KillDisk malware. Finally a DoS (Denial-of-Service) attack was launched against the customer call-center.

Generally, the following three main steps structure a cyberattack:

1. Discovery
   a. Characterize systems.
   b. Find weakness and vulnerabilities.
2. **Attack**: Exploit vulnerable people, processes and components.
3. **Intrusion**: Data Exfiltration, Denial of service, Command and control operations. The common intrusion methods are: weak authentication, network scanning / probing, removable media, brute force intrusion, abuse if access authority, spear fishing, SQL injection.

3.2. Cyber threats

Numerous threats can be highlighted within the cybersecurity in ITC:

- **Data Loss**: Production data can be lost (for instance erasing the database).
- **Data Integrity**: The data accuracy can be falsified.
- **Sensitive Data Recovery**: Sensitive data such is the case of BoM (Bill of Material) for industries can be recovered and used for external purposes.
- **Data Availability**: The SCADA data can be compromised and made inaccessible for users (Nicholson et al., 2014).
- **Machine Control**: The attackers can take control over the machines, which can in turn be harmful for both the industrial equipment and humans.
- **HMI Compromise**: The data displayed on HMI screens can be fake, as the data can be altered with the compromised one.
- **PLC Re-programming**: If accessed, the PLC can be reprogrammed to cause damage. The PLC can be also reprogrammed as a Logic Bomb by changing the password (Govin et al., 2017).

4. EXISTING SOLUTIONS

This section is dedicated to proposing the recommended solutions to face to cybersecurity threat in industrial systems. These solutions are structured in the following four categories:

Figure 2. An overview of ICS cybersecurity threats

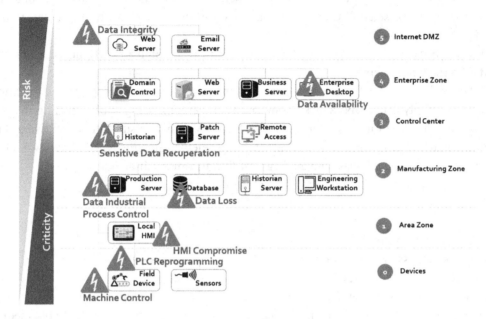

Category 1: Structuring and organizing the hardware disposition.
Category 2: Daily practices dealing with the industrial control system use.
Category 3: Monitoring and improving the system security.
Category 4: Recovering the system after an attack.

The following subsections will further explore into more detail each of the aforementioned categories.

4.1. STRUCTURING AND ORGANIZING THE HARDWARE DISPOSITION - PLANT CYBERSECURITY EFFECTIVENESS

The installation should be structured through the principles of responsibility separation. It generally consists of separating the following levels: shop floor, exploitation and office networks, so that a threat at one level does not impact the other layers.

Then, ICS has to be designed taking into consideration the security aspect, to provide robust security.

4.1.1. Zooning

The IEC 62 443 (Phinney, 2013), formerly the ISA 99 (ISA, 2007), standard recommends the structuring of the installation through zones. For instance, an industrial zone onto which the SCADA is connected, the PLC, the machines, etc. and another one dedicated for office use (internet navigation, etc.).

The data exchange between zones can be reinforced using a firewall to control its traffic. The firewalls enable:

- Separating different zones.

- Monitoring and logging the system events.
- Ensuring the use of authentication to enable access.
- Monitoring the network traffic and blocking unauthorized communications.

Furthermore, data diodes can be used to cut non-authorized access. The data diode can also be considered for better security reinforcement by blocking the data exchange from one zone to another.

Moreover, the external access (e.g. for maintenance purposes) should be supervised and idle external access points should be blocked. The VPN can provide a solution by providing secure external access.

Although it enables the prevention of suspicious network propagation, it does not block all attacks and causes some limits for remote access, such as in the case of on-call contract.

Furthermore, unnecessary services should be deactivated and even removed.

4.1.2. Security Perimeter

In order to improve the plant's security, logical and physical security is required. More precisely, the logical security should be ensured by locking the system by an authentication mechanism. Moreover, the physical security consists in locking the electrical cabinet, the PLC, etc. in order to limit access only to authorized personnel.

Note that, corporate authentication, authorization, and account management practices can be problematic for ICS, as they are always active.

According to (Nelso & Chaffin, 2011), the highest percentage of vulnerabilities is due to ICS software. In fact, authentication weakness can lead to fatal consequences at the installation.

4.1.3. DMZ Usage

To secure the different devices within the network, a demilitarized zone (DMZ) can also be considered. The DMZ, an intranet hidden from the plant network, can be used as a security layer to isolate ICS and corporate networks (Mahan et al., 2011).

4.1.4. PLC configuration

While programming a PLC, the non-used port should be closed so that it won't provide an opened door for cyberattacks. A simple research provided by Shodan, a search engine dedicated for IoT, reveals that a great number of PLC connected to the internet are exposed to external access by cyberattacks (Kaspersky Security Intelligence, 2016).

Modern ICS Equipment exploits IP protocols to connect to networks. Furthermore, they can be remotely access by solution providers for support purpose. Then, they expose security holes for cyberattacks.

For instance, using Shodan, a research engine initially dedicated to IoT, we find a surprising number of known vulnerability which cybercriminals can easily take over control (Kaspersky Security Intelligence, 2016).

4.1.5. VLAN

Virtual Networks have to be used within the Zooning principle. Their intrusion is more difficult for external interfering.

Virtual Machines are recommended to use as they (1) reduce capital management, (2) manage device recovery, and (3) running multiple guest OS.

4.1.6. Firewall

Firewalls are systems (software or hardware) that control and monitor the network traffic on a device or of the network. It can be a hosted-based firewall (for instance integrated to the operating system) or a network firewall. It is generally used as a barrier between trusted network (e.g. office network) and external network (e.g. Internet).

It enables to: (1) Establish domain separation, (2) monitor and log the system and the traffic event, (3) ensure the user authentication to access, and (4) disable unauthorized connections. Different techniques are used to ensure its roles (CSSP, 2009):

- Filtering the network packets.
- Circuit level gateways: the firewall allow only specific sessions to communicate.
- Proxy level gateways to limit the type of applications and protocols that communicate across security boundaries (FTP, HTTP, etc.).
- State full inspection by keeping the trace of the state of the connection crossing the firewall.

Despite of its importance, the firewall and antiviruses are not sufficient (Johnsen et al., 2009).

Figure 3. Firewall implantation onto an ICS architecture

4.1.7. Data Diode

Data diode are one-way communication out / into the plant. It is considered as a powerful security method. It is hardware designed to be the only way of communication. It transfers the data out of the protected network. Physically, the data diode are separated into two halves with a diode on each side working together to create a dual diode (KIM, 2017) (Stevens & Pope, 1999). In some sector its use is mandatory, such is the case of the NRC (i.e. Nuclear Regulatory Commission) recommendations.

Scada Network Improvement

The SCADA presents a major potential security breach point, mainly for the following reasons:

- Access control.
- Data encryption.
- Security application deployment.

During the past few years, the connections to the SCADA have increased dramatically. Moreover, the SCADA have also moved from using proprietary protocols to standards ones (Sommestad et al., 2010). As a consequence, SCADA systems are more exposed to security vulnerabilities, to whom they have never been exposed before.

Many reference points address this cybersecurity weak points and propose solutions such as: (Ralston et al., 2007; Ten et al., 2008; Hallaq et al., 2018). In this chapter, we adopt the recommendations elaborated by the US Energy Department, which proposes 21 recommendations to secure the SCADA systems.

Figure 4.Data diode use for disabling controlling the plant from other layers

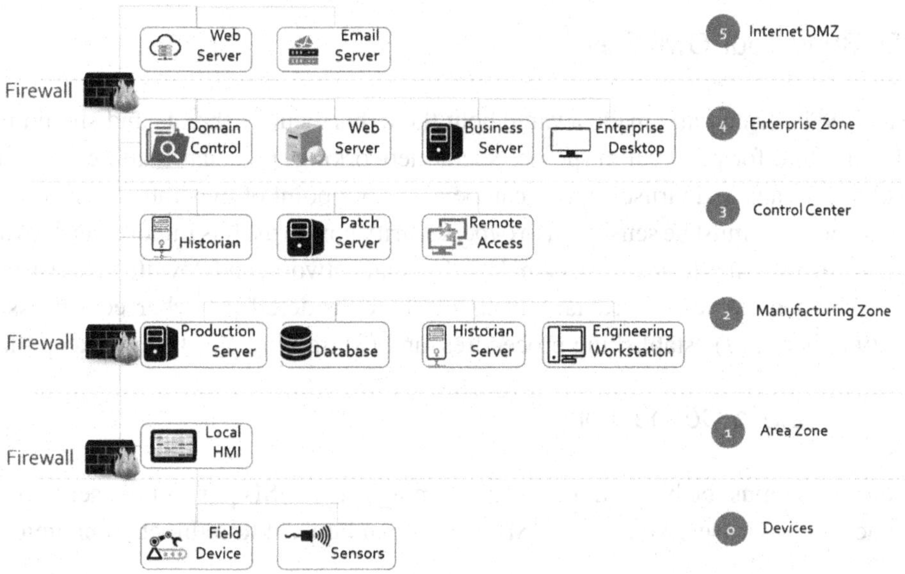

Figure 5. Steps to improve SCADA networks cybersecurity

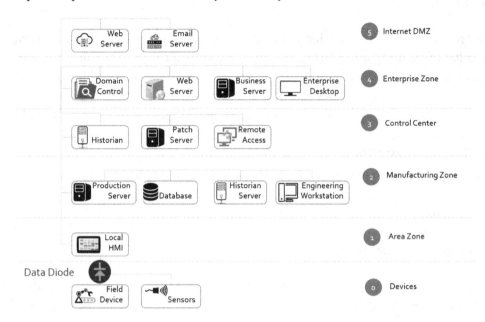

4.2. Daily Practices

The cybersecurity requires not only to implement good practices at the deployment phase, but it also represents a continuous network supervising. Many tools, freewares and sharewares, exist. The ICS network supports other network protocols such as the classical ones: ModBus Tcp, Profinet, e.g. The network supervision is mainly related to packet loss analysis, packet replication detection, bandwidth supervision.

Furthermore, a process should be adopted and implemented within the production site. Many recommendations on this topic exist in the literature. The main steps are: problems identification, installation protection, threat detection, and response to the threat.

4.2.1. BYOD: Bring Your Own Device

The users have to be informed and made aware about the cybersecurity threats and should not use the shop floor infrastructure for personal purposes (social networking, personal mailing, etc.) in order to avoid downloading Trojans and viruses which can be a starting point of cyberattack intrusions.

The users and operators must be sensitized to cybersecurity concerns. It is important not to use professional laptops and smartphones to access personal mail, social network, and download untrusted contain.

Moreover, the human element is crucial and should be considered for cybersecurity issues by (1) adopting security policies, (2) establishing procedures, and (3) training the staff and keep them aware.

4.2.2. Blocking Useless Connection

Useless port connection must be blocked. For instance, plugging a USB port is not useful in preventing an undesirable access or viruses. Malicious USB drivers can be used to redirect communication, alter network configuration, send malicious packet, etc. Note that, it is the case of memory card and extension cards, as well as for USB flash drives.

4.2.3. Internal Process

The ICS should also have a clear workflow to protect against cyberattacks. The main steps can be (Stouffer et al., 2007):

1. **Identify:** Develop the organizational understanding to manage cybersecurity risk to systems, assets, data, and capabilities.
   - Risk Management.
   - Risk analysis strategy.
   - Material Inventory.
2. **Protect**: Develop and implement the appropriate safeguards to ensure delivery of critical infrastructure services.
   - Access Control.
   - Training & collective consciousness.
   - Data Security.
   - Internal Procedure and process of data protection.
3. **Detect**: Develop and implement the appropriate activities to identify the occurrence of a cybersecurity event.
   - Anomaly and event.
   - Continuous monitoring of security.
4. **Reaction**: Develop and implement the appropriate activities to take action regarding a detected cybersecurity event.
   - Action plan - recovery plan.
   - Communication.
   - Analysis.
   - Improvement.
5. **Recovery**: Develop and implement the appropriate activities to maintain plans for resilience and to restore any capabilities or services that were impaired due to a cybersecurity event.
   - Recovery plan.
   - Improvement.
   - Communication.

4.3. Monitoring and Improving the System Security

In order to monitor the network, Intrusion Detection System (IDS) can be used to detect abnormal or suspicious activity on a machine (host) and/or the network. The IDS are divided into three families:

- Network Based Intrusion Detection System (NIDS) are dedicated to monitoring network security.
- HostBased Intrusion Detection System (HIDS) are dedicated to host security monitoring.
- Hybrid IDS that exploits NIDS and HIDS for monitoring hosts and the network.

There are tools supporting industrial protocols for intrusion detection and prevention.

As example, we can cite the OSSEC tool (Open Source SECurity), an open source HIDS. It:

- Performs log analysis.
- Checks file integrity.
- Ensures policy monitoring.
- Real time alerts.
- **Includes a Root Kit**: A kit to sustain access.
- Runs on most Operating system.
- Ensure signature-based detection.

4.4. Recovering the System After an Attack

A better strategy against cyberattacks requires adopting a strategy to recovery the system in case of cyberattacks. First of all, it consists at clearly identifying the problem to contain it. The identification of the problem include to identify:

- The place of the attack (loss of data, system shutdown, etc.).
- The type of attack (logic bomb, data corruption, etc.).
- The impacted assets (a server, an PLC, etc.) in order to isolate it from the network to minimize the attack impact by preventing the attack to be propagated through the network.

Internal monitoring process as mentioned earlier is useful to easily identify the attacks different aspects.

Then the problem have to be reported to different stakeholders. Next, relevant measure should to be taken (upgrade PLC firmware, reload machines program, scan the network, change the password, etc.).

Finally, lessons should be taken from the attack to improve the security of the whole system for long term that the attacks could not be reproduced by strengthening the cybersecurity measures.

5. CONCLUSION AND PERSPECTIVES

The ICS experts are faced with a new challenge: the security issue. The cyberattacks can be hazardous as they can cause considerable damage. Unless the standards and different publications (scientific, security agencies, etc.) are not put into use, the simple security aspect alone is not sufficient to protect the manufacturing infrastructure.

The main goal of this chapter is to highlight the importance of this aspect and introduce existing solutions to face to this challenge.

This issue is intensified mainly through the industry 4.0 that is based on CPS (Cyber Physical Systems) and that is interconnected through different protocols (Wifi, Sigfox, MQTT, etc.). The topic of cybersecurity of ICS will continue to increase over the coming years as more devices depend on interconnectability. One such example are autonomous vehicles (Miller and Valasek, 2015), or even modern vehicles, which depend ever more on their connectability with other devices. As IoT devices calculation capacities are limited and does not support encryption protocols for better security, more work is required for optimizing the security of such systems.

REFERENCES

Chen, T., & Abu-Nimeh, S. (2011). Lessons from stuxnet. *Computer, 44*(4), 91–93. doi:10.1109/MC.2011.115

CSSP, D. (2009). Recommended Practice: Improving Industrial Control Systems Cybersecurity with Defense-In-Depth Strategies. US-CERT Defense In Depth (October 2009) Google Scholar.

Formby, D., Durbha, S., & Beyah, R. (2017). *Out of control: Ransomware for industrial control systems.* RSA.

Galloway, B., & Hancke, G. P. (2013). Introduction to Industrial Control Networks. *IEEE Communications Surveys and Tutorials, 15*(2), 860–880. doi:10.1109/SURV.2012.071812.00124

Hallaq, B., Nicholson, A., Smith, R., Maglaras, L., Janicke, H., & Jones, K. (2018). CYRAN: a hybrid cyber range for testing security on ICS/SCADA systems. In Cyber Security and Threats: Concepts, Methodologies, Tools, and Applications (pp. 622-637). IGI Global.

Hermann, M., Pentek, T., & Otto, B. (2016). Design Principles for Industrie 4.0 Scenarios, In *Proceedings 2016 49th Hawaii International Conference on System Sciences (HICSS),* pp. 3928-3937. Koloa, HI, 2016, 10.1109/HICSS.2016.488

ISA (2007). ANSI/ISA–99.00.01–2007 Security for Industrial Automation and Control Systems Part 1: Terminology, Concepts, and Models, *International Society of Automation (ISA),* October 2007.

Johnsen, S., Skramstad, T., & Hagen, J. (2009, March). Enhancing the safety, security and resilience of ICT and SCADA systems using action research. In *Proceedings International Conference on Critical Infrastructure Protection* (pp. 113-123). Berlin, Germany: Springer. 10.1007/978-3-642-04798-5_8

Kaspersky Security Intelligence, The evolution of ransomware. Technical report, 07 2016.

Kim, W. (2017, November). Security Validation for Data Diode with Reverse Channel. In Critical Information Infrastructures Security: 11th International Conference, CRITIS 2016, Paris, France, October 10–12, 2016, Revised Selected Papers (Vol. 10242, p. 271). Springer.

Langner, R. (2011). Stuxnet: Dissecting a cyberwarfare weapon. *IEEE Security and Privacy, 9*(3), 49–51. doi:10.1109/MSP.2011.67

Litchfield, S., Formby, D., Rogers, J., Meliopoulos, S., & Beyah, R. (2016, September-October). Rethinking the Honeypot for Cyber-Physical Systems. *IEEE Internet Computing, 20*(5), 9–17. doi:10.1109/MIC.2016.103

Mahan, R. E., Fluckiger, J. D., Clements, S. L., Tews, C. W., Burnette, J. R., Goranson, C. A., & Kirkham, H. (2011). *Secure data transfer guidance for industrial control and SCADA systems (No. PNNL-20776). Pacific Northwest National Lab.* Richland, WA: PNNL. doi:10.2172/1030885

McLaughlin, S., Konstantinou, C., Wang, X., Davi, L., Sadeghi, A.-R., Maniatakos, M., & Karri, R. (2016). The Cybersecurity Landscape in Industrial Control Systems. *Proceedings of the IEEE, 104*(5), 1039–1057. doi:10.1109/JPROC.2015.2512235

Miller, C., & Valasek, C. (2015). Remote exploitation of an unaltered passenger vehicle. *Black Hat USA, 2015*, 91.

Nicholson, A., Janicke, H., & Cau, A. (2014). Position paper: Safety and security monitoring in ICS/SCADA systems, in *Proc. 2nd Int. Symp. ICS SCADA Cyber Security Res.,* pp. 61–66.

Phinney, T. (2013). IEC 62443: Industrial network and system security.

Ralston, P. A., Graham, J. H., & Hieb, J. L. (2007). Cyber security risk assessment for SCADA and DCS networks. *ISA Transactions, 46*(4), 583–594. doi:10.1016/j.isatra.2007.04.003 PMID:17624350

Sommestad, T., Ericsson, G. N., & Nordlander, J. (2010, July). SCADA system cyber security—A comparison of standards. In *Proceedings 2010 IEEE Power and Energy Society General Meeting,* (pp. 1-8). IEEE.

Stevens, M. W., & Pope, M. (1999). *An implementation of an optical data diode.* DSTO.

Stouffer, K., Falco, J., & Scarfone, K. (2011). Guide to industrial control systems (ICS) security. *NIST special publication, 800*(82), 16-16.

Stouffer, K., Zimmerman, T., Tang, C., Lubell, J., Cichonski, J., & McCarthy, J. (2017). *Cybersecurity framework manufacturing profile.* US Department of Commerce, National Institute of Standards and Technology. doi:10.6028/NIST.IR.8183

Ten, C. W., Liu, C. C., & Manimaran, G. (2008). Vulnerability assessment of cybersecurity for SCADA systems. *IEEE Transactions on Power Systems, 23*(4), 1836–1846. doi:10.1109/TPWRS.2008.2002298

Yannakogeorgos, P. A., & Lowther, A. B. (Eds.). (2013). *Conflict and Cooperation in Cyberspace: The Challenge to National Security.* CRC Press.

Yusuf, Y. Y., Sarhadi, M., & Gunasekaran, A. (1999). Agile manufacturing: The drivers, concepts and attributes. *International Journal of Production Economics, 62*(1-2), 33–43. doi:10.1016/S0925-5273(98)00219-9

ENDNOTES

[1] Internet of Things
[2] Supervisory Control And Data Acquisition,
[3] Manufacturing Execution System
[4] Cyber physical System
[5] Industrial Control System

Chapter 17
Study of Smartcards Technology:
Structure, Standards, Threats, Solutions, and Applications

Shaifali Narayan

National Institute of Technology, Kurukshetra, India

Brij B. Gupta

National Institute of Technology, Kurukshetra, India

ABSTRACT

Smart cards have gained popularity in many domains by providing different facilities in every domain. Such cards are beneficial for storing credentials and access information. The cards are easy to carry and provides easy and fast computations. The cards have certain limitations due to the possible attacks on them. This chapter gives an overview of the smartcards including its history, physical design, life cycle. It also provides an overview of the possible threats on smartcards and its application area.

1. INTRODUCTION

The development of smartcards allowed the user to carry the information securely and perform the operation easily. Smartcards based applications enables the storage, manipulations and transmission of the user data over the internet in a secure way. Smartcard based applications have gained popularity in both public and private sectors because of the convenience in usage, adaptability and other benefits. (Taherdoost, Hamed, Shahibuddin & Jalaliyoon, 2011) discussed that smartcards are the intelligent token which is identical to the credit card along with the integrated circuit present in its body. It contains memory unit and has computational capability which make it resistant to attack. These cards are cost effective and multifunction, which can be used for user identification and can also be used for physical and logical access (Chen & Shi, 2016).

DOI: 10.4018/978-1-7998-2242-4.ch017

Copyright © 2020, IGI Global. Copying or distributing in print or electronic forms without written permission of IGI Global is prohibited.

There are primarily four kinds of smartcards based on card reader interaction - contact, contactless, dual interface and hybrid cards (Gupta & Quamara, 2018). The chip on a smart card can be either an embedded memory chip or a microcontroller. Smart cards are intended to be resistant to manipulation and use encryption to protect data in memory. These microcontroller chip cards can execute on-card processing tasks and can manipulate data in the memory of the chip (Rouse, 2018). Smart card schemes have been shown to be more reliable than other machine-readable cards, such as magnetic stripe and barcode, with many studies indicating improvements in card read life and reader life showing much reduced system maintenance costs (CardLogix, 2010). Smart cards also provide essential system safety elements for information exchange across nearly any network type. From careless storage of user passwords to advanced system hacks, they safeguard against a complete spectrum of safety threats. The cost of managing password resets for an organisation or business is very high, making smart cards in these settings a cost-effective alternative.

The cards were used to provide user identification and can also be used for logical and physical access as they are the cost-effective multi-function cards. But with time, the application of smartcard got increased. With the ease provided by smartcards, they are now broadly used from secure payment applications like credit and debit cards, public transport system (Markantonakis, Mayes, Sauveron & Askoxylykis, 2008) to user identification and authentication applications like smart health cards (Aubert & Hamel, 2001; Hsu et al., 2011), employee cards (Chen & Shi, 2016), membership cards (Conlon and Whitacre, 2005), IoT (Vanderhoof, 2017; Gupta & Quamara, 2018); mobile based applications as Subscriber Identity Module (SIM) card for making paid television connections, purchasing goods, etc (Zkik, Orhanou & Hajji, 2017; Nedjah, Wyant, Mourella & Gupta, 2017; Gupta & Quamara, 2019; Tewari & Gupta, 2017; Gupta, Agarwal & Yamaguchi, 2016). For the smartcard-based applications to control the access, dynamic security policies were proposed (Gupta & Quamara, 2018).

International standards and requirements cover the technology of smart cards, with some focused-on apps specific to the industry. ISO / IEC is one of the world's technology standard bodies, including plastic cards. The primary standards for smart cards are ISO/IEC 7816, ISO/IEC 14443, ISO/IEC 15693 and ISO/IEC 7501 (CardLogix, 2010). Federal Information Processing Standards (FIPS) standards are intended to safeguard federal assets including systems for computers and telecommunications (QCard, n.d.). A standard for cards and readers proposed and enforced by Microsoft called the PC / SC specification. This proposal covers only CPU cards.

Apart from the benefits provided by smartcard, it also possesses certain threats as the cards depends on external devices for power and cock mechanism. Various logical, physical and data level threats are also a matter of concern and are needed to be addressed (Gupta, 2018; S. Gupta & B. Gupta, 2015; Jiang et al., 2018; Almomani, Gupta, Wan, Altaher & Manickam, 2013, Almomani, A., et. al., 2013). Before the understanding of the threats it is needed to understand the physical design and lifecycle of the smartcards, which is discussed in the next section.

2. PHYSICAL DESIGN

The structure of the smartcards can be divided into two parts – hardware and software. The hardware part provides the physical structure of the cards while the software part provides the details of the software which are installed in smartcards for the application working.

Figure 1. Contact card connections

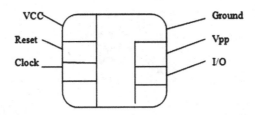

2.1 Details of Hardware

Smartcards are present in various forms and used as contact or contactless. Contact smartcards have a chip to perform working. Contactless smartcards are difficult to recognize as chip may be hidden inside the card (Hoon & Caytiles, 2011).

The different smartcard connections are: - Vcc and ground- for power supply, Reset- to hard restart all the processes, Clock- for external clock signal which is the heartbeat of the internal process, Vpp – provide higher EEPROM programming voltage, I/O – provide bidirectional communication between smartcard and terminal.

Smartcards are small embedded computer in the shape of credit card. It consists of a 8-bit CPU and small memory – 4Kb RAM, 16 Kb EEPROM, 64 Kb ROM. RAM is needed for performing fast computation and response. ROM is the area where the operating system and other basic software like encryption algorithms and security keys are stored. EEPROM is helpful in running the application.

2.2 Details of Software

Operating system of smartcard uses lifecycle management which restricts the operations that the card can perform. Data are stored in a nested file system and file and directories and the application data are stored in the EEPOM. Java cards are the popular operating system of the smartcards that uses the security concept of java. It is flexible for application design. The commands and the input are given as an input to the chip and after processing it the output command and the result is sent back. The process takes place in a half-duplex format and this along with restricted bit rate prevents the card from data attack.

Figure 2. CPU-Memory Connections

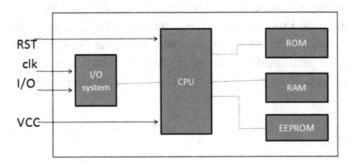

Figure 3. Smartcard lifecycle

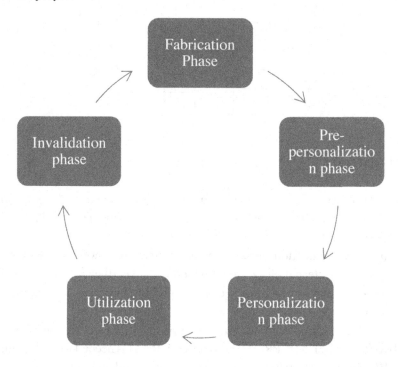

3. LIFECYCLE

Lifecycle of the smartcard is divided into five phases, which differs from the java cards at stage 3 and 4. It is possible to download data files and applications to the card many times.

1. **STAGE 1- Fabrication Phase**: This phase refers to the chip manufacturing where the chip is created and tested. It also consists of a fabrication key which helps in protecting it from fraud activities till the time it is successfully placed on the plastic card. The key is unique, and it is generated from master manufacturer key. Once all the steps are done, it is ready to be delivered to the manufacturer.
2. **STAGE 2 - Pre-personalization Phase**: Mainly this phase is for supplier where they built connections between the chip and the circuit. Personalization key replaces the fabrication key. Card access is provided by using logical address.
3. **STAGE 3 - Personalization Phase**: Main actor of this phase is card issuer. Logical data structures are created and data files, user id and pin are stored in the card.
4. **STAGE 4 - Utilization Phase**: Card holder uses the card and security policies restrict the access.
5. **STAGE 5 - Invalidation Phase**: Card can be in this phase because of two reasons. One by writing application which initiates the invalidation lock to individual or master file. After which only the read operation can be performed. Other way is when control system irreversibly blocks the access as both blocking and unblocking pins are blocked and all the operations are blocked including reading.

4. SMARTCARDS STANDARDS

The ISO promotes the establishment of voluntary norms through a process open to all parties. ISO / IEC is one of the world's leading technology standard bodies, including plastic cards. The primary standards for smart cards are - ISO/IEC 7816, ISO/IEC 14443, ISO/IEC 15693 and ISO/IEC 7501, which are discussed below.

1. ISO/IEC 7816: - ISO / IEC 7816 is a sequence of norms that specify integrated circuit cards and interchange use of such cards. These cards are identification cards designed for the exchange of data proposed between the outside world and the card's integrated circuit. The card provides information (computing result, stored data) and/or changes its content (data storage, event memorization) because of an information exchange. ISO/IEC 7816 part 1, 2, 3, 10 deals with synchronous card and 12 with USB cards. Other parts are independent of physical interface technology.

2. **ISO/IEC 14443:** The ISO / IEC 14443 standard for Near Field Communication (NFC) describes the proximity card requirements frequently used for identifying purposes (Sabella, 2016). It consists of 4 parts. ISO/IEC 14443-1:2008 define PICC's physical features, frequently referred to as proximity cards. ISO/IEC 14443-2:2010 Specifies the features of the power and two-way communication fields to be given between proximity coupling devices (PCDs) and proximity cards or items (PICCs). ISO/IEC 14443-3:2011 define how the method of communication starts, continues and finishes. ISO/IEC 14443-4:2008 define a protocol for messaging to be used to communicate with proximity cards.

3. **ISO/IEC 15693**: It is an ISO standard for vicinity cards, i.e. cards that can be read more distantly than proximity cards (Nedjah et al., 2017). Normally, such cards can be read out by a reader without powering themselves, as the reader will provide the card with the required energy over the air (wireless). It operates at the 13.56 MHz frequency, and offer maximum read distance of 1–1.5 meters.

4. **ISO/IEC 7501**: ISO / IEC 7501 outlines standards for travel documents readable by machine and has provided a clear suggestion on topology of smart cards. ISO/IEC 7501-1:2008 is for machine readable passport, ISO/IEC 7501-2:1997 is for machine readable visa, ISO/IEC 7501-3:2005 is for machine readable official travel documents.

5. THREATS ON SMARTCARDS

The increased application area of the card, leads into many security threats on them. The card becomes an authentication element in different authentication schemes. The attacks on such a factor can result from the damage or loss of the card for a while and allow the attacker to copy its secret. The security threats on smartcards can be divided into four categories- logical attack, physical attack, side channel attack and data level security attack (Schneier & Shostack, 1999; Witteman, 2002). The attacks are discussed in detail below.

4.1 Logical Attack

Application logic is the system flow that is supposed to be used to perform any operation (Jiang, et al., 2018; Gupta, B. B., et al, 2015; 2018; 2016). The section on Logical Attacks focuses on the abuse or exploitation of the logic flow of an application. Logical attack mainly includes finding and exploiting

Figure 4. Types of attacks on smartcards

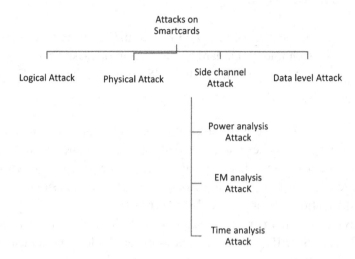

software bugs using normal communication channel. For example - hidden commands, buffer overflow to read past end of file, try to abuse file access privileges, exploit weakness in crypto protocol, malicious applet on multi- application smartcard. Different ways of logical attack on the smartcards are discussed below:

1. **Hidden Command**: Commands which are used to modify or retrieve data within the card. And such commands are active because of the initialization or execution phase of previous application.
2. **Parameter Poisoning and Buffer Overflow**: Misinterpretation of the parameter of commands could lead to different result.
3. **File Access**: The command access permission determines the security procedure to access a file. Access permissions can be confusing if there are multiple applications running under single operating system.
4. **Malicious Applet**: The security of a smartcard can be compromised if we use it on a rogue application.
5. **Communication Protocol**: The data transfer and communication between a terminal and a smartcard are directed by a communication protocol which controls the data flow control and the error recovery.
6. **Crypto-protocol, Design and Implementation**: Cryptographic protocols are mainly designed to control cryptographic operations and they should be designed carefully to avoid fall back with transaction.

Case Study 1: Offline dictionary attack on password protected smartcard: - For a strong authentication of the application, user selected passwords are used. If these passwords are too long they are hard to remember and if they are too small they are eligible for dictionary attack. So, it is needed that schemes should be developed that helps in protecting from the offline dictionary attack. Password based remote authentication was studied by (Gong, Lomas, Needham & Saltzer, 1993) where they tried to protect against offline dictionary attack by making use of asymmetric key algorithms. A more common way to pass the secret key is to make use of the symmetric key and encrypt the secret key with the user password and then store it on the smartcard. But this will not protect from offline dictionary attack. Instead, a counter could be set, and the smart card would be allowed to only sign a specified number of message and then it will be destroyed by itself.

The password protected smartcards are vulnerable to logical attacks. The smart card is more like a USB memory stick that holds password protection credentials for the user. There are various attacks possible on password protected smartcards and make the cards vulnerable to various security issues. For example – Denial of Service (DDoS) attacks (Al-Qerem, Alauthman, et al., 2019; Alieyan, Almomani et al., 2019; Dahiya & Gupta, B. B., 2019), Replay attack, Eavesdropping, Impersonation, Man-in-the-middle, Password guessing, Stolen smart card, Malicious card reader, and Partition attack.

To avoid logical attack, some of the countermeasures are proposed which are listed below:

1. **Structured Design**: Software should be created in block format so that it could easily be validated.
2. **Formal Verification**: Proper mathematical model for verification.
3. **Testing**: Validating it by using different test case.
4. **Standardization of Interface and Application**: Reuse the software whose security is already proven.
5. **Convergence to Java Card Operating System**: Java is much more secure than any other operating system. Using the java-based cards, secure the data as compare to other OS based cards.

4.2 Physical Attack

Many semiconductor chips used in a wide range of applications require protection against physical attacks or tamper resistance. Such attacks presume that direct access to the chip is possible with either electrical connections to signal wires or some measurements. Physical attack is the one where the attacker tries to destroy the packaging of the card to gain some information about the data stored on the card. These are also called as the invasive attack. Chip protection helps to prevent prospective hackers from executing and benefiting from unauthorized access. There are certain general tempering methodologies used to exploit the cards to extract confidential information discussed below together with other memory read attacks.

4.2.1 General Tampering Methodology

Some of the basic tampering methodologies which are used to perform physical attack on the smartcards are discussed below. The aim of these methodologies is to extract the sensitive data stored on the chip by tampering the chip.

a)   De – packaging

The physical attacks involve the tampering with the card to gain information about the data in the card. In this the chip are removed from the card and all the other particles attached with the chip are removed to make the silicon surface fully exposed.

b)   Layout –Reconstruction

After de-packing the next step is to map it. The attacker makes use of the various tools like high resolution camera and microscope to find out the layout of the various layers of the chip.

c)   Manual Micro-probing

The i/o signals, clock, power is provided to the chip to operate the processor using the pins to override the processor signals.

d)   Using Advanced Beam Technology

Like Ion beam, electron beam testers, Infrared rays will be used in addition with the current tools to gather the information without making any damage to it.

5.2.2 Attacks on Memory Reading

Keys and Memory reading attack is the attack where the attacker tries to find out the keys and user data stored in the memory of the chip of the smart card. Under the Keys and memory reading following are the possible techniques to get the data: - Reading ROM, Reviving and using the test mode, Memory contents reading by Bus probing, Key retrieval using by probing single bus bits, Key retrieval Rom overwriting, EEPROM writing, gate destruction, and memory remanence. EEPROM alteration is another method to capture the data stored in the card. The write operation in EEPROM could be affected due to unusual voltage and temperature, data could be captured by making changes to the voltage to microprocessor. EEPROM alteration by UV light, and EEPROM Alteration by voltage changing are some of the common used techniques to capture the data.

4.3 Side Channel Attacks

Cryptographic algorithm includes various keys, hash functions that form a set of primitives that are the building blocks of the target to be achieved (Zhou & Feng, 2005). Almost all the attacks on cryptographic system targets the weakness in implementation and deployment of mechanism and the cryptographic algorithm used. This weakness will either allow completely bypassing or weakening the strength of security solutions. Cryptographic algorithms are either implemented in the software or the hardware that interacts at the time of the process. The attackers can monitor these interactions and may result in information useful in cryptanalysis. This type of information is side channel attack and the attack is known as side channel attack.

Traditional cryptographic algorithm provide security where the attacker has access black box access to the information, but security of these algorithm may completely break if the attacker tries to tamper the secret key. The side channel cryptanalysis takes the advantage of implementation specific characteristic to recover secret parameter. The side channel attacks that mainly focus smartcards to gain some knowledge about the information are – Power analysis attack, Timing attack, and EM(Electromagnetic) analysis attack. These attacks are discussed below along with some possible countermeasures.

4.3.1 Types of Side Channel Attacks

A)   Power Analysis Attack

Smartcards primarily helps in authentication and making a transaction secure. It uses multiple symmetric and asymmetric algorithms to secure the data. These algorithms are highly secure but the devices on which these cards are operated are prone to side channel attack like smartcards CMOS (Complementary Metal-Oxide Semiconductor) gate-based microprocessor. CMOS gate have 3 sources of power leakage -current in transistor, short-circuit current while switching the gated during the simultaneous NMOS and PMOS conduction, and the last is dynamic power consumption because of charging and discharging of the load capacitance (Mahanta, Azad & Khan, 2015). According to (Messerges, Dabbish & Sloan, 2002), simple and differential power analysis are the two different types of power analysis attack discussed below.

a)   **Simple Power Analysis:** Implements direct power consumption interpretation while cryptographic operation from the device. SPA can get the device information and the secret key. Random input provided to cryptographic device and then visually checks power consumption. Attacker mainly computes the power consumption in waveform and can store the data by making use of digital oscilloscope and process the whole information to get secret data.

b)   **Differential Power Analysis:** Provides passive power consumption for the module. Commonly used power model in DPA are *Hamming distance model and hamming weight model.* In hamming distance, the power consumption is calculated by counting the number of transition 1®0 and 0®1 while executing the cryptographic algorithm. While in the hamming weight only the number of 1's in data are needs to be examined to find traces of power

To avoid power analysis attack, some of the countermeasures are proposed which are listed below:

1.   Avoiding the use of procedures that make use of secret key for conditional balancing can reduce the expose of SPA characteristics.
2.   Balancing power consumption to a constant value by using dummy register and gate.
3.   Adding noise to power consumption measurement.
4.   Correlation among power traces can be prevented by modifying the algorithm.
    B)   Electromagnetic Analysis Attack

These are the side channel attack performed by measuring electromagnetic radiations that are emitted from device while performing signal analysis on it (Li, Markettos & Moore, 2005). They are mainly non-invasive and passive in nature. Differential electromagnetic analysis is used to analyse EM transmission of a smartcard while performing operations. It involves hypothesizing the secret key to measure the EM traces and dividing them into portions as per the result and then calculating average of each portion to remove noise and finally calculating differential trace. A false secret key means differential trace is close to zero else it will have peaks which indicate the points where the key bits' values are changed. Below is discussed a real-world EM attack on contactless smartcard.

a)   The raw traces are collected between the last command bit sent to reader and the first answer bit received. So digital processing is applied to find the patterns.

b)   First rectify the raw traces, and then pass it to a Finite Impulse Response (FIR) filter. High-pass Infinite Impulse Response (IIR) filter helps in removing the constant amplitude offset.

c)   Select a demodulated pattern trace. This pattern is then located in all subsequent traces by finding the shift that minimizes the squared difference between the reference and the trace to align.

d)   In case of a synchronous clock in the device the alignment with one different pattern is sufficient to completely align the whole trace. But in this experiment the operations were asynchronous which means alignment can be wrong where portions do not belong to the referenced pattern.

To avoid power analysis attack, some of the countermeasures are proposed which are listed below.

1.   To hide the correlation between the changing data and the side channel information.

2.   Examine data dependent EM characteristics of a secure processor to assess their security from EM attack

C)   Timing Attack

Timing attack is a way to obtain user secret data by measuring the time it takes to perform the cryptographic operations (Bar-EI, 2005). A timing attack is a security vulnerability that allows an attacker to detect weaknesses in a computer or network system's protection by observing time taken by the system to respond to various inputs. This attack mainly focuses on time variants in performing the operation. There are some basic assumptions which are made to perform this attack. These assumptions are discussed below.

a)   The running time of a cryptographic module depends on its key.

b)   By adding noise, it could be made less feasible. Software approach for making attack less feasible by computing two set of conditions must take equal amount of time.

c)   Challenge response protocol is ideal for timing attack.

d)   With some known errors time can be calculated. Small the error less time required.

e)   The individual operation time cannot be measured in the practice. Only the total execution time can be measured, and the statistical methods are applied to deduce the secret key.

f)   Open SSL is a well-known free crypto library which is used on Apache web server to provide SSL function. But experiments are performed that demonstrate that the RSA private keys can be revealed from an open SSL based web server over a local network.

To avoid power analysis attack, some of the countermeasures are proposed which are listed below:

1.   Make operational parameter independent of the input data. The feasibility of this approach depends on the operation.

2.   Use of blinding is also recommended as it increases 2%-10% overhead.

3.   Another approach could be to eliminate branch processing in the implementation algorithm so that encryption time is equivalent.

4.   Currently used counter measures are noise injection and branch equalization.

4.3.2 Case Studies

Case Study 1: Relay attack on cards – To reduce the fraud rate chip and pin cards were introduced, which relies on 'challenge and response' for the security of the data. Despite the protections, there are still vulnerabilities. (Drimer & Murdoch, 2013) illustrated a real relay attack on smartcards. For the attack there are four characters involved – Alice, Bob, Carol and Dave. Alice is an innocent customer, Bob is the crook, Carol is Bob's accomplice and Dave is an honest merchant. Alice is a customer of a restaurant and Bob is the waiter in that restaurant. Carol is present in a jewellery shop whose merchant is Dave. When Alice inserts his card into an untrusted terminal, Carol is informed by an SMS to insert her card in a trusted terminal. All communication from the shop terminal of jewellers will be sent to Alice's card via Carol's card and Bob's terminal, and vice versa. Alice leaves the restaurant believing he has paid $20 for a meal, when his claim would show $2000 for a diamond. Alice will not be paid for the meal because the malicious terminal will never interact with the bank. The study shows how by using a malicious terminal, relay attack can be performed on the smartcards.

Case Study 2: EM side channel attack on contactless smartcards – (Kasper, Oswald & Paar, 2009) introduces a low-cost hardware to perform side channel attack on contactless smartcards. Practically check the effectiveness of the methods developed by examining the security of consumer contactless smartcards using strong cryptography, identifying protocol vulnerabilities and identifying vulnerability to side-channel attacks. Performed practical real-world EM attacks in a black-box scenario on consumer contactless smartcards. In addition, verified that a standard DES is used to encrypt the challenge by performing a full authentication and reproducing the responses of the cryptographically enabled contactless smart card under attack on the PC. To obtain the relevant side-channel data, recorded raw traces and digitally perform demodulation using a straightforward, incoherent demodulation approach.

4.4 Data Level Security Attack

Information security is the implementation of policies by handling its storage and allocation to guarantee data security and privacy. Security of information has both technical and social consequences (CardLogix, 2010). All data networks deal with the following key components when implementing a safety scheme: hardware, software, personnel and data. Data security includes data integrity, non-repudiation, authentication, auditing and logging, and authorization. To secure the data confidentiality, cryptography is an important method (CardLogix, 2010). The use of encryption to safeguard data against unlawful disclosure is confidentiality. Using an algorithm, plain text is converted to cipher text, then decrypted back to plain text using the same method. Cryptography is the technique by which information can be converted from a human readable form to a modified form, and then back to its initial readable form, making unlawful access hard. The following methods are used for cryptography: Ensure information privacy through data encryption, ensures uniqueness of data by checking that data is "original" and not the "original" copy. The sender attaches to the "initial" information a unique identifier and receiver of the information then checks this unique identifier, and Ensures data integrity by acknowledging the unlawful manipulation of information

Effective security system planning takes into consideration the need for approved customers to readily access data, while taking into consideration the many threats this access poses to information integrity and security (CardLogix, 2010). An organisation should look carefully at two fields when evaluating the threats to your information: internal attacks and external attacks. A typical inner attack conduct is the introduction of viruses and the attempted formatting of network disks. By deploying employee cards logging an employee into the scheme and recording the employee's time, date and machine, a business will automatically discourage such attacks. External attacks typically target the weakest link in the safety armor of a company. Other kinds of issues that may threaten your assets include: Analysis, Delegated Services, Installation and Deployment, Management, Training, Infrastructure Costs (Software and Hardware), and Audits and Upgrades.

5. APPLICATIONS

The smartcards have gained popularity in many areas over the time due to their ease and feasibility. Some of the applications of smartcards are discussed below:

1. **Banking Application**: Replacing the traditional magnetic stripe-based credit or debit card is the most prominent use of smart card in banking implementation (Cronin & College, 1998). The MasterCard and VISA are an example.
2. **Ecommerce and Retail**: Smart card can be used to store data such as account details of a person, transaction details, and by acting as a credit card can be used to buy products online (M'Raihi & Yung, 2001). Some distributors may also use smart cards to store points for a specific client and provide repeated clients with rewards.
3. **Telecommunications**: Developing SIM card or Subscriber Identity Module is the most prominent use of smart card technology. A SIM card provides each user with distinctive identification and provides each subscriber with access to the network and manages their authentication (Casadei, Savoldi & Gubian, 2006).
4. **Domestic**: The most commonly used domestic smart card is the DTH smart card. This card offers approved access to satellite data. The card with which we can access the facilities of Direct to Home TV is simply a smart card. The data within a smart card is encrypted and decrypted.
5. **Secured Physical Access**: Besides providing security of information, smartcards are also used to protect services and equipment by restricting access only to permitted users (Kisi, n.d.; Guillou, 1984). In addition, smart cards can help protect corporate information networks like logical access control as compared to physical access control when entering a facility (FacilitiesNet, n.d.).
6. **Healthcare**: Embedded with a programmable computer chip, the wallet-sized medical smart card stores and transmits the clinical, insurance coverage and biographical data of a cardholder (RW, 2000). Smart health cards can enhance patient information's safety and privacy, provide a safe carrier for portable medical documents and decrease health fraud (Secure Technology Alliance, n.d.). These card data access can also be secured using biometric features of patients (Marohn, 2006).
7. **Internet of Things (IoT)**: Smart Card Alliance is in favour of adding embedded security in IoT devices (Secure Technology Alliance, n.d.). To support features like PKI and strong encryption algorithms, an IoT device should incorporate safe hardware components. According to (Smith, 2019; Yang, Cai, Wei, Lu & Choo, 2016), it is possible to use smart cards to log in to the IoT server and for authentication purpose.

6. FUTURE WORK

Smart cards have multiple functions that can be an ID, a credit card, a stored-value cash card, and a repository of personal information like phone numbers or medical history. The card has security vulnerabilities regarding confidentiality, integrity and information accessibility including unauthorized remote monitoring, exploitation of communication protocols, denial of service (attack) attacks. To secure cards from such vulnerability, optimum solutions must be developed. The problems of privacy and the free cross-border exchange of data also restrict e-commerce development. Blockchain is a growing technology and combining it with smartcard technology is a perfect match for proper management of cryptographic data of applications and needs optimum solutions to be built for the same. With the development of contactless smartcards, it is majorly used in payment system. Many risk factors are associated with contactless payment cards which leads to fraud activities. Secure schemes need to be developed to secure the cards from fraud activities.

7. CONCLUSION

With the benefits already in existence, smartcards have gain popularity in both the private and public sector across the world, with the services provided by it in the real time. However, security attacks on confidentiality, integrity and data availability in smart card-based systems exists. This chapter provided a brief introduction to smartcard technology and highlighted the physical structure, lifecycle and standards available in smartcards. Also, elaborated various threats to the smartcards at different levels along with their countermeasures. The chapter has also discussed some of the case studies regarding the attacks on the smartcards. In addition, discussed the application area of smartcards with the growing need of user in every area. The future research area shows various development that are needed smartcards to secure them from vulnerabilities which leads to fraudulent activity in different areas.

REFERENCES

Al-Qerem, A., Alauthman, M., Almomani, A., & Gupta, B. B. (2019). IoT transaction processing through cooperative concurrency control on fog–cloud computing environment. *Soft Computing*, 1–17.

Alieyan, K., Almomani, A., Anbar, M., Alauthman, M., Abdullah, R., & Gupta, B. B. (2019). DNS rule-based schema to botnet detection. *Enterprise Information Systems*, 1–20. doi:10.1080/17517575.2019.1644673

Almomani, A., Gupta, B. B., Wan, T. C., Altaher, A., & Manickam, S. (2013). Phishing dynamic evolving neural fuzzy framework for online detection zero-day phishing email. *arXiv preprint arXiv:1302.0629*.

Aubert, B. A., & Hamel, G. (2001). Adoption of smart cards in the medical sector: The Canadian experience. *Social Science & Medicine*, *53*(7), 879–894. doi:10.1016/S0277-9536(00)00388-9 PMID:11522135

Bar-El, H. (2005). Known attacks against smartcards.

Casadei, F., Savoldi, A., & Gubian, P. (2006). Forensics and SIM cards: An Overview. *International Journal of Digital Evidence*, 5(1), 1–21.

Chen, S. (2016). *Trust Management for a Smart Card Based Private eID Manager* (Master's thesis, NTNU).

Chen, S. (2016). Trust Management for a Smart Card Based Private eID Manager (Master's thesis, NTNU).

Conlon, J., & Whitacre, J. (2005). U.S. Patent Application No. 11/047,593.

Cronin, M. J. (1998). *Banking and Finance on the Internet*. John Wiley & Sons.

Dahiya, A., & Gupta, B. B. (2019). A PBNM and economic incentive-based defensive mechanism against DDoS attacks. *Enterprise Information Systems*, 1–21. doi:10.1080/17517575.2019.1700553

Drimer, S., & Murdoch, S. J. (2013). *Chip & PIN (EMV) relay attacks*. Computer Laboratory University of Cambridge.

Gong, L., Lomas, M. A., Needham, R. M., & Saltzer, J. H. (1993). Protecting poorly chosen secrets from guessing attacks. *IEEE Journal on Selected Areas in Communications*, *11*(5), 648–656. doi:10.1109/49.223865

Guillou, L. C. (1984, April). Smart cards and conditional access. In *Workshop on the Theory and Application of of Cryptographic Techniques* (pp. 480-489). Berlin, Germany: Springer.

Gupta, B., Agrawal, D. P., & Yamaguchi, S. (Eds.). (2016). *Handbook of research on modern cryptographic solutions for computer and cyber security*. IGI Global. doi:10.4018/978-1-5225-0105-3

Gupta, B. B. (Ed.). (2018). *Computer and cyber security: principles, algorithm, applications, and perspectives*. CRC Press.

Gupta, B. B., & Quamara, M. (2018). An identity-based access control and mutual authentication framework for distributed cloud computing services in IoT environment using smart cards. *Procedia Computer Science*, *132*, 189–197. doi:10.1016/j.procs.2018.05.185

Gupta, B. B., & Quamara, M. (2018, October). A Dynamic Security Policies Generation Model for Access Control in Smart Card Based Applications. In *Proceedings International Symposium on Cyberspace Safety and Security* (pp. 132-143). Cham, Switzerland: Springer. 10.1007/978-3-030-01689-0_11

Gupta, B. B., & Quamara, M. (2019). *Smart Card Security: Applications, Attacks, and Countermeasures* (p. 118). CRC Press, Taylor & Francis. doi:10.1201/9780429345593

Gupta, B. B., & Quamara, M. (n.d.). A taxonomy of various attacks on smart card–based applications and countermeasures. *Concurrency and Computation: Practice and Experience*, e4993.

Gupta, S., & Gupta, B. B. (2015). BDS: browser dependent XSS sanitizer. In Handbook of Research on Securing Cloud-Based Databases with Biometric Applications (pp. 174-191). IGI Global. doi:10.4018/978-1-4666-6559-0.ch008

Hsu, M. H., Yen, J. C., Chiu, W. T., Tsai, S. L., Liu, C. T., & Li, Y. C. (2011). Using health smart cards to check drug allergy history: The perspective from Taiwan's experiences. *Journal of Medical Systems*, *35*(4), 555–558. doi:10.100710916-009-9391-5 PMID:20703535

Jiang, F., Fu, Y., Gupta, B. B., Lou, F., Rho, S., Meng, F., & Tian, Z. (2018). Deep learning based multi-channel intelligent attack detection for data security. *IEEE Transactions on Sustainable Computing*.

Kasper, T., Oswald, D., & Paar, C. (2009, August). EM side-channel attacks on commercial contactless smartcards using low-cost equipment. In *Proceedings International Workshop on Information Security Applications* (pp. 79-93). Berlin, Germany: Springer. 10.1007/978-3-642-10838-9_7

Ko, H., & Caytiles, R. D. (2011). A review of smartcard security issues. 보안공학연구논문지, *8*(3), 359-370.

Li, H., Markettos, A. T., & Moore, S. (2005, October). A security evaluation methodology for smart cards against electromagnetic analysis. In *Proceedings 39th Annual 2005 International Carnahan Conference on Security Technology* (pp. 208-211). IEEE.

M'Raïhi, D., & Yung, M. (2001). E-commerce applications of smart cards. *Computer Networks*, *36*(4), 453–472. doi:10.1016/S1389-1286(01)00166-9

Mahanta, H. J., Azad, A. K., & Khan, A. K. (2015, January). Power analysis attack: A vulnerability to smart card security. In *2015 International Conference on Signal Processing and Communication Engineering Systems* (pp. 506-510). IEEE. 10.1109/SPACES.2015.7058206

Markantonakis, K., Mayes, K., Sauveron, D., & Askoxylakis, I. G. (2008, October). Overview of security threats for smart cards in the public transport industry. In *IEEE International Conference on e-Business Engineering, 2008. ICEBE'08.* (pp. 506-513). IEEE. 10.1109/ICEBE.2008.91

Marohn, D. (2006). Biometrics in healthcare. *Biometric Technology Today*, *14*(9), 9–11. doi:10.1016/S0969-4765(06)70592-6

Messerges, T. S., Dabbish, E. A., & Sloan, R. H. (2002). Examining smart-card security under the threat of power analysis attacks. *IEEE Transactions on Computers*, *51*(5), 541–552. doi:10.1109/TC.2002.1004593

Nedjah, N., Wyant, R. S., Mourelle, L. M., & Gupta, B. B. (2017). Efficient yet robust biometric iris matching on smart cards for data high security and privacy. *Future Generation Computer Systems*, *76*, 18–32. doi:10.1016/j.future.2017.05.008

Schneier, B., & Shostack, A. (1999, May). Breaking up is hard to do: modeling security threats for smart cards. In *USENIX Workshop on Smart Card Technology, Chicago, IL,* Retrieved from Error! Hyperlink reference not valid.

Taherdoost, H., Sahibuddin, S., & Jalaliyoon, N. (2011). Smart card security; Technology and adoption. *International Journal of Security*, *5*(2), 74–84.

Tewari, A., & Gupta, B. B. (2017). Cryptanalysis of a novel ultra-lightweight mutual authentication protocol for IoT devices using RFID tags. *The Journal of Supercomputing*, *73*(3), 1085–1102. doi:10.100711227-016-1849-x

Vanderhoof, R. (2017). *Smart Card Talk*. Alliance, SC.

Witteman, M. (2002). Advances in smartcard security. *Information Security Bulletin*, 7, 11–22.

Yang, Y., Cai, H., Wei, Z., Lu, H., & Choo, K. K. R. (2016, July). Towards lightweight anonymous entity authentication for IoT applications. In *Proceedings Australasian Conference on Information Security and Privacy* (pp. 265-280). Cham, Switzerland: Springer. 10.1007/978-3-319-40253-6_16

Zhou, Y., & Feng, D. (2005). Side-Channel Attacks: Ten Years After Its Publication and the Impacts on Cryptographic Module Security Testing. *IACR Cryptology ePrint Archive, 2005*, 388.

Zkik, K., Orhanou, G., & El Hajji, S. (2017). Secure mobile multi cloud architecture for authentication and data storage. [IJCAC]. *International Journal of Cloud Applications and Computing*, 7(2), 62–76. doi:10.4018/IJCAC.2017040105

Compilation of References

"WEKA," accessed 2017. [Online]. Available: https://www.cs.waikato.ac.nz/ml/weka/

Abdel-Karim, A. (n.d.). Performance Analysis of Data Encryption Algorithms.

Abdelsayed, S., Glimsholt, D., Leckie, C., Ryan, S., & Shami, S. (2003, December). An efficient filter for denial-of-service bandwidth attacks. In GLOBECOM'03. IEEE Global Telecommunications Conference (IEEE Cat. No. 03CH37489) (Vol. 3, pp. 1353-1357). IEEE.

Abouelmehdi, K., Beni-Hassane, A., & Khaloufi, H. (2018). Big healthcare data: Preserving security and privacy. *Journal of Big Data*, *5*(1), 1–18. doi:10.118640537-017-0110-7

Abraham, A., Grosan, C., & Chen, Y. (2005). *Cyber Security And The Evolution Of Intrusion Detection Systems*. Information Management & Computer Security - IMCS. 1. . doi:10.26634/jfet.1.1.968

Abusnaina, A., Khormali, A., Alasmary, H., Park, J., Anwar, A., Meteriz, U., & Mohaisen, A. (2019). Examining Adversarial Learning against Graph-based IoT Malware Detection Systems. *Cornell University – Computer Science – Cryptography and Security, 2019*.

Academy of Medical Sciences (AMS). (2006). *Personal Data for Public Good: Using Health Information in Medical Research*. London, UK: AMS.

Acar, A., Aksu, H., & Selcuk Uluagac, A. A. (2018). A Survey on Homomorphic Encryption Schemes: Theory and Implementation. *ACM Computing Surveys*, *51*(4), 79. doi:10.1145/3214303

Adat, V., & Gupta, B. B. (2017, April). A DDoS attack mitigation framework for internet of things. In *Proceedings 2017 International Conference on Communication and Signal Processing (ICCSP)*, (pp. 2036-2041). IEEE. 10.1109/ICCSP.2017.8286761

Adat, V., Dahiya, A., & Gupta, B. B. (2018, January). Economic incentive-based solution against distributed denial of service attacks for IoT customers. In *Proceedings 2018 IEEE International Conference on Consumer Electronics (ICCE)* (pp. 1-5). IEEE.

Adat, V., Dahiya, A., & Gupta, B. B. (n.d.). *Economic Incentive Based Solution Against Distributed Denial of Service*.

Adat, V., & Gupta, B. B. (2018). Security in Internet of Things: Issues, challenges, taxonomy, and architecture. *Telecommunication Systems*, *67*(3), 423–441.

Advisory, C. E. R. T. CA-1996-21, Carnegie Mellon University. (2014). Retrieved from https://www uxsup.csx.cam.ac.uk/pub/webmirrors/www.cert.org/advisories/CA-1996-21.html

Advisory, C. E. R. T. CA-1997-28, Carnegie Mellon University. (2014). Retrieved from https://resources.sei.cmu.edu/asset_files/whitepaper/1997_019_001_496176.pdf

Aggarwal, A., Rajadesingan, A., & Kumaraguru, P. (2012). PhishAri: Automatic realtimephishing detection on twitter, eCrime Res. Summit, eCrime, pp. 1–12.

Aguilar-Melchor, C., Fau, S., Fontaine, C., Gogniat, G., & Sirdey, R. (2013). Recent advances in homomorphic encryption: A possible future for signal processing in the encrypted domain. *IEEE Signal Processing Magazine, 30*(2), 108–117. doi:10.1109/MSP.2012.2230219

Ahmad, T., Ahmad, S., & Jamshed, M. (2016). A knowledge based Indian agriculture: With cloud ERP arrangement. In *Proceedings of the 2015 International Conference on Green Computing and Internet of Things, ICGCIoT 2015* (pp. 333–340). 10.1109/ICGCIoT.2015.7380484

Ahmad, T., Ahmad, S., Jamshed, M., Sherwani, F. K., Ali, R., & Khan, W. … Qaisar, T. M. (2017). An ISM approach for analyzing the enablers in India's makerspace platforms. In *Proceedings 2017 14th Learning and Technology Conference.* 10.1109/LT.2017.8088121

Ahmad, T., Haque, M., & Khan, A. M. (2018). An Energy-Efficient Cluster Head Selection Using Artificial Bees Colony Optimization for Wireless Sensor Networks. doi:10.1007/978-3-319-96451-5_8

Ahmed, E., DeLuca, B., Hirowski, E., Magee, C., Tang, I., & Coppola, J. F. (2017, May). Biometrics: Password replacement for elderly? In *Proceedings 2017 IEEE Long Island Systems, Applications, and Technology Conference (LISAT),* (pp. 1-6). IEEE.

Airehrour, D., Vasudevan Nair, N., & Madanian, S. (2018). Social Engineering Attacks and Countermeasures in the New Zealand Banking System: Advancing a User-Reflective Mitigation Model. *Information, 9*(5), 110. doi:10.3390/info9050110

Akıncı, A. N. (2017). Avrupa Birliği Genel Veri Koruma Tüzüğü'nün Getirdiği Yenilikler ve Türk Hukuku Bakımından Değerlendirilmesi [*Evaluation of General Data Protection Regulation in the aspect of Turkish Law and Regulations*]. Paperwork Number-6, Kalkınma Bakanlığı, Yayın No: 2968.

Al Quhtani, M. (2017). Data Mining Usage in Corporate Information Security: Intrusion Detection Applications, *Business Systems Research, 8*(1), 51–59.

Ala'M, A. Z., & Faris, H. (2017, April). Spam profile detection in social networks based on public features. In *Proceedings 2017 8th International Conference on Information and Communication Systems (ICICS),* (pp. 130-135). IEEE.

Aldawood, H., & Skinner, G. (2018). Challenges of Implementing Training and Awareness Programs Targeting Cyber Security Social Engineering. In *International Conferences on Cyber Security and Communication Systems,* Melbourne, Australia. Academic Press.

Aldawood, H., & Skinner, G. (2018). Educating and Raising Awareness on Cyber Security Social Engineering: A Literature Review. In the *Proceedings of IEEE International Conference on Teaching, Assessment, and Learning for Engineering (TALE).* Australia: IEEE.

Aldawood, H., & Skinner, G. (2019). Contemporary Cyber Security Social Engineering Solutions, Measures, Policies, Tools, and Applications: A Critical Appraisal, *International Journal of Security (IJS), 10*(1), p. 15.

Al-Duwairi, B., & Govindarasu, M. (2006). Novel hybrid schemes employing packet marking and logging for IP traceback. *IEEE Transactions on Parallel and Distributed Systems, 17*(5), 403–418.

Alghamdi, B., Watson, J., & Xu, Y. (2016, October). Toward detecting malicious links in online social networks through user behavior. In *Proceedings IEEE/WIC/ACM International Conference on Web Intelligence Workshops (WIW),* (pp. 5-8). IEEE. 10.1109/WIW.2016.014

Alhajri, R., Zagrouba, R., & Al-Haidari, F. (2019). Survey for Anomaly Detection of IoT Botnets Using Machine Learning Auto-Encoders. *International Journal of Applied Engineering Research, 14*(10), 2417-2421.

Alheeti, K. M. A., Gruebler, A., & McDonald-Maier, K. D. (2015). An intrusion detection system against malicious attacks on the communication network of driverless cars. In *Proceedings 2015 12th Annual IEEE Consumer Communications and Networking Conference, CCNC 2015.* 10.1109/CCNC.2015.7158098

Alieyan, K., Almomani, A., Anbar, M., Alauthman, M., Abdullah, R., & Gupta, B. B. (2019). DNS rule-based schema to botnet detection. *Enterprise Information Systems*, 1–20. doi:10.1080/17517575.2019.1644673

Al-Kasassbeh, M. (2011). Network intrusion detection with wiener filter-based agent. *World Applied Sciences Journal, 13*(11), 2372–2384.

Al-Kasassbeh, M. (2017). An Empirical Evaluation For The Intrusion Detection Features Based On Machine Learning And Feature Selection Methods. *Journal of Theoretical and Applied Information Technology, 95*(22).

Al-Kasassbeh, M. (2018). A Novel Hybrid Method for Network Anomaly Detection Based on Traffic Prediction and Change Point Detection. *Journal of Computational Science, 14*(2).

Al-Kasassbeh, M., & Adda, M. (2009). Network fault detection with Wiener filter-based agent. *Journal of Network and Computer Applications, 32*(4), 824–833. doi:10.1016/j.jnca.2009.02.001

Al-Kasassbeh, M., Al-Naymat, G., & Al-Hawari, E. (2016). Towards Generating Realistic SNMP-MIB Dataset for Network Anomaly Detection. *International Journal of Computer Science and Information Security, 14*(9), 1162–1185.

Allan, N. (2018). *Behavioral Malware Detection by Data Mining*. Lambert Academic Publishing.

Almomani, A., Gupta, B. B., Wan, T. C., Altaher, A., & Manickam, S. (2013). Phishing dynamic evolving neural fuzzy framework for online detection zero-day phishing email. *arXiv preprint arXiv:1302.0629.*

Almomani, A., Alauthman, M., Albalas, F., Dorgham, O., & Obeidat, A. (2018). An online intrusion detection system to cloud computing based on NeuCube algorithms. [IJCAC]. *International Journal of Cloud Applications and Computing, 8*(2), 96–112. doi:10.4018/IJCAC.2018040105

Almseidin, M., Al-kasassbeh, M., & Kovacs, S. (2019). Fuzzy Rule Interpolation and SNMP-MIB for Emerging Network Abnormality. *International Journal on Advanced Science, Engineering and Information Technology, 9*(3).

Almseidin, M., Piller, I., Al-Kasassbeh, M., & Kovacs, S. (2019). Fuzzy automaton as a detection mechanism for the multi-step attack. *International Journal on Advanced Science, Engineering, and Information Technology, 9*(2).

Al-Naymat, G., Al-Kasassbeh, M., & Al-Hawari, E. (2018). Exploiting SNMP-MIB Data to Detect Network Anomalies using Machine Learning Techniques. In *Proceedings of SAI Intelligent Systems Conference*. Academic Press.

Al-Naymat, G., Al-Kasassbeh, M., & Al-Hawari, E. (2018). Using machine learning methods for detecting network anomalies within SNMP-MIB dataset. *Int. J. Wireless and Mobile Computing, 15*(1), 67–76. doi:10.1504/IJWMC.2018.10015860

Alomari, E., Manickam, S., Gupta, B. B., Anbar, M., Saad, R. M., & Alsaleem, S. (2016). A survey of botnet-based ddos flooding attacks of application layer: Detection and mitigation approaches. In Handbook of Research on Modern Cryptographic Solutions for Computer and Cyber Security (pp. 52–79). IGI Global.

Alomar, N., Alsaleh, M., & Alarifi, A. (2017). Social authentication applications, attacks, defense strategies and future research directions: A systematic review. *IEEE Communications Surveys and Tutorials, 99*.

Alom, Z., Bontupalli, V. R., & Taha, T. M. (2015). Intrusion detection using deep belief network and extreme learning machine. [IJMSTR]. *International Journal of Monitoring and Surveillance Technologies Research, 3*(2), 35–56. doi:10.4018/IJMSTR.2015040103

Al-Qerem, A., Alauthman, M., Almomani, A., & Gupta, B. B. (2019). IoT transaction processing through cooperative concurrency control on fog–cloud computing environment. *Soft Computing*, 1–17.

Alrubaian, M., Al-Qurishi, M., Rahman, S. M. M., & Alamri, A. (2015). A novel prevention mechanism for Sybil attack in online social network, *Proceedings 2015 2nd World Symp. Web Appl. Networking, WSWAN 2015*, pp. 1–6. 10.1109/WSWAN.2015.7210347

Alsaadi, T. (2015). *Internet of Things: Features, Challenges, and Vulnerabilities. International Journal of Advanced Computer Science and Information Technology.* IJACSIT.

Alsaleh, M., Alarifi, A., Al-Salman, A. M., Alfayez, M., & Almuhaysin, A. (2014, December). Tsd: Detecting sybil accounts in Twitter. In *Proceedings 2014 13th International Conference on Machine Learning and Applications (ICMLA),* (pp. 463-469). IEEE.

Amazon Elastic Compute Cloud (Amazon EC2), Amazon. (n.d.). Available from https://aws.amazon.com/ec2/. Accessed on Sept 2018.

Amichai-Hamburger, Y. (2017). *Internet psychology: The basics.* Routledge. doi:10.4324/9781315622163

Andersen, D. G. (2003, March). Mayday: Distributed Filtering for Internet Services. In *USENIX Symposium on Internet Technologies and Systems* (Vol. 4).

Anderson, T., Roscoe, T., & Wetherall, D. (2004). Preventing Internet denial-of-service with capabilities. *Computer Communication Review, 34*(1), 39–44.

Anwar, S., Mohamad Zain, J., Zolkipli, M. F., Inayat, Z., Khan, S., Anthony, B., & Chang, V. (2017). From intrusion detection to an intrusion response system: Fundamentals, requirements, and future directions. *Algorithms, 10*(2), 39. doi:10.3390/a10020039

Applegate, S. D. (2009). Social engineering: Hacking the wetware! *Information Security Journal. Article, 18*(1), 40–46.

Argyraki, K., & Cheriton, D. R. (2009). Scalable network-layer defense against internet bandwidth-flooding attacks. [ToN]. *IEEE/ACM Transactions on Networking, 17*(4), 1284–1297.

Arjunwadkar Narayan, M., & Parvat, T. J. (2015). An Intrusion Detection System,(IDS) with Machine Learning (ML) Model Combining Hybrid Classifiers. *connections, 1*(3).

Armbrust, M., & et al. (2009). *Above the clouds: a berkeley view of cloud computing.* Berkeley: University of California.

Armknecht, F., Boyd, C., Carr, C., Gjøsteen, K., Jäschke, A., Reuter, C. A., & Strand, M. (2015). A guide to fully homomorphic encryption. *IACR* 1192.

Armknecht, F., Katzenbeisser, S., & Peter, A. (2013). Group homomorphic encryption: Characterizations, impossibility results, and applications. *Designs, Codes, and Cryptography, 67*(2), 209–232. doi:10.100710623-011-9601-2

ASERT Team. NETSCOUT "OMG - Mirai Minions are Wicked". Link available at https://www.netscout.com/blog/asert/omg-mirai-minions-are-wicked

Atkins, B., & Huang, W. (2013). A study of social engineering in online frauds. *Open Journal of Social Sciences, 1*(3), 23–32. doi:10.4236/jss.2013.13004

Atkinson, R., & Kent, S. (1998). Security architecture for the internet protocol.

Atun, R., Aydin, S., Chakraborty, S., Sümer, S., Aran, M., Gürol, I., ... Akdağ, R. (2013). Universal Health Coverage in Turkey: Enhancement of Equity. *Lancet, 382*(9886), 65–99. doi:10.1016/S0140-6736(13)61051-X PMID:23810020

Aubert, B. A., & Hamel, G. (2001). Adoption of smart cards in the medical sector: The Canadian experience. *Social Science & Medicine, 53*(7), 879–894. doi:10.1016/S0277-9536(00)00388-9 PMID:11522135

AuYoung, A., Chun, B., Snoeren, A., & Vahdat, A. (2004, October). Resource allocation in federated distributed computing infrastructures. In *Proceedings of the 1st Workshop on Operating System and Architectural Support for the On-demand IT InfraStructure* (Vol. 9).

AWS Elastic Beanstalk, Amazon Web Services, Amazon. (n.d.). Available from https://aws.amazon.com/elasticbeanstalk/. Accessed on Sept 2018.

Aziz, A., Amin, M., Ismael, O. A., & Bu, Z. (2017). U.S. Patent No. 9,756,074. Washington, DC: U.S. Patent and Trademark Office.

Azmoodeh, A., Dehghantanha, A., & Choo, K. K. R. (2018). Robust malware detection for internet of (battlefield) things devices using deep eigenspace learning. *IEEE Transactions on Sustainable Computing, 4*(1), 88-95.

Azmoodeh, A., Dehghantanha, A., Conti, M., & Choo, K. K. R. (2018). Detecting crypto-ransomware in IoT networks based on energy consumption footprint. *Journal of Ambient Intelligence and Humanized Computing, 9*(4), 1141-1152.

Azure: Microsoft's Cloud Platform, Microsoft Corporation. (n.d.). Available from https://azure.microsoft.com/en-in/. Accessed on Sept 2018.

Bafna, A., & Kumar, S. (2012). ProActive Approach for Generating Random Passwords for Information Protection. *Procedia Technology, 4*, 129–133. doi:10.1016/j.protcy.2012.05.018

Baig, Z. A., & Binbeshr, F. (2013). Controlled Virtual Resource Access to Mitigate Economic Denial of Sustainability (EDoS) Attacks Against Cloud Infrastructures, in *Proceedings of the 2013 International Conference on Cloud Computing and Big Data, CLOUDCOM-ASIA '13*, pp. 346–353. IEEE Computer Society, Washington, DC. doi:10.1109/CLOUDCOM-ASIA.2013.51

Bailey, M., Cooke, E., Jahanian, F., Xu, Y., & Karir, M. (2009, March). A survey of botnet technology and defenses. In Proceedings 2009 Cybersecurity Applications & Technology Conference for Homeland Security (pp. 299-304). IEEE.

Baranwal, G., & Vidyarthi, D. P. (2015). A fair multi-attribute combinatorial double auction model for resource allocation in cloud computing. *Journal of Systems and Software, 108*, 60–76.

Bar-El, H. (2005). Known attacks against smartcards.

Barrett, D. J., Silverman, R. E., & Byrnes, R. G. (2005). *SSH, the Secure Shell: The definitive guide.* O'Reilly Media.

Basu, S., Bardhan, A., Gupta, K., Saha, P., Pal, M., Bose, M., . . . Sarkar, P. (2018, January). Cloud computing security challenges & solutions-A survey. In *Proceedings 2018 IEEE 8th Annual Computing and Communication Workshop and Conference (CCWC)*, (pp. 347-356). IEEE. 10.1109/CCWC.2018.8301700

Bayardo, R. J., & Agrawal, R. (2005). Data privacy through optimal k-anonymization. *IEEE 23rd International Conference on Data Engineering, ICDE*, 217-228. doi: 10.1109/ICDE.2005.42

Bazrafshan, H., & Fard, H. (2013). A Survey on Heuristic Malware Detection Techniques. In *Proceedings of the 5th Conference on Information and Knowledge Technology (IKT)*. 10.1109/IKT.2013.6620049

BehavioSec, Inc. (2019). Continuous Authentication through Passive Behavioral Biometrics. Retrieved October 1, 2019, from http://behaviosec.com

Behl, A. (2011, December). Emerging security challenges in Cloud computing: An insight to Cloud security challenges and their mitigation. In Proceedings 2011 World Congress on Information and Communication Technologies (WICT), (pp. 217-222). IEEE.

Beloglazov, A., & Buyya, R. (2010, May). Energy efficient resource management in virtualized cloud data centers. In *Proceedings of the 2010 10th IEEE/ACM international conference on cluster, cloud and grid computing* (pp. 826-831). IEEE Computer Society. 10.1109/CCGRID.2010.46

Belouch, M., El Hadaj, S., & Idlianmiad, M. (2018). Performance evaluation of intrusion detection based on machine learning using apache spark. In Procedia Computer Science. doi:10.1016/j.procs.2018.01.091

Bernardi, C. (2017). A fuzzy-based process mining approach for dynamic malware detection. In *Proceedings of the IEEE International Conference on Fuzzy Systems*. 10.1109/FUZZ-IEEE.2017.8015490

Bhattasali, C. R., & Chaki, N. (2013). Study of Security Issues in Pervasive Environment of Next Generation Internet of Things. In *Proceedings of the 12th International Conference on Information Systems and Industrial Management (CISIM)*. 10.1007/978-3-642-40925-7_20

Bhumika, P., & Bhushan, K. (2019). Fog Computing: Concepts, Applications, and Countermeasures Against Security Attacks, *Handbook of Research on Cloud Computing and Big Data Applications in IoT,* pp. 302-329, IGI Global.

Bhushan, K., & Gupta, B. B. (2018). A novel approach to defend multimedia flash crowd in cloud environment. *Multimedia Tools and Applications*, *77*(4), 4609–4639.

Bhushan, K., & Gupta, B. B. (2019). Distributed denial of service (DDoS) attack mitigation in software defined network (SDN)-based cloud computing environment. *Journal of Ambient Intelligence and Humanized Computing, 10*(5), 1985–1997.

Bhushan, K., & Gupta, B. B. (2019). Network flow analysis for detection and mitigation of Fraudulent Resource Consumption (FRC) attacks in multimedia cloud computing. *Multimedia Tools and Applications*, *78*(4), 4267–4298.

Bhuyan, M. H., Bhattacharyya, D. K., & Kalita, J. K. (2013). Network anomaly detection: Methods, systems and tools. *IEEE Communications Surveys and Tutorials*, *16*(1), 303–336.

Bhuyan, M. H., Kashyap, H. J., Bhattacharyya, D. K., & Kalita, J. K. (2013). Detecting distributed denial of service attacks: Methods, tools and future directions. *The Computer Journal*, *57*(4), 537–556.

BioCatch. (2019). Less friction, Less fraud. Retrieved October 1, 2019, from https://www.biocatch.com/

Blightman, K., Griffiths, S. E., & Danbury, C. (2013). Patient confidentially: When can a breach be justified? *Continuing Education in Anaesthesia, Critical Care & Pain, 14*(2), 52–55. doi:10.1093/bjaceaccp/mkt032

Bo, C., Zhang, L., Li, X. Y., Huang, Q., & Wang, Y. (2013). SilentSense: Silent User Identification Via Touch and Movement Behavioral Biometrics. In *Proceedings 19th Annual International Conference on Mobile Computing & Networking*, 187-190. 10.1145/2500423.2504572

Boneh, D., Di Crescenzo, G., Ostrovsky, R., & Persiano, G. (2004, May). Public key encryption with keyword search. In *Proceedings International conference on the theory and applications of cryptographic techniques* (pp. 506-522). Berlin, Germany: Springer.

Boshmaf, Y., Logothetis, D., Siganos, G., Lería, J., Lorenzo, J., Ripeanu, M., & Beznosov, K. (2015, February). Integro: Leveraging Victim Prediction for Robust Fake Account Detection in OSNs. In NDSS (Vol. 15, pp. 8-11).

Breda, F., Barbosa, H., & Morais, T. (2017). Social engineering and cyber security. In the *Proceedings of International Technology, Education, and Development Conference*, 4204-4211. Valencia, Spain, 10.21125/inted.2017.1008

Breitenbacher, D., Homoliak, I., Aung, Y. L., Tippenhauer, N. O., & Elovici, Y. (2019). HADES-IoT: A Practical Host-Based Anomaly Detection System for IoT Devices. In *Proceedings of the ACM Asia Conference on Computer and Communications Security (AsiaCCS '19)*. 10.1145/3321705.3329847

Brij, B. (2019). *Gupta, Quan Z. Sheng, Machine Learning for Computer and Cyber Security: Principle, Algorithms, and Practices* (p. 352). CRC Press, Taylor & Francis.

Brito, T. B., & Trevisan, E. F., E. F. C., & Booter, R. C. (2011). A Conceptual Comparison Between Discrete and Continuous Simulation to Motivate the Hybrid Simulation Technology. In *Proceedings of the 2011 Winter Simulation Conference*, 3915-3927. Academic Press.

Broownlee, J. (2016, March 16). Supervised and Unsupervised Machine Learning Algorithms. Retrieved October 1, 2019, from https://machinelearningmastery.com/supervised-and-unsupervised-machine-learning-algorithms/

Bryant, R. E. (1986). Graph-based algorithms for boolean function manipulation. *IEEE Transactions on Computers*, *100*(8), 677–691.

Burch, H., & Cheswick, B. (2000, December). Tracing Anonymous Packets to Their Approximate Source. In LISA (pp. 319-327).

Buyya, R., Shin, Y., Venugopal, S., Broberg, J., & Brandic, I. (2009). Cloud computing and emerging it platforms: vision, hype, and reality for delivering computing as the 5th utility, 25, 599–616, 2009. *Future generation computing system*, 599-616.

Cabrera, J. B., Lewis, L., Qin, X., Lee, W., Prasanth, R. K., Ravichandran, B., & Mehra, R. K. (2001, May). Proactive detection of distributed denial of service attacks using mib traffic variables-a feasibility study. In *2001 IEEE/IFIP International Symposium on Integrated Network Management Proceedings*. Integrated Network Management VII. Integrated Management Strategies for the New Millennium (pp. 609-622). IEEE.

Calheiros, R. N., Ranjan, R., Beloglazov, A., De Rose, C. A., & Buyya, R. (2011). Cloudsim: A Toolkit For Modeling And Simulation Of Cloud Computing Environments And Evaluation Of Resource Provisioning Algorithms. *Software, Practice, & Experience*, *41*(1), 23–50. doi:10.1002pe.995

Cambiaso, E., Papaleo, G., Chiola, G., & Aiello, M. (2013). Slow DoS attacks: Definition and categorisation. *International Journal Trust Management Computer Communication*, *1(3-4)*, 300–319.

Canetti, R., Halevi, S., & Katz, J. (2003, May). A forward-secure public-key encryption scheme. In *International Conference on the Theory and Applications of Cryptographic Techniques* (pp. 255-271). Berlin, Germany: Springer.

Carlin, A., Hammoudeh, M., & Aldabbas, O. (2015). Intrusion detection and countermeasure of virtual cloud systems-state of the art and current challenges. *International Journal of Advanced Computer Science and Applications*, *6*(6). doi:10.14569/IJACSA.2015.060601

Casadei, F., Savoldi, A., & Gubian, P. (2006). Forensics and SIM cards: An Overview. *International Journal of Digital Evidence*, *5*(1), 1–21.

Case Studies, E. R. T. (n.d.). DDoS Case Study: DDoS Attack Mitigation Boston Children's Hospital. Available at https://security.radware.com/ddos-experts-insider/ert-case-studies/boston-childrens-hospital-ddos-mitigation-case-study/

Cervantes, P., & Nogueira, S. (2015). Detection of Sinkhole Attacks for Supporting Secure Routing on 6LoWPAN for Internet of Things. In *Proceedings IFIP/IEEE International Symposium on Integrated Network Management (IM)*. 606 – 611. 10.1109/INM.2015.7140344

Chaabouni, N., Mosbah, M., Zemmari, A., Sauvignac, C., & Faruki, P. (2019). Network Intrusion Detection for IoT Security based on Learning Techniques. *IEEE Communications Surveys and Tutorials*.

Chadi, R. I. M. A. N., & Pierre, E. (2015). Comparative Analysis of Block Cipher-Based Encryption Algorithms: A Survey. Information Security and Computer Fraud, 3(1).

Chahal, K., & Eldabi, T. (2010). A multi-perspective comparison between system dynamics and discrete event simulation, *Journal of Business Information Systems*, pp. 4-17.

Chailloux, A. (2018). *Relativistic commitment and zero-knowledge proofs. Seventeenth Bellairs CryptoWorkshop 2018, Mar 2018*. Barbados: Holetown.

Charbathia, S., & Sharma, S. (2014). A Comparative Study of Rivest Cipher Algorithms, *International Journal of Information & Computation Technology, 4*(17). pp. 1831-1838.

Chaudhari, P., & Das, M. L. (2019). *Privacy Preserving Searchable Encryption with Fine-grained Access Control*. IEEE Transactions on Cloud Computing. doi:10.1109/TCC.2019.2892116

Chaudhary, P., Gupta, B. B., & Yamaguchi, S. (2016, October). XSS detection with automatic view isolation on online social network. In *Proceedings 2016 IEEE 5th Global Conference on Consumer Electronics,* (pp. 1-5). IEEE. 10.1109/GCCE.2016.7800354

Chaudhary, D., Bhushan, K., & Gupta, B. B. (2018). Survey on DDoS attacks and defense mechanisms in cloud and fog computing. [IJESMA]. *International Journal of E-Services and Mobile Applications, 10*(3), 61–83.

Chawla, V., & Nagpal, R. S. R. (2015). The RC7 Encryption Algorithm, *International Journal of Security and Its Applications 9*(5), pp. 55-60.

Chawla, A., Lee, B., Fallon, S., & Jacob, P. (2018, September). Host based intrusion detection system with combined cnn/rnn model. In *Proceedings Joint European Conference on Machine Learning and Knowledge Discovery in Databases* (pp. 149-158). Springer, Cham.

Chen, R., & Park, J. M. (2005, October). Attack Diagnosis: Throttling distributed denial-of-service attacks close to the attack sources. In *Proceedings 14th International Conference on Computer Communications and Networks, 2005. ICCCN 2005.* (pp. 275-280). IEEE.

Chen, R., Park, J. M., & Marchany, R. (2006). NISp1-05: RIM: Router interface marking for IP traceback. In Proceedings IEEE Globecom 2006 (pp. 1-5). IEEE.

Chen, R., Park, J. M., & Marchany, R. (2006). TRACK: A novel approach for defending against distributed denial-of-service attacks. Technical P~ eport TR ECE—O6-02. Dept. of Electrical and Computer Engineering, Virginia Tech.

Chen, S. (2016). *Trust Management for a Smart Card Based Private eID Manager* (Master's thesis, NTNU).

Chen, Y., Hwang, K., & Ku, W. S. (2006). Distributed Change-Point Detection of DDoS Attacks Over Multiple Network Domains. Proc. IEEE Int. Symp. Collaborative Technologies and Systems, pp. 543–550. Las Vegas, NV, May 14–17, IEEE CS.

Chen, C. L. (2009). A new detection method for distributed denial of-service attack traffic based on statistical test. *Journal of Universal Computer Science, 15*, 488–504.

Chen, T., & Abu-Nimeh, S. (2011). Lessons from stuxnet. *Computer, 44*(4), 91–93. doi:10.1109/MC.2011.115

Chhabra, M., & Gupta, B. B. (2014). Research Article An Efficient Scheme to Prevent DDoS Flooding Attacks in Mobile Ad-Hoc Network (MANET). *Research Journal of Applied Sciences, Engineering and Technology, 7*(10), 2033–2039.

Chhabra, M., Gupta, B., & Almomani, A. (2013). A novel solution to handle DDOS attack in MANET. *Journal of Information Security, 4*(3), 165.

Chiang, Z. (2016). *Fog and IoT: An Overview of Research Opportunities*. IEEE Internet of Things Journal.

Chiappetta, A. (2019). *Survey on Industrial Internet of Things (IoT) Threats and Security. In Handbook of Research on Cloud Computing and Big Data Applications in IoT* (pp. 330–366). IGI Global.

Cho, V., & Ip, W. H. (2018). A Study of BYOD adoption from the lens of threat and coping appraisal of its security policy. *Enterprise Information Systems, 12*(6), 659–673. doi:10.1080/17517575.2017.1404132

Chu, C., & Brockmeyer, M. (2010). Mobile Agents and Eventually Perfect Predicate Detection: An Intelligent General Approach to Monitoring Distributed Systems. In A. Hăkansson, R. Hartung, & N. T. Nguyen (Eds.), *Agent and Multi-agent Technology for Internet and Enterprise Systems. Studies in Computational Intelligence* (Vol. 289). Berlin, Germany: Springer. doi:10.1007/978-3-642-13526-2_12

Cisco WebEx, Cisco. (n.d.). Available from https://www.webex.co.in/. Accessed on Sept 2018

Conlon, J., & Whitacre, J. (2005). U.S. Patent Application No. 11/047,593.

Conti, M., Poovendran, R., & Secchiero, M. (2012, August). Fakebook: Detecting fake profiles in on-line social networks. In *Proceedings of the 2012 International Conference on Advances in Social Networks Analysis and Mining (ASONAM 2012)* (pp. 1071-1078). IEEE Computer Society. 10.1109/ASONAM.2012.185

Corbett, J. C. (2013). Spanner: Google's Globally Distributed Database. *ACM Transactions on Computer Systems*, 31.

Costa, A., Yelshyna, A., Moriera, T. C., Andrade, F., Julian, V., & Novais, P. (2017). A legal framework for an elderly healthcare platform: A privacy and data protection overview. *Computer Law & Security Review, 33*(5), 647–658. doi:10.1016/j.clsr.2017.03.021

Couch, L. W., II. (2013). Digital and Analog Communication Systems, 8th Edition, Prentice Hall, 2013.

Couillard, G., Denefle, P., Gissot, C., Grossin, B., Guépratte, C., Hilali, I., Lamarsalle, L., London, T., Manaud, N., Olivier, P., Prados, P., Sclison, S., Szwarcensztein, K., & Umhoefer, C. (2015, November). *Unlocking the Full Potential of Data Analytics for the Benefit of All*. Paris, France: Healthcare Data Institute.

Council of Canadian Academies. (2015, May). *Accessing health and health-related data in Canada. The expert panel on timely access to health and social data for health research and health system innovation*. IHE Innovation Forum, Edmonton, Canada.

Council of Europe. (2015, June). *Health-related issues in the case-law of the European Court of Human Rights*. Thematic Report. Retrieved from https://www.echr.coe.int/Documents/Research_report_health.pdf

Country Case Study: Turkey. (2016). *Top Markets Report Health IT Country Case Study*. International Trade Administration, United States of America. Retrieved from https://www.trade.gov/topmarkets/pdf/Health_IT_Turkey.pdf

CRM Salesforce Cloud, Salesforce Inc. (n.d.). Available from https://www.salesforce.com/in/?ir=1. Accessed on Sept 2018

Cronin, M. J. (1998). *Banking and Finance on the Internet*. John Wiley & Sons.

CSSP, D. (2009). Recommended Practice: Improving Industrial Control Systems Cybersecurity with Defense-In-Depth Strategies. US-CERT Defense In Depth (October 2009) Google Scholar.

Cui, J., Zhou, H., Zhong, H., & Xu, Y. (2018). AKSER: Attribute-based keyword search with efficient revocation in cloud computing. *Information Sciences, 423*, 343–352. doi:10.1016/j.ins.2017.09.029

Custer, B., Sears, A., Dechesne, F., Georgieva, I., Tani, T., & Hof, S. (2019). *EU Personal Data Protection in Policy and Practice*. Springer, Asser Press. doi:10.1007/978-94-6265-282-8

da Costa, K. A., Papa, J. P., Lisboa, C. O., Munoz, R., & de Albuquerque, V. H. C. (2019). Internet of Things: A survey on machine learning-based intrusion detection approaches. Computer Networks, 151, 147-157. Elsevier.

Dahiya, A., & Gupta, B. B. (2018). Importance of Providing Incentives and Economic Solutions in IT Security. In Machine Learning for Computer and Cyber Security: Principle, Algorithms, and Practices. (p. 320). MLCCS.

Dahiya, A., & Gupta, B. B. (2019). A PBNM and economic incentive-based defensive mechanism against DDoS attacks. *Enterprise Information Systems*, 1–21. doi:10.1080/17517575.2019.1700553

Dantone, M., Bossard, L., Quack, T., & Van Gool, L. (2011, November). Augmented faces. In *Proceedings 2011 IEEE International Conference on Computer Vision Workshops (ICCV Workshops),* (pp. 24-31). IEEE. 10.1109/IC-CVW.2011.6130218

Dasgupta, D., & Gonzalez, F. A. (2001). An Intelligent Decision Support System for Intrusion Detection and Response. doi:10.1007/3-540-45116-1_1

Dash, T. (2017). A study on intrusion detection using neural networks trained with evolutionary algorithms. *Soft Computing, 21*(10), 2687–2700. doi:10.100700500-015-1967-z

David, I., Siordia, O. S., & Moctezuma, D. (2016, November). Features combination for the detection of malicious Twitter accounts. In *Proceedings of the 2016 IEEE International Autumn Meeting on Power, Electronics, and Computing (ROPEC),* (pp. 1-6). IEEE. 10.1109/ROPEC.2016.7830626

DDoS Attack Types and Mitigation Methods, Incapsula Inc. (2019). Retrieved from http://www.incapsula.com/ddos/ddos-attacks/. Accessed on Jan 2019.

De Donno, M., Dragoni, N., Giaretta, A., & Spognardi, A. (2017, September). Analysis of DDoS-capable IoT malwares. In 2017 Federated Conference on Computer Science and Information Systems (FedCSIS) (pp. 807-816). IEEE.

De Hert, P. (2017). Courts, privacy and data protection in Belgium: Fundamental rights that might as well be struck from the Constitution. In M. Brkan, & E. Psychogiopoulou (Eds.), Courts, Privacy and Data Protection in the Digital Environment. Edward Elgar Publishing. doi:10.4337/9781784718718.00011

Degtyar, R., Peri, J. M., Thakkar, J. B., Whittenberger, K. M., Miller, M., Thadani, N. I., & Zaytsev, A. A. (2008). Method and apparatus for building metadata driven software development kit. U.S. Patent 7, 321, 894.

Department of Information Technology-Government of India. (2006). *Indian Computer Emergency Response Team Handling Computer Security Incidents Intrusion Detection System* (CERT). In *Security Guideline CISG 2003-06*. India: Ministry of Electronics & Information Technology.

Depren, O., Topallar, M., Anarim, E., & Ciliz, M. K. (2005). An intelligent intrusion detection system (IDS) for anomaly and misuse detection in computer networks. *Expert Systems with Applications, 29*(4), 713–722. doi:10.1016/j.eswa.2005.05.002

Deshpande, P., Sharma, S. C., Peddoju, S. K., & Junaid, S. (2018). HIDS: A host-based intrusion detection system for cloud computing environment. *International Journal of System Assurance Engineering and Management, 9*(3), 567–576. doi:10.100713198-014-0277-7

Deutschmann, I., Nordström, P., & Nilsson, L. (2013). Continuous Authentication Using Behavioral Biometrics. *IT Professional, 15*(4), 12–15. doi:10.1109/MITP.2013.50

Developers, A. (2019). Distribution Dashboard. Retrieved October 1, 2019, from https://developer.android.com/about/dashboards/

Developers, A. (2019). Sensors Overview. Retrieved October 1, 2019, from https://developer.android.com/guide/topics/sensors/sensors_overview

Developers, A. IntentService. (2019). Retrieved October 1, 2019, from https://developer.android.com/reference/android/app/IntentService

Devmane, M. A., & Rana, N. K. (2014, May). Detection and prevention of profile cloning in online social networks. In Proceedings Recent Advances and Innovations in Engineering (ICRAIE), 2014 (pp. 1-5). IEEE. doi:10.1109/ICRAIE.2014.6909237

Dey, R., Jelveh, Z., & Ross, K. (2012, March). Facebook users have become much more private: A large-scale study. In *Proceedings 2012 IEEE International Conference on Pervasive Computing and Communications Workshops (PERCOM Workshops),* (pp. 346-352). IEEE. 10.1109/PerComW.2012.6197508

Deyan, G. (2019, March 28). 60+ Smartphone. *Stat, 2019.* Retrieved from https://techjury.net/stats-about/smartphone-usage/

Dietz, C., Steinberger, W., & Antzek, A., Pras. (2018). IoT-Botnet Detection and Isolation by Access Routers. *Proceedings of the 9th International Conference on the Network of the Future.* 10.1109/NOF.2018.8598138

Dinakarrao, S. M. P., Sayadi, H., Makrani, H. M., Nowzari, C., Rafatirad, S., & Homayoun, H. (2019, March). Lightweight Node-level Malware Detection and Network-level Malware Confinement in IoT Networks. In *Proceedings 2019 Design, Automation, & Test in Europe Conference & Exhibition* (pp. 776-781). IEEE.

Ding, X., Zhang, L., Wan, Z., & Gu, M. (2010). A brief survey on de-anonymization attacks in online social networks, *Proc. - Int. Conf. Comput. Asp. Soc. Networks, CASoN'10,* pp. 611–615. 10.1109/CASoN.2010.139

Dittrich, D. (1999). The 'Stacheldraht' Distributed Denial of Service Attack Tool. Technical Report. University of Washington, Seattle, WA. Retrieved from https://staff.washington.edu/dittrich/misc/stacheldraht.analysis.txt

Dittrich, D. (1999). The DoS project's "trinoo" distributed denial of service attack tool, Retrieved from https://staff.washington.edu/dittrich/misc/trinoo.analysis. Accessed on January, 2019.

Dittrich, D. (1999). The Tribe Flood Network Distributed Denial of Service Attack Tool. Technical Report. University of Washington, Seattle, WA. Retrieved from https://staff.washington.edu/dittrich/misc/tfn.analysis.txt

Dittrich, D., Weaver, G., Dietrich, S., & Long, N. (2000). The 'mstream' distributed Denial of Service Attack Tool. Technical Report. University of Washington, Seattle, WA. Retrieved from https://staff.washington.edu/dittrich/misc/mstream.analysis.txt

Dmitrienko, A., Blinov, A., & Novikov, V. (2011). Distributed smart system for monitoring the state of complex technical objects. *Measurement Techniques.* pp. 235-239. . doi:10.100711018-011-9713-0

Dom, B., Ruvolo, J., & Tewari, G. (2004). U.S. Patent Application No. 10/323,568.

Donkervoet, B., & Agha, G. (2006). Reflecting on Aspect-Oriented Programming, Metaprogramming, and Adaptive Distributed Monitoring. In *Proceedings 5th International Symposium FMCO 2006*, (pp. 246-265). Berlin, Germany: Springer.

Dowling, S., Schukat, M., & Melvin, H. (2017). A ZigBee honeypot to assess IoT cyberattack behaviour. In *Proceedings 28th Irish Signals and Systems Conference*, 1-6. 10.1109/ISSC.2017.7983603

Dragoi, V., Richmond, T., Bucerzan, D., & Legay, A. (2018). Survey on Cryptanalysis of Code-Based Cryptography: from Theoretical to Physical Attacks. In *Proceedings 2018 7th International Conference on Computers Communications and Control (ICCCC)*.

Dragotti, P. L., Vetterli, M., & Blu, T. (2007). Sampling Moments and Reconstructing Signals of Finite Rate of Innovation: Shannon Meets Strang-Fix. *IEEE Transactions on Signal Processing, 55*(5), 1741–1757. doi:10.1109/TSP.2006.890907

Drimer, S., & Murdoch, S. J. (2013). *Chip & PIN (EMV) relay attacks*. Computer Laboratory University of Cambridge.

Duhan, S., & Khandnor, P. (2016). Intrusion detection system in wireless sensor networks: A comprehensive review. In *Proceedings 2016 International Conference on Electrical, Electronics, and Optimization Techniques (ICEEOT)* (pp. 2707-2713). IEEE. 10.1109/ICEEOT.2016.7755187

Duque, S., & Omar, M. N. Bin. (2015). Using Data Mining Algorithms for Developing a Model for Intrusion Detection System (IDS). In Procedia Computer Science. doi:10.1016/j.procs.2015.09.145

Durga Bhavani, A., & Soundarya P. M. (2012). Optimized Elliptic Curve Cryptography, *International Journal of Engineering Research and Applications (IJERA), 2*(5), pp. 412–419.

Dutta, U. K., Razzaque, M. A., Al-Wadud, M. A., Islam, M. S., Hossain, M. S., & Gupta, B. B. (2018). Self-adaptive scheduling of base transceiver stations in green 5G networks. *IEEE Access: Practical Innovations, Open Solutions, 6*, 7958–7969. doi:10.1109/ACCESS.2018.2799603

Dworkin, M., Barker, E., & Nechvatal, J. (2001). Advanced encryption standard (AES). *Federal Inf. Process. Stds.(NIST FIPS)-197*.

Ebrahim, M., Khan, S., & Khalid, U. B. (2013). Symmetric Algorithm Survey: A Comparative Analysis, *International Journal of Computer Applications, 61*(20).

Eckhardt, J., & Miouhlbauer, T. (2012, Feb 15). Enhancing Safety and Security of Distributed Systems through Formal Patterns. Retrieved from http://ceur-ws.org/Vol-834/paper6_essosds2012.pdf

EDUCBA. (2019). Top 32 most important cyber security tools you must aware, Retrieved August 21, 2019 from https://www.educba.com/32-most-important-cyber-security-tools/

Egele, M., Stringhini, G., Kruegel, C., & Vigna, G. (2017). Towards detecting compromised accounts on social networks. *IEEE Transactions on Dependable and Secure Computing*, (1), 1–1.

Ehatisham-ul-Haq, M., Azam, M. A., Loo, J., Shuang, K., Islam, S., Naeem, U., & Amin, Y. (2017). Authentication of Smartphone Users Based on Activity Recognition and Mobile Sensing. *Sensors (Basel), 17*(9), 2043. doi:10.339017092043 PMID:28878177

Eichhenhofer, J., & Gusy, C. (2017). Courts, privacy and data protection in Germany: Informational self-determination in the digital environment. In M. Brkan, & E. Psychogiopoulou (Eds.), Courts, Privacy and Data Protection in the Digital Environment. Edward Elgar Publishing. doi:10.4337/9781784718718.00013

ElevenPaths. (2019). Honeypotting, un oído en Internet. Retrieved October 9, 2019, from https://empresas.blogthinkbig.com/informe-ciberseguridad-honeypotting-un-oido-en-interne/

El-Latif, A. A. A., Abd-El-Atty, B., Hossain, M. S., Rahman, M. A., Alamri, A., & Gupta, B. B. (2018). Efficient quantum information hiding for remote medical image sharing. *IEEE Access: Practical Innovations, Open Solutions, 6*, 21075–21083. doi:10.1109/ACCESS.2018.2820603

Elmisery, A. M., Sertovic, M., & Gupta, B. B. (2017). Cognitive Privacy Middleware for Deep Learning Mashup in Environmental IoT, 2169-3536 (c) 2017 *IEEE Transactions.*

Elngar, A. A., El, D. A., Mohamed, A., & Ghaleb, F. F. M. (2013). *A Real-Time Anomaly Network Intrusion Detection System with High Accuracy.* Inf. Sci. Lett; doi:10.12785/isl/020201

Elrawy, M. F., Awad, A. I., & Hamed, H. F. (2018). Intrusion detection systems for IoT-based smart environments: a survey. *Journal of Cloud Computing, 7*(1), 21.

Erşahin, B., Aktaş, Ö., Kılınç, D., & Akyol, C. (2017, October). Twitter fake account detection. In *Proceedings of the 2017 International Conference on Computer Science and Engineering (UBMK),* (pp. 388-392). IEEE. 10.1109/UBMK.2017.8093420

Essentials of Machine Learning Algorithms. Analytics Vidhya, accessed 2017. [Online]. Available:https://www.analyticsvidhya.com/blog/2017/09/common-machine-learning-algorithms

European Court of Human Rights. (1997). The Court's case-law No.22009/93, Z. v. Finland, February 25, 1997, Available at https://hudoc.echr.coe.int/eng#%22itemid%22:[%22002-9432%22]

European Court of Justice. (2003). Judgment of November 6, 2003, Case C-101/01 – Bodil Lindqvist, 50 and 51.

European Court of Justice. (2014), Judgment of April 29, 2014, Case No. 52019/07 – L.H. v. Latvia.

European Union. (2016). Regulation (EU) 2016/679 of the European Parliament and of the Council of 27 April 2016 on the Protection of Natural Persons with Regard to the Processing of Personal Data and on the Free Movement of Such Data, and Repealing Directive 95/46, *Official Journal of the European Union.* Retrieved from http://eurlex.europa.eu/legal-content/EN/TXT/PDF/?uri=CELEX:32016R0679

Facebook, accessed 2017. [Online]. Available: http://www.facebook.com/

Faghani, M. R., & Nguyen, U. T. (2014, August). A study of clickjacking worm propagation in online social networks. In *Proceedings 2014 IEEE 15th International Conference on Information Reuse and Integration (IRI),* (pp. 68-73). IEEE. 10.1109/IRI.2014.7051873

Fan, W., Kevin, L., & Rong, R. (2017). Social engineering: IE based model of human weakness for attack and defense investigations. *IJ Computer Network and Information Security, 9*(1), 1–11. doi:10.5815/ijcnis.2017.01.01

Farhaoui, Y. (2016). How to secure web servers by the intrusion prevention system (IPS)? *International Journal of Advanced Computer Research, 6*(23), 65–71. doi:10.19101/IJACR.2016.623028

Farsi, A. L., & West, D. J. Jr. (2006). Use of electronic medical records in Oman and physician satisfaction. *Journal of Medical Systems, 30*(1), 17–22. doi:10.100710916-006-7399-7 PMID:16548410

Fei, T. L., Ming, K., & Zhou, Z. (2008). Isolation forest. In *Proceedings Eighth IEEE International Conference on Data Mining (ICDM),* 413-422. Academic Press.

Feinstein, L., Schnackenberg, D., Balupari, R., & Kindred, D. (2003, April). Statistical approaches to DDoS attack detection and response. In *Proceedings DARPA information survivability conference and exposition* (Vol. 1, pp. 303-314). IEEE.

Ferguson, P. (2000). Network ingress filtering: Defeating denial of service attacks which employ IP source address spoofing.

Fernandes, D. A., Soares, L. F., Gomes, J. V., Freire, M. M., & Inácio, P. R. (2014). Security issues in cloud environments: A survey. *International Journal of Information Security*, *13*(2), 113–170. doi:10.100710207-013-0208-7

Fire, M. (2012). Strangers Intrusion Detection - Detecting Spammers and Fake Profiles in Social Networks Based on Topology Anomalies, pp. 26–39.

Fire, M., Goldschmidt, R., & Elovici, Y. (2014). Online social networks: Threats and solutions. *IEEE Communications Surveys and Tutorials*, *16*(4), 2019–2036. doi:10.1109/COMST.2014.2321628

Florencio, D., & Herley, C. (2007, May). A large-scale study of web password habits. In *Proceedings of the 16th international conference on World Wide Web* (pp. 657-666). ACM. 10.1145/1242572.1242661

Formby, D., Durbha, S., & Beyah, R. (2017). *Out of control: Ransomware for industrial control systems*. RSA.

Fraunholz, D., Krohmer, D., Anton, S. D., & Schotten, H. D. (2017). Investigation of cyber-crime conducted by abusing weak or default passwords with a medium interaction honeypot. In *2017 International Conference on Cyber Security and Protection of Digital Services (Cyber Security)*, 1-7. 10.1109/CyberSecPODS.2017.8074855

Fridman, L., Weber, S., Greenstadt, R., & Kam, M. (2017). Active Authentication on Mobile Devices via Stylometry, Application Usage, Web Browsing, and GPS Location. *IEEE Systems Journal*, *11*(2), 513–521. doi:10.1109/JSYST.2015.2472579

Fruhlinger, J. (2018). The Mirai botnet explained: How teen scammers and CCTV cameras almost brought down the internet, CSO Blog [Online]. Available at https://www.csoonline.com/article/3258748/security/the-mirai-botnet-explained-how-teen-scammers-and-cctv-cameras-almost-brought-down-the-internet.html. Accessed on Jan, 2019.

Furht, B., & Escalante, A. (2010). *Handbook of cloud computing* (Vol. 3). New York: Springer. doi:10.1007/978-1-4419-6524-0

Galán-García, P., Puerta, J. G. D. L., Gómez, C. L., Santos, I., & Bringas, P. G. (2016). Supervised machine learning for the detection of troll profiles in twitter social network: Application to a real case of cyberbullying. *Logic Journal of the IGPL*, *24*(1), 42–53.

Galloway, B., & Hancke, G. P. (2013). Introduction to Industrial Control Networks. *IEEE Communications Surveys and Tutorials*, *15*(2), 860–880. doi:10.1109/SURV.2012.071812.00124

Gantz, J., & Reinsel, D. (2011). Extracting value from chaos. *IDC iview*, 1-12.

Garbade, M. J. (2019). Seven best cyber security tools, Retrieved from https://www.cybrary.it/0p3n/7-cyber-security-pentesting-tools/

Gascon, H., Uellenbeck, S., Wolf, C., & Rieck, K. (2014). Continuous Authentication on Mobile Devices by Analysis of Typing Motion Behavior. *Lecture Notes in Informatics (LNI), Proceedings - Series of the Gesellschaft fur Informatik (GI)*. Academic Press.

Gavrilis, D., & Dermatas, E. (2005). Real-time detection of distributed denial-of-service attacks using RBF networks and statistical features. *Computer Networks and ISDN Systems*, *48*, 235–245.

Geng, X., Huang, Y., & Whinston, A. B. (2002). Defending wireless infrastructure against the challenge of DDoS attacks. *Mobile Networks and Applications*, *7*(3), 213–223.

Geng, X., & Whinston, A. B. (2000). Defeating distributed denial of service attacks. *IT Professional*, *2*(4), 36–42.

Geric, S., & Vidacic, T. (2012). XML Digital Signature and its Role in Information System Security, *MIPRO* 2012, May 21-25, 2012, Opatija, Croatia.

Gil, T. M., & Poletto, M. (2001). MULTOPS: A Data-Structure for Bandwidth Attack Detection. *In Proc. 10th Conf. USENIX Security Symp., Vol. 10*, Berkeley, CA, August 13–17. 3. USENIX.

Glave, J. (1998). Smurfing cripples ISPs, in Wired Technology News [online]. Retrieved from http://www.wired.com/news/news/technology/story/9506.html

Goga, O., Venkatadri, G., & Gummadi, K. P. (2014). Exposing impersonation attacks in online social networks.

Goldman, J. (1998). Protecting privacy to improve health care. *Journal of Health Affairs, 17*(6), 47–60.

Goldstein, M., & Uchida, S. (2016). A Comparative Evaluation of Unsupervised Anomaly Detection Algorithms for Multivariate Data. *PLoS One, 11*(4). doi:10.1371/journal.pone.0152173 PMID:27093601

Gong, N. Z., & Wang, D. (2014). On the security of trustee-based social authentications. *arXiv preprint arXiv:1402.2699.*

Gong, L., Lomas, M. A., Needham, R. M., & Saltzer, J. H. (1993). Protecting poorly chosen secrets from guessing attacks. *IEEE Journal on Selected Areas in Communications, 11*(5), 648–656. doi:10.1109/49.223865

Google App Engine, Google Inc. (n.d.). Available from http://Cloud.google.com/appengine. Accessed on Sept. 2018.

Google Compute Engine, Google Inc. (n.d.). Available from https://Cloud.google.com/compute/. Accessed on Sept 2018.

Google. +, accessed 2017. [Online]. Available: https://plus.google.com/

Gou, Z., Yamaguchi, S., & Gupta, B. B. (2017). Analysis of various security issues and challenges in cloud computing environment: a survey. In Identity Theft: Breakthroughs in Research and Practice (pp. 221-247). IGI Global. doi:10.4018/978-1-5225-0808-3.ch011

Greavu-Serban, V., & Serban, O. (2014). Social engineering a general approach. *Informatica Economica, 18*(2), 5.

Greenleaf, G. (2018, May). *Global Convergence of Data Privacy Standards and Laws: Speaking Notes for the European Commission Events on the Launch of the General Data Protection Regulation (GDPR)*. Brussels & New Delhi, May 25, 2018. University of New South Wales Law Research Paper No. 18-56.

Guillou, L. C. (1984, April). Smart cards and conditional access. In *Workshop on the Theory and Application of of Cryptographic Techniques* (pp. 480-489). Berlin, Germany: Springer.

Gulihar, P., & Gupta, B. B. (2018, July). Cooperative Mitigation of DDoS Attacks Using an Optimized Auction Scheme on Cache Servers. In *Proceedings International Conference on Advanced Informatics for Computing Research* (pp. 401-412). Springer, Singapore.

Gupta, B. B. (2018). Computer and cyber security: principles, algorithm, applications, and perspectives. Boca Raton, FL: CRC Press, Taylor & Francis.

Gupta, B. B. (Ed.). (2018). Computer and cyber security: principles, algorithm, applications, and perspectives. Boca Raton, FL: CRC Press.

Gupta, B. B. (n.d.). An efficient KP design framework of attribute-based searchable encryption for user level revocation in cloud. Concurrency and Computation: Practice and Experience, e5291.

Gupta, B. B., & Dahiya, A. (n.d.). An Auction Based Incentivized Scheme for DDoS Attacks, *Journal of Information Technology Research (JITR),* IGI Global, (Accepted, In press),

Gupta, B. B., & Harish, S. A. (2019). A Risk-Transfer based DDoS Mitigation Framework for Cloud Environment, *4th International Conference Information, Communication & Computing Technology (ICICCT-2019), Scopus Indexed Springer CCIS Conference Proceeding,* JIMS Rohini, Delhi (Accepted, In Press).

Gupta, B. B., & Quamara, M. (2018, October). A Dynamic Security Policies Generation Model for Access Control in Smart Card Based Applications. In *Proceedings International Symposium on Cyberspace Safety and Security* (pp. 132-143). Cham, Switzerland: Springer. 10.1007/978-3-030-01689-0_11

Gupta, B. B., & Quamara, M. (n.d.). A taxonomy of various attacks on smart card–based applications and countermeasures. *Concurrency and Computation: Practice and Experience*, e4993.

Gupta, B. B., & Sheng, Q. Z. (Eds.). (2019). Machine Learning for Computer and Cyber Security: Principle, Algorithms, and Practices. Boca Raton, FL: CRC Press.

Gupta, B. B., Agrawal, D. P., & Wang, H. (2019). Computer and Cyber Security: Principles, Algorithm, Applications, and Perspectives. Boca Raton, FL: CRC Press.

Gupta, B. B., Agrawal, D. P., & Yamaguchi, S. (2016). Handbook of Research on Modern Cryptographic Solutions for Computer and Cyber Security. IGI Global.

Gupta, B. B., Dharma, P. A., & Yamaguchi, S. (Eds.). (2016). Handbook of Research on Modern Cryptographic Solutions for Computer and Cyber Security. IGI Global.

Gupta, B. B., Joshi, R. C., & Misra, M. (2009). Defending against distributed denial of service attacks: issues and challenges. *Information Security Journal: A Global Perspective 18*(5), 224-247.

Gupta, B. B., Joshi, R. C., & Misra, M. (2012). Distributed denial of service prevention techniques. *arXiv preprint arXiv:1208.3557.*

Gupta, B. B., Misra, M., & Joshi, R. C. (2012). An ISP level solution to combat DDoS attacks using combined statistical based approach. *arXiv preprint arXiv:1203.2400.*

Gupta, S., & Gupta, B. B. (2015). PHP-sensor: a prototype method to discover workflow violation and XSS vulnerabilities in PHP web applications, *Proceedings of the 12th ACM International Conference on Computing Frontiers*, pp. 1-8, Italy: ACM NY. 10.1145/2742854.2745719

Gupta, A., Stahl, D. O., & Whinston, A. B. (1996). Economic issues in electronic commerce. In R. Kalakota, & A. B. Whinston (Eds.), *Readings in Electronic Commerce* (pp. 197–227). MA: Addison Wesley.

Gupta, A., Stahl, D. O., & Whinston, A. B. (1999). The economics of network management. *Communications of the ACM, 42*(9), 57–57.

Gupta, B. B. (2011). *An Introduction to DDoS Attacks and Defense Mechanisms: An Analyst's Handbook*. Lap Lambert Academic Pub.

Gupta, B. B. (2016). Analysis Of Various Security Issues And Challenges In Cloud Computing Environment. *Survey (London, England).*

Gupta, B. B. (2018). *Computer and cyber security: principles, algorithm, applications, and perspectives. Boston*, MA: Auerbach Publications.

Gupta, B. B. (2019). *Modern Principles, Practices, and Algorithms for Cloud Security* (p. 344). Hershey, PA: IGI Global.

Gupta, B. B. (Ed.). (2018). *Computer and cyber security: principles, algorithm, applications, and perspectives*. UK: CRC Press, Taylor & Francis.

Gupta, B. B., Agrawal, D. P., & Wang, H. (2019). *Computer and Cyber Security: Principles, Algorithm, Applications, and Perspectives*. Boca Raton, FL: CRC Press, Taylor & Francis Group.

Gupta, B. B., & Ali, S. T. (2019). Dynamic Policy Attribute Based Encryption and its Application in Generic Construction of Multi-Keyword Search. [IJESMA]. *International Journal of E-Services and Mobile Applications, 11*(4), 16–38.

Gupta, B. B., & Badve, O. P. (2017). GARCH and ANN-based DDoS detection and filtering in cloud computing environment. *International Journal of Embedded Systems, 9*(5), 391–400.

Gupta, B. B., & Badve, O. P. (2017). Taxonomy of DoS and DDoS attacks and desirable defense mechanism in a cloud computing environment. *Neural Computing & Applications, 28*(12), 3655–3682.

Gupta, B. B., & Badve, O. P. (2017). Taxonomy Of Dos And Ddos Attacks And Desirable Defense Mechanism In A Cloud Computing Environment. *Neural Computing & Applications, 28*(12), 3655–3682. doi:10.100700521-016-2317-5

Gupta, B. B., & Gulihar, P. (2020). Taxonomy of Payment Structures and Economic Incentive Schemes in Internet. [JITR]. *Journal of Information Technology Research, 13*(1), 150–166. doi:10.4018/JITR.2020010110

Gupta, B. B., & Gupta, A. (2018). Assessment of Honeypots: Issues, Challenges and Future Directions. [IJCAC]. *International Journal of Cloud Applications and Computing, 8*(1), 21–54.

Gupta, B. B., Gupta, S., & Chaudhary, P. (2017). Enhancing the Browser-Side Context-Aware Sanitization of Suspicious HTML5 Code for Halting the DOM-Based XSS Vulnerabilities in Cloud. *International Journal of Cloud Applications and Computing.* doi:10.4018/ijcac.2017010101

Gupta, B. B., & Quamara, M. (2018). An identity-based access control and mutual authentication framework for distributed cloud computing services in IoT environment using smart cards. *Procedia Computer Science, 132,* 189–197. doi:10.1016/j.procs.2018.05.185

Gupta, B. B., & Quamara, M. (2019). *Smart Card Security: Applications, Attacks, and Countermeasures* (p. 118). CRC Press, Taylor & Francis. doi:10.1201/9780429345593

Gupta, B. B., & Sheng, Q. Z. (2019). *Machine Learning for Computer and Cyber Security: Principle, Algorithms, and Practices.* CRC Press. doi:10.1201/9780429504044

Gupta, B., Agrawal, D. P., & Yamaguchi, S. (Eds.). (2016). *Handbook of research on modern cryptographic solutions for computer and cyber security.* IGI Global. doi:10.4018/978-1-5225-0105-3

Gupta, B., Gupta, S., & Chaudhary, P. (2017). Enhancing the browser-side context-aware sanitization of suspicious HTML5 code for halting the DOM-based XSS vulnerabilities in cloud. [IJCAC]. *International Journal of Cloud Applications and Computing, 7*(1), 1–31. doi:10.4018/IJCAC.2017010101

Gupta, B., Gupta, S., & Chaudhary, P. (2017). Enhancing the browser-side context-aware sanitization of suspicious html5 code for halting the dom-based xss vulnerabilities in cloud. *International Journal of Cloud Applications and Computing,* 1–31.

Gupta, M., Kochhar, S., Jain, P., & Nagrath, P. (2019). Hybrid recommender system using A-priori algorithm. In *Proceedings International Conference on Sustainable Computing in Science, Technology and Management,* 26-28. Academic Press.

Gupta, S., & Gugulothu, N. (2018). Secure nosql for the social networking and e-commerce based bigdata applications deployed in cloud. [IJCAC]. *International Journal of Cloud Applications and Computing, 8*(2), 113–129. doi:10.4018/IJCAC.2018040106

Gupta, S., & Gupta, B. B. (2015). BDS: browser dependent XSS sanitizer. In *Handbook of Research on Securing Cloud-Based Databases with Biometric Applications* (pp. 174–191). IGI Global. doi:10.4018/978-1-4666-6559-0.ch008

Hallaq, B., Nicholson, A., Smith, R., Maglaras, L., Janicke, H., & Jones, K. (2018). CYRAN: a hybrid cyber range for testing security on ICS/SCADA systems. In Cyber Security and Threats: Concepts, Methodologies, Tools, and Applications (pp. 622-637). IGI Global.

Halvorsen, J., Waite, J., & Hahn, A. (2019). Evaluating the Observability of Network Security Monitoring Strategies With TOMATO. *IEEE Access: Practical Innovations, Open Solutions, 7*, 108304–108315. doi:10.1109/ACCESS.2019.2933415

Hartigan, J. A., & Wong, M. A. (1979). Algorithm AS 136: A k-means clustering algorithm. *Journal of the Royal Statistical Society. Series A (General), 28*(1), 100–108.

Hayes, B. (2008). Cloud computing. *Communications of the ACM, 51*(7), 9–11. doi:10.1145/1364782.1364786

Heartfield, R., & Gan, D. (2016). Social Engineering in the Internet of Everything. Cutter IT Journal, 29(7), 20-29.

Hermann, M., Pentek, T., & Otto, B. (2016). Design Principles for Industrie 4.0 Scenarios, In *Proceedings 2016 49th Hawaii International Conference on System Sciences (HICSS)*, pp. 3928-3937. Koloa, HI, 2016, 10.1109/HICSS.2016.488

Hernandez, C., Pedraza, L. F., & Salgado, C. (2013). A proposal of traffic model that allows estimating Throughput mean values, *Proceedings of 27th International Conference on Advanced Information Networking and Applications Workshops*, Washington, DC: IEEE Computer Society. 10.1109/WAINA.2013.216

High Court of Australia. (1992). The Court's case-law No. 2 SCR 138., Mclnerney v. MacDonald, June 11, 1992, Available at https://scc-csc.lexum.com/scc-csc/scc-csc/en/item/884/index.do

High Court of Australia. (1996). The Court's case-law No. 186 CLR 71, Breen v. Williams, September 6, 1996, Available at http://www.julieclarke.info/publications/1998breen.pdf

HOIC. Sourceforge.net. (2019). Retrieved from http://sourceforge.net/projects/hoic/

Hossain, M. S., Muhammad, G., Abdul, W., Song, B., & Gupta, B. B. (2018). Cloud-assisted secure video transmission and sharing framework for smart cities. *Future Generation Computer Systems, 83*, 596–606. doi:10.1016/j.future.2017.03.029

Hrestak, D., & Picek, S. (2014). Homomorphic encryption in the cloud. In *2014 37th International Convention on Information and Communication Technology, Electronics, and Microelectronics (MIPRO'14)*. pp. 1400–1404. IEEE.

Hsu, M. H., Yen, J. C., Chiu, W. T., Tsai, S. L., Liu, C. T., & Li, Y. C. (2011). Using health smart cards to check drug allergy history: The perspective from Taiwan's experiences. *Journal of Medical Systems, 35*(4), 555–558. doi:10.100710916-009-9391-5 PMID:20703535

Huang, Y., Geng, X., & Whinston, A. B. (2007). Defeating DDoS attacks by fixing the incentive chain. *ACM Transactions on Internet Technology, 7*(1), 5.

Hu, B., Liu, Q., Liu, X., Peng, T., Wang, G., & Wu, J. (2017, May). DABKS: Dynamic attribute-based keyword search in cloud computing. In *2017 IEEE International Conference on Communications (ICC)* (pp. 1-6). IEEE. 10.1109/ICC.2017.7997108

Hu, D., & Ning, Q. (2017). Survey on Fog Computing: Architecture, Key technologies, Applications and Open Issues. *Journal of Network and Computer Applications, 98*, 27–42. doi:10.1016/j.jnca.2017.09.002

Huertas, A., García, F. J., Gil, M., & Martínez, G. (2016). SeCoMan: A Semantic-Aware Policy Framework for Developing Privacy-Preserving and Context-Aware Smart Applications. *IEEE Systems Journal, 10*(3), 111–1124.

Huertas, A., Gil, M., García, F. J., & Martínez, G. (2014). Precise: Privacy-aware recommender based on context information for cloud service environments. *IEEE Communications Magazine, 52*(8), 90–96. doi:10.1109/MCOM.2014.6871675

Huertas, A., Gil, M., García, F. J., & Martínez, G. (2014). *What Private Information Are You Disclosing? A Privacy-Preserving System Supervised by Yourself* (pp. 1221–1228). Paris, France: IEEE Intl Conf on High Performance Computing and Communications.

Huertas, A., Gil, M., García, F. J., & Martínez, G. (2016). MASTERY: A multicontext-aware system that preserves the users' privacy. In *Proceedings NOMS IEEE/IFIP Network Operations and Management Symposium*, 523-528.

Huertas, A., Gil, M., García, F. J., & Martínez, G. (2017). Preserving patients' privacy in health scenarios through a multicontext-aware system. *Annales des Télécommunications*, 72(9-10), 577–587. doi:10.100712243-017-0582-7

Hussain, F., Hussain, R., Hassan, S. A., & Hossain, E. (2019). Machine Learning in IoT Security: Current Solutions and Future Challenges. *Cornell University – Cryptography and Security.*

Hwang, K., Dave, P., & Tanachaiwiwat, S. (2003). NetShield: Protocol Anomaly Detection with Datamining Against DDoS Attacks. *Proc. 6th Int. Symp. Recent Advances in Intrusion Detection*, pp. 8–10. Pittsburgh, PA, September 8–10, Springer.

Hwang, K., & Li, D. (2010). Trusted Cloud computing with secure resources and data coloring. *IEEE Internet Computing*, 14(5), 14–22. doi:10.1109/MIC.2010.86

Idziorek, J., Tannian, M., & Jacobson, D. (2012, June). Attribution of fraudulent resource consumption in the Cloud. In *Proceedings 2012 IEEE 5th International Conference on Cloud Computing (CLOUD)*, (pp. 99-106). IEEE. 10.1109/CLOUD.2012.23

Institute of Medicine. (2009). *Beyond the HIPAA Privacy Rule: Enhancing Privacy, Improving Health Through Research.* Washington, DC: The National Academies Press.

ISA (2007). ANSI/ISA–99.00.01–2007 Security for Industrial Automation and Control Systems Part 1: Terminology, Concepts, and Models, *International Society of Automation (ISA),* October 2007.

Jain, A. K., & Gupta, B. B. (2017). Phishing detection: Analysis of visual similarity-based approaches. *Security and Communication Networks.*

Jain, S., Lang, J., Gong, N. Z., Song, D., Basuroy, S., & Mittal, P. (2015). New directions in social authentication. *Proc. USEC.*

Jalili, R., Imani-Mehr, F., Amini, M., & Shahriari, H. R. (2005). Detection of Distributed Denial of Service Attacks Using Statistical Pre-Processor and Unsupervised Neural Networks. *Proc. Int. Conf. Information Security Practice and Experience*, pp. 192–203. Singapore, April 11–14, Springer.

Javed, A., Bletgen, D., Kohlar, F., Durmuth, M., & Schwenk, J. (2014, June). Secure fallback authentication and the trusted friend attack. In *Proceedings 2014 IEEE 34th International Conference on Distributed Computing Systems Workshops (ICDCSW)* (pp. 22-28). IEEE. 10.1109/ICDCSW.2014.30

Jeswani, D., Natu, M., & Ghosh, R. K. (2012). Adaptive Monitoring: A Framework to AdaptPassive Monitoring using Probing, In *Proceedings of 8th International Conference on Network and Service Management (CNSM 2012)*, Las Vegas, NV. Academic Press.

Jiang, F., Fu, Y., Gupta, B. B., Lou, F., Rho, S., Meng, F., & Tian, Z. (2018). Deep Learning based Multi-channel intelligent attack detection for Data Security, 2377-3782 (c) 2018 *IEEE transactions.*

Jiang, F., Fu, Y., Gupta, B. B., Lou, F., Rho, S., Meng, F., & Tian, Z. (2018). *Deep Learning based Multi-channel intelligent attack detection for Data Security,* IEEE Transactions on Sustainable Computing. DOI:. doi:10.1109/TSUSC.2018.2793284

Jiang, F., Fu, Y., Gupta, B. B., Lou, F., Rho, S., Meng, F., & Tian, Z. (2018). Deep learning based multi-channel intelligent attack detection for data security. *IEEE transactions on sustainable computing*, 1-1.

Jiang, F., Fu, Y., Gupta, B. B., Lou, F., Rho, S., Meng, F., & Tian, Z. (2018). Deep learning based multi-channel intelligent attack detection for data security. *IEEE transactions on Sustainable Computing*.

Jiang, F., Fu, Y., Gupta, B. B., Lou, F., Rho, S., Meng, F., & Tian, Z. (2018). Deep learning based multi-channel intelligent attack detection for data security. *IEEE Transactions on Sustainable Computing*.

Jiang, L., Tan, R., Lou, X., & Lin, G. (2019, April). On Lightweight Privacy-Preserving Collaborative Learning for Internet-of-Things Objects. In *Proceedings of the 19th International Conference on Internet of Things Design and Implementation*. (pp. 70-81). ACM. 10.1145/3302505.3310070

Jiao, L., Li, J., Xu, T., Du, W., & Fu, X. (2016). Optimizing Cost For Online Social Networks On Geo-Distributed Clouds. *IEEE/ACM Transactions on Networking*, *24*(1), 99–112. doi:10.1109/TNET.2014.2359365

John, A., & Sivakumar, T. (2009). Ddos: Survey of traceback methods. *International Journal of Recent Trends in Engineering*, *1*(2), 241.

Johnsen, S., Skramstad, T., & Hagen, J. (2009, March). Enhancing the safety, security and resilience of ICT and SCADA systems using action research. In *Proceedings International Conference on Critical Infrastructure Protection* (pp. 113-123). Berlin, Germany: Springer. 10.1007/978-3-642-04798-5_8

Johnson, R., Hoeller, J., Arendsen, A., Risberg, T., & Kopylenko, D. (2005). *Professional java development with the spring framework*.: John Wiley & Sons.

Jorquera, J. M., Sánchez, P. M., Fernández, L., Huertas, A., Arjona, M., De Los Santos, S., & Martínez, G. (2018). Improving the Security and QoE in Mobile Devices through an Intelligent and Adaptive Continuous Authentication System. *Sensors (Basel)*, *18*(11), 3769. doi:10.339018113769 PMID:30400377

Joshi, R. C., & Gupta, B. B. (2019). *Security, Privacy, and Forensics Issues in Big Data* (p. 452). Hershey, PA: IGI Global.

Jun, K., & Kang, S. (2004). Adaptive and Distributed Fault Monitoring of Grid by Mobile Agents, In *Third International Conference on Grid and Cooperative Computing(GCC 2004)*. (pp. 975-978). China: Springer-Verlag Heidelberg.

Jutte, D. P., Roos, L. L., & Brownell, M. D. (2011). Administrative record linkage as a tool for public health research. *Annual Review of Public Health*, *32*(1), 91–108. doi:10.1146/annurev-publhealth-031210-100700 PMID:21219160

K. Chahal, J., & Kaur, A. (2016). A Hybrid Approach based on Classification and Clustering for Intrusion Detection System. *International Journal of Mathematical Sciences and Computing*. doi:10.5815/ijmsc.2016.04.04

Kalkan, K., & Alagöz, F. (2016). A distributed filtering mechanism against DDoS attacks: ScoreForCore. *Computer Networks*, *108*, 199–209.

Kambourakis, G., Kolias, C., & Stavrou, A. (2017, October). The mirai botnet and the IoT zombie armies. In MILCOM 2017-2017 IEEE Military Communications Conference (MILCOM) (pp. 267-272). IEEE.

Kang, M. S., Gligor, V. D., & Sekar, V. (2016, February). SPIFFY: Inducing Cost-Detectability Tradeoffs for Persistent Link-Flooding Attacks. In NDSS.

Karimazad, R., & Faraahi, A. (2011). An Anomaly-Based Method for DDoS Attacks Detection Using RBF Neural Networks. *Proc. Int. Conf. Network and Electronics Engineering*, Singapore, pp. 44–48. IACSIT Press.

Kasinathan, P., & Spirito, V. (2013). Denial-of-Service Detection in 6LoWPAN-based Internet of Things. In *Proceedings of the International Conference on Wireless and Mobile Computing, Networking and Communications*. Academic Press.

Kasinathan, P., Costamagna, G., Khaleel, H., Pastrone, C., & Spirito, M. A. (2013, November). DEMO: An IDS Framework for Internet of Things Empowered by 6lowpan. In *Proceedings of the 2013 ACM SIGSAC Conference on Computer & Communications Security*. 1337 – 1340. 10.1145/2508859.2512494

Kasper, T., Oswald, D., & Paar, C. (2009, August). EM side-channel attacks on commercial contactless smartcards using low-cost equipment. In *Proceedings International Workshop on Information Security Applications* (pp. 79-93). Berlin, Germany: Springer. 10.1007/978-3-642-10838-9_7

Kaspersky Security Intelligence, The evolution of ransomware. Technical report, 07 2016.

Kaufman, L. M. (2009). Data security in the world of Cloud computing. *IEEE Security and Privacy*, 7(4), 61–64. doi:10.1109/MSP.2009.87

Kauser, S., Rahman, A., Khan, A. M., & Ahmad, T. (2019). Attribute-based access control in web applications. In Advances in Intelligent Systems and Computing. doi:10.1007/978-981-13-1819-1_36

Kaushik, S., & Gandhi, C. (2019). Ensure Hierarchal Identity Based Data Security in Cloud Environment. [IJCAC]. *International Journal of Cloud Applications and Computing*, 9(4), 21–36. doi:10.4018/IJCAC.2019100102

Kayem, A. V., & Meinel, C. (2017). Clustering Heuristics for Efficient t-closeness Anonymisation. In *Proceedings International Conference on Database and Expert Systems Applications.*pp. 27-34. Cham, Switzerland: Springer. 10.1007/978-3-319-64471-4_3

Kazanjian, R. K., Drazin, R., & Glynn, M. A. (2017). Implementing strategies for corporate entrepreneurship: a knowledge-based perspective. Strategic entrepreneurship: Creating a new mindset, 173-199.

Keane, J. K. (2019). Kojoney2 SSH medium-interaction honeypot. Retrieved October 5, 2019, from https://github.com/madirish/kojoney2

Keller, M., Blench, M., Tolentino, H., Freifeld, C. C., Mandl, K. D., Mawudeku, A., ... Brownstein, J. S. (2009). Use of unstructured event-based reports for global infectious disease surveillance. *Emerging Infectious Diseases*, 15(5), 689–695. doi:10.3201/eid1505.081114 PMID:19402953

Kenda, K., & Mladenic, D. (2018). Autonomous Sensor Data Cleaning in Stream Mining Setting. *Business Systems Research*, 9(2), 69–79. doi:10.2478/bsrj-2018-0020

Kenkre, P. S., Pai, A., & Colaco, L. (2015). Real time intrusion detection and prevention system. In *Proceedings of the 3rd International Conference on Frontiers of Intelligent Computing: Theory and Applications (FICTA) 2014* (pp. 405-411). Springer, Cham. 10.1007/978-3-319-11933-5_44

Kent, S., & Atkinson, R. (1998). RFC 2402: IP authentication header.

Kessler, G. (2014). An Overview of Cryptography.

Khan, A., Choromanski, K., Pothen, A., Ferdous, S. M., & Halappanavar, T. A. (2018). Adaptive Anonymization of Data using b-Edge Cover. In *Proceedings SC18: International Conference for High Performance Computing, Networking, Storage and Analysis*, Dallas, TX. IEEE. doi: 10.1109/SC.2018.00062

Khan, N., & Gorde, K. S. (2015). Data security by video steganography and cryptography techniques.

Khan, H. (2019). *Recent Advancements in Intrusion Detection Systems for the Internet of Things*. Hindawi Security and Communication Networks. doi:10.1155/2019/4301409

Kheirkhah, E., Mehdi, S., Jahanshahi, H. A., & Acharya, H. (2013). An experimental study of SSH attacks by using honeypot decoys. *Indian Journal of Science and Technology*, 6(12), 5567–5578.

Kim, M. S., Kong, H. J., Hong, S. C., Chung, S. H., & Hong, J. W. (2004, April). A flow-based method for abnormal network traffic detection. In *Proceedings 2004 IEEE/IFIP network operations and management symposium* (Vol. 1, pp. 599-612). IEEE.

Kim, W. (2017, November). Security Validation for Data Diode with Reverse Channel. In Critical Information Infrastructures Security: 11th International Conference, CRITIS 2016, Paris, France, October 10–12, 2016, Revised Selected Papers (Vol. 10242, p. 271). Springer.

Kim, Y., Lau, W. C., Chuah, M. C., & Chao, H. J. (2004, March). PacketScore: Statistics-based overload control against distributed denial-of-service attacks. In Proceedings IEEE INFOCOM 2004 (Vol. 4, pp. 2594-2604). IEEE.

Kim, C. H. (2012). Improved Differential Fault Analysis on AES Key Schedule. *IEEE Transactions on Information Forensics and Security*, 7(1), 41–50. doi:10.1109/TIFS.2011.2161289

King, B. B., & Morda, D. (2001). *CERT Coordination Center, CERT Advisory CA-2001-20 Continuing Threats to Home Users. Technical Report CA-2001-20*. Pittsburgh, PA: Carnegie Mellon Software Engineering Institute; Retrieved from https://seclists.org/cert/2001/14

Kiruthiga, S., & Kannan, A. (2014, April). Detecting cloning attack in Social Networks using classification and clustering techniques. In *Proceedings of the 2014 International Conference on Recent Trends in Information Technology (ICRTIT)*, (pp. 1-6). IEEE. 10.1109/ICRTIT.2014.6996166

Klosek, J. (2011). *Protecting your health privacy: A citizen's guide to safeguarding the security of your medical information*. Santa Barbara, CA: Praeger.

Ko, H., & Caytiles, R. D. (2011). A review of smartcard security issues. 보안공학연구논문지, 8(3), 359-370.

Koll, D., Schwarzmaier, M., Li, J., Li, X. Y., & Fu, X. (2017). Thank You for Being A Friend: An Attacker View on Online-Social-Network-Based Sybil Defenses, *Proc. - IEEE 37th Int. Conf. Distrib. Comput. Syst. Work. ICDCSW 2017*, no. i, pp. 157–162. 10.1109/ICDCSW.2017.67

Koontz, L. (2017). What is Privacy? In Information Privacy in the Evolving Healthcare Environment (Second Edition). Boca Raton, FL: CRC Press.

Kottler, S. (2018). "February 28th DDoS Incident Report" an official report by Github. Link available at https://github.blog/2018-03-01-ddos-incident-report/

Kumar, B. S., Ch, T., Raju, R. S. P., Ratnakar, M., Baba, S. D., & Sudhakar, N. (2013). Intrusion Detection System- Types and Prevention. *International Journal of Computer Science and Information Technologies*, 4(1), 77–82.

Kumar, M. G. V., & Ragupathy, U. S. (2016). A Survey on Current Key Issues and Status in Cryptography, *IEEE WiSPNET 2016 conference*.

Kumar, G. R., Mangathayaru, N., & Narsimha, G. (2016). An approach for intrusion detection using novel gaussian based kernel function. *Journal of Universal Computer Science*.

Kumar, Z., Wang, K., & Kumar, J. (2019). A Multimodal Malware Detection Technique for Android IoT Devices Using Various Features. *IEEE Access: Practical Innovations, Open Solutions*, 7, 64411–64430. doi:10.1109/ACCESS.2019.2916886

Laboratory, L. (1998). Darpa intrusion detection data sets (1998). Retrieved from http://Www.Ll.Mit.Edu/Mission/Communications/Ist/Corpora/Ideval/Data/Index.Html

Lancini, M. (2013, April). Social authentication: Vulnerabilities, mitigations, and redesign. In *Proc. DeepSec Conf.* (pp. 476-492).

Lane, D. C. (2000). You Just Don't Understand Me. Working Paper, London School of Economics, Operational Research Group.

Laney, D. (2001) 3D data management: Controlling data volume, velocity and variety. *META Group Research Note,* 1-6.

Langner, R. (2011). Stuxnet: Dissecting a cyberwarfare weapon. *IEEE Security and Privacy, 9*(3), 49–51. doi:10.1109/MSP.2011.67

Lau, F., Rubin, S. H., Smith, M. H., & Trajkovic, L. (2000). Distributed denial of service attacks. In IEEE International Conference on Systems, Man, and Cybernetics, 2000, vol. 3. pp. 2275–2280. Nashville, TN.

Law on Ratification of the Convention for the Protection of Human Rights and Fundamental Freedoms and the Additional Protocol. (1950), (ECHR), adopted by law [6366, 10 March 1954] OJ 8662, 19 March 1954. Retrieved from http://www.coe.int/en/web/conventions/search-on-treaties/-/conventions/chartSignature/3

Law on The Turkish Medical Association of 1953. Retrieved from http://www.mevzuat.gov.tr/MevzuatMetin/1.3.6023.pdf (Turkish).

Lee, B., Amaresh, S., Green, C., & Engels, D. (2018). Comparative study of deep learning models for network intrusion detection. *SMU Data Science Review, 1*(1).

Lee, S.-W., & Seo, D. I. (2015). Authentication method and apparatus for detecting and preventing source address spoofing packets. U.S. Patent No. 8,966,609. Feb. 24, 2015.

Lee, K., Kim, J., Kwon, K. H., Han, Y., & Kim, S. (2008). DDoS attack detection method using cluster analysis. *Expert Systems with Applications, 34,* 1659–1665.

Lee, R. M., Assante, M. J., & Conway, T. (2014). German steel mill cyber attack. *Industrial Control Systems, 30,* 62.

Lewis, S. (2011). How has health services research made a difference? *Healthcare Policy, 6*(Special Issue), 74–79. PMID:24933375

Li, N., Li, T., & Venkatasubramanian, S. (2007). t-closeness: Privacy beyond k-anonymity and l-diversity. In *Proceedings IEEE 23rd International Conference on Data Engineering, ICDE,* 106-115. doi: 10.1109/ICDE.2007.367856

Li, W. (2004). Using genetic algorithm for network intrusion detection. In *Proceedings of the United States Department of Energy Cyber Security Group 2004 Training Conference,* Kansas City, KS. Academic Press.

Li, C., Zhang, Z., & Zhang, L. (2018). A Novel Authorization Scheme for Multimedia Social Networks Under Cloud Storage Method by Using MA-CP-ABE. [IJCAC]. *International Journal of Cloud Applications and Computing, 8*(3), 32–47. doi:10.4018/IJCAC.2018070103

Lichodzijewski, P., Nur Zincir-Heywood, A., & Heywood, M. I. (2003). Host-based intrusion detection using self-organizing maps. doi:10.1109/ijcnn.2002.1007776

Li, F., Clarke, N., Papadaki, M., & Dowland, P. (2011). Behaviour Profiling for Transparent Authentication for Mobile Devices. In *Proceedings 10th European Conference on Information Warfare and Security, ECIW. (p. 307). Academic Conferences International Limited.*

Li, H., Markettos, A. T., & Moore, S. (2005, October). A security evaluation methodology for smart cards against electromagnetic analysis. In *Proceedings 39th Annual 2005 International Carnahan Conference on Security Technology* (pp. 208-211). IEEE.

Li, J., Lin, X., Zhang, Y., & Han, J. (2016). KSF-OABE: Outsourced attribute-based encryption with keyword search function for cloud storage. *IEEE Transactions on Services Computing, 10*(5), 715–725. doi:10.1109/TSC.2016.2542813

Li, L., Liu, Y. A., Liu, K. M., & Ming, Y. A. N. G. (2009). Pricing in combinatorial double auction-based grid allocation model. *Journal of China Universities of Posts and Telecommunications*, *16*(3), 59–65.

Li, L., Gu, T., Chang, L., Xu, Z., Liu, Y., & Qian, J. (2017). A ciphertext-policy attribute-based encryption based on an ordered binary decision diagram. *IEEE Access: Practical Innovations, Open Solutions*, *5*, 1137–1145. doi:10.1109/ACCESS.2017.2651904

Limwiwatkul, L., & Rungsawang, A. (2004) Distributed Denial of Service Detection Using TCP/IP Header and Traffic Measurement Analysis. In *Proc. IEEE Int. Symp. Communications and Information Technology*, pp. 605–610. Sapporo, Japan, October 26–29. IEEE CS.

Ling, L., Xu, G., & Wu, F. (2017). *Security Vulnerabilities of Internet of Things: A Case Study of the Smart Plug System.* IEEE Internet of Things Journal.

LinkedIn. accessed 2017. [Online]. Available: http://www.linkedin.com

Lippmann, R. P., & Cunningham, R. K. (2000). Improving intrusion detection performance using keyword selection and neural networks. *Computer Networks*, *34*(4), 597–603. doi:10.1016/S1389-1286(00)00140-7

Litchfield, S., Formby, D., Rogers, J., Meliopoulos, S., & Beyah, R. (2016, September-October). Rethinking the Honeypot for Cyber-Physical Systems. *IEEE Internet Computing*, *20*(5), 9–17. doi:10.1109/MIC.2016.103

Liu X, Liu K, Guo L, Li X, Fang Y. (2013). A game-theoretic approach for achieving k-anonymity in location-based services. In *Proceedings 2013 INFOCOM IEEE*, 2985-2993. doi:10.1109/INFCOM.2013.6567110

Liu, Z., Jin, H., Hu, Y. C., & Bailey, M. (2017). Fine-Grained Endpoint-Driven In-Network Traffic Control for Proactive DDoS Attack Mitigation. *arXiv preprint arXiv:1709.05710.*

Liu, X., Yang, X., & Lu, Y. (2008, August). To filter or to authorize: Network-layer DoS defense against multimillion-node botnets. ACM. *Computer Communication Review*, *38*(4), 195–206.

Li, X., Wang, E., Yang, W., & Ma, J. (2016). DALP: A demand-aware location privacy protection scheme in continuous location-based services. *Concurrency and Computation*, *28*(4), 1219–1236. doi:10.1002/cpe.3613

LOIC. Sourceforge.net. (2019). Retrieved from http://sourceforge.net/projects/loic/

Lu, W., Hu, X., Li, X., & Wei, Y. (2016). A new method of QoS prediction based on probabilistic latent feature analysis and cloud similarity. *International Journal of High Performance Computing and Networking, 9*(1-2), 52-60.

Lunt, C. (2012). U.S. Patent No. 8,302,164. Washington, DC: U.S. Patent and Trademark Office.

Luo, J. Z., Jin, J. H., Song, A. B., & Dong, F. (2011). Cloud computing: Architecture and key technologies. *Journal of Communication*, *7*(7), 3–21.

M'Raïhi, D., & Yung, M. (2001). E-commerce applications of smart cards. *Computer Networks*, *36*(4), 453–472. doi:10.1016/S1389-1286(01)00166-9

Machanavajjhala, A., Gehrke, J., Kifer, D., & Venkitasubramaniam, M. (2006). l-diversity: Privacy beyond k-anonymity. In *Proceedings 22nd International Conference on Data Engineering, ICDE*, 24-24. doi: 10.1145/1217299.1217300

Maeda, W., Suzuki, Y., & Nakamura, S. (2016). Fast text anonymization using k-anonyminity. *Proceedings of the 18th International Conference on Information Integration and Web-based Applications and Services, ACM*, 340-344. doi: 10.1145/3011141.3011217

Mahajan, R., Bellovin, S. M., Floyd, S., Ioannidis, J., Paxson, V., & Shenker, S. (2002). Controlling high bandwidth aggregates in the network. *Computer Communication Review, 32*(3), 62–73.

Mahan, R. E., Fluckiger, J. D., Clements, S. L., Tews, C. W., Burnette, J. R., Goranson, C. A., & Kirkham, H. (2011). *Secure data transfer guidance for industrial control and SCADA systems (No. PNNL-20776). Pacific Northwest National Lab.* Richland, WA: PNNL. doi:10.2172/1030885

Mahanta, H. J., Azad, A. K., & Khan, A. K. (2015, January). Power analysis attack: A vulnerability to smart card security. In *2015 International Conference on Signal Processing and Communication Engineering Systems* (pp. 506-510). IEEE. 10.1109/SPACES.2015.7058206

Mahdavinejad, R., Barekatain, A., & Barnaghi, S. (2018). *Machine learning for internet of things data analysis: a survey.* Digital Communications and Networks. doi:10.1016/j.dcan.2017.10.002

Mamta, G., & Gupta, B. B. (2019a). An efficient KP design framework of attribute-based searchable encryption for user level revocation in cloud. *Concurrency and Computation,* e5291. doi:10.1002/cpe.5291

Mananet, Reverse Firewall, Retrieved from http://www.cs3–inc.com/pubs/Reverse FireWall.eps.

Mandal, A. K., Parakash, C., & Tiwari, A. (2012). Performance evaluation of cryptographicalgorithms: DES and AES, *in IEEE Students Conference on Electrical, Electronics, and Computer Science,* pp. 1–5.

Mandal, P. C. (2012). Evaluation of performance of the Symmetric Key Algorithms: DES, 3DES, AES and Blowfish. *Journal of Global Research in Computer Science Department of Computer Application, 3,* 67–70.

Manjunath, K., Chiplunkar, N. N., & Nagesh, H. R. (2016). Framework of Security Mechanisms for Monitoring AdaptiveDistributed Systems, *IOSR Journal of Computer Engineering (IOSR-JCE)e-, 18*(4), Ver. I, pp. 25-36.

Mankins, D., Krishnan, R., Boyd, C., Zao, J., & Frentz, M. (2001, December). Mitigating distributed denial of service attacks with dynamic resource pricing. In *Proceedings Seventeenth Annual Computer Security Applications Conference* (pp. 411-421). IEEE.

Manna, A., & Al-kasassbeh, M. (2019). Detecting network anomalies using machine learning and SNMP-MIB dataset with IP group. *The 2nd International Conference on New Trends in Computing Sciences.* Academic Press.

Mansouri, Y. (2017). *Brokering algorithms for data replication and migration across cloud-based data stores.* Melbourne: The University Of Melbourne.

Mansouri, Y., Nadjaran Toosi, A., & Buyya, R. (2017). Cost optimization for dynamic replication and migration of data in cloud data centers. *IEEE Transactions On Cloud Computing,* 705-718.

Mansouri, Y., Nadjaran Toosi, A., & Buyya, R. (2017). Data storage management in cloud environments: taxonomy, survey, and future directions. *Acm computing survey (ACM CSUR),* 50.

Marchessault, G. (2011). The Manitoba Centre for Health Policy: A case study. *Health Policy (Amsterdam), 6*(Special Issue), 29–43. PMID:24933371

Markantonakis, K., Mayes, K., Sauveron, D., & Askoxylakis, I. G. (2008, October). Overview of security threats for smart cards in the public transport industry. In *IEEE International Conference on e-Business Engineering, 2008. ICEBE'08.* (pp. 506-513). IEEE. 10.1109/ICEBE.2008.91

Marohn, D. (2006). Biometrics in healthcare. *Biometric Technology Today, 14*(9), 9–11. doi:10.1016/S0969-4765(06)70592-6

Marston, S., Li, Z., Bandyopadhyay, S., Zhang, J., & Ghalsasi, A. (2011). Cloud computing—The business perspective. *Decision Support Systems*, *51*(1), 176–189. doi:10.1016/j.dss.2010.12.006

Maske, S. A., & Parvat, T. J. (2016, August). Advanced anomaly intrusion detection technique for host based system using system call patterns. In *Proceedings 2016 International Conference on Inventive Computation Technologies (ICICT)* (Vol. 2, pp. 1-4). IEEE. 10.1109/INVENTIVE.2016.7824846

Mason, J. (2018, Jan. 10). Cyber Security trends and challenges, Retrieved from https://www.globalsign.com/en-in/blog/cybersecurity-trends-and-challenges-2018/

Massie, M. L., Chun, B. N., & Culler, D. E. (2004). *The ganglia distributed monitoring system: design, implementation, and experience, Parallel Computing* (pp. 817–840). Elsevier; doi:10.1016/j.parco.2004.04.001

Mateen, M., Iqbal, M. A., Aleem, M., & Islam, M. A. (2017, January). A hybrid approach for spam detection for Twitter. In *Proceedings 2017 14th International Bhurban Conference on Applied Sciences and Technology (IBCAST)*, (pp. 466-471). IEEE. 10.1109/IBCAST.2017.7868095

Mathur, M., & Kesarwani, A. (2013). Comparison Between Des, 3DES, RC2, RC6, Blowfish And AES, *Proceedings of National Conference on New Horizons in IT – NCNHIT*.

McInnes, L., Healy, J., & Melville, J. (2018). UMAP: Uniform manifold approximation and projection for dimension reduction. *The Journal of Open Source Software*, *3*(29), 861. doi:10.21105/joss.00861

McLaughlin, S., Konstantinou, C., Wang, X., Davi, L., Sadeghi, A.-R., Maniatakos, M., & Karri, R. (2016). The Cybersecurity Landscape in Industrial Control Systems. *Proceedings of the IEEE*, *104*(5), 1039–1057. doi:10.1109/JPROC.2015.2512235

Medical Statute of Deontology of 1960. Retrieved from http://www.mevzuat.gov.tr/MevzuatMetin/2.3.412578.pdf (Turkish).

Mehmood, T., & Rais, H. B. M. (2016). Machine learning algorithms in context of intrusion detection. In *2016 3rd International Conference on Computer and Information Sciences, ICCOINS 2016 - Proceedings*. 10.1109/ICCOINS.2016.7783243

Melese, S. Z., & Avadhani, P. S. (2016). Honeypot system for attacks on SSH protocol. *International Journal of Computer Network and Information Security*, *8*(9), 19. doi:10.5815/ijcnis.2016.09.03

Mell, P., & Grance, T. (2011). The NIST definition of Cloud computing.

Memos, V. A., Psannis, K. E., Ishibashi, Y., Kim, B. G., & Gupta, B. B. (2018). An Efficient Algorithm for Media-based Surveillance System (EAMSuS) in IoT Smart City Framework. *Future Generation Computer Systems*, *83*, 619–628. doi:10.1016/j.future.2017.04.039

Menezes, A. J., van Oorschot, P. C., & Vanstone, S. A. (2016). A Handbook of Applied cryptography, Taylor and Francis Inc. Boca Raton, FL: CRC Press.

Meng, W., Tischhauser, E. W., Wang, Q., Wang, Y., & Han, J. (2018). When intrusion detection meets blockchain technology: A review. *IEEE Access: Practical Innovations, Open Solutions*, *6*, 10179–10188. doi:10.1109/ACCESS.2018.2799854

Messerges, T. S., Dabbish, E. A., & Sloan, R. H. (2002). Examining smart-card security under the threat of power analysis attacks. *IEEE Transactions on Computers*, *51*(5), 541–552. doi:10.1109/TC.2002.1004593

Michelin, R. A., Zorzo, A. F., Campos, M. B., Neu, C. V., & Orozco, A. M. (2016, December). Smartphone as a biometric service for web authentication. In *Proceedings 2016 11th International Conference for Internet Technology and Secured Transactions (ICITST)*, (pp. 405-408). IEEE. 10.1109/ICITST.2016.7856740

Miles, E., Ferguson, P., & Warner, J. (2019, March 5). Three Families in Three Days – Revisiting Prolific Crimeware To Improve Network Detection: Emotet. Retrieved January 1, 2020, from https://atr-blog.gigamon.com/2019/02/28/revisiting-prolific-crimeware-to-improve-network-detection-emotet/

Miller, C., & Valasek, C. (2015). Remote exploitation of an unaltered passenger vehicle. *Black Hat USA, 2015*, 91.

Ministry of Health Turkey, Department of Health Informatics. (2016). Ministry of Health Turkey, Department of Health Informatics. Retrieved from https://sbsgm.saglik.gov.tr (Turkish).

Min, V. (2015). Design and Evaluation of Feature Distributed Malware Attacks against the Internet of Things (IoT). In *Proceedings of the 20th International Conference on Engineering of Complex Computer Systems*. 10.1109/ICECCS.2015.19

Mirkoviac, J., Prier, G., & Reiher, P. (2002) Attacking DDoS at the Source. In *Proc. 10th IEEE Int. Conf. Network Protocols*, pp. 1092–1648. Paris, France, November 12–15, IEEE CS.

Mirkovic, J., Reiher, P., & Robinson, M. (2003, August). Forming alliance for DDoS defense. In *New Security Paradigms Workshop* (pp. 18-21).

Mishra, A., Gupta, B. B., & Joshi, R. C. (2011). A comparative study of distributed denial of service attacks, intrusion tolerance and mitigation techniques. In *Proceedings - 2011 European Intelligence and Security Informatics Conference, EISIC 2011*. 10.1109/EISIC.2011.15

Mishra, A., Gupta, B. B., & Joshi, R. C. (2011). A comparative study of distributed denial of service attacks, intrusion tolerance and mitigation techniques. In *Proceedings 2011 European Intelligence and Security Informatics Conference*. (pp. 286-289). IEEE.

Mislove, A., Viswanath, B., Gummadi, K. P., & Druschel, P. (2010). *You are who you know: inferring user profiles in online social networks* (pp. 251–260). Wsdm. doi:10.1145/1718487.1718519

Mitchell, R., & Chen, R. (2015). Behavior rule specification-based intrusion detection for safety critical medical cyber physical systems. *IEEE Transactions on Dependable and Secure Computing, 12*(1), 16–30. doi:10.1109/TDSC.2014.2312327

Mitnick, K. D., & Simon, W. L. (2011). *The art of deception: Controlling the human element of security*. John Wiley & Sons.

Mittal, H., Jain, M., & Banda, L. (2013). Monitoring Local Area Network using Remote Method Invocation. *International Journal of Computer Science and Mobile Computing, 2*(Issue. 5), 50–55.

Mizrak, A. T., Savage, S., & Marzullo, K. (2008). Detecting compromised routers via packet forwarding behavior. *IEEE Network, 22*(2), 34–39.

Mnasouri, Y., & Buyya, R. (2016). To Move Or Not To Move: Cost Optimization In A Dual Cloudbased Storage Architecture. *Journal of Network and Computer Applications, 75*, 223–235. doi:10.1016/j.jnca.2016.08.029

Modi, C., Patel, D., Borisaniya, B., Patel, A., & Rajarajan, M. (2013). A survey on security issues and solutions at different layers of Cloud computing. *The Journal of Supercomputing, 63*(2), 561–592. doi:10.100711227-012-0831-5

Modi, C., Patel, D., Borisaniya, B., Patel, H., Patel, A., & Rajarajan, M. (2013). A survey of intrusion detection techniques in Cloud. *Journal of Network and Computer Applications, 36*(1), 42–57. doi:10.1016/j.jnca.2012.05.003

Modiri, A., Dehghantanha, N., & Parizi, K. (2018). *Fuzzy Pattern Tree for Edge Malware Detection and Categorization in IoT*. Journal Of System Architecture.

Moore, A. (2005). Intangible property: Privacy, power, and information control. In M. Adam (Ed.), Information Ethics: Privacy, property, and power. Seattle, WA: University of Washington Press.

Motwani, R., & Nabar, S. U. (2008). Anonymizing unstructured data. *arXiv preprint arXiv:08* doi:10.5582.2008

Muralidhar, S., Lloyd, W., Roy, S., Hill, C., Lin, E., Liu, W., ... & Kumar, S. (2014). F4: Facebook's warm blob storage system. *Usenix symposium on operating systems design and implementation (OSDI 14)* (pp. 383–398). Broomfield: USENIX.

Nagasundaram, S., & Aissi, S. (2017). U.S. Patent No. 9,665,722. Washington, DC: U.S. Patent and Trademark Office.

Najari, L. (2014). Malware detection using data mining techniques. *International Journal of Intelligent Information Systems.*

Nandhini, M., & Das, B. B. (2016, March). An assessment and methodology for fraud detection in online social network. In *Proceedings Second International Conference on Science Technology Engineering and Management (ICONSTEM),* (pp. 104-108). IEEE. 10.1109/ICONSTEM.2016.7560932

Nedjah, N., Wyant, R. S., Mourelle, L. M., & Gupta, B. B. (2017). Efficient yet robust biometric iris matching on smart cards for data high security and privacy. *Future Generation Computer Systems, 76*, 18–32. doi:10.1016/j.future.2017.05.008

Nespoli, P., Zago, M., Huertas, A., Gil, M., Gómez, F., & García, F. J. (2018). A Dynamic Continuous Authentication Framework in IoT-Enabled Environments. In *IoTSMS'18: Proceedings of the 5th International Conference on Internet of Things: Systems, Management, and Security*, Valencia, Spain. 10.1109/IoTSMS.2018.8554389

Nespoli, P., Zago, M., Huertas, A., Gil, M., Gómez, F., & García, F. J. (2019). PALOT: Profiling and Authenticating Users Leveraging Internet of Things. *Sensors. Special Issue on Sensor Systems for Internet of Things, 19*(12), 2832.

Nguyen, M. H., Ho, D. N., Luu, D. H., Moldovyan, A. A., & Moldovyan, N. A. (2011, August). On functionality extension of the digital signature standards. In *Proceedings The 2011 International Conference on Advanced Technologies for Communications (ATC 2011)* (pp. 6-9). IEEE.

Nicholson, A., Janicke, H., & Cau, A. (2014). Position paper: Safety and security monitoring in ICS/SCADA systems, in *Proc. 2nd Int. Symp. ICS SCADA Cyber Security Res.,* pp. 61–66.

Nissenbaum, H. (2004). Privacy as Contextual Integrity. *Washington Law Review (Seattle, Wash.), 79*, 101–139.

Niu B, Li Q, Zhu X, Cao G, Li H. (2014). Achieving k-anonymity in privacy-aware location-based services. In *Proceedings 2014 INFOCO IEEE*, 754-762. doi:10.1109/INFOCOM.2014.6848002

Nubera eBusiness S. L. (2010). *Top 10 Network Cybersecurity tools for Enterprises*, Retrieved Sept 27, 2019 from https://www.coranet.com/top-10-network-cybersecurity-tools/

O'Keefe, C. M., Westcott, M., O'Sullivan, M., Ickowicz, A., & Churches, T. (2016). Anonymization for outputs of population health and health services research conducted via an online data center. *Journal of the American Medical Informatics Association, 24*(3), 544–549. doi:10.1093/jamia/ocw152 PMID:28011594

Obeidat, I., Hamadneh, N., Alkasassbeh, M., Almseidin, M., & AlZubi, M. (2019). Intensive Pre-Processing of KDD Cup 99 for Network Intrusion Classification Using Machine Learning Techniques. *International Journal of Interactive Mobile Technologies, 13*(1).

OConnor, T. J., Enck, W., & Reaves, B. (2019, May). Blinded and confused: uncovering systemic flaws in device telemetry for smart-home internet of things. In *Proceedings of the 12th Conference on Security and Privacy in Wireless and Mobile Networks* (pp. 140-150). ACM.

OECD. (2013). *Strengthening Health Information Infrastructure for Health Care Quality Governance: Good Practices, New Opportunities, and Data Privacy Protection Challenges. OECD Health Policy Studies.* Paris, France: OECD Publishing.

OECD. (2015). *Health Data Governance: Privacy, Monitoring, and Research, OECD Health Policy Studies*. Paris, France: OECD Publishing.

Ogiela, M. R. (2019). Cognitive Solutions for Security and Cryptography, Cognitive Systems Research, 55, 258-261.

Ogiela, M. R., & Ogiela, L. (2016). On using Cognitive Models in Cryptography. In *Proceedings IEEE AINA 2016 - The IEEE 30th International Conference on Advanced Information Networking and Applications*, pp. 1055-1058.

Ogiela, L. (2017). *Cognitive information systems in management sciences*. Elsevier, Academic Press.

Ojenan, T. (2017). Courts, privacy and data protection in Finland: Making privacy and data protection real with a little help from the courts. In M. Brkan, & E. Psychogiopoulou (Eds.), Courts, Privacy and Data Protection in the Digital Environment. Edward Elgar Publishing. doi:10.4337/9781784718718.00012

Olakanmi, O. O., & Dada, A. (2019). An Efficient Privacy-preserving Approach for Secure Verifiable Outsourced Computing on Untrusted Platforms. *International Journal of Cloud Applications and Computing, 9*(2), 79–98. doi:10.4018/IJCAC.2019040105

Omar, G. A., & Guirguis, S. K. (2018). A Survey on Cryptography Algorithms. *International Journal of Scientific and Research Publications, 8*(7).

Omar, S., Asri, Md., Jebur, H., & Benqdara, S. (2013). Machine Learning Techniques for Anomaly Detection: An Overview. *International Journal of Computers and Applications, 79*(2).

Oosterhof, M. (2019). Cowrie SSH honeypot (based on Kippo). Retrieved October 5, 2019, from https://github.com/cowrie/cowrie

Ouaguid, A., Abghour, N., & Ouzzif, M. (2018). A novel security framework for managing Android permissions using blockchain technology. [IJCAC]. *International Journal of Cloud Applications and Computing, 8*(1), 55–79. doi:10.4018/IJCAC.2018010103

Padayachee, K. (2014). Aspectising honeytokens to contain the insider threat. *IETF Information Security, 9*(4), 240–247. doi:10.1049/iet-ifs.2014.0063

Padilha, R. (2018). Proposta de Um Método Complementar de Compressão de Dados Por Meio da Metodologia de Eventos Discretos Aplicada. In *Um Baixo Nível de Abstração. Dissertação (Mestrado em Engenharia Elétrica)*. Campinas, SP, Brasil: Faculdade de Engenharia Elétrica e de Computação, Universidade Estadual de Campinas.

Panhuis, W. G., Paul, P., Emerson, C., Grefenstette, J., Wilder, R., Herbst, A. J., ... Burke, D. S. (2014). A Systematic Review of Barriers to Data Sharing in Public Health. *BMC Public Health, 14*(1), 144. doi:10.1186/1471-2458-14-1144 PMID:25377061

Pan, S., Morris, T., & Adhikari, U. (2015). Developing a Hybrid Intrusion Detection System Using Data Mining for Power Systems. *IEEE Transactions on Smart Grid, 6*(6), 3104–3113. doi:10.1109/TSG.2015.2409775

Papadopoulos, C., Lindell, R., Mehringer, J., Hussain, A., & Govindan, R. (2003, April). Cossack: Coordinated suppression of simultaneous attacks. In *Proceedings DARPA Information Survivability Conference and Exposition* (Vol. 1, pp. 2-13). IEEE.

Pappa, G. L., Freitas, A. A., & Kaestner, C. A. A. (2002). Attribute Selection with a Multi-objective Genetic Algorithm. doi:10.1007/3-540-36127-8_27

Park, K., & Lee, H. (2001, August). On the effectiveness of route-based packet filtering for distributed DoS attack prevention in power-law internets. ACM. *Computer Communication Review, 31*(4), 15–26.

Parno, B., Wendlandt, D., Shi, E., Perrig, A., Maggs, B., & Hu, Y. C. (2007, August). Portcullis: Protecting sconnection setup from denial-of-capability attacks. ACM. *Computer Communication Review, 37*(4), 289–300.

Parreño, M., Moorsel, A., & Castruccio, S. (2017). Smartphone Continuous Authentication Using Deep Learning Autoencoders. In *Proceedings 15th International Conference on Privacy, Security and Trust*, 147-1478. Academic Press.

Patel, V. M., Chellappa, R., Chandra, D., & Barbello, B. (2016). Continuous User Authentication on Mobile Devices: Recent Progress and Remaining Challenges. *IEEE Signal Processing Magazine, 33*(4), 49–61. doi:10.1109/MSP.2016.2555335

Patila, P., & Narayankarb, P., Narayan, D. G. C., & Meena, S. M. (2015). A Comprehensive Evaluation of Cryptographic Algorithms: DES, 3DES, AES, RSA and Blowfish, *International Conference on Information Security & Privacy (ICISP2015)*, December 11-12, 2015, Nagpur, India. Academic Press.

Pauna, A., & Bica, I. (2014). RASSH-Reinforced adaptive SSH honeypot. In *Proceedings 10th International Conference on Communications*, 1-6.

Pecorella, T., Brilli, L., & Mucchi, L. (2016). The role of physical layer security in IoT: A novel perspective. Information, 7(3), 49.

Peltier, T. R. (2016). *Information Security Policies, Procedures, and Standards: guidelines for effective information security management*. Auerbach Publications. doi:10.1201/9780849390326

Peng, J., Choo, K. K. R., & Ashman, H. (2016). User profiling in intrusion detection: A review. *Journal of Network and Computer Applications, 72*, 14–27. doi:10.1016/j.jnca.2016.06.012

Phinney, T. (2013). IEC 62443: Industrial network and system security.

Pillai, B., Mounika, M., Rao, P. J., & Sriram, P. (2016). Image steganography method using k-means clustering and encryption techniques. In *Proceedings 2016 International Conference on Advances in Computing, Communications, and Informatics (ICACCI)*. pp. 1206-1211. IEEE.

Ping of Death. (2019). Cloudflare blog. Available at https://www.cloudflare.com/learning/ddos/ping-of-death-ddos-attack/. Accessed on Jan 2019.

Plageras, P., & Stergiou, W. (2018). Efficient IoT-based Sensor BIG Data Collection-Processing and Analysis in Smart buildings. *Future Generation Computer Systems, 82*, 349–357. doi:10.1016/j.future.2017.09.082

Polakis, I., Ilia, P., Maggi, F., Lancini, M., Kontaxis, G., Zanero, S., ... Keromytis, A. D. (2014, November). Faces in the distorting mirror: Revisiting photo-based social authentication. In *Proceedings of the 2014 ACM SIGSAC Conference on Computer and Communications Security* (pp. 501-512). ACM. 10.1145/2660267.2660317

Pop, F., Arcalianu, A., Dobre, C., & Cristea, V. (2011). Enhanced Security for Monitoring Services in Large Scale Distributed Systems, *IEEE International Conference on Computer Communication and Processing (ICCP 2011)*, pp. 549-556. Cluj-Napoca, Romania, 10.1109/ICCP.2011.6047929

Post, R. (2001). Three concepts of privacy. *The Georgetown Law Journal, 89*(6), 2087–2089.

Praveena, A., & Smys, S. (2017, January). Prevention of inference attacks for private information in social networking sites. In *Proceedings 2017 International Conference on Inventive Systems and Control (ICISC)*, (pp. 1-7). IEEE. 10.1109/ICISC.2017.8068648

Premkamal, P. K., Pasupuleti, S. K., & Alphonse, P. J. A. (2020). Efficient Escrow-free CP-ABE with Constant Size Ciphertext and Secret Key for Big Data Storage in Cloud. [IJCAC]. *International Journal of Cloud Applications and Computing, 10*(1), 28–45. doi:10.4018/IJCAC.2020010103

Pritts, J. (2008). *The Importance and Value of Protecting the Privacy of Health Information: Roles of HIPAA Privacy Rule and the Common Rule in Health Research*. Washington, DC: Institute of Medicine.

Priyanka, S., & Singh, K. R. (2016). Cyber Attacks On Intrusion Detection System, *International Journal of Information Sciences and Techniques (IJIST), 6*(1/2).

Prokofiev, A. O., Smirnova, Y. S., & Surov, V. A. (2018, January). A method to detect Internet of Things botnets. In *Proceedings 2018 IEEE Conference of Russian Young Researchers in Electrical and Electronic Engineering (EIConRus)* (pp. 105-108). IEEE 10.1109/EIConRus.2018.8317041

Puri, R. (2003). Bots & botnet: An overview. *SANS Institute, 3,* 58.

Qiu, S., Liu, J., Shi, Y., & Zhang, R. (2017). Hidden policy ciphertext-policy attribute-based encryption with keyword search against keyword guessing attack. *Science China. Information Sciences, 60*(5), 052105. doi:10.100711432-015-5449-9

R. Lemos. (2017,Nov). Expect a New Battle in Cyber Security: AI versus AI. Symantec Publications.

Rahmani, H., Sahli, N., & Kammoun, F. (2009) Joint Entropy Analysis Model for DDoS Attack Detection. In *Proc. 5th Int. Conf. Information Assurance and Security*, Vol. 02, pp. 267–271. Xian, China, August 18–20. IEEE CS.

Rai, N. (2014). Genetic Algorithm Based Intrusion Detection System. *International Journal of Computer Science and Information Technologies, 5*(4), 4952-4957.

Ralston, P. A., Graham, J. H., & Hieb, J. L. (2007). Cyber security risk assessment for SCADA and DCS networks. *ISA Transactions, 46*(4), 583–594. doi:10.1016/j.isatra.2007.04.003 PMID:17624350

Rama Krishna, A., Chakravarthy, A. S. N., & Sastry, A. S. C. S. (2016). Variable Modulation Schemes for AWGN Channel based Device to Device Communication. *Indian Journal of Science and Technology, 9*(20), DOI: 10.17485 / ijst / 2016 / v9i20 / 89973.

Ramanathan, S., Mirkovic, J., Yu, M., & Zhang, Y. (2018, December). SENSS Against Volumetric DDoS Attacks. In *Proceedings of the 34th Annual Computer Security Applications Conference* (pp. 266-277). ACM.

Rams, T., & Pacyna, P. (2013). A Survey of Group Key Distribution Schemes With Self-Healing Property. *IEEE Communications Surveys and Tutorials, 15*(2), 820–842. doi:10.1109/SURV.2012.081712.00144

Rapid 7. (2019). Public data of the honeynet deployed by the company Rapid 7 in Heisenberg. Retrieved October 7, 2019, from https://opendata.rapid7.com/heisenberg.cowrie/

Rathore, M. M., Ahmad, A., & Paul, A. (2016). Real time intrusion detection system for ultra-high-speed big data environments. *The Journal of Supercomputing, 72*(9), 3489–3510. doi:10.100711227-015-1615-5

Raza, W., Wallgren, L., & Voigt, T. (2013). Svelte: Real – time Intrusion Detection in the Internet of Things. *Ad Hoc Networks, 11*(8), 2661–2674. doi:10.1016/j.adhoc.2013.04.014

Rehman, U. U., Khan, W. A., Saqib, N. A., & Kaleem, M. (2013, December). On detection and prevention of clickjacking attack for osns. In *Proceedings 2013 11th International Conference on Frontiers of Information Technology (FIT)*, (pp. 160-165). IEEE. 10.1109/FIT.2013.37

Republic of Turkey Prime Ministry Investment Support. Promotion Agency. (2017). *Legal Guide to Investing in Turkey*, CMS, p. 113. Retrieved from http://www.invest.gov.tr/en-US/infocenter/publications/Documents/Legal-Guide-to-Investing-in-Turkey.pdf

Rimal, B. P., Choi, E., & Lumb, I. (2009, August). A taxonomy and survey of cloud computing systems. In *2009 Fifth International Joint Conference on INC, IMS and IDC* (pp. 44-51). IEEE. 10.1109/NCM.2009.218

Riman, C., & Pierre, E. (2015). Comparative Analysis of Block Cipher-Based Encryption Algorithms: A Survey. Information Security and Computer Fraud, 3(1).

Riman, C., & Abi-Char, P. E. (2015). Comparative Analysis of Block Cipher-Based Encryption Algorithms: A Survey. *Information Security and Computer Fraud, 3*(1), 1–7.

Rivest, R. L. S., & Adleman, L. (1978). A Method for Obtaining Digital Signatures and Public Key Cryptosystems. Comm. ACM, 21, 120-26.

Rivest, R. L., & Robshaw, M. J. B. (1998). The Security of the RC6 Block Cipher. *Version 1.0* – August.

Rodrigo,, N., & CALHEIROS, R. R. (2011). CLOUDSIM: A toolkit for modeling and simulation of cloud computing environments and evaluation of resource provisioning algorithms. *Software, Practice, & Experience*, 23–50.

Rodríguez, P., Bautista, M. A., González, J., & Escalera, S. (2018). Beyond one-hotencoding: Lower dimensional target embedding, *Image and Vision Computing*, 75, 21-31.

Roos, L. L., Brownell, M., Lix, L., Roos, N. P., Walld, R., & MacWilliam, L. (2008). From health research to social research: Privacy, methods, approaches. *Social Science & Medicine, 66*(1), 117–129. doi:10.1016/j.socscimed.2007.08.017 PMID:17919795

Rosenberg, J., Coronel, J. B., Meiring, J., Gray, S., & Brown, T. (2019). Leveraging ElasticSearch to improve data discoverability in science gateways. In Practice and Experience in Advanced Research Computing on Rise of the Machines Learning, 19. doi:10.1145/3332186.3332230

Rossow, C. (2014). *Amplification Hell: Revisiting Network Protocols for DDoS Abuse*. NDSS.

Rothstein, M. A. (2007). Health Privacy in Electronic Age, *The Journal of Legal Medicine, Oct-Dec; 28*(4), 487–501.

Rubinstein, Y. D., Brill, J. A., Bejar, A., Frank, J. H., & Breger, D. (2017). U.S. Patent No. 9,626,725. Washington, DC: U.S. Patent and Trademark Office.

Sadasivam, G. K., Hota, C., & Anand, B. (2018). Honeynet data analysis and distributed SSH brute-force attacks. In Towards Extensible and Adaptable Methods in Computing, 107-118. doi:10.1007/978-981-13-2348-5_9

Sadasivam, G. K., Hota, C., & Anand, B. (2018). Detection of severe SSH attacks using honeypot servers and machine learning techniques. *Software Networking, 2017*(1), 79–100. doi:10.13052/jsn2445-9739.2017.005

Sahoo, S. R., & Gupta, B. B. (2018). Security Issues and Challenges in Online Social Networks (OSNs) Based on User Perspective. In Computer and Cyber Security (pp. 591-606). Auerbach Publications.

Sahoo, S. R., & Gupta, B. B. (2019). Classification of various attacks and their defence mechanism in online social networks: A survey. *Enterprise Information Systems, 13*(6), 832–864.

Sahoo, S. R., & Gupta, B. B. (2019). Hybrid approach for detection of malicious profiles in twitter. *Computers & Electrical Engineering, 76*, 65–81. doi:10.1016/j.compeleceng.2019.03.003

Saifullah, A. M. (2009). Defending Against Distributed Denial-of-Service Attacks with Weight-Fair Router Throttling. Technical Report 2009-7. Computer Science and Engineering, Washington University, St. Louis, MO.

Saini, B., & Somani, G. (2014, March). Index page based EDoS attacks in infrastructure cloud. In *International Conference on Security in Computer Networks and Distributed Systems* (pp. 382-395). Berlin, Germany: Springer.

Samimi, P., Teimouri, Y., & Mukhtar, M. (2016). A combinatorial double auction resource allocation model in cloud computing. *Information Sciences, 357*, 201–216.

Sánchez, P., Huertas, A., Fernández, L., Martínez, G., & Wang, G. (2019). Securing Smart Offices through an Intelligent and Multi-device Continuous Authentication System. In *Proceedings of the 7th International Conference on Smart City and Informatization*. Guangzhou, China: Springer Computer Science Proceedings.

Saracino, A., Sgandurra, D., Dini, G., & Martinelli, F. (2018). Madam: Effective and efficient behavior-based android malware detection and prevention. *IEEE Transactions on Dependable and Secure Computing, 15*(1), 83–97. doi:10.1109/TDSC.2016.2536605

Savage, S., Wetherall, D., Karlin, A., & Anderson, T. (2000, August). Practical network support for IP traceback. ACM. *Computer Communication Review, 30*(4), 295–306.

Saveetha, P., Arumugam, S., & Kiruthikadevi, K. (2014). Cryptography and the Optimization Heuristics Techniques, *International Journal of Advanced Research in Computer Science and Software Engineering, 4*(10), 408–413.

Schneier, B., & Shostack, A. (1999, May). Breaking up is hard to do: modeling security threats for smart cards. In *USENIX Workshop on Smart Card Technology, Chicago, IL,* Retrieved from Error! Hyperlink reference not valid.

Schuba, C. L., Krsul, I. V., Kuhn, M. G., Spafford, E. H., Sundaram, A., & Zamboni, D. (1997, May). Analysis of a denial of service attack on TCP. In *Proceedings, 1997 IEEE Symposium on Security and Privacy, 1997.* (pp. 208-223). IEEE. 10.1109/SECPRI.1997.601338

Schwiderski, S. (1996, April). *Monitoring the Behaviour of Distributed Systems* (Doctoral Thesis). Retrieved from https://www.microsoft.com/en-us/research/wp-content/uploads/2016/02/scarlets-scarletschwiderskiphd.pdf

scikit-learn developers. (2019). Scikit-learn: machine learning in Python. Retrieved October 1, 2019, from http://scikit-learn.org/stable/index.html

Scriptzteam. (2019). Public repository in GitHub. Retrieved October 8, 2019, from https://github.com/scriptzteam/REALTiME-SSH-HoneyPot_v1.1

Seo, D., Lee, H., & Perrig, A. (2011, October). PFS: Probabilistic filter scheduling against distributed denial-of-service attacks. In *Proceedings 2011 IEEE 36th Conference on Local Computer Networks* (pp. 9-17). IEEE.

Seo, D., Lee, H., & Perrig, A. (2013). APFS: Adaptive probabilistic filter scheduling against distributed denial-of-service attacks. *Computers & Security, 39*, 366–385.

Sethi, S., & Sarangi, S. R. (2017). Internet of Things – Architectures, Protocols and Applications. *Hindawi – Journal of Electrical and Computer Engineering, 2017*, 1–25. doi:10.1155/2017/9324035

Shafahi, M., Kempers, L., & Afsarmanesh, H. (2016, December). Phishing through social bots on Twitter. In *Proceedings 2016 IEEE International Conference on Big Data (Big Data)*, (pp. 3703-3712). IEEE. 10.1109/BigData.2016.7841038

Shaheen, Y. K., & Al-kasassbeh, M. (2019). A Proactive Design to Detect Denial of Service Attacks Using SNMP-MIB ICMP Variable. *The 2nd International Conference on New Trends in Computing Sciences*. Amman, Jordan.

Shahzad, F. (2014). State-of-the-art survey on cloud computing security Challenges, approaches and solutions. *Procedia Computer Science, 37*, 357–362. doi:10.1016/j.procs.2014.08.053

Shamsolmoali, P., & Zareapoor, M. (2014, September). Statistical-based filtering system against DDOS attacks in cloud computing. In *Proceedings 2014 International Conference on Advances in Computing, Communications and Informatics (ICACCI)* (pp. 1234-1239). IEEE.

Shankar Sriram, V. S., Dinesh, S., & Sahoo, G. (2010). Multiplication Based Elliptic Curve Encryption Scheme with Optimized Scalar Multiplication (MECES), International Journal of Computer Applications, 1(11), pp. 65–70.

Shankar, K., & Eswaran, P. (2015). ECC Based Image Encryption Scheme with aid of Optimization Technique using Differential Evolution Algorithm. *International Journal of Applied Engineering Research, 10*(5), 1841–1845.

Shankar, K., & Eswaran, P. (2016). *An Efficient Image Encryption Technique Based onOptimized Key Generation in ECC Using Genetic Algorithm, Artificial Intelligence and Evolutionary Computations in Engineering Systems* (pp. 705–714). India: Springer.

Shapiro, M., Johnston, D., Wald, J., & Mon, D. (2012). *Patient-Generated Health Data. White Paper* (Prepared for Office of Policy and Planning, Office of the National Coordinator for Health Information Technology), RTI International, Research Triangle Park, NC.

Sharafaldin, I., Lashkari, A. H., & Ghorbani, A. A. (2018). Toward generating a new intrusion detection dataset and intrusion traffic characterization. In *Proceedings 4th International Conference on Information Systems Security and Privacy*, 108-116. 10.5220/0006639801080116

Sharma, S. (2017). Activation functions: Neural networks. *Towards Data Science.*

Sharma, V. (2017). Cap. getting started with Kibana. *Beginning Elastic Stack, Apress*, 29-44.

Sharma, J., & Saxena, K. (2012). Cloud security challenges. *International Journal Computer Science and Information Technologies, 3*(3).

Sharma, K., & Gupta, B. B. (2018). Taxonomy of distributed denial of service (ddos) attacks and defense mechanisms in present era of smartphone devices. [IJESMA]. *International Journal of E-Services and Mobile Applications, 10*(2), 58–74.

Sharpe, R., Warnicke, E., & Lamping, U. (2015). Wireshark User's Guide, Retrieved from http://www.wireshark.org/docs/wsug_html_chunked/

Shenker, S., Clark, D., Estrin, D., & Herzog, S. (1996). Pricing in computer networks: Reshaping the research agenda. *J. Telecommunications Policy, 20*(3), 183–201.

Shi, W., Yang, J., Jiang, Y., Yang, F., & Xiong, Y. (2011). SenGuard: Passive user identification on smartphones using multiple sensors. In *Proceedings IEEE 7th International Conference on Wireless and Mobile Computing, Networking and Communications (WiMob)*, 141-148. IEEE.

Shi, L., & Song, L., Ye. (2019). Energy Audition based Cyber-Physical Attack Detection System in IoT. *Proceedings of the ACM Turing Celebration Conference.* 10.1145/3321408.3321588

Siddique, K., Akhtar, Z., Khan, F. A., & Kim, Y. (2019). KDD Cup 99 Data Sets: A Perspective on the Role of Data Sets in Network Intrusion Detection Research. *Computer, 52*(2), 41–51. doi:10.1109/MC.2018.2888764

Singh, G., Singla, A. K., & Sandha, K. S. (2012). Superiority of Blowfish Algorithm in Wireless Networks. *International Journal Computer Applications, 44*(11), pp. 23-26.

Singh, S., Iqbal, M. S., & Jaiswal, A. (2015). Survey on Techniques Developed using Digital Signature: Public key Cryptography, *International Journal of Computer Applications, 117*(16), pp. 0975 – 8887.

Singhal, N., & Raina, J. P. S. (2011). Comparative Analysis of AES and RC4 Algorithms for Better Utilization. *International Journal of Computer Trends and Technology*, 177–181.

Singla, B., & Bertino, E. (2019). How Deep Learning Is Making Information Security More Intelligent. *IEEE Security and Privacy, 17*(3), 56–65. doi:10.1109/MSEC.2019.2902347

Skottler. (2018). February 28 DDoS Incident Report, Github Report. Available at https://githubengineering.com/ddos-incident-report/

Snapp, S. R., Brentano, J., Dias, G., Goan, T. L., Heberlein, L. T., Ho, C. L., & Levitt, K. N. (2017). DIDS (distributed intrusion detection system)-motivation, architecture, and an early prototype.

SOC eSentire. (2017). Annual threat report. Retrieved October 5, 2019, from https://www.esentire.com/resource-library/2017-annual-threat-report

Sochor, T., & Zuzcak, M. (2014). Study of internet threats and attack methods using honeypots and honeynets. In *Proceedings International Conference on Computer Networks*, 118-127. 10.1007/978-3-319-07941-7_12

Social Insurance and Universal Health Insurance Law of 2006, (GHI). Retrieved from http://turkishlaborlaw.com/images/turkish-social-security-law/social-security-law-5510.pdf

Solove, D. J. (2006). A taxonomy of privacy. *University of Pennsylvania Law Review, 154*(3), 516–518. doi:10.2307/40041279

Sommestad, T., Ericsson, G. N., & Nordlander, J. (2010, July). SCADA system cyber security—A comparison of standards. In *Proceedings 2010 IEEE Power and Energy Society General Meeting,* (pp. 1-8). IEEE.

Somya, B. P., & Ahmad, T. (2016). Methods and techniques of intrusion detection: A review. In Communications in Computer and Information Science. doi:10.1007/978-981-10-3433-6_62

Soni, A., & Agrawal, S. (2013). Key Generation Using Genetic Algorithm for Image Encryption, *International Journal of Computer Science and Mobile Computing (IJCSMC), 2*(6), pp. 376– 383.

Sonja, M., Ioana, G., Miaoging, Y., & Anna, K. (2018). Understanding value in health data ecosystems: A review of current evidence and ways forward. *Rand Health Quarterly, 7*(2), 3. PMID:29416943

Souri, H. (2018). *A state-of-the-art survey of malware detection approaches using data mining techniques.* Human-Centric Computing and Information Sciences. doi:10.118613673-018-0125-x

Spitzner, L. (2003). *Honeypots: Tracking hackers* (p. 1). Reading: Addison-Wesley.

Sreelaja1, N. K., & Vijayalakshmi Pai, G. A. (2011). Swarm intelligence based key generation for stream cipher, *Security and Communication Networks, 4*(2), 181–194.

Srinivas, B. L., Shanbhag, A., & D'Souza, A. S. (2014). A Comparative Performance Analysis of DES and BLOWFISH Symmetric Algorithm. *IJIRCCE.*

Stein, G., Chen, B., Wu, A. S., & Hua, K. A. (2007). Decision tree classifier for network intrusion detection with GA-based feature selection. doi:10.1145/1167253.1167288

Stergiou, C., Psannis, K. E., Kim, B. G., & Gupta, B. (n.d.). Secure integration of IoT and cloud computing. *Future Generation Computer Systems.* 964 - 975.

Stergiou, C., Psannis, K. E., Gupta, B. B., & Ishibashi, Y. (2018). Security, privacy, & efficiency of sustainable cloud computing for big data & IoT. *Sustainable Computing: Informatics and Systems, 19,* 174–184.

Stergiou, C., Psannis, K. E., Kim, B. G., & Gupta, B. (2018). Secure integration of IoT and cloud computing. *Future Generation Computer Systems, 78,* 964–975. doi:10.1016/j.future.2016.11.031

Stevens, M. W., & Pope, M. (1999). *An implementation of an optical data diode.* DSTO.

Stolfo, S. J. (1999). KDD cup 1999 dataset. *UCI KDD Repository.* Retrieved from http://kdd.ics.uci.edu/

Stouffer, K., Falco, J., & Scarfone, K. (2011). Guide to industrial control systems (ICS) security. *NIST special publication, 800*(82), 16-16.

Stouffer, K., Zimmerman, T., Tang, C., Lubell, J., Cichonski, J., & McCarthy, J. (2017). *Cybersecurity framework manufacturing profile*. US Department of Commerce, National Institute of Standards and Technology. doi:10.6028/NIST.IR.8183

Su, J., Vasconcellos, V. D., Prasad, S., Daniele, S., Feng, Y., & Sakurai, K. (2018, July). Lightweight classification of IoT malware based on image recognition. In *Proceedings 2018 IEEE 42nd Annual Computer Software and Applications Conference (COMPSAC)* (Vol. 2, pp. 664-669). IEEE. 10.1109/COMPSAC.2018.10315

Subashini, S., & Kavitha, V. (2011). A survey on security issues in service delivery models of cloud computing. *Journal of Network and Computer Applications*, *34*(1), 1–11. doi:10.1016/j.jnca.2010.07.006

Subba, B., Biswas, S., & Karmakar, S. (2016, March). A neural network based system for intrusion detection and attack classification. In *Proceedings 2016 Twenty Second National Conference on Communication (NCC)* (pp. 1-6). IEEE. 10.1109/NCC.2016.7561088

Sugandhi, R., Pande, A., Chawla, S., Agrawal, A., & Bhagat, H. (2015, December). Methods for detection of cyberbullying: A survey. In *Proceedings 2015 15th International Conference on Intelligent Systems Design and Applications (ISDA),* (pp. 173-177). IEEE. 10.1109/ISDA.2015.7489220

Sun, A., Ji, T., & Wang, J. (2016). Cloud platform scheduling strategy based on virtual machine resource behaviour analysis. *International Journal of High Performance Computing and Networking*, *9*(1-2), 61-69.

Sun, W., Yu, S., Lou, W., Hou, Y. T., & Li, H. (2014, April). Protecting your right: Attribute-based keyword search with fine-grained owner-enforced search authorization in the cloud. In *Proceedings IEEE INFOCOM 2014-IEEE Conference on Computer Communications* (pp. 226-234). IEEE.

Sung, A., Abraham, A., & Mukkamala, S. (2005). *Cyber-Security Challenges: Designing Efficient Intrusion Detection Systems and Anti-Virus Tools*. Enhancing Computer Security with Smart Technology.

Sweeney, L. (2002). k-anonymity: A model for protecting privacy. *International Journal of Uncertainty, Fuzziness, and Knowledge-based Systems*, *10*(5), 557–570. doi:10.1142/S0218488502001648

Szegedy, C., *Toshev, A., & Erhan, D.* (2015). Deep Neural Networks for Object Detection.

Taherdoost, H., Sahibuddin, S., & Jalaliyoon, N. (2011). Smart card security; Technology and adoption. *International Journal of Security*, *5*(2), 74–84.

Takase, K., & Kato, O. (2019). A prototype implementation and evaluation of the malware detection mechanism for IoT devices using the processor information. *International Journal of Information Security*. doi:10.100710207-019-00437-y

Tang, C., & Hefferman, W. (2015). A Hierarchial Distributed Fog Computing Architecture for Big data Analysis in Smart Cities. In *Proceedings of the ASE BigData & Social Informatics. Academic Press.*

Tatar, M., Mollahaliloglu, S., Sahin, B., Aydın, S., Maresso, A., & Hernandez-Quevedo, C. (2011). Turkey: Health System Review. *Health Systems in Transition*, *13*(6), 21. Retrieved from http://www.euro.who.int/__data/assets/pdf_file/0006/158883/e96441.pdf PMID:22455830

Ten, C. W., Liu, C. C., & Manimaran, G. (2008). Vulnerability assessment of cybersecurity for SCADA systems. *IEEE Transactions on Power Systems*, *23*(4), 1836–1846. doi:10.1109/TPWRS.2008.2002298

Terry, N. P., & Francis, L. P. (2007). Ensuring the privacy and confidentiality of electronic health records. *University of Illinois Law Review*, *2*, 681–736.

Tesink, S. (2007). *Improving intrusion detection systems through machine learning*. In Proceedings of ILK Research Group Technical Report Series no. 07--02. Academic Press.

Tewari, A., & Gupta, B. B. (2017). A lightweight mutual authentication protocol based on elliptic curve cryptography for IoT devices. *International Journal of Advanced Intelligence Paradigms*, 9(2-3), 111–121.

Tewari, A., & Gupta, B. B. (2017). Cryptanalysis of a novel ultra-lightweight mutual authentication protocol for IoT devices using RFID tags. *The Journal of Supercomputing*, 73(3), 1085–1102. doi:10.100711227-016-1849-x

Tewari, A., & Gupta, B. B. (2018). A lightweight mutual authentication approach for RFID tags in IoT devices. *International Journal of Networking and Virtual Organisations*, 18(2), 97–111.

Thaseen, I. S., & Kumar, C. A. (2014). Intrusion detection model using fusion of PCA and optimized SVM. In *Proceedings of 2014 International Conference on Contemporary Computing and Informatics, IC3I 2014*. 10.1109/IC3I.2014.7019692

The Circular of Ministry of Health. (2015, February). Number: 2015/5. Retrieved from https://dosyaism.saglik.gov.tr/Eklenti/23257,enabizgenelge20155pdf.pdf?0 (Turkish).

The Circular of Ministry of Health. (2016, July 15). Number: 2016/10. Retrieved from https://dosyamerkez.saglik.gov.tr/Eklenti/4283,hasta-mahremiyetine-saygi-gosterilmesi-2016-10pdf.pdf?0 (Turkish).

The Constitution of the Republic of Turkey (Turkiye Cumhuriyeti Anayasası) [2709, October 18, 1981] OJ repeated, November 9, 1982. Retrieved from https://global.tbmm.gov.tr/docs/constitution_en.pdf (English).

The Constitutional Court of the Republic of Turkey, Individual Application, Decision number 2014/14189, Date: 25.10.2017.

The General Board of Penalty, Supreme Court, E.2012/12-1584, K:2014/312.

The Patient Rights Directive of 1998, Retrieved from http://mevzuat.basbakanlik.gov.tr/Metin.Aspx?MevzuatKod=7.5.4847&MevzuatIliski=0&# (Turkish)

Thomas, R., Mark, B., Johnson, T., & Croall, J. (2003). NetBouncer: Client-Legitimacy-Based High-Performance DDoS Filtering. Proc. 3rd DARPA Information Survivability Conf. and Exposition, pp. 111–113, Washington, DC, USA, April 22-24. IEEE CS.

Tozer, E. P. (2012). *Broadcast Engineer's Reference Book* (1st ed.). FOCAL PRESS. doi:10.4324/9780080490564

Tripathi, S., Gupta, B., Almomani, A., Mishra, A., & Veluru, S. (2013). Hadoop based defense solution to handle distributed denial of service (ddos) attacks. *Journal of Information Security*, 4(3), 150.

Tsai, W. T., Sun, X., & Balasooriya, J. (2010, April). Service-oriented Cloud computing architecture. In *Proceedings 2010 Seventh International Conference on Information Technology: New Generations (ITNG)*, (pp. 684-689). IEEE. 10.1109/ITNG.2010.214

Turkey's National Health Information System Portal (Saglik-Net). Retrieved from http://www.sagliknet.saglik.gov.tr/giris.htm (Turkish)

Turulja, L., & Bajgoric, N. (2018). Knowing Means Existing: Organizational Learning Dimensions and Knowledge Management Capability. *Business Systems Research*, 9(1), 1–18. doi:10.2478/bsrj-2018-0001

Twitchell, D. P. (2007). Social engineering in information assurance curricula. In *Proceedings of the 2006 Information Security Curriculum Development Conference, InfoSecCD '06*. Academic Press.

Twitter, accessed 2017. [Online]. Available: http://www.twitter

U.S. Department of Transportation. (2019). *Cybersecurity and Intelligent Transportation Systems, A Best Practice Guide* (Publication Number- FHWA-JPO-19-763). USA: Office of the Assistant Secretary for Research and Technology.(www.its.dot.gov/index.htm)

Valli, C., Rabadia, P., & Woodward, A. (2013). Patterns and patter - An investigation into SSH activity using Kippo honeypots. In *Australian Digital Forensics Conference*, 141-149.

Van der Maaten, L. (2014). Accelerating t-SNE using tree-based algorithms. *Journal of Machine Learning Research*, *15*(1), 3221–3245.

Vanderhoof, R. (2017). *Smart Card Talk*. Alliance, SC.

Veridium Ltd. (2019). Biometric Authentication Technology - Fingerprint, Face, Camera, Sensors. Retrieved October 1, 2019, from http://veridiumid.com/biometric-authentication-technology/mobile-authentication

Verisign, Distributed Denial of Service Trends Report, Retrieved from https://www.verisign.com/en_IN/security-services/ddos-protection/ddos-report/index.xhtml

Vijay. (2019). Most Powerful Cyber Security Software Tools. Software Testing Help, Retrieved from https://www.softwaretestinghelp.com/cybersecurity-software-tools/

Vissers, T., Somasundaram, T. S., Pieters, L., Govindarajan, K., & Hellinckx, P. (2014). DDoS defense system for web services in a cloud environment. *Future Generation Computer Systems*, *37*, 37–45.

Wallgren, R., Raza, S., & Voigt, T. (2013). Routing Attacks and Countermeasures in the RPL-Based Internet of Things. *International Journal of Distributed Sensor Networks*, *9*(8). doi:10.1155/2013/794326

Wang, H., Jin, C., & Shin, K. G. (2007). Defense against spoofed IP traffic using hop-count filtering. *IEEE/ACM Transactions on Networking (ToN)*, *15*(1), 40-53.

Wang, W., Chen, L., Shin, K. G., & Duan, L. (2014, April). Secure cooperative spectrum sensing and access against intelligent malicious behaviors. In *Proceedings IEEE INFOCOM 2014-IEEE Conference on Computer Communications* (pp. 1267-1275). IEEE.

Wang, X., Cao, J., & Wang, J. (2016). A dynamic cloud service selection strategy using adaptive learning agents. *International Journal of High Performance Computing and Networking*, *9*(1-2), 70-81.

Wang, H., Dong, X., & Cao, Z. (2017). Multi-value-independent ciphertext-policy attribute-based encryption with fast keyword search. *IEEE Transactions on Services Computing*, 1. doi:10.1109/TSC.2017.2753231

Wang, K., Qi, X., Shu, L., Deng, D. J., & Rodrigues, J. J. (2016). Toward trustworthy crowdsourcing in the social internet of things. *IEEE Wireless Communications*, *23*(5), 30–36.

Wang, K., Xu, Y., Wong, R. C. W., & Fu, A. W. C. (2010). Anonymizing temporal data. In *Proceedings International Conference on Data Mining, ICDM, IEEE*, 1109-1114. doi: 10.1109/ICDM.2010.96

Wang, Q., Li, M., Tang, Y., & Ni, M. (2019). Source-Load Coordinated Reserve Allocation Strategy Considering Cyber-Attack Risks. *IEEE Access*, *7*, 111332–111340. doi:10.1109/ACCESS.2019.2934646

Wayman, J., Jain, A., Maltoni, D., & Maio, D. (2005). An Introduction to Biometric Authentication Systems. In *Biometric Systems* (pp. 1–20). London, UK: Springer. doi:10.1007/1-84628-064-8_1

Weagle, S. (n.d.). New Report Points to Alarming DDoS Attack Statistics and Projections. Available at https://www.corero.com/blog/736-new-report-points-to-alarming-ddos-attack-statistics-and-projections.html. Accessed on Jan, 2019.

Weka 3. (2019). Data Mining Software in Java. Retrieved October 1, 2019, from https://www.cs.waikato.ac.nz/ml/weka/

Wiczer, J., Wiczer, M. B., & Hills, V. (2015). Improving Energy Efficiency Using Customized Monitoring Tools, In *Proceedings of 17th Metalcasting Congress, Modern Casting*, pp. 36-39. Academic Press.

Wilder, B. (2012). *Cloud architecture patterns: Using Microsoft Azure*. O'Reilly Media, Inc.

Winkler, I. (2016, January 13). The threat of shoulder surfing should not be underestimated. Retrieved October 1, 2019, from https://www.csoonline.com/article/3021882/security/the-threat-of-shoulder-surfing-should-not-be-underestimated.html

Witteman, M. (2002). Advances in smartcard security. *Information Security Bulletin*, 7, 11–22.

Wood, G., & Ethereum. (2014). A secure decentralised generalised transaction ledger. *Ethereum Project Yellow Paper*.

Wu, L., Garg, S. K., & Buyya, R. (2011, May). SLA-based resource allocation for software as a service provider (SaaS) in cloud computing environments. In *Proceedings of the 2011 11th IEEE/ACM International Symposium on Cluster, Cloud, and Grid Computing* (pp. 195-204). IEEE Computer Society.

Wu, Z., Butkiewicz, M., Perkins, D., Katz-Bassett, E., & Madhyastha, H. V. (2013). Spanstore: cost-effective geo-replicated storage spanning multiple cloud services. Acm sigcomm (pp. 292-308). Farminton, PA: ACM.

Wu, J. H., Kao, H. Y., & Sambamurthy, V. (2016). The integration effort and E-health compatibility effect and the mediating role of E-health synergy on hospital performance. *International Journal of Information Management*, 36(6), 1288–1300. doi:10.1016/j.ijinfomgt.2016.09.002

Wu, X., Zhu, X., Wu, G. Q., & Ding, W. (2014). Data mining with big data. *IEEE Transactions on Knowledge and Data Engineering*, 26(1), 97–107. doi:10.1109/TKDE.2013.109

Wu, Z., & Madhyastha, H. (2013). Understanding The Latency Benefits Of Multi-Cloud Webservice Deployments. *Computer Communication Review*, 43(1), 13–20. doi:10.1145/2479957.2479960

Xiao, L., Wan, X., Lu, X., Zhang, Y., & Wu, D. (2018). IoT security techniques based on machine learning. *IEEE Signal Processing Magazine*.

Xiao, L., & Sun, M. (2019). *Malware Detection based on Deep Learning of Behavioural Graphs*. Hindawi – Mathematical Problems in Engineering.

Xiao, Z., Song, W., & Chen, Q. (2012). Dynamic resource allocation using virtual machines for cloud computing environment. *IEEE Transactions on Parallel and Distributed Systems*, 24(6), 1107–1117. doi:10.1109/TPDS.2012.283

XOIC. Sourceforge.net. (2019). Retrieved from http://sourceforge.net/projects/xoic/

Yaar, A., Perrig, A., & Song, D. (2004, May). SIFF: A stateless Internet flow filter to mitigate DDoS flooding attacks. In Proceedings IEEE Symposium on Security and Privacy, 2004. 130–143. IEEE.

Yan, T., Zeng, S., Qi, M., Hu, Q., & Qi, F. (2019). *Cyber security detection and monitoring at IHEP private cloud for web services*. EPJ Web of Conferences. 214. 07016. 10.1051/epjconf/201921407016

Yang, M., Yu, Y., Bandara, A. K., & Nuseibeh, B. (2014, September). Adaptive sharing for online social networks: A trade-off between privacy risk and social benefit. In *Proceedings of the 2014 IEEE 13th International Conference on Trust, Security, and Privacy in Computing and Communications (TrustCom)*, (pp. 45-52). IEEE. 10.1109/TrustCom.2014.10

Yang, X. L. A. L. X., & Wetherall, D. (2008). Passport: Secure and adoptable source authentication.

Yang, Y., Cai, H., Wei, Z., Lu, H., & Choo, K. K. R. (2016, July). Towards lightweight anonymous entity authentication for IoT applications. In *Proceedings Australasian Conference on Information Security and Privacy* (pp. 265-280). Cham, Switzerland: Springer. 10.1007/978-3-319-40253-6_16

Yang, X., Wetherall, D., & Anderson, T. (2005, August). A DoS-limiting network architecture. ACM. *Computer Communication Review*, 35(4), 241–252.

Yang, Y., Chen, F., Chen, J., Zhang, Y., & Yung, K. L. (2019). A secure hash function based on feedback iterative structure. *Enterprise Information Systems*, *13*(3), 281–302. doi:10.1080/17517575.2018.1564942

Yannakogeorgos, P. A., & Lowther, A. B. (Eds.). (2013). *Conflict and Cooperation in Cyberspace: The Challenge to National Security*. CRC Press.

Yassin, W., Udzir, N. I., Muda, Z., & Sulaiman, M. N. (2013). Anomaly-Based Intrusion Detection Through K- Means Clustering and Naives Bayes Classification. In *Proceedings of the 4th International Conference on Computing and Informatics, ICOCI 2013*. Academic Press.

Yau, D. K., Lui, J. C., Liang, F., & Yam, Y. (2005). Defending against distributed denial-of-service attacks with max-min fair server-centric router throttles. *IEEE/ACM Transactions on Networking*, *13*(1), 29–42.

Ye, J., & Mo, J. (2015). U.S. Patent No. 9,009,232. Washington, DC: U.S. Patent and Trademark Office.

Ye, Y. M., Pan, C. C., & Yang, G. K. (2016). An Improved Location-Based Service Authentication Algorithm with Personalized K-Anonymity. In *Proceedings China Satellite Navigation Conference, 2016 CSNC*. pp. 257-266. Singapore, Springer. doi: 10.1007/978-981-10-0934-1_23

Yegireddi, R., & Kumar, R. K. (2016, November). A survey on conventional encryption algorithms of cryptography. In *Proceedings 2016 International Conference on ICT in Business Industry & Government (ICTBIG)* (pp. 1-4). IEEE.

Yi, H., & Zhang, Y. (2010). Research of campus network security system based on intrusion detection, In *the Proceedings of International Conference on Computer Design and Applications*, Qinhuangdao, China. Academic Press.

Yi, H., Jung, H., & Bae, S. (2017). Deep Neural Networks for traffic flow prediction. In *Proceedings 2017 IEEE International Conference on Big Data and Smart Computing (BigComp)* (pp. 328-331). IEEE.

Yin, C., Zhang, S., Xi, J., & Wang, J. (2017). An improved anonymity model for big data security based on clustering algorithm. *Concurrency and Computation*, *29*(7). doi:10.1002/cpe.3902

Yin, G., & Wei, G. (2010). Application Design of Data Packet Capturing Based on Sharpcap, In *Proceedings of Fourth IEEE International Joint Conference on Computational Sciences and Optimization*, Washington, DC: IEEE Computer Society.

Yu, S., Zhou, W., Guo, S., & Guo, M. (2016). A feasible IP traceback framework through dynamic deterministic packet marking. *IEEE Transactions on Computers*, *65*(5), 1418–1427.

Yu, J., Lee, H., Kim, M.-S., & Park, D. (2008). Traffic flooding attack detection with SNMP MIB using SVM. *Computer Communications*, *31*(17), 4212–4219. doi:10.1016/j.comcom.2008.09.018

Yu, S. (2016). Big privacy: Challenges and opportunities of privacy study in the age of big data. *IEEE Access: Practical Innovations, Open Solutions*, *4*, 2751–2763. doi:10.1109/ACCESS.2016.2577036

Yusuf, Y. Y., Sarhadi, M., & Gunasekaran, A. (1999). Agile manufacturing: The drivers, concepts and attributes. *International Journal of Production Economics*, *62*(1-2), 33–43. doi:10.1016/S0925-5273(98)00219-9

Yu, Z., Gao, C. Z., Jing, Z., Gupta, B. B., & Cai, Q. (2018). A practical public key encryption scheme based on learning parity with noise. *IEEE Access: Practical Innovations, Open Solutions*, *6*, 31918–31923. doi:10.1109/ACCESS.2018.2840119

Zaidi, K., Milojevic, M. B., Rakocevic, V., Nallanathan, A., & Rajarajan, M. (2016). Host-based intrusion detection for vanets: A statistical approach to rogue node detection. *IEEE Transactions on Vehicular Technology*, *65*(8), 6703–6714. doi:10.1109/TVT.2015.2480244

Zaman, S., & Grosu, D. (2012, June). An online mechanism for dynamic vm provisioning and allocation in clouds. In *Proceedings 2012 IEEE Fifth International Conference on Cloud Computing* (pp. 253-260). IEEE.

Zaman, S., & Grosu, D. (2013). Combinatorial auction-based allocation of virtual machine instances in clouds. *Journal of Parallel and Distributed Computing, 73*(4), 495–508.

Zargar, S. T., Joshi, J., & Tipper, D. (2013). A survey of defense mechanisms against distributed denial of service (DDoS) flooding attacks. *IEEE Communications Surveys and Tutorials, 15*(4), 2046–2069.

Ženko, Z., Mulej, M., & Potocan, V. (2017). Knowledge-cum-values Management belongs to the Way out from Global Crisis. *Business Systems Research, 8*(1), 113–123. doi:10.1515/bsrj-2017-0009

Zhang, M., Duan, Z., Li, Q., & Chu, H. (2016). Transformation from business process models to BPEL with overlapped patterns involved. *International Journal of High Performance Computing and Networking, 9*(1-2), 82-92.

Zhang, Q., Li, Z., & Song, C. (2011). The Improvement of digital signature algorithm based on elliptic curve cryptography. *IEEE Transactions.*

Zhang, J., Li, H., Liu, X., Luo, Y., Chen, F., Wang, H., & Chang, L. (2015). On efficient and robust anonymization for privacy protection on massive streaming categorical information. *IEEE Transactions on Dependable and Secure Computing*, 507–520. doi:10.1109/TDSC.2015.2483503

Zhang, M., Wang, L., Jajodia, S., Singhal, A., & Albanese, M. (2016). Network diversity: A security metric for evaluating the resilience of networks against zero-day attacks. *IEEE Transactions on Information Forensics and Security, 11*(5), 1071–1086. doi:10.1109/TIFS.2016.2516916

Zhang, X., Zheng, H., Li, X., Du, S., & Zhu, H. (2014). You are where you have been: Sybil detection via geo-location analysis in OSNs, *Proceedings 2014 IEEE Glob. Commun. Conf. GLOBECOM, 2014*, 698–703.

Zhang, Z., Sun, R., Zhao, C., Wang, J., Chang, C. K., & Gupta, B. B. (2017). CyVOD: A novel trinity multimedia social network scheme. *Multimedia Tools and Applications, 76*(18), 18513–18529. doi:10.100711042-016-4162-z

Zheng, Q., Xu, S., & Ateniese, G. (2014, April). VABKS: verifiable attribute-based keyword search over outsourced encrypted data. In *Proceedings IEEE INFOCOM 2014-IEEE Conference on Computer Communications* (pp. 522-530). IEEE. 10.1109/INFOCOM.2014.6847976

Zheng, Q., Wang, X., Khurram Khan, M., Zhang, W., Gupta, B. B., & Guo, W. (2017). A lightweight authenticated encryption scheme based on chaotic scml for railway cloud service. *IEEE Access: Practical Innovations, Open Solutions, 6*, 711–722. doi:10.1109/ACCESS.2017.2775038

Zhou, Y., & Feng, D. (2005). Side-Channel Attacks: Ten Years After Its Publication and the Impacts on Cryptographic Module Security Testing. *IACR Cryptology ePrint Archive, 2005*, 388.

Zhu, Q., Fung, C., Boutaba, R., & Basar, T. (2012). GUIDEX: A game-theoretic incentive-based mechanism for intrusion detection networks. *IEEE Journal on Selected Areas in Communications, 30*(11), 2220–2230.

Zhu, W., Luo, C., Wang, J., & Li, S. (2011). Multimedia cloud computing. *IEEE Signal Processing Magazine, 28*(3), 59–69. doi:10.1109/MSP.2011.940269

Zighra. (2019). Smart Identity Defense. AI-Powered Continuous Authentication and Fraud Detection. Retrieved October 1, 2019, from https://zighra.com/

Zissis, D., & Lekkas, D. (2012). Addressing Cloud computing security issues. *Future Generation Computer Systems, 28*(3), 583–592. doi:10.1016/j.future.2010.12.006

Zkik, K., Orhanou, G., & El Hajji, S. (2017). Secure mobile multi cloud architecture for authentication and data storage. [IJCAC]. *International Journal of Cloud Applications and Computing, 7*(2), 62–76. doi:10.4018/IJCAC.2017040105

Zyskind, G., Nathan, O., & Pentland, A. (2015). Enigma: Decentralized computation platform with guaranteed privacy, *arXiv preprint arXiv:1506.03471.*

About the Contributors

B. B. Gupta received PhD degree from Indian Institute of Technology Roorkee, India in the area of information security. He has published more than 50 research papers in international journals and conferences of high repute. He has visited several countries to present his research work. His biography has published in the Marquis Who's Who in the World, 2012. At present, he is working as an Assistant Professor in the Department of Computer Engineering, National Institute of Technology Kurukshetra, India. His research interest includes information security, cyber security, cloud computing, web security, intrusion detection, computer networks and phishing.

Tameem Ahmad received M.Tech. degree in Computer Science & Engineering with specialization in Software Engineering and B.Tech. degree in Computer Science & Engineering. Currently, he is working as an Assistant Professor in Department of Computer Engineering, Aligarh Muslim University, Aligarh. He has also worked in Cognizant Technology Solutions. His research areas of interest are Soft Computing, Natural Language Processing, Database Systems and Data Warehousing.

Mouhammd Alkasassbeh graduated from the school of computing, Portsmouth University, UK in 2008. He is currently a full professor in the Computer Science Dept. Princess Sumaya University for Technology. His research interests include Network Traffic Analysis, Network Fault Detection, Classification Network Fault and abnormality and Machine learning in the area of computer networking and network security.

Mohd Asad Anwar completed my bachelor degree in engineering from UPTU and master degree in engineering from Aligarh Muslim University.

Rangel Arthur holds a degree in Electrical Engineering from the Paulista State University Júlio de Mesquita Filho (1999), a Master's degree in Electrical Engineering (2002) and a Ph.D. in Electrical Engineering (2007) from the State University of Campinas. Over the years from 2011 to 2014 he was Coordinator and Associate Coordinator of Technology Courses in Telecommunication Systems and Telecommunication Engineering of FT, which was created in its management. From 2015 to 2016 he was Associate Director of the Technology (FT) of Unicamp. He is currently a lecturer and advisor to the Innovation Agency (Inova) of Unicamp. He has experience in the area of Electrical Engineering, with emphasis on Telecommunications Systems, working mainly on the following topics: computer vision, embedded systems and control systems.

Vaibhav Bhatia is a software developer, who has a keen interest in developing applications that respect the privacy and ease the life of a day to day technology user.

Rajkumar Buyya is Professor and Future Fellow of the Australian Research Council, and Director of the Cloud Computing and Distributed Systems (CLOUDS) Laboratory at the University of Melbourne, Australia. He is also serving as the founding CEO of Manjrasoft, a spin-off company of the University, commercializing its innovations in Cloud Computing. He has authored over 425 publications and four textbooks including "Mastering Cloud Computing" published by McGraw Hill and Elsevier/Morgan Kaufmann, 2013 for Indian and international markets respectively. He is one of the highly cited authors in computer science and software engineering worldwide. Microsoft Academic Search Index ranked Dr. Buyya as the world's top author in distributed and parallel computing between 2007 and 2012. Software technologies for Grid and Cloud computing developed under Dr. Buyya's leadership have gained rapid acceptance and are in use at several academic institutions and commercial enterprises in 40 countries around the world. Dr. Buyya has led the establishment and development of key community activities, including serving as foundation Chair of the IEEE Technical Committee on Scalable Computing and five IEEE/ACM conferences. These contributions and international research leadership of Dr. Buyya are recognized through the award of "2009 IEEE Medal for Excellence in Scalable Computing" from the IEEE Computer Society, USA. Manjrasoft's Aneka Cloud technology developed under his leadership has received "2010 Frost & Sullivan New Product Innovation Award" and "2011 Telstra Innovation Challenge, People's Choice Award".

Bhanu Chander, Research scholar at Pondicherry University, India. Completed his Graduate degree in Computer science and engineering from Acharya Nagarjuna University, India and Completed his Post Graduate Degree from Central University of Rajasthan, India. His main research fields are Machine learning, Data Security, Cryptography, Wireless sensor network, and Deep learning.

Selem Charfi has obtained his Ph.D at the University of Valenciennes (France) in 2013. His research concerns human-computer interaction (HCI), agent-based architecture models of interactive systems, software engineering and HCI evaluation, with application to the supervision of transport systems. He is co-author of several papers in international conferences. He is involved in several research networks and projects. He worked also in the domain of industrial computer-science and mainly at the MES systems. Actually he is involved as a system technical architect for a transport ticketing system elaboration. His main research interest are: HCI - Human Computer Interaction, H2C - Human Computer Confluence, Indutry 4.0 and Big Data.

Chhavi Chaturvedi is a Master's Scholar in Cyber Security at National Institute of Technology, Kurukshetra, India. She is Completed her bachelor's degree in Computer Engineering from Government Women Enfineering College, Ajmer.

Niranjan N Chiplunkar did his BE in Electronics and Communication from National Institute of Engineering Mysore in the year 1986 and M.Tech in Computer Science and Engineering from MIT, Manipal. He acquired his Ph.D. in Computer Science and Engineeing from SJ College of Engineering of Mysore University in 2002. Prof. Niranjan has more than 25 years of teaching experience. He served as Lecturer and then as Reader in the Dept. of Computer Science and Engg. at MIT Manipal from 1987 to 1996, from 1996 to June 2012 he worked at NMAM Institute of Technology, Nitte as a Professor in the Computer Science & Engineering Department. From 2003, he was heading the Department of CSE and was Vice Principal of the Institute and from 2010, he was also holding additional charge of Dean(Academics) Dr.Niranjan has written one Text book on autoCAD for VLSI published by NMAMIT Publications in 2007 and one more on "VLSI CAD" published by PHI Learning, New Delhi in 2011. He has edited two International and one national level conference Proceedings. Prof. Chiplunkar has been awarded with Bharatiya Vidya Bhavan National Award for the Best Engineering College Principal - 2014 by Indian Society for Technical Education. He has also been awarded with "Excellent Achievement Award" from Centre for International Cooperation on Computerization, Govt. of Japan in March 2002. During 2007, he has been given "Distinguished Alumnus" award by the Manipal University. His Biodata has been published in "Marqui's Who's Who in the World in 2009 issue. Prof. Niranjan has been awarded with appreciation certificates from EMC (India) and IEEE Bangalore Chapter for his contribution towards EMC Academic Alliance initiative and IEEE Student Branch activities as a Branch counselor at NMAMIT, Nitte, respectively. Prof. Chiplunkar has presented more than 60 technical papers in National and International Conferences and journals. He has successfully guided two Ph.D. Scholar under VTU, 1 Ph.D Scholar under VIT, Vellur and is currently guiding 5 Ph.D students towards their Ph.D. thesis. He is a Fellow of Institution of Engineers (India) and member of several other Professional bodies like IEEE, CSI, and ISTE. He is on the examination boards of various Universities in India. Dr. Niranjan has successfully completed TWO funded research projects - one from AICTE, New Delhi and another from DST, Govt. of India on "Network on Chip Architecture design(Project cost:Rs.4.6lakhs - 2 years) and Multicore software framework development(Project cost: Rs.15.96lakhs - 2 years) respectively. Prof. Niranjan has organized 5 ISTE-Short Term Training Programmes, Three International Conferences, 4 National Conferences and several workshops. Dr.Niranjan has visited countries like Japan (during Jan-March 2002, March 2013),, Srilanka (during 2004), UAE (during 2005 and 2006), Singapore, Malaysia (during December 2007 & 2012), Qatar (during May 2008 and June 2009), USA (during June 2008 & October 2013), Thailand(during April 2010) and Shanghai, China (during March 2011) on different official assignments. He has taken part in EMC world conference at Las Vegas in June 2008 and has visited Stanford University and University of California at SandDiego. He was the ISO Management representative and TEQIP nodal officer of NMAMIT, Nitte. Prof. Niranjan was the President of Rotary Club of Nitte during 2006-07.

Veli Durmuş is PhD in Healthcare Management. He has received his B.Sc. degree both in Law and in Public Administration. Also, he has M.Sc and Ph.D. degree in Healthcare Management. Dr. Durmuş has professionally over 16 years experience in health services as a paramedic and a health officer. Dr. Durmuş's research interests have focused mainly on health law, health policy and management, and also he has many published articles and books.

Reinaldo França was in Computer Engineering in 2014. Currently, he is an Ph.D. degree candidate by Department of Semiconductors, Instruments and Photonics, Faculty of Electrical and Computer Engineering at the LCV-UNICAMP working with technological and scientific research as well as in programming and development in C / C ++, Java and .NET languages. His main topics of interest are simulation, operating systems, software engineering, wireless networks, internet of things, broadcasting and telecommunications systems

Manuel Gil Pérez is Assistant Professor in Department of Information and Communications Engineering of the University of Murcia, Spain. His research focuses on cybersecurity, trust management, privacy-preserving data sharing, and security operations in highly dynamic scenarios.

Misbahul Haque received M.Tech. degree in Computer Science & Engineering with specialization in Software Engineering and B.Tech. degree in Computer Engineering. Currently, he is working as an Assistant Professor in Department of Computer Engineering, Aligarh Muslim University, Aligarh.

Alberto Huertas Celdrán is an Irish Research Council Government of Ireland Postdoctoral research fellow associated with the TSSG, WIT. Huertas Celdran received M.Sc. and Ph.D. degrees in Computer Science from the University of Murcia, Spain. His scientific interests include medical cyber-physical systems (MCPS), Brain-Computer Interfaces (BCI), cybersecurity, data privacy, continuous authentication, semantic technology, context-aware systems, and computer networks.

Yuzo Iano has a BS (1972), Master's degree (1974) and a Ph.D. degree (1986) in Electrical Engineering from the State University of Campinas, Brazil. Since then he has been working in the technological production field, with 1 patent granted, 8 patent applications filed, and 36 projects completed with research and development agencies. Successfully supervised 29 doctoral theses, 49 master's dissertations, 74 undergraduate and 48 scientific initiation work. He has participated in 100 master's examination boards, 50 doctoral degrees, author of 2 books and more than 250 published articles. He is currently Professor at the State University of Campinas, Brazil, Editor-in-Chief of the SET International Journal of Broadcast Engineering and General Chair of the Brazilian Symposium on Technology (BTSym). He has experience in Electrical Engineering, with knowledge in Telecommunications, Electronics and Information Technology, mainly in the field of audio-visual communications and data.

Saurav Jindal has worked as a research scholar at Punjab Engineering College, Chandigarh. His research interests include Distributed Computing, Privacy and Security.

José María Jorquera Valero is a predoctoral fellow in Cybersecurity and Cyberdefence Research Lab at Murcia University. Jorquera Valero received BSc. and M.Sc. degrees in Computer Science from the University of Murcia, Spain. His scientific interests include computer networks, Machine Learning, cybersecurity, data privacy, and continuous authentication.

Gayathri K S is currently working as an Assistant Professor in the Department of Computer Science, Mar Baselios College of Engineering and Technology (MBCET), Thiruvananthapuram, Kerala. Having 7 years teaching experience and 2 years industrial experience.

Manjunath Kotari did his Bachelor of Engineering in Computer Science&Engineering from R.V.College of Engineering, Bangalore. Dr. Kotari obtained his M.Tech in Computer Science and Engineering from NMAM Institute of Technology, Nitteand completed his Ph.D from VTU, Belagavi in the area of Distributed Systems & Network Security. Dr. Manjunath has been served 12 years in various capacities at N.M.A.M. Institute of Technology, Nitte and from last 8 years Dr. Kotari working as Professor & Headin the Department of Computer Science and Engineering at Alva's Institute of Engineering & Technology, Moodbidri. Dr. Kotari has published more than 35 technical papers in International Journals/

National and International Conferences. His areas of interests are Network Security, VLSI CAD and Computer Architecture. He has co-ordinated several Faculty Development Programmes at NMAMIT, Nitte and AIET, Moodbidri. Also, attended several workshopsand conferences across various engineering colleges in INDIA. He is member of BOE/BOS in various universities. Also a Member of VTU-LIC (Local Inquiry Committee). Dr. Kotari is a Member of Computer Society of India(CSI), Institution of Electrical & Electronics Engineers(IEEE), Life Member of Indian Society for Technical Education(ISTE) and Indian Society for Training & Development (ISTD) He is a Co-author for the TWO Technical Book titled "CAD for VLSI" and "VLSI CAD" authored by Dr. Niranjan N Chiplunnkar, Principal NMAMIT, Nitte and this book was published by PHI Learning Pvt. Ltd,NewDelhi. He has compiled several course materials for "Sikkim Manipal University". He is a Regular Reviewer for the SN Applied Sciences (SNAS), InderScience Journal and other International Journals/Conferences. He is guiding 5-to -6 projects per year for the both PG and UG students. "Network Gaming for Mobile" has got "BEST PROJECT OF THE YEAR 2006-07" by KSCST. He has chaired the sessions of several State level and National/International level technical paper presentations. He has delivered Invited Lectures in various topics like Cloud Computing, Distributed Computing, Storage Area Networks, Advanced Multimedia Computing, Requirements Engineering and Ethical Hacking etc in the various institutes. He happily got married to Ms. Jaya on 4th May 2003 and Blessed with a kids Master "ARJUN"and Master "ASHWIN".

Yaser Mansouri is a Fellow researcher in the Computer Science and Engineering Department at Qatar University. He received his PhD from Cloud Computing and Distributed Systems (CLOUDS) Laboratory, Department of Computing and Information Systems, the University of Melbourne, Australia. He was awarded International Postgraduate Research Scholarship (IPRS) and Australian Postgraduate Award (APA) supporting his PhD studies. He received his BSc degree from Shahid Beheshti University and his MSc degree from Ferdowsi University of Mashhad, Iran in Computer Science and Software Engineering. His research interests cover the broad area of Distributed Systems, with special emphasis on data replication and management in data grids and data cloud systems. Specifically, he is interested in designing new data placement algorithms and analyzing their performances.

Gregorio Martínez Pérez is Full Professor in Department of Information and Communications Engineering of the University of Murcia, Spain. His scientific activity is devoted to cybersecurity, privacy, and networking, working on different national and European IST research projects on these topics.

Ana Carolina Borges Monteiro is a Ph.D. student at the Faculty of Electrical and Computer Engineering (FEEC) at the State University of Campinas - UNICAMP, where she develops research projects regarding health software with emphasis on the development of algorithms for the detection and counting of blood cells through processing techniques. digital images. These projects led in 2019 to a computer program registration issued by the INPI (National Institute of Industrial Property). She holds a Master's degree in Electrical Engineering from the State University of Campinas - UNICAMP (2019) and graduated in Biomedicine from the University Center Amparense - UNIFIA with a degree in Clinical Pathology - Clinical Analysis (2015). In 2019, he acquired a degree in Health Informatics. Has experience in the areas of Molecular Biology and management with research animals. Since 2017, she has been a researcher at the FEEC/UNICAMP Visual Communications Laboratory (LCV) and has worked at the Brazilian Technology Symposium (BTSym) as a member of the Organizational and Executive Committee and as a member of the Technical Reviewers Committee. In addition, she works as a reviewer at the Health magazines of the Federal University of Santa Maria (UFSM - Brazil), Medical Technology Journal MTJ (Algeria) and Production Planning & Control (Taylor & Francis). Interested in: digital image processing, hematology, clinical analysis, cell biology, medical informatics, Matlab and teaching.

Shaifali Narayan is currently pursuing her Master's degree in Cyber Security from National Institute of Technology, Kurukshetra, India. She received her Bachelor's degree in Computer Science and Engineering from Invertis University, Bareilly, India, in 2015.Her current research are Security in Internet of Things (IoT), authentication in smart card technology and data privacy.

Poonam Saini received her Ph.D. degree in Computer Engineering from National Institute of Technology, Kurukshetra, India in 2013 and M.Tech from UIET, Kurukshetra University, Kurukshetra, India in 2006. She has received B. Tech. in Information Technology from Kurukshetra University, Kurukshetra, India in 2003. She is currently working as Assistant Professor in Computer Science and Engineering at Punjab Engineering College, Chandigarh, India. Her research interest includes Fault-Tolerant Distributed Computing Systems, Mobile Computing, Blockchain, Machine Learning, Big Data Analytics and Security.

Pedro Miguel Sánchez is a PhD student in Computer Science at the University of Murcia. Pedro Miguel Sánchez received M.Sc. and Bachelor degrees in Computer Science from the University of Murcia, Spain. His scientific interests include Machine learning, cybersecurity, data privacy, continuous authentication and computer networks.

Abhik Setia is a technology enthusiast programmer, interested in building modern solutions to improvise our day to day activities in life.

Tony Thomas is an Associate Professor at the Indian Institute of Information Technology and Management- Kerala, India. He received his master's and Ph.D. degrees from IIT Kanpur. After completing his Ph.D., he pursued postdoctoral research at the Korea Advanced Institute of Science and Technology, Daejeon, South Korea. He later worked as a member of research staff at the General Motors Research Lab, Bangalore, India, and the School of Computer Engineering, Nanyang Technological University, Singapore. His current research interests include malware analysis, biometrics, cryptography, machine learning, IoT security, cyber threat prediction and visualization, digital watermarking, multimedia security and digital forensics.

Mert Uydacı is Professor, Ph.D. in Marketing and Advertising. He has received his B.Sc. degree in Business Administration. Also, he has M.Sc. and Ph.D. in Production Management and Marketing. Professor Uydacı's research interests have focused primarily on marketing in healthcare, health policy and management, and he also has many published national and international articles and books. The latest published book is "Green Marketing".

Index

T

Z

Purchase Print, E-Book, or Print + E-Book

IGI Global's reference books are available in three unique pricing formats:
Print Only, E-Book Only, or Print + E-Book.
Shipping fees may apply.

www.igi-global.com

Recommended Reference Books

ISBN: 978-1-5225-8876-4
© 2019; 141 pp.
List Price: $135

ISBN: 978-1-5225-8100-0
© 2019; 321 pp.
List Price: $235

ISBN: 978-1-5225-7847-5
© 2019; 306 pp.
List Price: $195

ISBN: 978-1-5225-6313-6
© 2019; 349 pp.
List Price: $215

ISBN: 978-1-5225-7628-0
© 2019; 281 pp.
List Price: $220

ISBN: 978-1-5225-5855-2
© 2019; 337 pp.
List Price: $185

Do you want to stay current on the latest research trends, product announcements, news and special offers?
Join IGI Global's mailing list today and start enjoying exclusive perks sent only to IGI Global members.
Add your name to the list at **www.igi-global.com/newsletters.**

Publisher of Peer-Reviewed, Timely, and Innovative Academic Research

www.igi-global.com   Sign up at www.igi-global.com/newsletters   f facebook.com/igiglobal   t twitter.com/igiglobal   t linkedin.com/igiglobal

Ensure Quality Research is Introduced to the Academic Community

Become an IGI Global Reviewer for Authored Book Projects

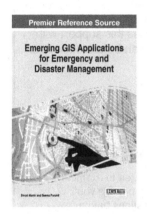
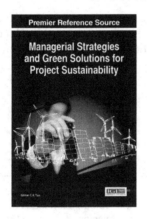

The overall success of an authored book project is dependent on quality and timely reviews.

In this competitive age of scholarly publishing, constructive and timely feedback significantly expedites the turnaround time of manuscripts from submission to acceptance, allowing the publication and discovery of forward-thinking research at a much more expeditious rate. Several IGI Global authored book projects are currently seeking highly-qualified experts in the field to fill vacancies on their respective editorial review boards:

Applications and Inquiries may be sent to:
development@igi-global.com

Applicants must have a doctorate (or an equivalent degree) as well as publishing and reviewing experience. Reviewers are asked to complete the open-ended evaluation questions with as much detail as possible in a timely, collegial, and constructive manner. All reviewers' tenures run for one-year terms on the editorial review boards and are expected to complete at least three reviews per term. Upon successful completion of this term, reviewers can be considered for an additional term.

If you have a colleague that may be interested in this opportunity,
we encourage you to share this information with them.

IGI Global Proudly Partners With eContent Pro International

Receive a 25% Discount on all Editorial Services

Editorial Services

IGI Global expects all final manuscripts submitted for publication to be in their final form. This means they must be reviewed, revised, and professionally copy edited prior to their final submission. Not only does this support with accelerating the publication process, but it also ensures that the highest quality scholarly work can be disseminated.

English Language Copy Editing

Let eContent Pro International's expert copy editors perform edits on your manuscript to resolve spelling, punctuaion, grammar, syntax, flow, formatting issues and more.

Scientific and Scholarly Editing

Allow colleagues in your research area to examine the content of your manuscript and provide you with valuable feedback and suggestions before submission.

Figure, Table, Chart & Equation Conversions

Do you have poor quality figures? Do you need visual elements in your manuscript created or converted? A design expert can help!

Translation

Need your documjent translated into English? eContent Pro International's expert translators are fluent in English and more than 40 different languages.

Hear What Your Colleagues are Saying About Editorial Services Supported by IGI Global

"The service was very fast, very thorough, and very helpful in ensuring our chapter meets the criteria and requirements of the book's editors. I was quite impressed and happy with your service."

– Prof. Tom Brinthaupt,
Middle Tennessee State University, USA

"I found the work actually spectacular. The editing, formatting, and other checks were very thorough. The turnaround time was great as well. I will definitely use eContent Pro in the future."

– Nickanor Amwata, Lecturer,
University of Kurdistan Hawler, Iraq

"I was impressed that it was done timely, and wherever the content was not clear for the reader, the paper was improved with better readability for the audience."

– Prof. James Chilembwe,
Mzuzu University, Malawi

Email: customerservice@econtentpro.com   **www.igi-global.com/editorial-service-partners**

www.igi-global.com

Celebrating Over 30 Years of Scholarly
Knowledge Creation & Dissemination

InfoSci®-Books

A Database of Over 5,300+ Reference Books Containing Over 100,000+ Chapters Focusing on Emerging Research

GAIN ACCESS TO **THOUSANDS** OF REFERENCE BOOKS AT **A FRACTION** OF THEIR INDIVIDUAL LIST **PRICE**.

InfoSci®-Books Database

The **InfoSci®-Books** database is a collection of over 5,300+ IGI Global single and multi-volume reference books, handbooks of research, and encyclopedias, encompassing groundbreaking research from prominent experts worldwide that span over 350+ topics in 11 core subject areas including business, computer science, education, science and engineering, social sciences and more.

Open Access Fee Waiver (Offset Model) Initiative

For any library that invests in IGI Global's InfoSci-Journals and/or InfoSci-Books databases, IGI Global will match the library's investment with a fund of equal value to go toward **subsidizing the OA article processing charges (APCs) for their students, faculty, and staff** at that institution when their work is submitted and accepted under OA into an IGI Global journal.*

INFOSCI® PLATFORM FEATURES

- No DRM
- No Set-Up or Maintenance Fees
- A Guarantee of No More Than a 5% Annual Increase
- Full-Text HTML and PDF Viewing Options
- Downloadable MARC Records
- Unlimited Simultaneous Access
- COUNTER 5 Compliant Reports
- Formatted Citations With Ability to Export to RefWorks and EasyBib
- No Embargo of Content (Research is Available Months in Advance of the Print Release)

*The fund will be offered on an annual basis and expire at the end of the subscription period. The fund would renew as the subscription is renewed for each year thereafter. The open access fees will be waived after the student, faculty, or staff's paper has been vetted and accepted into an IGI Global journal and the fund can only be used toward publishing OA in an IGI Global journal. Libraries in developing countries will have the match on their investment doubled.

To Learn More or To Purchase This Database:
www.igi-global.com/infosci-books

eresources@igi-global.com • Toll Free: 1-866-342-6657 ext. 100 • Phone: 717-533-8845 x100

www.igi-global.com

Printed in the United States
By Bookmasters

Printed in the United States
By Bookmasters